Golddiggers, Farmers, and Traders in the "Chinese Districts" of West Kalimantan, Indonesia

Mary Somers Heidhues

Golddiggers, Farmers, and Traders in the "Chinese Districts" of West Kalimantan, Indonesia

SOUTHEAST ASIA PROGRAM PUBLICATIONS
Southeast Asia Program
Cornell University
Ithaca, New York
2003

Cornell Southeast Asia Program Publications
640 Stewart Avenue, Ithaca, NY 14850-3857

Studies on Southeast Asia No. 34

Printed in the United States of America

ISBN 0-87727-733-8

Cover: Cover design by Judith Burns, Publications Services, Cornell University
Cover map: "Pontianak, Capital of the Residency of Borneo's West Coast, and Environs" from a manuscript of Commissioners Francis and Tobias, ca. 1822, in *Kaart van Nederlands Ostindië in 8 Bladen*, ed. Gijsbert Franco von Derfelden de Hinderstein (The Hague: Imprimerie de l'État, 1842) p. 7, map 18. Reproduction, Niedersächsische Staats- und Universitätsbibliothek, Göttingen.

TABLE OF CONTENTS

Table of Contents   5

List of Maps   7

List of Plates   8

Acknowledgments   9

Introduction   11

Chapter One: The Setting: The Peoples and their Histories   16

Chapter Two: Chinese Society and the Dutch to the First "Kongsi War"   47

Chapter Three: From 1850 to the End of the Kongsis   85

Chapter Four: Demographic and Economic Change: From Gold Miners to
Settlers and Traders, 1860-1940   126

Chapter Five: Community and Political Life in Prewar Times   163

Chapter Six: War and Indonesian Independence   197

Chapter Seven: Community under Duress   235

Epilogue: Repeated Violence and Uncertain Outcome   273

Glossary of Foreign Terms   279

Bibliography   283

Index   303

MAPS

Map One: West Kalimantan, showing the Chinese Districts   16

Map Two: Southeastern China, indicating approximate home areas of   30
Chinese of West Kalimantan

Map Three: Major Chinese Settlements in 1810   49

Map Four: Territories of the major kongsis, circa 1822   57

Map Five: Pontianak and environs, circa 1822, showing the   70
Chinese settlements

Map Six: Important sites in the Second Kongsi War   88

Map Seven: Dispersal of Chinese Population after the Kongsi Wars   126

Map Eight: West Kalimantan in 1967, showing areas of rebel activity   247
and "Dayak Raids"

PLATES

Plate 1: Chinese woman using *dulang*, about 1937   34

Plate 2: Chinese coolies and their boss in Borneo, circa 1890   56

Plate 3: Diagram of the Lanfang Kongsi Hall in Mandor in 1822   59

Plate 4: Chinese, probably from West Borneo, circa 1890   62

Plate 5: *Pasar* (marketplace) of Pemangkat, circa 1920   90

Plate 6: Gate to Chinese Temple on site of former kongsi hall   101

Plate 7: Picture of Lo Fong Pak, Chinese Temple, Sungai Purun   110

Plate 8: Ruins of temple to commemorate Lanfang Kongsi, Mandor   113

Plate 9: Chinese vegetable garden near Pontianak, 1998   133

Plate 10: *Pasar* (marketplace) of Capkala, circa 1920   139

Plate 11: Sultan of Sambas, 1919   164

Plate 12: Chinese stores rebuilt after fires of 1930s, circa 1949   166

Plate 13: Henry de Vogel, M. Hzn., Resident of West Borneo   178

Plate 14: Water containers in the Chinese quarter of Pontianak, circa 1920   180

Plate 15: Harbor of Pontianak, circa 1935   195

Plate 16: Mandor Memorial: Japanese soldiers humiliate women   204

Plate 17: Mandor Memorial: Multi-ethnic resistance to the Japanese   205

Plate 18: The Sultan of Pontianak with Resident K. A. James, circa 1920   206

Plate 19: The Mandor Memorial to victims of the Japanese massacre   209

Plate 20: *Pasar*, Anjungan, 2000   251

Plate 21: Lo Fong Pak memorial, Mandor, 2000   254

Plate 22: Wildcat gold miners near Mandor, 2000   263

PLATES

Plate 15 ...

Plate 16 ...

Plate 17 ...

Plate 18 ...

Plate 19 ...

Plate 20 ...

Plate 21 ...

Plate 22 ...

ACKNOWLEDGMENTS

Over the years during which this book took shape, many people have aided me with their writings, discussions, advice, assistance, and consolation. Those whose writings have contributed will find their names in the bibliography. I am grateful especially to colleagues and critics Sharon Carstens, Charles Coppel, Myra Sidharta, Claudine Salmon, Thee Kian Wee, Mona Lohanda, Ming Govaars-Tjia, Yuan Bingling, and Mély G. Tan; and in Pontianak, among others, Tangdililing, Hengky, Buyung Rivai and Eta, Hendry Jurnawan, and Melanie Susanto, even where we may differ.

Special thanks are due for material and intellectual help to Emeritus Prof. Bernhard Dahm, former head of Southeast Asia Studies, University of Passau, who acted as sponsor for the project in 1995-1997, during which time I benefited from a grant from the German Research Society (Deutsche Forschungsgemeinschaft). Without that support, it would never have seen the light of day. Prof. Dahm followed the project through to completion; he and Claudine Salmon, an anonymous reader in Ithaca, and especially Sharon Carstens, who put a careful eye to the text more than once, have offered helpful criticism, without bearing responsibility for any of my missteps. The editors of Cornell's Southeast Asia Program displayed patience and professionalism in dealing with a complex and sometimes messy task.

In 1995-1996 I was a Guest of the Rector at the Netherlands Institute of Advanced Study, Wassenaar. I am grateful to the Rector for this opportunity and to the staff, especially the library staff, for their support. In the summer of 1993, when the project was just taking shape, I was a Luce Visiting Scholar at Ohio University, Athens. There, Lian The-Milliner helped me find my way into the history of Chinese in Borneo, including those of Sarawak, whose experiences sometimes resembled, or even touched, those of Chinese in West Kalimantan.

The most important archives and libraries used were in the Netherlands, where I experienced unfailing patience and cooperation. These were, roughly in order of the time I spent in them: the library of the Royal Institute of Linguistics and Geography (KITLV); the National Archives (Algemeen Rijksarchief); the Netherlands Institute for War Documentation (NIOD); a private archives in Den Bosch; the Leiden University Library; and that of the Royal Institute for the Tropics, Amsterdam.

In particular, I thank the Indonesian National Archives (Arsip Nasional) and its staff for access to its valuable collection, as well as the Indonesian Institute for the Sciences (Lembaga Ilmu Pengetahuan Indonesia), which facilitated my research in Indonesia.

The libraries of Cornell University (Kroch Library, Echols Collection) and of the University of Göttingen (Niedersächsische Staats- und Universitätsbibliothek) and their personnel also aided the study. Cornell is a depository for many contemporary materials on West Kalimantan. During a brief visit to London, the author also consulted material in The British Library, India Office Library and Records (IOLR).

For drawing the maps, I am grateful to Birgit Heidhues. None of these persons or institutions bears responsibility for errors I have made.

A special word of thanks goes to my children for their implicit and explicit support. Once delightful distractions, they are now valued companions.

INTRODUCTION

This study is a history of a single province of Indonesia, West Kalimantan, and within the history of that huge territory, concentrates on what was once called the "Chinese Districts" and the town of Pontianak. The high proportion of the inhabitants who were ethnic Chinese imprinted a special cultural stamp upon these districts, giving them their name. By concentrating on the Chinese minority in that area during the nineteenth and twentieth centuries, this study aims to remedy a lack of information—and some misinformation—about an important minority concentration in Indonesia, retrieving where possible a record that is fast disappearing.

The story of the Chinese gold-mining kongsis of West Borneo (as West Kalimantan was called during the colonial era) and of the Dutch colonial attempts to suppress them is, at least superficially, widely known. What happened after the protracted struggles of the nineteenth century is, however, less known, and often difficult to reconstruct.

The Chinese of West Kalimantan are a unique group among Indonesia's Chinese minority, contrasting with the prevalent image of Chinese as economically successful businessmen. Most of them are, unlike the subjects of many recent studies, neither *towkays* nor tycoons, drawing attention because of their economic "success" as entrepreneurs and big businessmen. A few people in West Kalimantan may fit this description, but they are not typical of the community, which is made up for the most part of small traders, shop owners, farmers, and fishermen. Many Chinese in the province are poor, some even living at the subsistence level.

Nor are West Kalimantan's Chinese "sojourners," to use a term popularized by Wang Gungwu. They are long-term settlers, some of them with roots that go back to the eighteenth century, yet over the years, outsiders have branded them aliens because they held to a culture perceived as foreign. Superficially, they appear to have remained very "Chinese," above all retaining the use of the Chinese language over generations, in contrast to the long-resident ethnic Chinese of Java, who adopted Malay and other local languages, losing the ability to speak a Chinese language.

Nor is their presence, unlike Chinese settlement in some parts of the Indonesian Archipelago, a result of Dutch colonialism. The Dutch East India Company did, indeed, encourage Chinese to come and populate its newly-established headquarters in Batavia after 1619, while Dutch and other Western enterprises brought Chinese coolies in the nineteenth and early twentieth centuries to work mines and plantations, especially in the islands outside of Java. Chinese migrants arriving in West Kalimantan usually organized their own migration, using their own networks. In the early days, local Malay rulers encouraged them to come, but neither colonial authorities, who occasionally tried to cut off immigration, nor Western enterprises, promoted their coming.

Above all, the Chinese in West Kalimantan are a significant minority, numbering perhaps four hundred thousand persons, well over 10 percent of the population of the province. This region has been, historically, together with eastern Sumatra, Bangka-Belitung, and the Riau archipelago, one of four major concentrations of ethnic Chinese in Indonesia outside Java.

The first migration of Chinese to West Kalimantan remains difficult to document, but their history soon involves the attempts of the various indigenous and colonial polities in the region to suppress and control them, often through violence. Such attempts begin with the relations between Chinese-dominated mining communities and the Malay rulers of Sambas and Mempawah, who encouraged them to come to the island but then found the miners too powerful to control. Dutch colonial efforts followed, their exertions lasting for much of the nineteenth century. Batavia was determined to eliminate the special organizations of the Chinese—which it saw as establishing independent Chinese-dominated states within the colonial realm—at first by force, then, in the twentieth century, by administrative measures. At the same time, the Dutch recognized the "usefulness" of the Chinese settlers who had acquired a key position in the economy of West Borneo. During World War II, the Japanese occupied the territory and asserted supremacy over its peoples, trying brutally but unsuccessfully to break the Chinese economic grip on the territory and to subject the community to Japanese rule. Most recently, the Indonesian state extended its activities to West Kalimantan, seeking not only to control the political and economic activities of the ethnic Chinese, but attacking their cultural autonomy as well. In attempting to subordinate the minority, it too resorted to violence, putting an end to the history of the Chinese Districts by driving ethnic Chinese from rural areas of the province in 1967.

A second theme of this history is how strong community organization helped the Chinese to face, and sometimes to surmount, external threats. Like other Chinese communities abroad, those of West Kalimantan maintained a variety of bodies for internal control and the achievement of common purposes. At first, these were the famous kongsis, shareholding partnerships that ran the mines and—this is another unique attribute of West Kalimantan—governed extensive territories with all the trappings of independent states, including a kind of democratic governance that gave much of the community its say in political decisions. After the last of the kongsis was abolished in 1884, there followed a plethora of voluntary organizations with political (parties and "reading rooms"), social (language and hometown organizations, surname associations) economic (chambers of commerce, traders' and producers' associations), and cultural (schools, temple boards) purposes, not to mention the "secret societies," sworn brotherhoods whose activities strongly colored outsiders' perceptions of the community. Although most of these organizations were dissolved under the Suharto government after 1965, some have survived. Others are currently being reconstituted. This organizational proliferation helped to maintain cultural autonomy in a non-Chinese environment.

Some years ago, referring to the period before 1942, I called Chinese society in West Kalimantan "Little China in the Tropics,"[1] emphasizing their attempts, so

---

[1] Mary Somers Heidhues, "Little China in the Tropics: The Chinese in West Kalimantan to 1942," in *South China: State, Culture and Social Change during the 20th Century*, ed. L. M. Douw and P. Post (Amsterdam: North-Holland for Royal Netherlands Academy of Arts and Sciences, 1996), pp. 131-138. For rural Chinese communities in Southeast Asia, Mary Somers Heidhues,

typical for diaspora communities, to re-create the homeland abroad. Living in relatively compact and homogeneously Chinese settlements helped the Chinese of West Kalimantan to build something like a "little China." Yet they were "in the tropics" and the physical and social environment extracted its price. Houses were built of local materials and sometimes, as in local custom, on elevated foundations. Farming methods and, as will be shown in chapter three, fighting methods had to change. So did the rhythm of life, customary activities, even food and dress. They lived among, and often with, other non-Chinese peoples. In the end, the expansion of state power decisively limited the freedom to recreate any kind of "China" within Indonesia's borders. These people were "in the *Indonesian* tropics," with strongly limited freedom to develop a "little China."

Even if the minority in West Kalimantan deviates from the image of "rich and economically powerful," its economic activities form the third theme of this history. Chinese traders and farmers held a central place in the region's economy and contributed to the introduction of new crops and their adoption by native producers. West Borneo's economy in precolonial and colonial times had a strong export orientation and a propensity for smuggling. It still does. The economy of the province is highly centrifugal, not bound to Java (the administrative center of colonial and independent Indonesia), but linked to places beyond its borders like Singapore, Sarawak, and other destinations abroad. The centrifugal nature of West Kalimantan's economy is one of the reasons for recurrent conflict with the center.

Writing the history of this community is no simple task. There are no existing internal histories of the community as such, only of one of the kongsis. Most Chinese-language sources that might illuminate the community's past have been lost, probably irretrievably, because of lack of interest, an aggressive climate, and, above all, because of repression and violence. A few Chinese-language references survive, but they stem mostly from outsiders. Consequently, the following chapters rely on written sources, above all colonial documents and other materials in Dutch and Indonesian, to extract the history of the region and its people. In addition, the author visited Pontianak and the former Chinese Districts a number of times between 1963 and 2000. Until the end of that period, relying primarily on written sources offered the only possibility for reconstructing local history; neither the Indonesian government nor the author's personal situation would have permitted the kind of long-term field study that might provide deeper information on more recent developments in West Kalimantan. That will be a task for others, in a more open political environment, to complete. They will perhaps use this study for historical background.

A significant part of this work deals with Hakka Chinese, allowing a comparison with Bangka, with its miners and farmers, and with Hakkas in China and places abroad, especially their relations with indigenous peoples. Hakkas dominated the Chinese Districts and later moved as traders into the interior. As S. T. Leong, Sharon Carstens, and other scholars of "Hakkaology" have shown, this group of Han Chinese has shown a strong ability to preserve Chinese culture and Hakka identity in hostile surroundings, especially through their language. At the same time, Hakkas have, even in China, displayed a readiness to work together

"Chinese Settlements in Rural Southeast Asia: Unwritten Histories," in *Sojourners and Settlers: Histories of Southeast Asia and the Chinese in Honour of Jennifer Cushman*, ed. Anthony Reid (St Leonards: Allen and Unwin for Asian Studies Association of Australia, 1996), pp. 164-182.

with non-Chinese peoples.[2] The Chinese of West Kalimantan, especially the Hakkas (Teochiu dominate the urban community of Pontianak), often formed alliances with the Dayaks or indigenous peoples of the island, both through economic activities and through family relations. Thus, although Hakkas retained their language and identity, they often lived near to or at the level of indigenous peoples.

The author does not speak more than a little Mandarin Chinese, and no Hakka or Teochiu whatsoever. This was not the handicap it might have been for a more field-centered project. Especially during the more recent visits to Kalimantan, it was easy to converse with people in Indonesian, not least because Chinese-language schools had been closed down in 1965-1966 and replaced by education in Indonesian, although most Chinese still use Chinese languages in familiar settings.

Finally, although emphasizing the ethnic Chinese element in its population, this text should be a contribution to the social and economic history of West Kalimantan. The different ethnic groups of West Kalimantan, admittedly, have different histories, but this history tries to place the ethnic Chinese in the context of the past of the entire province and its people.

SPELLING, NAMES, MEASURES

Finding a reasonably consistent—or at least comprehensible—orthography for this text was no mean challenge.

Chinese Terms

First of all, the word "Chinese." Naturally, there are significant differences between residents of China and persons of Chinese descent living in Indonesia. Any term that would make this clear, even "ethnic Chinese," would simply be too clumsy to repeat each time I refer to the subject of this study. Therefore, the people of West Kalimantan who are of Chinese origin will be termed "Chinese," and it should be clear to the reader who is meant, and that most of these people are, today, Chinese Indonesians.

Chinese terms and proper names are presented in the following chapters as closely as possible to the way they are presented in the documents. The decision to follow the usage of the time and place is certainly open to challenge. The Dutch wrote down what they thought they heard, with no thought of a consistent orthography. The differences in pronunciation between Hakkas, Teochius, and some regional differences add to the confusion. Nevertheless, Mandarin Chinese was not understood by most Chinese in West Kalimantan before the twentieth century and to Mandarinize their names from an earlier era is to insert them into a national Chinese sphere to which they did not belong. Using local spellings puts these people in local history.

---

[2] See Leong Sow-theng, *Migration and Ethnicity in Chinese History: Hakkas, Pengmin, and their Neighbors,* ed. Tim Wright, introduction by G. William Skinner (Stanford: Stanford University Press, 1997); Sharon A. Carstens, "Pulai: Memories of a Gold Mining Settlement in Ulu Kelantan," *Journal of the Malaysi an Branch, Royal Asiatic Society* 53,1 (1980): 50-67 and Sharon A. Carstens, "Form and Content in Hakka Malaysian Culture," in *Guest People: Hakka Identity in China and Abroad,* ed. Nicole Constable (Seattle and London: University of Washington Press, 1996), pp. 124-148.

This does not solve all problems. Not only are many terms hard to decode in handwritten and sometimes even in printed sources; in a single document a person's name may be spelled in three different ways. How incomprehensible the results may be is shown by the military historian Hooyer,[3] who writes of the activities of "To Spoen," apparently unaware that this is the same as "Fosjoen (M. *heshun*)" and deciphers "Kioe Liong (*jiu long*, nine dragons)" as "Kioe Siong." I have opted for the most likely spelling, following the documents. The reader should beware that "oe" is pronounced "u" and, in words like "kapthai" and "laothai," "th" is pronounced like "t." However, for better understanding and consistency, a transcription in Mandarin Chinese follows (in *pinyin*) wherever possible, and there is a glossary of foreign words and their transcriptions, as far as they are known, at the end of the text.

Translations are mine, except as noted.

Malay/Indonesian Names and Place Names

Malay/Indonesian orthography has changed over the years. Indonesian personal and place names will, wherever possible, be given in modern spellings (*ejaan yang disempurnakan*). Some places in West Kalimantan that formerly had Chinese names now have Indonesian names, but in discussing the period of Chinese settlements, the older names will be used; I have tried to modernize the spelling. Otherwise, Indonesian prevails. Dutch names and terms are as found in the documents. For the colonial period, the name "West Borneo" is used. Today, Borneo usually applies to the entire island, Kalimantan to the Indonesian part of it. After independence, Indonesians called the province West Kalimantan, Kalimantan Barat, or Kalbar, and I follow that usage.

Currencies, Weights, and Measures

"Dollars" and "$" refer before the twentieth century to Spanish/Mexican silver dollars, the most widely accepted currency in the area during the eighteenth and nineteenth centuries.

"Rp" are Indonesian Rupiah. Their value in US dollars has fluctuated since independence, from 15 Rp to the US dollar in the 1950s to over 10,000 in recent times.

Dutch guilders, "*f*" (florin), were worth about US$.40 in the pre-World War II years. During the nineteenth century, there was a discrepancy between copper guilders, worth 100 *duit* or cents, and silver guilders, which were worth 120 *duit*. The Chinese quickly recognized the difference and acted accordingly.

Weights and measures were often not standardized. They are explained, as far as possible, in the text and glossary. In mining times, gold was often simply weighed in silver dollars.

---

[3] G. B. Hooyer, *De krijgsgeschiedenis van Nederlandsch-Indië van 1811-1894*, Vol. 2 (The Hague: van Cleef and Batavia: Kolff, 1896), p. 16.

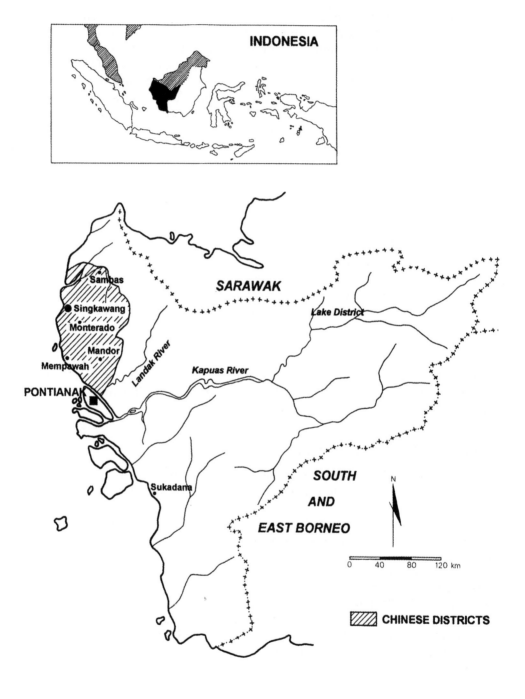

Map One. West Kalimantan, showing the Chinese Districts.

CHAPTER ONE

THE SETTING: THE PEOPLES AND THEIR HISTORIES

Today, boundaries clearly define where West Kalimantan begins and ends. The borders of Kalimantan Barat, Indonesia's fourth largest province, enclose an area of 146,807 square kilometers (roughly four times the size of the Netherlands) and a population in 1999 of about 3,850,000.[1] One of the world's largest islands, Borneo, which took its name from the Sultanate of Brunei, is bounded on the north and west by the South China Sea, on the south by the Java Sea, and on the east by the Straits of Makassar and the Sulawesi or Celebes Sea; the equator bisects it. When Indonesians call the Indonesian part of the island "Kalimantan," to most of them the name signifies "river of precious stones," although the term probably meant "land of raw sago" (*lamanta*), a product that grows abundantly in its swampy areas.[2]

Historically, the island of Borneo has been relatively impervious to outside influences. Dense tropical forest inhibited communication and colonization, and its immense land mass is hard to access from the coastal areas. Few bays or sheltered inlets offer ships a safe anchorage; sand bars obstruct the mouths of the great rivers that provide a path into the interior, making it difficult or impossible for larger ships to enter. The rivers themselves, because of low water levels in the dry season, rapids, or excessive rain in wet seasons, may not be navigable for much of the year.

Kalimantan, with well over two-thirds of the total area of the island of Borneo, was in colonial times a part of the Netherlands Indies. Sarawak and Sabah in the north form East Malaysia, part of the Federation of Malaysia; they were formerly under British rule. The Sultanate of Brunei, Brunei Darussalam, is a smaller, independent state (once a British protectorate) in the north, sharing no common border with Indonesia.

With that, the boundaries appear to be very clear. In the era of the Netherlands Indies, the Dutch divided their Borneo territory into two residencies, South and East Borneo and West Borneo or Borneo's Western Division

---

[1] West Borneo's geographic features are described, for example, in J. C. F. van Sandick and V. J. van Marle, *Verslag eener spoorwegverkenning in Noordwest-Borneo* (Batavia: Albrecht, 1919). More information is in G. L. Uljee, *Handboek voor de Residentie Westerafdeeling van Borneo* (Weltevreden: Visser & Co., 1925), and, in a nutshell, in Denys Lombard, "Guide Archipel IV: Pontianak et son arrière-pays," *Archipel* 28 (1984): 77-97.

[2] Victor T. King, *The Peoples of Borneo* (Oxford: Blackwell, 1993), p. 18. For an introduction to Borneo, see King, *Peoples*, pp. 1-28; Jan B. Avé and Victor T. King, *Borneo: The People of the Weeping Forest: Tradition and Change in Borneo* (Leiden: National Museum of Ethnology, 1986), pp. 7-8.

(*Westerafdeeling*). A final correction to the latter's borders was made in 1894,[3] while the border of the northern territories—now part of Malaysia—was delineated in 1884, 1891, and 1912.[4] After Indonesian independence, Kalimantan became a single province, but this changed in 1957, when what had been the Western Division in colonial times became the province (or first-level region) of West Kalimantan or Kalimantan Barat.[5] The former colonial territory of South- and East Borneo now forms three provinces: South, East, and Central Kalimantan. Yet, however well-defined the borders, even the international borders, people continue to cross them easily and events have often spilled across them. (See map one.)

The geographical subject of this study is not the entire province of Kalimantan Barat. It concentrates on the capital city of Pontianak, together with what was once called the "Chinese Districts," because the population of Chinese origin exercised such a strong influence on the area and its development. These districts reached north from Pontianak along the coast toward Sambas and the Sarawak border, following the more fertile river valleys for tens of kilometers inland. They formed part of the old native principalities of Sambas, Mempawah, and Pontianak. Technically, the Chinese Districts were, in the late nineteenth century, the two administrative districts of Sambas and Monterado (the capital of the Monterado district later moved to Singkawang), but in practice the areas of strong Chinese influence included Pontianak itself and the entire area west of the principality of Landak and north of the Kapuas River, including the former gold-mining regions dominated by Chinese mining organizations. In contemporary administrative terminology, this includes the municipality (*kotamadya*) of Pontianak and parts of the districts (*kabupaten; kabupaten* and *kotamadya* are second-level regions) of Pontianak and Sambas. (The capital of *kabupaten* Sambas—Singkawang—was due to separate from Sambas to become a *kotamadya* at the time of writing. The new capital of this *kabupaten* would be the town of Sambas.)

The Chinese began to settle in this area in considerable numbers about the middle of the eighteenth century. In the 1920s, Pontianak and the Chinese Districts, a fraction of the area of West Borneo, were home to two-thirds of the population of the residency and an estimated 90 percent of its ethnic Chinese.[6] A similar concentration prevails today.

PAST BOUNDARIES

Just as no clear territorial boundaries separated precolonial Southeast Asian polities, the peoples who inhabited the western part of Borneo in precolonial times

---

[3] Jacob Ozinga, *De economische ontwikkeling der Westerafdeeling van Borneo en de bevolkingsrubbercultuur* (Wageningen: Gebr. Zomer en Keuning, 1940), p. 84.

[4] Graham Irwin, *Nineteenth-Century Borneo: A Study in Diplomatic Rivalry* (Singapore: Donald Moore Books, 1967), pp. 206-207; see also *Koloniaal Verslag* (1891): 2 (Bijlage, Verslag der Handelingen van de Staaten-Generaal [Appendix, Minutes of the Estates-General] [title varies], 1866-1923).

[5] Harlem Siahaan, *Golongan Tionghoa di Kalimantan Barat: Tinjauan ekomonis historis* (Jakarta: Leknas-LIPI, mimeo, 1974), pp. 37-38.

[6] H. Zondervan, "De economische ontwikkeling van Nederlandsch-Borneo," *Indische Gids* 50,1 (1928): 611-612. Although 90 percent may be an exaggeration, the concentration remains.

did not define their space according to the artificial borders of modern times. O. W. Wolters's description of traditional Southeast Asian realms certainly applied to West Borneo:

> There were no "borders" in the modern sense but only porous peripheries . . . . ecological factors kept ethnic groups in habitation zones where they could live comfortably. There were, of course, vital economic interdependencies such as upstream and downstream, forest and agricultural peoples, forest collectors, and port polities.[7]

More important than borders were the coastal and riverine centers of power; among those on the island of Borneo, the northern seaport of Brunei was one early focus of trade. This Islamic sultanate claimed hegemony over other port centers, so that in time the whole island came to be called by its name. In the seventeenth and especially the eighteenth centuries, other harbor polities came onto the scene, and some of them challenged Brunei's dominance. Banjarmasin was the trading center for the south. There, and in the southern part of the West Coast, influences from Java were more important than those of Brunei or of neighboring Malay areas.

In the seventeenth century, Sukadana was the most important port in the West, apparently because it controlled an entrance to the great Kapuas River system that dominates the western part of the island. Landak, inland on the River Landak, the major tributary of the Kapuas, monopolized the source of diamonds in the region. These two principalities had been linked to the Javanese realm of Majapahit, and, in the seventeenth century, the Sultanate of Banten in West Java claimed authority over them. Sukadana was hardly a metropolis; the port may have had no more than five thousand inhabitants at its peak.[8]

Larger Malay port cities in Sumatra or along the Malay Peninsula (like Palembang in the early period of Srivijaya or Melaka in the fifteenth century) were primarily entrepôts, where traders exchanged products brought from far away, as well as collecting and exchanging local goods. Bornean ports tended, because of their less central location on international sea lanes, to be dependent only on the exchange of local goods for imported products. China was a prominent customer. Visitors and traders from China reached the island well before the thirteenth century, although the number who settled certainly was very small in early times. Borneo's exports, jungle and marine products, were exchanged for salt, rice, textiles, and other consumer goods. Early on, Borneo's minerals—gold and diamonds—must also have entered international commerce.[9]

---

[7] O. W. Wolters, "Southeast Asia as a Southeast Asian Field of Study," *Indonesia* 59 (October 1994): 10. As van Goor points out, even the Dutch government was not willing, "until far into the nineteenth century... to indicate exactly where its territorial claims ended." See J. van Goor, "Seapower, Trade and State Formation: Pontianak and the Dutch 1780-1840," in *Trading Companies in Asia, 1600-1830*, ed. J. van Goor (Utrecht: HES Uitgevers, 1986), p. 85.

[8] Ozinga, *Economische ontwikkeling*, pp. 27-28; Valentijn, at the beginning of the eighteenth century, estimated that the town had six hundred houses, cited in Dr. [John] Leyden, "Sketch of Borneo," *Verhandelingen van het Bataviaasch Genootschap van Kunsten en Wetenschappen* (1814), pp. 1-64, repr. in *Notices of the Indian Archipelago and Adjacent Countries* (1837), p. 99.

[9] Compare the distinction between the two kinds of ports in Anthony Reid, *The Lands below the Winds*, vol. I of *Southeast Asia in the Age of Commerce 1450-1680*, (New Haven: Yale University Press, 1988), pp. 57, 60.

Lesser coastal kingdoms to the north of Sukadana competed for trade. Archaeological discoveries in the area around Sambas indicate that this region participated in international trade as early as the eighth to tenth centuries. Its location in the northwest of the island and a relatively good anchorage favored the area (the capital was not situated in its present location), which also benefited from the export of gold.[10] Farther south were other principalities—some coastal, like Mempawah, some farther inland—each with a relatively well-defined center but only a vague boundary. Marriage and family bonds reinforced political relationships within kingdoms, as well as relationships to outside kingdoms like Banten or Riau; nonetheless these alliances were fluid and often short-lived.

Essential to these small principalities was their geographical situation at or near the mouths of rivers. Borneo's great rivers, which arose in the low mountains toward the center of the island, acted as its highways. In the early nineteenth century, only footpaths crossed the island's jungles where the rivers failed to penetrate; in the 1830s, the territory had "no carriage road in the whole country, nor a single horse or beast of burthen."[11] River basins also form Borneo's major regions: in the east, the Mahakam and its tributaries are the route to the interior, while the Barito river system defines southern Borneo and the Kapuas River and its tributaries the western part. Rulers established control of major or subsidiary river sheds, of their trade and traffic, and of the people who lived along the banks by setting up headquarters near the river mouth. Like most other Malay principalities, those of western Borneo were really "only an aggregation of river settlements."[12]

Rulers of coastal harbors placed themselves just far enough upstream to defend themselves against pirate attacks from the sea and to gain a sheltered anchorage. In fact, the immediate coastal area was hardly inhabited. Swampy and subject to frequent flooding, and exposed to attack from marauders, the coasts were largely ill-suited for dwelling or cultivation.

A pattern of *hilir* (downstream) and *hulu* (upstream) relations enabled rulers to support their realms to a significant extent through trade. Smaller potentates would settle farther upriver, each with control of the trade passing their vantage point at the mouth of a tributary, but with only partial control of their territory. They paid tribute to, and traded with, rulers situated downriver. Most of the downstream rulers and their immediate subjects were, by the eighteenth century, Muslims and speakers of Malay. The upriver people might not be Malay or Muslim at all; these groups were commonly called Dayaks. This water-aligned system of tributaries, both hydraulic and political, was common among Malay sultanates in Borneo, parts of Sumatra, and the Malay Peninsula.

---

[10] On archeological finds in Sambas, see for example, E. Edwards McKinnon, "The Sambas Hoard: Bronze Drums and Gold Ornaments Found in Kalimantan in 1991," *Journal of the Malaysian Branch, Royal Asiatic Society* 67,1 (1994): 9-28. Earlier studies include Tan Yeok Seong, *Notes and Views on Sambas Treasures* (Singapore: Nanyang Book Company, 1948); Roland Braddell, "A Note on Sambas and Borneo," *Journal of the Malayan Branch, Royal Asiatic Society* 22,4 (1949): 1-15; and Tom Harrisson, "Gold and Indian Influences in West Borneo," *Journal of the Malayan Branch, Royal Asiatic Society* 22,4 (1949): 33-110.

[11] George Windsor Earl, *The Eastern Seas, or Voyages and Adventures in the Indian Archipelago* (London: W. H. Allen 1837, repr. Singapore: Oxford University Press, 1971), p. 222.

[12] J. R. Logan, "Traces of the Origin of the Malay Kingdom of Borneo Proper," *Journal of the Indian Archipelago* 2 (1848): 513.

River sheds did not necessarily confine the inhabitants to a defined territory, however. Footpaths in the *hulu* connected one river area with another and offered upstream people a means of circumventing the authority of a downstream ruler if he became too demanding. Sometimes, port rulers extended their influence to other ports, moving upriver or by sea along the coast, thereby gaining influence over neighboring river sheds.[13]

Trade and power relations brought the Malay coastal principalities of western Borneo into a wider zone of principalities. The seas linked them to Malay kingdoms elsewhere, like Johor-Riau, Kedah, and Siak, or to the islands of Bangka and Belitung. They also brought first Indian and then Islamic influences to the island; Chinese and Arab traders visited, as did traders from nearer locations. For the coastal dwellers, their Malay identity and Islamic religion connected them to a world encompassing much of the Malay-Indonesian archipelago.

Malay royal chronicles (*hikayat*) and genealogies (*silsilah*) represent the Bornean polities as part of a wider space that reaches from Sulawesi to Sumatra and the Malay Peninsula. The region is united by a common culture, although it is divided by rivalries in trade and warfare. The elite confirmed the unifying aspects of language, religion, and customs through intermarriage. Their chronicles refer to the same heroes and events; even their language is remarkably uniform, however much spoken Malay may have varied from place to place.[14] After the introduction of Islam, this space expanded ideally to include the entire Islamic world, with Mecca as its center, but in the images of Bornean Malay chronicles, Mecca remained a distant and symbolic center,[15] and the Malay World itself was the focus of power and interaction.

THE PEOPLES

Three major ethnic groups—today people speak of "three pillars"—have dominated the history of West Kalimantan: Dayak, Malay, and Chinese. Writing on ethnic and national identities in Southeast Asia often stresses that ethnicity is not necessarily the result of physical appearance or genetic inheritance; ethnicity is also the result of social and environmental processes and, to some extent, it is an

---

[13] This model of upstream-downstream relations is based on Bennet Bronson, "Exchange at the Upstream and Downstream Ends: Notes toward a Functional Model of the Coastal State in Southeast Asia," in *Economic Exchange and Social Interaction in Southeast Asia*, ed. Karl L. Hutterer (Ann Arbor: Michigan Papers on Southeast Asia, 1977), pp. 39-52. Muhammed Gade Ismail, "Politik perdagangan Melayu di kesultanan Sambas, Kalimantan Barat: masa akhir kesultanan 1808-1818" (M.A. thesis, Universitas Indonesia, 1985) applies the model of Bronson to power relations in Sambas in the early nineteenth century; see also Muhammed Gade Ismail, "Trade and State Power: Sambas (West Borneo) in the Early Nineteenth Century," in *State and Trade in the Indonesian Archipelago*, ed. G. J. Schütte (Leiden: KITLV Press, 1994), pp. 143-44 and, for a general view of *hulu-hilir* relations in Sumatra, J. Kathirithamby-Wells, "*Hulu-hilir* Unity and Conflict: Malay Statecraft in East Sumatra before the Mid-Nineteenth Century," *Archipel* 45 (1993): 77-95.

[14] A. C. Milner, *Kerajaan: Malay Political Culture on the Eve of Colonial Rule* (Tucson: University of Arizona Press, 1982), pp. 3-4, passim.

[15] See Denys Lombard, "Vers la conception d'un espace géographique et d'un temps linéaire," in *Le carrefour javanais: Essai d'histoire globale*, Vol. II, *Les réseaux asiatiques* (Paris: Éditions de l'École des Hautes Études en Sciences Sociales, 1990), pp. 196-200, where he discusses the vision of space in the *Hikayat Hang Tuah*.

artificial construct.[16] Especially in precolonial times, people might change or, as Wolters says,[17] manipulate their ethnic identities. Even as late as the mid-nineteenth century, colonial reports occasionally complain that individuals are "more Chinese than Malay" or "more Malay than Chinese," suggesting that people often failed to stay put in the ethnic boxes the administrators assigned them.[18]

Certainly, the colonial powers endeavored to classify and solidify ethnic identities. For most people, however, and at most times, being Chinese, Malay, or Dayak meant that a person differed from members of other designated groups in multiple ways: by appearance, clothing, language, religion, housing, and occupation. To most people, the boundaries defining these three identities were tangible, even if boundary crossing took place. A Dayak might, by adopting Malay language, dress, and religion, become Malay, *masuk Melayu* (literally, "enter Malayhood"). He might then be considered a Malay and no longer Dayak—although converts frequently retained identifiable Dayak cultural traits.

In addition, Borneo's society is characterized, even in recent times, by a high degree of ethnically linked economic specialization, which reinforces identities and makes the lines separating groups more impermeable. Only in most recent times has such specialization become less distinct, but it has in no way disappeared. Ethnicity may sometimes be a matter of choice, but certain long-lasting and established "primordial" qualities also define ethnicity, and even sub-ethnic identities, as they are experienced and understood in western Borneo.[19]

---

[16] Benedict Anderson, *Imagined Communities: Reflections on the Origin and Spread of Nationalism* (London: Verso, 1983) sees nations as at least partly constructed, influenced by popular literature and the press, among other factors. Those who see ethnicity as flexible and not determined include Fredrik Barth, "Introduction," in *Ethnic Groups and Boundaries*, ed. Fredrik Barth (London: Allen and Unwin, 1969), pp. 9-38, and the "situational" approach of contributions to Charles F. Keyes, ed., *Ethnic Change* (Seattle: University of Washington Press, 1982), and Judith Nagata, "What is a Malay? Situational Selection of Ethnic Identity in a Plural Society," *American Ethnologist* 1,2 (1974): 331-350. On the other hand, Anthony D. Smith, *The Ethnic Origins of Nations* (Oxford: Blackwell, 1986) believes ethnic identities are persistent and long-lived. On the ethnic identity of the Chinese in Indonesia, see, among others, Mary Somers Heidhues, "Identity and the Minority: Ethnic Chinese on the Indonesian Periphery," *Indonesia Circle* 70 (1996): 181-192, and Mary Somers Heidhues, "Chinese Identity in the Diaspora: Religion and Language in West Kalimantan, Indonesia," in *Nationalism and Cultural Revival in Southeast Asia: Perspectives from the Centre and the Region*, ed. Sri Kuhnt-Saptodewo et al. (Wiesbaden: Harrassowitz, 1997), pp. 201-210. For ethnicity in Borneo, see Victor T. King, *Ethnic Classification and Ethnic Relations: A Borneo Case Study* (Hull: Centre for South-East Asian Studies, University of Hull, 1979).

[17] "In some areas, there was a considerable degree of bilingualism and opportunities for manipulating one's identity. Bilingualism signifies that people with different origins had learnt to live together." Wolters, "Southeast Asia," p. 10.

[18] Monthly reports from West Borneo, Short Report, Assistant Resident of Sambas, August 1853, located in Arsip Nasional Republik Indonesia (ANRI), Jakarta, colonial archives, Borneo's Westerafdeeling (BW) 6/1 (90). There are scattered references to persons of double ethnic identity, for example a Chinese official mentioned in Political Report, West Borneo, 1866, ANRI BW 2/4 (224).

[19] Smith, *Ethnic Origins of Nations*. On ethnic specialization in Borneo, see King, *Ethnic Classification*, p. 19 and King, *Peoples*, pp. 38-39. Sub-groups of the major ethnic groups also differed from one another, having their own "ethnic boundaries," as will be seen in the case of the ethnic Chinese.

DAYAKS

While Dayaks are generally considered to be the "indigenous" people of the island, the name "Dayak" nevertheless covers a multiplicity of groups who constitute about 40 percent of the current population of the province.[20] The name, which may mean something like "uplander" or possibly even "slave," applies to non-Muslim peoples with differing cultures. Although some persons regard "Dayak" as a pejorative term, or see "Daya" as more polite, the name is widely used both by non-Dayaks and by people indigenous to the island, and, among the latter, it is currently favored by young intellectuals and political leaders as the term that best describes their own ethnicity.

Traits that distinguish certain Dayak groups from others[21]—for example, differences in their language or social systems, or differences in the extent to which they cultivate wet rice or dry rice or subsist as nomadic collectors, or whether they live in long houses, and so on—can be very significant to the people themselves, and they are certainly important to anthropologists. However, it is very difficult to identify Dayak sub-groups in the sources (many of them Dutch reports) that will be used for this discussion, since these documents often ignore such distinctions. Furthermore, among the Dayak groups living nearer the coast and those who maintain frequent contact with Malays and Chinese, group identity may became blurred.[22] If, in the following discussion, the Dayaks seem to be stereotypically portrayed and sketched as bit players, this is a result, in part, of a vagueness that characterizes both the available sources and the changeable identities of the sub-groups themselves.

In the coastal kingdoms, members of the Malay courts and other associates of the rulers held authority over Dayaks, including the right to their labor and taxes, through appanages. The *Hikayat Upu Daeng Menambun*, a Malay history of Mempawah, describes how this was done. In this case, an inheritance is being divided, and people ask about

> the Dayak of Mempawah, Pebahar and Malingsam, in order to apportion them correctly. For from of old it had been the custom that the Pangeran Mangku [one of the princes of the Mempawah court] ruled over the Sekayuk Pebahar Dayak, and the man who became Panembahan [Mempawah's ruler] over the Sekayuk Mempawah.[23]

When, in the late nineteenth century, the Dutch extended their authority to places where few Malay courts existed, they began to rule some Dayak groups of the

---

[20] John McBeth and Margot Cohen, "Murder and Mayhem: Ethnic Animosity Explodes in Bloodshed," *Far Eastern Economic Review*, February 20, 1997, p. 27.

[21] Often named for the river area where they lived, Dayaks who moved might or might not take their name with them. Report of Major Andresen, 1852, cited in E. B. Kielstra, "Bijdrage tot de geschiedenis van Borneo's Westerafdeeling," Part IV, *Indische Gids* 11,1 (1889): 951.

[22] Ozinga, *Economische ontwikkeling*, p. 32.

[23] Fritz Schulze, *Die Chroniken von Sambas und Mempawah: Einheimische Quellen zur Geschichte West-Kalimantans* (Heidelberg: Julius Groos, 1991), p. 63 (Malay transliteration); p. 115 (German translation). The *Tuhfat al-Nafis* also refers to this; see Raja Ali Haji bin Ahmad, *The Precious Gift (Tuhfat al-Nafis): An Annotated Translation by Virginia Matheson and Barbara Watson Andaya* (Kuala Lumpur: Oxford University Press, 1982), pp. 77-78, 81.

interior directly. Otherwise, they relied on Malay appanage holders to control them.[24]

The Dayaks who lived near the coast or along major rivers are sometimes called "Malayic Dayaks," because of cultural and language affinity to Malays. The boundary between them could be especially porous in this environment, with many Dayaks crossing over to become more "Malay" without completely deserting their Dayak past. Some "Malay" rulers also acquired legitimacy or extended their power by marrying into Dayak ruling families, as did Daeng Menambun of Mempawah.[25]

Usually, Malay nobles or retainers who were holders of appanages mobilized the Dayaks to provide the Malay rulers with labor and supplies, including fighting men for the court in wartime, and useful goods like rice or, for foreign trade, jungle products. After the eighteenth century, the rulers often used—or tried to use—Dayak fighters to subdue the Chinese.[26]

Ideally, under the *hulu-hilir* system, which governed much of Malay-Dayak relations, trade and tribute were mutually beneficial: Malays could not live and forage in the forest; Dayaks, as a rule, avoided seafaring and lacked the external relations necessary for trade abroad. Over time, however, the Dayak appear to have become the weaker of the two partners in this relationship,[27] and many colonial officials and other observers felt the Malay-Dayak relationship was purely exploitative.

Examples of this unequal relationship between Malay rulers and Dayaks under colonial rule abound. In 1851, for example, Dayaks paid the ruler of Sambas or his appanage holders a *hasil* (yield, crop) of at least five to ten guilders annually, in cash, produce, or gold dust, as well as rice at the harvest. The ruler profited from trade with the interior and from time to time expected extra "gifts."[28]

In 1873, the Gado Dayak of Mempawah complained that the Malay authorities were assessing onerous fines not sanctioned by custom. If they laid out *ladang* (dry fields) too close to paths, or set fire carelessly to surrounding plots, the fine was fifteen guilders. Although traditional Dayak punishments for adultery existed, the ruler instead demanded a month of forced labor from those brought to justice for this violation; even offenses like stealing fruit attracted his attention.

---

[24] The Dutch took control over the Dayaks of Lara-Bengkayang from a member of the Sambas court in 1823, but they returned it to the court later. T. A. C. van Kervel, D. W. J. C. van Lijnden, "Bijdrage tot de kennis van Borneo: De hervorming van den maatschappelijken toestand ter westkust van Borneo," *Tijdschrift voor Nederlandsch Indië* 15,1 (1853): 186. Pontianak seems to have had few or no appanages; members of court were given a salary by the sultan. J. J. K. Enthoven, *Bijdragen tot de Geographie van Borneo's Wester-Afdeeling* (Supplement, *Tijdschrift van het Koninklijk Aardrijkskundig Genootschap, 1901-1903*) (Leiden: Brill, 1903), p. 851.

[25] This discussion of ethnic groups in West Kalimantan draws especially from King, *Ethnic Classification* (he adopts the term "Malayic Dayaks" from A. Hudson) and King, *Peoples*. On Mempawah, see Schulze, *Chroniken von Sambas und Mempawah*, pp. 19-20, and below.

[26] P. M. van Meteren Brouwer, "De geschiedenis der Chineesche Districten der Wester-Afdeeling van Borneo van 1740-1926," *Indische Gids* 49,2 (1927): 1063.

[27] C. Kater, "Aanteekeningen op Prof. Veth's 'Westerafdeeling van Borneo', 5de boek van het tweede deel," *Indische Gids* 5,1 (1883): 12. Although he felt the colonial system had tipped the balance in favor of the Malays, Kater wrote, "In general [Veth's] description of the Malay is too dark, that of the Dayak too rose-colored."

[28] R. C. van Prehn Wiese, "Aantekeningen betreffende Borneo's Westkust," *Tijdschrift voor Indische Taal-, Land- en Volkenkunde* 10,1 (1861): 140-141.

He assessed every family two guilders for a new ironwood fence being built around his palace, and demanded a contribution for his wife's funeral.[29]

A later example cites a tax or *hasil-Dayak* of *f*7.50 per family, assessed in cash. Adult males had to provide twenty days of corvée labor. Ten percent of the value of natural products exported (this was called *sepuluh-satu*, out of ten, one) went to the ruler, and he, or the appanage holders, also demanded additional "voluntary" contributions.[30]

Without political organization beyond the level of *kampung* or settlement, dependent on imported goods like salt,[31] the Dayaks had little chance for successful confrontation with outsiders. Apart from "weapons of the weak" like adulteration, short-weighing, foot-dragging, pleading insolvency, and other strategies,[32] the Dayak had few effective methods for defending themselves against exploitation. When pressed too hard, they might resort to violence against neighboring Malay settlements or simply flee. In the case of the Gado Dayaks, violence had brought the matter to the attention of colonial authorities.

The Dutch regarded the Chinese, too, as exploiters of the Dayaks. The Chinese began, in the eighteenth and early nineteenth centuries, to displace the Malay aristocracy as the trading partners and patrons of the Dayaks. Whether the Chinese immigrants "drove out" the Dayaks from their territory as they came to settle in West Borneo is a more complicated question. In 1859, an official came upon a group of Dayaks who had fled from attacks by Chinese gold miners in the 1840s, who were then living far in the interior on the border with Sarawak, in a miserable settlement plagued by disease and meager harvests. Their flight had only brought them more suffering.[33] But this seems to have been an exception; more often the Dayaks stayed near Chinese settlements.

Protecting the Dayaks from rapacious rulers, appanage holders, and Chinese exploiters provided a reason for expansion of Dutch colonial rule. Governor-General Rochussen, in his 1851 farewell address, made the "uplift and protection" of the

---

[29] Report of Resident, Pontianak, February 10, 1873, in Algemeen Rijksarchief, The Hague (ARA), Archief Ministerie van Koloniën, 1850-1900 (1932), 2.10.02 V. 13.5.1873 (76).

[30] This example is from Ngabang, Landak, in 1883. J. ten Haaft, Memorie van Overgave (memorandum of transfer), Landak, 1934, ARA 2.10.39, MvO KIT 984, p. 73. Inventaris van de Memories van Overgave, 1849-1962, Westerafdeeling Borneo, MMK (Ministerie van Koloniën) 260-265 and KIT-Collectie, KIT 980-992. See the similar listing for Sambas Dayaks in Muhammed Gade Ismail, "Politik perdagangan," pp. 99-101. It could be argued that the oppression of the Dayaks became worse under colonial rule, because Dutch support of the rulers changed the balance of power, but that is a matter for another study.

[31] Salt normally had to be imported to Borneo. Humidity and rainfall were too high to permit salt production by evaporation, even in the coastal areas. Some salt springs do exist in the interior. See J. H. Crockewit, "De zoutbron aan de Spauk-rivier, landschap Sintang, residentie Westerafdeeling van Borneo," *Natuurkundig Tijdschrift voor Nederlandsch-Indië* 12,2 (1856): 85-90.

[32] To borrow the title of James C. Scott's study of resistance by the powerless, *Weapons of the Weak: Everyday Forms of Peasant Resistance* (New Haven: Yale University Press, 1985).

[33] Report of Assistant Resident van Gaffron, ARA 2.10.02 V. 22.5.62 (38). This description fits the Dayaks of Lara who were driven from Bengkayang (Lara) by the Chinese. The troubles lasted from the beginning of 1842 to October 1843 (see also chapter two).

Dayak a major goal of policy for the West Coast.[34] Another Dutchman, Baron von Hoëvell, publisher of an influential colonial journal and man of the church who never even saw the island, thought the Dayak were "benevolent, tractable, hospitable, not averse to work, and simple," adding, "This good and strong people is entirely entangled in the serpents' coils of the Malays."[35]

The Dutch resolution to "protect" the Dayaks led in subsequent decades to the imposition of measures against the Malay rulers, and for the Chinese, to the enactment of restrictions on settlement outside the towns:

> Certainly the Dayaks are left open to all kinds of abuses on the part of these [Chinese] people, and for this reason the settlement of Chinese outside of the residential quarters set aside for their nation should be prevented as far as possible, although their visiting various parts of this region for the purpose of trade may take place freely and without hindrance.[36]

Did the writer see the contradiction in what he was proposing?

In spite of their reputation as exploiters, the Chinese also forged close and mutually beneficial links with the Dayaks. A mid-nineteenth century report says of some Dayaks, "they would rather attach themselves to the Chinese than to the Malays."[37] Conflicts with the Chinese were not typical: the Chinese in Monterado frequently invited the neighboring Dayaks to their feasts and into their houses.[38]

These Dayaks were distancing themselves, it seems, from the political and cultural influences of the Malay power holders, using the presence of the Chinese to gain more freedom for themselves. There are repeated references to intermarriage, and a report adds "sometimes the Dayaks adopt many of the Chinese customs"; some even spoke Chinese. Chinese men would marry Dayak women (Chinese and part-Chinese women usually married only Chinese men).[39] Especially after the dissolution of the Chinese mining organizations, Dayaks worked in Chinese-operated gold mines.[40] As late as the 1940s, Dayaks were still adopting some

---

[34] J. J. Rochussen, "Redevoering, gehouden bij de overgave van het bestuur aan den heer Duymaer van Twist, in den Raad van Indië, op den 12den Mei 1851," *Tijdschrift voor Nederlandsch Indië* 18,1 (1856): 56.

[35] W. R. Baron von Hoëvell, "Onze roeping op Borneo," *Tijdschrift voor Nederlandsch Indië* 14,2 (1852): 188-89. Compare the invective of W. L. de Sturler, *Voorlezing over den innerlijken Rijkdom onzer Oost-Indische bezittingen in verband met den oorsprong en den aard der zedelijke en maatschappelijke gesteldheid der bevolking van die gewesten* (Groningen: J. Oomkens, 1849), pp. 13-16, against the Chinese who with their usury "have laid an iron yoke" on the Dayak and should be forced to desist.

[36] Political Report for 1872, Resident (Van der Schalk) of Pontianak, March 13, 1873, ANRI BW 2/10 (230). For more on residence restrictions in the twentieth century, see chapter five.

[37] E. A. Francis, *Herinneringen uit den levensloop van een "Indisch" ambtenaar van 1815 tot 1851* (Batavia: van Dorp: 1856-1860), 1: 238. Many other sources confirm the affinity between Dayaks and Chinese.

[38] E. de Waal, *West Borneo*, vol. 8 of *Onze Indische Financien*, ed. E. A. G. J. van Delden (The Hague: M. Nijhoff, 1907), p. 25, referring to a letter of van de Graaft.

[39] The report, from ca. 1858, is cited in Kielstra, "Bijdrage," Part XIX, *Indische Gids* 14,1 (1892): 1265. On language, see for example G. L. Uljée, *Handboek*, p. 48.

[40] H. E. D. Engelhard, "Bijdragen tot de kennis van het grondbezit in de Chineesche Districten," *Bijdragen tot de Taal-, Land- en Volkenkunde* 51,7 (1900): 256. Usually Dayak laborers were less expensive than Chinese coolies.

Chinese customs: many spoke some Chinese; some maintained house altars in the Chinese style; and some women wore Chinese slacks instead of short skirts or sarongs. In addition, Dayaks imitated the immigrants' rice-growing methods, laying out rain-fed *sawahs* (wet rice fields) and sometimes even beginning to irrigate them.[41]

Over the period of Chinese settlement in West Borneo, from the eighteenth to the twentieth century, Chinese immigrants had formed links with many of these "original" inhabitants of the island. These links were sometimes profitable, giving the Dayaks more liberty from Malay overlords and introducing new economic possibilities, but at other times the two sides and their interests clashed. The Malays, and later the Dutch, used certain groups of Dayaks to put down the Chinese; other Dayak groups sided with them. Just as ethnic boundary crossing existed, so did ethnic alliances shift, and no group presented a monolithic front with, or against, another.

This insight cannot, however, be gained from Dayak sources. In the past, Dayak cultures were non-literate. Their histories were transmitted orally. However important these memories were, and are, to Dayak societies, they are not helpful in constructing a history of the Chinese in West Kalimantan.

MALAYS

Malays represent perhaps 40 percent of the current population of West Kalimantan, being roughly equal in numbers to the Dayaks. Like other ethnic groups, Malays were not a homogenous community. Historically, differences in status created social divisions. Members of the courts, most of them relatives of the ruler or of his important retainers, formed one distinct social group. Others groups included, for instance, freemen, craftsmen, soldiers, peasants, fishermen. Malays, as Muslims, were usually free of taxes and corvée. *Masuk Melayu*, "becoming a Malay," was possible in theory for anyone who chose to follow Islam and Malay customs, but recently converted Dayaks or people of mixed Malay-Dayak origin were not always accepted as full Malays in the nineteenth century; such people were often distinguished as *anak bumi*, children of the land, or *orang sungai*, people of the river.[42]

An 1832 account outlines a more extensive social differentiation among Malays, with *raja* (princes, rulers), *priyayi* (their children, the upper nobility), *mantri* (nobles and officials), *panggawa* (servants of the state), *anak sungai* or *anak desa* (children of the river or village, free farmers), *anak dagang* (traders, usually non-Malay outsiders), *orang berutang* or *kawan* (debtors or retainers), and *budak* (slaves). Important administrative officials were close relatives of the ruler. The principality of Sambas, for example had a sultan, six *mantri raja* (court officials), who were the Pangerans (*pangeran*, prince) Bandahara, Pakunegara, Temenggung, Sumadilaga, Sumadisastra, and Laxamana. Then followed four *kiai* (Islamic

---

[41] General Memorandum, Sub-district Bengkayang, District Singkawang, by M. Waisvisz, July 12, 1938-May 20, 1941, ANRI BB 287, 38-39.

[42] Ismail, "Politik perdagangan," p. 90. Some Western sources use *anak sungai*, cf. Kielstra, "Bijdrage," Part IV, *Indische Gids* 11,1 (1889): 951. Conversion of Dayaks was not a primary goal of Malay rulers, since it would deprive them of taxable subjects. See General Report for 1880, ANRI BW 5/11 (26).

teachers), four *orang kaya* (nobles), and an *imam* (an Islamic official). The crown prince, if there was one, might be called Pangeran Ratu.[43]

Trade was the basis of the rulers' wealth; they also assumed title to the lands and their people.[44] Princes and relatives of the sultans depended on favors and appanages from these rulers for their income. If they were not satisfied, members of the royal family might challenge the ruler's position, resort to piracy, or squeeze their Dayak subordinates. Even non-noble Malays seldom worked the land; many were fishermen or craftsmen. Only a few were subsistence farmers.[45] The courts obtained rice from Dayaks or through external trade.

Among, or culturally related to, the "Malays" were other groups that are sometimes subsumed under that name. In the early eighteenth century, Bugis adventurers from Sulawesi entered the area, allying with the royal houses like Mempawah and Sambas. Like Malays, they were Muslims, fitting well into Malay society, but they had their own language, customs, and economic roles. During the following century, other Bugis followed the first adventurers and became, not just nobles or retainers, but settlers and traders. Most members of this ethnic group now live in the neighborhood of Pontianak.

In time, other immigrants from the surrounding islands joined them, including Javanese (recalling the historic connections of Sukadana and Landak to Majapahit and later to Banten), Madurese, Minangkabaus, and others. Common to these groups was their adherence to Islam. In the twentieth century, small numbers of non-Islamic peoples from the Indonesian archipelago also migrated to West Kalimantan, and the name *pribumi*, indigenous, came to include all autochthonous Indonesians—the Muslim and non-Muslim immigrants, the Malays, and the Dayaks—but not, at least until the late twentieth century, the Chinese.

The Arabs made up a special group. They were of foreign origin, but since they were Muslims, the men intermarried easily with Malays. After the founding of the Sultanate of Pontianak by an Arab house, Arabs, as rulers and subjects of the rulers, acquired a kind of "honorary Malay" status. Like Malays, they were free of certain taxes or, in colonial times, of restrictions on landholding. This "honorary Malay" status contradicted their legal status in colonial times. In the rest of the colony, persons of Arab descent were "Foreign Asiatics,"[46] but in West Borneo, Arabs were seen as natives.

---

[43] E. A. Francis, "Westkust van Borneo in 1832," *Tijdschrift voor Neêrland's Indië* 4,2 (1842): 14-17; Ismail, "Politik perdagangan," pp. 77-82. Compare Andresen's list of four princes: Ratu, Tommonggeng, Paku Negara, and Bendahara, cited in Kielstra, "Bijdrage," Part IV, *Indische Gids* 11,1 (1889): 951. Van Prehn Wiese, "Aantekeningen," pp. 138-139, also has a list, slightly different from this, for Sambas. Given the length of Francis's list, one wonders if all posts were filled, or if the informant might have described an ideal situation.

[44] That the land belonged to the ruler, as God's representative on earth, seems to have been less a traditional arrangement than one enforced by colonial policy.

[45] Kielstra, "Bijdrage," Part IV, *Indische Gids* 11,1 (1889): 953; Ozinga, *Economische ontwikkeling*, p. 34.

[46] Foreign Asiatics, in colonial times, included Chinese, Arabs, and Indians, even if born in the Indies. They enjoyed some privileges that natives did not, but were subject to other legal restrictions; see below.

Malay Histories of West Borneo

Authors of Borneo's Malay histories attempted to locate their realms in a Malay-Islamic world and to underline their legitimacy. Illustrious ancestry and political prowess reflected glory on the rulers, while the presence of Chinese immigrants was of no significance to these writers, and therefore goes unrecorded.

According to one royal genealogy, *Silsilah Raja-Raja Sambas*, the early rulers of Sambas descended from a brother of the Sultan of Brunei who migrated first to Sukadana, where he married the sister of its reigning sultan, and then to Sambas itself. This chronicle, which reports that Sambas was also a tributary of Johor, thus places this principality in a triangle of influence between Brunei, Johor, and Sukadana.[47]

Mempawah, too, seems to have been a "breakaway" polity from Brunei. Its court history, *Hikayat Upu Daeng Menambun*, claims another point of origin: the Bugis adventurers who spread through the Archipelago after the Dutch occupied Makassar in 1667.[48] This *hikayat* recounts the tale of five Bugis brothers who traveled through the Malay world; one became *yang dipertuan muda*[49] of Riau-Johor, while the others dispersed. The second brother, Upu Daeng Menambun, visited Sukadana, where he married a daughter of the sultan whose mother came from the ruling family of Mempawah.[50] Later, this Daeng Menambun moved to Mempawah and became its ruler or *panembahan*. Both this *hikayat* and the *Tuhfat al-Nafis* (The Precious Gift), which was composed in Johor, relate the story of the five adventurers, thereby placing Mempawah in a web of relationships like that of the Sambas court. Yet Mempawah's connections reach more widely, to Makassar, Sumatra, Java, Riau and the Malay Peninsula.[51] The influence of the five Bugis, according to the chronicles, extended to Sambas as well, where the youngest brother, Upu Daeng Pamase, married a sister of its sultan.[52]

However richly these chronicles may relate Malay histories, they relegate the Dayak to an unimportant role, and the Chinese to invisibility. Only one longer Malay text deals with the role of the Chinese, and that is a nineteenth-century work called *Syair Perang Cina di Monterado*. Written in the environs of the court of Mempawah, it describes the war between 1850 and 1854 against the Chinese gold miners of Monterado from a pro-Malay—and pro-Dutch—perspective. Its account of the war contributes to chapter three.

---

[47] Schulze, *Chroniken von Sambas und Mempawah*, pp. 141-161.

[48] Ibid., p. 14.

[49] Literally, "younger ruler," a kind of second king.

[50] Some sources indicate that this woman was not a "Malay," but a Dayak. This account would thus illustrate the Islamization of Mempawah through the influence of Sukadana and the arrival of the Bugis.

[51] Schulze, *Chroniken von Sambas und Mempawah*, pp. 35-86; see also Raja Ali Haji bin Ahmad, *The Precious Gift*.

[52] Schulze, *Chroniken von Sambas und Mempawah*, p. 160.

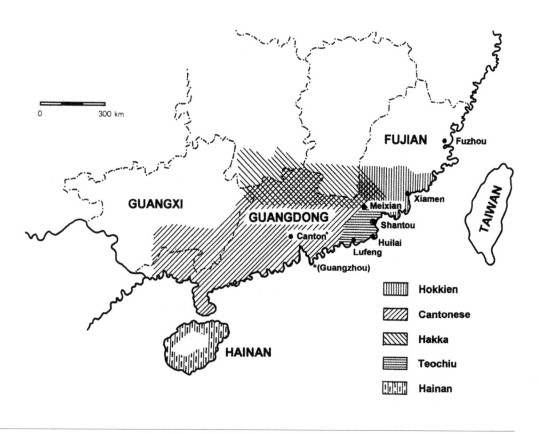

Map Two. Southeastern China, indicating approximate home areas of Chinese of West Kalimantan.

CHINESE

The most populous group of immigrants not native to the Archipelago was made up of the Chinese. They, too, were a variegated group. Although nearly all Chinese in West Kalimantan came from the southern Chinese province of Guangdong (with a few Hokkiens from Fujian), their languages—Hakka, Teochiu, Cantonese, Hainanese, and others—were mutually unintelligible. To most outside observers, the Chinese appeared as a homogeneous group, but the divisions among them were great enough to enable the Dutch to apply "divide and rule" tactics to subdue them, as will be seen in later chapters.

The two largest groups in West Borneo were the Teochiu (M. Chaozhou), who came from the northeastern coastal area of Guangdong, around the port city of Swatow (Shantou), and the Hakkas, who migrated primarily from inland Guangdong's hilly areas or from poorer lowland parts of the province, where they often lived mixed with other language groups. Hakkas also lived in inland Fujian province (Tingzhou), but few if any Fujian Hakkas migrated to West Borneo.

Differences between Hakkas and Teochius should not be exaggerated; both are Han Chinese, both speak a southern Chinese language. Hakkas opened new land in China, sometimes with the help of local minority people, farmed less fertile areas, and migrated readily to new sites—hence the name Hakka (M. *kejia*), which means "guest people." In Borneo, too, they were pioneers. Teochiu tended to concentrate in urban areas and in trade, while Hakkas worked in mines and agriculture, and later became small traders in the interior. Even today Teochius (who in colonial documents are often called "Hoklo" [M. *fulao*]) are the most numerous group among the Chinese population in the city of Pontianak and the regions to the south of it, while Hakkas are the major group in the north, especially in the former Chinese Districts. (See map two: Chinese homelands of Hakka, Teochiu, etc.) The most numerous group among the Chinese in Java, the Hokkiens, were relatively few on the island, although a few prominent Hokkien families lived in Pontianak, as well as representatives of other speech groups, in particular the Hainanese.

Table 1.1
Sub-ethnic or Speech Groups among Chinese in West Borneo
1930 Census

Hakka	38,313
Teochiu	21,699
Cantonese	2,961
Hokkien	2,570
Other	1,257
Total	66,700 (of these, 16,669 were born abroad)

Source: Based on 1930 Census.[53]

---

[53] W. L. Cator, *The Economic Position of the Chinese in the Netherlands Indies* (Oxford: Blackwell, 1936), p. 96.

In addition to those Chinese enumerated above, 41,298 more ethnic Chinese were merely enumerated according to sex and approximate age. Most of them were Hakkas as well.

Colonial officials were at first ignorant of regional and linguistic differences among the Chinese settlers and depended, until the first Dutch translators for Chinese appeared in the 1860s, on other Chinese for information about their compatriots. The word "Hakka," for example, was not used in colonial documents in the early nineteenth century; the Dutch referred to the miners and others as "mountain" or "hill people." To illustrate the confusion, the first Commissioner for Borneo, Nahuys van Burgst, then Resident of Yogyakarta, wisely took a Chinese interpreter with him when he first visited the West Coast in 1818. The man, Tan Djin Sing, was said to speak Chinese, Javanese, Malay, Dutch, and English (it is unlikely that he spoke Hakka, although he probably was able to communicate with the predominantly Teochiu Chinese of Pontianak).[54] Thanks to Tan or to other, non-Hakka Chinese, Dutch officials soon held the general opinion that the predominant group among the miners, the "mountain people," were raw and hardly civilized, the "dregs" of the Chinese nation, and that they needed to be controlled with a heavy hand. This opinion certainly reflected feelings current among non-Hakka Chinese, both in South China and abroad, especially in the nineteenth century. In China, the Hakkas engaged in warfare against some of the Cantonese, and they formed the backbone of the Taiping Rebellion in China which lasted more than a decade, from 1850-64.[55]

Compared to the Malays, who were so clearly ranked by a social and political hierarchy, the Chinese, lacking hereditary titles, appeared to be rather egalitarian. In mining areas, leaders were usually elected, perhaps on the basis of physical prowess or organizational talent. Elsewhere, social status was closely linked to wealth.[56] Even in the twentieth century, when Chinese education expanded rapidly, wealth remained the most important criterion for community leadership, although education, especially schooling in China, was also valued.

---

[54] P. J. Veth, *Borneo's Wester-Afdeeling: Geographisch, statistisch, historisch, vorafgegaan door eene algemeene schets des ganschen eilands* (Zaltbommel: Joh. Nomanen Zoon, 1854-1856), 2: 35-36, 45. The interpreter was the Kapitan Cina of Yogyakarta, that is, its head of the Chinese. He was known later by the name Raden Tumenggung Secadiningrat. For Tan Djin Sing, see *The British in Java 1811-1816: A Javanese Account*, ed. Peter Carey (Oxford: Oxford University Press for the British Academy, 1992), pp. 483-485, note 399; and Peter Carey, "Changing Javanese Perceptions of the Chinese Communities in Central Java, 1755-1825," *Indonesia* 37 (April 1984): 28-32. A recent, but not always reliable, biography of Tan claims that he was actually of noble Javanese descent, adopted and raised by a Chinese family; see T. S. Werdoyo, *Tan Jin Sing, dari Kapiten Cina sampai Bupati Yogyakarta* (Jakarta: Pustaka Utama Grafiti, 1990), pp. xx, 1-2. Carey's sources show that Europeans easily identified Tan as a Chinese and that he was not of Javanese origin. Probably he spoke Hokkien, which is close to Teochiu.

[55] P. H. van der Kemp, "Montrado tijdens het herstel van ons gezag in 1818," *Koloniaal Tijdschrift* 9 (1920): 277. De Groot wryly remarks that "One should never... believe either Hakkas or Hoklos, when they claim that the other group is the refuse of their nation." J. J. M. de Groot, *Het kongsiwezen van Borneo: Eene verhandeling over den grondslag en den aard der Chineesche politieke vereenigingen in de koloniën* (The Hague: M. Nijhoff, 1885), pp. 79-80 note 1.

[56] W. A. van Rees, *Montrado: Geschied- en krijgskundige bijdrage betreffende de onderwerping der Chinezen op Borneo, naar het dagboek von een Indisch officier over 1854-1856* (Bois-le-Duc: Müller, 1858), pp. 49-51. About mining organizations, see chapter two. The Chinese abroad did not inherit noble titles and, in general, could not achieve prominence in government office.

Legally, the Dutch considered all ethnic Chinese, including those born in the Archipelago and those of mixed descent, to be "Foreign Asiatics" (*Vremde Oosterlingen*), a term normally applied to those of Arab descent (although not in Pontianak) and to immigrants from India as well.[57] The colonial authorities developed a variety of restrictions to keep the Chinese from becoming "natives." Before colonial rule, Chinese had occasionally blended into other ethnic groups in Borneo. Chinese traders who became attached to local courts might adopt Malay titles and even convert to Islam, as they did in Palembang, for example, and conceivably some Chinese traders did the same at Malay courts on the West Coast. Isolated individuals in the interior sometimes melted into Dayak society, though this rarely happened. Once colonial administration was in place in the mid-nineteenth century, the opportunities for Chinese immigrants and their descendants to cross the defined ethnic and political boundaries certainly diminished.

Chinese Society in West Borneo

Although some Chinese traders had visited Brunei and other Bornean principalities for centuries, the first Chinese to arrive in West Borneo in large numbers came in the mid-eighteenth century to mine gold. As miners, the Chinese competed with Malays and Dayaks, who had done the mining before them, but Chinese methods were more efficient for working all but the smaller, more remote deposits.

Malay rulers, who had encouraged the Chinese to immigrate, nonetheless restricted the newcomers. The new miners' first agreements with the local rulers forbade them to engage in agriculture (this was done to insure that the immigrants would buy rice and imported necessities from the rulers at high prices), but farming was an essential part of mining, and, in the eighteenth century, land was plentiful, even in coastal areas, so that the Malay edicts were largely ineffectual. The Chinese opened land for rice and other crops. As farmers, the Chinese and the Dayaks did not usually compete for land. In general, Dayaks farmed higher, drier territory, often on hillsides, which was more suitable for *ladang* cultivation.[58] The Chinese preferred lowlands with ample water for planting wet rice. Both cultivation systems changed over time: some Dayaks switched from dry-field to wet rice cultivation, and the introduction of cash crops like pepper and rubber made higher terrain useful for the Chinese, too. By the twentieth century, suitable land would become scarcer and competition between the two groups would increase.

Although the Chinese seldom became "Dayak," marriages between Dayak women and Chinese men led the wives, in a way, to *masuk Cina*, "become Chinese." These wives would adopt Chinese dress and raise their children as Chinese. The Chinese who took women from nearby Dayak groups might take the entire family

---

[57] This formal distinction dates from the mid-nineteenth century, but laws restricting Chinese assimilation existed before then. See above, note 46.

[58] E. Doty and W. J. Pohlman, "Tour in Borneo, from Sambas through Montrado to Pontianak and the Adjacent Settlements of Chinese and Dayaks, during the Autumn of 1838," *Chinese Repository* 8 (1839): 295, 298, report that Dayaks prefer to work the uplands. Ozinga makes a similar observation; see *Economische ontwikkeling*, pp. 7-9.

of in-laws "under their protection."[59] These links, as well as trade relations, may have encouraged certain Dayaks to learn one of the Chinese languages and adopt other Chinese customs.

Plate 1. Chinese woman using *dulang* to separate flecks of gold from sand, about 1937. Photograph taken by Karl Helbig. © Roemer-und Pelizaeus-Museum Hildesheim. Foundation Helbig. By permission.

In nineteenth-century mining communities, virtually all the women were of mixed origin; a Western observer judged them to be "prettier" than pure Malays or Javanese. They wore a kind of Chinese dress: blue cotton trousers that reached below the knee and a matching jacket closed on the side with silver buttons. A pair of leather clogs with thick wooden soles completed the attire. On holidays, the ladies wore silken clothes and golden jewelry, while the wealthiest sported golden buttons, Chinese shoes, and stockings. Unlike more cloistered Chinese women in most parts of the Indies, these women had comparative freedom to see and be seen by strangers; in fact, according to reports, they were not shy at all.[60] Furthermore, they were a commercial asset to their partners, at least to those who were traders,

---

[59] Earl, *Eastern Seas*, pp. 293-294. Although Earl means this in a positive sense, the Chinese practice of acquiring Dayak women through indebtedness aroused Dutch objections.

[60] Rees, *Onderwerping der Chineezen*, p. 49; W. H. Senn van Basel, "Eene Chineesche nederzetting op Borneo's Westkust," *Tijdschrift voor Nederlandsch Indië* 3,1 (1874): 388-389. Among others, during her visit to Borneo, the Viennese traveler Ida Pfeiffer also noted the frequency of intermarriage and the Chinese preference for Dayak women over Malays. See Ida Pfeiffer, *Meine zweite Weltreise* (Vienna: Gerold's Sohn, 1856), p. 68.

as they might manage the shops while the men went about other activities.[61] In 1861, years after the closing of the Monterado *kongsi*, women were observed going to wash the remains of the gold-bearing sand, wearing dark blue slacks and jacket and a sort of red turban under a miners' hat. They headed for the mines carrying their *dulangs* (wok-shaped pans for washing the gold) and singing "mountain songs," a typical Hakka pastime.[62] If these women were not "pure" Chinese by descent, they had become culturally so.

Where the communities became more settled, daughters were born, and there, intermarriage between Chinese men and Dayak women became less common. This seems to have been the case even in the early nineteenth century:

> When the Chinese first came to this area, they married only with the daughters of the Dayaks. Only later, when the population had grown, did they start to arrange marriages among themselves and they rarely took Dayak women for their wives.[63]

After the war with Monterado in the 1850s, the administration intervened to make it illegal for Chinese men to acquire Dayak women as payment for debt. In addition, a Chinese man who "legally" acquired a Dayak wife was supposed to pay *f*120, a substantial sum, to the Malay ruler or appanage holder of her community, as reimbursement for the "loss." A few years later, an official complained that such fees left the Chinese bachelors prey to unspeakable "immorality," and in 1861 authorities withdrew the measures requiring bride payments.[64] Toward the end of the century, especially in coastal regions, more women were immigrating from China. Through immigration and reproduction, Chinese communities became more balanced between males and females, and intermarriage with local people became rare, except in areas where Chinese males were comparatively isolated, as in the interior. Interethnic marriage appears to have picked up slightly in recent decades, especially among Christians.[65]

---

[61] See the account in Earl, *Eastern Seas*, pp. 208-209 and that of a visit to Mandor in R. C. van Prehn, "Aantekeningen betreffende Borneo's Westkust," *Tijdschrift voor Indische Taal-, Land- en Volkenkunde* 7 (1858): 22-32 and ANRI BW 28/33.

[62] M. von Faber, "Schets van Montrado in 1861," *Tijdschrift voor Indische Taal-, Land- en Volkenkunde* 13 (1846): 465. At the time, the mining population was declining. About one-third were too old or sick to pay taxes, and less than one-third of the men and all the women were born locally. In the twentieth century, Chinese women in West Borneo often wore Malay-style sarongs like those of *peranakan* Chinese women of Java. See, among others, photograph no. 3 in G. A. de Mol, "Vier groote Landbouwwerktuigen van de Chineezen in West-Borneo," *Sin Po*, Special Issue, 618 (February 2, 1935). The author, who first visited Pontianak and Singkawang in 1963, was also surprised to find Chinese women dressed in sarongs, unlike Chinese women in Malaya, who at the time preferred Chinese slacks, often brightly patterned ones.

[63] Xie Qinggao, *Hailu*, cited in Yuan Bingling, *Chinese Democracies: A Study of the Kongsis of West Borneo (1776-1884)* (Leiden: Research School of Asian, African and Amerindian Studies, CNWS, Universiteit Leiden, 2000), p. 309. The account is from the 1820s, if not considerably earlier.

[64] Political Report, 1858, by Resident, West Borneo, ANRI BW 1/9 (216); Political Report, 1859, ANRI BW 1/10 (217); Secret Political Report, 1860, West Borneo, ANRI BW 1/11 (218); Political Report, West Borneo, 1861, ANRI BW 1/12 (220).

[65] For a contemporary study of intermarriage in the former Chinese Districts, see Andreas Barung Tangdililing, "Perkawinan antar suku bangsa sebagai salah satu wahana pembauran bangsa: Studi kasus perkawinan antara orang Daya dengan keturunan Cina di Kacamatan

Although the Chinese tended to retain a Chinese language, bilingualism was common. Not infrequently, Chinese spoke both Hakka and Teochiu.[66] Many Hakkas came from the upland areas of regions like Hepo (called Hoppo) in Jieyang, or from Lufeng, Haifeng, Fengshun, and Huilai; these so-called *pansanhok* (*banshanke*, literally, "half-mountain Hakka," that is, half-Hakka, half-Hoklo or Teochiu) were generally conversant in both languages before they left China.[67] The *pansanhok* dominated the northern and central part of the Chinese Districts; around Pontianak and Mandor, Hakkas from the Hakka "capital" of Meixian in Guangdong, who are said to speak more "pure" Hakka, predominated. This division in Hakka dialects (and places of origin) was related to the boundaries of the mining organizations, as will be seen.

In the second half of the nineteenth century, Chinese traders began to move into the interior, trading in forest products purchased from Dayak collectors. Upcountry, a local wife—a trader might have two wives, a local one in the interior, and one settled in his urban base—was an important business asset. For small gifts, traders could easily win the Dayak woman's consent to cohabit.[68] Significantly, Chinese traders in the interior learned Dayak languages, just as many Dayaks who lived near Chinese settlements learned to speak Chinese, usually Hakka.[69]

Malay remained the language of the coastal towns, used by all ethnic groups. In these towns, many local-born Chinese spoke Malay, Dayaks used it at the marketplace, and Dutch colonial administrators, many of them unable to cope with

---

Samalantan, Kabupaten Sambas, Kalimantan Barat" (PhD Dissertation, Universitas Indonesia, 1993).

[66] Often called "dialects," these are better described as "languages." Unfortunately, linguists have yet to explore contemporary language use in West Kalimantan.

[67] S. H. Schaank, "De kongsis van Montrado, Bijdrage tot de geschiedenis en de kennis van het wezen der Chineesche vereenigingen op de Westkust van Borneo," *Tijdschrift voor Indische Taal-, Land- en Volkenkunde* 35,5/6 (1893): 509-517, describes the "Pan-San-Hok" and their important position in the area Lara-Lumar. They also dominated the Monterado kongsi. For a recent communication on *banshanke*, see Huang Kunzhang, "Taiguodi 'banshanke'," *Huaren Life Overseas* 2 (1987): 14. I thank Prof. Huang for this clarification. Cf. also Leonard Blussé and Ank Merens, "Nuggets from the Gold Mines: Three Tales of the Ta-kang Kongsi of West Kalimantan," in *Conflict and Accommodation in Early Modern East Asia: Essays in Honour of Eric Zürcher*, ed. Leonard Blussé and Harriet T. Zurndorfer (Leiden: E. J. Brill, 1993), pp. 289ff. (Misled by the word *hok* in Schaank's account, this article calls them *panshan fu*.) De Groot, *Kongsiwezen*, pp. 64-66 assumes that all people of Lufeng, Haifeng, and so on, are Hoklos (Teochiu). It is Schaank who distinguishes them, drawing on what people around Monterado, Lara, and Lumar called themselves; they were Hakkas from a Teochiu area.

Leo J. Moser, *The Chinese Mosaic: The Peoples and Provinces of China* (Boulder: Westview Special Studies on East Asia, 1985), pp. 243, 252, says that Hakkas migrated from core Hakka areas in western Fujian (Tingzhou), southern Jiangxi, and possibly the neighborhood of Meixian to the *coastal* areas of Guangdong, while Schaank also emphasizes their presence in upland Hepo in Jieyang district. See also De Groot, *Kongsiwezen*, p. 66. Moser also distinguishes a (coastal) Luhai (Lufeng-Haifeng) dialect of Hakka, but places speakers from Fengshun and Huilai, for example, linguistically closer to Meixian. Schaank, who spent several years as an official in the Monterado area, also wrote about the locally spoken Lufeng dialect. See S. H. Schaank, *Het Loeh-Foeng-Dialect* (Leiden: Brill and Amsterdam: Meulenhoff, 1897).

[68] Political Report, 1873, ANRI BW 2/11 (231).

[69] For one example, see W. L. Ritter, *Nacht en morgen uit het Indische leven* (Amsterdam: Van Kesteren, 1861), pp. 30-31, which describes a Dayak who fled from his people but found work with the headman of a mining kongsi because he spoke some Chinese. Even today, some non-Chinese in West Kalimantan claim to understand Hakka.

other local tongues, propagated it.[70] Bi- and multi-lingualism was frequent, despite ethnic boundaries.

HAKKAS AND HAKKA TRADITIONS

Hakkas are a southern Chinese speech group; Hakka speakers reside most commonly in Guangdong and Fujian province and, because they frequently migrate within China, in a few other Chinese provinces (Guangxi, Sichuan) as well. In rural West Borneo, people from the core Hakka areas like Meixian and Dapu, together with others from Teochiu-speaking areas, who were of Hakka migrant origin and therefore bilingual (Hakka-Teochiu), predominated. Other southern Chinese groups, like Hainanese or Hokkien, were represented among the coolies, but, given the numerical predominance of Hakkas in the mining and agricultural areas, not only their language but their values would have been dominant (especially since Hakkas are defined, above all, by their language[71]). Pontianak remained a Teochiu settlement, however, and so did the area to the south of it, which was outside the Chinese Districts.

Hakkas often claim they were forced from a northern Chinese homeland by barbarian attacks during the Song Dynasty, or earlier, which led them to move southward. Arriving in already thickly populated areas of the southeast, they settled on higher ground, eking out a living from less fertile land, something that made them hard-working, in their own eyes and those of others.

Hakkas, among the Han Chinese, are defined by their language, but also by their apparent hardiness, clannishness (according to the reports of others), and willingness to take on back-breaking tasks in mining or agriculture. In both China and Southeast Asia, Hakkas are stereotyped as "rural and poor,"[72] even though today some Hakkas may be urban and wealthy. The Hakka residents of West Kalimantan are (or were) significantly rural, and many remain poor, in contrast to ethnic Chinese elsewhere in Indonesia, who live in the cities and tend to be relatively well-off.

Outside of China, Hakkas frequently settled in farming or mining areas, and less often in cities, which earned them the title of "pioneers." Borneo was obviously an appropriate terrain for such pioneers, and so were the islands of Bangka and Belitung, where, from the eighteenth to twentieth centuries, Hakkas

---

[70] Anonymous, "Verslag eener reis naar Montrado, gedaan in het jaar 1844," *Tijdschrift voor Neêrland's Indië* 9,3 (1847): 70. (The author is probably D.L. Baumgart, Assistant Resident of Sambas from 1842-1844, but he is not named in the text.) Compare P. Adriani, *Herinneringen uit en aan de Chineesche districten der Wester-Afdeeling van Borneo, 1879-1882: Schetsen en indrukken* (Amsterdam: Campagne en Zoon, 1898), p. 135 (for Singkawang); Memorie van Overgave, W. J. ten Haaft, Landak, 1934, ARA 2.10.39, KIT 984, pp. 46-47.

[71] Myron L. Cohen, "The Hakka or 'Guest People': Dialect as a Sociocultural Variable in Southeast China," in *Guest People: Hakka Identity in China and Abroad*, ed. Nicole Constable (Seattle: University of Washington Press, 1996), pp. 36-79 gives a clear exposé of this argument. See also Mary S. Erbaugh, "The Secret History of the Hakkas: The Chinese Revolution as a Hakka Enterprise," *China Quarterly* 132 (December 1992): 937-968, and Mary S. Erbaugh, "The Hakka Paradox in the People's Republic of China: Exile, Eminence, and Public Silence," in *Guest People*, pp. 196-231. On Hakka identity, see Moser, *Chinese Mosaic*, pp. 250-54.

[72] Nicole Constable, "Introduction," in *Guest People*, pp. 22-23.

predominated among the tin miners.[73] Most of the Hakkas in rural areas remained farmers and laborers, although in Malaysian cities, where many settled, they were often artisans, (traditional) pharmacists, and pawnbrokers.[74] Perhaps goldsmiths could also be added to the list, a trade linked, of course, to the gold mines.

Among the Hakka, gender roles were less strongly defined than among other Chinese; Hakka women participated freely in agricultural labor, although not in community affairs. Accustomed to arduous work in the fields, Hakka women did not bind their feet, and may have been more independent than their non-Hakka sisters.[75] No observers report foot binding in Borneo. "The Chinese women . . . are all large footed," says Earl about Monterado, who added that these women nevertheless had well-proportioned and dainty feet.[76] Non-Chinese women (especially Dayak) who married Chinese men seem to have been rapidly assimilated into the culture of their husbands. Significantly, non-Hakka wives of Hakka men living in other regions also readily accepted and sustained the culture. In China and Hong Kong, for example, non-Hakka Chinese women who married into Hakka villages quickly learned the dominant language, according to reports, and families maintained Hakka identity over generations, despite these intermarriages.[77] This certainly matches the experiences of Hakka families in Borneo who were able to integrate local wives into their Chinese society.

Although the walled and fortified multi-storied dwellings of Hakka villages of Fujian and elsewhere in southeastern China are well-known and often used as evidence to prove that the Hakka's group identity was generally clannish and inward-looking,[78] many Hakkas, especially in Guangdong, because of their status as poor migrants, lived in dispersed settlements.[79] Even the kongsis did not build such elaborate common dwellings—only the so-called kongsi house was fortified by an outer wall and thicket. (See Plate 3, page 59.) Hakka farmers in Borneo sometimes lived in scattered settlements. Only in the twentieth century did they move to more concentrated villages. In the early decades of the century, they were pressured to resettle by the colonial rulers, who wanted the Chinese to live where

---

[73] Another early Hakka mining settlement was located in Pulai, Kelantan, Malaysia, founded in the seventeenth or early eighteenth century by gold miners who then switched to subsistence agriculture, taking local wives from the surrounding non-Muslim communities. In Pulai, Hakkas were economically conservative but politically radical (especially during the early post-World War II years). Later chapters will examine the political radicalism of the Chinese communities in West Borneo. See Sharon A. Carstens, "Pulai: Memories of a Gold Mining Settlement in Ulu Kelantan," *Journal of the Malaysian Branch of the Royal Asiatic Society* 53,1 (1980): 50-67.

[74] Sharon A. Carstens, "Form and Content in Hakka Malaysian Culture," in *Guest People*, pp. 124-129.

[75] Constable, "Introduction," pp. 25-28.

[76] Earl, *Eastern Seas*, p. 292. Adriani, *Chineesche districten*, pp. 132-134, gives a long account of foot binding in China, but says he never saw evidence of it in the Indies. Lily-footed women did, of course, migrate to the Indies, especially in the early twentieth century. The author saw a number of such women at a festival in Sukabumi, West Java, in the 1960s. They were born in China before the custom died out there, but they were not Hakkas.

[77] Cohen, "The Hakka," p. 66.

[78] The official souvenir of the Hakka World Congress of 1996 was an ashtray in the shape of a fortress village. However, in parts of Fujian, Hokkiens may also live in fortified circular dwellings. See Glen Dudbridge, *China's Vernacular Cultures*, Inaugural Lecture, University of Oxford, June 1, 1995 (Oxford: Clarendon Press, 1996), p. 23.

[79] Cohen, "The Hakka," pp. 48-51 and passim.

they could be easily supervised. Later, in the 1960s, the Indonesian government forced them into concentrated settlements (see chapter seven).

Scholars believe today that interaction with minority, non-Han groups in the mountains of Guangdong and Fujian formed Hakka identity. Hakka migrations within China brought them into contact with such minorities, especially when they were forced to settle in marginal, less populated areas. Most important was the minority called She. The Hakka took She women as wives, integrating them into Hakka life, and used the She, slash-and-burn farmers, to assist, for example, in clearing mountain forests for planting.[80] These interactions suggest that the Hakka were not so clannish, since they proved capable of cooperating with and learning from the minority groups with whom they came in contact.

Similar patterns shaped Hakka relations with the Dayak who lived in neighboring areas of Borneo. They married Dayak women, but incorporated them and their offspring into Hakka culture. They used the skills of the local people to help clear mining sites of trees and brush, as they had worked with the She in the homeland. They adjusted their housing to the local environment, using wood for building and thatch or ironwood shingles for roofing. Occasionally they borrowed local agricultural practices.[81] The ability to interact with non-Chinese peoples would also prove to be an asset when Hakka traders moved into the interior of Borneo in the late nineteenth century (a move that will be discussed in chapter four).

Orientations and Organizations

For much of the period dealt with in this study, the cultural and political center of West Borneo's Chinese society was South China, while its commercial center was Singapore. Borneo was peripheral to both of these.

Despite the contemporary dimensions of the Chinese minority in West Kalimantan, with a substantial population of over 400,000 persons,[82] nearly all studies of this ethnic group have concentrated on the gold mining activities of

---

[80] "Hakkas invited the poor from among the She people... to clear the forests by the slash-and-burn technique." Sow-theng Leong, *Migration and Ethnicity in Chinese History: Hakkas, Pengmin, and their Neighbors*, ed. Tim Wright (Stanford: Stanford University Press, 1997), pp. 47, also p. 99. She people even came to depend on the Hakka (especially near Fuzhou and Quanzhou, Fujian Province, in the seventeenth century) for jobs. Leong has shown convincingly that this symbiosis was at the beginning of a crystallization of Hakka identity in China, and Sharon Carstens has encouraged me to see the parallel to ethnic relations in Borneo. Similarly, the Hakka miners of Bangka used local people to clear the forests at mining sites, see Mary F. Somers Heidhues, *Bangka Tin and Mentok Pepper: Chinese Settlement on an Indonesian Island* (Singapore: Institute of Southeast Asian Studies, 1992).

[81] According to G. William Skinner, "The Chinese Minority," in *Indonesia*, ed. Ruth T. McVey (New Haven: Human Relations Area Files, 1963), p. 104, Hakkas adopted agricultural implements from the people of Borneo.

[82] McBeth, "Murder and Mayhem," p. 27, estimates that the Chinese were 12 percent of the population. Their share in the population declined during the 1990s because of outmigration, especially to Java, and for other reasons. Some returned temporarily to the province after the May 1998 riots in the capital (see chapter seven and epilogue). A recent source, citing official data from the office of the provincial government, says Chinese were 17 percent of the population, but this seems high. *Kompas*, January 26, 2001. The Census of 2000 promised an official count of ethnic groups, the first since 1930, but results were not available at the time of this writing.

Chinese in the nineteenth century and the mining organizations called kongsis. These kongsis were religious, economic, and political institutions which acted almost as independent states. (A closer look at their activities follows in chapter two.)[83]

Most previous studies have thus looked at the community from the inside and paid little attention to its relations with the rest of West Kalimantan's society. On the surface, these relations appear highly problematic. Outsiders, above all Indonesians from outside Kalimantan, have perceived the Chinese minority as a stubborn and exclusive group, clinging to alien customs and loyalties and resisting both contact with and cultural influences from surrounding peoples. Considered to be "the Chinese among the [Indonesian] Chinese," the Chinese of Kalimantan, measured against an imaginary scale of degrees of "assimilation," are consistently placed at the extreme end among those who resist assimilation.[84] Many writers mention how different the West Kalimantan Chinese are, or were, from those of Java.[85] One observer, however, has emphasized the positive side of their distinctiveness and offers a reason for it:

> All over the Indonesian archipelago, the West Kalimantan Chinese were probably the only Chinese colonists who were for a few decades at liberty to develop their own social, political, cultural, and other institutions, relatively free from any outside influence such as a strong colonial state with its centralizing policies . . . [86]

Yet the mining organizations alone, in spite of their tradition of independence and self-governance, were not the only factors that inclined the Chinese community of Kalimantan to independence and that explain why this community was so little influenced by the cultures surrounding it. At least three other factors are of importance:

1) The composition of the Chinese minority itself, both from an ethnic and a class perspective, was significant. Unlike Java's predominantly Hokkien and commercially oriented minority, which lived in business contact with local people, Kalimantan's Chinese included a significant proportion of miners and small

---

[83] Twentieth-century studies of the kongsis include Barbara E. Ward, "A Hakka Kongsi in Borneo," *Journal of Oriental Studies* 1,2 (1954): 358-370; James C. Jackson, *The Chinese in the West Borneo Goldfields: A Study in Cultural Geography* (Hull: University of Hull Publications, Occasional Papers in Geography, 1970); Wang Tai Peng, "The Word Kongsi: A Note," *Journal of the Malaysian Branch, Royal Asiatic Society* 52,1 (1979): 102-105; Wang Tai Peng, *The Origins of Chinese Kongsi* (Petaling Jaya: Pelanduk Publications, 1994); Quirijn S. Langelaan, *De Chinezen van Sambas, 1850* (Master's thesis, University of Amsterdam, 1984); and Mary Somers Heidhues, "Chinese Organizations in West Borneo and Bangka: *Kongsi* and *Hui*," in *"Secret Societies" Reconsidered: Perspectives on the Social History of Early Modern South China and Southeast Asia*, ed. David Ownby and Mary Somers Heidhues (Armonk: M. E. Sharpe, 1993); and Yuan, *Chinese Democracies*.

[84] Skinner, "Chinese Minority," places West Kalimantan's Chinese at the far end of the scale, although he shows that they have "locally-rooted" elements. More recent studies are cited in chapter seven.

[85] See also Eddi Elison, "Kesukaran WNA Cina untuk jadi WNI di Kalbar: Ada yang jadi WNI lewat calo, tapi dihukum," *Selecta* 876 (July 3, 1978): 44, "In any respect, Chinese in Kalimantan Barat are very different from Chinese in other regions."

[86] Onghokham, "The Chinese of West Kalimantan," *Globalink* 1,3 (March-May 1996).

farmers, both residing in relatively isolated, relatively homogeneous settlements, with less interaction with local people. In turn, many of these were Hakkas, a self-conscious minority within China and abroad.

2) The nature of the host society influenced the Kalimantan Chinese minority. It is important to situate the Chinese in the surrounding environment. West Kalimantan's society is not only ethnically divided, as previously mentioned, but ethnic groups tend to fill specific "slots" in the economy. Such specialization of economic activity reinforces ethnic distinctions.

3) Government policies regarding the Kalimantan Chinese minority varied through the years, ranging from laissez-faire policies to intimidation and violence. Once the Netherlands claimed authority in the area, establishing it by force i f necessary, its presence modified minority life, yet left much of its cultural autonomy intact. After independence, the Indonesian state became a forceful intruder, but its most intrusive policy, the promotion of assimilation, had only limited effectiveness.

Chinese Sources and Images of Borneo

The Chinese produced what are probably the earliest representations of Borneans as they looked to others. A scroll attributed to a Tang Dynasty (618-906 CE) painter depicts envoys from Borneo and Champa (a historical realm or realms in southern Vietnam) bringing tributary gifts to the Emperor. They are carrying birds and bright feathers, strange animals, and curious forms of petrified wood. Stranger still are the wiry half-naked, barefoot bearers themselves.[87] Their appearance seems to confirm their lack of what Chinese would consider to be culture.

Other, better known, representations can be found in the written accounts of China's court historians and geographers, most of whom probably cited visitors to Brunei. At the latest, Chinese knew of the city and island from the sixth century. Still later, there is ample evidence of visits from China. A thirteenth-century tombstone stands in the north of the island,[88] and relics of early trade—snuff bottles, jars, and other typically Chinese objects—confirm contact.

Whereas the officials, artists, and chroniclers in China's imperial capital could assign Borneo to the category of the remote and insignificant, for the traders of South China, Borneo was a valuable and interesting trading partner. China's wares were in demand there: silk and golden thread to clothe its nobility, simpler textiles for the common folk, or huge ceramic pots, called *tempayan*, used locally as prestige objects, to store water for the dry season, and (by non-Islamic peoples) as burial jars. For their part, Chinese buyers sought *damar* and other resins for paints and lacquers; animal products like *bezoar* (gallstones of wild pigs) for their presumed medical and sexual powers; beeswax for candles; birds' nests, seafood, and

---

[87] *Chinese Art Treasures from the Chinese National Palace Museum and the Chinese National Central Museum* (Geneva: Éditions d'Art Albert Skira, 1961), pp. 34-35. According to art historians, the painting, attributed to Yen Li-pen (d. 673), may have been painted by a later artist, but it goes back at least to the eleventh century, from the date of an inscription it bears. Not all the aliens are so lightly dressed; some wear flowing robes and sandals, but they are clearly not from Borneo.

[88] Wolfgang Franke (with Chen Tieh Fan), "A Chinese Tomb Inscription of A.D. 1264, Discovered Recently in Brunei," in *Brunei Museum Journal* 3,1 (1973): 91-99.

honey for the kitchen; and balsamic camphor for pharmaceutical use. By the eighteenth century, Chinese traders visiting Borneo also sought gold.

What image of Borneo prevailed in the minds of the gold miners who sailed there in the eighteenth century? Did they dream of making a fortune from the "old gold mountain" (*laojinshan*), as they called the future Chinese Districts, where the best deposits were found?[89] Were they simply seeking an escape from the social and economic upheavals that unsettled their homelands? Or did they have no choice because they were impressed into service? The only Chinese-language sources that might deal with these questions are from the nineteenth century, decades after the first mines were established, and they offer comparatively little information, whereas older descriptions provide mostly sailing directions and shopping lists of local products.

Yuan Bingling has recently made available in English a translation of what may be the earliest extant Chinese text about the mines of Borneo's West Coast. First published in about 1820 and reprinted several times since, *Hailu* or *Records of Overseas* by Xie Qinggao[90] describes widespread gold deposits. Similar, earlier tales may have lured fortune-seekers to Borneo, but the details about the first decades of mining remain obscure.

More helpful are a few internal records of the mining experience on Borneo. De Groot has transmitted a chronicle of one mining settlement, the well-known Lanfang Kongsi of Mandor, in Chinese and in Dutch translation, with his comments.[91] He himself expressed some doubts about the text as a historical source, feeling that his informants from Lanfang may have suppressed some information, especially information concerning their more stormy relations with the colonial power.[92] The Lanfang chronicle is probably the best-known text on West Borneo's history, having been re-published in English[93] and, in Chinese, read and immortalized by the Hakka researcher Lo Hsiang-lin (Luo Xianglin).[94] The chronicle is not so much a history of the kongsi as an outline of its leadership, and it is, as a historical source, "fairly disappointing."[95]

The attention given to Lanfang is in a sense ironic. Larger and more powerful was the Thaikong (M. Dagang) Kongsi of Monterado. S. H. Schaank, another trained sinologist and colonial servant, collected both oral and written material

[89] Schaank, "Kongsis van Montrado," p. 506. There were two other "gold mountains": San Francisco was *jiujinshan*, "age-old gold mountain," and Australia was the *xinjinshan*, the "new gold mountain."

[90] Translated in Yuan, *Chinese Democracies*, pp. 305-310. Xie, who traveled extensively in the South Seas during the late eighteenth century, became blind before dictating his recollections, and his scribes may have added other information to his account.

[91] De Groot, *Kongsiwezen*. De Groot, later a professor in Leiden, served as a Chinese translator in West Borneo shortly before the Lanfang Kongsi was dissolved in 1884. (See chapter three.)

[92] De Groot, *Kongsiwezen*, pp. 26-27, note 1. See also Blussé and Merens, "Nuggets from the Gold Mines," pp. 288-289, which confirms that there were more troubles than the chronicle relates.

[93] Ward, "Hakka Kongsi."

[94] Lo Hsiang-lin (Luo Xianglin), "A Chinese Presidential System in Kalimantan," *Sarawak Museum Journal*, 9,15-16 (1960): 670-674. Yuan Bingling has also translated de Groot's work into Chinese.

[95] Yuan Bingling, *Chinese Democracies*, p. 281.

from Chinese living around Monterado; he published his account of that important kongsi in 1893.[96]

Recently, Blussé and Merens found and translated three documents originating from Monterado in about 1850, two in Chinese (with Malay translations) and one in Malay.[97] These materials reveal the rivalry that existed between the miners' organizations competing for access to ore deposits. Although they briefly mention the Malay aristocracy, threats from Dayak neighbors, and/or battles with the colonial government, these sources still cast comparatively little light on wider inter-ethnic relations.[98] Some Chinese-language materials exist in the Indonesian National Archives and, recently, some Chinese manuscripts from gold mining times have come to light in the Leiden University Library,[99] but they share the limitations of the other accounts.

In more recent times, the Chinese of Kalimantan produced their own sources, including daily newspapers and books.[100] Many of these were lost in the violence of the Japanese period and the 1960s. The Indonesian government forbade open display of Chinese characters after 1966, and otherwise indicated its suspicion of anything written in Chinese. As a result, materials were hidden, lost, or deliberately destroyed. The humid climate, destructive to written materials, and lack of interest did the rest. The contribution of Chinese sources to this study is, in the end, a small one.

EUROPEANS

Europeans never developed the kind of relationship with West Borneo that they had with Java or even with parts of Sumatra. There was no "Indisch" group of settlers with a strong attachment to the local landscape and culture, as there was in Java. For one thing, the numbers of Europeans were too small. In 1860, only 104 Europeans lived in the entire residency, and that had only increased to 1,077 by 1930.[101] Military and administrative postings to the island were often of short duration, and the residency sometimes functioned as a "penal colony" for civil servants.[102] Private businessmen were few in number, and their economic enterprises

---

[96] Schaank, "Kongsis van Montrado." Schaank partly corrects de Groot's account.

[97] Chinese documents had to be translated into Malay so colonial officials could read them. Yuan Bingling has since located the Chinese version of the third account; see *Chinese Democracies*, p. 282.

[98] Blussé and Merens, "Nuggets from the Gold Mines."

[99] Yuan Bingling kindly directed me to these materials, nearly all of which are accompanied by Dutch or Malay translations, in the Leiden University Library, Department of Western Manuscripts, Hoffmann collection (BPL 2186 N-O).

[100] Claudine Salmon has collected a number of coolie novels, one of which might refer to the situation in Kalimantan, but the place names are fictionalized by the author, so it is difficult to confirm the connection. See Claudine Salmon, "Taoke or Coolies? Chinese Visions of the Chinese Diaspora," *Archipel* 26 (1983): 179-210.

[101] *Koloniaal Verslag* (1860); also Nederlandsch-Indië, Departement van Economische Zaken, Volkstelling [Census] 1930 (Batavia: Landsdrukkerij), cited in Ozinga, *Economische ontwikkeling*, pp. 98-99. These numbers may exclude members of the military temporarily stationed in the residency. In the latter year, "European" included Eurasians.

[102] M. Buys, *Twee maanden op Borneo's Westkust: Herinneringen* (Leiden: Doesburgh, 1892), p. 3. Buys describes the situation in the 1880s.

usually failed quickly, for a variety of reasons. Thus, there was no European contingent comparable to that of East Sumatra's plantation belt. Visits by explorers were relatively brief. Only missionaries spent longer stretches of time in Borneo, but they were thinly dispersed.

However numerically unimportant, the Europeans did not see themselves as intruders. Not only did missionaries evince a strong sense of commitment, some colonial officials saw themselves as protective, paternal figures. The nineteenth-century Resident (the highest official in the province) Cornelis Kater remained in West Borneo for decades, spending virtually his entire Indies career there. Yet for the Europeans, even more so than for the Asian immigrants, home remained elsewhere.

Western Sources and Images of Borneo

Given the limited number of non-European sources that treat the Chinese in Kalimantan (see discussion above), it is hardly surprising that this account relies heavily upon Dutch archival and printed materials, most of them well catalogued and readily accessible to curious scholars. These sources use a chronology and images familiar to Western researchers, and, most importantly, they are the only reports that offer a view of all ethnic groups and their relations to one another.

Their prevailing viewpoint is, admittedly, that of outsiders and administrators. Both the Dutch and later Indonesian-language materials often portray the Chinese community from a hostile perspective, from the standpoint of competitors in a battle for control and suppression. Yet, these sources are almost all that exists, so that the researcher must rely on them, while noting their biases and hidden agendas.

Official accounts begin with the establishment of the Dutch in the area in 1818—with a few reports from an earlier station in Pontianak in the 1780s—and follow its story to 1950, when Dutch officials turned over the province to a newly independent Indonesia. After that, most published sources are Indonesian materials—as late as 1997, West Kalimantan was only beginning to establish its own provincial archives. Dutch sources thus form the backbone and much of the flesh of this study, bringing together the divergent histories of the province's inhabitants. It is the author's task to divest them, as far as possible, of colonial, personal, and temporal distortions in order to produce as coherent and objective an account as possible.

That European representations of Borneo can mislead is easily shown. Early accounts of the island, whether from explorers or colonial officials, saw the lush rainforest and its seemingly inexhaustible fertility and believed it would produce untold wealth. Yet Borneo, and especially the western part, proved to be a difficult challenge for hopeful entrepreneurs; it had few good harbors; dense vegetation inhibited land travel; and even river transport was, depending on the season, difficult or impossible, making exploitation of the island's supposed rich resources extremely difficult. Even the soil was relatively infertile, and precious ores were not plentiful.

Just as Europeans misperceived the local terrain, they also misperceived the local people. Local peoples often seemed as dangerous and forbidding as the jungle itself. The interior was the land of pagans and headhunters. The Dayaks lived in common dwellings called long houses, hunted with spears, raised pigs, and openly displayed the skulls they had taken from their enemies.[103] A "primitive" people, as judged by Europeans, the Dayaks fascinated explorers, who were interested in their customs and artifacts, and aroused the zeal of missionaries, who were eager to take charge of their spiritual welfare. Typically, even modern accounts of Borneo, whether from researchers or tourists, concentrate on the people of the interior.

Biases against other ethnic groups in Borneo appear in European representations as well. In the pursuit of business, Malay traders might also raid ships for booty and for slaves, and Europeans therefore tagged them as dangerous or devious.[104] Although the colonial power worked closely with the Malay rulers, their attitude to those rulers vacillated between paternalism and scorn. On the one hand, the colonial policy of indirect rule, which maintained native rulers at their posts, was useful and economical, requiring relatively few European officials and peace-keepers, but it meant cooperating with these Malay rulers. While some officials respected the Malay sultans and *panembahans* as potential allies and, above all, as the "natural" rulers of the population, others, especially those in the capital city of Batavia, saw them as lazy, degenerate, addicted to idleness and gambling (or worse), vindictive, and an impediment to progress.[105]

The initial Western response to the Chinese seems to have been surprise that they were there at all. Early visitors to the West Coast already found Chinese quarters in most towns, apart from the sizable number in the mining territories. Soon, the enterprise and talent of the Chinese attracted admiration, but other observers complained that Chinese trading practices hoodwinked the innocent Dayaks. At the same time, Europeans feared that these Chinese might be planning to incorporate West Borneo into China—after all, the Europeans were trying to incorporate the region into *their* colony. During the entire colonial and postcolonial eras, the Chinese were almost never administered by people who spoke their language or made an effort to understand their traditions.

European officials, missionaries, adventurers, and visitors provide most of the sources on which this work is based. Dayak sources are oral, while Malay and Chinese sources are often incomplete. Even though Western sources are biased and in many ways incomplete, they nevertheless enable us to compose a long-needed history of an important and unique Southeast Asian Chinese minority community.

---

[103] Not only Europeans relished accounts of headhunters. Xie Qinggao (cited in Yuan, *Chinese Democracies*, pp. 309-310) also writes, "When they obtain a human head, they hang it over their gate."

[104] On precolonial slavery in Southeast Asia, compare Reid, *Age of Commerce*, pp. 129-136, and Milner, *Kerajaan*, p. 18. James F. Warren, *The Sulu Zone, 1768-1898: The Dynamics of External Trade, Slavery, and Ethnicity in the Transformation of a Southeast Asian Maritime State* (Singapore: Singapore University Press, 1981) discusses the Sulu pirates and slave-raiders, but not those of western Borneo. Westerners especially condemned enslavement of other Westerners captured by pirates, but many castigated all slave-holding arrangements.

[105] Hoëvell, "Onze roeping," p. 191.

CHAPTER TWO

CHINESE SOCIETY AND THE DUTCH TO THE FIRST KONGSI WAR

The nineteenth century saw the Dutch position in the Indonesian archipelago change from that of a mercantile power with trading stations only in the major ports and minimal territorial involvement (except in Java and the Spice Islands) to an administrative power that asserted wide territorial claims. Rivalry with the British and internal weakness had driven the Dutch East India Company (VOC, Vereenigde Oostindische Compagnie) to bankruptcy at the end of the eighteenth century, and the Netherlands government took over its interests. Although the VOC had made contact with West Borneo, and even maintained a presence there sporadically, it was only in July 1818 that the Dutch established a permanent station at Pontianak and began to assert authority over the entire territory. Although they were able to cooperate with important Malay rulers in their endeavor, their political and economic initiatives soon brought them into conflict with the Chinese.

Between 1811 and 1816, during the Napoleonic Wars, the British had occupied Java and other Dutch outposts in the Indies, challenging Dutch supremacy in the region. Even after the withdrawal of the British, the two nations continued their competition for influence in the Malay world.[1] In addition to securing their claim to Borneo, the Dutch hoped to exploit the island's apparently limitless wealth for profit. Furthermore, they needed to protect shipping from pirates, many of whom lived or found hiding places along Borneo's coast, where some freebooters were cooperating closely with local rulers. All these factors, and the invitation of the sultans,[2] prompted the Dutch to "return" to West Borneo in 1818.

---

[1] P. J. Veth, *Borneo's Wester-Afdeeling: Geographisch, statistisch, historisch, vorafgegaan door eene algemeene schets des ganschen eilands* (Zaltbommel: Nomanen Zoon, 1854-1856), 1: xlvi, 343-383; J. van Goor, "Seapower, Trade and State Formation: Pontianak and the Dutch 1780-1840," in *Trading Companies in Asia, 1600-1830*, ed. J. van Goor (Utrecht: HES Uitgevers, 1986), p. 88. On Anglo-Dutch rivalry in nineteenth-century Borneo, see Graham Irwin, *Nineteenth-Century Borneo: A Study in Diplomatic Rivalry* (The Hague: M. Nijhoff, 1955; reprint, Singapore: Donald Moore Books, 1967).

[2] In March 1817, the Sultan of Sambas urged the Dutch to come to his aid; shortly after, the Sultan of Pontianak also invited them to return. P. H. van der Kemp, "Palembang en Banka in 1816-1820," *Bijdragen tot de Taal-, Land- en Volkenkunde* 6,7 (1900): 704; P. H. van der Kemp, "De Vestiging van het Nederlandsch gezag op Borneo's Westerafdeeling in 1818-1819," *Bijdragen tot de Taal-, Land- en Volkenkunde* 76 (1920): 118-121; Muhammad Gade Ismail, "Politik perdagangan Melayu di kesultanan Sambas, Kalimantan Barat: masa akhir kesultanan 1808-1818" (Master's thesis, Universitas Indonesia, 1985), p. 60. On the early history of Pontianak, see, among others, J. van Goor, "A Madman in the City of Ghosts: Nicolaas Kloek in Pontianak," *Itinerario* 2 (1985): 196-211; van Goor, "Seapower, Trade, and State Formation"; Mary Somers Heidhues, "The First Two Sultans of Pontianak," *Archipel* 56 (1998): 273-294,

GOLD AND THE CHINA TRADE

During the British interregnum of 1811-1816, Lieutenant Governor T. S. Raffles had sent a request to Pontianak for information about conditions in West Borneo. There an English ship captain or trader named J. Burn, who had lived in Pontianak since at least 1808, wrote a lengthy account of the town, its surroundings, its two rulers, and its economy. Published in part in Batavia in 1814, and reprinted in Singapore in 1837, Burn's description must have whetted Raffles's appetite, and later that of the Dutch, for intervention in West Borneo, for it included details of the area's valuable products—above all, gold.[3] Raffles later enthused, "Large colonies of Chinese have established themselves [in Borneo . . . The amount of gold they export annually] has been estimated at not less than half a million sterling."[4]

Gold is found widely in Borneo, although usually in small quantities. Some rivers carry gold-bearing sand, making it possible to pan for gold dust. Gold was one of the commodities traded by the *hulu* people to their appanage holders and to the coastal rulers. Rulers surrounded themselves with golden jewelry, cups, bowls, and other luxury items. Their clothing, too, *kain songket*, was of cloth interwoven with gold thread.[5]

It is unknown how much gold was sent to destinations in China, South Asia, or Southeast Asia, and how much was retained by local rulers. Because Sumatra and the Malay Peninsula also produced the precious metal, tracing the trade is difficult, but apparently China was a major destination. In 1779, W. A. Palm, the VOC representative stationed in Pontianak, heard from the sultan that Chinese junks, which arrived there with coarse cloth, annually carried off the weight of

and Veth, *Borneo's Wester-Afdeeling*, vol. 1, passim, and vol. 2 (Zaltbommel: Nomanen Zoon, 1854 and 1856), passim.

[3] J. Burn, manuscript on Pontianak (British Library, India Office and Records, European Manuscripts, Eur E 109, dated February 12, 1811 and March 12, 1811); Sophia Raffles, *Memoir of the Life and Public Services of Sir Thomas Stamford Raffles* (London: John Murray, 1830), pp. 40, 46-47. Burn's two accounts run to 151 manuscript pages and are probably the source of most of Raffles's information (and perhaps misinformation) on the area. Cf. Veth, *Borneo's Wester-Afdeeling*, 1: 372-375. Burn's account is partly reproduced in Dr. [John] Leyden, "Sketch of Borneo," *Verhandelingen van het Bataviaasch Genootschap van Kunsten en Wetenschappen* 7 (1814): 1-64, partly reprinted in *Notices of the Indian Archipelago and Adjacent Countries*, ed. J. H. Moor (Singapore: n.p., 1837; reprint, London: Frank Cass, 1968), pp. 93-109. On Burn and other British visitors to West Borneo, see also F. Andrew Smith, "Missionaries, Mariners and Merchants: Overlooked British Travellers to West Borneo in the Early Nineteenth Century," paper presented to Seventh Biennial Conference, Borneo Research Council, Kota Kinabalu, July 15-18, 2002.

[4] Thomas Stamford Raffles, manuscript (British Library, India Office and Records, European Manuscripts, Eur D 199, ca. 1817), pp. 213-214; compare John Crawfurd, *History of the Indian Archipelago* (Edinburgh: Constable, 1820), p. 482, which estimates, unrealistically, that there are 200,000 Chinese in Borneo. Monterado, he reports, has six thousand workers, who annually produce over a pound of gold each.

[5] In 1851, even the Sultan of Sintang, miles upriver from the more prosperous coastal principalities, wore a gold-brocaded cap and vest (Ida Pfeiffer, *Meine zweite Weltreise*, [Vienna: Gerold's Sohn, 1856], 1: 125). Compare the description of the Sultan of Tidore in Leonard Y. Andaya, *The World of Maluku: Eastern Indonesia in the Early Modern Period* (Honolulu: University of Hawaii Press, 1993), pp. 62-64, who displayed golden water jars, drank from golden cups, and wore gold-embroidered silk or cotton garments. Yellow, and therefore gold, was the sign of royalty.

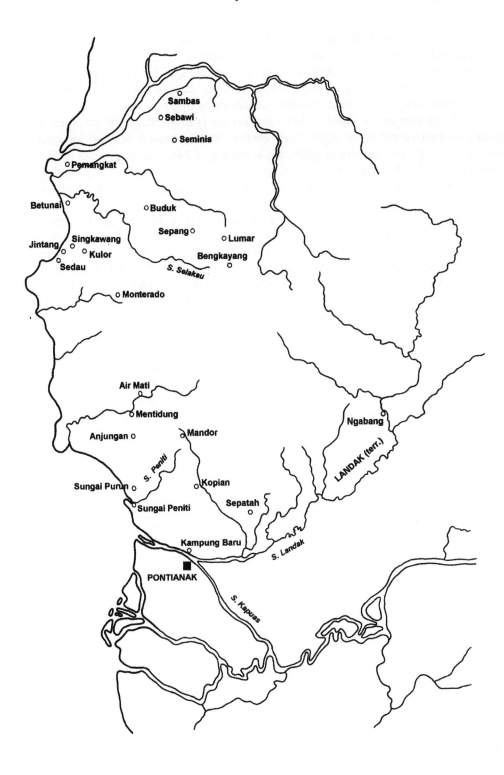

Map Three. Major Chinese Settlements in 1810.

four thousand *reals* in gold.[6] By 1822, most of the gold was certainly going to China, but a considerable amount also went to British traders in exchange for opium, textiles, and iron. The rest was sent to Siam and exchanged for salt, opium, and textiles; gold also went, mostly in Bugis ships, to Java, for cash or for oil, tobacco, and cloth.[7] Soon, Singapore joined the other destinations of gold exports.[8]

Little information exists about China's market for gold. Perhaps the prosperity of China's southern coast in the eighteenth century had increased demand for gold imports, used for jewelry or kept in gold bars as savings. China was the source of the gold thread used by the Malays for their fine textiles, so some gold was probably re-exported from China to Southeast Asia in this form, or in other finished products.

However, nineteenth-century observers indicate that gold was not the most desired item traded between Borneo and China. Burn lists the products exported from Pontianak in 1811, mostly on Chinese junks. The traders loaded birds' nests, beeswax, rattans, Borneo camphor, a kind of ebony, tin from Bangka, sometimes opium (which was also imported from elsewhere), a reddish wood used for dyeing (gaharu-wood), *bêche de mer* and *trepang* from the sea, in addition to considerable quantities of gold. In Burn's experience, the Chinese preferred natural products to gold, accepting the metal only when they could not get enough of them.[9]

The gold collected in West Borneo—normally in the form of gold dust—was usually sold in terms of silver dollars, the price depending on the presumed purity of the gold, which differed according to where it was mined. The dust sold for about twenty-three to twenty-five silver dollars for a *bungkal*, a *bungkal* being the weight of two silver dollars. Upriver, the price was as low as sixteen silver dollars

---

[6] Four thousand *reals* or silver dollars by weight of gold might be worth forty to fifty thousand silver dollars; see below on weighing gold. *Batav. Inkomende brieven overgekomen in 1779* (Letters received in Batavia in 1779) ARA, VOC 3524, Book 25, part 3, no. 21. Much later, in 1885-86, the Chinese of Mandor were selling embroidery made from golden thread, which, although popular with the *peranakan* and *baba* communities of Malaya and the Archipelago, was also sold to Europeans in Borneo. General Report for 1885, located in Arsip Nasional Republik Indonesia (ANRI), Jakarta, colonial archives, Borneo Westerafdeeling (BW) 5/16 (31) and General Report for 1886, ANRI BW 5/17 (32).

[7] Veth, *Borneo's Wester-Afdeeling*, 2: 110, citing a report of Commissioner J. H. Tobias.

[8] E. A. Francis, *Herinneringen uit den levensloop van een 'Indisch' ambtenaar van 1815 tot 1851* (Batavia: Van Dorp, 1856), 1: 251.

[9] Burn, p. 68. Burn's report is probably the most extensive source on trade, and, with the exception of Palm's reports, the earliest. Standard sources on China's trade, including a recent study of maritime interests, Jane Leonard, *Wei Yuan and China's Rediscovery of the Maritime World* (Cambridge: Harvard University Press, 1984), mention silver but not gold. China never coined gold, so it was not of interest for minting, as copper and, after the seventeenth century, silver were. Merchants thus preferred payments in silver rather than gold. The Chinese used gold for jewelry, and gold bars, occasionally, as money. Niels Steensgard pointed out, in conversation, that China actually exported gold in the seventeenth century.

Most Chinese provinces had some gold deposits, usually alluvial. The Chinese learned early to separate gold dust by directing a stream of water over the pay dirt in a wooden sluice box. It is unknown if they ever used mercury to separate the gold (now a common, and extremely toxic, procedure). Only in Southeast Asia, where labor was scarce, did Chinese miners use water to remove topsoil, a technique common in Borneo and also in tin mining in Bangka. See Peter J. Golas, "Mining," Part 13 of *Chemistry and Chemical Technology*, Vol. V, *Science and Civilization in China*, ed. Joseph Needham (Cambridge: Cambridge University Press, 1999), pp. 112, 254-255, 258-259.

per *bungkal*.[10] From China, junks brought tea, raw and woven silk, coarse earthenware, sugar candy, iron pots and other Chinese products, and a great deal of "painted paper" (probably joss paper, temple money used by Chinese in religious ceremonies).[11] While the cargo of a junk from Canton (M. Guangzhou) might be worth 25,000 to 30,000 dollars, those from Amoy or elsewhere carried less.[12]

Gold was, therefore, *a* major but not *the* major export of West Borneo. To the British and Dutch, however, it symbolized the supposed riches of the entire island.

CHINESE GOLD MINING

As early as 1740, the Panembahan of Mempawah, or perhaps the Sultan of Sambas, had decided to import Chinese laborers to mine gold. Probably, the first area to be opened was along the Sungai Duri, where the claims of these two kingdoms met.[13] No records remain, but Commissioner Tobias wrote in 1822 that the first settlement had been in Sambas, in the neighborhood of Seminis, and that it had been established in about 1740.[14]

All the people of Borneo did some gold mining, and gold was found there for centuries. Why was it necessary to import Chinese miners? Burn explains:

[The Dayaks] cultivate Paddy, and many of them search and [pan] Gold Dust, but this though it may naturally be supposed a simple and easy business is really not the case, the Chinaman far surpassing them in this art, which not only requires great personal Labour but perseverance and attention.[15]

---

[10] Burn, p. 78. One conversion says there are 550 *bungkal* in a *picul*, which is about sixty-two kilograms, so a *bungkal* would weigh about 113 grams.

[11] Compare the list of exports in the 1830s: rattan, wax, ebony and ironwood, gold dust from Mandor, and diamonds from Landak. Exports, especially for China, were tortoise shell, camphor, birds' nests, and pepper, while diamonds went mostly to Java, and gold to Java, Singapore, and China. From China came silks, nankeen (cotton), Chinese tobacco, tea, pickled vegetables, fruits, fish, offering or wrapping paper, iron pots and pans, coarse earthenware bowls, plates, and water vessels, and other goods. Francis, *Herinneringen*, 1: 251-252.

[12] Burn, pp. 81-82.

[13] P. M. van Meteren Brouwer, "De geschiedenis der Chineesche Districten der Wester-Afdeeling van Borneo van 1740-1926," *Indische Gids* 49,2 (1927): 1057, says Mempawah brought in some twenty Chinese from Brunei to the river Sungai Duri around 1740. J. T. [sic] Willer, "Eerste proeve eener kronijk van Mempawa en Pontianak," *Tijdschrift voor Indische Taal-, Land- en Volkenkunde* 3 (1855): 524-525, gives the impression that the Mempawah mines were only opened at the end of the 1760s; the earlier date is from S. H. Schaank, "De kongsis van Montrado, Bijdrage tot de geschiedenis en de kennis van het wezen der Chineesche vereenigingen op de Westkust van Borneo," *Tijdschrift voor Indische Taal-, Land- en Volkenkunde* 35,5/6 (1893): 506. Some accounts say Sambas began using Chinese laborers first. See Veth, *Borneo's Wester-Afdeeling*, 1: 297-299.

[14] Report of Schwaner on Hostilities with the Chinese of Sambas, 1846 (with a copy of Tobias's report from April 10, 1822), ANRI BW 18/2 (195). On the earliest period of Chinese gold mining in Borneo, see Yuan Bingling, *Chinese Democracies: A Study of the Kongsis of West Borneo (1776-1884)* (Leiden: Research School of Asian, African, and Amerindian Studies, CNWS, Universiteit Leiden, 2000), chapters one and two.

[15] Burn, p. 12.

Chinese mining technology and labor organization produced more gold than did the rather desultory methods of native laborers, who worked as miners when agricultural tasks, fishing, hunting, and collecting in the forest did not occupy them. The Chinese mined in larger groups, they made use of simple machines (including the so-called chain-pallet pump) in order to work on a larger scale, and their use of machines, access to capital, and control of labor made possible more continuous operation of the mines.[16] They also used water power to supplement manpower:

> The Chinese . . . avail themselves of . . . the mines abandoned by the Daya or Malayu. A tank is formed or a small stream is dammed up; and a channel being cut in the direction of the vein, the sluices are opened, and the superior strata are entirely cleared away by the velocity of the stream, and the Arèng [pay dirt] being discovered the sluice is shut. The Arèng having been dug out is washed, by exposure to the repeated action of water conducted along wooden troughs fixed in an inclined plane . . . [17]

The Malay rulers must have expected that increased production of gold from Chinese miners would profit them. They had encouraged Chinese immigration for this reason and planned to treat the immigrant Chinese in about the same way they treated the Dayaks of the *hulu*. The court would supply salt and rice, opium, and a few other necessities, at prices the rulers themselves set. The Chinese were not to engage in agriculture or to own firearms; they would not import or export anything themselves. They would deliver tribute in gold as payment for being allowed to work the mines. In addition, all Chinese immigrants would pay a tax on entering Borneo, and an even higher one when they left.

But these miners were not Dayaks. The Dayaks lived in small and relatively isolated communities with few outside ties, and so were comparatively easy to control. The Chinese laborers were better organized and connected. Their kongsis—the same organizations that enabled the Chinese to mine more efficiently—also enabled them to defy Malay authority, and their ties abroad gave them an additional advantage. Soon they were evading virtually all the provisions of the agreements with the native rulers.

The Chinese could circumvent the rulers' ports by using parallel rivers to reach the sea, bringing in men, goods, or weapons, and exporting gold. The region of Sambas, for example, was drained by a number of rivers, not just the Sambas Kecil

---

[16] Mary Somers Heidhues, *Bangka Tin and Mentok Pepper: Chinese Settlement on an Indonesian Island* (Singapore: Institute of Southeast Asian Studies, 1992), pp. 11-12, explains Chinese mining technology as used in the tin mines in Bangka. Except for the smaller scale of operations in Borneo, and the fact that, unlike tin ore, the gold dust usually was not smelted, the technology used, with water wheels, dams, sluices, and bores, was the same. See also Francis, *Herinneringen*, 1:253; James C. Jackson, "Mining in Eighteenth-Century Bangka: The Pre-European Exploitation of a 'Tin Island'," *Pacific Viewpoint* 10,2 (1969): 28-54; James C. Jackson, *The Chinese in the West Borneo Goldfields: A Study in Cultural Geography* (Hull: University of Hull Publications, Occasional Papers in Geography, 1970); and J. H. Kloos, "Vorkommen und Gewinnung des Goldes auf der Insel Borneo," *Tijdschrift voor Nederlandsch Indië* 4,2 (1866): 212-214.

[17] Anonymous, "Memoir on the Residency of the North-West Coast of Borneo," from *Singapore Chronicle*, October and November, 1827 in *Notices of the Indian Archipelago and Adjacent Countries*, ed. J. H. Moor (Singapore: n.p., 1837, reprint, London: Frank Cass, 1968), p. 8.

where its sultan lived. Indeed, many Chinese settlements, like Paniraman, Sungai Pinyu, Sungai Raya, Selakau, and Sedau, sprang up along the coast near the mouths of secondary rivers. The Chinese of the *hulu* had founded their own *hilir*. They also utilized "Dayak trails," footpaths connecting river sheds; in fact, they improved them to facilitate overland travel.[18] Contrary to their agreements, they planted rice and vegetables in the more fertile valleys, thus rendering themselves less dependent on the court's offerings, which were overpriced and frequently unavailable.[19] They intimidated and even killed the Dayaks the rulers sent to "control" them, and they put other Dayaks to work in agriculture or mining.

Links of trade and indebtedness between the Chinese and the Dayaks bypassed the Malay appanage holders. One Dutch resident claimed that the Chinese had actually "alienated the Dayak from the Malay and were in many respects beneficial for them."[20] While there is evidence that the Chinese and the Dayaks fought each other, they also maintained friendly relations.[21] The growing ties between Chinese and Dayaks, and the consequent decline of official trade, weakened the sultan's hold over appanage holders at court, who under other conditions had received benefits from him. All this led rulers and members of court to turn to piracy.[22]

Disputes that arose over control of gold and trade in the late eighteenth century and thereafter were not simply ethnic conflicts. Some Dayak groups sided with the Malay rulers and later the Dutch, while others fought alongside the Chinese. The Dayaks also used the presence of the Chinese to gain more economic, political, and cultural independence. In areas where the Chinese were settling, relationships became not dyadic—between Dayak clients and Malay patrons—but plural.

Court intrigues also disregarded ethnic divisions. Chinese miners in Sambas paid their taxes properly for some years after their arrival, but when a new sultan succeeded to the throne, his oldest brother, the Pangeran Anom, who had lived among the Chinese for five years, adopting Chinese dress and, apparently, their

---

[18] Francis, *Herinneringen*, 1: 305; W. L. Ritter, *Indische herinneringen, aantekeningen en tafereelen uit vroegeren en lateren tijd* (Amsterdam: Van Kesteren, 1843), p. 127. Along one path, there was even a Chinese inn. E. Doty and W. J. Pohlman, "Tour in Borneo, from Sambas through Montrado to Pontianak and the Adjacent Settlements of Chinese and Dayaks, during the Autumn of 1838," *Chinese Repository* 8 (1839): 299-300, 306.

[19] A. Azahari, *De ontwikkeling van het bevolkingslandbouwbedrijf in West-Kalimantan* (Bogor: 1950), p. 66, thinks that the sultan's monopoly of rice deliveries laid the foundation for Chinese agriculture, but, in practice, Chinese mines often maintained vegetable gardens and pigsties (Heidhues, *Bangka Tin*, p. 61). Of course vegetable gardening had a long tradition in China.

[20] Resident Willer in a letter of August 22, 1851, cited in E. B. Kielstra, "Bijdrage tot de geschiedenis van Borneo's Westerafdeeling," Part II, *Indische Gids* 11,1 (1889): 519.

[21] Ismail, "Politik perdagangan," p. 55.

[22] Ibid, pp. 2-3, 51, 98, 108-110, 167. See also Muhammad Gade Ismail, "Trade and State Power: Sambas (West Borneo) in the Early Nineteenth Century," in *State and Trade in the Indonesian Archipelago*, ed. G. J. Schutte (Leiden: KITLV Press, 1994) pp. 141-149, where this is argued concisely. Additionally, he attributes the breakdown of *hulu-hilir* relations in the late eighteenth century to the presence of foreign, especially British, traders, who wished to avoid the Malay courts to buy gold and other goods (see Ismail, "Politik perdagangan," p. 110).

religion and customs,[23] himself incited the Chinese of Monterado to stop paying taxes to the sultan. This Pangeran Anom later succeeded to the throne, but, unfortunately for him, the Chinese were now so independent that they paid their tax (one thousand dollars worth of gold) to their former ally only once.[24]

Clearly, between their arrival in the mid-eighteenth century and the early nineteenth century, the Chinese miners had become independent of the Malay authorities. Their independence was facilitated, in part, by the problems of the terrain and the nature of Malay principalities, with their centralized authority, weak periphery, and lack of territorial control. But the challenging landscape and the character of the Malay courts were not the only factors at play. The Chinese had gained independence by utilizing strong and relatively stable territorial organizations, the kongsis.

THE KONGSIS

The Chinese loan word kongsi (M. *gongsi*) has wide currency in the Malay-Indonesian world for any common undertaking or partnership, especially one in which the participants pool their financial contributions. In contemporary Southeast Asia, a kongsi is a firm or public company, "any kind of association, from a club to a limited company."[25] In West Borneo, by the time the Dutch arrived, these early cooperative units had taken on the character of states.

The early miners of West Borneo probably first organized their labor in small groups, choosing their own leaders and dividing the profits of mining between the members. This kind of cooperative venture has a long tradition in China and among the Chinese in Southeast Asia. It enabled businessmen, traders, and miners to pool capital and, where necessary, to manage labor, since their potential share in the profits motivated the workers to stay on the job. Thus, kongsi is a generic, non-specific term, even when applied to the situation in West Borneo. Possible meanings include:

—A kongsi, especially in mining areas, can be a group of a few to as many as several dozen members, who agree to contribute capital or labor, each member having a share (*hun*, Mandarin *fen*), and to divide profits among themselves.[26]

---

[23] True, the Pangeran was a Malay Muslim, but he was an eighteenth-century man, who did not think in strict ethnic and religious categories.

[24] Ritter, *Indische herinneringen*, pp. 119-121; T. A. C. van Kervel and D. W. J. C. van Lijnden, "Bijdrage tot de kennis van Borneo: De hervorming van den maatschappelijken toestand ter westkust van Borneo," *Tijdschrift voor Nederlandsch Indië* 15,1 (1853): 188-189. Ritter was in Borneo from 1826-1834, the last seven years as Assistant Resident of Sambas. These accounts say the miners came about 1760. See also Veth, *Borneo's Wester-Afdeeling*, 1: 367-370. Francis, a contemporary of Ritter, repeats the story about the Pangeran Anom (*Herinneringen*, 1: 320-322), as do Doty and Pohlman, "Tour in Borneo," pp. 303-304.

[25] Barbara E. Ward, "A Hakka Kongsi in Borneo," *Journal of Oriental Studies* 1,2 (1954): 359n; compare J. L. Vleming, *Het Chineesche zakenleven in Nederlandsch-Indië* (Weltevreden: Landsdrukkerij, 1926), pp. 57-70.

[26] Yuan, *Chinese Democracies*, p. 3, follows Schaank ("Kongsis van Montrado") in calling these lowest-level kongsis *hui*, associations. Again, *hui* is a generic term with many possible meanings and will be used here—except when in the name of an association—to refer to what are commonly called "secret societies." Yuan also suggests that the shared capital of such a group may be called kongsi, although I have not found that usage in works on West Borneo. Yuan

Such a group usually worked a single mine site. To observers, they represented a kind of "economic democracy,"[27] but little is known of the earliest organizations.

—In the gold-mining territory of West Borneo—and this seems unique in Chinese experience—there were associations or federations of mining kongsis. These might incorporate hundreds or even thousands of persons at several mine sites. They maintained an assembly hall (*tjoengthang*, M. *zongting*, general or central hall),[28] and representatives of major constituent kongsis were responsible for daily government. They are called "republics" and "democracies" in the nineteenth-century sources. The three major federations in West Borneo were:

- Fosjoen (M. Heshun), in Monterado.
- Lanfang (M. Lanfang), in Mandor, and
- Samtiaokioe (M. Santiaogou), which for a time was a member of Fosjoen in Monterado, but moved away in 1819. (See map four.)

—The name kongsi was also applied to the head of the kongsi and to his residence, which was the headquarters of the federation.

—Brotherhoods or "secret societies" also used the term. The influential secret society Ngee Heng or Ngee Hin (M. *yixing*) of Singapore and Malaya, which also appeared in Borneo, called itself officially Ngee Hin Kongsi. After the kongsis in Borneo were dissolved, "society" activity soon flared up.

While mining and commercial kongsis existed wherever Chinese settled, West Borneo seems to be unique in having associations that grew by incorporation of several such entities to control and govern sizable territories. In contrast, the Malay sultanates were not territorial realms; they controlled not land, but people and revenue. The individual mining kongsis merged and re-merged during the late eighteenth and early nineteenth centuries, forming federations that conducted themselves as "states," and, indeed, up to the 1850s, the major Chinese kongsi federations were the only "states" on the West Coast of Borneo. Neither the native principalities nor the Dutch colonial power had comparable organizations, infrastructures, or power.

The miners had formed larger groupings out of smaller kongsis in order to withstand the challenges of the environment, the hostility of the Dayaks, and the predations of the Malay sultans. This consolidation was not necessarily a peaceful

---

associates the term closely with "management," and, indeed, "common management" is a possible literal translation of kongsi.

[27] Wang Tai Peng, *The Origins of Chinese Kongsi* (Petaling Jaya: Pelanduk, 1994); Carl A. Trocki, *Opium and Empire: Chinese Society in Colonial Singapore, 1800-1910* (Ithaca: Cornell University Press, 1991), esp. pp. 15-49; compare Mary Somers Heidhues, "Chinese Organizations in West Borneo and Bangka: *Kongsi* and *Hui*," in *"Secret Societies" Reconsidered: Perspectives on the Social History of Early Modern South China and Southeast Asia*, ed. David Ownby and Mary Somers Heidhues (Armonk: M. E. Sharpe, 1993), pp. 66-88 and below.

[28] Hall is a usual translation for the word *thang* (M. *ting*), but, as de Groot emphasizes, "this building is also clearly an ancestral temple." J. J. M. de Groot, *Het kongsiwezen van Borneo: Eene verhandeling over den grondslag en den aard der Chineesche politieke vereenigingen in de koloniën* (The Hague: M. Nijhoff, 1885), p. 120.

Plate 2. Chinese coolies and their boss in Borneo, circa 1890.
Credit: KITLV, Leiden, number 6548. By permission.

process. As Siahaan[29] has shown, inter- and intra-kongsi conflicts were a permanent feature of the West Coast landscape.

Of the three major kongsi federations that existed on Borneo's West Coast, the powerful Monterado federation of kongsis, called Fosjoen Tjoengthang (M. Heshun Zongting),[30] was often called the "irreconcilable enemy" of the colonial government, although for years the two sides lived at peace. The largest, and by Dutch times dominant, kongsi among Fosjoen's members was Thaikong (M. Dagang), a name meaning "big harbor" or "big river," probably chosen because of its location near the Sungai Raya, the great river. A second member, Samtiaokioe (M. Santiaogou, three-branch ditch, referring to the open pit from which gold-bearing earth was dug), left Fosjoen, after some disputes, in 1822, but other, smaller kongsis remained with Thaikong.[31] The best-known kongsi, Lanfang of Mandor, made its peace with the Dutch in 1823, but its loyalty to the colonial administration was more ambiguous than colonial officials realized. Lanfang outlived the other major kongsis, surviving until 1884, when it was dissolved.

---

[29] Harlem Siahaan, "Konflik dan perlawanan kongsi Cina di Kalimantan Barat 1770-1854" (PhD dissertation, Universitas Gadjah Mada, 1994).

[30] The name *heshun* probably means "harmonious and prosperous," although the Matthews Dictionary translates the combination as "civil and obliging" or "pleasant." *Zongting* is a general or central hall, but had many functions. Yuan, *Chinese Democracies*, pp. 271f, lists "a parliament, an executive council, a presidency, an army headquarters, and a public congress hall . . . also a temple." Most sources refer to it as the "kongsi house" and, in fact, it was also the dwelling of the headman and his family. See illustration.

[31] Schaank, "Kongsis van Montrado," pp. 557-558. On Monterado's version of the split, see Leonard Blussé and Ank Merens, "Nuggets from the Gold Mines: Three Tales of the Ta-kang [Dagang] Kongsi of West Kalimantan," in *Conflict and Accomodation in Early Modern East Asia: Essays in Honour of Erik Zürcher*, ed. Leonard Blussé and Harriet Zurndorfer (Leiden: E. J. Brill, 1993), pp. 284-321, and in more detail, Yuan, *Chinese Democracies*, pp. 96-102. Smaller kongsis are shown on map three.

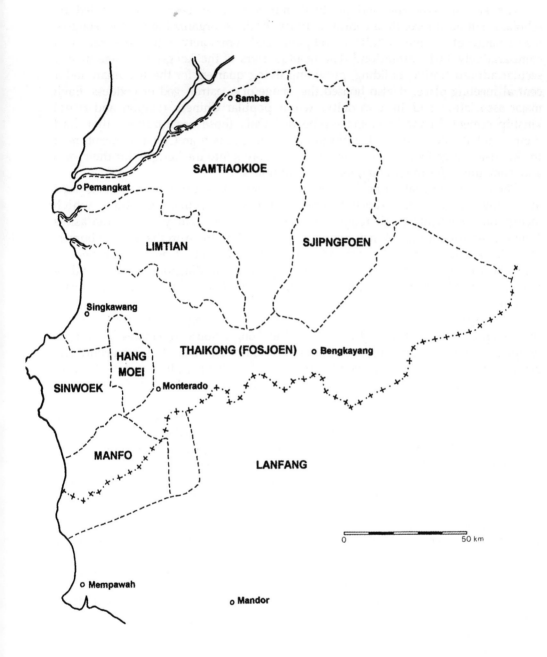

Map Four. Territories of the major kongsis, circa 1822. Smaller kongsis were partly absorbed by Fosjoen. The x-dotted line separates Sambas from Mempawah.

The kongsis' economic and political functions have been widely noted by scholars, but until recently a central activity of these organizations—the kongsis' maintenance of a common hall for religious and community activities—received comparatively little attention.[32] The headquarters of the kongsi was more than a secular administrative building, providing living quarters for the headman and a central meeting place; it also housed the image of a patron god or goddess. Each major association had its own deity, while popular Chinese religion and ritual kinship cemented kongsi membership bonds.[33] Only those organizations that had their own hall, altar, and god could initiate immigrants from China as members of the kongsis. Large federations thus initiated laborers into the kongsis for their own and, sometimes, for the smaller, independent mines.[34]

The initiation ritual for new miners was apparently similar to the rituals used at the founding of a new Taoist temple or of a new settlement in China, which incorporated elements of folk religion. Immigrants to Borneo may have taken ashes from the incense-burners of their home temples, adding them to the incense burners at their new location.[35] This act, accompanied by taking of an oath, formed a symbolic kinship, making the new members (who in the diaspora were devoid of family) "ritual brothers," recalling the ritual brotherhood of the so-called "secret societies."

The diagram of the "kongsi house" of the Lanfang Kongsi in Mandor[36] confirms this religious aspect: the central part of the kongsi house resembles a Chinese temple, as they are found all over China and Southeast Asia. The open court, the atrium pond, and the exterior pond with a small bridge are all features of larger temples. The image of the main deity resides at the center rear.[37] (See diagram from Veth, below.)

The Dutch were aware of the presence of images in kongsi houses, but, impressed by the fortifications surrounding them, they regarded them as military or administrative headquarters, not religious centers. Typically, European visitors describing a kongsi hall spoke of a fort (indeed it was heavily fortified) or even a "*raadhuis,*" a city hall.[38] This misunderstanding led to trouble after the dissolution of Lanfang Kongsi in 1884 (as will be illustrated in chapter three).

---

[32] See Yuan, *Chinese Democracies*, for a remedy of this situation. She also notes (p. 3) that the term kongsi is sometimes used for common descent groups, if, for example, they maintain a clan temple.

[33] See also H. van Dewall, "Opstand der Chinezen van Menteradoe, Westkust-Borneo 1853-54," manuscript, KITLV collection H 83, and below, for the activities of patron deities.

[34] Schaank, "Kongsis van Montrado," pp. 526-528; cf. Yuan, *Chinese Democracies*, pp. 16, 34.

[35] On this practice in Taoism, see Kristofer Schipper, *Tao: De levende religie van China* (Amsterdam: Meulenhoff, 1998, 4th ed.), pp. 36-37. In Mandarin, it is called *fenxiang*.

[36] Veth, *Borneo's Wester-Afdeeling*, 1: 324.

[37] My understanding of temples has benefited from Schipper, *Tao*, pp. 33-37, as well as from Yuan, *Chinese Democracies*. For a collection of temple and tomb epigraphs in West Kalimantan, see Wolfgang Franke (with Claudine Salmon and Anthony Siu), *Bali, Kalimantan, Sulawesi, Moluccas*, volume 3 of *Chinese Epigraphic Materials in Indonesia* (Singapore: South Seas Society, 1997), pp. 46-185.

[38] For example, R. C. van Prehn Wiese, "Aantekeningen omtrent de Wester-Afdeeling van Borneo," *Tijdschrift voor Indische Taal-, Land- en Volkenkunde* 10,1 (1861): 124.

If popular religion formed the social cement of the kongsis, their primary task remained to import miners and to export gold. The religious qualities of kongsis did

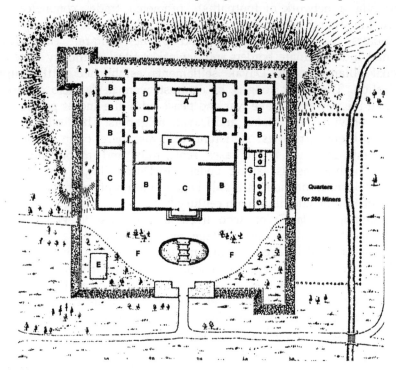

Key.   A: Altar of Toapekong
       B: Rooms for *kapitan*, clerks
       C: Hall for Public Meetings
       D: Rooms for Guests
       E: Storerooms
       F: Open spaces, atrium, with ponds

Plate 3. Diagram of the Lanfang Kongsi Hall in Mandor in 1822. [39]

not subtract from their obvious economic, political, and administrative functions. Unlike modern Westerners, nineteenth-century Chinese did not think in separate religious and secular categories; their religion was as much about this world as the next, and gods, mediums, and processions could be expressions of state and individual power as much as were armies, judicial procedures, or administrative structures.[40] Kongsis were multi-functional.

In spite of their rivalries and weaknesses, in all of West Borneo from 1819 to 1850, large kongsis like Lanfang and Fosjoen established control over territory,

---

[39] Based on P. J. Veth, *Borneo's Wester-Afdeeling: geographisch, statistisch, historisch, vorafgegaan door eene algemeene schets des ganschen eilands*, Vol. 1 (Zaltbommel: Joh. Nomanen Zoon, 1854), p. 323

[40] Compare Jean DeBernardi, "Epilogue: Ritual Process Reconsidered," in "*Secret Societies Reconsidered,* " ed. Ownby and Heidhues, esp. pp. 216-219.

regularly chose their leaders, dealt with criminal and civil offenses, meted out corporal punishment, maintained a standing army, improved overland communications (via a network of footpaths), promoted trade, commerce, and industry, collected taxes and tolls, minted coins, set up schools, and regularly held religious ceremonies to insure solidarity and public welfare. The Malay principalities had indeterminate borders and a weak central authority based on shifting personal alliances. The Dayak settlements established little supra-village organization. The major kongsis, by contrast, were in de facto control of their land and had the power to make war and peace with the Indies government, with one another, or with their Malay and Dayak neighbors. They often built a network of forts in their territories, stationing officials there or in subordinate towns and settlements, and they levied taxes, rents, tolls, and import and export duties, even from native vessels sailing under the Dutch flag.[41] The colonial authorities in West Borneo, for their part, only began to attempt many of the tasks expected of a "state" in the late nineteenth century.[42]

The Dutch Sinologist De Groot, who lived and worked in West Borneo, propagated the idea that kongsis were "village republics" (having a "democratic spirit"),[43] a conclusion which drew on his understanding of Chinese village organization.[44] Certainly the kongsis evidenced many similarities to Chinese village life, but there were differences, too. Participation was carefully limited to favor newcomers (those born in China) over longtime residents or *petompang*,[45] those of mixed blood and locally born, thus inverting usual village practice. Voting rights were reserved to miners, whereas villages in China were dominated by agriculturists. Finally, the commercial interest—gold mining—overrode other local interests, just as the miners outvoted other inhabitants.

The use of the term "republic" for the kongsis also deserves scrutiny, for Dutch authors of the nineteenth century often used the word "republic" simply to mean a political body without a king or hereditary ruler. Certainly the Monterado Kongsi, which elected its leaders every four months (although some remained in office or rotated among positions of leadership), was republican in organization, and, as far as the miner-voters were concerned, democratic. Little information exists about the internal organization of Samtiaokioe, but the situation in Lanfang differed considerably from that in Monterado. In Lanfang, leaders remained in office for

---

[41] Most of these activities are mentioned in the Report of former Resident Willer. ANRI BW 28/25 (82). See also Kielstra, "Bijdrage," Part I, *Indische Gids* 11,1 (1889): 349; and Schaank, "Kongsis van Montrado," pp. 571-587, 597-606.

[42] W. R. Baron von Hoëvell, in "Onze roeping op Borneo," *Tijdschrift voor Nederlandsch Indië* 14,2 (1852): 193, refers to the colonial administration in West Borneo before 1851 as "completely imaginary."

[43] De Groot, *Kongsiwezen*, p. 140. Compare: "Indeed the kongsis were...oligarchic republics in the full meaning of the word. In a direct way, the little man had nothing to contribute, unless it be at the election of a new village head" (p. 127). However, he argues that "public opinion" tended to hold the bosses in check, at least before colonial times, and blames the Dutch for altering this balance of power (pp. 127, 130).

[44] It is tempting to compare de Groot's idea of village republics with the ideal image that many colonial writers had of "village democracies." De Groot is certainly more sober in his assessment of village power relations, however, and "village democracy," although it survived into the twentieth century among politicians, has now lost currency among academics.

[45] The word comes from *bantangfan* (M.), "half-Chinese-barbarian," referring to those of mixed parentage. See Yuan, *Chinese Democracies*, p. 70.

years, and their successors were often sons or close relatives. Furthermore, the internal organization of all the kongsis changed as they grew larger or came under the influence of the Dutch (as was the case with Lanfang after 1823). De Groot's designation of the kongsis as democratic, then, should be weighed with care.

Whatever their constitution, the markedly independent and powerful kongsis enraged the colonial authorities. As perceived by the Dutch, these Chinese organizations had arrogated to themselves powers to which they were not entitled, including access to land, while colonial policy dictated that the land belonged to the sultans and not to the Chinese, who were merely entitled to use it if they paid a tax or rent. The Chinese punished crimes cruelly, even with the death sentence, on their own authority. They avoided the taxes and monopolies set up by the Dutch. Insofar as they were democratic, they could only remain democratic by resisting the rule of an outside authority. Finally, the kongsis had extended their influence into the nearby Dayak villages, who had to pay tribute to the kongsi or to buy from Chinese traders on credit, a system that easily put them into debt-slavery, according to colonial observers. The Chinese used indebtedness to acquire the children or wives of the Dayaks as their servants.[46] From the Dutch perspective, the Malay principalities could be tolerated, more because of their weakness than their virtues; Chinese organizations, whatever their virtues, were intolerable because of their strength.

THE KONGSIS AT WORK

Little is known of the earliest settlements of gold miners. Palm, the agent of the VOC in Pontianak, visited a gold mine near Landak in 1779, but it may have been worked by natives.[47] Burn's 1811 account reports on mining technology and gold production, but it makes little mention of the organization.

The first Chinese miners were probably recruited by the traders and ship captains from China who had long had contacts with West Borneo. To work the mines, forming cooperative units was really a necessity, given the grueling but relatively unskilled work to be performed, and the need to divide responsibilities and profits. Small-scale mining in China was organized on a similar cooperative basis; shareholding endeavors also have a long tradition in South China mercantile and seagoing communities.[48] Accounts of Chinese mining in the tin mines of Bangka show the importance of cooperative forms: miners shared work and chose their officers—headman, cook, and treasurer-clerk—at regular intervals. Headmen of Bangka mines who had served their term would return to being ordinary miners. Members divided shares in the undertaking among the working miners and the mine officials; when a season's work was completed and the metal sold, each shareholder participated in the profits.[49] The names of many West

---

[46] Kervel and van Lijnden, "Bijdrage," pp. 191-193.

[47] C. L. M. Radermacher, "Beschrijving van het eiland Borneo, voor zoover hetzelfde tot nu bekend is," *Verhandelingen van het Bataviaasch Genootschap van Kunsten en Wetenschappen* 2 (1780): 125, 147-148. The earliest reports of the Kapuas area were from Palm, who supplied Radermacher with information.

[48] Wang, *Origins of Chinese Kongsi*, pp. 14-47. Yuan, *Chinese Democracies*, points out that the miners in such small groups probably were relatives or close acquaintances.

[49] For a description of cooperative mining in Bangka, see Heidhues, *Bangka Tin*, pp. 37-40, and Heidhues, "Chinese Organizations."

Borneo kongsis reflect their origin as shareholding groups. Examples are the Sjipngfoen (M. Shiwufen) or "Fifteen Shares," the Sjipsamfoen (M. Shisanfen), "Thirteen Shares," and so on.[50] Members often bound themselves together by an oath, as did members of Chinese "secret societies,"[51] but the primary goal of the mining kongsis was commercial, not conspiratorial.

Plate 4. Chinese, probably from West Borneo, circa 1890. Credit KITLV, Leiden, number 6549. By permission.

Mines also needed capital to bring in workers. Given the simple technology involved, recruiting and transporting workers was the major expense incurred in mining operations. Few special skills were required, and most of the simple machines involved could be constructed from locally available materials. However, a steady supply of fresh labor was absolutely essential for operating the mines, given the high rates of death, sickness, departure (many miners chose to return to China), and other forms of attrition. This was especially true as the mines grew larger, employing one or two hundred workers, and the investment in waterworks, dams, and sluices grew.[52]

The need for recruiting laborers limited the cooperative nature of mining. Only when new miners had worked off the debt for their passage could they become shareholders. Those who provided passage and turned over new arrivals to the kongsis—often urban businessmen performed these functions—were in practice

---

[50] Schaank, "Kongsis van Montrado," pp. 522-523.

[51] Ibid., pp. 585-586, cites an example of such an oath. In contrast to the society initiation, according to Schaank, in mining kongsis no blood was spilled to promise loyalty.

[52] Crawford, *History*, 3: 475-476. Jackson, *Chinese in the West Borneo Goldfields*, pp. 34-37 gives details, with a sketch, of the pump and waterworks. See also Heidhues, *Bangka Tin*, p. 13, for an early drawing of a tin mine using a pump. Tin mines were on a larger scale than gold mines.

lending capital to the mines. In return, they might be awarded shares in the mines, representing the labor of miners they had furnished. In a history of Monterado, Schaank emphasized that the smaller mines depended on the larger kongsis, which had links to the coastal harbors, to provide them with new laborers.[53] Although small mines may have started as cooperative, familial endeavors, over the course of years they might become dependent on outsiders for labor and capital, just as the economy of the larger mines became more complex and less egalitarian. Drawing on an informant who had worked in Borneo for years, an observer noted this difference in 1820:

> The great mines are wrought by companies of persons of property and capital, who employ monthly labourers. The smaller mines, on the other hand, are worked by the mere labourers who at once conduct the operative parts, and share the proceeds on terms of perfect equality.[54]

New kongsis were being formed constantly; others were abandoned as sites were exhausted or became unprofitable, and the miners decided to try their luck elsewhere. As a result, the area of exploitation expanded outward from the initial sites in Sambas and Mempawah territory. At the same time, struggles for the control of deposits, land, and water continued.

With the expansion and exhaustion of sites, smaller kongsis were often absorbed by larger ones. That is what happened in 1776, when the Fosjoen Tjoengthang consolidated fourteen kongsis in the Monterado area into a single body. The two most powerful members of this new federation were the above-mentioned Thaikong, with gold fields west and southwest of Monterado, and Samtiaokioe, with fields farther to the north. (See map three.)

If members of small kongsis were friends or relatives of each other, the larger ones were more diverse. However, some groups and some families dominated. Most of the Thaikong Chinese were from Lufeng and Huilai on Guangdong's coast, the main surnames were Ng (M. Wu), Wong (M. Huang), and Tjhang (M. Zheng). In Samtiaokioe, dominant family surnames were Tjoe (M. Zhu) and Woen (M. Wen). Like Thaikong's, most of Samtiaokioe's miners came from Lufeng and Huilai; these people were *pansanhok*.[55] Lanfang men were predominantly from Meixian (the Hakka "heartland") or from Dapu, both in upland Guangdong. Nevertheless, none of the major kongsis drew their laborers from a single source; other speech groups, even Hokkiens or Cantonese, were represented, too.

When Fosjoen was formed, another seven kongsis were working in Lara, near the present town of Bengkayang.[56] As existing sites were depleted, the Chinese

---

[53] Schaank, "Kongsis van Montrado," p. 528. Veth also refers to supplying of miners in return for shares (*Borneo's Wester-Afdeeling*, 1: 303). It was a common practice elsewhere, too.

[54] Crawfurd, *History*, 3: 474-475.

[55] See chapter one, "Chinese Society in West Borneo," for this term. To underline the predominance of Hakkas from coastal Guangdong, or *pansanhok*, in 1915 a list of one hundred contributors to a Chinese nationalist organization in Capkala, in the heart of Thaikong territory, included twenty-two from Lufeng and fifteen from adjacent Huilai; three were Hepo-Jieyang Hakkas. Meixian and Dapu were only thirteen altogether. A few contributors were from non-Hakka areas; only one was Teochiu.

[56] Schaank, "Kongsis van Montrado," pp. 523-526. Bengkayang was close to Lara but belonged in 1823 to Samtiaokioe. In the following years of prosperity, the Lara Kongsi became allies of

opened new mines in the region around Seminis, Sepang,[57] and Lumar. A new kongsi of Hakkas from Hoppo (M. Hepo[58]) in Jieyang called Limthian (M. Lintian) Kongsi, grew up in Buduk some time after this.[59]

Food supplies also led to conflicts among early mine settlements. In 1775, just before Fosjoen was consolidated, Monterado had defeated an attempt by a nearby Chinese agricultural kongsi called Thien Thi Foei (M. Tiandihui[60]) to monopolize the supplies of food for the miners. This agricultural kongsi disappeared, while another agricultural endeavor, Lanfanghui, which had similarly challenged the Monterado miners, moved out of the neighborhood, finally settling in Mandor, where it concentrated on mining operations.[61]

The local rulers of Sambas and Mempawah had long since ceased to control external kongsi trade; they had no influence on Chinese activity in agriculture, nor could they prevent them from acquiring arms and ammunition. Despite their agricultural activities, however, the kongsis still needed to import some rice from abroad, as well as tobacco, salt, and opium. For that, they could utilize the harbor settlements they controlled, especially in the environs of Singkawang.[62]

Lanfang Kongsi

One Chinese text from the nineteenth century relates the history of the Lanfang Kongsi of Mandor. Its founder, Lo Fong Pak (M. Luo Fangbo), who seems to have been associated with Lanfanghui, the agricultural kongsi that had clashed with Monterado, arrived in Borneo in 1772 from Meixian, or Jiayingzhou, as it was then known, Guangdong, with a number of followers. (The kongsi chronicle speaks of "100 families," but the immigrants were very probably unaccompanied males.) In 1777, the year after Fosjoen was founded, Lo established a new mining kongsi at Mandor, on the territory of the Panembahan of Mempawah, not far from the

---

Monterado, although they remained independent until at least 1837, when they came completely under Thaikong. Van Meteren Brouwer, "Geschiedenis," p. 1069, calls Bengkayang "Larah Sam Thiaoe Keoe," while the rest of Lara was "Larah Thai Kong."

[57] Sepang is called Sepawang in some sources.

[58] Hoppo is in Jieyang, Chaozhou Prefecture. Schaank also identifies people from there as *pansanhok*. The Hakka had migrated to Hoppo since the fifteenth century; see also Wolfgang Franke, "The Sovereigns of the Kingdoms of the Three Mountains, San Shan Guowang, at Hepo and in Southeast Asia: A Preliminary Investigation," in *Collected Papers: International Conference on Chinese Studies* (Kuala Lumpur: n.p., 1994), p. 373.

[59] Schaank, "Kongsis van Montrado," pp. 528-534; 555, 580. Veth, *Borneo's Wester-Afdeeling*, 1: 304 is more vague about the relationship of Lara-Bengkayang and Thaikong.

[60] This is the name of a famous Chinese "secret society" or brotherhood, the "Heaven and Earth Society."

[61] Yuan (*Chinese Democracies*, pp. 40, 42-45) speculates about the nature of this kongsi and its links to the sworn brotherhoods or "secret societies." She believes the original agricultural kongsis called Tiandihui and Lanfanghui may have been close to a secret society in their early years. She links Lanfang and its name "orchid fragrance" with symbolism of the Heaven and Earth Society (Tiandihui). Society rites and symbols may have had a life of their own, being used to solidify intra-group ties without implying organizational relations, but Yuan's speculation remains plausible.

[62] Schaank, "Kongsis van Montrado," pp. 566-567. On Mandor, compare R. C. van Prehn "Aantekeningen betreffende Borneo's Westkust," *Tijdschrift voor Indische Taal-, Land- en Volkenkunde* 7 (1858): 22-32; and ANRI BW 28/33.

Kapuas River. Lo's retention of the name "Lanfang" connects him and his associates with the defeated Lanfang farming operation near Monterado.[63] Schaank believes that its defeat by Monterado was the reason Lo moved across the Sungai Peniti to the territory of Mempawah, where he initially remained hostile to Fosjoen.

The establishment of Lanfang took place not long after the founding of Pontianak in 1771. According to archival sources, the initial growth of this kongsi was related to the new sultanate's activities, and Sultan Abdurachman, the founder of Pontianak, soon claimed hegemony over the kongsi territory, although it belonged to Mempawah at first. In 1787, the Mandor territory fell decisively to Pontianak.[64] Lanfang now developed economic ties with that city. Chinese laborers going to the mines passed through the port of Pontianak (instead of Mempawah), and the sultan profited from their comings and goings. Kampung Baru, across the river from the sultan's headquarters, grew up as a settlement subordinate to the kongsi. However, Lanfang, although it survived as a kongsi until 1884, was never as powerful as Thaikong. (See map four.)

Another version of the founding of Lanfang, apparently from Malay sources, suggests that, in 1788, a collection of smaller kongsis existed in the Mandor area, and it was "Tiko Jengut" (a nickname of founder Lo Fong Pak[65]) who consolidated these organizations, creating the Langfang Kongsi, which he subsequently led until 1795. Headman Lo expelled the weaker kongsis to Karangan, leaving only Lanfang in Mandor. From there, Lanfang Kongsi began to expand toward Landak in the nineteenth century.[66]

KONGSIS AS TERRITORIAL ORGANIZATIONS

Kongsi federations included not only mines, but also substantial towns like those of Monterado or Mandor. Usually the *pasar* or market consisted of a street lined on both sides with rows of shops; in Monterado, other streets intersected the main one. At the end of the *pasar* stood the central kongsi headquarters or *tjoengthang* (M. *zongting*). This substantial building was built of ironwood with wooden shingles; other houses were usually roofed with cheaper *alang-alang* grass. In the *thang* complex, bachelor miners lived in simple barracks; the kongsi headmen occupied the main building. The complexes were surrounded by an earthen wall topped by a bamboo thicket for defense. (See Plate 3.)

---

[63] The history of Lanfang translated by de Groot gives the impression that Lo Fong Pak came from China directly to Pontianak, but Schaank already casts doubt on this version. De Groot, *Kongsiwezen*, pp. 8-9; Schaank, "Kongsis van Montrado," pp. 519-520. Lo arrived in 1772, founding the kongsi five years later. See also van Meteren Brouwer, "Geschiedenis," pp. 1058-1063, and Historical Note on the Kongsi Lanfang in ARA 2.10.02 V. 31.5.86 (36).

[64] Historical Note, ARA V. 31.5.86. During this time, a representative of the Dutch was stationed in Pontianak (above). The dispute involved an altercation between Sambas and Mempawah and the intervention of Pontianak; because Mempawah was unable to pay certain debts to him, Sultan Abdurachman was able to put his son on Mempawah's throne, but the Mempawah ruling line was later restored by the Dutch. On the early years of Pontianak, see Heidhues, "First Two Sultans."

[65] Tiko is from *dage*, big brother, in this case the boss of a kongsi (or "secret society"), and *jengut* is Malay for "beard." The picture of Lo Fong Pak in Sungai Purun's temple (described in Franke, *Chinese Epigraphic Materials*, 3: 180-182) indeed shows a man with a flowing beard. See Plate 7, p. 110.

[66] Willer, "Eerste proeve," p. 544. See also account of Landak below.

As the center of kongsi life, the *thang* offered room for assemblies of the miners and for religious offerings. Many contemporary towns—Pemangkat is an example—follow this typical layout. In Pemangkat, the commercial area extends along a single street in the plain (with a few intersecting streets), while on the mountain that dominates the town are the temples to Dabogong and, farther up the hill, to Tianhou; the former is probably located on the site of the former kongsi hall that was destroyed in the fighting of 1851.[67] (See Plate 5, page 90.) Adjacent to the temple is a school, which was once a Chinese school.[68]

The major kongsis were linked with dependent towns along the coast, including ports like Pemangkat and Singkawang—where goods from Singapore could be brought and coolies transported—and farming settlements, or fishing villages. Monterado had Singkawang, Samtiaokioe had Pemangkat, the Buduk Kongsi (later an ally of Thaikong) probably used Sebangkau, and, at first, Mandor used the harbor of Sungai Peniti[69] and other locations, like Kuala Mempawah, until it shifted its business to Pontianak. (See map five from 1820s on page 70, which gives some indication of this relationship.) These coastal settlements supplied food and outside linkages that were essential to survival—and to escaping the sultans' grasp.

KONGSI TOWNS

As the numbers of miners in the gold fields increased, it became necessary to accommodate and serve them, not only with agricultural products, but also with urban activities. As a result, towns allied to kongsis expanded, with settlements of craftsmen, shops, and services. A visitor to the town of Monterado in 1851 counted the enterprises that served the mines and mineworkers: four ironsmiths, five goldsmiths, two tinsmiths, eight bakers, ten pig butchers, fifty fishmongers, four carpenters, eighty barbers and the same number of tailors, three lantern-makers, and four schoolmasters. Health care was in the hands of thirty doctors and fifteen pharmacies, and, for recreation, the town had twenty-eight opium dens, ten gambling houses, and two restaurants.[70]

---

[67] Dabogong is god of wealth and virtue, often the patron of a mine; Tianhou or Mazi is a patroness of fishermen, sailors, and those who trade at sea.

[68] On Chinese settlements in West Kalimantan, see Johannes Widodo, "The Pattern of Chinese Settlements in Western Kalimantan," *Journal of the South Seas Society* 54 (December 1999): 114-117, who calls them "introverted." In the nineteenth century, many farmers lived in a more scattered fashion, outside the towns.

[69] The history of Lanfang remarks that Lo Fong Pak, after differences with the Teochius in Pontianak, took over a mine on the Sungai Peniti near Mandor, making that his base. If the above analysis holds, the "differences" that provoked the move to settle in Mandor may have been the struggle between Monterado and the first Lanfang around 1774, not a struggle with Pontianak. De Groot, *Kongsiwezen*, p. 9.

[70] Van Prehn Wiese, "Aantekeningen Wester-Afdeeling," p. 123. He does not mention brothels. Items traded included textiles, baked goods, fruits, and lightly salted fish brought daily from Singkawang. This same author visited Mandor in 1851, where he counted a similar variety of activities, but smaller in number. See R. C. van Prehn, "Aantekeningen betreffende Borneo's Westkust," p. 26, and ANRI BW 28/33. In 110 houses there were two distillers, three opium dens, five ironsmiths, three goldsmiths, and two schoolteachers, among others. Only the gambling houses (twenty-three) were more numerous than in Monterado.

Of special importance were the kongsis' coastal towns, which enabled them to import and export goods free from Malay or Dutch control. Just as Pontianak was the largest Malay-dominated town, Singkawang became the largest of the towns dependent on kongsis, as an early account confirms:

> Singkawang is a sizable *kampung,* consisting of a long street with low, wooden houses, which serve as shops for the sale of rice, meat and other daily needs, or for smoking opium. A kongsi house [hall, temple] is off to one side of the street. The Chinese living here, in contrast to the mineworkers, are for the most part married, either directly with Dayak women or with women descended from Chinese unions with Dayak women. In the neighborhood are fine rice paddies and the men spend a lot of time farming, while the shops, in their absence, are tended by the women.[71]

Surveying Asian commerce at the end of the eighteenth century, W. Milburn confirmed the interest of British traders in dealing with such coastal towns, noting the attractions of Sinkawang in particular:

> There is a place called Singkawang, between Pontiana and Sambass, peopled with Chinese in considerable numbers, which has lately been much resorted to by our ships . . . . [In Mempawah] there are a great number of Chinese merchants . . . . Momparva is one of the best markets in the East for opium, as a considerable trade is carried on in the Chinese junks, and by the proas [*perahu,* small sailing vessels] from the neighboring places and islands.[72]

Singkawang was located about thirty kilometers from the mining headquarters, Monterado, and was subordinate to it until the Kongsi War of 1850-1854. Chinese farmers in the neighborhood had introduced a number of crops from China,[73] and reports describe a thriving agricultural region. The path to Singkawang along the coast took visitors through "an extensive valley, teeming with cultivation" and "a series of gardens, which, in addition to many kinds of culinary vegetables, produced sugar cane, maize, plantains, and a variety of fruits."[74]

Later descriptions confirm the nature of the settlement. The population along the coast, both men and women, were of sturdy, "peasant" stock, the women dressed in long, wide slacks of blue cotton. They, as well as some of the men, wore "straw hats of an amazing size, so that not only the head, but the whole body was

---

[71] Veth, *Borneo's Wester-Afdeeling,* 1: 104, drawing on accounts of George Windsor Earl, *The Eastern Seas, or Voyages and Adventures in the Indian Archipelago* (London: W. H. Allen, 1837; reprint, Singapore: Oxford University Press, 1971) and de Stuers, who was there in the 1820s. Singkawang's market burned down several times, and it is difficult to imagine the old town when visiting the present-day one.

Veth's report that the women could manage the shops in their spouses' absence is another possible indication that Hakka kongsi culture was able to accommodate flexible gender roles, as noted in chapter one.

[72] W. Milburn, *Oriental Commerce* (London: Black, Parry and Co., rev. ed. 1825), pp. 413, 418. These comments date from around 1800.

[73] Burn, p. 110.

[74] Earl, *Eastern Seas,* p. 280. The area around Singkawang is better suited to agriculture than other, mostly swampy, coastal areas.

protected from sun and rain."[75] Outside the town, against the slope of a hill, was a Chinese temple that the townspeople visited for prayer and for picnics.[76]

Another active Chinese port town was Pemangkat. A few decades after the war with Monterado of 1850-54 had driven away most of its residents, a visitor found that activity in the town, which served as a Chinese commercial settlement and a harbor for the Sambas region, had resumed. The mountain that dominated the town was completely covered by rice paddies and other plantings, and the valley appeared prosperous, its inhabitants industrious.[77]

Bengkayang was an inland town, located about five hundred meters above sea level and perhaps founded only in the nineteenth century. In addition to being a center of gold mining (it is the successor to the kongsi town, Lara), Bengkayang controlled the access to the paths leading from mining communities like Monterado and Mandor to Sarawak. It would gain importance in the twentieth century as a center for the rubber trade.

CHINESE SETTLEMENT IN PONTIANAK AND MALAY-RULED TOWNS

Apart from the kongsi settlements, there was a sizable population of Chinese settlers living in Pontianak and other Malay-dominated towns. By 1811, according to the account of Burn, Pontianak was already an emporium for the West Coast and a service center for the Lanfang Kongsi, having

> ... ten thousand Chinese, but few of them possessed of much property above the sum of twenty thousand [silver] dollars, as they are frequently remitting to China, the Chinese are Merchants, Mechanicks, and Laborers, they cultivate the Ground, search for Gold Dust, distill Arack, make Sugar, and trade to the Interior, and to the ... different Races to the Northward and Southward, but in particular to the place called Monterado and Slackaw [Selakau] which in fact is almost one and the same place a little way to the Northward of Mempawa where there is about thirty thousand Chinese settled, and are supplied from Pontiana with Opium, Piece Goods, Iron and China ... were it not for the Chinese, Pontianak would be of little value.[78]

A Dutch official who arrived a dozen years later confirmed Burn's assessment of the town's Chinese activities:

---

[75] M. Buys, *Twee maanden op Borneo's Westkust: Herinneringen* (Leiden: Doesburgh, 1892), pp. 172-173. These may be the typical hats worn by Hakka women in the fields in China. Buys found them far too heavy for European heads. Many Bornean people also wore wide hats, however.

[76] P. Adriani, *Herinneringen uit en aan de Chineesche districten der Wester-Afdeeling van Borneo, 1879-1882: Schetsen en indrukken* (Amsterdam: Campagne en Zoon, 1898), p. 93. This appears to be the Fudeci, with the adjacent Guanyin temple (or its forerunner), described by Franke, *Chinese Epigraphic Materials*, 3: 152-153. "Picnics" might be the Chinese practice of offering food at graves or temples. Interestingly, the Chinese cemetery of Singkawang is also called "Gongsishan" (kongsi mountain) cemetery (p. 168).

[77] Adriani, *Chineesche districten*, pp. 58-60. See Plate 5.

[78] Burn, pp. 67, 68. Later figures show that the Chinese were far fewer, only about one-third of the city's population; perhaps the author here is including Chinese in Mandor and the environs of Pontianak in the ten thousand.

[The Chinese] are the ones who exercise the crafts and trades in Pontianak and, as a result, the smiths, carpenters, dyers, planters, etc., of this place [are Chinese]. And one also finds many traders among them . . . . Without exaggeration one can say that the kingdom of Pontianak produces nothing but gold dust, mined by the Chinese.[79]

Chinese junks sailed annually to Pontianak, bringing goods from China, while a few smaller ones came from Siam. After a stay of several months, Chinese ships departed laden with a great quantity of local goods, above all gold.

Yet however important the Chinese were for the town, according to Burn, they were neither as frugal, as hard working, nor as wealthy as some one thousand Bugis traders, who shared Pontianak with about three thousand Malays and a hundred Arabs. The typical Chinese laborer spent his money on good food, gambling, and opium; the exceptional few saved for their return to China or remitted their money to relatives in China.[80] Virtually all Chinese arrivals were indentured laborers, in debt for their passage. Some acquired property locally, some returned to China, but most stayed on. If they were lucky, they gained a wife and settled down; if unlucky, they lost their earnings in gambling and opium.[81]

The Chinese *pasar* or market formed the commercial center of the city on the left bank of the Kapuas, but across the Landak River from Pontianak was Kampung Baru, also a Chinese settlement (it was subordinate to the Lanfang Kongsi of Mandor). Currently called Siantan, it is a center of Pontianak's industry. Urban Chinese quarters were thus separate from the Malay settlements and the *kampungs* of Arabs and Bugis close to the sultan's palace on the island between the rivers Kapuas and Landak. This pattern of segregated settlement was repeated on a smaller scale in other towns. (See maps three and five.)

By 1811, Pontianak had become an established gateway for immigrants from China bound for the town or for Lanfang Kongsi. However, Burn's report shows that the numbers of immigrants who chose to sail from China to Borneo were declining; in the first years of the 1800s, up to fifteen junks had arrived annually carrying men eager to work in the mines, but by 1811 Pontianak could only expect to welcome two or three such ships per year.[82] Because of the monsoon, the ships came at only one time of the year, and in West Borneo they came only to Pontianak. Sambas and Mempawah had lost their function as ports of entry for new mine laborers. Fewer arrivals meant less income for both the Malay rulers, because Chinese returning to China had to pay fifteen dollars exit tax, while those entering on the junks, which "when they arrive are always crowded with new settlers," paid an immigration tax of one dollar per person.[83]

What was behind the decline: had gold production dropped? Was the danger of piracy or the British-Dutch rivalry inhibiting trade, forcing junks to land only at the relatively sheltered harbor of Pontianak? It seems none of these factors was decisive. Instead, the decline in immigration reflected a looming economic reality.

---

[79] Francis, *Herinneringen*, 1: 244, 250, describing the situation in 1832.

[80] Burn, pp. 67-70.

[81] Ibid., p. 106.

[82] Ibid., pp. 67, 71.

[83] Ibid., pp. 68, 81-83.

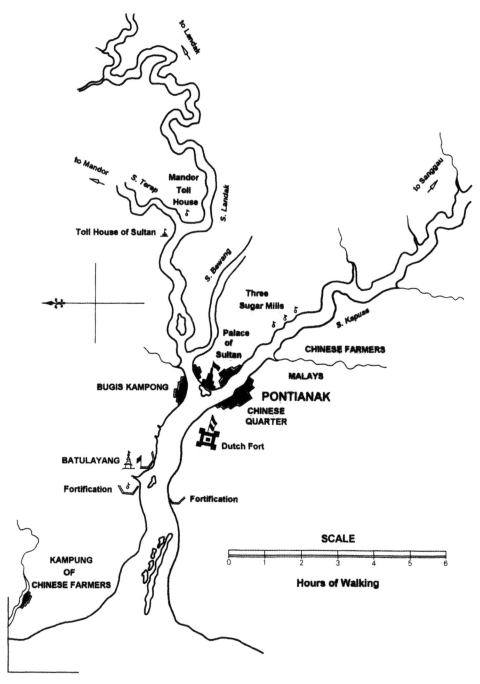

Map Five. Pontianak and environs, circa 1822, showing the Chinese settlements, some of them linked to the Mandor Lanfang Kongsi. [84]

---

[84] Drawn from a manuscript of Commissioners Francis and Tobias, ca. 1822, in *Kaart van Nederlands Ostindië in 8 Bladen*, ed. Gijsbert Franco von Derfelden de Hinderstein (The Hague, Amsterdam: Imprimerie de l'État, 1842) p. 7, map eighteen. Reproduction, Niedersächsische Staats- und Universitätsbibliothek, Göttingen. The original is reproduced on the cover of this book.

Some mines, according to the account of 1811, were already in financial trouble, a sign of more problems to come.

Other Settlements

Burn's report of 1811 also gives an inventory of the upriver states and their Chinese populations. (Burn probably relied on hearsay for this information, but his is the only contemporary account with such detail.) As it shows, the Chinese had penetrated the interior of Borneo as miners and as traders. Sanggau, up the Kapuas River, produced the best gold dust on the island. About five to six hundred Chinese settlers lived in the area, along with approximately the same number of Malays. Sanggau produced two *piculs* (a *picul* is about sixty-two kilograms) of high-quality gold dust annually, selling for $52,800 in silver dollars. In spite of a high tariff on exports of gold, the ruler of Sanggau only collected a few thousand dollars yearly, however, for producers easily evaded his controls. He did better with his own trading activities. Most of Sanggau was still covered by jungle, except where cleared by the Chinese for mining.[85] Tayan had some gold and a few dozen Chinese, who also forged the iron found there into pots or into simple weapons.[86]

Other settlements upriver included Sebadau, a predominantly Dayak settlement, with one hundred Chinese, one thousand Dayaks, and about fifty Malays. This town produced a relatively small amount (fifty *bungkals*) of gold. "Billiton"—not the island of Belitung, but Belitang—above Sebadau and Sanggau on the Kapuas River, had no Chinese living there. Sintang, far inland on the Kapuas, was supposed to have sixty thousand Dayaks, one thousand Malays, and 1,700 Chinese in residence, and to produce about four *piculs* of gold dust at a value of about $100,000 annually. (These population figures, and the estimated production, may be exaggerated.) Sintang was linked by trails with rivers leading to Banjarmasin and Brunei. (Compare map seven, p. 126.) Although there were other small settlements of Chinese along the Kapuas River, none had yet penetrated as far as the so-called lake district, where the Dayaks were the only miners.[87]

The principality of Landak, earlier famous for its diamonds, on the Landak River, which flows into the Kapuas River at Pontianak, had a Malay *panembahan*. He claimed authority over five to six thousand Dayaks (the ruler did not bother to count beyond this number), two hundred Malays, fifty Bugis, and three hundred "natives of Bantam," (that is, Banten, West Java) who had migrated to Landak while Banten was the overlord of Landak in the eighteenth century. There were about one hundred Chinese working there, and its gold production reached about twelve thousand dollars annually. Burn thinks this was potentially the richest deposit of gold in all Borneo, but the mines were less productive than those in some other regions because the ruler was determined to limit production (this according to Burn). Chinese miners (probably from Lanfang) had repeatedly attempted to enter the area by force, but the ruler of Landak

---

[85] Ibid., pp. 14-16, 109, 119.

[86] Ibid., pp. 105-107.

[87] Ibid., pp. 130-137. On the Kapuas lake district, where many Malays settled (or many Dayaks had become Malays), see J. J. K. Enthoven, *Bijdragen tot de Geographie van Borneo's Wester-Afdeeling* (Supplement, *Tijdschrift van het Koninklijk Aardrijkskundig Genootschap*, 1901-1903) (Leiden: Brill, 1903). See map one, p. 16.

successfully repelled them, conscious of the fate of Monterado and Selakau, which had formerly been subject to the Sultan of Sambas but fell under Chinese control.[88] Since Landak's diamonds were more important than its gold, and Chinese were not good diamond miners, the *panembahan* could manage without them. Conflict between the Malays ruling Landak and the Chinese who wished to mine there flared up again in the 1840s.

Chinese miners were also causing trouble for the Sultan of Sambas in 1811. Realizing that Sambas was weak, the Chinese had rebelled against the Sultan, partly "instigated by emissaries from Pontianak."[89] They had reduced their annual payments to Sambas to $1,500, and sometimes paid nothing. Burn thinks Sambas had lost control over the gold mining settlements around Monterado through the ruler's own incompetence.

THREE GROUPS OF CHINESE

The Chinese community could be divided into three major groups based on their residence and profession. The first group was composed of the gold miners, who made the mine organization or kongsi their home. Most of them, being single, lived in the bachelor quarters of the headquarters or at the mines themselves; most were immigrants and transients. The mine bosses, although better situated and perhaps even living with wives and families, also belonged to this group.

The second group was made up of the Chinese who were associated with the mining kongsis, but not as miners. They might be farmers or petty traders, living in the small *pasars* (market settlements) that served the mining communities. The non-mining people of the kongsis were often locally born and of mixed descent, or they were former miners. Both of these groups were predominately Hakkas or *pansanhok*.[90] Fishing or trading communities along the coast, like Singkawang, Pemangkat, or Sungai Pinyu, also provided the inland kongsis with a landing place for rice, salt, and other (illicit, by the government's definition) imports. The Chinese settlement of Mempawah, Kuala Mempawah, was subject to the Lanfang Kongsi of Mandor; that of Kampung Baru, across the river from Pontianak, was also a dependency of Lanfang. Other mining organizations had their own settlements, subject to their own officials.[91] Chinese farmers were highly skilled, frugal, and diligent; the entire family contributed to production. Although many were subsistence farmers, their income was often linked to the production of market

---

[88] Burn, pp. 140-144.

[89] It is entirely in keeping with the character of Pontianak's sultan that he meddled in his neighbors' affairs—unless, of course, the emissaries were Chinese. Another account (chapter one) says the Chinese were assessed $1,000 annually.

[90] See chapter one for a description of Chinese language differences and on *pansanhok*.

[91] Compare de Waal's slightly different categories. E. de Waal, *West Borneo*, Vol. 8 of *Onze Indische financien*, ed. E. A. G. J. van Delden (The Hague: M. Nijhoff, 1907), pp. 20ff. Van Prehn Wiese, "Aantekeningen," describes a visit to such kongsi-dependent towns in 1851-52. Sungai Pinyu, for example, had a *kapitan* from Mandor, who was assisted by a *laothai* (M. *laoda*). Sungai Duri was part of Thaikong, with a *tjaktjoe* (M. *zhazhu*), serving the same function as the *laothai*. See also anonymous, "De held van Pemangkat," *Tijdschrift voor Nederlandsch Indië* 13,1 (1851): 68.

crops, and their relation to the monetary economy differentiated them from most other peoples of the island.[92]

The urban dwellers, traders, craftsmen, and laborers constituted a third group. All accounts agree that Chinese dominated the trade and industry of the residency. They lived in the Chinese *kampung*s of Pontianak and Sambas and sometimes in smaller towns like Ngabang in Landak. Although as urban traders and craftsmen they served the multi-ethnic urban communities and sometimes were connected to the courts, they might also be associated with the mining communities; urban Chinese might advance money or sell provisions to the upland miners. These were usually long-term or permanent settlers. Most of them seem to have been Teochius.

THE COMING OF THE DUTCH, 1818

That Borneo's Malay rulers—in particular the reigning Sultan of Pontianak—still felt dependent on the Dutch twenty years after the VOC had departed from West Borneo astonished Burn. A few years later, when the British had scarcely retreated from Dutch possessions, the rulers of Sambas and Pontianak appealed to the Dutch to return. The Sultan of Sambas wrote such an appeal to the Resident of Semarang in March 1817. His letter shows that he felt threatened both by his own nobles and by Pontianak (not to mention by his poor relationship with the Chinese miners), and motivated by, in his words, the "wretched and lamentable conditions in a land that for some time has been in ruins."[93]

In his letter, the Sultan of Sambas argued that the "Company" (as people of the Indies called the Dutch colonial authority long after the VOC had been dissolved) now had an opportunity to prove its good will by providing him with a stout warship, guns, and ammunition. (The Sultan had also invited the British to come help him, but he neglected to mention that fact in his letter to Batavia.) In their reply, the Dutch promised protection if the sultan would sign an appropriate contract with them, but said nothing about arms deliveries. A few months later, the Sultan of Pontianak followed this example; desiring to renew his old friendship with the Netherlands, he, too, invited the Dutch to "return."[94]

Why were the West Coast sultans so eager to befriend the Dutch? Clearly, their situation was perilous. The Dutch commissioner for West Borneo wrote in 1819:

> . . . this ruler [the Sultan of Sambas] had asked the Dutch to occupy Sambas in order to escape the threat that the powerful Chinese might . . . perhaps even at some time depose him altogether.[95]

---

[92] Cf. Azahari, *Ontwikkeling*, p. 62. The classic essay on Chinese facility with money is Maurice Freedman, "The Handling of Money: A Note on the Background to the Economic Sophistication of Overseas Chinese," in *The Study of Chinese Society: Essays by Maurice Freedman*, ed. G. William Skinner (Stanford: Stanford University Press, 1979), pp. 22-26.

[93] Text of letter in van der Kemp, "Palembang en Banka," p. 704; see also Kemp, "Vestiging," pp. 114-116. The ruins, of course, were partly the result of British reprisals.

[94] Van der Kemp, "Vestiging," pp. 118-121; Ismail, "Politik perdagangan," p. 60.

[95] Report of Commissioner Nahuys, Banjarmasin, March 7, 1819, cited in "De bevestiging van het nederlandsch gezag op Borneo, en de vermeerdering der inkomsten van dat eiland voor de schatkist," *Tijdschrift voor Nederlandsch Indië* 12,2 (1850): 169 (probable author is W. H.

And later, a historian reviewing the situation confirmed this assessment and found that

> Conditions in Sambas were bad enough, but in Pontianak they were no better, even there the authority of the ruler was undermined by the Chinese, there, too, all prosperity had vanished.[96]

Muhammad Gade Ismail, who studied the position of Sambas from 1808 to 1818, believed that local rulers turned to the Dutch because the presence of Chinese gold miners in the interior had critically weakened *hulu-hilir* bonds. Unable to collect taxes from the Dayaks and unable to enforce their authority over the Chinese, the rulers could not accumulate the wealth they needed to pacify their noble relatives and finance their own considerable expenses. The Chinese, who now had easy access to the coast, were refusing to pay tribute and circumventing royal trading monopolies. The rulers had no choice but to turn to piracy themselves or to collude in the acts of piracy carried out by their relatives at court. This, in turn, brought conflict with the European powers. The Sultan of Sambas and his colleagues in Mempawah and Pontianak hoped the Dutch would at last help enforce their authority over the Chinese.[97]

But not only the Chinese were to blame for the rulers' plight. Mutual rivalries among the sultanates also prompted them to turn to the Westerners for help. Pontianak's sultan controlled only the town; he had little authority over the Dayaks, although he could collect duties on items exported from the Kapuas area and, probably, engage in piracy on the side. He might use the Dutch to extend his power to other territories or to keep his followers in line.[98] Similar motives prevailed elsewhere among Malay rulers eager to see "the Company" return to Borneo.

THE LOCAL RULERS

Even while they were soliciting assistance from the Dutch, the Sultans of Sambas and Pontianak also invited the British to establish themselves in their territory. As it happened, the Dutch arrived first, reaching Pontianak on July 21, 1818.[99] The Dutch located their headquarters there, initially under Commissioner J. van Boeckholtz, who installed smaller garrisons in Sambas and Mempawah, and raised the flag in Landak. The second Sultan of Pontianak, Syarif Kassim, himself

---

Muntinghe); and in P. H. van der Kemp, "Montrado tijdens het herstel van ons gezag in 1818," *Koloniaal Tijdschrift* 9 (1920): 278.

[96] E. B. Kielstra, "West Borneo," *Onze Eeuw* 16,2 (April 1916): 42; compare Francis, *Herinneringen*, 1: 320-322.

[97] See Muhammad Gade Ismail, "Politik perdagangan," p. 168, and Muhammad Gade Ismail, "Trade and State Power," pp. 144-148.

[98] Willer, "Eerste proeve," p. 523; Burn, manuscript, pp. 57-59; Van Goor, "Madman," p. 205; Heidhues, "First Two Sultans," pp. 281-285; 289-293.

[99] Ismail, "Politik perdagangan," p. 60. A British force arrived two weeks later, but the sultan promptly sent it packing. Van der Kemp, "Vestiging," pp. 131-33.

a former ruler of Mempawah, conveyed his warmest expressions of friendship to Batavia.[100]

During the first thirty years they "administered" West Borneo, the Dutch never mustered a force sufficient to assert control over even the coastal regions of their territory. They depended on the cooperation of the native rulers, which they usually received, although the rulers sometimes engaged in prolonged foot-dragging. They had almost no knowledge of the terrain, and no one who could explain to them the interests of either the Dayaks or the Chinese. The quality of their officials often left much to be desired, and even their goals were often in doubt.

According to the first contracts established between the Dutch and various local principalities, signed soon after the Dutch arrival, the Malay rulers were to relinquish all authority over the Chinese, making them "direct subjects" of the colonial authorities, but their authority over the Malays and the Dayaks would remain untouched. For the Chinese (and other foreigners, excepting Arabs, who were subjects of the sultans), the Dutch were simply applying the policy of direct rule which they had used to deal with the Chinese in Java and expected to work equally well in Borneo.[101] In time, they appointed Chinese officers to act as intermediaries with Chinese populations of the towns they controlled, but these officials had no influence on the mining kongsis, which enjoyed de facto independence from external authority.

Subsequent contracts with the native rulers—they were revised repeatedly, either because they were unacceptable to Batavia or because a new ruler had come to the throne—essentially "bought" the compliance of the sultans by offering them a substantial retainer, which would be derived mostly from taxes the Dutch would collect from the Chinese. Pontianak signed away half its revenue (mostly taxes on trade) to the Dutch, but in turn the sultan was rewarded with an income of ƒ42,000 in 1822, a sum which was increased to ƒ45,000 the following year. In contrast, Sambas received ƒ12,000 and Mempawah ƒ8000;[102] these smaller amounts underline the relative importance of the new capital of the West Coast in comparison with its neighbors. The Dutch planned to collect duties on imports and exports, impose a head tax on the Chinese population, auction off revenue farms,[103] especially those on use of opium (consumed mainly by Chinese workers), and manage a salt monopoly. The first agreements, succeeded by others, some of which survived until World War II, also left the native rulers with minor sources of income from appanages and personal claims on the Malays or the Dayaks.

---

[100] Van der Kemp, "Vestiging," pp. 134-37 (with text of Syarif Kasim's letter, p. 141).

[101] Even the VOC contract with Pontianak in 1779 provided for direct rule by the Dutch over the Chinese. See Veth, *Borneo's Wester-Afdeeling*, 1: 262; 2: 37-38, 44-45. In 1819, however, the commissioner to Borneo, Nahuys, was ignorant of the existence of the previous contract. The Javanese model for dealing with the Chinese included using the institution of Chinese officials to collect taxes and administer community affairs. In Borneo, however, there was no important *peranakan*, Malay-speaking element, to cooperate with the Dutch.

[102] Van Goor, "Seapower, Trade, and State Formation," p. 87; van der Kemp, "Vestiging," p. 144; Veth, *Borneo's Wester-Afdeeling*, 2: 37-39, 49-54.

[103] Revenue farms were rights to collect duties or taxes on certain products or activities (opium, alcohol, gambling, the slaughter of pigs, and so on). "Farmers" paid an agreed sum to the government for the right, and collected fees from the public themselves, pocketing any difference. Usually, these farms were auctioned to the highest bidder for a given time.

The arrangement could not work. The new authorities had exaggerated ideas of profits to be expected from taxes and revenue farms, and they overestimated the number of Chinese who would pay the head tax. Batavia mistakenly expected the salt monopoly alone to bring in thousands.[104] The exaggerated expectations of the Dutch are surprising, since the colonial administrators must have known—or should have known—that the sultans had been unable to enforce their levies on the Chinese for years.[105]

THE SITUATION OF THE CHINESE

Clearly, the Dutch had something to offer the rulers, but did they have anything to offer the Chinese? Apparently not, as Dutch historian P. J. Veth pointed out:

> It is hard to deny that the Chinese on Borneo's West Coast owed everything to themselves, to their own industry, and nothing to the Government, and that the times that preceded the restoration of our authority on Borneo's West Coast had clearly taught that they did not need the protection we wanted to sell them for such a high price.[106]

Having guaranteed the native rulers (and their sizable courts) a living and committed themselves to support that system, and to cover the additional expenses of Western administrators, the Dutch had to make the Chinese pay up—but the Chinese had no interest in doing so. They soon understood that they were expected to bear a disproportionate amount of the costs of the Dutch and Malay administrations, while receiving little in exchange. Most onerous was the personal head tax, especially for the kongsi Chinese, who were unaccustomed to paying taxes. Previously, any expenses or duties, including payments to the sultans, had been simply deducted from kongsi profits, not assessed individually.[107]

Seeds of Conflict

False expectations on the part of the Dutch were one source of conflict, but there were other problems on the Bornean frontier. From the first decades of the nineteenth century, the mines were in trouble and hostilities frequent. Among the

---

[104] Extract from *Batavia Courant* of June 5, 1819 in British Library, India Office Library and Records, Mackenzie Collection, Vol. 14, pp. 113-114. The act is dated May 14, 1819 and extends the monopoly on salt, already effective in Java, to Pontianak, Mempawah, and Sambas. All salt had to be purchased from the government. It was extremely difficult to make salt from seawater in Borneo because of the high humidity. The many rivers carry so much fresh water to the sea that, for example, fresh water is found in the ocean several kilometers from the mouth of the Kapuas; see G. L. Uljée, *Handboek voor de Residentie Westerafdeeling van Borneo* (Weltevreden: Visser & Co, 1925), p. 17.

[105] Van der Kemp, "Vestiging," pp. 144, 156 (letter of Elout). There was talk of seventy thousand Chinese, although Raffles's estimate of fifty thousand was already generous.

[106] Veth, *Borneo's Wester-Afdeeling*, 2: 59. Like other colonial authors, Veth speaks of the "restoration" of Dutch authority, assuming it had been firmly established in the area in the 1790s.

[107] Report from Pontianak: Question of Travel Passes for Chinese, ARA V. 30.1.66 (42).

twenty-one "most important" conflicts in West Borneo between 1770 and 1854, as listed by Indonesian historian Harlem Siahaan, in only six did Chinese miners fight directly against the colonial government; of the remaining fifteen, six were among the kongsis themselves, and the rest between the kongsis and the local population.[108] Many others were not recorded.

Exhaustion of the gold deposits on their territories was probably the major factor in the inter-kongsi conflicts.[109] The atmosphere of violence prevailing in the absence of a strong authority was not unlike that in some parts of the southeastern Chinese homeland, where inter-clan and inter-village feuds (M. *xiedou*) were common in the nineteenth century.[110]

Kongsis were also divided internally, between miners and townspeople or farmers. Of course the system of recruiting laborers from certain defined areas and of relying on initiation rituals and cooperative agreements, all strengthened by the trappings of brotherhood, bound the members of a kongsi strongly to one another and tended to create an environment that incited rivalries between different kongsis. Yet, although some conflicts may have been determined by members' place of origin in China and rivalries established along ethnic or geographical divisions, the most bitter rivals—the miners of Samtiaokioe and those of Thaikong—were both so-called *pansanhok*.[111] It appears that the more fundamental problem was the competition for resources, gold sites, and water supplies, all of which were scarce and dwindling.[112] As early as 1822, Commissioner Tobias noted ominously that Thaikong, the keystone of Fosjoen, had only four larger mines left.[113]

Fewer junks laden with immigrant mine workers were coming to Borneo, the population was declining, and the gold produced was not enough to support the remaining miners, especially in Mandor and parts of Monterado.[114] The only other alternative for the kongsis was to expand their territory, but that led to hostilities with other kongsis, or with the Dayaks and the Malays who still worked the more remote gold sites.

General reports of hostilities during this period should not be taken to prove that relations between the kongsis and the Dutch were universally bad. True, the urban Chinese were more cooperative with the colonial administration, but even the kongsis were often able to work with colonial officials. The mining communities

---

[108] Harlem Siahaan, "Konflik dan perlawanan," p. 22. A contemporary source, on the other hand, insists the Chinese of Monterado had challenged the colonial government on eight occasions before 1850. See unidentified fragment in Report on the Chinese in West Borneo, 1850-53, ANRI BW 28/28 (79).

[109] As listed in Siahaan, "Konflik dan perlawanan," p. 22.

[110] Blussé and Merens, "Nuggets from the Gold Mines," p. 290.

[111] R. C. van Prehn, Relaas van den oorlog met de oproerige Chinezen ter West-Kust van Borneo, beginnende in 1850 (Western manuscripts, Leiden University Library, BPL 2472) p. 34, points out that the Thaikong who attacked Samtiaokioe in 1850 were of the same "tribe" as the defenders. Schaank ("Kongsis van Montrado," pp. 514, 525) confirms this.

[112] Jackson, *Chinese in the West Borneo Goldfields*, pp. 57-61.

[113] Report of Tobias January 28, 1822, ANRI BW 18/2 (195).

[114] Monterado was thought to be losing miners and producing too little gold to pay the rest adequately. In 1831, Mandor was already making little profit. Mines of Lara and Lumar however, had top quality gold and made plenty of profit, as did mines of Sepang, Seminis, and Buduk, the former two belonging to Samtiaokioe. They might bring in ƒ2,500,000 per year, in one estimate. See also Report to Governor General, June 28, 1831, ANRI BW 19/13 (150).

were not homogeneous groups, and they reacted in different ways to Dutch advances. Between 1833 and 1850, the Monterado Kongsi regularly paid at least some of the head taxes assessed on its members.[115] When a Dayak killed a Lumar Chinese in 1849, the Assistant Resident of Sambas asked Thaikong to mediate the matter. This non-violent solution avoided a potential series of retributions between kongsis and Dayak groups; Chinese headmen came to Sambas to thank the official, invited him to visit their territory, and promptly paid their outstanding taxes.[116]

Nor did conflicts between the Chinese and other groups split inevitably along ethnic lines. The Malays and the Dayaks might be allies of the Chinese, or their enemies. Some Malays, like Mas Buyang, a nephew of the Mempawah rulers and Pontianak and head of a settlement on the Sungai Duri, were willing smugglers for the Chinese kongsis, and were "strongly suspected of always having helped" them.[117] The Dayaks, too, might fight for the kongsis, or against them. The process of subjecting Chinese settlers to colonial rule lasted from 1818 to 1885; repercussions extended into the twentieth century. Even these Kongsi Wars did not involve decades of constant fighting. Some Chinese were enemies, some allies, while others shifted from one status to another.

Burn's report of the sharp decline in the China trade should have warned his readers that the kongsis were already suffering from depletion of their gold sites. The consolidation of the mines and incorporation of smaller kongsis, as in the formation of Fosjoen in 1776, may have been a symptom of weakness, not strength. The numbers of Chinese, probably never more than fifty thousand adult males, were declining in the nineteenth century. In 1828, one Dutch investigator thought no more than sixteen thousand Chinese men then lived in all of the West Coast, and the total number of Chinese was about 27,000. He estimated that the total population of the West Coast might be over half a million, with over 370,000 Dayaks and 138,000 Malays.[118] These figures—admittedly a guess—represent the results of three years of efforts to obtain a realistic count of the population.

But even while the kongsis were being weakened by the depletion of their resources and manpower, they had enough strength, of a certain kind, to concern the Dutch authorities who hoped to govern and tax them. The kongsis were not only accustomed to political independence, they were also increasingly self-sufficient. Salt and opium, which the Dutch hoped to turn into lucrative revenue monopolies, were necessities for the miners, but they had found their own supplies. They bypassed the Dutch as they had bypassed the rulers. The establishment of Singapore as a free port in 1819 opened an ideal source for smuggled opium and weapons, while salt came in quantity from southern Siam and the Malay

---

[115] Reports on Chinese on West Coast of Borneo, ANRI BW 29/9 (83). The source of this report is not further identified. See also anonymous, "De verwikkelingen van het Nederlandsch-Indisch Gouvernement met de Chineesche bevolking op Westelijk Borneo toegelicht," *Tijdschrift voor Nederlandsch Indië* 15,2 (1853): 386, citing the general reports of the residency for 1848 and 1849. Because of the difficulties of taking a census and differences about the actual numbers of miners, after 1833 the head tax was assessed against kongsis as a lump sum.

[116] De Waal, *Onze Indische Financien*, 8: 27.

[117] Van Prehn Wiese, "Aantekeningen," pp. 112-113.

[118] J. H. Tobias, "Bevolkingsstaat der verschillende rijken op de Westkust van Borneo," *De Nederlands Hermes* 3,12 (1828): 31-33.

Peninsula; it was also of better quality and cheaper than that available from the government.[119]

Singapore would rapidly develop into a trading entrepôt, a way station for migrants going to and from China, and a center of Chinese identity and politics apart from the Mainland. It maintained that role into the twentieth century, providing a new external focus for the Chinese of West Borneo.

FIRST CONTACTS

Soon after their arrival, Dutch officials decided to visit the kongsi centers. The first to reach Monterado, the headquarters of the Fosjoen federation with its two strongest members, Thaikong and Samtiaokioe, was the Resident of Mempawah, C. J. Prediger, who erroneously believed Monterado to be subject to Mempawah's *panembahan*, and therefore situated in his district. In fact, because most of its territory was north of the Sungai Duri, Monterado had been under the rule of Sambas since 1784—if it paid any tribute to anyone.

Meanwhile, the Resident of Sambas, Georg Müller, tried to compel Fosjoen Kongsi to send a representative to Sambas to acknowledge the authority of the Dutch there. When his attempts proved unsuccessful, he decided to visit the kongsi himself, arriving at "Santagiau" in late November 1818. (As mentioned earlier, Samtiaokioe was part of Fosjoen, but did Müller even know where he was?) Here, he raised the Dutch flag and told the kongsi people to pay taxes, above all a head tax, to him in Sambas. Ignorant of Prediger's intentions toward the kongsi, he then departed.[120]

Prediger arrived in Monterado a few days later, on December 1, 1818. After signing an agreement similar to the one they had already made with Müller, the Monterado Chinese insisted on sending a delegation to Sambas to report the matter to the sultan, leaving Prediger behind in Monterado. The delegation slyly intimated to the ruler that this foreigner was trying to get hold of the kongsi for Mempawah, thereby arousing the sultan's jealousy. Meanwhile, Prediger, feeling threatened, attempted to leave Monterado, but the Monterado Chinese made him return the copy of the agreement first. Back in Mempawah, Prediger felt justified in calling the Chinese "most faithless and profit-seeking creatures."[121]

A small contingent of Dutch troops had remained in Monterado. When the delegation from Fosjoen arrived in Sambas, Müller, outraged by Prediger's behavior, immediately departed for Monterado, and then ordered the few Dutch soldiers left there by Prediger to "surrender" to him, lower the Dutch flag, and raise it again, before the eyes of the mystified Chinese.[122]

---

[119] Francis, *Herinneringen*, 1: 325-326; on salt see also Jacob Ozinga, *De economische ontwikkeling der Westerafdeeling van Borneo en de bevolkingsrubbercultuur* (Wageningen: N. V. gebr. Zomer en Keuning, 1940), p. 15. On the salt trade in the Archipelago to 1813, see Gerrit Knaap and Luc Nagtegaal, "A Forgotten Trade: Salt in Southeast Asia, 1670-1813," in *Emporia, Commodities and Entrepreneurs in Asian Maritime Trade, c. 1400-1750*, ed. Roderich Ptak and Dietmar Rothermund (Stuttgart: Franz Steiner Verlag, 1991), pp. 127-157.

[120] Van der Kemp, "Vestiging," p. 283. Müller's temperament later sealed his fate; in 1825 he was killed on a brash trip to the interior.

[121] Cited in Van der Kamp, "Montrado," p. 285.

[122] Ibid., pp. 283-287.

This comedy of errors did not leave a favorable impression on the Chinese. Müller was a habitual hothead who did not even speak decent Malay, much less Chinese.[123] But Monterado's representatives were not being completely honest either. When the highest Dutch official, Commissioner A. G. Nahuys van Burgst, tried to patch up the quarrel, asking leaders of several kongsis to meet him in Sambas in January 1819, the leaders demurred, explaining that Chinese New Year celebrations (January 26) would prevent them from making the visit. When they failed to appear by January 28, Nahuys expressed his impatience. The kongsi officials pleaded that they still could not come because the settling of accounts for the gold mines was not finished (which was true, although Nahuys perceived it as a false excuse) and that since the Chinese were under the protection of the Sultan of Sambas, it would suffice for the Dutch to settle all outstanding matters with him.[124] Given the independence of the kongsi from this ruler, what the Chinese suggested was certainly disingenuous, if not devious. Meanwhile, in April 1819, Prediger found himself under attack in Mempawah by Chinese from the nearby coastal settlements of Sungai Raya and Sungai Pinyu, and from Monterado itself.

The scene shifts to Pontianak, where, at the end of 1819, men of the Lanfang Kongsi in Mandor attacked the Dutch garrison in Pontianak. The troops were able to beat them back. Both there and in Mempawah, the Dutch found that the sympathies and allegiances of the local rulers, disturbingly, inclined toward the kongsis.[125]

Until mid-century, the Dutch were only strong enough to establish posts in those places where they were welcome. In cities like Pontianak and Sambas, the Chinese population accommodated itself to Dutch rule.[126] In the interior, Chinese kongsis and much of the Dayak population existed independently of the Dutch, and, in the north, the British soon challenged Dutch hegemony over the island. In 1822, the First Kongsi War broke out.

THE FIRST KONGSI WAR: DIVIDING THE GOLD FIELDS

The term "Kongsi Wars" actually refers to three periods of warfare (1822-24, 1850-54, and 1884-85) linked by long-term tensions. What prevailed most of the time between 1819 and 1849 was not war, but an unstable peace. Before 1849, the colonial government had other priorities that prevented it from devoting much attention to the independent kongsis, and, since mining and immigration from China were declining, time was on the Dutch side. Substantial force would be necessary to subdue the Chinese; this was not available. After 1857, the region fell quiet again, but then conflict flared in Mandor in 1884.[127]

---

[123] Veth, *Borneo's Wester-Afdeeling*, 2: 99.

[124] Van der Kemp, "Montrado," pp. 289-290.

[125] Van Meteren Brouwer, "Geschiedenis," pp. 1065-1066; one explanation was that the Sultan of Pontianak was indebted to the Mandor Chinese.

[126] In 1848, it was estimated that five hundred Chinese lived in Sambas and 1,700 in Pontianak. De Waal, *Onze Indische Financien*, 8: 20-21, citing contemporary sources. De Waal divides the Chinese into three groups: in the towns, in the interior, in the kongsis. However, those in the interior and in some of the towns were mostly kongsi people at this time.

[127] Compare anonymous, "De bevestiging van het nederlandsch gezag."

An exception to Batavia's disengagement strategy was the campaign of 1822-24. In late 1821, Commissioner J. H. Tobias had come from Java to put matters in West Borneo to rights, and he urged Batavia to make a show of force against the kongsis. In 1823, about three hundred men under Lt. Col. H. J. J. L. de Stuers cowed Mandor into submission and attacked the more powerful Fosjoen federation in Monterado.[128]

The Dutch presence on the coast may have aggravated a split in Fosjoen—or the split may have occurred for other reasons. In June, 1822, the Samtiaokioe members of the Fosjoen federation in Monterado decided, in the words of the Thaikong Kongsi, "suddenly in the dead of night, without any reason, [to] collect their gold and steal away."[129] Were they looking for better grounds or simply opting out of a federation that was losing money, while they themselves still controlled productive sites in Sepang and Seminis?[130] (Sepang's gold was also purer than Monterado's and fetched a higher price.[131]) Samtiaokioe members later told the Dutch that a Thaikong man had murdered one of their people. The murderer was caught and sentenced to death, but his comrades had freed him and the Fosjoen council had failed to grant justice to Samtiaokioe. At the time, the Lumar (M. Sjipngfoen or Shiwufen, Fifteen Shares) and Buduk (M. Limtian or Lintian) Kongsis also deserted Fosjoen.[132] Samtiaokioe then sought help against Thaikong's wrath from the Sultan of Sambas and from the Dutch, who replied by sending troops. Making no inquiries to discover Thaikong's side of the story, apparently, the Dutch troops fought their way to Monterado, reducing the central hall or *thang* (M. *ting*) to ashes in April 1823.[133]

Commissioner Tobias now tried to make peace by dividing the warring kongsis, leaving the Monterado-Sungai Raya area under Thaikong and its allies.[134] Samtiaokioe was assigned the region to the north of Monterado, including Sepang. Pemangkat would be Samtiaokioe's port and its rice bowl, as the port town of Singkawang was for Monterado. (See map four, page 57.) The Chinese quarter of

---

[128] Veth, *Borneo's Wester-Afdeeling*, 2: 116-123. De Stuers's full title was Lt. Col. Jhr. H. J. J. L. Ridder de Stuers; he later rose to major general in the colonial army.

[129] See the document in Blussé and Merens, "Nuggets from the Gold Mines," pp. 295-296; Schaank, "Kongsis van Montrado," pp. 538; and Siahaan, "Konflik dan perlawanan," pp. 339ff.

[130] These two sites were still doing well in 1831. See Report to Governor General, June 28, 1831, ANRI BW 19/13 (150).

[131] W. A. van Rees, *Montrado: Geschied- en krijgskundige bijdrage betreffende de onderwerping der Chinezen op Borneo, naar het dagboek van een Indisch officier over 1854-1856* (Bois-le-Duc: Müller, 1858), p. 87.

[132] Francis, *Herinneringen*, 1: 317. Francis would not have had direct information about the events, but his version better explains why the whole kongsi of Samtiaokioe, the most populous and oldest of the Fosjoen kongsis, had to leave Monterado behind.

[133] Veth, *Borneo's Wester-Afdeeling*, 2: 180. See correction in Schaank, "Kongsis van Montrado," p. 540n.

[134] See details in Kervel, "Bijdrage," pp. 171-181; notes on this document are also found in Report about Opposition among the Chinese in Sambas, 1846, ANRI BW 18/2 (195); Siahaan, "Konflik dan perlawanan," pp. 343-352; Blussé and Merens, "Nuggets from the Gold Mines," p. 312; Veth, *Borneo's Wester-Afdeeling*, 1: 103, and 2: 84-85. Veth believes the reason for the split was conflict over mine sites. Perhaps Samtiaokioe told Francis about the perversion of justice to make its case more appealing to the Dutch. For Thaikong's version, see Yuan, *Chinese Democracies*, pp. 98-102.

Sambas town would be independent of the kongsis, directly under the colonial government; this decision was made in part because an important temple that belonged to both kongsis was located in Sambas town.[135] In January 1824, Fosjoen paid its head taxes to the Dutch, and peace seemed assured on the West Coast.[136] Nonetheless, Tobias's ability to enforce his authority depended on a strong presence of Dutch troops.

In September 1824, however, the rump Fosjoen drove off the Dutch troops in Singkawang, who were planning another march on Monterado to chastise the kongsi. Chinese from Thaikong threatened other Dutch positions again a few months later. Reinforcements had hardly arrived in Borneo in 1825 when they were diverted to Java because of the outbreak of the Java War. Not surprisingly, Fosjoen again asserted its independence, and colonial forces could do little. Thaikong and its allies were not strong enough to drive the Dutch from the coast, but the remaining colonial force was far too weak to subdue Thaikong.[137] Furthermore, although Samtiaokioe controlled more people and better sites, it would prove to be militarily weaker than Thaikong.[138]

THE 1830s AND 1840s

A do-nothing approach characterized Dutch activity of the next decades. From a position of weakness, colonial officials vacillated. The head tax on Chinese settlers was abolished in favor of increased customs duties. The head tax was later reinstated.

Relations with the kongsis continued to be strained. Samtiaokioe was not submissive either, and in 1832, in an altercation with the Dutch that concerned smuggling, some of its people murdered a Dutch official. Batavia replied by sending a new commissioner to the area, who negotiated another truce.[139] From 1838 to 1846, colonial officials were not even supposed to enter the interior. Only two assistant residents remained in the territory, joined by an occasional commissioner from Batavia and a skeleton military presence.[140]

Recognizing the colonial power's weakness, the kongsis became delinquent in their tax payments. By 1841, Lanfang had an unpaid backlog of ƒ16,000, Monterado

[135] Veth, *Borneo's Wester-Afdeeling*, 2: 127-129.

[136] General Report on Residency of Sambas for 1823, by M. van Grave, ARA, Collectie Schneither, 2.21.007.57 (23); "Kronijk van Nederlandsch Indië, loopende van af het jaar 1816: De jaren 1824 en 1825," *Tijdschrift voor Neêrland's Indië* 7,2 (1845): 166-173; C. L. Blume, "Toelichtingen aangaande de nasporingen op Borneo van G. MÜLLER," *De Indische Bij* I (1843): 123; Kielstra, "West Borneo," pp. 45-46. This story is repeated in E. B. Kielstra, "West Borneo," in *De Indische Archipel: Geschiedkundige schetsen*, ed. E. B. Kielstra (Haarlem: De Erven F. Bohn, 1917), pp. 251-293.

[137] Veth, *Borneo's Wester-Afdeeling*, 2: 419ff; "Kronijk van Nederlandsch Indië," pp. 548-551; cf. D. J. van Dungen Gronovius, "Verslag over de Residentie Borneo's Westkust, 1827-1829," *Tijdschrift voor Nederlandsch Indië* 5,1 (1871): 32; and van Meteren Brouwer, "Geschiedenis," pp. 1072-1073.

[138] Ritter, *Indische herinneringen*, p. 125.

[139] Francis, *Herinneringen*, 1: 327-330.

[140] De Waal, *Onze Indische Financien*, 8: 11. Exceptions to the travel ban were made for purposes of exploration; see, for example, ibid., 8: 16.

*f*42,426, Sepang (Samtiaokioe) *f*2,799, and Lara *f*1,600.[141] Smuggling, especially with Singapore, was endemic. West Borneo was costing the treasury far more than it brought in. The contracts with the sultans guaranteed them substantial annual subsidies, and, lacking Chinese taxes, the stipends had to be paid from the colonial purse.

Fosjoen's problems also persisted. In 1837, two other kongsis left the remaining federation at Fosjoen; Thaikong was now alone in Monterado. The kongsi soon attacked Samtiaokioe's valuable sites, especially Sepang, in an attempt to claim them, and Samtiaokioe pleaded with the Dutch for support, as it had in 1822.

Trouble between the Dayaks and the Chinese arose. In 1842, Chinese miners in Lara took over a Dayak gold mine, driving Dayak miners away; the Dayaks replied by burning some Chinese dwellings, and in response the Chinese murdered about forty Dayaks. The Dayaks again retaliated by burning some hundred houses. The Malay appanage holder, Pangeran Jaya of Sambas, encouraged his Dayaks to resist, but Chinese from Thaikong joined the fray, fighting off the Sambas forces with the help of the Dayaks from Selakau. Years later, an official visited the Dayaks who had been driven from the Lara territory and found them living near the Sarawak border in great poverty.[142]

In 1844, Assistant Resident D. L. Baumgardt visited Monterado without incident, remaining four days. He was welcomed, as were all official visitors, with music, banners, and cannon salutes.[143] He noted that Thaikong leaders received some Dayaks with great hospitality; but they also demanded satisfaction from any who rebelled.[144] Summing up his experiences, he concluded that the kongsis understood what the Dutch had in mind:

> There can be no doubt that the Chinese know . . . that the Netherlands government is a powerful organization, able to, whenever it really will, confront all the Chinese in Borneo together with the Dayaks and Malays, and if necessary to destroy them. But on the other hand, the same Chinese realize the advantage of their present state of independence, a privilege that they have only secured after much trouble and difficulty . . . . they told me openly that they did not come to this coast to wage war, but to increase their fortune.[145]

---

[141] Dagregister van den kommissaris-inspecteur (Donker) voor de Westkust van Borneo, June 10-August 13, 1841, cited in Kervel, "Bijdrage," p. 185.

[142] Report of Travel to Sarawak and Brunei Borders, by Assistant Resident of Sambas H. van Gaffron, December 12, 1859, ARA V. 22.5.62 (38).

[143] J. J. Rochussen, "Verwikkelingen met de Chinesen op de Westkust van Borneo," in *Toelichting en verdediging van eenige daden van mijn bestuur in Indië, in antwoord op sommige vragen van J. P. Cornets de Groot van Kraaijenburg,* ed. J. J. Rochussen (The Hague: Van Cleef, 1853), p. 34. When in 1842 the Dayaks of Lara rose against the Chinese, the Assistant Resident of Sambas was told to keep out of the dispute. It was probably this same man, D. L. Baumgardt, Assistant Resident of Sambas in 1842-44, who was the 1844 visitor to Monterado. He was unable to follow his plan to travel to Lara because the path had fallen into disrepair since the Dayak troubles. Thaikong later allowed some Dayak families to return. See also "Verslag eener reis naar Montrado, gedaan in het Jaar 1844," *Tijdschrift voor Neêrland's Indië* 9,3 (1847): 63-65 (probable author is Baumgart); De Waal, *Onze Indische Financien,* 8: 12, 14, 24-27.

[144] De Waal, *Onze Indische Financien,* 8: 24-27.

[145] "Verslag eener reis," pp. 68-69. The reference to waging war means the "constant attacks" from the Dayaks, not going to war with the Dutch.

The Lanfang Kongsi, with its headquarters in Mandor, also faced declining gold production by the 1830s, yet other miners were entering its territory to look for gold. In 1842, at about the same time as the Thaikong-Lara altercations, Lanfang Kongsi men attempted to move into Landak, especially in the area of Perigi (see map six), but the Panembahan of Landak organized Malay-Dayak resistance.[146] Because Landak's sites were so promising, however, miners from Lanfang and elsewhere continued to infiltrate the territory. Fighting resumed in 1846, but the Sultan of Pontianak was able to arbitrate a solution.

Colonial authorities regarded the presence of Chinese settlers in Landak as highly detrimental to Dayak welfare and supported the *panembahan* in resisting Chinese settlement in his territory.[147] Only in 1851 did the Lanfang Kongsi headman win Landak's permission for the Chinese to open some mines and to settle in its capital, Ngabang.[148]

Finally, a new player entered the fractious scene. In 1839, James Brooke, an Englishman who had served the Sultan of Brunei, settled in Sarawak, where he set up an independent territory, challenging the Dutch assumption that they controlled all of Borneo. His subsequent establishment as Rajah of Sarawak led the Dutch to fear that the West Coast, too, might attract British intervention, or that the Sultan of Sambas, unhappy because of kongsi unrest, might turn to Brooke for support. As a result, the Dutch now began more systematic exploration of the territory and resolved to deal more assertively with both Chinese kongsis and recalcitrant natives.[149]

---

[146] Siahaan, "Konflik dan perlawanan," p. 366; van Meteren Brouwer, "Geschiedenis," p. 1075; see also Resident Willer's account of Landak-Mandor relations, ANRI BW 28/25 (82).

[147] Unsigned draft, apparently a justification of his policies by former Resident Willer, ANRI BW 28/28 (79). Willer is incensed at Chinese treatment of the Dayaks. Disorder was always an impetus to intervention; see De Waal, *Onze Indische Financien*, 8: 12-13, and his brief account of the hostilities (8: 64-65). See also the account in de Groot, *Kongsiwezen*, p. 34 and that in Francis, *Herinneringen*, 1: 301-304. Dutch relations with Landak were often tense, but the authorities usually supported its efforts to prohibit Chinese settlement or to limit it to the capital town of Ngabang.

[148] Van Meteren Brouwer, "Geschiedenis," p. 1079.

[149] This argument is developed in Irwin, *Nineteenth-Century Borneo*, especially pp. 129ff.; see also de Waal, *Onze Indische Financien*, 8: 12-18; anonymous, "Borneo en de Heer Rochussen," *Tijdschrift voor Nederlandsch Indië* 16,1 (1854): 30.

CHAPTER THREE

FROM 1850 TO THE END OF THE KONGSIS

After years of minimal investments of funds and forces in West Borneo, in 1849, Governor General J. J. Rochussen (1846-51) adopted a more interventionist policy. In that year, he divided Borneo into two residencies, West Borneo and South and East Borneo, an administrative division they retained until near the end of the colonial period.[1] In February 1850, a new Resident, T. J. Willer, arrived in West Borneo.[2] Assistant Resident R. C. van Prehn was assigned to Sambas. The colonial lion was without teeth, however: at mid-century less than two hundred troops were stationed in Sambas and Pontianak combined, many of them unfit to fight.[3] New troops were unavailable, and the Dutch were unsure how far their purported allies, the native rulers, would support them in a showdown with the kongsis.

On the other hand, Batavia was in a stronger position than in 1819, with more manpower at its disposal, thanks to a lull in colonial wars. The navy had new weapons: steam-driven vessels[4] that would enable it to patrol the coast and weaken the kongsis by reducing smuggling. For the moment, however, only token forces were available.

MOVING TOWARD SHOWDOWN WITH THAIKONG

Large-scale smuggling by the kongsis shattered Dutch complacency. Singapore had become an inexhaustible source of opium, weapons, and other goods. The profit on a smuggled chest of 150 pounds of opium was estimated at seven hundred to a thousand guilders, and how many chests reached the West Coast was anyone's guess. Pangeran Ratu Tua Mangkunegara, a nephew of the Sultan of Sambas, had acquired the official opium revenue farm for Monterado, but he claimed that he

---

[1] E. de Waal, *West Borneo*, vol. 8 of *Onze Indische financien*, ed. E. A. G. J. van Delden (The Hague: M. Nijhoff, 1907), p. 18; de Waal dates this "conversion" to Rochussen's predecessors, from the time of the Landak war in the 1840s, see pp. 12-14.

[2] E. B. Kielstra, "West Borneo," *Onze Eeuw* 16,2 (April 1916): 239. Willer had previously served among the Mandailing Batak in Sumatra.

[3] Anonymous, "De verwikkelingen van het Nederlandsch-Indisch Gouvernement met de Chineesche bevolking op Westelijk Borneo toegelicht," *Tijdschrift voor Nederlandsch Indië* 15,2 (1853): 276; *Regeeringsalmanak*, various years.

[4] W. L. de Sturler, *Vorlezing over den innerlijken Rijkdom onzer Oost-Indische bezittingen in verband met den oorsprong en den aard der zedelijke en maatschappelijke gesteldheid der bevolking van die gewesten* (Groningen: J. Oomkens, 1849), p. 26, emphasizes the need for low draft, steam-driven vessels to fight pirates. Previously, pirates or smugglers easily escaped sailing vessels by rowing away when the wind changed.

earned a meager thirty-six guilders from the farm annually, because so much illicit opium entered the area. In 1849, he pleaded with the Dutch to defend his rights.[5]

Furthermore, so little salt was being traded by the official monopoly at Sambas that the real consumption of the area was unknown.[6] Siamese or Chinese junks sometimes brought salt as ballast, which was then sold to the people by local traders.[7] The Dutch determined to intervene in this trade in order to salvage a potential source of revenue. Although all the kongsis smuggled such products, Thaikong bore the brunt of the blame.

Despite signs of increasing tension, the first inflammatory incident, in May 1850,[8] might have been ignored or settled with a fine under other circumstances, but instead, as a result of the colonial response, it helped incite a renewed war with Thaikong. The colonial authorities had tried to seize a small craft, a *sampan pukat*[9] loaded with opium, salt, and gunpowder, that was trying to enter the river at Sedau (near Singkawang), the main route for clandestine traffic to Monterado. Resident Willer blockaded the vessel, using a Dutch frigate temporarily in the vicinity. He demanded that the Chinese at the nearby fort of Jintang, a Thaikong town, turn over the vessel and pay a fine. After a brief standoff, the *sampan* slipped out to sea and the frigate sailed off, leaving Willer to try to recover his authority.[10]

---

[5] According to Quirijn S. Langelaan, "De Chinezen van Sambas, 1850" (Master's thesis, University of Amsterdam, 1984), p. 54, the pangeran was a brother of the sultan.

[6] J. J. Rochussen, "Verwikkelingen met de Chinesen op de Westkust van Borneo," in *Toelichting en verdediging van eenige daden van mijn bestuur in Indië, in antwoord op sommige vragen van J. P. Cornets de Groot van Kraaijenburg* (The Hague: van Cleef, 1853), p. 35; anonymous, "De held van Pemangkat," *Tijdschrift voor Neêrland's Indië* 13,1 (1851): 69; Kielstra, "West Borneo," pp. 239-40; anonymous, "Verwikkelingen," pp. 371, 392. For the early salt trade, see Gerrit Knaap and Luc Nagtegaal, "A Forgotten Trade: Salt in Southeast Asia, 1670-1818," in *Emporia, Commodities and Entrepreneurs in Asian Maritime Trade, c. 1400-1750*, ed. Roderich Ptak and Dietmar Rothermund (Stuttgart: Franz Steiner Verlag, 1991), p. 173, and, for the modern salt trade in Thailand, L. A. Peter Gosling, "Contemporary Malay Traders in the Gulf of Thailand," in *Economic Exchange and Social Interaction in Southeast Asia: Perspectives from Prehistory, History, and Ethnography*, ed. Karl L. Hutterer (Ann Arbor: Michigan Papers on Southeast Asia, 1977), pp. 76, 80. Salt also entered from Sarawak; see Graham Irwin, *Nineteenth-Century Borneo: A Study in Diplomatic Rivalry* (The Hague: M. Nijhoff, 1955, reprint, Singapore: Donald Moore Books, 1967), p. 69; *Koloniaal Verslag* (1849): 173.

[7] P. J. Veth, *Borneo's Wester-Afdeeling: Geographisch, statistisch, historisch, vorafgegaan door eene algemeene schets des ganschen eilands* (Zaltbommel: Joh. Nomanen Zoon, 1856), 2: 109.

[8] For a recent account of the events of 1850, see Langelaan, "Chinezen van Sambas," pp. 45-62, 69-91; and Yuan Bingling, *Chinese Democracies: A Study of the Kongsis of West Borneo (1776-1884)* (Leiden: Research School of Asian, African and Amerindian Studies, SNWS, Universiteit Leiden, 2000), pp. 160-165.

[9] *Pukat* means net. The vessel is also called a *perahu pukat*. De Waal, *Onze Indische financien*, 8: 28, quotes a source that says the boat had a crew of forty-two and was well-armed, but he doubts it was so large; that would be a huge crew for a mere *sampan*.

[10] R. C. van Prehn, Relaas van den oorlog met de oproerige Chinezen ter West-Kust van Borneo, beginnende in 1850 (Western manuscripts, University of Leiden Library, BPL 2472), pp. 1-14, offers a detailed account by a participant. See also anonymous, "Verwikkelingen," p. 277; "Borneo en de heer Rochussen," *Tijdschrift voor Nederlandsch Indië* 16,1 (1854): 31-33. Also *Koloniaal Verslag* (1850): 20-21. Thaikong, apologizing for the problem, had suggested to the Dutch that they might take the *perahu* after it put out to sea, but the Dutch failed to understand what this meant. If the craft were lost at sea, Thaikong would not be liable for the loss. If it

The next incidents involved the two mutually hostile kongsis. Skirmishes between Thaikong and Samtiaokioe soon broke out near Sambas; a larger attack by Thaikong forces seemed imminent. Samtiaokioe sought help from the Assistant Resident of Sambas, van Prehn, but he could offer no military support. The Sultan of Sambas then called up Dayak forces, under the command of the Malays, to attack the Thaikong Chinese. His troops avoided Thaikong and fell instead upon some nearby farming settlements that belonged to the kongsis of Lumar and Buduk, which until then had been neutral in the rivalry between Thaikong and Samtiaokioe. Several farmers[11] were killed, their houses were burned, and some of their women were brought to the sultan. These two kongsis then turned to Thaikong for help, blaming Samtiaokioe for instigating the brutality.

The altercation now drew in the Dutch. Samtiaokioe later complained to the Dutch that Thaikong had attacked them first. Thaikong blamed the headman of Sepang, a Samtiaokioe man, for setting loose the Dayak, and accused Assistant Resident van Prehn of complicity in the affair.[12] The military commander of the province, Major A. J. Andresen,[13] wrote soon after:

> I have seen the now uninhabited areas of Bawan and Planggouw. Whether so many defenseless farmers were so brutally murdered there as some Malays, Dayaks, and Chinese relate, I cannot tell for sure; but it is true that extensive rice fields have reverted to fields of alang-alang, and instead of the many houses that once stood in this place, you find only half-charred posts here and there.[14]

Andresen, who had recently arrived, believed that the vicious response of Thaikong against Samtiaokioe and its settlements, supported by men from Lumar and Buduk, must have been a result of these incidents.

---

were destroyed in Sedau, as the Dutch planned, Thaikong would have to reimburse its Singapore owners. De Waal, *Onze Indische financien*, 8: 29-31.

[11] A Chinese letter cited in Yuan, *Chinese Democracies*, pp. 166-169, says eighty families, with few exceptions, were wiped out. These farmers apparently lived in dispersed settlements.

[12] Langelaan, "Chinezen van Sambas," pp. 58-62, and Yuan, *Chinese Democracies*, p. 168, believe that Assistant Resident van Prehn agreed to the attack against Lumar-Buduk. They cite a report of the later Commissioner Prins from 1853. Prins, however, retained van Prehn in office until 1855 and van Prehn's own account says he and Willer had told the sultan that the Dayaks might fight defensively, but should not start a war. The attacks on Buduk and Lumar, in his version, came after Thaikong people were found preparing for war by building forts in those territories (Relaas van den oorlog, pp. 13, 18-20); subsequently, van Prehn admitted "unleashing" the Dayaks against Thaikong (p. 30).

[13] Andresen had been in Sambas since 1851, according to C. G. Toorop, "De krijgsverrichtingen in de Chineesche districten," *Indisch Militair Tijdschrift* 2 (1932): 905. He was then a major but was named lieutenant colonel in 1853. Sources usually refer to him by the higher rank, in Dutch, "Overste." Andresen's request to remain in West Borneo in 1855 as a civilian official was refused. He served as commissioner for South and East Borneo, and as military commander there until 1859, when he was discharged. "Stamboeken Indische Ambtenaren," ARA 2.10.36.015 Stamboek L 247. The village names are as given in Dutch sources; their exact location is unknown.

[14] Note of military commander Major Andresen of December 18, 1852, cited in E. B. Kielstra, "Bijdrage tot de geschiedenis van Borneo's Westerafdeeling," Part IV, *Indische Gids*, 11,1 (1889): 960.

Map Six. Important sites in the Second Kongsi War.

Thaikong, with more armed men than Samtiaokioe, now overran the Samtiaokioe settlements of Sepang, Seminis, Sebawi, and, in August 1850, the harbor town of Pemangkat. Some four thousand Samtiaokioe people fled to Sarawak, where their kongsi already controlled a few settlements, and the kongsi reconstituted itself on the territory governed by the English Rajah James Brooke. These immigrants formed the core of a Hakka Chinese community around Bau, not far from the border to Dutch territory, where they mined gold. Another estimated two thousand Samtiaokioe refugees scattered throughout Dutch Borneo, some ending in Lanfang territory.

Oblivious to—or ignoring—Samtiaokioe's machinations, influential circles in Batavia blamed Thaikong. For Batavians, the attacks constituted evidence of Thaikong's greedy intentions toward Samtiaokioe's gold fields and rice paddies. In fact, more than the competition for resources fueled the deep, mutual hatred that divided the kongsis from each other. Raids on each other's territory had left dead and wounded, and hundreds of refugees. Resident Willer, better aware of the involvement of both sides, saw the only hope of peace in eliminating both kongsis and installing direct civil administration, with firm Dutch control over all Chinese.

An initial contingent of troops soon arrived from Java, and in late 1850 the Dutch blockaded the coastline, cutting off Thaikong's supplies. In September 1850, Batavia, fearing Thaikong might threaten Sambas from its position in Pemangkat, sent a number of ships and a few hundred fresh troops under Lt. Col. Sorg to retake the town. Fiercely defending its position at the foot of Mt. Pemangkat (which the Chinese called Elephant Mountain), Thaikong lost hundreds of men. (See Plate 5.) The town was reduced to ashes, but civilian casualties were few; most of the population had fled before the battle.[15] Although they occupied the fortified kongsi temple briefly, the Dutch forces finally had to withdraw, while Sorg himself was wounded and died. Some colonial military praised the battle as a victory, but in reality it was a fiasco.[16] A military history of the battle overlooks its disastrous outcome for the Dutch:

> After a wild fight, for which there is no comparable example in the military history of the Netherlands Indies, he [Sorg] defeated a well-dug-in enemy, nine times the strength of his forces.[17]

---

[15] Pemangkat is described in E. Doty and W. J. Pohlmann, "Tour in Borneo, from Sambas through Montrado to Pontianak and the Adjacent Settlements of Chinese and Dayaks, during the Autumn of 1838," *Chinese Repository* 8 (1839), pp. 283-284; it was only founded in about 1829, that is, after Samtiaokioe split with Thaikong and could not use Singkawang as a harbor. At the time of the visit in 1838 over a thousand people lived in the town. On Elephant Mountain, see Schaank, "De kongsis van Montrado, Bijdrage tot de geschiedenis en de kennis van het wezen der Chineesche vereenigingen op de Westkust van Borneo," *Tijdschrift voor Indische Taal-, Land- en Volkenkunde* 35,5/6 (1893): 554. W. A. van Rees, *Wachia, Taykong en Amir* (Rotterdam: H. Nijgh, 1859) p. 144, says there were four hundred Thaikong dead after the battle.

[16] Yuan, *Chinese Democracies*, 172-177 and 199-206, shows how Dutch accounts turned the poor but brutal showing at Pemangkat into a "glorious feat."

[17] Quotation from anonymous, "Verwikkelingen," p. 320 and sketch maps included there. Also van Rees, *Wachia*, pp. 113-145; G. B. Hooyer, *De krijgsgeschiedenis van Nederlandsch-Indië van 1811-1894* (The Hague: Van Cleef and Batavia: Kolff, 1897) Vol. 3: 8-12. Some Europeans cherished a myth that Chinese would run away when attacked. Although Samtiaokioe's men

Plate 5. *Pasar* (marketplace) of Pemangkat, with mountain in the background, circa
1920. Credit: Division of Rare & Manuscript Collections, Cornell University.

Colonial reinforcements sent in mid-November failed to clear the remnants of the
Thaikong soldiers from the mountain, where they overlooked all movements in the
Dutch-occupied town and harbor. Although the people of Sambas expected an
attack after the battle in Pemangkat, Thaikong's goal had probably been
primarily to cut off Samtiaokioe from imports and from the rice growing in
Pemangkat's fields. In that they succeeded.[18]

Negotiations

If the battle of Pemangkat failed to subdue Thaikong, the naval blockade was
more effective. Reports of distress in Monterado soon reached Dutch territory,
although the kongsi put up a brave front. In early December 1850, some of
Thaikong's men, with others from Buduk and Lumar, its new allies, decided to
negotiate for peace, and they wrote to Batavia that Samtiaokioe had provoked
the attack on Pemangkat. As for the incident at Sedau, the *sampan pukat* had
merely taken refuge from adverse winds. Unimpressed, officials in the capital
rejected Thaikong's impudence; it had written to the colonial administration
directly, as one state to another (*als rijk tot rijk*).[19] Resident Willer, lacking the

---

did, occasionally, do just that, Thaikong certainly put up a battle. The estimate of their strength,
however, seems exaggerated.

[18] Anonymous, "Verwikkelingen," pp. 280, 339; Hooyer, *De krijgsgeschiedenis,* pp. 8-12;
Toorop, "Krijgsverrichtingen," pp. 900-901, 903-904. Toorop mistakenly calls the Samtiaokioe
Chinese Teochiu; Doty and Pohlman insist that they were mostly Hakkas. Probably, most were
pansanhok like the Thaikong people (see chapter two).

[19] Anonymous, "Verwikkelingen," pp. 364-368; cf. Schaank, "Kongsis van Montrado," p. 553.

forces to destroy the kongsis, was more impressed by the initiative.[20] He had the kongsi "delegates," who had presented themselves in Pontianak, beg Dutch pardon by solemnly bowing to the Dutch flag, offering incense and candles at the flagpole. He also demanded a fine from the three kongsis of a *picul* (about sixty-two kilograms) of gold, a great burden given their financial state.[21]

Willer's plan went farther. He wished to install a new administration for the mining territories, including those of Samtiaokioe. Kongsi members would nominate four candidates for a new headman or regent[22] for this administration, from whom the Dutch would choose a single official, who would be subject to the Assistant Resident of Sambas. The regent would receive a salary and would bear, like the head of Lanfang Kongsi, the Chinese title of *kapthai* (M. *jiatai*, great *kapitan*). He would have the right to appoint some lesser officials, but the heads of smaller towns (*laothai*, M. *laoda*) would be elected. All the Sambas kongsis (but not Lanfang, which was mostly in Pontianak territory) would give up their seals of authority. Willer regarded the seals as signs of "statehood." The gold mines themselves would become independent economic entities. The new regent's administration would have control of the opium farm and the salt monopoly in former Thaikong territory and would be called Fosjoen Tjoengthang (M. Heshun Zongting, The United Hall of Fosjoen), perhaps to avoid the name "kongsi."[23] Fosjoen was the name of the union to which both Thaikong and, before 1819, Samtiaokioe, as well as other, smaller kongsis, belonged.

Meanwhile, Willer accompanied three men from the hostile kongsis, led by Tjang Ping (M. Zheng Hong) of Thaikong, to Batavia in February 1851, to ask the governor-general's "forgiveness." The coastal blockade was relaxed, permitting some rice and salt to reach the interior, and Thaikong's troops withdrew from the Pemangkat area.[24] Willer, however, not only lacked the troops to enforce his plan, but his superiors in Batavia also distrusted Thaikong, feeling obliged to look out for the interests of the Malay rulers and those of Samtiaokioe (although the latter had moved to Sarawak).

Batavia thought Willer had been duped and that Thaikong was using the lull to recuperate; officials believed the break in the fighting had been the result not of repentance, but rather of the rainy season. Also, the agreement would be deleterious to the Sultan of Sambas, who was inexplicably called "one of the

---

[20] As Yuan Bingling points out, Willer could not even give orders to the troops that were in Borneo, for he had to depend on Batavia for all military decisions (*Chinese Democracies*, p. 161).

[21] Since the mines had been shut down for months because of the fighting, this penalty could be paid over twenty years. Kielstra, "Bijdrage," Part I, *Indische Gids* 11,1 (1889): 324.

[22] Comparable to the district head or regent (now called *bupati*) in Java.

[23] Text in anonymous, "Verwikkelingen," pp. 358-362; see also account in Rochussen "Verwikkelingen met de Chinesen," pp. 43-46; Kielstra, "Bijdrage," Part I, *Indische Gids* 11,1 (1889): 324-329.

[24] Kielstra "Bijdrage," Part I, *Indische Gids* 11,1 (1889): 322-329; anonymous, "Verwikkelingen," pp. 355-357, with the minutes of a meeting between Willer and kongsi representatives on January 27, 1851 in Pontianak, reprinted pp. 358-362. Governor General Rochussen also refers to the visit of the kongsi representatives; J. J. Rochussen, "Redevoering, gehouden bij de overgave van het bestuur aan den heer Duymaer van Twist, in den raad van Indië, op den 12den Mei 1851," *Tijdschrift voor Nederlandsch Indië* 18,1 (1856), p. 56. He was especially concerned in this matter, he asserts, to protect the Dayak from Malay and Chinese exploiters.

government's oldest allies" in a Dutch report. In reality they feared that the sultan, whom they considered to be untrustworthy in general, might desert his Dutch "allies" and seek alliance with Brooke in Sarawak. Willer's successor, Commissioner A. Prins, who arrived on the scene in February 1853, eventually exiled the sultan to Java. Sambas was no friend of the Dutch.[25]

Batavia also objected to Willer's cavalier treatment of Samtiaokioe, but Willer knew Samtiaokioe was no innocent victim. The important thing was to repopulate the territory deserted when Samtiaokioe had fled to Sarawak, and he thought people from Thaikong could do so.[26]

The governor-general finally received the three Chinese led by Tjang Ping at the end of March 1851, then sent the party back to Borneo, satisfied that the "imperious Chinese have pleaded for forgiveness."[27] Resident Willer returned to Pontianak in late April, hoping that the Dutch military could still defend Samtiaokioe's remaining territory, in particular gold-rich Sepang,[28] in another looming confrontation with Thaikong forces.

The year 1851 passed relatively peacefully; negotiations with the kongsis dragged on to the end of 1852. Neither Willer nor Tjang Ping and the other delegates had backing for a decisive solution. Batavia remained skeptical about the resident's plans, while in Monterado opposition to Tjang was mounting.[29]

The negotiators had acted without the miners, the most powerful group in the kongsi, although they had shown the Dutch a document with a seal, which Willer believed was an authorization to act for Thaikong. They did have support from the town-dwellers, who probably bore the brunt of the Dutch blockade.[30]

The miners were still demanding that Sepang be awarded to Thaikong. The kongsi's outstanding debts of ƒ80,000 (to shareholders or others who advanced money for mining or for warfare, and probably to suppliers in Singapore) should be repaid before the kongsis were dissolved, or the fine (a *picul* in gold) handed over. The miners also wanted the new regent's term of office to last four months, equal to the term of the kongsi headman, but the Dutch held out for a year. Ignoring continued resistance from Monterado, Willer ceremoniously installed Tjang Ping as

---

[25] E. B. Kielstra, "West Borneo," in *De Indische Archipel: Geschiedkundige schetsen*, ed. E. B. Kielstra (Haarlem: De Erven F. Bohn, 1917), p. 283. In 1853, the sultan and his brother were replaced and exiled to Java. See also Kielstra, "Bijdrage," Part I, *Indische Gids* 11,1 (1889): 330 and especially Part II, *Indische Gids* 11,1 (1889): 524-526, which quotes Willer's assessment at length ("He is weak of mind and body: both were destroyed early and now, in the long run, by opium..."); anonymous, "Verwikkelingen," pp. 383-384.

[26] For some of Samtiaokioe's machinations, apart from the attack on Buduk (above), see van Prehn, Relaas van den oorlog, pp. 34ff.; anonymous, "Verwikkelingen," pp. 389-390. Yuan dwells on these at length (*Chinese Democracies*, passim).

[27] Rochussen, "Redevoering" p. 56. Here, Rochussen ignored the advice of the more experienced Francis, who thought the only way to deal with the Chinese was to defeat them militarily. See "Borneo en de heer Rochussen," p. 29.

[28] Kielstra, "Bijdrage," Part II, *Indische Gids* 11,1 (1889): 529.

[29] As mentioned, Willer also had no authority over the military in his residency. Importantly, Tjang Ping was not the headman of Thaikong. Yuan (*Chinese Democracies*, p. 205) calls his office "accountant" (*tsjoe koe sian*, M. *cai ku xian*). Tjang himself was not a wealthy man, but he seems to have been a successful military leader of kongsi forces.

[30] Wang Tai Peng, *The Origins of Chinese Kongsi* (Petaling Jaya: Pelanduk Publications, 1994), p. 94 ascribes the desire for peace to the "towkay elite," which exaggerates the wealth of the townsmen.

Regent of Fosjoen in June 1851. The flags and cymbals accompanying the ceremony could not disguise the fact that an important part of Thaikong would not support Tjang.[31]

The new governor-general, A. J. Duymaer van Twist (May 1851-May 1856), correctly foresaw that the "ultra-democratic" elements in Thaikong—the miners themselves—would not accept the peace as negotiated. Willer returned to Batavia in August 1851, only to be snubbed by the new governor-general. A new military commander, Major Andresen, had arrived in West Borneo in early 1851,[32] but troops remained scarce. Finally, back in Pontianak in March 1852, the resident made initial arrangements for Tjang Ping and his associates to be awarded the opium farm for Monterado, which would insure, he thought, ample funds for the new Fosjoen administration, enable the payment of the fines assessed on Thaikong by the Dutch, and leave a profit for the colonial treasury as well. Any profitable opium farm, however, depended on suppression of smuggling, which would have raised the price of the drug and aroused miner opposition.

Back in Pontianak, Willer tried to dissolve both Thaikong and Samtiaokioe by commanding them to turn over their official seals to the Dutch for destruction. Tjang at first appeared willing to cooperate. Thaikong's members assembled to discuss these proposals at the beginning of December 1852. One thousand men had participated in the meeting, but only one-fifth of those present supported Tjang. Some 70 percent were miners, both laborers and shareholders, while 30 percent were farmers and shop owners. The *"lansaai"* (M. *lanzai*, riff-raff, presumably the miners) had appeared in great numbers and dominated the meeting. They rejected Willer's opium plan, refused to hand over the seals for destruction, and accused Tjang Ping of wanting to become a "mandarin" (*koanjin*, M. *guanren*) for the Dutch. Finally, the men consulted an oracle of Sam-Bong-Jak,[33] the god of the upper temple in Monterado. Next to the central hall, Monterado had "upper" and "lower" halls, called Sjongbok and Habok (M. Shangwu and Xiawu, Upper and Lower House),[34] Through a medium, the deity advised compliance with the

---

[31] Anonymous, "De toenemende verwikkelingen op Borneo," *Tijdschrift voor Nederlandsch Indië* 15,2 (1853): 137.

[32] Kielstra, *Indische Archipel*, p. 282.

[33] San-wang-ye or Sanshan Guowang, the Kings of the Three Mountains, are worshipped in the Chaozhou area of Guangdong and especially by Hoppo (Hepo) Hakkas, in China and abroad. Probably, the hall belonged to a kongsi of Hoppo Hakkas who had joined Fosjoen at some time. On the three deities, see Schaank's history of Limtian (Buduk) Kongsi in "Kongsis van Montrado," pp. 559-560, and Wolfgang Franke, "The Sovereigns of the Kingdoms of the Three Mountains, San Shan Guowang, at Hepo and in Southeast Asia: A Preliminary Investigation, " in *Collected Papers: International Conference on Chinese Studies* (n.p.: Kuala Lumpur, 1994), pp. 376-377; and his "Notes on Chinese Temples and Deities in Northwestern Borneo," in *Sino-Malaysiana, Selected Papers on Ming and Qing History and on the Overseas Chinese in Southeast Asia by Wolfgang Franke, 1942-1988* (Singapore: South Seas Society, 1989), pp. 384-385. One of the kongsi flags pictured in P. J. Veth, *Borneo's Wester-Afdeeling*, 1: 324, displays this name. Schaank translated "Bong Jak" or "Wong-dja" (M. *wangye*) as "royal prince," but the character *ye* also means "father" and is used for a god. Compare the account of Sanshan Gongwang in Claudine Salmon and Denys Lombard, *Les Chinois de Jakarta: Temples et vie collective* (Paris: Cahier d'Archipel, 1977), p. 49.

[34] Monterado had three kongsi houses, arranged in a rough triangle, each about a fifteen minutes' walk from the others. These were probably halls of former member kongsis of Fosjoen, and each had its own patron god. The central one, the *thang* (M. *ting*, hall), was the "reception house" and probably served all of Fosjoen as its central temple. A second, older one, was the

government, turning over the seal and, at least openly, accepting a new seal and flag from the government.[35]

Meanwhile, sensing trouble, Tjang Ping sent his wife and children to Sambas town for safekeeping. On December 21, 1852, Tjang, accompanied by a number of prominent men and members of other kongsis, appeared in Pontianak. Tjang had apparently promised to back the kongsi demands in negotiations, for the miners demanded retention of Sepang for Thaikong and direct election of the headmen (not merely nomination by the kongsi and selection by the Dutch). Tjang knew this would be unacceptable to Willer.

Tjang's position did not improve when Willer decided to cancel the opium plan and auctioned off Monterado's opium farm on December 24, 1852. In the end it was sold, although for a higher price, to Tjang and his colleague from Monterado, the wealthy Eng Tjong Kwee (M. Wu Changgui), together with the Kapthai of Mandor, Lioe A Sin (M. Liu Asheng), and Lioe's brother-in-law, Then Sioe Ling, Kapitan of the Hakkas in Pontianak.[36] In early January 1853, delegates arrived from Monterado, carrying what they said was the official seal[37] of Thaikong, with the news that a kongsi gathering had finally decided to surrender the seal to the Dutch.[38]

PREMATURE REQUIEM FOR A KONGSI

On January 14, 1853 some thirty invited guests and hundreds of townspeople gathered on the banks of the Kapuas River in Pontianak to watch the public burning of the seal of the Thaikong Kongsi.[39] Representatives of the Chinese

---

former kongsi house of Samtiaokioe, and another the new kongsi house of Thaikong. See anonymous, "Verslag eener reis naar Montrado, gedaan in het jaar 1844," *Tijdschrift voor Neêrland's Indië* 9,3 (1847): 70. Given its association with Tianhou, Habok might be the former headquarters of Samtiaokioe; the patron of Sjongbok was Sanshan Guowang.

[35] H. van Dewall, Opstand der Chinezen van Menteradoe, Westkust-Borneo, 1853-54, manuscript, KITLV collection, H 83, pp. 2-5. Van Dewall was a military man who became acting assistant resident at Monterado in 1854. He apparently gathered a great deal of information about the events of 1852-54. Oracles were a frequent feature of decision-making. When the oracle of Monterado failed to speak, people went for advice to the oracle of Lumar: "Tian Loo," (p. 13) probably the goddess Tian Hou, who is widely revered in West Kalimantan today. For more on kongsis and gods, see below.

[36] Political Report for 1858, dated March 31, 1859, Arsip National Republik Indonesia (ANRI), Jakarta, colonial archives, BW 1/9 (216).

[37] The seal or *cap* (at the time spelled *tjap*) was, to Willer, the symbol of the political authority of the kongsi. But such a seal had other functions. Gold dust was filled into paper packets marked with the *cap* of the kongsi to certify both its weight and its place of origin, which in turn indicated its degree of purity, Monterado gold ore being less pure than that of other kongsis but not, the *cap* guaranteed, adulterated. George Windsor Earl, *The Eastern Seas, or Voyages and Adventures in the Indian Archipelago* (London: W. H. Allen, 1837, reprint, Singapore: Oxford University Press, 1971), p. 287. Without the seal, Monterado's production would be, for a time at least, worth little.

[38] See the summary in de Waal, *Onze Indische financien*, 8: 37ff. The opium farm for 1853 cost ƒ30,000 more than in 1852, but this probably reflected the expectation of peace and the end of smuggling.

[39] This ceremony, and the long negotiations preceding it in December 1852 and January 1853, are described in Conferences with Chinese in Pontianak in December 1852 and January 1853 and Reports to Governor General, ANRI 31/8 (87), with a copy of van Prehn's seating

community of Pontianak and a delegate from the Lanfang Kongsi were present. The Sultan of Pontianak delegated the Pangeran Bendahara to attend, promising to pray for "blessings for your endeavor." Some other Moslems appeared in their capacity as local officials.

Resident Willer, with the help of two Chinese *kapitan*s from Pontianak, the Chinese interpreter and Kapitan of Sambas, Assistant Resident of Sambas van Prehn (who handled most of the protocol), and the residential secretary, had carefully scheduled each stage of the ceremony. An unforeseen downpour delayed the opening, but at 10:30, the solemnities began.

In the first act, Tja Mien, a priest of Sjongbok (the upper house or hall) in Thaikong, as officiant, assisted by two Chinese priests from Pontianak, brought the Thaikong seal, together with incense sticks, to the ritual incense burner (*hionglo*, M. *xianglo*) for cremation. At this point, Europeans were to remove their hats, Chinese to bow. From the Kapuas River, the ship Doris fired a three-gun salute. The ashes of the seal, shielded from the sun by the resident's golden umbrella, were then carried to the river, accompanied by the priest, Tjang Ping (as new regent/*kapthai*), and several Europeans. The Doris closed with another salute.

In the next stage of the ceremony, more Western and secular in character, Tjang and other new Chinese officers took an oath of loyalty to the King, the Netherlands, and the colonial government (accompanied by another salute from the Doris). The new flags and seals they received underlined their status as employees of the colonial government. As the Dutch flag was raised, the Doris fired twenty-one guns.

The final act of the day was the dedication, with appropriate ritual and incense, of the new seal of what was to be a commercial body, without political or judicial authority, the Sjong-Ha-Bok Kongsoe (M. *Shangxiawu Gongsuo*, Office or Association of the Upper and Lower House). This association was formed to run the mines formerly governed by Thaikong.[40] The dedication, Willer thought, would assure that a new *toapekong* (M. *dabogong*, patron spirit of the kongsi), having departed from the ashes of the old seal, would reside in the new seal to sanction and protect the new commercial body. Three salvos from the Doris closed the day's ceremony. After an exchange of congratulations, some sixty Chinese and European guests entered the residence for a celebratory meal.

Batavia, informed by a triumphant Willer, was amazed. The governor-general,[41] appalled by Willer's "mysticism," promptly dispatched his cabinet secretary, Prins, to serve as commissioner to Borneo and to assess Willer's state of mind. Arriving in Pontianak, Prins quickly demoted the resident to inactive status,

arrangements for the event. J. W. Young, "Bijdrage tot de geschiedenis van Borneo's Westerafdeeling," *Tijdschrift voor Indische Taal-, Land- en Volkenkunde* 38 (1895): 499-550, describes the ceremony and reproduces the plan.

[40] Sjongbok and Habok were the upper and lower kongsi houses, besides the central hall in Monterado. P. M. van Meteren Brouwer, "De geschiedenis der Chineesche Districten der Wester-Afdeeling van Borneo van 1740-1926," *Indische Gids* 49,2 (1927): 1085, treats the hall as headquarters of the Thaikong Kongsi. Sjongbok and Habok are, for him, "commercial bodies" (cf. de Waal, *Onze Indische financien*, 8: 55). In reality, these were two additional houses or halls, probably from formerly associated kongsis (see above).

[41] Who was A. J. Duymaer van Twist.

giving precedence to the military commander, Andresen, who later became resident.[42]

Background to the Ceremony

Why did Willer resort to "mysticism"? Determined to dissolve Thaikong and end mutual feuding between it and Samtiaokioe, yet lacking adequate military forces, he had asked the leaders of the warring kongsis simply to turn over their seals and declare the kongsis, which he saw as political and economic entities, disbanded. Samtiaokioe's local branch appeared willing to comply, but it insisted that, since Samtiaokioe had always been loyal to the Dutch (a questionable assertion), Thaikong must be the first to dissolve itself. In any case, most of the members of the Samtiaokioe kongsi were now in Sarawak, out of reach of Dutch authority.[43]

Thaikong leaders, for their part, insisted that their seal could not be destroyed or given to the Dutch. It was the property of the kongsi's *toapekong*—as Willer called it, the "guardian angel." The *toapekong* was an emanation of "Njoek-fong-thay-ti" (M. *Yuhuang Dadi*, the World-spirit, the Jade Emperor). Yet each kongsi had its own *toapekong,* and a kongsi's seal belonged to its *toapekong* alone, and the *toapekong*s of different kongsis might be mutual enemies.

Given the situation and the beliefs of the kongsis regarding their seals, Willer decided to have Thaikong's seal burned. One of his papers bears a marginal note explaining that, on an altar in the open air, the seal (*cap*), symbol of collective identity, and the *toapekong* himself would ascend to heaven in the smoke, and the ashes, now deconsecrated, could be disposed of in flowing water. The name of kongsi, now officially dead, could not be resurrected without calling down the wrath of the spirits.[44] Willer's "theology," whether learned from Tjang Ping and his colleagues or from informants in Pontianak, seems to accord with popular Taoist traditions.[45] In any case, Willer hoped this would end the conflict between the Dutch and Thaikong and between Thaikong and Samtiaokioe (which would also have to offer up its seal, presumably at a later date).

Engaged in negotiations with the resident since mid-December of 1852, perhaps the Chinese participants had come around to his point of view. Their motives are not recorded. Perhaps they recognized Dutch strength. Certainly the Dutch

---

[42] Van Prehn, former Assistant Resident of Sambas, was made responsible for civil affairs but subject to Andresen. The *Regeeringsalmanak* shows that Willer and van Prehn had assumed office in 1850. Willer left in 1853; van Prehn was still listed as assistant resident in 1855, but became acting resident as well. According to de Waal *(Onze Indische financien,* 8: 69), Prins named Andresen in August 1854 as resident, which he remained until February 1856.

[43] At one point, they offered to reconstitute themselves with the name "Samtai Tjongthang (M. Sanda Zongting, Three-great Central Hall), which Willer rejected as an echo of the former name. See Yuan, *Chinese Democracies,* pp. 196ff for some of the problems.

[44] Note by Willer, which appears to be a draft of a Memorie van Overgave, ANRI Borneo-W 28/28 (79).

[45] Compare the references to the Jade Emperor (M. Yuhuang Shangdi) in Kristofer Schipper, *Tao: De levende religie van China,* 4th ed. (Amsterdam: Meulenhoff, 1998), pp. 42, 118. Years later, Dutch officials would adopt another ritual to preserve peace: meetings of "reconciliation" among hostile Dayak groups as a means to stop headhunting. No one complained about their "mysticism."

blockade was causing hardship, for even if it failed to seal off the coast completely, a reduction in imports of necessities would have driven up prices, and, indeed, reports reached Pontianak of difficulties in Monterado. Peace would reopen the area to trade and profit, and Tjang Ping may have looked forward to his new office of regent-*kapthai*. His associate Eng Tjong Kwee would be vice-regent. Another incentive offered by the Dutch was the opium farm, but, as mentioned above, in the end Tjang and Eng had to share the Monterado farm with two Mandor Chinese.

Men like Tjang and Eng may even have been eager to get rid of the kongsi, despite their protests. Thaikong could not afford to continue the war. It was deep in debt, owing at least ƒ80,000, and, according to some accounts, perhaps even double that sum.[46] Would creditors continue to provide capital for running the mines? Tjang and Eng may even have feared that, given the hopeless situation, the miners themselves might revolt against the townspeople.

Under these circumstances, the ceremonial dissolution of the kongsi was the preferred solution for all the parties involved. Both sides had to engage in a certain amount of play-acting for the benefit of their own constituencies, showing appropriate deference to both the Dutch authorities and the Chinese gods. Unfortunately, neither Batavia nor the rank-and-file of the kongsi were convinced by the charade, though for different reasons.

Thaikong Reacts, Batavia Acts

The flaw in Willer's strategy was not so much his resort to symbolic behavior, but his apparent ignorance of how the rest of the kongsi would react. In August 1851, Tjang Ping had told Willer that virtually all the traders and farmers of Monterado were on his side, but only one-third of the miners were in accord with him; now the division was even less favorable.[47] The Chinese year was ending, and after two weeks of New Year celebrations, on February 22, 1853, the kongsi would elect new leaders. During the holidays, mine work ceased. Miners converged on Monterado town to celebrate, to settle the mine accounts of the past four months, and to elect new officials. They would outnumber—and outvote—the townspeople.[48]

After Willer's ceremony, Tjang Ping wisely found an excuse to go to Sambas instead of returning to Monterado. Voters there had repudiated his policy and chosen new kongsi officials who were determined to reject the Dutch terms. They imprisoned and mistreated a relative of Tjang Ping, who died in captivity. There

---

[46] Conference of January 18, 1853, ANRI 31/8 (87); anonymous, "Toenemende verwikkelingen," p. 137; compare Kielstra, "Bijdrage," Part I, *Indische Gids* 11,1 (1889): 338.

[47] As the meeting of December 1852 showed (above). Kielstra, "Bijdrage," Part II, *Indische Gids* 11,1 (1889): 505-506. The meeting in early January that resulted in turning over the seal was probably one of townspeople only (de Waal, *Onze Indische financien*, 8: 55). Townspeople were not able to vote in kongsi affairs, unless they owned shares in the kongsi.

[48] Rochussen, "Verwikkelingen met de Chinesen," p. 52, insists that the only persons allowed to vote were the *parit chiongs*, or bosses of the mines, but the number of voters was several hundred or even a thousand, which means that most miners did vote. Only the non-shareholders among the miners, who were still paid a monthly wage, were not allowed to vote.

was no way to reconcile the kongsi, and a military denouement was rapidly becoming inevitable.[49]

In March 1853, military reinforcements, denied to Willer for so long, arrived from Java. They occupied Sepang, the prized mining area, in April. Thaikong and its allies, consulting their oracles, determined that this was the best time to mount an attack on Sepang, and mine work stopped. Liao Njie (or Ngie) Liong (M. Liao Erlong, Liao the Second Dragon, probably a pseudonym) assumed command of the troops, bearing a rattan whip and a yellow flag with the word *lin*, that is, "command," printed on it. "Banners" of 108 troops each, four from Monterado, and one each from Lumar, Lara, Buduk, and Singkawang, took to the field. In the first clashes, victory went to the Dutch, but in May, Thaikong forces occupied a devastated Sepang. They haughtily rejected Dutch offers for negotiations.

By March 1854, the prevailing sentiment was, "Now fear of Chinese, mixed with hate of Chinese, ruled the day."[50] Batavia resolved to eliminate Thaikong and its allies.

The navy tightened its already strict blockade, and some 1,700 additional, relatively well-equipped, troops joined the March 1853 arrivals. The Sultan of Sambas provided 1,400 coolies for transporting equipment; the Sultan of Pontianak contributed seagoing vessels.[51]

Troubles with the Dayaks near Sintang threatened in April, and a contingent of Dutch troops sailed up the Kapuas River to deal with them, postponing a move against Thaikong. Finally, colonial troops, marching overland from Betunai on the Selakau River[52] and backed by maritime forces, took Singkawang on May 18, 1854. Liao Njie Liong, his men, and the townspeople had deserted the town; the colonial invaders turned Singkawang's kongsi hall into their supply depot. Delegations from Thaikong's allies, the kongsis of Buduk, Lumar, and Lara, soon arrived at Singkawang to offer their submission. Thaikong appeared to be isolated.

The agricultural area around Singkawang offered the troops generous supplies of pigs, ducks, hens, and produce of field and tree, but almost all settlements were abandoned when the troops arrived. From Singkawang, the forces moved, mostly overland, past Kulor, where Liao and his men had torched the market before withdrawing. Where some inhabitants remained, as in Jintang, they assured the military they were innocent of cooperation with Thaikong.[53]

---

[49] Note of former Resident Willer, ANRI Borneo-W, 28/25 (82); anonymous, "Toenemende verwikkelingen," p. 138.

[50] Kielstra, *Indische Archipel*, p. 284.

[51] Hooyer, *De krijgsgeschiedenis*, p. 21.

[52] Betunai was a fortified settlement on the side of Thaikong, only a few miles from Singkawang, but separated from it by extremely difficult, uncleared terrain. The Selakau River was navigable for steam vessels for some distance and preferable to Sedau (south of Singkawang) as a landing site; Singkawang could not be approached by ships at all. Toorop, *De Krijgsverrichtingen*, p. 905; A. J. A. Gerlach, *Fastes militaires des Indes-Orientales néerlandaises* (Zaltbommel: Noman, 1859), 1: 648-652. (See map six.)

[53] Letter, Inspector of Navy to Governor General, June 19, 1854, ARA 2.10.02 V. 29.8.54 no. 11 (362) and W. R. Berghuis, Rapport aangaande de verrichtingen van Z. M. zeemagt ter Westkust van Borneo durende de krijgs-operatiën tegen Singkawang, Montrado, enz., manuscript, 1854, KITLV collection, H254, pp. 6-8 and the same author's Stukken met betrekking tot de expeditie ter Westkust van Borneo in 1854, manuscript, KITLV collection, H354, stress the role of the naval forces; cf. Hooyer, *De krijgsgeschiedenis*, p. 23; Kielstra, *Indische Archipel*, p. 285. The description reflects the sheer agony of overland travel: troops sank in mud over their knees,

Nevertheless, town and village people adjusted quickly to the new situation. When military commander Andresen fortified the kongsi hall of Singkawang, many Chinese offered their labor. Before long, the Dutch were using Chinese coolies for transport, because they were sturdier than Malays or Dayaks, willing to work for cash, and able to deliver the goods reliably.[54]

When the Dutch column reached Monterado on June 2, the townspeople, having prevented Liao's men from setting fire to the *pasar*, surrendered, kneeling in front of their houses, dressed in white garments, to greet the incoming troops.

Accepting the surrender, the troops made their quarters in the kongsi halls: the central *thang*, and Sjongbok, and Habok, the upper and lower house.[55] Andresen thought that the surrender of the townspeople meant that resistance had ended,[56] but the hostile faction, leaving the town, occupied the surrounding hills. They fired on Monterado, set up small forts (*bentengs*) along the paths to other settlements, and weeks later they reduced the *pasar* and most of the town of Monterado to ashes. The colonial troops had to move out, fighting for one village after another, yet they were unable to capture the ringleaders. Thaikong had been destroyed only to reappear, first as Kioe Long (M. Jiulong, Nine Dragon) Kongsi, then under the banner of the Ngee Hin (M. Yixing) Society or Sam Tiam Fui (M. Sandianhui), both names of "secret societies" or sworn brotherhoods. This brotherhood or *hui* met secretly, at night, and conscripted new members, while the Chinese who cooperated with the Dutch became targets for reprisals and threats; some were even killed.[57]

In September 1854, military operations cleared the town of Bengkayang of rebels, and the situation now appeared to favor the Dutch. This time the population did not flee at the approach of troops. About two thousand refugees from Lara were in the area of Bengkayang, but they now began to rebuild their town, turning in their weapons. People were returning to the other towns as well, reconstructing the *pasars* and working the fields and mines. However, Landak still harbored some two thousand refugees, some of them rebels. Two rebel leaders were

---

hacked through dense vegetation, and tripped over fallen trees. Part of the force could go by boat, but the Chinese blocked the rivers with chains and logs. Only the Singkawang-Kulor stretch was easily traversed. The settlements of Singkawang, Sedau, Sungai Raya, Kulor, Jintang, and Tengahan were all subject to the Thaikong Kongsi. See "Verslag eener reis," pp. 64, 72.

[54] Letter, Inspector of Navy to Governor General, June 19, 1854, ARA 2.10.02 V. 29.8.54, (11); Summary of reports and letters from West Borneo, ARA 2.10.02 V. 1.12.54, no. 4 (385). The Chinese insisted on having no escort, and usually performed well, unless they were carrying alcoholic beverages, which tended to disappear.

[55] Van Dewall, "Opstand," pp. 25-27; Gerlach, *Fastes militaires*, p. 658. The intention of the white garments signaled surrender, and white flags were flown, but the Chinese associate white clothing with mourning. The *thang*, Sjongbok and Habok were, as described above, temples and seats of kongsi government. See also the description of Monterado in Hooyer, *De krijgsgeschiedenis*, p. 23; and Yuan, *Chinese Democracies*, pp. 72ff.

[56] Unrest in West Borneo, with two letters of Lt. Kol. A. J. Andresen, ARA 2.10.02 V. 17.8.1854 (3).

[57] W. A. van Rees, *Montrado: Geschied- en krijgskundige bijdrage betreffende de onderwerping der Chinezen op Borneo, naar het dagboek van een Indisch officier over 1854-1856* (Bois-le-Duc: Müller, 1858), pp. 218-219, 234. Sandianhui, the "Three Dots Society," was a variant of the Tiandihui, the "Heaven and Earth Society." Although they behaved conspiratorially in Borneo and in China, the societies operated openly in Singapore for decades.

captured with the help of the *kapthai* of the Lanfang Kongsi. He delivered them up as soon as the Dutch persuaded the refugees in Landak, who threatened his territory, to depart.[58]

AFTER THE WAR

The imposition of Dutch control meant taxes and corvée. Most onerous was the annual head tax of three guilders on all adult males. Payment was a precondition for obtaining identification papers, and any Chinese man without papers could be arrested on suspicion of supporting the rebels. Able-bodied men had to work one day in seven on public works, constructing roads from Singkawang to Monterado, Sepang, and Lara. Delinquents, if caught, worked for four days in a row. The authorities also called in all weapons, even those needed for hunting. Finally, the Dutch canceled all Dayak debts to the Thaikong Chinese.

Compulsory smallpox vaccinations also aroused resistance. The Chinese had their own inoculations, but the Dutch insisted only their method would work. Those who could show no vaccination scar faced arrest.[59] The aggressive behavior of Madurese soldiers, a mainstay of the colonial troops, proved to be yet another source of friction.[60]

Increasingly, the colonial power tried to force the Chinese to live in concentrated settlements, at *pasars*, or in *kampungs* near major roads and paths. They ordered the Chinese who had erected huts in the jungle to move to settlements within fourteen days; after that, patrols composed of Dayaks and police would seek out and destroy any structures they found. According to the Dutch, it was time for the Chinese to "live an orderly life" again, subject to colonial control.[61]

Hunting down the remnants of what they believed to be a secret society, which they blamed for harassing the Chinese who were willing to cooperate, the Dutch executed some captured rebels and deported others to Java, but many escaped to Sarawak. Spies led troops to the headquarters of the rebels, who now called themselves Ngee Hin-Lanfang Kongsi,[62] in June. There, the Dutch captured

---

[58] Summary of reports and letters from West Borneo, ARA 2.10.02 V. 1.12.54 (4); Kielstra, "Bijdrage," Part IX, *Indische Gids* 11,2 (1889): 2145-2148. Van Meteren Brouwer, "Geschiedenis," p. 1077, thinks Lanfang was on the side of Samtiaokioe against Thaikong, but, as will be seen, the kongsi played a flexible and self-interested role.

[59] Van Rees, *Onderwerping der Chinezen*, pp. 214, 221, 226, 229-230; Kielstra, "Bijdrage," Part IX, *Indische Gids* 11,2 (1889): 2140. The Chinese had long used so-called "variolation" to immunize against smallpox and were reluctant to try the unfamiliar Western method.

[60] Van Meteren Brouwer, "Geschiedenis," p. 1087.

[61] Van Rees, *Onderwerping der Chinezen*, pp. 245-246. This recalls the use of concentrated settlements and identity cards in the campaign against pro-Communist rebels in Malaya after 1948. In fact, the Dutch had also concentrated peasant settlements after the Java War (1825-30) and the much smaller Amir Rebellion on Bangka in 1851.

[62] Note the name of the Lanfang Kongsi of Mandor, combined with that of a major brotherhood (Ngee Hin or Yixing) in Singapore. Comparing a recently discovered account in Leonard Blussé and Ank Merens, "Nuggets from the Gold Mines: Three Tales of the Ta-kang Kongsi of West Kalimantan," in *Conflict and Accommodation in Early Modern East Asia: Essays in Honour of Erik Zürcher*, ed. Leonard Blussé and Harriet T. Zurndorfer (Leiden: E. J. Brill, 1993), pp. 284-321 with the account in J. J. M. de Groot, *Het kongsiwezen van Borneo: Hene verhandeling over den grondslag en den aard der Chineesche politieke vereenigingen in de koloniën* (The Hague: M. Nijhoff, 1885) passim., Yuan believes Mandor headman Liu A Sin not only smuggled goods to Monterado during the hostilities, but sheltered and supported rebels within Lanfang territory,

Plate 6. Gate to Chinese temple on site of former kongsi hall, Pemangkat, 1998.
Credit: the author.

military supplies and secret society paraphernalia, a *toapekong* image, and membership lists. This raid broke the back of the resistance, although remnants survived.[63]

In August 1855, the new road between Singkawang and Monterado was completed. Work on the road stopped for ten weeks to allow time for planting, then civil reconstruction began in earnest. In 1856, the old territory of Thaikong was quiet, while Samtiaokioe had withdrawn to Sarawak. A final incident was an attack on Dutch forces in Lumar in June of that year. It was perhaps provoked by local headmen who resented losing control of opium sales, but the immediate cause was the Dutch decision to destroy the old kongsi hall of Sjipngfoen, the symbol of Lumar's former "independence." Rebel attackers, mostly from the mines, occupied the kongsi hall, burning the market before stronger Dutch forces drove them off. The townspeople of Lumar cooperated with the Dutch, and there were no repercussions among Chinese elsewhere, but some three hundred people fled to Sarawak.[64]

Liao Njie Liong was never caught. Apparently he escaped to Toho in Lanfang territory, remaining there for months with the knowledge of Lanfang's Kapthai Lioe A Sin. From there, people said, he escaped to Sarawak, hidden in a coffin,

---

although he undermined Thaikong in other ways (*Chinese Democracies*, pp. 257-259). See also discussion of Lanfang below.

[63] Van Meteren Brouwer, "Geschiedenis," p. 1089.

[64] Political Report for 1856, dated April 30, 1857. ANRI BW nr. 1/7 (214); Van Rees, *Onderwerping der Chinezen*, pp. 268-269, 304-318; anonymous, "Nieuwe onlusten op Borneo: door +++, dd 12 Oct 1856," *Tijdschrift voor Nederlandsch Indië* 18,2 (1856): 322.

although there was a price of five hundred silver dollars on his head.[65] Andresen believed Liao had joined a "secret society" in China and was trying to establish the brotherhood in Borneo. As long as the Monterado kongsi existed, its strong discipline had prevented him from starting a new organization; when Thaikong ceased to exist, then Liao was free to make an attempt.[66]

Major Andresen, promoted to Lieutenant Colonel during the war but relieved of duty in West Borneo in February 1856, returned to the Netherlands with a panel inscribed "Fosjoen Tjoengthang," which had hung above the door of the *thang* of Monterado. He offered it to his king as a sign of the sovereign's authority over the Chinese of former Thaikong.[67]

The Thaikong area never recovered. The population declined: many people migrated, either into the interior or, more often, toward farming and trading settlements near the coast. For a time, Monterado was capital of an assistant residency, but in 1880, even that moved to Singkawang.[68] Chinese immigration was prohibited from 1853-56, but permitted thereafter; nevertheless new arrivals dried up. Many mines were played out, and, without the kongsi, who would finance immigration? At the end of the nineteenth century, a visitor found two women washing gold near Monterado; their income reached only one quarter of a guilder daily, and that only if they worked intensely.[69]

SARAWAK

The battles with Thaikong led indirectly to the Sarawak Rebellion of 1857. Hakka Chinese from Bau, resisting Rajah James Brooke's attempts to enforce a government opium monopoly, attacked Kuching, killing a number of Europeans, while Brooke narrowly escaped with his life.[70] Although Bau was peopled by Samtiaokioe refugees, the rebellion broke out soon after a group of refugees arrived from Lumar in 1856 (possibly joined by some Thaikong diehards who had been forced to leave Mandor and Landak).

Brooke rallied the support of loyal Malays and Dayaks from Sarawak, who pursued the rebel Chinese, forcing some two thousand of them to flee across the

---

[65] The other four leading headmen of the uprising were known to be Wong Kim Nauw, Lo Kong Njian, Phang Lim, and Lim Sam On. Letters of Andresen, ARA 2.10.02 V. 17.8.54 (3). See also Blussé and Merens, "Nuggets from the Gold Mines," p. 313; van Dewall, "Opstand," p. 27; Gerlach, *Fastes militaires*, pp. 663ff.; van Rees, *Onderwerping der Chinezen*, p. 168; Yuan, *Chinese Democracies*, pp. 246-255.

[66] Letter of Andresen cited in Kielstra, "Bijdrage," Part X, *Indische Gids* 12,1 (1890): 463. Memorie van Overgave, Kroesen, cited in Kielstra, "Bijdrage," Part XVIII, *Indische Gids* 12,1 (1890): 2208. On kongsi relations with *hui*, see the discussion below.

[67] Andresen's Letters to King from Breda, ARA 2.10.02 V. 6.7.57 (12) and ARA 2.10.02 V. 25.8.57 (43). It would be interesting to know where the panel might be; some of the papers Andresen brought to the Netherlands found their way to the Leiden University Library, Hoffmann Collection (Western Manuscripts, BPL 2186, N-O).

[68] Van Meteren Brouwer, "Geschiedenis," p. 1092.

[69] M. Buys, *Twee maanden op Borneo's Westkust: Herinneringen* (Leiden: Doesburgh, 1892), pp. 179-180.

[70] For the rebellion, see Spenser St. John, *Life in the Forests of the Far East* (London: Smith, Elder and Co., 1862, repr. Singapore: Oxford University Press, 1986), pp. 337-364; and Craig A. Lockard, "The 1857 Chinese Rebellion in Sarawak," *Journal of Southeast Asian Studies* 9,1 (1978): 85-98. Lockard sees Brooke's policies as an important factor in provoking the rebellion.

border to Dutch territory. Many of them headed for Pemangkat, the rice bowl abandoned in the fighting with Thaikong. By 1858, so many Chinese had returned that nearly half of the valley of Pemangkat was again under cultivation and the population was increasing steadily. The border remained porous, however. About the same time, a few hundred West Borneo Chinese left to work the gold and antimony mines in Sarawak, and cross-border migration continued thereafter;[71] indeed, it continues today.

The Dutch, although they sided with Brooke in the uprising, welcomed the returning Chinese with open arms in the hope that they would help restore the devastated economy of the Pemangkat region. Conveniently, the *toapekong* of the old kongsi Samtiaokioe was waiting for the returnees in Sambas.[72]

LANFANG SURVIVES

One major kongsi, not the largest and certainly not the most "democratic," survived. The Mandor Chinese of the Lanfang Kongsi had made peace with the Dutch in 1823, and the relationship held, even though Mandor had not maintained perfect neutrality when the Dutch were fighting to subdue Thaikong.[73]

At the time of the kongsi's establishment in 1777, traffic to Mandor followed the Sungai Peniti through Mempawah territory; a footpath linked the river to Mandor.[74] As Pontianak grew more important, Lanfang became dependent on that harbor, using the Sungai Terap and the Landak and Kapuas Rivers for most of its communications. New coolies debarked in Pontianak or boarded Chinese junks there for their return to China. The kongsi most likely established links to the newly founded sultanate as well.[75]

If Mandor became more integrated with Pontianak, and less so with Mempawah, it also maintained links with its subordinate coastal kongsi settlements. Its policy of seeking understanding with the Dutch, or appearing to do so, significantly allowed the Lanfang Kongsi to exist for three decades after colonial power had wiped out all other such organizations—or the kongsis had expired for other reasons.

---

[71] Political Report for 1857, dated March 31, 1858, ANRI BW 1/8 (215).

[72] On the relations between the kongsis and Sarawak, see "Kultuur- en industrie-ondernemingen op Borneo," *Tijdschrift voor Nederlandsch Indië* 20,2 (1858): 399-400. For the Dutch side of the revolt, see Verbaal [Report], ARA 2.10.02 V. 5.6.1857 (46). The *toapekong* had been in the palace of the former Sultan of Sambas since 1851; finally it was taken to Seminis. Kielstra, "Bijdrage," Part XI, *Indische Gids* 11,2 (1889): 691.

[73] Blussé and Merens, "Nuggets from the Gold Mines," pp. 313-316; Yuan, *Chinese Democracies*, pp. 257-259.

[74] E. A. Francis, *Herinneringen uit den levensloop van een 'Indisch' ambtenaar van 1815 tot 1851*, (Batavia: van Dorp, 1856), 1: 253. Compare de Groot, *Kongsiwezen*, pp. 9, 13-14, on the role of the Peniti River.

[75] See Mary Somers Heidhues, "The First Two Sultans of Pontianak," *Archipel* 56 (1998): 273-294. Only in 1787 was the core Mandor territory recognized by the Dutch as part of Pontianak, not Mempawah, but that would not have stood in the way of earlier contacts. Some Lanfang Kongsi Chinese still lived on Mempawah territory.

Relations with the Dutch

After some initial altercations, the Lanfang Kongsi and the colonial authorities established a "special relationship." The head of the kongsi was called *kapthai*, replacing the usual title for a kongsi headman, which was *tiko* or *thaiko* (M. *dage*, big brother, boss). The colonial authorities claimed the right to confirm the kongsi's choice for this office (a system they had tried unsuccessfully to introduce in Thaikong thirty years later). In 1824, the resident in Pontianak even approved a loan of ƒ20,000 to Lanfang to expand its mines.[76]

Administratively, Kampung Baru, across the Kapuas River from Pontianak, was, like many other kongsi towns, a part of the Mandor kongsi. The Hakkas who lived there celebrated kongsi holidays, especially the feast of founder Lo Fong Pak. The Lanfang Kongsi also had a base in the city of Pontianak, in the *pasar*, where it had built a hall, the Lanfang Futhang (M. *futing*, auxiliary hall), perhaps as early as 1820. In 1851, given the troubles with Thaikong and official mistrust of anything that seemed like a secret society, its public festivals ceased. By 1856, the *toapekong* had been removed from the building.[77] In 1859, festivities resumed in the hall, renovated thanks to the initiative of Kapthai Lioe A Sin and his school friend and brother-in-law, Then Sioe Lin, Kapitan of the Hakkas in Pontianak from 1853 to 1877.[78]

Decline of Lanfang

With the dissolution of the other kongsis in 1854, the days of Lanfang were numbered, although the authorities still regarded Kapthai Lioe as a trustworthy ally. Lioe was, among other things, the opium farmer both for his kongsi and for parts of West Borneo, together with Kapitan Then Sioe Lin, and these two also participated in the 1853 opium farm for the former kongsi area of Monterado.[79]

In 1857, colonial authorities began to curtail the kongsi's independence, although they stopped short of abolishing it, as they had Thaikong. They withdrew Lanfang's own opium farm, restored the head tax on its adult males, confirmed that members must pay certain taxes to the native rulers, and forbade (again) the kongsi to exercise influence over Dayaks.[80] A few months later, some dissatisfied kongsi members fomented a rebellion against Kapthai Lioe. The malcontents formed a "secret society," conspiring to get rid of him, but Lioe

---

[76] Historical Note on the Lanfang Kongsi, ARA 2.10.02 V. 31.5.86 (36).

[77] Political Report for 1856, ANRI BW 1/7 (214).

[78] The Treasury of the Lanfang Futhang, note of civil and military authority, Pontianak, ARA 2.10.10 Mailrapporten (MR) 1885: 293. By this time, there were *kapitan*s for the major speech groups in Pontianak. Some accounts call Then Sioe Lin the father-in-law of Lioe, but most favor brother-in-law. For more on this hall, see chapter six.

[79] Report on Chinese Society in West Borneo, 1852, letter of van Prehn to Resident, Pontianak, December 27, 1852. Letter of Resident to Governor-General, Pontianak, December 31, 1852, ANRI BW 28/32 (77). The opium farm was auctioned to Then Sioe Lin with Lioe A Sin of Mandor as guarantor for ƒ145,200. On the office of *kapitan*, see also chapter six.

[80] Van Meteren Brouwer, "Geschiedenis," p. 1090.

prevailed, turning most of the captured rebels over to the colonial authorities.[81] This convinced the Dutch that Lioe was indispensable.[82]

In 1874, the Lanfang Chinese living in Mempawah territory formed a society to resist paying taxes to the local ruler, but the matter ended when Kapthai Lioe intervened.[83] Two years later, Lioe resigned in favor of his son, Lioe Liong Kwon, but in 1880 the son died, and the father resumed leadership of the now financially insolvent kongsi. The gold sites were exhausted, and many Chinese turned to farming or trade, or moved away. Lioe was in frail health, keeping the kongsi afloat partly out of his own pocket. In 1873, the *kapthai* was already so indebted to a Malay money lender that he lost control of the West Borneo opium farm and had to join a partnership with his creditor.[84] Three years later, the government offered Lioe a substantial interest-free credit of *f*100,000 to shore up Lanfang.[85]

The population decline reflected material conditions. Mandor had over four thousand inhabitants in the late 1860s.[86] In 1871, only twenty-seven miners worked for the kongsi, out of nearly two thousand adult men, while nearly six hundred were farmers. Twelve years later, in 1883, Lioe counted 2,725 (adult) men spread over the territory of the kongsi, about 1,200 of whom paid the head tax. The coastal kongsi settlement of Sungai Pinyu was already more populous than Mandor town.[87] Inexplicably, one Dutch source, ignoring the kongsi's financial state, claims that Mandor was "always known as the only decently administered principality in the residency," contrasting it with the Malay principalities.[88] The kongsi may have been better administered than the native principalities, but it was moribund nonetheless.

In 1880, Lioe officially agreed to have the kongsi disbanded upon his death, a solution that colonial officials had favored since the abolition of Thaikong.[89] The territory on which the Lanfang people had lived, farmed, and mined would return to the native rulers of Mempawah, Pontianak, and Landak. The Chinese inhabitants, like all other Chinese in the province, would then be directly ruled by Dutch or Dutch-appointed officials.

---

[81] Political Report for 1857, ANRI BW 1/8 (215). Lioe delivered thirty-three supposed conspirators into the hands of the Dutch and said two others had been killed. It is unclear whether the conspirators were protesting against Lioe's collaboration with the Dutch or against him as leader. Lanfang people actually paid less tax if they moved to Dutch territory, which many now did. Political Report for 1861, March 1, 1862, ANRI BW no. 1/12 (220); Secret Political Report for 1860, February 1, 1861, ANRI BW 1/11 (218).

[82] J. J. M. de Groot, "Lioe A Sin van Mandohr," *Tijdschrift voor Nederlandsch Indië* 10 (1885): 42.

[83] Kielstra, "Bijdrage," Part XXIV, *Indische Gids* 15,1 (1893): 956.

[84] Political Report for 1866, ANRI BW 2/4 (224); Political Report for 1873, ANRI BW 2/11 (231).

[85] *Koloniaal Verslag* (1876): 19. The account in de Waal suggests that the loan was rejected (*Onze Indische financien*, 8: 67).

[86] Political Report for 1868, ANRI BW 2/6 (226).

[87] Letters, Pontianak to Batavia, ARA 2.10.10 MR 1884: 720; Historical Note on the Lanfang Kongsi, ARA 2.10.02 V. 31.5.86 (36).

[88] Kielstra, *Indische Archipel*, p. 286.

[89] General Report for 1884, ANRI, BW 5/15 (30). A government decree (*besluit*) of August 3, 1880, no. 14, confirmed this arrangement.

End of Lanfang and War

Dutch, Chinese and Malay officials, even guests from Java, had attended Kapthai Lioe's seventy-first birthday celebration in December 1883.[90] He died less than a year later, on September 22, 1884, in his quarters in the Lo Fong Pak Hall in Pontianak.[91] Despite the fact that he had a history of poor health, his death was unexpected.[92]

Resident Cornelis Kater, a man with more than three decades of experience in Borneo,[93] accompanied the body to Mandor for burial with honors on October 1, demonstrating respect for the deceased, although Lioe's coffin was not displayed in the kongsi headquarters, as befitted a headman, in the view of the Chinese. Refusing the plea of the *kapthai's* widow and of the town's prominent Chinese that Lioe's son, En Kwon, at the time still a minor, be the new *kapthai*, Kater insisted that the kongsi had ceased to exist, according to the agreement of 1880. All objects connected with Lanfang, including the "soul tablet" of founder Lo Fong Pak, had to be removed from the headquarters or *thang*.

Kater installed a *controleur*[94] with a handful of native police in the kongsi headquarters; this group was to become the colonial administration of Mandor. The authorities appointed a number of Chinese officers to oversee the former Lanfang territory, many of them former kongsi officials. The tablet of Lo Fong Pak and the image of kongsi patron god Guan Di were housed, after a perfunctory ceremony, in provisional quarters on October 6; other kongsi paraphernalia were confiscated. Two days later, Resident Kater, leaving behind some money for the construction of a new temple to house the religious images, returned to Pontianak. Meanwhile, the townspeople honored the gods in their temporary homes.[95]

---

[90] De Groot, "Lioe A Sin."

[91] Lioe was born in 1812 in Jiayingzhou (Mailrapport, October-November 1884, ARA 2.10.10 MR 1884: 684; de Groot, "Lioe A Sin," p. 34). In Mandor, rumors arose that he was poisoned or took poison himself in despair over the situation of the kongsi, but his death was apparently from natural causes. Lioe's quarters were in the Lanfang Hall described above.

[92] Letter of Andresen cited in Kielstra, "Bijdrage," Part X, *Indische Gids* 12,1 (1890): 463. Memorie van Overgave, Kroesen, cited in Kielstra, "Bijdrage," Part XVIII, *Indische Gids* 12,2 (1890): 2208. On kongsi relations to *hui*, see the discussion below.

[93] Kater, according to his official record (Stamboeken Indische Ambtenaren, ARA 2.10.36.015 Stamboek I 470), was born in 1824 in South Holland and came to Surabaya in 1850. His first posting in West Borneo was in the following year; he died in Bandung in 1891. He was resident from 1867 to 1871, and after returning from leave, from 1873 to 1885 (he took another leave in 1882-1884). He is the author of several articles on the Dayaks and Bugis in the residency. A biography of Kater would reveal much about Borneo policies in these decades. See also de Waal, *Onze Indische financien*, 8: 9.

[94] *Controleur* was the rank immediately below assistant resident.

[95] *Koloniaal Verslag* (1885): 17ff., is the source for the following account where no other source is given. See also, from Kater's successor, General Report for 1884, ANRI, BW 5/15 (30), and Report, Disorder in West Borneo and Discharge of Resident Kater, ARA 2.10.02 V. 22.4.85 (48); Kielstra, *Indische Archipel*, pp. 286-287. On Kater's permission that Guan Di or Guan Gong, as the patron deity is called, but not the tablets of kongsi founder Lo Fong Pak, could remain in the *thang*, see the journal of Resident Kater, October-December 1884, ARA MR 1885:22. In November 1884, a letter from kongsi adherents (ARA 2.10.10 MR 1885:684) complains to the Governor General about Kater. For the opinion of Kater's successor, see Short Report, March 15-April 15, 1885 and Letter to Governor General, May 15, 1885, both in ARA 2.10.10 MR 1885:252; and Reasons for Rebellion, ARA 2.10.10 MR 1885:370. Moving a deity or *toapekong* was not necessarily a matter for religious specialists. See Short Reports, 1879, ANRI BW

Kater must have thought that he had dispatched the situation quickly and gracefully, but this was because he did not fully comprehend the significant role of religious ritual in kongsi affairs. He was oblivious to the supernatural quality of the hall, which he considered to be merely the residence of the now-dead *kapthai* and an administrative building. Putting a *controleur* into the house and removing the gods was regarded by the people of Lanfang as an act of desecration, but Kater believed he was asserting the Netherlands' political supremacy through these actions. In spite of his long experience on the West Coast, Kater joined the ranks of colonial officials whose ignorance of Chinese custom led to disaster. Unsurprisingly, a rebellion followed.

Without warning, on the morning of October 23, a band of Chinese claiming to represent the now-defunct kongsi appeared at the *pasar* of Mandor, penetrated the former headquarters, and killed the *controleur* and three policemen. They re-installed the effigy of Guan Di and the tablets of Lo Fong Pak. The revolt then spread, and news soon reached Pontianak. On November 3, 1884, some 150–200 Chinese attackers were beaten back from Bengkayang.[96] Some Chinese from the coastal towns quietly sent their families to Sarawak or Singapore and Monterado's residents fled; Pontianak was near panic. Rumors circulated that the "dreaded secret society" Sam Tiam Fui (M. Sandianhui, which was linked to the Heaven and Earth Society, Tiandihui) was behind the rebellion. Kater feared that the entire area of the Chinese Districts, as the former territories of Monterado were now called, might rise against the Europeans.[97]

The rebels were led by "Liong Lioe Njie (or Ngie)"—perhaps the name meant "Lioe the Second Dragon," referring to Thaikong rebel leader Liao Njie Liong, who was said to have returned from Sarawak. Indeed, an old man with a white beard had been sighted in Mandor.[98] In fact, the leader of the rebels was Lioe Pang Liong, a former clerk of the Lanfang Kongsi, whose name lent itself to confusion with that of the pseudonymous rebel of thirty years before. Meanwhile, the rebels, who were using a seal of the Ngee Hin (M. Yixing) Society, an influential brotherhood in Singapore, had blocked the river route to Mandor from Pontianak.[99]

6a/11 (115), about the unceremonious removal of the Lim family gods to a new temple in Pontianak in 1879.

[96] Bengkayang was on the route to Sarawak, a strategic location. See St. John, *Life in the Forests*, pp. 335-337. In the twentieth century, Chinese often traveled from Sarawak overland via Jagoi-Seluas-Sanggau-Bengkayang. See Letter (circa 1933) ANRI BB 1233.

[97] Kielstra, "Bijdrage," Part XXV, *Indische Gids* 15,1 (1893): 974. The account in Kielstra provides a good summary of the subsequent events.

[98] Entry for October 29, 1884, journal of Resident Kater, ARA 2.10.10 MR 1885:22.

[99] A traditional Chinese celebration in Pontianak on December 25-30 was almost forbidden by the authorities, who feared unrest. (Secret Letter, Resident Kater to Governor General, December 18, 1884, ARA 2.10.10 MR 1884: 796; Report on Military Activity to Chief, War Department, December 9, 1884, ARA 2.10.10 MR 1884: 788; Journal of Resident Kater, ARA 2.10.10 MR 1885:22; Journal, Resident Kater, entry of December 17, 1884, ARA 2.10.10 MR 1885:71.) In fact, it passed quietly. (Letter, Resident Kater to Governor General, December 13, 1883, forwarding journal entries for December, ARA 2.10.10 MR 1885:49). The feast was called *tjatjau* or *tatjau*; it may have been a temple feast or so-called "birthday" of its patron. Permission was needed because Resident Kater had forbidden fireworks, *wayang*, and public gambling since October, when troubles broke out in Mandor. Using the Ngee Hin brotherhood's seal suggested that the rebels had contact with Singapore, but an informant later told the Dutch that the Ngee Hin paraphernalia used were bogus. Report, Causes of Mandor Rebellion, June 12, 1885, ARA 2.10.10 MR 1885:374. On the Ngee Hin in Singapore, see Carl A. Trocki, *Opium*

Resident Kater telegraphed Batavia—via Singapore, as there was no direct line—for reinforcements from Java. On November 7, two companies arrived from Java, but the troops were needed to protect interior Chinese settlements like Monterado and Bengkayang, so Kater requested an additional two hundred men.[100] On November 11, several hundred rebels again attacked Bengkayang, suffering heavy losses.[101] The Dutch finally cleared the Bengkayang area of the rebels, who also left the Monterado area, never to return. The Monterado Chinese themselves took no part in the rebellion.

The center of hostilities now moved to the border area between former Thaikong and Lanfang territories, along the Mempawah River. Rebels occupied Mentidung in early November and fortified Air Mati, blocking the approach to Mandor from the Mempawah side.[102] Rebels returned in January 1885 to Mentidung, capturing some heavy arms.[103] Anjungan seemed to be free of rebels. Coastal Lanfang Kongsi towns like Sungai Pinyu remained quiet, although several youths from there were rumored to have joined the rebellion. Officials bravely asserted that most Chinese who supported the rebels did so out of fear, not sympathy.[104]

Now colonial troops were ready to attack Mandor, but, before they did, a peace party emerged, led by Kapthai Lioe's widow. Kater believed she was playing a double game. She seems to have been in contact with the rebels, but later allied herself with those favoring reconciliation, even writing to the Sultan of Pontianak to ask him to mediate. She and the peace faction told the Dutch that five to six hundred rebels were situated near Mandor. They urged Kater to call off any attack, because they feared the rebels would then burn the *pasar*, but Kater and his military commander, Lt. Col. J. A. Vetter, delayed their approach only long enough to have the peace party remove fortifications around the town.

On November 26, 1884, colonial troops entered Mandor without encountering resistance and reoccupied the kongsi headquarters. Civil administration resumed, investigation of the murders began, and in December some troops returned to Java.[105] On December 11, the religious images were again removed from the *thang*.[106]

---

and Empire: Chinese Society in Colonial Singapore, 1800-1910 (Ithaca: Cornell University Press, 1991).

[100] Journal of Resident Kater, October 26, 1884, ARA 2.10.10 MR 1885:22.

[101] Letters, War Department to Governor General, and Telegram from Resident Kater of November 20, 1884, ARA 2.10.10 MR 1884:720; Journal of Resident Kater, November 12-15, 1884, ARA 2.10.10 MR 1885:22.

[102] Letter from Military Commander, Pontianak, November 19, 1884, ARA 2.10.10 MR 1884: 720. At the end of November, troops found Mentidung deserted, and reoccupied it, assisted by auxiliaries provided by the Panembahan of Mempawah and by Sanking and Sembaya Dayaks. Kielstra, "Bijdrage," Part XXV, *Indische Gids* 15,1 (1893): 978.

[103] Journal of Resident Kater, Entry, January 28, 1885, ARA 2.10.10 MR 1885:71.

[104] Journal of Resident Kater, October-December 1884, ARA 2.10.10 MR 1885:22 and other comments. Colonial officials frequently resorted to this explanation, but in this case it is likely that intimidation was actually a factor.

[105] For a summary, see Kielstra, "Bijdrage," Part XXV, *Indische Gids* 15,1 (1893): 971-986, and for the military activities, Toorop, "Krijgsverrichtingen," pp. 911ff. More detail is in Letter of November 5, 1884, ARA 2.10.20 MR 1884:676; Letter from Military Commander, Pontianak, October 31, 1884, ARA 2.10.10 MR 1884:684; Letter, Military Commander, Pontianak to War Department, December 9, 1884, ARA 2.10.10 MR 1884:788; and Journal of Resident Kater, ARA 2.10.10 MR 1885:22.

[106] Letter, Military Commander, Pontianak, December 20, 1884, ARA 2.10.10 MR 1885:3.

THE MANDOR REBELLION AND DAYAK-CHINESE RELATIONS

Rebels also made contact with sympathetic Dayak groups. In particular, a Sepatah Dayak headman, Pa Gunang, of Jelutung, Landak, hid two rebel leaders, while his *kampung* fought off a Dutch patrol. Commander Vetter favored immediate reprisals against them, but Kater urged caution, fearing the uprising might then spread to other Dayaks of Landak, leading to a general uprising that might unite Chinese rebels and Dayaks, threatening Dutch rule in the entire province. In January 1885, when troops did attack Pa Gunang's *kampung*, they found neither headman nor rebels, but Pa Gunang's son was killed in the fighting, and the old man subsequently joined the rebels, adopting the purported rebel leader Liong Lioe Njie as his "son."[107]

Meanwhile, Resident Kater pressed the Malay appanage holder to intervene and order Pa Gunang to Ngabang, the capital of Landak. The old man was told to send any Chinese rebels to Ngabang. This demand produced no results, but Kater later realized that Pa Gunang was no threat to the general order, in any case.[108]

At the same time, around Mandor, Dayaks, who were familiar with the jungles, were helping the Chinese rebels ambush colonial patrols, while sickness and isolation—supply lines to Pontianak were cut—threatened the small Dutch garrison. The kongsi headquarters where the troops were quartered had no water, because the enemies had drained its reservoir.[109]

Kater now asked the rulers of Sambas, Pontianak, and Mempawah to recruit Malays, Bugis, and especially Dayaks, to beef up the colonial forces. The Panembahan of Mempawah provided, among others, Sanking and Sembaya Dayaks to help occupy and defend Mentidung. Military commander Vetter felt such auxiliaries were just more mouths to feed from scarce supplies; he wanted to use the Dayaks as scouts with regular army patrols, while Kater hoped that they could fight independently.[110] Just as some Chinese were rebels and some remained quiet, the Dayaks also fought on both sides of the conflict, depending on whether their ties of affinity or dependence lay with Malays or Chinese.

---

[107] See various references in Journal of Resident Kater, ARA 2.10.10. MR 1885:22; Letters from Kater and Military Commander Vetter, ARA 2.10.10 MR 1885:34, MR 1885:49, and MR 1885:71. Pa Gunang was also head of the Tamila Dayaks, who in turn had three *negris* or territories, one of which was Samarua, where Jelutung was located. Report, Causes of Mandor Rebellion, June 12, 1885, ARA 2.10.10 MR 1885:374. Pa Gunang's aid ended at moral support, although the Sepatah and Menyukei Dayaks continued to assist or conceal the rebels.

[108] The acting Panembahan of Landak was not very cooperative with the authorities; he only acted against Pa Gunang (below) when Kater's successor threatened military intervention in Landak.

[109] This account follows closely the summary in the General Report for 1884, ANRI BW 5/15 (30). See also Letter, War Department to Governor General, November 24, 1884, ARA 2.10.10 MR 1884: 720; Letter to Governor General, December 31, 1884, and Journal of Resident Kater, ARA 2.10.10 MR 1885:49 (on Pa Gunang); Journals of Military Commander Vetter and Resident Kater, January 1885, ARA 2.10.10 MR 1885:71, and Vetter's letter from Mandor, February 16, 1885, in ARA 2.10.02 V. 22.4.85 (48).

[110] Journal of Resident Kater, Entry of January 16, 1885 and others, ARA 2.10.10 MR 1885:71; Vetter's assessment of the situation is also in Disorders in West Borneo, ARA 2.10.02 V. 22.4.85 (48). The two men kept up an acrimonious correspondence with each other and with Batavia.

Kater's interest in using the Dayaks may have been due to his greater knowledge of their customs; he was "deeply immersed in knowledge of native conditions"; someone "who knows the native thoroughly, ever his friend, often his confidant."[111] This sympathy seems to have been in inverse proportion to his understanding of the Chinese, as his behavior in Mandor showed.

On February 5, 1885, reinforcements from Java arrived again; most were headed for Mandor. A detachment also occupied the temple at another Lanfang town, Sungai Purun. Kater insisted that they be there to prevent smuggling and to calm the people along the coast.[112]

Plate 7. Picture of Lo Fong Pak, Chinese Temple, Sungai Purun.
Credit: the author, 2000.

Dayak Violence against Chinese

Kater soon realized that his policy of employing Dayaks as soldiers was misconceived. On February 9, Dayak auxiliaries from Mempawah were in the process of flushing out rebels to the west of Mandor when they attacked Chinese

---

[111] Cited in de Waal, *Onze Indische financien*, 8: 9. After the war with Monterado, Kater helped the Dutch extend their rule into the interior Dayak territory.

[112] Journal of Military Commander, West Borneo, Entries for February 9, 10, 12, 1885, ARA 2.10.10 MR 1885:119; Short Report, January 15-February 15, 1885, ARA 2.10.10 MR 1885:132bis; Short Report, May 15-June 15, 1885, ARA 2.10.10 MR 1885:401. Sungai Purun was one of the coastal settlements that belonged to Lanfang Kongsi (cf. chapter two).

settlements near Anjungan, which had not even been involved in the rebellion. Refugees from along the Mempawah River, mostly women and children, began arriving in Mandor. They reported that the Dayaks were burning Chinese settlements and taking heads, a custom often—and not completely inaccurately—attributed to Dayak warriors. In the following days, the Dayaks torched the houses of Chinese near Mandor itself. Victims fled to the coastal towns like Sungai Purun, Sungai Peniti, and Sungai Pinyu, or to Mandor. The authorities remonstrated with the Panembahan of Mempawah but failed to stem the violence. Later, the *controleur* of Mandor counted the victims: 248 houses burned and twenty-six persons killed, including three women and four children. One Chinese man who had fled the rebels and who returned to find his family dead committed suicide. Among the settlements destroyed was Anjungan.[113]

Thereafter, the Dutch used Dayaks only in places where they could directly supervise them. Kater, appalled by the violence, wrote bitterly that the Dayak preferred to make war against the Chinese in the forest rather than be exposed to enemy fire alongside colonial soldiers.[114]

> The Dayaks of Mampawah, whom I requested in order to harass and drive out the Chinese who make the paths insecure, I feared as much, have gone over to murdering and have, so far as they dared, destroyed a number of settlements and murdered several Chinese. . . . I need not say, prospects of a land where this occurs are very sad.[115]

Meanwhile, frustrated by lack of communication with Mandor, military commander Vetter built, using prisoners and native labor, a wide road from Pontianak to Kopian, some two hours' walking distance from Mandor, so that troops and supplies could reach the interior by land. The enemy could easily block the river, water travel was often difficult, and the overgrown banks offered cover for attacks on approaching vessels. Road building proceeded excruciatingly slowly, drawing troops away from the task of mopping up the rebels and leaving garrisons undermanned. Only in August 1885 was the twenty-mile road finished. Meanwhile, Kater and Vetter drew an exasperated Batavia into their disputes over strategy.[116] First they had clashed over how to deal with Pa Gunang, Kater believing he understood how to bring the Dayak away from the rebels, then they disagreed on using Dayak auxiliaries. In the end, both had to go.

---

[113] Journal of Resident Kater, Entry of January 20, 1885, ARA 2.10.10 MR 1885:71; compare ARA 2.10.10 MR 1885:132bis.

[114] Mailrapport, 1885, ARA 2.10.10 MR 1885:71; Short Report, 1885, ARA 2.10.10 MR 1885:132bis. This report deals with events from January 15 to February 15, 1885.

[115] Letter of Resident Kater, February 12, 1885, ARA 2.10.10 MR 1885:455, cited in ARA 2.10.02 V. 31.5.86 (36).

[116] This lengthy correspondence, which dragged on until Kater was discharged, is in the Letters of Kater and Vetter in ARA 2.10.10 MR 1885:34; ARA 2.10.10 MR 1885:49; ARA 2.10.10 MR 1885:58; and ARA 2.10.10 MR 1885:464.

Kater and Vetter Replaced

Tired of the bickering, colonial authorities decided to appoint a military man as both commander and resident. Col. A. Haga, Chief of the General Staff, took office in mid-March 1885. Kater retired, having spent virtually his entire career in West Borneo and having been its resident, interrupted only by home leave, since 1867.[117] Vetter was kept on, but not as commander.

Peace soon followed. Many rebels, finding jungle life unbearable, surrendered. Lioe Pang Liong, a former clerk of the kongsi and an early initiator of the uprising, was captured in early 1885.[118] Lesser rebels were pardoned on surrender, while others were either sentenced to jail or executed. The former farming settlements of the Lanfang Kongsi, clustered in a fertile valley, were ruined and deserted.[119] By April 1885, however, people were returning to harvest their crops and eventually to rebuild their homes. In June 1885, informants had provided the Dutch with detailed reports of the formative meetings of the rebellion, not only naming the participants and their ranks, but describing the initiation ceremony itself.[120]

Pa Gunang himself finally came to Pontianak and performed, on May 1, 1885, a ceremonial oath of submission to Dutch authority.[121] The old man then returned to his village, where the rebels had lost a sanctuary. As a result, the threat of a Chinese-Dayak alliance ended.[122]

Less than six months after his arrival, Haga could declare the area pacified. Most of the refugees had returned to their homes, and over a hundred families already had permanent dwellings. Chinese along the coast began planting coconuts, a sign that they intended to remain in West Borneo for some time.[123]

By September 1885, civilian rule was restored, and Lt. Col. Vetter was reappointed as the military commander of West Borneo; expeditionary troops left for Java. A garrison of a hundred men remained in Mandor until December 1888.[124]

---

[117] Kater was honorably discharged from the colonial service "because his time of service was completed," according to *Indisch Besluit* of February 27, 1885. See his personal record, ARA 2.10.36.015 Stamboek I 470 and Disorders in West Borneo, ARA 2.10.02 V. 22.4.85 (48). His immediate replacement was Col. Haga, who became civil and military governor.

[118] Short Report, April 15-May 15, 1885, ARA 2.10.10 MR 1885:319; Reasons for Rebellion, ARA 2.10.10 MR 1885:370; *Koloniaal Verslag* (1886): 10. The new Resident, Kroesen, was a military man with the rank of major, but he was not military commander. Lioe Pang Liong was sentenced to death in June 1885. See Report, Causes of Mandor Rebellion, ARA 2.10.10 MR 1885: 374.

[119] Reports, Civil and Military Commander Haga, West Borneo, April 1885, ARA 2.10.10 MR 1885:240; Short Report, Commander Haga, March 15-April 15, 1885, ARA 2.10.10 MR 1885:252.

[120] Reasons for Rebellion, ARA 2.10.10 MR 1885:370. See also General Report for 1885, ANRI, BW 5/16 (31). In all, eight rebels were executed, four of them in Mandor.

[121] Telegram, May 1, 1885, ARA 2.10.10 MR 1885:268; Letters, April-May 1885, ARA 2.10.10 MR 1885:293. Here, the Dutch had no problems with using Dayak "mysticism," unlike their previous resistance to using Chinese symbols.

[122] Reasons for Rebellion, ARA 2.10.10 MR 1885:370.

[123] Short Report, March 15-April 15, 1887, ARA 2.10.10 MR 1887:219; Report, Resident A.H. Gijsberts, ARA 2.10.10 MR 1887:454. It took several years for these trees to bear fruit, so they were a sure sign of plans to remain.

[124] Kielstra, "Bijdrage," Part XXIV, *Indische Gids* 15,1 (1893): 986; *Koloniaal Verslag* (1885): 10; *Koloniaal Verslag* (1889): 16.

Although many rebels were captured, a few probably made their way to Sarawak. At least one of these was extradited to Dutch territory in 1889.[125]

In Mandor, the Dutch provided funds to build a new temple, paying ƒ3,000 to the Mandor Chinese for the old kongsi headquarters building, which was to be demolished, and adding two hundred guilders for guard houses in Kopian that they had seized.[126] The new temple would house images and tablets of Kwan-Ya (M. Guan Di), Lo Fong Pak, and the Thay Pak Kong (*toapekong*, M. *dabogong*), as well as tablets for all the *kapthais* of the former kongsi. In October 1885, these objects were carried in a solemn procession to the new temple, and about three hundred Chinese, far fewer than in kongsi times, participated in a festive meal at the *pasar*. That evening a theater (*wayang*) performance and gambling, both important features of religious holidays, crowned the festivities.[127]

Plate 8. Ruins of temple to commemorate Lanfang Kongsi, Mandor, dedicated in October 1885. The board on the left says "Long live the son of heaven." Credit: the author, 2000.

---

[125] Letter of H. N. Stuart concerning visit to Kuching, Pontianak, October 10, 1889, ARA 2.10.10 MR 1889:730.

[126] Letter of Haga on Reorganization of Lanfang Territory, ARA 2.10.02 V. 31.5.86 (36). The government paid a total of ƒ3,278.75, covering construction costs.

[127] Report of Civil and Military Commander Haga, ARA 2.10.10 MR 1885:685; Short Report, August 15-September 15, 1886, ARA 2.10.10 MR 1886:636; Report of Resident's Visit to Mandor, October 10-14, 1886, ARA 2.10.10 MR 1886:719; Report, Resident A. H. Gijsberts, ARA 2.10.10 MR 1887:454; General Report 1885, ANRI BW 5/16 (31); General Report 1886, ANRI BW 5/17 (32).

Having participated in the dedication of the temple, the new resident praised the results in a letter to Batavia: "The whole structure is simple but very tidy [*netjes*], without being overloaded, and pleasantly impresses the viewer."[128]

Religious ceremonies soon centered on the new building.[129] In 1886, another ceremony followed, an act of reconciliation between the Dayaks who had attacked the Chinese homesteads and the Mandor Chinese.[130] The appearance in 1887 of a "secret society" in Pontianak, recruited by a man from Singapore, and other apparently conspiratorial activity, uncovered the following year, disturbed the peace only briefly.[131]

CAUSES OF REBELLION, END OF KONGSI WARS

Was Kater correct in thinking that a secret society had organized the rebellion? Could such a conspiracy plausibly have been organized in these months because Lanfang's discipline no longer held such societies in check? Or did Kater's own behavior actually cause the outbreak? The former kongsi members expressed their opinions clearly:

> This happened because the resident drove out our Kwan-Ya [Guan Di] and Lo Thay Pak [Lo Fong Pak] to another place and took possession of the *thang*.
>
> The heads of the people urgently requested that the Kwan-Ya and Lo Thay Pak not be moved, but the resident refused stubbornly . . . Since it was inevitable, on October 6 the Kwan Ya and Lo Thay Pak were taken to the *pasar*. All wept and could not contain their sorrow.[132]

I asked people about the reason for the troubles and all answered that it was because the resident had not fulfilled the wish of the whole population for the return of the *thang*, because he had ordered the removal of the Kwan Ya and Lo Thay Pak, . . . because he did not want to have the coffin of the

---

[128] Report of Resident's Visit to Mandor, October 10-14, 1886, ARA 2.10.10 MR 1886:719. The wooden temple was already in ruins in mid-1994, and by 2000 only a few pillars remained. See Plate 8. The nearby memorial to Lo Fong Pak, built of concrete in the twentieth century, still stands, and remains of offerings indicate that visitors occasionally worship there. By 2000, however, wildcat gold miners had dug up and inundated the paths leading to the memorial. Compare Wolfgang Franke, Claudine Salmon and Anthony Siu, *Bali, Kalimantan, Sulawesi, Moluccas*, vol. 3 of *Chinese Epigraphic Materials in Indonesia* (Singapore: South Seas Society, 1997), pp. 90-97, for a description of the remains of the temple and a photograph taken in 1974.

[129] *Koloniaal Verslag* (1886): 11; General Report for 1886, ANRI, BW, 5/17 (32).

[130] General Report for 1886, ANRI BW 5/17 (32); *Koloniaal Verslag* (1887): 11.

[131] Letters from Resident Gijsberts about Chinese Secret Society, Pontianak, February 18, 1887, ARA 2.10.10 MR 1887:117A; Letter, March 20, 1887, ARA 2.10.10 MR 1887:158C; Letter, April 14, 1887, ARA 2.10.10 1887:218; Letter of Resident Gijsberts, ARA 2.10.10 1888:454; *Koloniaal Verslag* (1887): 11; *Koloniaal Verslag* (1888): 15.

[132] From a poster of the Lanfang rebels found on February 14, 1885, referring to the murder of the *controleur*, and from a Mandor diary, both cited in ARA 2.10.10 MR 1885:252; compare Letter from Members of Kongsi Lanfang, Enclosure, ARA 2.10.10 MR 1884:709.

deceased *kapthai* in the *thang* and the burial had to take place in haste. The whole population was unhappy about that, and this led to the affair.[133]

The debate over which agents and events were most responsible for the rebellion remained controversial. Kater's analysis was clear: he blamed secret societies like the Sam Tiam Fui for the unrest.[134] Yet reports show that secret societies were effectively subdued during most of these years. Secret society activity had disturbed the kongsi in 1857, but Kapthai Lioe had suppressed it. Societies had turned up in Mempawah and in Pemangkat in 1875, but the authorities quickly intervened, punishing their leaders.[135] Kater believed he had evidence of society activity in Mandor in early 1884 and felt that the dissolution of the kongsi and the occupation of the *thang* were irrelevant to the outbreak. Others were not convinced by his arguments. The head of the War Department disagreed. For him, the provocation lay "in the way in which the resident brought Lanfang under our administration." According to this opinion, the Mandor dissidents had sought support from a society only after Kater had subjugated Lanfang, or perhaps they may have already been members. This support enabled the society to gain more members.[136] Haga, Kater's successor, also a military man, was equally convinced that the resident's behavior had provoked the rebellion.[137]

The reports of society activity that Kater cited claimed that the organizers sought to recruit Hoklo (Teochiu) Chinese. Did this group plan to turn against the Dutch as well? Although the activities of the rebels extended to Bengkayang and Mentidung, all attacks were directed from the Mandor area. Support for the rebels came only from the former Lanfang region; no evidence surfaced of a broadly organized society with branches throughout the Chinese population of the West Coast. Rumors that the Chinese of other areas were preparing to join the rebellion remained rumors. Captured correspondence from the Mandor rebels to other Chinese showed them urging their compatriots to form a society, not calling on them to act out of loyalty to an existing one. Haga concludes that no society had planned hostilities against the government before the death of the *kapthai*, because there was no reason for it.[138] All this seems to confirm that Kater's act of expelling the gods from the *thang* and occupying it with an administrative official had provoked the violence. The society had served to organize opposition, not to create it.

The complaints cited—complaints about perfunctory treatment of the deceased *kapthai*, seizure of the *thang*, the expulsion of the deities—were reiterated in Chinese letters to native rulers that tried to win sympathy for the Chinese position or convince them to intervene with the Dutch. These arguments also appeared in posters directed to potential Chinese supporters of the rebellion. The

---

[133] Letter from the widow of Kapthai Lioe to the Sultan of Pontianak on October 30, 1884 cited in Letter, Pontianak to Governor General, May 19, 1885, in ARA 2.10.10 MR 1885:252. Notice that Lioe's widow did not mention the dissolution of the kongsi itself as a cause for the rebellion.

[134] Sandianhui or "Three Drops Society," see above.

[135] General Report 1875, ANRI BW 5/6 (21).

[136] Letter to Governor General, Batavia, November 24, 1884, ARA 2.10.10 MR 1884:720.

[137] Letter of Haga to Governor General, May 19, 1885, ARA 2.10.10 MR 1885:252.

[138] Ibid.

rebels themselves claimed that they had been constantly disturbed by the cries of the disinherited ghosts and deities, until they were driven to murder the *controleur*.[139]

On August 12, 1885, four rebel leaders were executed in Mandor. Lioe Pang Liong, asking in vain to speak to Col. Haga, left a final message:

> . . . now that I must die, I want to tell him [Haga] that the cause of the rebellion was only a result of the removal of the Kwan Ya and Lo Thay Pak. . . . I am not an enemy of the government, therefore I will die for the Lanfang Kongsi.

In Pontianak, a poster appeared with a Chinese poem promising revenge for Lanfang in eighteen years. The year 1903, however, passed without incident.[140] Finally, as an expression of gratitude, the new, government-appointed, officials of Mandor offered four inscribed golden plates to the four main colonial officials of the residency. Haga returned them promptly with the remark that the population should keep what little it had.[141]

Former Lanfang Kongsi territory was now divided among the native principalities of Pontianak, Mempawah, and Landak. Kampung Baru (later Siantan) became part of the town of Pontianak, while the settlement of Pakoktin, also formerly part of Mandor, joined Mempawah town.[142] The Chinese, although direct subjects of the government, were also required to pay some taxes, especially for land use, to the native rulers.

With that, the Kongsi Wars had ended. Given the complex ethnic and political alliances, it would be inaccurate to characterize the altercations called the Kongsi Wars simply as wars of resistance by the Chinese against Dutch colonialism. Even some people from Thaikong Kongsi, the most prominent enemy of the colonial power, pleaded for peace or asked the Dutch for help.

Nevertheless, not one of the kongsis was whole-heartedly committed to an alliance with the Dutch. Assistant Resident van Prehn had a nasty dispute with members of Samtiaokioe in Sambas in 1851. Lanfang played a waiting game and probably gave rebel Liao Njie Liong a chance to escape to Sarawak. Even Kapthai Lioe A Sin, whom the Dutch considered to be a dependable supporter of their interests, had intrigued against them.[143]

---

[139] Letter from Members of Kongsi Lanfang, enclosure, ARA 2.10.10 MR 1884:709.

[140] Translation of poster by Moll and letter of Haga, August 17, 1885 (with quotation from Lioe), ARA 2.10.10 MR 1885:464.

[141] Letter of Haga, August 27, 1885, ARA 2.10.10 MR 1885:568. One inscription read, "Thanks to your great virtues this land is again reunited and bound together like a bundle of grass. You have protected the population of this land, therefore we offer you this thin golden plate, without assuming it is retribution for your goodness. For the Civil and Military Commander of West Borneo. With reverent greetings, the Kapitan of Mandor [Lo Thong] in the name of the whole people."

[142] General Report, 1884, ANRI, BW. 5/15 (30). As of January 1, 1888, the Afdeeling (district) Mandor was dissolved and the area divided between the native rulers. General Report for 1886 of Resident Gijsberts, dated March 28, 1887, ANRI, Borneo-W, 5/17 (32). Kampung Baru and Pakoktin had Lieutenants of the Chinese, so they were sizable settlements. Note on reorganization of Mandor administration, undated, ARA 2.10.02 V. 31.5.86 (36). Pakoktin seems to be another name for Kuala Mempawah.

[143] See items in Blussé and Merens, "Nuggets from the Gold Mines."

In addition, trouble with the Chinese tended to develop into trouble with other ethnic groups. Again, Dayaks were involved in the wars on both sides. Nor were the local rulers dependable allies of the Dutch, in spite of their contracts, as difficulties in Sambas and Mempawah show. The *Syair Perang Cina di Monterado*[144] indicates that Mempawah eagerly supported the Dutch against Chinese "treason," but the ruler was actually a reluctant helper. Only after the Dutch had provided sizable amounts of food and weapons was the Panembahan ready to join the fight as a whole-hearted supporter of the Dutch side.

AT WAR WITH THE KONGSIS

A closer look at warfare against the kongsis tells more about the tactics chosen by both sides, their use of allies across ethnic boundaries, and the influence that the terrain and surroundings had on choice of methods.

The Dutch

Colonial warfare in the tropics was a grim and, in human terms, costly business, and troops faced natural obstacles as well as human enemies.[145] They waded knee-deep (or deeper) in swamp muck. Disease was a greater problem than enemy fire, which in fact caused few deaths. Brackish water, mosquitos, and poor conditions bred fevers, while most of those wounded—and many died of relatively light wounds—fell victim not to bullets, but to sharpened bamboo spears called *ranjus*, which were especially effective when used in concealed traps. In the battle for Monterado, for example, twenty men were wounded by *ranjus*, eight by gunfire.[146]

A major difficulty for the Dutch was how to obtain a steady supply of ammunition and provisions on an island where there were no major roads until after the 1850s. In the Singkawang area, they could collect booty in the form of pigs and chickens, but elsewhere, the men needed to bring their own supplies. Hundreds of troops required an innumerable contingent of bearers, coolies, and, to clear the paths, woodcutters. Dayaks and Malays, supplied by the sultans, were unsatisfactory as bearers; those who carried goods to Monterado were completely exhausted when they arrived. Of 1,400 Malay coolies sent by the Sultan of Sambas in May of 1854, three hundred were dead by November.[147] After 1854, the desperate Dutch went over to using paid "voluntary" Chinese coolies. They proved adept at carrying beverages, biscuits, and bacon, the staple food of the army, and, although

---

[144] Arena Wati, *Syair Perang Cina di Monterado* (Bangi: Penerbit Universiti Kebangsaan Malaysia, 1989), written to commemorate the second Kongsi War, describes the ruler of Mempawah as a whole-hearted ally of the Dutch against Chinese "treason." In the colonial documents, however, the Panembahan appears as a reluctant helper. Only after the Dutch had provided sizable amounts of food and weapons was he ready to join the fight as a firm ally of the Dutch.

[145] Letter, Inspector of Navy to Governor General, June 19, 1854, ARA 2.10.02 V. 29.8.54 (11).

[146] In the battle for Monterado, for example, twenty men were wounded by *ranjus*, eight by gunfire. See the Letters of Andresen, ARA 2.10.02 V. 17.8.1854 (3); Kielstra, "Bijdrage," Part XXV, *Indische Gids* 15,1 (1893): 983; Hooyer, *Krijgsgeschiedenis*, p. 31. The environment was the greater enemy.

[147] Letter from Prins, Commissioner for West Borneo, Pontianak, July, 14, 1854, ARA 2.10.02 V. 20.9.54 (22).

they demanded wages, they were a better bargain than men impressed into service by the sultans. The Chinese worked without military escort, as their headmen had guaranteed that they would not assist the enemy or steal the supplies. By late 1854, many "well-intentioned" Chinese ended their cooperation with the Dutch to protest impressment (the act of seizing...for public service) of coolie labor, violence from colonial troops, and the "liberties" the troops took with Chinese women.[148]

Naval blockades made a major contribution to the Dutch efforts, especially in the war with Monterado. The steamships available to the navy could cut off or inhibit supplies to the rebels, for rice, salt, opium, and ammunition had to be imported.[149]

When rebellion threatened, Dayak auxiliaries were extremely useful to the Dutch. After the Lumar attack in 1856, it was sufficient to threaten pursuit by Dayaks to convince most of the population to return to the town. Commissioner Prins, in 1854, was delighted with the idea of using Dayaks from Mempawah to search for and attack Chinese rebels; he later remarked, "To threaten the Chinese with the Dayaks appears to us to be a sensible measure." When, a few months after the burning of Monterado, the Chinese who had not joined the rebels began returning to the town and to their fields, Andresen ascribed the turnaround to the Dutch strategy of using Dayaks to seek them out in their forest hiding places.[150] However, using Dayaks against the Chinese meant encouraging the Dayaks to take heads and use other methods the Dutch might not wish to employ, as Kater learned.

The *Syair Perang Cina di Monterado* also goes to some length to show that the Dutch had assented in permitting the Dayaks to plunder the Chinese during the hostilities of the 1850s. According to this account, allowing plunder (*rampas*) was the condition for Dayak participation. The document adds that the Dutch expressed their admiration of the brave Dayak leaders and fighting men to the Malay nobles of the court of Mempawah.[151] In the Mandor fighting in 1885, the unleashing of the Dayak allies resulted in cruel and indiscriminate attacks on the rural population; revulsion at the suffering of the noncombatants, as noted, was one reason for the Dutch decision to remove Resident Kater from office.

The Chinese

More evidence about Chinese-Dayak relations and about Chinese adaptation to their new environment is reflected in their warfare, and colonial documents offer many details about military practice. The kongsis utilized a creative mix of tactics learned in China—especially some that Hakka participants in the Taiping Rebellion (1850-1864) had utilized—as well as tactics adapted to the local environment, some of which they learned from Dayak allies. Almost universally, as soon as trouble arose, the Chinese would begin building small earthen stockades, and the civilian population would flee. The authorities would then insist the

[148] Reports from Commissioner Prins, ARA 2.10.02 V. 1.11.54 (34); Summary of Reports from West Borneo, ARA 2.10.02 V. 1.12.54 (4); Hooyer, *Krijgsgeschiedenis*, p. 25.

[149] Berghuis, Rapport, p. 11; van Dewall, Opstand, p. 21.

[150] Reports from Prins, ARA 2.10.02 V. 1.11.54 (34); "Nieuwe onlusten," pp. 325-326.

[151] Wati, *Syair Perang Cina di Monterado*.

fortifications be leveled and the population returned to their *kampungs*. If they complied, the administration could be fairly confident that people would remain quiet. On the other hand, the population could prove uncooperative:

> Absolutely nowhere did they [the Chinese rebels] stand and fight against our troops, and when we tried to get information from the well-disposed inhabitants about their hiding places, they only replied that the evil-doers had fled into the forest.[152]

The *bentengs* attracted particular admiration:

> The fortifications of the enemy were masterfully chosen. They stretched out along a large part of the path, defended each other, and one of them, which was very substantial, served especially to block the crossing over the river, which was ten meters wide.[153]

Two rows of tree trunks filled with earth were a typical fortification for a kongsi headquarters. These stockades, and most *bentengs* as well, permitted the defenders to excape quickly if needed, because many fortifications were closed on only three sides. According to a 1824 account, in order to build such a fortress, two or three hundred men with laminated wooden shields would plant their shields into the ground and, protected in this manner, would throw up, rapidly and with "surprising skill," an earthen fortification. Paths or approaches might be blocked by a typical Southeast Asian weapon, the *ranju*, dug into the ground.[154]

As long as they were successful and confident of victory, the account continues, the Chinese would hold out behind their stockades, but if the defense were breached, instead of resisting, they would flee. The Dayak, too, would not defend a fortification; instead, they preferred to ambush their enemy along narrow paths, as did many Chinese rebels.[155]

The Chinese in Kalimantan often adopted war tactics from the local people; at times, they were even said to wear Dayak clothing.[156] They used the *tjanto* or *canto*, a simple, locally made, long-barreled gun, which could be fired from the shoulder or placed on a stand like a small cannon, but was inaccurate at a distance beyond a few hundred paces. Another firearm was the locally made portable cannon called *lila*, as well as homemade Dayak-style firearms. Lances, heavy swords, daggers, sticks, and clubs complemented guns.[157] Andresen remarked after

---

[152] *Koloniaal Verslag* (1885): 22.

[153] From a report of 1854 cited in Kielstra, "Bijdrage," Part IX, *Indische Gids* 11,2 (1889): 2131.

[154] Report on West Borneo, Resident of Sambas van Grave, December 20, 1824, ARA 2.21.007.57 (123) [in French]; Kielstra, "Bijdrage," Part XXV, *Indische Gids* 15,1 (1893): 983.

[155] Letter from military commander Vetter to Resident Kater, January 29, 1885, ARA 2.10.10 MR 1885:34.

[156] Journal of Resident Kater, Entry for January 30, 1885 (citing an informant), ARA 2.10.10 MR 1885:71.

[157] Report on West Borneo, Resident of Sambas van Grave, December 20, 1824, ARA 2.21.007.57 (123); Toorop, "Krijgsverrichtingen," pp. 885-888; W. L. Ritter, "De kanonneerboot," *De Kopiist* 1,10 (1842): 349; W. L. Ritter, *Indische herinneringen, aantekeningen en tafereelen uit vroegeren en lateren tijd* (Amsterdam: Van Kesteren, 1843), p. 126; anonymous, "Nieuwe onlusten," p. 323.

the fall of Monterado that the rebels had few firearms; most of them were armed with staves (*stokken*).[158]

The contrast between the fighting in Borneo and in the "Chinese War" on Java in the 1740s is noteworthy. In Java, the Chinese did not resort to guerrilla methods, since they were unable to melt into the countryside or count on the support of the village population.[159] Although they also fought open battles in Borneo, the Chinese there preferred fortifications (*benteng* or *kubu*) built on a Southeast Asian pattern; to attack, they utilized primitive booby traps made with gunpowder and ambushed enemy columns moving along narrow paths, as did the Dayaks.

A military historian describes how Thaikong organized to meet the Dutch threat in August 1850. Colonial forces faced up to seven thousand fighting men, members of the kongsi, who were well-armed, trained, and paid a regular salary. In addition there were "Pins" (probably M. *bing*, soldier), troops who were unpaid and performed mostly coolie services, and who were not necessarily armed. The regular soldiers were organized in *khie* (M. *ji*, flag, banner, or pennant) of about eighty men under a *tjong-saai* (M. *zongshuai*, commander). The *tjong-lin* (M. *zonglin*, general) took over administration of the kongsi federation in time of war, overseeing the provision of food and ammunition. (This seems to have been Tjang Ping's role, so he was not just a bookkeeper.) Flags accompanied the warriors. Thaikong's strength was exceptional. Samtiaokioe had only about one-third the number of troops, in comparison, and failed to organize military logistics efficiently, something that cost it dearly when Thaikong attacked it.[160]

Some of the kongsi battle tactics were also used in China. During the Taiping Rebellion, which was nearly concurrent with the Second Kongsi War, the rebels proved adept at constructing pontoon bridges. In Borneo, the Thaikongs crossed rivers with "ferries and rafts."[161] The ability of the Taipings, who were led in China by Hakkas, to construct fortifications is well-known. With the help of miners who had worked underground, they built tunnels to undermine enemy bastions as well as strong fortifications to defend their towns.[162] In Borneo,

---

[158] Cited in report from Commissioner Prins to Governor General, Sambas, August 22, 1854, ARA 2.10.02 V. 1.11.54 (34).

[159] In Java, the Chinese used ambushes, trenches, and fortifications, but their major tactic seems to have been laying siege to a town. Their numbers were, of course, greater than those of the Bornean rebels, and some battles took place at sea. As for melting into the countryside, Remmelink emphasizes that their hairstyles would have made them most conspicuous (in fact, the Chinese tucked their pigtails under a cap, as the cover illustration of his book shows). See Willem Remmelink, *The Chinese War and the Collapse of the Javanese State, 1725-1743* (Leiden: KITLV Press, 1994) pp. 136, 146, 157.

[160] Van Rees, *Wachia, Taykong*, pp. 108-109.

[161] Van Prehn, Relaas van den oorlog, p. 39. He notes earlier in the same text that the Thaikongs must be prevented from constructing a floating bridge to cross the Sebangkau River to attack Pemangkat (p. 33).

[162] Johnathan D. Spence, *God's Chinese Son: The Taiping Heavenly Kingdom of Hong Xiuquan* (New York and London: W. W. Norton, 1996), esp. p. 165. Underground passages and sieges played no role in the Kongsi Wars, but the Lanfang history mentions underground digging. It places this battle in Sepatah-Landak, where Thaiko Lo [Fong Pak] ordered that his enemy be attacked by "digging under the ground." See de Groot, *Kongsiwezen*, p. 15. Another version is in J. J. K. Enthoven, *Bijdragen tot de Geographie van Borneo's Wester-Afdeeling* (Supplement, *Tijdschrift Aardrijkskundig Genootschap, 1901-1903*) (Leiden: E. J. Brill, 1903), pp. 745, 806-807, who received his information in about 1900. His report attributes these tactics to Eng Njan Tsjin, called "Njie Koh" (*erge*, second brother), who was a "general" of Lo Fong Pak. In

however, neither manpower nor materials existed that would enable members of a kongsi to fortify entire settlements; gold miners worked in open pits, not below ground. The kongsis had to adapt their means of fighting to local conditions, which explains why their women and children fled the towns at the first sign of a conflict and the remaining soldiers learned quickly to construct and rely on temporary earth stockades. Full-fledged sieges like those of the Taipings or the Chinese rebels in Java were inappropriate.

Another weapon was fire. Kongsi halls were constructed of wood, and buildings around them were often covered with thatch from *nipa* (palms) or *alang-alang* grass, so fire could devastate them. When the Dutch themselves occupied kongsi halls, Chinese attackers effectively used a kind of Asian Molotov cocktail: clay pots wrapped in flammable material and attached to a fuse, filled with gunpowder and metal splitters or gunshot.[163]

As noted, when Dutch forces neared a settlement, the population usually fled. The Dutch ascribed their flight to their cowardice, but it may have been merely an acknowledgement of military reality; defending the often scattered houses or the tinder-box marketplaces was hopeless. Often, these settlements were put to the torch by the rebels themselves.

Other methods also inhibited Dutch troop movements. Fortifications blocked or flanked the approaching paths, which were so narrow that two men, at most, could walk abreast. Guerrilla forces often positioned themselves to ambush approaching columns of troops. In peacetime, the narrow paths between settlements were often improved, and wooden plank walkways made them easier to traverse; in wartime, planks could be removed.

For defense along the rivers, the Chinese felled trees or laid chains of rattan or metal to block the movement of boats—complicating a journey already made difficult by banks that were overgrown with low-hanging trees and rivers that were often shallow, narrow, and winding. Felling trees to block rivers was a Dayak tactic, too.[164] In 1853, the Singkawang River was closed with ironwood posts, hammered into the riverbed; defenders on both banks, ensconced in small *bentengs*, prevented their removal.[165]

Sometimes Dayak assistance was not voluntary.[166] While the Dayaks of Mempawah had proven to be ready allies of the Dutch against the Chinese, the

---

Enthoven's version, the Chinese were said to be fighting on behalf of the Sultan of Pontianak. Sultan Kasim asked Dutch help against Tayan in 1817, well after Lo Fong Pak's death in 1803; see Heidhues, "First Two Sultans," p. 292.

[163] Report on West Borneo, Resident of Sambas van Grave, December 20, 1824, ARA 2.21.007.57 (123). Van Grave calls the object a Congrève, after a French military man. See also Letter, Inspector of Navy to Governor General, June 19, 1854, ARA 2.10.02 V. 29.8.54 (11), about the clay pots used to start fires; and letter of Andresen to Army Commander in Batavia, Monterado, August 19, 1854, ARA 2.10.02 V. 1.11.54 (34), describing a "Chinese mine" or booby trap. See also Toorop, "Krijgsverrichtingen," pp. 880-929; and Hooyer, *Krijgsgeschiedenis*, pp. 1ff.

[164] Kielstra, "Bijdrage," Part XIX, *Indische Gids* 14,1 (1892): 1266-1267, referring to a rebellion of Dayaks near Ngabang in 1859. They had felled large trees to block a river.

[165] Anonymous, "De expeditie tegen de Chinezen op Borneo," *Tijdschrift voor Nederlandsch Indië* 16,2 (1854): 71.

[166] "The whole mob was made up of, according to the Lieutenant Colonel [Andresen], not more than about 800 men, among them various Dayaks, who can be assumed, as in the past, to have

Dutch avoided forging alliances with Sambas Dayaks, especially those of Lara (Bengkayang) and elsewhere, because they judged the Sambas Dayaks had lived too long "under the Chinese yoke" to be trusted. Besides, an old feud between the Dayaks of Mempawah and those of Lara made it unwise to bring them together in a single contingent.[167] Apart from their military usefulness for the Chinese, Dayaks were masters at chopping down trees, something Chinese were not adept at doing. The Chinese had employed them in this capacity, as noted above, to clear the mine sites.[168]

SUPERNATURAL AID IN WAR

The Malay-language history of the Monterado war notes the names of eight *panglima* or "generals" of the Thaikong forces who led them to battle:

> Their names were Mee Ong and Boon Cha/Soo Tek with Teen Sai Ja/Koon Yam Nyong and Koon Ya/Peet Sai Ja and Tee Ja.[169]

This puzzling listing, made more puzzling by the transcription into and from Jawi, refers not to human military officers (*panglima*), but to the gods of the participating kongsis. Mee Ong is the patroness of sailors, Mazu or Tianhou *niang* (honorific for a goddess). Teen Sai Ja and Tee Ja are, respectively, Tianshi *ye* (Heavenly Master; *ye* is an honorific) and, possibly, the Jade Emperor (Tianye). Koon Yam Nyong is the merciful Guan Yin *niang*, Koon Ya, the god of war and commerce, Guan Gong *ye*. The three deities known as Sanshan Guowang, honored in Buduk and in the upper hall of Monterado,[170] may be hidden behind the names of the other gods, as may another figure, Tudi, the Earth God, or—as he is formally known—Fude Zhengshen, the Spirit of Wealth and Virtue, probably the most popular of all deities in West Borneo. (He is familiarly called *toapekong*, M. *dabogong*.)

The gods, perhaps physically present in the form of images or as tablets, were accompanied by mediums or oracles who, in trances, related the gods' wishes to the fighting men.[171] The medium of Monterado's Sjongbok (upper house) for the Sam-Bong-Jak (M. Sanshan Guowang), and the medium of Habok (lower house) for the goddess Moa Njong (M. Mazu or Tianhou) accompanied the force, and other local deities, Tie-Jak (M. Guan Di?) and Kon Njim Njong (M. Guan Yin), came with their oracles.[172] The oracles were, apparently, placed close to the commanding officers during battle, ready for consultation.

---

been forced to join the Chinese." Letter of Prins to Governor General, Sambas, August 22, 1854, ARA 2.10.02 V. 1.11.54 (34).

[167] Letter of Andresen to Army Commander in Batavia, Monterado, August 19, 1854, in ibid.

[168] Van Rees, *Onderwerping der Chinezen*, p. 240. See also chapter one in this volume, "Hakkas and Hakka Traditions."

[169] Wati, *Syair Perang Cina*, p. 87, verse 243.

[170] See Franke, "Sovereigns of the Kingdoms." The Limtian Kongsi in Buduk, populated by Hepo Hakkas, honored these three gods. Limtian (Lintian) is a former name for Hepo.

[171] Compare the list of gods in Yuan, *Chinese Democracies*, pp. 38-43. A similar account is in van Dewall, *Opstand*. This was a literal "Gott mit uns."

[172] See note 34 for more on these gods and goddesses and their role in the kongsi. Spellings vary.

SOCIETIES AND KONGSIS

De Groot[173] has pointed out that "secret societies" surfaced after the abolition of the kongsi federations and suggested that the kongsis had served to keep them in check, while the removal of kongsi rule gave them free rein. Certainly the kongsis minimized opposition activity by enforcing their rule strictly.

Such societies in West Borneo were, however, locally limited. Colonial officials were trained to recognize "secret societies" from the work, in particular, of Gustaaf Schlegel,[174] which, appearing in 1866, described their oaths, the "catechism" of initiation questions, and their organization in detail. Whenever they found society paraphernalia or other evidence, officials quickly linked such finds to a society. Yet they never found proof of concrete ties with China or Singapore beyond evidence concerning activities of the few immigrants who, already initiated in the rites themselves, propagated them for others in the colony.

Each of the *"hui* conspiracies," including the conspiracy of 1912 discussed in chapter five, was a response to a particular provocation: the abolition of Thaikong and the introduction of taxes and road-building duties; the abolition of Lanfang; the desecration of the kongsi hall after the death of the Lanfang *kapthai*; the introduction of new taxes and demands, including demands for corvée labor, imposed by the authorities. In 1912, greatly increased demands for taxes and corvée provoked resistance again. In these situations, rebels assured one another of their loyalty by using the oaths and symbols widely known among southern Chinese and widely utilized to bind people together. Like the kongsis, societies drew on Chinese popular religion and its symbols.[175] These traditions and symbols were not the cause of the rebellious activity, but its organizing principles.

LANFANG'S DEMISE

Meanwhile, Lanfang's population, estimated at about 7,500 in the first half of the nineteenth century, had dropped to 1,060 by the end of the century. Mandor itself had begun to decay, according to witnesses; even its road—built by Vetter at such a high cost—was unusable by 1900.[176]

De Groot had argued that, since the colonial government had no trouble governing native peoples indirectly, through their own headmen and under a

---

[173] De Groot, *Kongsiwezen*, pp. 171-180, strongly rebutted Veth and Hoffmann (whom he cites on p. 173) that the kongsis themselves were built on the model of "secret societies," but he attributed the appearance of societies after 1855 to the dissolution of the kongsis, and the experience of 1884 in Mandor, at first glance, seems to confirm his opinion.

[174] Gustave Schlegel, *Thian Ti Hwui: The Hung-league or Heaven-Earth League: A Secret Society with the Chinese in China and India* (Batavia: Lange & Co. 1866). This book was, it seems, required reading for colonial officials, especially for Chinese language officers, who often cited it.

[175] Compare the contributions to David Ownby and Mary Somers Heidhues, eds., *"Secret Societies" Reconsidered: Perspectives on the Social History of Early Modern South China and Southeast Asia* (Armonk: M. E. Sharpe, 1993), especially Ownby's introduction (pp. 3-33) and Heidhues, "Chinese Organizations in West Borneo and Bangka: *Kongsi* and *Hui*," pp. 68-88.

[176] Enthoven, *Bijdragen*, pp. 817-819.

system that was appropriate for them, it was foolishly stubborn to insist that the Chinese be ruled directly.[177] Yet he himself admitted that Kapthai Lioe had consumed most of his wealth during the war with Monterado, spending over ƒ120,000 arming his men, and another large sum in gold to improve Chinese settlements in Landak. When the mines petered out, Lioe tried to encourage plantations, but they, too, failed, leaving him in debt. The Lanfang Kongsi had ceased to be a going concern long before Kapthai Lioe's death. Lanfang, in the end, had to go because it was bankrupt.

Like Thaikong before it, Lanfang could no longer earn enough from mining to meet its own expenses (and de Groot must have known this in 1883, when he left Pontianak). Lioe A Sin had kept the association afloat by feeding his own funds into it—funds that he earned, where possible, from the opium farm. When the revenue farm declined sharply in value after 1850, Lanfang never recovered, nor did Lioe.[178]

Were the kongsis eliminated because they were too "democratic"? Thaikong fit this model best; its frequent elections of officials displeased the Dutch, who wanted to negotiate with a more stable partner. One account of these elections, however, shows that the same officials were often rotated among offices,[179] although this was in the last, wartime days of the kongsi.

Lanfang seems to have had a strong central leadership from its beginning, and this was certainly the case after 1823. Then relations with the Dutch changed the role of the *kapthai,* increasing his authority as the head of the kongsi.[180] Lanfang also appears to have been less "democratic" than most other kongsis, because of the infrequency of its elections. While Monterado had frequent elections for its headmen, who held office for only four months, Lanfang was a more autocratic institution.[181] Its different organization may have enabled it to come to a quicker and more lasting settlement with the Dutch, who in turn reinforced Lanfang's autocracy. Lanfang's leaders served for life, or until they resigned or left the territory. As a result, the Dutch could confirm a man in office and have the assurance that, in the normal run of things, they would be dealing with him for several years. The *kapthai* was the person who represented the kongsi to the administration. He was responsible to it and, at the same time, could expect its support, as did Lioe A Sin. He did not need to consult with the population. Instead, he depended on the Dutch and also represented the Dutch. This dependence became

---

[177] De Groot, *Kongsiwezen,* pp. 127ff.

[178] De Groot, "Lioe A Sin," pp. 34-40. While de Groot's book (*Kongsiwezen*) pleads for the retention of kongsis, he surely realized that the state of kongsi finances made their continued existence impossible.

[179] Van Dewall, Opstand.

[180] Historical Note on the Lanfang Kongsi, ARA 2.10.02 V. 31.5.86 (36); compare Memorie van Overgave of Kroesen in Kielstra, "Bijdrage," Part XVIII, *Indische Gids* 12,1 (1890): 2185ff. Kroesen says Lanfang did not meet the fate of other kongsis in the 1850s "for the most part because of its less democratic form of government" (p. 2208). De Groot also, as noted, sees Lanfang changing after submitting to the Dutch and substituting a *kapthai* for its *tiko.*

[181] In 1851, van Prehn noted that the *kapthai* did have the books examined by a commission of elders once or twice a year; otherwise he was independent of control. Officials of Lanfang were chosen permanently and only replaced at their own request or for misdeeds. The mine bosses were elected every four months, but they had no political authority. See "Aantekeningen betreffende Borneo's Westkust," p. 23.

even more obvious after 1857, when the Dutch confirmed the existence of Lanfang and of Lioe as its head. The formerly "strict republican form of government of the kongsi, according to which the *kapthai* exercised only very little authority and had to consult the lesser headmen in all questions" was replaced by one which "made the kapthai the sole representative of the kongsi to the Government," one which made Lanfang even less of a "republic" and more of a "monarchy," under "autocratic paternalism."[182] Lioe sometimes consulted his headmen, but never, as far as is known, the entire mining force, much less the adult population. An assembly like those held in Thaikong in 1852-53 would have been unthinkable in Lanfang.

In time, the kongsi became, so to speak, Lioe's personal property. The name continued to exist, but in reality the lesser members of the kongsi administration were now no more than servants of the *kapthai*, and Lioe became like a native ruler, whose authority was only limited by that of the colonial power.[183]

The decline of the kongsis throughout the period described here resulted from a number of factors, including the kongsis' consumption of their own resource base as well as pressure from the Netherlands East Indies officials. It is unlikely that Batavia regretted the loss. For Batavia, these strong organizations, which adopted so many functions of a modern state, were very different partners from the native principalities. They were rivals of the colonial state itself. The kongsis had to go, because only one state, the colonial state, could exist in the Netherlands Indies.

The Dutch finally saw the end of the kongsis, but depopulation and impoverishment followed. Only at the end of the century did the Chinese again begin coming in significant numbers to the West Coast, and what drew them at that time was not so much gold, but new resources in the form of natural products and agricultural opportunities. While the Teochiu maintained their hold on Pontianak's trade, Hakkas also quickly moved into these new fields. The expansion of Dutch control of the interior in the final decades of the nineteenth century and the establishment of greater security made it worthwhile for this group of pioneering settlers to look for new opportunities there. Often, they preceded the colonial power in moving into remote areas. As a result, West Borneo became a major exporter of forest products, some agricultural goods, and later of smallholder rubber, as the following chapter shows. While the indigenous population, for the most part, gathered or produced these products, Chinese traders encouraged and organized their export to the world's consumers.

---

[182] General Report, 1884, by Haga, ANRI BW 5/15 (30). On the insistence of the headman of Monterado that he consult the other mine heads before making a decision, see Earl, *Eastern Seas*, pp. 284-285, 288, 290-292.

[183] Historical Note on the Lanfang Kongsi, ARA 2.10.02 V. 31.5.86 (36). Or, in the history's words, "Through our direct intervention the nature of the kongsi administration was entirely and wholly changed." The Kapthai "completely eclipsed" all other members of the administration of the kongsi. Here, this account makes use of a report of Interpreter for Chinese W. P. Groeneveldt, who traveled through Mandor on foot in 1875.

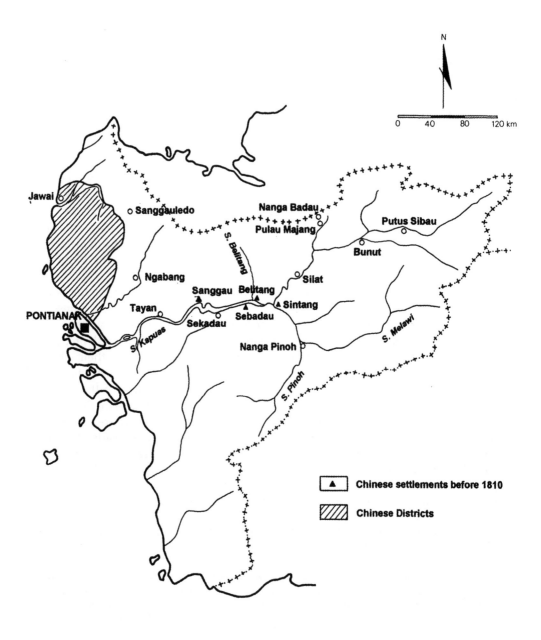

Map Seven. Dispersal of Chinese Population after the Kongsi Wars.

CHAPTER FOUR

DEMOGRAPHIC AND ECONOMIC CHANGE: FROM GOLD MINERS TO SETTLERS AND TRADERS, 1860-1940

The modern export-oriented economy of West Borneo, which dealt in both natural and agricultural products, took shape in the second half of the nineteenth century. Many of its characteristics are unchanged today: the economy remains predominantly agricultural and extractive, dependent on the export of raw materials. In the 1970s and 1980s, the lumber industry boomed, and, for a time, the production of mandarin oranges was an important activity, but both these sectors declined in the 1990s. No new industries have appeared to replace them, and rubber remains West Borneo's major agricultural export, as it was for most of the twentieth century. In this economy, the ethnic Chinese have occupied a key position, while Western investments and activities continue to be of negligible importance, as the following comments, separated by nearly eighty years, illustrate. In 1866, an observer looking at gold mining wrote:

> It is the Chinese who control almost all branches of industry in Borneo, and only through them do the foreign rulers of this distant region harvest the fruits of a land. . . . In every place where he can get a foothold, the Chinese turns wildernesses into fertile rice fields, he constructs pathways for the transport of local products, and he works to exploit mineral wealth with diligence and perseverance.[1]

Decades later, in 1925, another author described the Chinese traders' adept dealings with inland peoples, contrasting their advantageous situation with the more difficult situation of Western plantation and mine owners in this residency who sought to exploit local resources:

> The Chinese, thanks to his yearlong residence, knows the people and their needs; he is constantly in touch with them by means of the system of advances, his barter trade in the interior gives him a great advantage over the European, his *toko* [shop] no less. The Chinese works mainly with people who are already indebted to him, an enormous advantage compared to others who have to work with expensive, free, and often unwilling coolies.[2]

---

[1] J. H. Kloos, "Vorkommen und Gewinnung des Goldes auf der Insel Borneo," *Tijdschrift voor Nederlandsch Indië* 4,2 (1866): 208.

[2] G. L. Uljée, *Handboek voor de Residentie Westerafdeeling van Borneo* (Weltevreden: Visser & Co., 1925), p. 88.

The consistent role of the ethnic Chinese also characterizes West Borneo's economy.

The years from 1885 to 1942 were relatively peaceful times in which few disturbances arose, except for the troubles of 1912–14, described in the following chapter. This period not only allowed the Chinese to recover gradually from war and the destruction of the kongsis, but also provided opportunities for both settlers and immigrants to help develop an expanding economy.

From the time the Dutch began to investigate Borneo, they had described its potential in glowing terms. They supposed that the coastal region was unquestionably as fertile as Java and that the uplands would be suitable for growing coffee, pepper, and spices. Natural products like rattan, birds' nests, and beeswax were plentiful, not to mention gold, diamonds, and other minerals.[3] Yet, despite this apparent potential bounty, through most of the nineteenth century the residency of Borneo's West Coast failed to earn enough revenue to pay the costs of its own administration. The Chinese, as the most economically influential group, often bore the blame for Borneo's failure to meet revenue expectations. In reality, Borneo's soils were poor; its agricultural potential, natural resources, and probably even its population were more limited than early visitors thought.[4]

POPULATION CHANGE

At the end of the Monterado war in 1854, colonial authorities expected gold mining to resume, but many miners were departing of their own accord. The mines were unprofitable, having exhausted the possibilities of Chinese technology, and without the kongsis, the industry lacked entrepreneurs to provide capital and imported labor. The one remaining kongsi, Lanfang, was also in decline; its population had dropped drastically.

Maintaining the transient, largely adult male population of the mines had depended on constant replenishment from China. Immigration had declined because of the economic malaise after the Monterado War, unrest in South China, competition from gold-mining areas in California and Australia, and because no kongsi organization was available to manage it.

By the end of the century, however, the Chinese population was increasing, drawn by opportunities that had little to do with gold mining. A network of traders collected forest products for the international market; later, cash crops provided new opportunities. By 1915, smallholder rubber farming, spread primarily by Chinese traders and tended by Malays, Chinese, and later Dayaks, was getting results. Thus, a "complete" change took place in the economy of West Borneo during the quarter century before 1919.[5] Smallholder agriculture had developed on a large scale "without any encouragement from the administration."[6]

---

[3] For example, W. H. Muntinghe's report of 1821 in "De bevestiging van het nederlandsch gezag op Borneo, en de vermeerdering der inkomsten van dat eiland voor de schatkist," *Tijdschrift voor Nederlandsch Indië* 12,2 (1850): 62-64.

[4] Jacob Ozinga, *De economische ontwikkeling der Westerafdeeling van Borneo en de bevolkingsrubbercultuur* (Wageningen: N. V. gebr. Zomer en Keuning, 1940), pp. 3-4.

[5] J. C. F. van Sandick and V. J. van Marle, *Verslag eener spoorwegverkenning in Noordwest-Borneo* (Batavia: Albrecht, 1919), part 1, p. 6.

[6] An anonymous author ("De cultuur van hevea in West-Borneo," *Indische Gids* 41,2 [1919]: 1320) places the introduction of rubber in 1909-1910.

Population growth followed economic improvement. An observer wrote in 1925, ". . . there are few areas in the Indies . . . where prosperity [*welvaart*] is so great, a prosperity furthermore that was achieved through the area's own efforts."[7]

Population counts carried out in the twentieth century give more exact totals than the exaggerated estimates of numbers of Chinese, Dayaks, and others published earlier. Early estimates of Dayak population were guesses at best. As late as 1930, however, census-takers resorted to a simplified count in parts of the interior (where over forty thousand Chinese lived) and even these figures may not be completely correct.

Graph 4.1:
Population Growth, 1850-1930

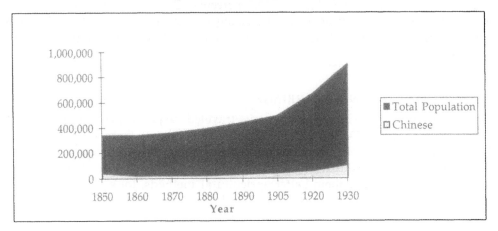

Graph 4.2:
Chinese as a Percentage of Total Population

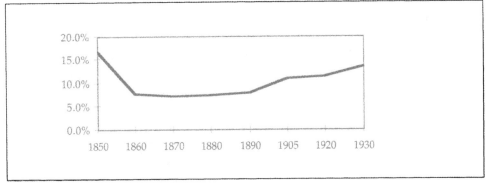

---

[7] Uljée, *Handboek*, p. 5.

In the first half of the 1800s, in disputes about head taxes, colonial bureaucrats tended to overestimate numbers of adult male Chinese, while kongsis tended to underestimate them. The twentieth-century geographer James C. Jackson reports over forty thousand Chinese in the area in the 1810s, and about fifty thousand in 1850;[8] both these totals are probably exaggerated. Once colonial authority was established in an area, head counts became more reliable. During the 1860s and early 1870s, the Chinese population hovered around 25,000; its proportion of the total population was 7.3 percent in 1860 and only reached 7.7 percent in 1890 (Graph 2).

After 1877, the Chinese population began to climb slowly, reaching nearly 28,000 at the end of the decade. By 1905, it was 48,348 (10.7 percent of total population), and by the time of the census of 1920, nearly 67,787 (11.2 percent). Ten years later, the figure was 107,998 (13.5 percent). Growth resulted partly from increased immigration, attracted by the changes in the economy, and partly from natural increase, as the balance of the sexes improved and more stable families formed.

IMMIGRATION AND INTERMARRIAGE

Prior to the 1850s, Chinese immigrants traveled on junks, arriving annually in December or January. During the Monterado War, Chinese immigration to West Borneo was forbidden, but a regulation of 1856 allowed limited numbers to enter.[9] Authorities began to feel that Chinese immigrants would have a positive influence on the Dayaks, teaching them better agricultural methods, for example, and that they would deal more fairly with them than did Malay, Bugis, or Arab traders. At the same time, authorities believed Chinese traders would have to be watched to insure that they did not arrive in excessive numbers or take advantage of local trading partners.[10]

Between early 1856 and March 1857, however, only 169 Chinese persons arrived. In 1858, 123 Chinese arrived, some of whom had spent years in Singapore. Most of this group settled in Pontianak, but a few others, Hakkas, still planned to try their luck at mining. On the other hand, hundreds were moving to Sarawak, where opium was cheaper and the corvée less onerous.[11] In 1868, Resident Kater pleaded to allow the free immigration of Chinese, above all in Monterado and Sambas, districts that still felt the effects of the war with Thaikong.[12]

---

[8] James C. Jackson, *The Chinese in the West Borneo Goldfields: A Study in Cultural Geography* (Hull: University of Hull Publications, Occasional Papers in Geography, 1970), pp. 24-26. A Chinese account by Xie Qinggao (translated in Yuan Bingling, *Chinese Democracies: A Study of the Kongsis of West Borneo [1776-1884]*, pp. 305-310) speaks of "several tens of thousands" of people from Fujian and Guangdong who mine gold and diamonds.

[9] *Koloniaal Verslag* (1856): 28, but see also Message from Kroesen, Pontianak, August 26, 1857, ARA V. 2.12.57, (2), where it appears that immigration of Chinese to West Borneo was still officially prohibited.

[10] Memorandum of transfer of Kroesen, 1858, cited in E. B. Kielstra, "Bijdrage tot de geschiedenis van Borneo's Westerafdeeling," Part XVIII, *Indische Gids* 12,2 (1890): 2190.

[11] Political Report for 1857, March 31, 1858, ANRI 1/8 (215); *Koloniaal Verslag* (1858): 11. The incoming miners were described as originating from the hills. The term "Hakka" only appears later in colonial accounts.

[12] Report cited in Kielstra, "Bijdrage," Part XXIII, *Indische Gids* 14,2 (1892): 2313-2314.

Figures on net immigration between 1875 and 1882 show that arrivals barely exceeded departures. Each year between 1887 and 1895, however, arrivals increased, so that there were a few hundred more immigrants than emigrants.[13] Between 1880 and 1900, the Chinese population increased by about 2 percent annually, climbing to over 3 percent after 1900. Limited transportation during World War I reduced the influx, but between the censuses of 1920 and 1930, annual population growth for the Chinese of West Borneo reached the unusually high rate of 4.77 percent, mostly because of immigration.[14] Some of this flow was reversed during the years of the global economic Depression immediately following this period.

Graph 4.3:
Chinese Immigrants to West Borneo, 1900-1933[15]

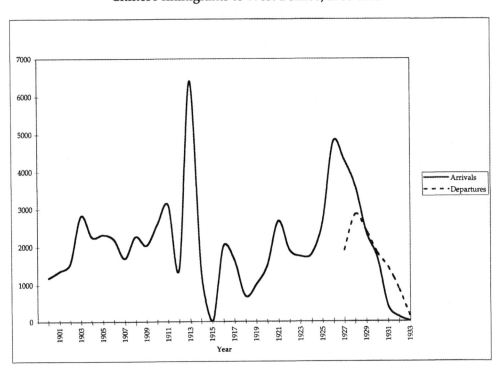

<hr/>

[13] The statistics in the *Koloniaal Verslag* also mention arrivals to and departures from destinations within the Netherlands Indies, but this is technically not immigration, and many of these may have been short-term visitors. J. J. K. Enthoven, *Bijdragen tot de Geographie van Borneo's Wester-Afdeeling* (Supplement, *Tijdschrift Aardrijkskundig Genootschap*, 1901-1903) (Leiden: Brill, 1903), pp. 858-859, remarks that most immigrants in 1900 remained in the Pontianak-Kampung Baru area, the latter as coolies in the lumber mills. Most were Teochiu. Enthoven guessed that most Chinese in Mandor and Sebadau were born locally, while most of those in the district of Pontianak (the 9,059 Chinese who lived in Pontianak town and 1,405 in the coastal fishing settlement of Sungai Kakap) were immigrants.

[14] Nederlandsch-Indië, Departement van Economische Zaken, [*Volkstelling 1930*], Vol. VII *Chineezen en andere vreemde oosterlingen in Nederlandsch-Indië* (Batavia: Landsdrukkerij, 1935), p. 43.

[15] Source: *Koloniaal Verslag and Indisch Verslag*, various years; *Volkstelling* 1930, Vol. VII, p. 49. Emigration figures for Foreign Orientals.

In the 1920s, immigrants had to prove they could earn a regular income and to pay a fee of one hundred guilders for an admission card before being allowed into the residency.[16] Probably many of them were laborers sponsored by their potential employers; a few were schoolteachers invited to teach in private Chinese schools. Much immigration resulted in only temporary residence, as the available statistics on emigration show. From 1929-1933, departures exceeded arrivals. A number of laborers and sharecroppers who had arrived to work as coolies on the larger rubber plantings were sent back to China when the owners decided to cut costs in response to a decrease in the price of rubber.

Although the number of Chinese in West Borneo surpassed 100,000 in 1930, rapid population growth did not continue into the 1930s, and the annual growth rate above 4 percent—as estimated for 1920-1930—proved to be exceptional. The Depression put an end to any rapid growth in the Chinese population, although immigration seemed to pick up again in the late 1940s and early 1950s (see chapter six).

On the other hand, the number of Chinese women and families among the population had increased. Immigration of women from China had been rare in kongsi times. In 1865, three wealthy Chinese brought a shipful of immigrants, mostly women, from China, but the ship was wrecked and most were killed.[17] Perhaps similar attempts were made to import females *en masse*, but we have no record of such attempts. Some Hakka women appear to have followed their menfolk to other destinations abroad by the 1860s,[18] but it is difficult to know if that happened in Borneo. Despite the limited numbers of Chinese women who crossed the water, the rate of Chinese intermarriage with Dayak wives was relatively low. Utilizing information from an 1877 census of Mandor-Lanfang, Resident Kater found only fifteen "pure" Dayak women out of a total of over 1,300 adult females who were cohabiting with Chinese.[19] Intermarriage between Chinese and Dayak was primarily a frontier phenomenon. In addition, after 1850, some forms of intermarriage were actively discouraged by the government. Colonial officials believed the Chinese were acquiring brides by encouraging Dayak men to run up debts and taking their daughters or wives in return for unpaid obligations. They forbade such Chinese-Dayak liaisons for indebtedness in 1854.[20]

This regulation may have been ineffectual, but it soon became irrelevant anyway; the number of women in Chinese communities was already growing as a result of demographic and economic changes. Wherever settled Chinese communities developed, enough women were born to provide men with wives. Furthermore, the continued opening of trade and agriculture after 1900 created opportunities that attracted whole families to West Borneo; these pursuits thus

---

[16] See Uljée, *Handboek*, p. 126, concerning conditions for admission about 1925. Earlier the fee had been *f*25. In the mid-1920s, an estimated 80 percent of immigrants stayed more than a few years in Borneo, but this clearly changed during the Depression.

[17] *Koloniaal Verslag* (1865): 16. Certainly the women were meant to be prostitutes, but the account does not mention the intentions of the financiers.

[18] See Mary F. Somers Heidhues, *Bangka Tin and Mentok Pepper: Chinese Settlement on an Indonesian Island* (Singapore: Institute of Southeast Asian Studies, 1992), p. 150; personal communication from Myra Sidharta.

[19] Historical Note on the Lanfang Kongsi, ARA 2.10.02 V. 31.5.86 (36). Of nearly five thousand inhabitants, about two thousand were adult males.

[20] Political Report for 1856, ANRI BW 1/7 (214). (See also chapter one.)

Plate 9. Chinese vegetable garden near Pontianak, 1998. Credit: the author.

differed from mining, which was largely a male occupation. As a result of increasing numbers of women, intermarriage became more unusual. In the 1930 census, only 230 non-Chinese women, mostly Dayaks, were listed as the wives of Chinese men in all of West Borneo.[21]

There is one more point to be made. When evaluating these numbers, one must remember that the statistics report only "legal" marriages and therefore provide only a limited perspective on the situation in the interior. A civil registry of marriages had been introduced for Chinese, but it was honored primarily in the breach.[22] The census figures provide no details about over 40,000 Chinese living in the interior, mostly Hakkas, who were simply enumerated and not asked about marital status. In fact, this was the group most likely to cohabit with Dayak women.

REDISTRIBUTION OF POPULATION

The first Chinese to settle in Borneo lived in court and harbor towns like Sambas or Sukadana. Miners lived where they mined; Monterado and Mandor grew up around the mining kongsi sites. As noted earlier, most kongsis also controlled coastal harbors. Functioning kongsis encompassed agricultural settlements as well, such as those around the harbor of Pemangkat, which served Samtiaokioe, or near

---

[21] *Volkstelling 1930*, Vol. VII, p. 291.

[22] The civil registry (*burgerlijke stand*) for marriages of Chinese residents was introduced in Borneo after 1925. Twenty years later, it still played little or no role in Chinese marriages. Note about Civil Registry in Pontianak from 1948, ARA 2.21.120:59. For information on marriage registration, see also chapter seven.

the harbor of Singkawang, which served Thaikong. Mandor ruled over a fertile farming valley near the town.

As the first mining sites were depleted, miners moved on. Settlements followed the deposits from Mandor into Landak, from Monterado toward Bengkayang. Both moves resulted, as chapter two has shown, in friction with Malay and Dayak neighbors, and sometimes with other Chinese. But the dominant trend was to move from mining to small-scale agriculture, from extraction to settlement. Where mines employing ten to thirty Chinese laborers previously dominated the landscape, now small houses, surrounded by gardens, with animals and other household property, were beginning to predominate. After 1854, the trend toward settled farming continued.[23] Population shifts took the Chinese away from the kongsi centers, either toward the coastal towns and into lands suitable for rice growing—or, later, coconut and rubber agriculture—or toward the interior, where they engaged in trade or small-scale mining.[24] Sometimes they engaged in multiple activities. Chinese expansion inland benefited from better security, thanks to the expansion of Dutch rule into the interior, but often the Chinese newcomers preceded the Dutch. According to a 1931 account, they settled wherever they felt conditions were advantageous:

> Outside of the centers where Chinese live, they have penetrated as farmers into the remotest corners of the sub-district [of Singkawang]. In their own peculiar manner, they take possession of the best pieces of land, without giving the slightest thought to the regulations made by the authorities on the matter of illegal occupation.[25]

Small groups of miners continued to pioneer new sites, but most sought their fortune elsewhere. Mandor and Monterado were sad relics of their former selves. The old mines were nearly useless, having been worked over not once, but several times. Abandoned *pagongs* (mine ponds) overflowed after rains, flooding the diggings and covering them with sand. The houses were deserted, the roads ruined and useless.[26]

Some Chinese leaving Mandor settled in the environs of Pontianak, as did many new arrivals from China; the urban society of West Borneo's most important port offered better chances of getting work as laborers or craftsmen there. Pontianak developed according to the pattern of its early days; in 1903, the city center was still organized as it had been described in the early nineteenth century. On the left bank of the Kapuas were the Chinese quarter and the European settlement, with public buildings, schools, and the military encampment. The Chinese quarter was located close to the river, partly reaching out, on posts, into the water. Dwellings, shops, and commercial buildings competed for space, ". . . in short, a real Chinese

---

[23] Compare the account in Political Report for 1859, ANRI BW 1/10 (217).

[24] Ozinga, *Economische ontwikkeling*, p. 220.

[25] Letter, Resident to Director of Binnenlands Bestuur, Pontianak, March 14, 1931, in ANRI BB 1233.

[26] Enthoven, *Bijdragen*, pp. 817-819. Enthoven surveyed the Kapuas area at the turn of the century, when Chinese trade with Dayaks in forest products was beginning to decline. Most Chinese shops he encountered in the upper Kapuas were quite poor, but he demonstrates that Chinese traders were already widespread before rubber was introduced as a cash crop. See the discussion of the introduction of rubber later in this chapter.

labyrinth, with a constant, industrious hustle and bustle, a great contrast to the calm and space of the European neighborhoods."[27]

In the style of Malay dwellings, the Chinese houses were connected to each other by wooden walkways. Shops and storerooms, filled with flammable commodities, were often prey to fire. As early as 1851, a fire destroyed the temple and several houses in the neighborhood, and fires occurred repeatedly in the major Chinese quarters throughout the next half century. The Dutch finally insisted that the Chinese build houses from stone, although this did not prevent the fires from recurring.[28] Every house was also a *toko* (shop), or a workshop. These shops, crammed with wares, gave an appearance of industry and even prosperity, even though the situation of the poor Chinese laborers who provided unskilled labor for the settlement drew the pity of onlookers.[29]

Some Malay houses were upriver from the Chinese quarter, but most Malays and others in Pontianak lived on the small peninsula formed by the junction of the Kapuas and the Landak Rivers. There a bridge connected the sultan's palace—a large wooden building—to the mosque. In a crowded, rather poor, urban *kampung* nearby lived Malays, Bugis, and Arabs. Others resided near the mouth of the Landak. In 1901, Pontianak had a population of 186 Europeans, about 5,500 Chinese, and about eleven thousand Javanese, Malays, and Bugis, in addition to three hundred Arabs.[30]

Teochius were the largest group among the Chinese in the town itself; some two thousand of the 4,449 Chinese were Teochiu (Hoklo) and 1,700 were Hakka. In Kampung Baru, with 1,036 Chinese, about 640 were Hakkas, while all of the 1,060 Chinese in Mandor were Hakkas.[31] Kampung Baru, which until 1884 belonged to Lanfang Kongsi, was the "industrial" center of the town. The area illustrated the economic development of the island as a whole. First, lumberyards and sawmills for construction and shipbuilding and a warehouse for stockpiling forest products grew up.[32] Then, in the late nineteenth century, coconut oil and copra factories were built. Finally, the rubber industry's smokehouses multiplied until they stretched out along the riverbank. Beyond the "industrial" area lived Chinese farmers and market gardeners.

---

[27] Ibid., p. 821.

[28] G. L. Uljée, "Pontianak, zijn economische beteekenis," *Tijdschrift voor Economische Geographie* 22,4 (April 15, 1931): 145. In Pontianak in 1991, a major fire in the Chinese business district caused loss of life and extensive property damage.

[29] Marius Buys, *Twee maanden op Borneo's Westkust: Herinneringen* (Leiden: Doesburgh, 1892), pp. 42-50. Buys devotes some space to the sturdiness of the Borneo Chinese, distinguishing them from those in Java who were "softened" by intermarriage with Javanese. Even those Chinese of mixed origin were still very "Chinese" in appearance.

[30] Enthoven, *Bijdragen*, p. 819.

[31] Ibid., p. 881.

[32] Buys, *Twee maanden*, pp. 59-61. At the time of Buys's visit in the 1880s, forest products like rattan, resins, and gutta-percha were loaded on rafts of heavy tree trunks and floated to Pontianak. Later the trees fed saw mills; see ibid., p. 71. For the importance of these products, see below. Compare the description in Uljée, "Pontianak," pp. 144ff.

Pontianak dominated trade, commerce, and administration in the residency; the Pontianak Chinese financed and exported major crops.[33] Singkawang became the second most vital port, while Sambas and Mempawah fell far behind. The Chinese quarter of Sambas, which also had its houses built out on poles along or into the river, was much smaller than that of Pontianak, and appeared, in the late nineteenth century, impoverished. Lacking solid ground for their vegetable patches, the inhabitants had planted their gardens out on floats in the water, and these, too had a neglected appearance.[34] For the Sambas area, coastal Pemangkat would become a regional trade center.

DISPERSAL TO THE INTERIOR

The movement to the coast and to agricultural areas was only part of the story of Chinese migration. Before the end of the eighteenth century, the Chinese had probably begun to mine in Sanggau and Tayan, along the Kapuas River. By 1866, Chinese mines had moved upriver, reaching Sintang and Silat. (See map seven.) Later, Chinese miners were found in Nanga Pinoh, Bunut, and Putus Sibau, far into the interior. Since gold deposits were widespread, but not rich, the need to open new sites had drawn Chinese miners farther and farther inland.[35]

Other Chinese moved into the interior to trade. By 1872, colonial officials noticed significant numbers of Chinese going to "isolated areas" in the interior. This trend attracted attention because it showed initiative, even daring, since much of the interior was just being incorporated under Dutch rule in the late nineteenth century. Traders who moved away from the coast were leaving the protection of colonial authorities.[36]

Chinese itinerant traders tended to be new arrivals, or *sinkeh* (M., *xinke*), yet they often quickly learned local Dayak languages. Local-born Chinese (Dutch sources call this group "*peranakan*," but "locally rooted" may be better[37]) lived in larger Chinese settlements and did not readily venture into the interior. Some

---

[33] Van Sandick and van Marle, *Spoorwegverkenning*, part 1, p. 21; Uljée, *Handboek*, p. 73. Gambier was grown on larger farms with hired Chinese or Dayak coolies; see A. Azahari, *De ontwikkeling van het bevolkingslandbouwbedrijf in West-Kalimantan* (Bogor: n.p., 1950), p. 77.

[34] Buys, *Twee maanden*, pp. 223-224; P. Adriani, *Herinneringen uit en aan de Chineesche districten der Wester-Afdeeling van Borneo, 1879-1882: Schetsen en indrukken* (Amsterdam: Campagne en Zoon, 1898), p. 72, calls this "little Venice." Sambas also had a temple connecting it to the mining kongsis.

[35] Kloos, "Vorkommen und Gewinnung," p. 207. As noted, Chinese mining methods readily exhausted deposits.

[36] E. de Waal, *West Borneo*, Vol. 8 of *Onze Indische financien*, ed. E. A. G. J. van Delden (The Hague: M. Nijhoff, 1907), pp. 68-69. Some, of course, had a wife in each location.

[37] G. William Skinner, "The Chinese Minority," in *Indonesia*, ed. Ruth McVey (New Haven: Human Relations Area Files, 1963), pp. 104-105. As used in Java, *peranakan* usually implies speaking a local language in daily use, which Chinese in Borneo did not. Skinner places all ethnic Chinese on a scale of local-rootedness, with the *peranakan* of Java representing the most rooted and acculturated, and those of Borneo the most oriented to Chinese culture. Chapter seven discusses this model. The opposite of *peranakan* is *totok*, "pure," but not necessarily foreign-born.

traders maintained a base in a town, moving to the interior for trade and remaining there for part of the year. Many were agents of firms in larger towns.[38]

Soon, traders on the Kapuas River increased their mobility by using small motor- or steam-driven boats to tow large, flat-bottomed freight transporters called *tongkangs*.[39] The lowest-level traders traveled overland carrying backpacks filled with their wares. In the 1950s, some *tengkulak* (middleman-dealers in export goods) lived entirely on their houseboats—sometimes on two boats bound together—on the rivers of Kalimantan.[40]

The Dayak easily entered into commercial relations with the Chinese: in 1885, it was said that Dayaks liked to shop at the market of Mandor, for example, and, as the Chinese moved into the interior, Chinese shops offered a kind of entertainment for visiting Dayaks seeking to buy and sell goods or just to socialize.[41] Dayaks often referred to the Chinese as *sobat*, which is frequently interpreted as "friend," although the meaning is uncertain. Friend or not, the Dayak knew what he could expect from his *tauke* (trader). A visitor to the Kapuas River in the 1880s wrote:

> These people [Chinese traders] are often established here for weeks and months in order to buy products from the Dayaks, which they have previously paid for by supplying salt and other necessities, and also some luxury items, like earthenware, tobacco, and arrack, which the Dayaks greatly like. The Dayaks in general follow the practice, widespread among natives of the Indies, of working and delivering for cash in advance . . . they seldom fail to meet their obligations.[42]

In 1896, a Chinese *pasar* of sixteen houses was built at Putus Sibau, the "uppermost" town on the Kapuas.[43] These territories were ruled directly by the Dutch—that is, without their being under native rulers or Malay aristocrats—and it was Chinese traders who opened them to commerce:

> Such posts as Putus Sibau, Nanga Badau, and Pulau Madjang all date from the years 1895-1905; and it was . . . Chinese trading posts that brought about the direct contact of the Dayaks with the commerce of the world . . .[44]

The Dutch presence offered some protection to Chinese miners and traders, but they were not dependent on it. In 1899, French trader Adolphe Combanaire

---

[38] General Memorandum, Bengkayang, M. Waisvicz, July 12, 1938-May 20, 1941, ANRI BB 287, p. 43.

[39] Ozinga, *Economische ontwikkeling*, p. 17.

[40] K. Tobing, *Kalimantan Barat* (Bandung: Masa Baru, ca. 1952), pp. 69, 72.

[41] Journal of Resident Kater, October-December 1884, ARA MR 1885:22 says Dayaks were so common at the *pasar* of Mandor that the government could use them as informants without attracting attention to them.

[42] Buys, *Twee maanden*, pp. 83-84.

[43] *Koloniaal Verslag* (1896): 21; *Encyclopaedie van Nederlandsch-Indië* (The Hague: M. Nijhoff and Leiden: Brill, 1927), p. 362.

[44] W. L. Cator, *The Economic Position of the Chinese in the Netherlands Indies* (Oxford: Blackwell, 1936), p. 169.

traversed Borneo from Sarawak to Banjarmasin, mostly on foot. Avoiding contact
with colonial authorities, he found Chinese coffee planters, miners, and traders
living far from the nearest Dutch station. On the Kapuas River below Sintang at
Belitang-Sepauk, Combanaire visited an isolated Chinese mine settlement a few
days' journey north of the Kapuas, on the Belitang River.[45] There, a former Chinese
trader, who had learned of the gold site from his Dayak customers, was employing
some fifteen Chinese laborers on a shareholding basis to work the mines. He
received, for "discovering" the terrain, half the proceeds; the workers' kongsi
divided the rest.[46] Providing the laborers with supplies on credit, he probably
managed to keep much of their profits as well. The mine, at the base of a hill, had
been thoroughly turned over, and a dam had been built to capture the water supply
and divert it to wash the gold from the soil. Having described this local
enterprise, Combanaire offers his opinion that only the Chinese combine desire for
profit, ability to work, and talent for organizing hydraulic works in the
combination needed to mine gold. He estimates that the miners earned two dollars
per day of work, a good return, but all mining ceased in the rainy season, at which
time the laborers would have to fend for themselves. This settlement was
provisioned by another Chinese trader who lived with his family a day's journey
away from the site. This trader's extensive property included a fine stand of
pepper vines, an arrack distillery, and a number of pigs.[47] He in turn acquired
provisions from Sintang, where small steamboats from Pontianak brought
merchandise in exchange for local products, especially forest products gathered by
Dayaks.[48]

Sintang was an important Kapuas town and an assistant residency. It had an
official Chinese quarter housing 650 residents, and that neighborhood assured its
status as a center for trade with the interior. Dayaks often brought gold dust, gutta-
percha, other native rubbers, ironwood, and natural resins directly to purchasers
there, while Chinese entrepreneurs living upriver used the town as a base for their
trade and enterprise. Sintang furnished all kinds of goods: salt, iron and tobacco,
"wine, beer, brandy, gin, butter, sardines, flour, potatoes, onions, fruit preserves,
cigars." All but a few of Sintang's Chinese, who like others in the interior were
Hakkas, merely eked out a living in petty trade; seldom did anyone really
prosper.[49]

---

[45] This, too, would have been a kongsi. Acording to Enthoven, *Bijdragen*, p. 583, ninety Chinese
lived at Belitang itself, in some three blocks of rather dilapidated wooden houses. He confirms
that gold-bearing grounds were in the neighborhood.

[46] This, of course, throws some light on how a small kongsi divided its gains.

[47] Adolphe Combanaire, *Au pays des coupeurs de têtes: À travers Bornéo* (Paris: Librarie Plon,
1910), pp. 87-88; 276. Lesley Potter introduced me to Combanaire, a lesser-known but very
entertaining traveler.

[48] Ibid., pp. 271-279. At times, low water made it impossible for freight to reach Sintang, and its
prices for imports soared. See Enthoven, *Bijdragen*, p. 478.

[49] *Regeringsalamanak voor Nederlandsch-Indië* (1902): 255-257; Enthoven, *Bijdragen*, pp. 479,
573. The list of goods is from Combanaire, *Au pays*, p. 304, whose supply of alcoholic beverages
not only gave him courage on his jungle travels, but also assured him of a welcome in Dayak
long houses.

Plate 10. *Pasar* (marketplace) of Capkala, circa 1920. In small towns, simple shophouses with *atap* (*nipa* palm) roofing were common.
Credit: Rare and Manuscript Collections, Cornell University Library.

Two other areas in the interior that proved attractive to Chinese were the "lake district" of the Kapuas River and Sekadau. A few Chinese controlled the export of salted fish from the productive "lake district," where the Kapuas River spilled over its banks to form huge reservoirs during wet weather. There about 40 percent of the population of about twenty thousand were Malays, an unusually high percentage for the interior regions, although many of them were of Dayak origin.[50] The lure of gold, not fish, brought the Chinese to Sekadau. Mines began to appear in the early nineteenth century, when the first Hakkas arrived there, expecting to get rich. By 1900 there were nearly six hundred Chinese in the area, and they were increasing rapidly in nearby areas, although few concentrations numbered more than several hundred inhabitants.[51] By the turn of the century, Chinese settlers, some golddiggers, but most of them petty tradesmen, had moved into the interior, often far beyond the reach of the colonial power. The commercial and political ramifications of this dispersal soon attracted the mistrust of the colonial authorities. While they were attending to the administrative implications, a new system of trade was developing in the residency.

---

[50] Enthoven, *Bijdragen*, pp. 91-93, 123-132, 154-174.

[51] Ibid., pp. 581-586.

STATE INTERVENTION: RESIDENCE

The relative ease with which these and other Chinese moved and settled in the interior of Borneo contrasts with the difficulties experienced by Chinese in Java, whose travel and settlement were more effectively restricted.[52] Although the laws outlining the so-called *wijkenstelsel* (quarter system) were designed to confine Chinese to legally recognized Chinese quarters, in Borneo this meant little. The resident could permit Chinese to live elsewhere for purposes of trade or agriculture. Often, Chinese who had, in fact, established permanent residences outside the *wijken* (quarters) were officially treated as "temporary" residents of their own homes, a convenient fiction for all involved. For years, the system was not enforced at all.[53]

In 1902, nearly ninety settlements, some of them very small, were designated as official Chinese quarters. In 1912, authorities in Borneo attempted to enforce settlement restrictions and to control travel more closely, ignoring the situation of many Chinese farmers who lived in their plots, but this provoked resistance (see chapter five). By 1922, only seventy-five Chinese quarters existed, but this did not mean that the population was becoming more concentrated; in fact, the opposite was the case.[54]

CHINESE TRADERS

. . . the Chinese . . . spread out . . . over all of West Borneo far into the deepest interior, where they settled as *taukes* . . . later, after pacification of the interior, the Chinese were free to settle wherever they chose. They opened *tokos*, favoring especially places where the rivers flowed together. . . . If the economic basis of the Malays (or Muslims) was obligatory trade, the Chinese retained a monopoly thanks to their system of giving advances. Now the Dayaks and the Chinese *taukes* live in an economic symbiosis, and it is an open question whether, on the whole, this condition is good or bad.[55]

---

[52] In Java, Foreign Orientals were obliged to live in specially designated settlements or quarters (*wijken*). Exceptions were always possible, however, for business purposes or other necessary activities.

[53] *Regeringsalamanak voor Nederlandsch-Indië* (1913): 494-495. This comment is repeated in Secret Report, Resident de Vogel to Governor-General, January 27, 1913, ARA V. 4.7.1914 (8). Compare Enthoven, *Bijdragen*, p. 573. According to Wouter Brokx, *Het recht tot wonen en tot reizen in Nederlandsch-Indië* (Bois-le-Duc: C. N. Teulings, 1925), pp. 138-142, only after 1855 did the question of residence restrictions for the Outer Islands appear. Travel passes were required in West Borneo after 1865, also for natives; this was relaxed after 1915, when local authorities were allowed to make their own rules (pp. 213-216). The regulations of 1866 and 1872 limited the right to residence in the Outer Islands, but it is not clear when they were applied to West Borneo. In any case, Staatsblad 1913, number 454, allowed holders of an entry permit (*toelatingskaart*) in West Borneo to reside where they wished; this was extended by a 1916 regulation (p. 189). Both travel and residence were later more strictly limited, as chapter five shows.

[54] *Regeringsalamanak voor Nederlandsch-Indië* (1902): 255-257; *Regeringsalamanak voor Nederlandsch-Indië* (1922): 655-656; Ozinga, *Economische ontwikkeling*, pp. 91-92 (citing Borel).

[55] F. H. van Naerssen, Verslag van mijn verblijf in Kalimantan Barat, (typescript, Echols Collection, Cornell University Library, 1949, part 2), p. 27.

In the interior, some Chinese traders used houseboats, while others resided in what the authorities recognized as "temporary" urban quarters. Their presence was not unwelcome. Dayaks understood well that they stood to benefit if more than one Chinese trader competed for their business and quickly learned how to get better prices for their goods by traveling an extra day to reach another trader.[56]

The strong position of Chinese traders in the residency arose from the peculiar structure of the West Bornean economy. The *hulu-hilir* relationship had developed in the past because the people of the interior were dependent on, or desired, imported goods like salt, tobacco, opium, cloth, beads, and sometimes rice. Until the late nineteenth century, the Malay courts and aristocracy had monopolized the trade, maintaining Dayak partners in a dependent relationship. In areas where there were few dependents, debtors, or slaves of the Malays, harvesting of forest products probably began only when Chinese entered the area. Like the Malay elite, Chinese traders made use of dependency relationships by advancing money to the Dayaks and keeping them in debt,[57] but they also opened new markets. Exports increased as a result, benefiting all parties, at least in the short run (although sometimes, as will be seen, excessive harvests of natural products threatened sustainability).

In the twentieth century, poor harvests in the interior and a concentration on the production of export goods rendered wide areas of the region dependent on imported rice. The lack of a local consumer goods industry meant that these goods had to come from other islands or from abroad. In this situation, Chinese traders found ample opportunity to put their talents to use. Although a good deal of importing and exporting was controlled by European trading concerns, the distribution of imports and the collection of most exports remained in Chinese hands. The Chinese traders lived close to local consumers; at the same time, their networks extended abroad to entrepôts like Singapore, Bangkok, or Saigon, where both essentials, like rice, and non-essential consumer goods could be purchased. Chinese businessmen had already become major rice importers by the 1880s, before Borneo became dependent on imported rice; their supplies rendered official government imports superfluous.[58] In 1891, for example, when the harvest failed because of bad weather, Chinese traders, without official prompting, brought in 219,999 *piculs* of rice from Siam.[59]

In the twentieth century, vital rice imports depended on export earnings. During the Depression, when export prices collapsed, a painful adjustment resulted. In general, as Ozinga noted in 1940, the presence of a Chinese trading network in the interior saved the Dayak from being forced to resort to inferior foods if the local rice harvest failed. The interior people could obtain rice from a Chinese shop,

[56] Enthoven, *Bijdragen*, p. 808.

[57] Ozinga, *Economische ontwikkeling*, pp. 218, 222; E. A. Ranken, "De niet-Europese bijdrage tot de economische ontwikkeling van West-Borneo, 1900-1940," in *Het belang van de buitengewesten: Economische expansie en koloniale staatsvorming in de buitengewesten van Nederlands-Indië, 1870-1942*, ed. A. H. P. Clemens and J. Th. Lindblad (Amsterdam: NEHA, 1989), using official accounts, paints a dark picture of Chinese traders and their exploitation of Dayaks, pp. 181-183, 201. Uljée, *Handboek*, speaks of a "permanent group of Malays and Dayaks who collect forest products with [cash] advances from Chinese," p. 78.

[58] Ozinga, *Economische ontwikkeling*, pp. 192-193; *Koloniaal Verslag* (1880): 193; *Koloniaal Verslag* (1891): 237.

[59] *Koloniaal Verslag* (1891): 237. A *picul* is about 62 kilograms or 130 pounds.

on credit if necessary, a situation that enhanced both the security and the quality of their food supply.[60] Although outsiders often worried about indebtedness among the Dayaks, in fact the system put the goods into their hands.[61]

SINGAPORE

The British colony of Singapore was the focus of most of West Borneo's export and import trade; even imports that originated elsewhere or goods that were underway to distant destinations traveled via this entrepôt. Almost from its foundation in 1819, Singapore dominated the foreign trade of the region, despite repeated attempts by the Dutch to direct trade toward Java. Only salt was a significant import from Java, thanks to the state salt monopoly. In their time, the Borneo kongsis had tried to avoid even that. Even "secret societies" had links to Singapore. Statistics show that West Borneo was one of the five Indies residencies that traded least with Java between 1924 and 1933 (and probably at other times as well).[62]

Attempting to wean the province from its economic dependence on the British colony and its people from dependence for credit on the Chinese, the authorities encouraged the Java Bank and other credit institutions to enter the region during the twentieth century. Of these, only the Java Bank survived the Depression and its catastrophic effects on export prices.[63]

Batavia's efforts offered neither flexible credit structures nor a market for exports. Singapore was a major source of both. Ships bringing rice from Siam or Vietnam to Borneo returned to Singapore loaded with export goods. Passenger service was frequent. In 1928, the state-owned KPM (Koninklijke Paketvaart Maatschappij, Royal Packet Company) ships bound for Singapore departed from Pontianak once every four days, while ships bound for Batavia were scheduled for departure only once every two weeks, a reflection of the relative importance of the two metropoles.[64] Smaller ships and boats, probably hundreds of them, complemented the steamer traffic. In the 1920s, letters to Europe were routed via Singapore, not Batavia, while a steamship ticket to Singapore was cheaper than one to Batavia.[65] Many Chinese transferred their profits or savings to Singapore; these transfers balanced the trade surplus in commodities that the residency accumulated through exports. Some of this money was probably remitted to China.

---

[60] Ozinga, *Economische ontwikkeling*, p. 226.

[61] As Richard C. Fidler, "Chinese-Iban Economic Symbiosis," *Southeast Asian Journal of Social Science* 6,1/2 (1978): 56-77, points out, that, despite their debts, the Dayaks in such relationships above all enjoyed the use of the purchases before having to meet their obligations to the traders. " . . . in the end it is the Iban who get possession of the . . . goods," p. 67.

[62] Lourens Jeroen Touwen, "Extremes in the Archipelago: Trade and Economic Development in the Outer Islands of Indonesia, 1900-1942" (PhD dissertation, Leiden University, 1997), pp. 45-46. From 1924-28, only 10 percent of its exports went to Java and about 22 percent of its imports came from Java. For the years 1929-33, the figures were similar.

[63] Ozinga, *Economische ontwikkeling*, pp. 193-194, 198, 231.

[64] Van Sandick and van Marle, *Spoorwegverkenning*, part 2, p. 222; H. Zondervan, "De economische ontwikkeling van Nederlandsch-Borneo," *Indische Gids* 50,1 (1928): 499.

[65] Uljée, *Handboek*, pp. 129, 133. KPM offered special rates for travel from the West Coast to Singapore, probably to compete with Chinese shipping. During the emergencies of the 1880s, Resident Kater had to telegraph Batavia via Singapore.

Singapore's position in trade and finance remained unchallenged long after Indonesian independence. The largest traders in West Borneo often moved, after a few years in Pontianak, to Singapore itself or to British Malaya, where they continued business. Many important traders on the West Coast were agents of ethnic Chinese firms established in Singapore.[66]

FOREST PRODUCTS

In the mid-nineteenth century, forest products were West Borneo's most important exports, next to gold. As the kongsis declined later in the century, natural products surpassed minerals in importance. In the early twentieth century, dwindling supplies became a problem as some natural resources became scarce. Shortly thereafter, before 1925, smallholder crops overtook natural products as the region's major export.[67]

This rapid change can be illustrated by comparing the values of various exports. In 1900-1904, forest products were the great majority of exports by value, followed by coconuts. Five years later, they were about half of exports, dwindling to less than one-fourth in 1910-14, while coconuts accounted for over half the value of all exports. By 1920-24, trade in forest products had declined, so that now these goods accounted for only a small fraction of exports, and they never again regained their earlier dominance.[68]

At the turn of the century, West Borneo contributed a significant share of the forest exports produced by the entire Dutch East Indies.

Graph 4.4:
Forest Produce Exports

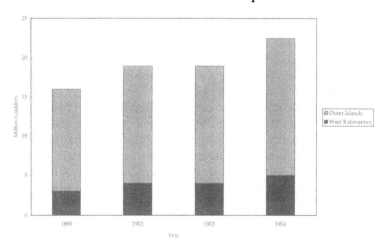

---

[66] Van Sandick and van Marle, *Spoorwegverkenning*, part 2, p. 218; Uljée, *Handboek*, pp. 88-89; Ozinga, *Economische ontwikkeling*, pp. 195-196. On postwar connections with Singapore, see Chan Kwok Bun and Claire Chiang See Ngoh, *Stepping Out: The Making of Chinese Entrepreneurs* (Singapore: Prentice Hall, 1994), pp. 71-73.

[67] Ozinga, *Economische ontwikkeling*, pp. 224-229.

[68] Ranken, "Niet-Europese bijdrage," p. 180.

In 1899, 1902, and 1903 (no figures are available for 1900-1901), West Borneo had the largest volume of exports of any single province of the Netherlands Indies. In 1904, the value of its forest exports climbed to over ƒ5,000,000, but it lost its position as the export leader, because South and East Borneo, larger and with relatively untouched reserves, especially of rattan, had bypassed it to become the largest exporter.[69]

Two changes took place in the traditional trade in forest products during the nineteenth century. First, the Dutch limited by contract the rights of Malay rulers to collect taxes and tribute from Dayaks. This greatly weakened the position of the rulers and their appanage holders in dealing with the Dayaks, and as a result they began to lose their privileged position as key traders. Second, the demand for forest products in international markets increased greatly.

A striking example of this change in consumer demand is the development of the international market for gutta-percha, a kind of latex produced by certain jungle trees (*Palaquium* and *Payena*) that was used in the nineteenth century as insulation for underwater telegraph cables and for some other purposes where plastics are used today. The market price for gutta-percha varied with fluctuations in cable-laying activity, so knowledge of international markets was important for traders. First collected systematically in Singapore in 1845, gutta-percha sources were soon depleted on that island, because trees were felled to extract the product. Collection expanded to neighboring areas, and each of them was soon worked out because of the profligate means of collection. It was difficult and impractical to tap—rather than cut down—the trees to obtain gutta-percha; one hundred trees might be felled to obtain a *picul* (about sixty-two kilograms) of latex. (Extraction methods later improved somewhat, but not enough to save the trees.) By 1870, market prices for gutta-percha had risen, and people were eagerly seeking it in the forests. Although some natives tried planting these trees in their home gardens, where they tended other fruit or nut trees, these efforts at husbandry had little effect, so that by the end of the century it appeared that the population of trees would be exterminated. Faced with this prospect, collectors and traders began adulterating the gutta-percha and searching for substitutes.[70]

Exports of gutta-percha and other products, like *jelutung* (a rubber-like, elastic tree product), which originated in Borneo and were destined for Singapore, began around 1848 and increased rapidly during the next twenty years.[71] Initially gutta-percha was gathered during the dry, slack agricultural season by Dayaks when they needed something to exchange for rice or other necessities. It is probable that trade initially followed traditional channels controlled by Malay sultanates. When demand for gutta-percha rose in the 1860s, however, the role of Chinese traders increased, too.[72]

---

[69] *Koloniaal Verslag*, 1899-1904.

[70] Lesley Potter, "A Forest Product out of Control: Gutta Percha in Indonesia and the Wider Malay World, 1845-1915," in *Paper Landscapes: Explorations in the Environmental History of Indonesia*, ed. Peter Boomgaard et al. (Leiden: KITLV Press, 1997), pp. 283-295; Ozinga, *Economische ontwikkeling*, pp. 137-143, 163, 237; see also Combanaire, *Au pays*. Gutta-percha was also used in golf balls.

[71] L. K. Wong, "The Trade of Singapore, 1819-1869," *Journal of the Malayan Branch, Royal Asiatic Society* 33,4 (1960): 1-315, cited in Potter, "Forest Product," p. 286. *Jelutung* is still used in chewing gum.

[72] Potter, "Forest Product," pp. 288 ff.; *Koloniaal Verslag* (1865): 216.

Graph 4.5:
Annual Exports of Jungle Rubber, Gutta-percha, and *Jelutung*, in *f*1000

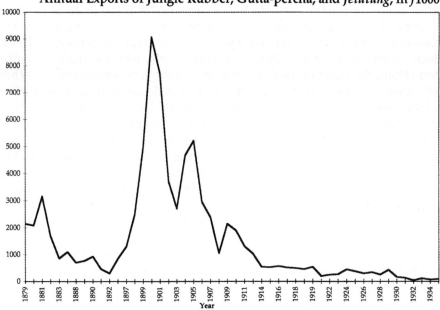

These and other official statistics show that both the amount and the value of authentic gutta-percha exports peaked in 1900. Thereafter, cheaper but naturally occurring products like *jelutung* replaced gutta-percha; by that time, the *Palaquium* and *Payena* trees, sources of gutta-percha, could only be found in remote areas. Nonetheless, the increasing numbers of Chinese traders in the interior had produced a significant shift in the economic status of the gatherers of forest products: increasing competition among traders permitted gatherers to claim better prices for their goods and to pay less for imported commodities.

After peaking in 1905, the value of jungle rubber dropped. In 1907, agricultural exports overtook those of forest products. By 1914, rubber cultivation dominated the economic activity of people in parts of the interior, and the harvesting of forest products had become a much less significant industry.[73]

Other forest products experienced similar boom and bust cycles. Rattan, derived from a variety of climbing palm that thrived in swampy areas, also has a long history of collection and export; its earliest use was for baskets and ropes (for example, to rope house beams together). Valued abroad as a material used in furniture production, rattan figured as a profitable export, but its use declined rapidly after 1927, when such furniture became unfashionable. Because there was such a great variety of rattans, some of which could be cultivated, this industry proved to be more stable and less environmentally destructive than gutta-percha harvesting. In time, however, much of the land where the climbing palms flourished was found to be suitable for rubber, so the palms were removed. The value of rattan exports fluctuated greatly, peaking in 1897 (at *f*1,318,000) and declining after that.[74]

---

[73] Ozinga, *Economische ontwikkeling*, pp. 229-230.

[74] Ibid., pp. 155-159.

An unusual forest product was *tengkawang* or illipé nut, which comes from a dipterocarp tree (L. *shorea spp.*). *Tengkawang* had many uses: an edible fat, it can be burned in lamps or candles, used to make cosmetics or soap, or as a machine lubricant. West Borneo produced nearly all the *tengkawang* of the Indies, but the fat was sometimes processed abroad. All exports went through Singapore, and most end products were sent to Western Europe. Unfortunately, like the trade in gutta-percha and rattan, the trade in *tengkawang* was fraught with uncertainties. When coconut oil, used as a lamp fuel, and petroleum, which could be used as fuel or machine lubricant, proved to be convenient substitutes for *tengkawang*, the price fell. Also, harvests of this wild nut varied greatly: only once every six years or so was there a bumper crop. Good years alternated erratically with scarce years, and a good local harvest might coincide with poor prices on the international market. In 1912 and 1914, exports reached nine thousand tons; in the latter year the crop brought a record value of f2,444,000. By 1935, the relatively high export of nearly five thousand tons had a value of only f248,000.[75]

Woodcutters began to work in the interior in the 1850s, especially in Sambas, but until World War II, the lumber industry remained relatively unimportant in West Borneo. It delivered wood to the local building industry and exported small amounts of lumber to Java or Japan. Malays and Dayaks provided the labor for felling trees, while Chinese engaged in trade and milling. Several sawmills were located in Kampung Baru. Some traders also constructed wooden *perahus* or *sampans*.[76]

Colonial officials noted the variety of goods being harvested from the forests of the interior, and in "boom" times, especially, when forest-gathering activities peaked, the Dutch feared that these pursuits were distracting Dayaks from food production. But in fact much of this effort was concentrated in the months when agricultural tasks were light. Although the thriving trade in export products did divert labor from the fields, failed harvests were usually the result of bad weather, not insufficient labor. Moreover, during the times when men roamed the jungle and felled the trees or gathered rattan in difficult terrain, women could do much of the agricultural work.

Although some Malays continued to purchase some forest products (Malay traders might also trade using goods bought on credit from the Chinese, as observed in Nanga Pinoh in 1903[77]), the Chinese dominated the export trade. Their network, centered in Singapore, reached to settlements like Sintang and to Chinese *pasars* in the interior. Since the Chinese traders often reached customers by boat, at the main

---

[75] Ibid., pp. 133-136; Uljée, *Handboek*, p. 79, says a good harvest comes once every seven years. Compare the more recent Charles M. Peters, "Illipe Nuts (*Shorea* spp.) in West Kalimantan: Use, Ecology, and Management Potential of an Important Forest Resource," in *Borneo in Transition: People, Forests, Conservation, and Development*, ed. Christine Padoch and Nancy Lee Peluso (Kuala Lumpur: Oxford University Press, 1996), pp. 230-244, which stresses the problem of commercial usage of a fruit that produces erratically. *Tengkawang* is currently used in cosmetics.

[76] Japanese traders who tried to export lumber from the West Coast of Borneo in the 1930s were forced to give up because of tension with the Chinese traders caused by the Sino-Japanese War. Ozinga, *Economische ontwikkeling*, pp. 159-163. Uljée, *Handboek*, p. 81; Zondervan, "Ontwikkeling van Nederlandsch-Borneo," p. 618. Some Kampung Baru mills belonged to Malays. See Plate 14.

[77] Enthoven, *Bijdragen*, p. 409.

harbors the goods could often be loaded directly from the boats onto oceangoing vessels.[78]

Trade in the interior was usually managed by barter; rice, tobacco, cloth, glass beads, and, clandestinely, salt[79] or weapons, were in greatest demand. In Belitang, one trader offered his customers petroleum, sugar, tobacco, salt, some textiles, and homemade arrack.[80] The availability of consumer goods encouraged more intensive forest-gathering.

CHINESE PENETRATION OF LANDAK

The subdistrict of Landak, which bordered on the Lanfang Kongsi and was known to be a source of diamonds as well as gold, illustrates the geographical and economic shifts made by the Chinese in their search for prosperity. A few Chinese mined gold in Landak in the early nineteenth century, but they had left when local nobles (probably appanage holders) became more aggressive and unfriendly.[81] In the 1840s, the Lanfang Kongsi warred with Landak. As a result, the territory became a kind of "buffer" between kongsi territory and the native-dominated interior.[82]

In 1850, Landak had five hundred Malay and nine thousand Dayak families living inside its borders. The Dayak lived in poor circumstances. Although the ruler of Landak still tried to resist Chinese penetration, an estimated (or overestimated) thousand Chinese miners were working in three kongsis positioned near the border between Landak and Lanfang's territory, for example in Perigi. The resentment left from the 1840s war with Landak and Dayak hostility made it necessary for the Lanfang miners to seek safety in numbers,[83] although this figure is probably too high. In 1854 a survey found only seventy-five Chinese men residing in Landak with their wives and children. A mere forty of them were working mines on the account of the Kapthai of Mandor (this estimate is probably too low).[84]

After the dissolution of the kongsis in the 1850s, more Chinese began to seep into Landak, by land and along the waterways, despite restrictions imposed by the Malay elite. Many of them found their way into the interior, though living in this frontier was still dangerous; some Chinese in isolated places were murdered, often by thieves.[85]

Landak was not one of the major areas for jungle products, but it did export some *tengkawang*. Chinese traders sometimes tried to drive Malays out of the trade in forest products. In Landak, they focused pressure on the nobility, but Landak's

---

[78] And vice versa. *Koloniaal Verslag* (1874): 215.

[79] Because of the government monopoly on salt.

[80] Combanaire, *Au pays*, pp. 86-87, 279.

[81] Anonymous, "Bijdrage tot de kennis der binnenlandsche rijken van het westelijk Borneo," *Tijdschrift voor Nederlandsch Indië* 11,1 (1849): 343-344.

[82] Memorandum of transfer, W. J. ten Haaft, Landak, 1934, ARA 2.10.39, MvO KIT 984, p. 30.

[83] O. van Kessel, "Statistieke aanteekeningen omtrent het stoomgebied der rivier Kapoeas (Wester-Afdeeling van Borneo)," *Indisch Archief* 1,2 (1850): 168-169.

[84] From a mining survey by Everwijn, which probably counted the few hundred miners of Perigi as part of Mandor. *Koloniaal Verslag* (1854): 158. This only partly accounts for the discrepancy.

[85] See for example, Short Reports, 1879, ANRI BW 6a/11 (115).

aristocrats seem to have enjoyed a relatively strong position in their dealings with the colonial regime, perhaps because of their history of controlling the diamond mines. As late as 1915, the Malay rulers still monopolized the *tengkawang* trade. A Chinese businessman in Singkawang, Lim Moi Lioek (M. Lin Meiliu), sent agents into the territory to try to take over the trade himself, but he was ultimately unsuccessful. The fact that his agents were Japanese complicated the situation, for some Malays denounced them as spies and had them arrested by the local military.[86] The matter became an international incident, and in the end, Lim failed to secure a foothold in Landak. We know this to be true because ten years later, in 1925, a local official reported that only Malays, not Chinese, traded with the Dayaks in Landak.[87]

Nevertheless, by 1919 there were 2,009 Chinese in Landak, including a *kapitan* of the Chinese residing in the main settlement of Ngabang. Seven lesser Chinese officers dealt with smaller settlements.[88] Typically, Chinese immigrants established river settlements downstream from Malays, where they were relegated because Malays feared contamination from pork. At this time, most of these settlements were concentrated in the area bordering the former territory of Lanfang Kongsi.[89] This suggests that most of the Chinese were urban traders and craftsmen, farmers and, possibly, miners, who did not carry on any extensive trade in the countryside. The 1920s saw the Chinese "making use of every opportunity to acquire rights to agricultural land, thereby driving many Malays into poverty."[90]

By 1934, Landak's Chinese had become "settled farmers and established traders." Although they constituted less than 5 percent of the population, their numbers had increased to over 3,100, not only as a result of immigration, but also due to natural increase. The substantial number of females per one thousand males (849.5) indicates that the Chinese in this area had become a settled population by the 1930s. There were only four Chinese officers governing the settlements in Landak, but smaller market places had informal headmen.[91] Apart from those residing in settlements around market places, many Chinese lived on farms, raising ducks, chickens, pigs, vegetables, fruits, and rice for home consumption or for sale.

---

[86] For some tantalizing details of the Landak incident, see among others, Letters, Investigation of Treatment of Japanese in Landak, ARA 2.10.36.04 V. 13.8.1915 (2); Correspondence, Landak Incident, V. 29.2.1916 (46), and further references in Decision on Landak Affair, ARA 2.10.36.04 V. 30.3.1916 (6) and telegram, V. 11.4.1916 (52), as well as secret reports in ARA 2.10.26.051 V. 5.11.1915 E13 and V. 26.11.1915 E14, and secret mail report in ARA 2.10.36.06 MR 1915:120x. Peter Post helpfully pointed me to this matter. The Japanese had the status of Europeans; Lim may have been trying to exploit their relative freedom to move about, a freedom which the Chinese did not have.

[87] Uljée, *Handboek*, p. 89.

[88] Memorandum of transfer, J. F. Later, Landak 1919, ARA 2.10.39 MvO KIT 981, p. 75.

[89] Van Sandick and van Marle, *Spoorwegverkenning*, part 1, pp. 67, 141.

[90] Uljée, *Handboek*, p. 97, cited in Zondervan, "Ontwikkeling van Nederlandsch-Borneo," p. 621. Uljée himself however felt that the Chinese should be allowed to open up the territory, while the Malays who lost land thereby would simply open more themselves; see G. L. Uljée, "Nog eens: De economische ontwikkeling van Nederlandsch-Borneo, in 't bijzonder von West-Borneo," *Indische Gids* 51,1 (1929): 379. This discussion about giving Chinese free rein to open the territory or confining them by means of passes and other measures to the towns continued for decades.

[91] Memorandum of transfer, W. J. ten Haaft, Landak, 1934, ARA 2.10.39 MvO KIT 984, pp. 27, 31; Memorandum of transfer, anonymous, Landak, ca. 1930, ARA 2.10.39 MvO KIT 982, p. 100.

Rubber and pepper were important cash crops; the Chinese farmers either concentrated on rubber-pepper-gambier or on rice. Most Chinese also traded in these products, but typically they had little capital. The large-scale traders and institutions that could provide substantial credit were located in Pontianak and Singapore. Ngabang was probably the chief Landak trading center. It had a good market and, since it was located at the upper limit of steam traffic on a major river, it was the focus for riverborne trade in the subdistrict.

Like most Chinese in the interior, the Chinese of Landak were almost all Hakkas. They were hard workers in agriculture, but it does not appear that farm work isolated or segregated them, for in the 1930s it was reported that they mixed easily with the Dayak. By this time, they must have been trading with the Dayak as well. Marriage and inheritance customs followed Chinese tradition; children of mixed parentage were raised as Chinese and spoke Chinese. Probably the existence of even a tiny community of Chinese helped integrate those of mixed parentage. Although all Chinese spoke Hakka, the local-born Chinese were usually also fluent in Malay. Immigrant Chinese, drawn to inland trading, often learned Dayak languages.[92]

SMALLHOLDERS AND TRADE

Landak exemplifies the Chinese migration toward the interior. The other migration of the Chinese, toward the coast, was associated with a transition to cash crop farming. The Chinese had established many farms along the coast or near mining centers by the mid-nineteenth century, settling in groups of ten to thirty families in fertile, well-watered valleys.[93] Their crops were often new to Borneo: they cultivated vegetables, pineapple, sugar cane, and, above all, wet rice, which they probably introduced to the island.[94] The number of Chinese farmers grew steadily, as illustrated by the chart below.

Graph 4.6:
Occupations of Foreign Orientals in West Borneo[95]

	1875	1887	1891	1895
Farmers	3,506	4,367	4,604	4,799
Miners	1,574	1,639	1,085	1,043
Traders	1,942	2,002	1,838	2,226
Craftsmen	650	---	5,602*	---

* includes coolies and employees; see text.

In 1875, out of all the Foreign Orientals registered in West Borneo as employed, 3,506 made a living from agriculture (not including those involved in fishing or animal husbandry), while 1,574 worked in mining. Wholesale or retail traders

---

[92] Memorandum of transfer, W. J. ten Haaft, Landak, 1934, ARA 2.10.39 MvO KIT 984, pp. 45-47.

[93] Kielstra, "Bijdrage," Part XVI *Indische Gids* 12,2 (1890): 1704-1705. This is a shortened version of a Memorandum of transfer by Major Andresen, written in 1856.

[94] Jackson, *Chinese in the West Borneo Goldfields*, pp. 38-41.

[95] Source: *Koloniaal Verslag*, various years.

numbered 1,942, and there were 650 registered craftsmen. By 1887, the number of farmers had climbed to 4,367. Miners numbered 1,639, traders 2,002. The 1891 survey, which tracked the occupations of 13,142 Foreign Orientals in the residency at the time (perhaps 90 percent of whom were Chinese, the rest being Arabs or Indians) shows how the occupations of the Chinese had changed. A substantial proportion, 43 percent (5,602) were craftsmen of various kinds, or coolies and employees, not including 170 household servants. A slightly smaller proportion, 35 percent (4,640) of Foreign Orientals were farmers, or they raised fish or animals. Only 1,085 persons (8 percent), all but two of them Chinese, gave their occupation as mining. An additional 1,838 (14 percent) of Foreign Orientals were engaged in trading, pawnshops, and money-lending. Government-related service engaged 156 Foreign Orientals; 163 worked for revenue farms. Of the fifty-seven teachers in non-religious private schools (religious private schools would be traditional Islamic schools), fifty-five were Chinese. Allowing for the presence of some non-Chinese in the category "Foreign Orientals," it is still clear that trade and crafts, whether workers were involved as independent entrepreneurs or as employees, and agriculture far superseded mining activity as the main occupation of West Borneo's Chinese population.[96] The importance of agriculture continued to increase, in fact. In 1895, the final year for which these statistics appear, there were 4,799 farmers, 1,043 miners, and 2,226 traders.[97]

Chinese agriculture in West Borneo was concentrated in the region stretching from Pontianak northward along the coast, including inland areas in the Chinese Districts like the Monterado area and Bengkayang. Chinese *sawah* (wet-rice fields, mostly rain-fed) produced good results, enough to enable those farmers to market some rice from each crop.[98] In time, the Malays, Bugis, and Dayaks living near Chinese farmers began to lay out wet-rice fields as well. The Chinese had also brought simple machines from China for threshing and milling their rice, and for crushing sugar cane. Local people adopted simpler versions of these machines as well.[99]

COCONUTS

Not the Chinese but the Bugis introduced the first important cash crop into the coastal area. Familiar with coconuts and in a position to import indentured workers ("slaves") to provide labor, the Bugis drained much of the coastal area near Pontianak, especially around Sungai Kakap, where thousands of kilometers of

---

[96] Since persons named only one occupation this does not reflect the widespread practice of multiple occupations (mining and farming, trading and farming). *Koloniaal Verslag* (1893): Appendix A. In 1900, Enthoven, *Bijdragen*, p. 865, found only one skilled goldsmith in the territory. In recent times, Pontianak alone has had several goldsmiths, perhaps a reflection of a tendency to put savings into gold, rather than inflationary currency. In Singapore, goldsmithing is a typical Hakka trade.

[97] *Koloniaal Verslag*, 1875-1895. Again, figures are for Foreign Orientals.

[98] Ozinga, *Economische ontwikkeling*, pp. 105-106; *Koloniaal Verslag* (1862): 214.

[99] See G. A. Mol, "Vier groote landbouwwerktuigen van de Chineezen in West-Borneo," *Sin Po* 618 (February 2, 1935, Special Issue). On the other hand, the Chinese also used native implements (G. William Skinner, "The Chinese Minority," in McVey, ed., *Indonesia*, p. 104). See also P. J. Veth, *Borneo's Wester-Afdeeling: Geographisch, statistisch, historisch, vorafgegaan door eene algemeene schets des ganschen eilands* (Zaltbommel: Joh. Nomanen Zoon, 1854), 1: 66.

parits (canals, ditches—the same word is used in the gold mine diggings) provided drainage and transportation. This activity probably began on a small scale before 1850.[100] Many Bugis grew prosperous during these years; at one time they were considered the wealthiest group in the residency, and coconut farming contributed substantially to their prosperity.[101]

As early as 1870, when the prosperity of the Bugis elite seemed exemplary, the Chinese were beginning to drive the Bugis out of the retail trade in coconuts and were themselves growing the crop. At first, their interest in coconuts was limited to buying nuts and producing coconut oil.[102] The trees and the land remained in the hands of Bugis, Arabs, and Malays, some of whom had substantial holdings; one Arab planter planned to expand to ninety thousand trees in 1872. Most coconut was made into oil and exported to Java, but in 1873, oil was also being sent to Singapore, and, by 1876, Singapore was the primary destination for this product.[103] A few years later, petroleum was replacing coconut oil for use in lamps, and coconut was mostly being exported as copra for processing in Singapore.[104] The process later reversed; by 1889, two coconut oil factories existed in Pontianak; until 1910 they were the only such factories operating in the Indies.[105] In 1946, the government estimated that 70 percent of coconut land was in Chinese hands, with about ten thousand small properties of up to three or four hectares and about one thousand larger holdings, all owned by Chinese farmers.[106] No Europeans had any coconut plantings worth noting.

International demand and the chance to use Singapore as a market gave the Chinese a decided advantage over other traders. At first, the Chinese had resisted growing tree crops because they feared tying down their capital for the many years (up to twenty) it took for trees to mature, but coconut plantings opened up in Pemangkat, Singkawang, and Monterado at the end of the 1850s, and this subsequently became a trend.[107] Around Pontianak, some Chinese bought existing groves from Bugis planters, while others opened new ones. They occupied land

---

[100] *Koloniaal Verslag* (1870): 10; *Koloniaal Verslag* (1871): 11. For a description of *parits*, see Zondervan, "Ontwikkeling van Nederlandsch-Borneo," pp. 606-607. *Koloniaal Verslag* (1859) reports that one Chinese farmer planted three thousand trees near Monterado and indicates interest in the cultivation in Chinese-dominated areas. Going from planting to production would have taken several years. Ozinga, *Economische ontwikkeling*, p. 114, claims that Governor-General Rochussen (1845-51) stimulated coconut growing, but many initiatives that came from the administration around that time (coffee, cotton, sugar) failed. The coastal areas, where coconuts thrived, only became safe for agricultural use when piracy was suppressed. See Azahari, *Ontwikkeling*, p. 71.

[101] The *haj* statistics show that prosperity from smallholder farming or trading was not confined to the Chinese. From forty-three pilgrims to Mecca in 1869, the number increased to 237 in 1880. General Report for 1880, Resident Kater, February 8, 1881, ANRI BW 5/11 (26).

[102] *Koloniaal Verslag* (1871): 197; Enthoven, *Bijdragen*, p. 814. Ranken ("Niet-Europese bijdrage," p. 199), and Touwen (*Extremes*, p. 155) attribute the early spread of coconut cultivation to Chinese initiative, which was imitated by Malays, but nineteenth-century sources show that Bugis were first.

[103] *Koloniaal Verslag* (1872): 186; *Koloniaal Verslag* (1873): 213; *Koloniaal Verslag* (1876): 199.

[104] *Koloniaal Verslag* (1883): 207; "Short Report," May 1881, ANRI BW 6a/12 (116).

[105] Ozinga, *Economische ontwikkeling*, p. 118.

[106] Azahari, *Ontwikkeling*, pp. 130-132.

[107] Veth, *Borneo's Wester-Afdeeling*, 2:185; *Koloniaal Verslag* (1859): 129-130; Ozinga, *Economische ontwikkeling*, p. 115. Modern coconut trees mature faster.

without giving a thought to its legal status, subsequently becoming the biggest producers in the coastal area north of Pontianak. Around 1915, they overtook the Bugis as coconut producers in the residency as a whole. By 1919, the whole coastal belt from Sungai Purun (thirty-six kilometers north of Pontianak) to Sungai Duri (ninety kilometers north) had become a single coconut grove, two to four kilometers wide, covering land where formerly rice had grown. Rice paddies were located inland, but they did not form a continuous belt.[108] Two decades later, the coconut belt had grown to be 360 kilometers long, extending from south of Sukadana to north of Pemangkat.[109] In addition, the Chinese drained much of the swampy area inside the triangle marked off by Pontianak-Mandor-Ngabang for agricultural use, and some parts of this land were planted with coconut trees.[110] By 1927, many Chinese had ventured further north and were planting coconuts around Jawai, a northern coastal town, an area the Dutch still considered insecure.[111]

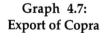

Graph 4.7:
Export of Copra

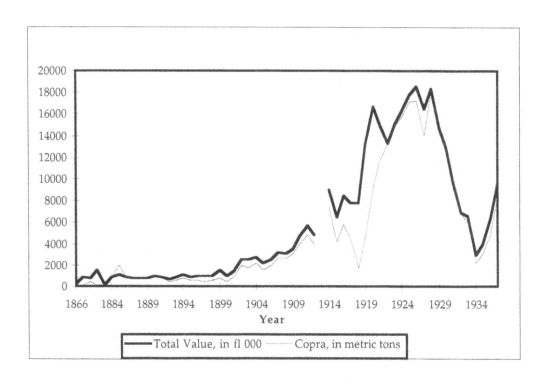

---

[108] Van Sandick and van Marle, *Spoorwegverkenning*, part 1, p. 96; Ozinga, *Economische ontwikkeling*, pp. 230-231.

[109] Cator, *Economic Position*, p. 168.

[110] Van Sandick and van Marle, *Spoorwegverkenning*, part 1, pp. 6-7.

[111] P. M. van Meteren Brouwer, "De geschiedenis der Chineesche Districten der Wester-Afdeeling van Borneo van 1740-1926," *Indische Gids* 49,2 (1927): 1098. Jawai is across the Sambas River from Pemangkat, in the direction of Paloh and Sarawak.

Nearly all coconut production, which was concentrated in coastal lowlands, was managed by smallholders.[112] The residency exported 20 percent of all copra coming from the Netherlands Indies in 1921, 19 percent in 1930, and only 14.5 percent in 1937. West Borneo's copra was not high quality, but the region was surpassed only by Menado in the amount it produced.[113] Coconuts remained an important export for decades, although, like other crops, they lost value during the Depression years.

OTHER EARLY CASH CROPS: PEPPER AND GAMBIER, SAGO

In hilly terrain, pepper was a major export crop even before the end of the nineteenth century. It was primarily a Chinese smallholder crop, one adopted only occasionally by native growers before World War II. Gambier was a second export crop grown mostly in the hills; it, too, was most often produced through Chinese effort, since gambier usually required plantation-style organization and labor. Both plants tended to exhaust the soil fertility or other resources in short order—pepper was also subject to diseases and pests—so that farmers were constantly forced to open new plots when the old fields became unproductive.

Yet despite these challenges, pepper farming increased in the 1880s around Pontianak, in Monterado and Landak, and in the upland regions of Sambas, especially near Bengkayang. Exports grew rapidly. Most growers managed only small plots, but they needed hired workers during the busiest seasons.[114] In the 1930s, problems with pests forced pepper growing to move to the Sanggauledo area.[115] Chinese-dominated Singkawang came to be the most important export harbor for this product.

The Chinese had experimented to improve pepper vines and increase their production, and they also experimented with different varieties of pepper. After 1892, they began to grow the more valuable, but more labor-intensive, white pepper.[116] West Borneo was second to Bangka-Belitung in white pepper exports for the Archipelago. Production declined in the late 1920s, although prices were high, probably because land and labor were more often invested in rubber. In 1935, world pepper prices collapsed, and only a few stands survived World War II.[117] Largely a native-grown product, sago was briefly exported from West Borneo beginning in the late nineteenth century. It never attained the importance of a dominant export crop that it commanded in Sarawak or North Borneo, however, and when rubber was introduced, producers lost interest in sago.[118]

---

[112] Zondervan, "Ontwikkeling van Nederlandsch-Borneo," p. 609, reports that in 1925 European concerns exported 311 tons of copra, smallholders 61,359 tons.

[113] Ozinga, *Economische ontwikkeling*, pp. 120-121.

[114] *Koloniaal Verslag*, 1892 and other years; Azahari, *Ontwikkeling*, p. 155. Cf. Zondervan, "Ontwikkeling van Nederlandsch-Borneo," p. 611.

[115] Azahari, *Ontwikkeling*, p. 82.

[116] Black pepper is picked green and dried unskinned. White pepper is allowed to ripen, then its skins are removed. Such intensive cultivation of pepper was called the "Bangka method"; see ibid., p. 155.

[117] Ozinga, *Economische ontwikkeling*, pp. 128-132.

[118] Ibid., pp. 111-113. In the interior it continued to serve as an emergency food.

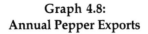

Graph 4.8:
Annual Pepper Exports

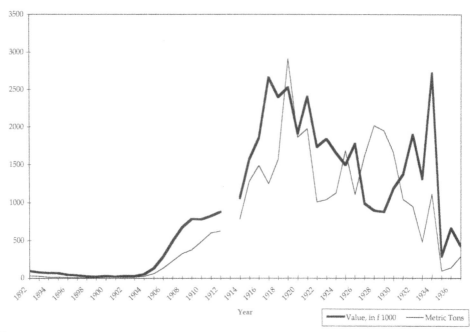

RUBBER

Rubber overtook coconuts in importance soon after rubber agriculture was introduced. Around the turn of the century, *hevea* seeds reached West Borneo from Singapore. In 1906 or 1907, the government began to distribute seeds to potential growers,[119] but seeds alone were of little value without a market. For a time, colonial specialists believed that rubber could grow only on tropical plantations managed by Europeans, because they expected that smallholders would fail to care for the trees properly. To their surprise, the trees planted by smallholders thrived, even if they were not clean-weeded or tapped according to "scientific" methods. High rubber prices after 1910 awakened widespread interest in the new crop, and the results were soon visible in the form of widespread planting.[120]

Throughout all of the Outer Islands, beginning in the 1910s, smallholder rubber production boomed, and smallholder production surpassed estate production in the late 1930s. In some provinces, and especially in West Kalimantan, rubber proved to

---

[119] Memorandum of transfer, J. Oberman, Resident of West Borneo, 1938, ARA 2.10.39 MvO MMK 265, Appendix III, p. 1; Ranken,"Niet-Europese bijdrage," p. 183; Ozinga, *Economische ontwikkeling*, p. 290. Acccording to local tradition, Haji Yusup of Kampung Saigon introduced rubber to West Kalimantan. Azahari, *Ontwikkeling*, p. 79. Hajis often brought new products from Singapore or elsewhere.

[120] Ozinga, *Economische ontwikkeling*, pp. 262-264, 289-290; Uljée, *Handboek*, p. 75. Ozinga's statistics for the entire Indies show that smallholders overtook the mostly Western-owned plantations in terms of area planted in 1932, but total smallholder exports were less than those of all plantations, although in the 1930s the difference was small. In 1935, smallholders exported more than plantation enterprises because they continued to tap when capital-dependent plantations shut down.

be quite profitable for smallholders—this was true especially from 1915-1928—and rubber farming quickly supplanted the gathering of forest products as a source of income.[121]

Encouragement came less from the state than from the Chinese, who spread rubber cultivation to native smallholders in the interior. They planted seeds brought from Singapore or cuttings from locally grown trees in flats filled with soil, placing these flats on the roofs of the boats that traveled upstream for trading. When the trader reached his destination, days or weeks later, the seedlings were ready for their recipients.[122]

By the 1920s, the rubber boom was in full swing. Ethnic Chinese took part in the industry as owners of rubber plots, tappers, smallholders, and traders.[123] Rubber became the major cash crop for Chinese, Malay, and, increasingly, Dayak farmers, and by about 1920, rubber cultivation had spread to the hilly interior lands of the Upper Kapuas, Upper Melawi, and Upper Pinoh.[124] In the Chinese districts in 1938, "every Chinese breadwinner has at least two plots, [one] for growing food and a rubber garden."[125] Many Chinese traders tended rubber plots as a sideline.

Because of the dramatic fall in rubber prices during the Depression, the authorities restricted the opening of additional rubber plots in 1934.[126] Hoping to dampen independent production by farmers, they also levied an export tax on the product, but supplies proved relatively stable, since smallholders tended to tap more when prices fell, in order to maintain their income, as had been their practice after prices dropped in 1926. Rather than cut back on production in hard times, farmers discharged their wage laborers and put family members to work tapping the trees. In this way, farmers could still generate some cash income, even though they had to produce more for it. Colonial officials often worried that the farmers' ambitious engagement in rubber cultivation prevented them from dedicating sufficient energy and land to the cultivation of food crops—they had asked similar questions of Dayaks engaged in forest-gathering activities—but there was little they could do beyond encouraging planters to provide for food crops.[127] When the prices of cash crops fell, farmers did turn back to subsistence farming. In reality,

---

[121] Jeroen Touwen, "Chinese Trade and Credit in the Outer Islands of Indonesia 1900-1940," Paper presented to Association of South-East Asian Studies Conference, London, April 1996, pp. 1-2. Touwen, *Extremes*, pp. 156-160, shows how Chinese traders encouraged local people to begin or expand rubber cultivation. Rubber does not really compete with food production in swidden agriculture; it complements it. See Michael R. Dove, "Smallholder Rubber and Swidden Agriculture in Borneo: A Sustainable Adaptation to the Ecology and Economy of the Tropical Forest," *Economic Botany* 47,2 (1993): 136-147.

[122] Memorandum of transfer, J. Oberman, Resident of West Borneo, 1938, ARA 2.10.39 MvO MMK 265, Appendix III, p. 1.

[123] Ranken, "Niet-Europese bijdrage," pp. 196-199.

[124] Azahari, *Ontwikkeling*, p. 79.

[125] Memorandum of transfer, J. Oberman, Resident of West Borneo, 1938, ARA 2.10.39 MvO MMK 265, Appendix II, p. 5.

[126] In connection with the International Rubber Restriction Scheme, see Touwen, *Extremes*, p. 161. Much ink has been spilled on production and export limitations and their effect on prices.

[127] Tobing, *Kalimantan Barat*, p. 36, comments on this problem years later when he remarks, "For the Indonesians, working in the *ladang* is a kind of emergency task. If the forest crops are profitable, they do not attend to their *ladangs*, and at the same time they go to tap rubber, collect gambir, jelutung, damar and other forest products to sell to Chinese *tengkulaks*."

however, the population could produce rubber and grow food crops at the same time, for the labor required for rubber was not so great that it interfered with the planting and tending of rice.[128]

Graph 4.9:
Annual Rubber Exports, Prewar[129]

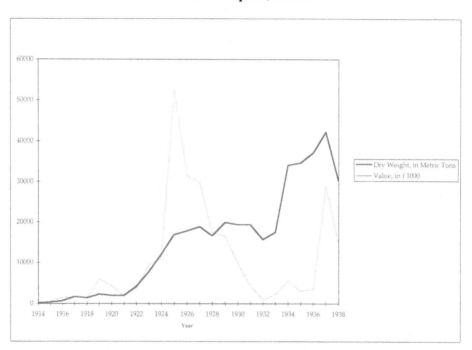

Only in early 1932, when the market price had fallen to a low of about ƒ0.06-0.07 per kilogram (meaning prices were only about ƒ0.045 in the interior), did the region's rubber production significantly drop. One-fourth of the population of the residency now depended on imported rice, one-third of which was purchased with rubber income in "normal" years. In the following year, 1933, rubber production climbed again, despite low prices, or rather, because of them.[130] In 1937, authorities introduced limited quotas and export coupons in the hope of maintaining better prices.[131] Restriction of rubber production and the imposition of special export taxes during the 1930s earned the government ƒ22,000,000—this was money that did not reach the growers. Some of these funds were used for public works to "open up" the province and for other projects designed to provide jobs and cash incomes to

---

[128] Ozinga, *Economische ontwikkeling*, pp. 348-349.

[129] Source: Ozinga, *Economische ontwikkeling*, pp. 293-294. The exports from 1925 to 1934 of dry rubber are certainly too low because of improper conversion to dry weight. Small amounts sent to Java are not included after 1919.

[130] Ibid., pp. 334-337. Rubber production in the Palembang region was much more sensitive to price changes. In 1932, production was half that of 1931, but it climbed quickly in the following years because of rising prices. In other words, the population of West Borneo was much more dependent on cash income from rubber. Touwen, *Extremes*, pp. 166-67, notes that rubber producers in the interior of Borneo had no alternative export crop.

[131] Ozinga, *Economische ontwikkeling*, pp. 247-248, 338ff.

residents.[132] One reason for "opening up" the residency, of course, was to enable the government to collect taxes more easily.

Except at the lowest level of retail trade, the Chinese dominated the marketing of rubber, while the Pontianak Chinese virtually monopolized the its export. After 1924, exports were also processed in Pontianak, and in later years, factories opened in Singkawang and Sambas. By the 1930s, first the Chinese, then others, were taking advantage of the technology that pressed the latex into sheets for smoking, using a device like an old-fashioned clothes wringer to squeeze the coagulated latex. These sheets commanded better prices than raw rubber. A few years later, larger smokehouses were turning out such good quality sheets that they could be sold directly to America and Europe, bypassing remillers in Singapore.[133]

In 1935-37, a "rubber census" found that there were over 8.7 million trees in the province, less than half of them being tapped (because they were too young, too old, or for other reasons). West Borneo had few plantation-sized properties, and its rubber industry functioned with almost no involvement of Western capital; its estimated potential production—the output it could produce if there were no restrictions or quotas—was over seventy thousand tons annually. In 1938, presumably after acreage was limited, 108,000 farmers in the territory still owned rubber plots. Some 5,400 hectares of these fields were contained in "plantations," most of which were relatively small plots held under the plantation law, but the vast majority of owners were smallholders.[134] Among the owners, eleven thousand were Chinese, just thirty were Europeans, thirty-three were Japanese, and 113 were other Foreign Asiatics. The majority of the owners—over 97,000—were Malays, Dayaks, or other native ethnic groups from the Archipelago.[135] The number of people who lived from producing, selling, and processing rubber, when family members are taken into account, must have comprised most of the population (over 800,000 in all) of the residency.[136]

West Borneo contributed significantly to total rubber exports in Indonesia, in spite of the trivial role of plantation production there. In 1934-36, the residency paid about one-fourth of the Indies' total export levy on rubber. In 1937, West Borneo had the largest share of the export quota for smallholders and produced over 21 percent of all rubber exports. In mid-1937, additional quotas were distributed by the government, and the lion's share went to South Sumatra (which included the residencies of Palembang, Lampung, and Bengkulen), with West Borneo in second place (16.03 percent), ahead of South- and East Borneo and Jambi. All other residencies had shares of less than 10 percent each.[137] During these years, the government's restrictions on production slightly improved the quality of the rubber, temporarily improving returns.

---

[132] Ibid., pp. 338-342.

[133] Ibid., pp. 295-299. The authorities favored this change, but local producers and exporters complied willingly.

[134] Cator, *Economic Position*, p. 172, estimated that 2 percent of exports were from "plantations."

[135] Some of these native owners may have been fronts for Chinese.

[136] Memorandum of transfer, J. Oberman, Resident of West Borneo, 1938, ARA 2.10.39 MvO MMK 265, Appendix III, p. 1; Ozinga, *Economische ontwikkeling*, pp. 292, 303-309, 318, 349. Figures differ slightly.

[137] Ozinga, *Economische ontwikkeling*, pp. 284-287, 314-315. This applies to smallholders only. The plantations, concentrated in eastern Sumatra, had other arrangements.

In 1937, total rubber income in the residency climbed by an estimated ƒ20,000,000 (compare graph 4.8).[138] In that year, prices fell again, although they recovered briefly after September 1939 when war broke out in Europe and export quotas were increased accordingly.[139]

Only coconuts could compete with rubber for land and labor, since they were even less labor-intensive, and they grew on coastal land less suitable for rubber. Better prices or income from other products could in no way compensate for the losses in rubber income after 1926. There were no substitutes. People cashed in their meager savings, and, in the end, reduced their standard of living. Many short-term immigrants, who had worked as coolies or sharecroppers, left Borneo after 1930, when the use of wage labor, imported or local, became too expensive, and farmers ceased hiring. Hired labor was even less desirable after rubber exports were limited. Against this background, it is not surprising that the early 1930s saw a significant emigration of the Chinese, most of them back to China.

STATE INTERVENTION: LANDHOLDING

Authorities were of two minds about Chinese trading and agricultural activity, especially when they considered the interior. On the one hand, they realized the importance of Chinese traders to native smallholders. On the other, they feared the Chinese might deprive natives of their land or otherwise cheat them. One answer was to restrict the Chinese settlers' and traders' access to land, another to require them to reside in urban areas. As Resident van der Schalk wrote in 1872:

> It is certain that the Dayaks are exposed to all kinds of vexations on the part of these people, and for these reasons the settlement of Chinese outside of the quarters reserved for their nation is resisted as much as possible, although their visiting the various parts of this district for the purpose of trade may take place freely and without obstruction.[140]

The state intervened in the economic development of the community by determining who had legal titles to property and by issuing leases. At the same time, Chinese farmers felt entitled to the land they had opened and worked:

> The Chinese farmer feels he is no stranger here. He feels himself more entitled to the land than the so-called Native, because the land occupied by him has normally been worked by his family for generations.[141]

The Chinese acquired land easily throughout the nineteenth century. They simply cleared and occupied a plot, with or without the knowledge of the native ruler (who was considered to be the owner of the land in colonial times). Later, they

---

[138] Memorandum of transfer, J. Oberman, Resident of West Borneo, 1938, ARA 2.10.39 MvO MMK 265, Appendix III, p. 41; Memorandum of transfer, P. Salm, Singkawang, 1937, ARA 2.10.39 MvO KIT 989, p. 25; Ozinga, *Economische Ontwikkeling*, pp. 280ff, 333-334.

[139] General Memorandum, Bengkayang, M. Waisvisz, July 12, 1938-May 20, 1941, ANRI BB 287, pp. 46-47.

[140] Political Report, 1872, Resident van der Schalk, ANRI BW 2/10 (230).

[141] Letter, Resident of West Borneo to Director, Civil Service, 1933, ANRI BB 1233.

acquired land by buying or renting it from natives, without inquiring into the legal implications. Especially in the neighborhood of Singkawang and along the roads, Chinese agriculture spread. True, the Dayaks' *ladangs* (dry rice fields) were more often located in hilly or isolated terrain, although this was changing.[142] By the turn of the century, good land in the area was becoming scarce, and in 1916 the government attempted to reserve agricultural land within the native states (that is, in those territories under native rulers, where over 90 percent of the Chinese lived[143]) for natives. This affected the status of the considerable lands already being worked by Chinese farmers. The government also limited the rights of Chinese to work land in other areas ruled directly by the Dutch (without the intervention of the Malay elite), which, in addition to Dayak lands in the interior and part of the town of Pontianak, included Meliau in Sanggau, Pontianak district, areas where many Chinese had settled by 1926.[144]

Nevertheless, the movement of the Chinese into agriculture presented the authorities with a fait accompli. Regulations were imposed after new problems had developed. At first, authorities allowed Chinese to obtain some agricultural land by lease for a limited time; they could lease plots of up to ten hectares for up to twenty years. By 1916, 25,000 plots had been assigned to Chinese in the territories of Sambas, Pontianak, and Mempawah alone. Chinese paid a quit rent (*hasil tanaman*) of one guilder per *bouw*[145] annually to the rulers. Some Chinese protested that ten hectares was too little for a plot to be viable, especially for tree crops, and in any case twenty years was too short a term for a proper lease (although it was true the lease could be extended on application).[146] Partly as a result of such protests, after 1916 new laws were instituted that enabled several thousand commercial crop smallholders to obtain fifty-year leases for long-term crops like coconuts or rubber. Five years later, agricultural laws were enforced more strictly, illegal occupation of land was made punishable, and the old quit rents were raised. Rules kept changing, and the farmers' understanding of the relevant legislation was often confused. In some cases, Chinese farmers had paid lump sums to natives to purchase their land, assuming these transactions were legally binding, when in fact, unbeknown to them, the law forbade them from purchasing native land. The Chinese could not understand the annual payments to the rulers at all.[147]

Later, some rental agreements were changed to long-term right of use (*recht van opstal*), which allowed Chinese farmers to build on their land or to mortgage it for

---

[142] H. E. D. Engelhard, "Bijdragen tot de kennis van het grondbezit in de Chineesche Districten," *Bijdragen tot de Taal-, Land- en Volkenkunde* 51 (1900): 258-259; compare chapter one.

[143] Cator, *Economic Position*, p. 162.

[144] Letter, Department of Interior to Governor General, ca. 1931, ANRI BB 1233.

[145] A *bouw* is about 7,100 square meters.

[146] See Ozinga, *Economische ontwikkeling*, who says many Chinese held multiple plots, but may be incorrect. A 1919 survey by Koppenol, acting Adjunct Inspector for Agricultural Affairs, identified 1,024 Foreign Orientals occupying land in Pemangkat and 2,414 in Singakwang, but very few had contracts for their land, and if they did, it was only right of use. Many Chinese, misunderstanding land rights and taxes, thought they had "bought" the land. In territories under local rulers, "sale" of land to Chinese was not absolutely forbidden until the twentieth century. Report, December 20, 1919, ANRI BB 1113.

[147] The best summary of these laws on Chinese and land is Cator, *Economic Position*, pp. 162-167.

credit.[148] "Illegal" occupation of land continued, however, despite repeated efforts to stop it. In 1931, the procedure for obtaining agricultural land was greatly simplified. By then, some sixteen thousand ethnic Chinese leaseholders had secured fifty-year leases for their holdings, while many others had negotiated leases for shorter periods. Agricultural land could now legally be rented to non-natives, a provision created especially for West Borneo.[149] The government adopted these provisions not so much to encourage and increase Chinese agricultural activity, but, after the fact, to meet the needs of a farming community that already existed.

WEST BORNEO'S ECONOMY ON THE EVE OF WORLD WAR II

West Borneo's economy had changed dramatically in the years since the Kongsi Wars. From a subsistence economy with small sectors engaged in mining or the export of natural products, it had become, first, an exporter of forest products, and subsequently a smallholder economy with coconut and rubber as its major exports.

The exploitation of forest products proved unsustainable; by the 1940s, only people in remote, mountainous areas still collected resins and native rubbers for sale.[150] The cultivation of coconuts and rubber quickly provided cash incomes for much of the population. High prices in the 1920s brought "real" prosperity to the residency; the Depression brought real suffering. The region's food production was insufficient for its population, and if exports fell, so did food supplies. Smallholders benefited greatly from exports, when they did well, but it was difficult or impossible for them to diversify their crops in a manner that would protect them from market fluctuations.[151]

During this transitional period, the Chinese played a major role. In their efforts, they were assisted by Bugis (in the case of coconut production) and of course by the native producers and consumers themselves. West Borneo proved inhospitable for European capital; investments came instead from Asian sources. Borsumij (Borneo-Sumatra Maatschappij, The Borneo-Sumatra Company) was established in Pontianak as an importer in 1901. Another import house, Geo. Wehry, set up a branch there in 1925. A number of Chinese trading houses, however, had established a presence in West Borneo before the turn of the century, in the 1880s or earlier. Even the powerful state-owned shipping company, KPM,

---

[148] Letter, Resident van Prehn to Director of Binnenlands Bestuur, February 13, 1931, ANRI BB 1233.

[149] Agricultural land was of course leased to plantations in eastern Sumatra under long-term leases, but this was supposedly unused, "*woeste*," land. When Chinese sought land in West Borneo, the authorities insisted that it was not "abandoned" but being used by Dayak shifting cultivators or others (which was also the case in much of eastern Sumatra). Memorandum of transfer, H. de Vogel, Resident, West Borneo, 1918, ARA 2.10.39 MvO MMK 261, pp. 56-59; Memorandum of transfer, K. H. van Prehn, Resident, West Borneo, 1933, ARA 2.10.39 MvO MMK 264, p. 16; and Letter of van Prehn, February 13, 1931, ANRI BB 1233; Cator, *Economic Position*, pp. 162-168; Ozinga, *Economische ontwikkeling*, pp. 42-46.

[150] General Memorandum, Bengkayang, M. Waisvisz, July 12, 1938-May 20, 1941, ANRI BB 287.

[151] Ibid. An activity that was increasing in importance, although still small, was the timber industry. Its resources, especially of ironwood, were already threatened in some areas, and the government had set aside reserves.

faced a major Chinese competitor, Thong-Ek, on the route to Singapore, as well as the Straits Steamship Company.[152]

The Chinese trading system of using advances stimulated the production of cash crops, but it tended to leave the native partners permanently in debt, instead of putting cash or savings into their hands. The limited attempts of the Dutch to improve the situation with a people's credit bank offered no real alternative to the Chinese as chief traders and moneylenders; efforts simply failed.[153]

A recent study of Chinese trading activity in the Outer Islands draws conflicting conclusions about the roles of Chinese credit and indigenous smallholders in the region. On the one hand, the study sees the credit system as having encouraged economic activity:

> Chinese credit was more an incentive than an impediment to indigenous entrepreneurship. It enabled peasants to plant and harvest new crops, even though it tied them to their credit-supplier. . . . The middleman earned a large slice of the total profits, but also opened up the regions and stimulated foreign exports . . . .

On the other hand, the same author feels the Chinese credit system hampered efforts to increase productivity:

> The credit system, which implied that money was often spent on direct consumptive expenditure even before the delivery of export products to the creditor was made, may have impeded investments [to increase] productivity.[154]

This conflict runs through all discussions of Chinese relations with native suppliers. From the evidence provided by a study of the 1920s, the effects appeared mostly positive. The "handbook" of 1925 speaks almost lyrically about the "new era" of agriculture and trade that had replaced gold mining.[155] In later years, this perspective changed. Temporarily prosperous, West Borneo in fact remained an area of limited resources and limited possibilities. The Chinese had made a major, but fragile, contribution to the economy, as the war years would show.

---

[152] Uljée, *Handboek*, pp. 88, 91, 94-95.

[153] Ibid., pp. 97-98.

[154] Touwen, *Extremes*, pp. 192, 197.

[155] Uljée, *Handboek*, p. 124.

CHAPTER FIVE

COMMUNITY AND POLITICAL LIFE IN PREWAR TIMES

Undesirable political activities seemed far removed from West Borneo at the turn of the century, and in 1909 a government representative could even say: "What is our verdict on the Borneo Chinese? Very positive."[1] But serious trouble with Chinese recurred between 1912 and 1914, a few years after this rather complacent report, so that the Chinese of West Borneo soon regained their old reputation of rebelliousness and unmanageability. This reputation, which had once been attributed to the kongsi miners, was now assigned by colonial pundits to the increasing numbers of Chinese migrants engaged in other economic pursuits as well, and especially to the Hakkas.

The colonial government tried to use Chinese officers to administer this minority, but because the Chinese population was now growing more rapidly, the government's efforts were largely unsuccessful. As a result, the influence of the colonial bureaucracy over the Chinese weakened. More important and influential than colonial policies or Chinese *kapitans* were the schools and temples that gave form to the community. It was these Chinese institutions, rather than Dutch colonial institutions, that most effectively governed and unified the Chinese communities in West Borneo.

ADMINISTRATION AFTER THE KONGSIS

After the Monterado wars, the number of colonial officials in the province increased rapidly, assistant residencies were reshaped, and control expanded far beyond the coastal bastions. This development made it necessary to assign new Chinese officials and assistants in a number of areas. Sambas, Monterado, and Sintang became assistant residencies, with *controleurs* posted at smaller towns.[2] Monterado, which included the territory of Thaikong and other kongsis, had, besides the assistant resident, four Dutch *controleurs* and a Chinese *kapthai* or regent, three *kapitans* in larger towns, and some thirty *laothais* in smaller ones, as well as a representative of the Sultan of Sambas, who was responsible for

---

[1] L. H. W. van Sandick, *Chineezen buiten China: Hunne beteekenis voor de ontwikkeling van Zuid-Oost-Azië, speciaal van Nederlandsch-Indië* (The Hague: M. van der Beek's Hofboekhandel, 1909), p. 313.

[2] E. de Waal, *West Borneo*, Vol. 8 of *Onze Indische financien*, ed. E. A. G. J. van Delden (The Hague: M. Nijhoff, 1907), p. 20. The numbers of *controleurs* increased to eight and then eleven by 1865.

Plate 11. Sultan of Sambas, 1919.   Credit: Collection of photographs from the
career of O. Horst as Administratief Officier, Controleur, and Assistent-Resident in
Riau, West Borneo, Bali and Lombok, 1912-1938.
Kroch Library Rare and Manuscript Collections, Cornell University Library.
By permission.

administering the native population.[3] In the 1880s, this district's capital was
moved to Singkawang, which had become more important than the former kongsi
headquarters in Monterado because the population was moving toward the coast.
(An indication of Mandor's comparative insignificance in the twentieth century is
that it was administered by a *laothai*, while Sungai Pinyu, a flourishing coastal
market center formerly part of Lanfang Kongsi, had a *kapitan*.[4]) Former
Samtiaokioe territory in Pemangkat and Seminis became part of the assistant
residency of Sambas.[5] As a result, most Chinese were now living in territories ruled
by native rulers, although they were directly subject to Dutch authority.

One of the long-term results of the 1912–14 disturbances (described in detail
below) was to enlarge temporarily the district of Singkawang. In 1914, an expanded
assistant residency of Singkawang was established, which included Singkawang,
Pemangkat, Bengkayang (formerly Lara and Lumar), Sambas, and Mempawah.
The assistant resident who governed this enlarged territory was a "civil and

---

[3] M. von Faber, "Schets van Montrado in 1861," *Tijdschrift voor Indische Taal-, Land- en
Volkenkunde* 13 (1864): 470. Von Faber was the Chinese interpreter in Pontianak in 1860. He
was one of the two first candidates trained in Chinese for colonial service. See Leonard Blussé,
"Of Hewers of Wood and Drawers of Water: Leiden University's Early Sinologists (1853-
1911)," in *The Leiden Oriental Connection*, ed. W. Otterspeer (Leiden: E. J. Brill, 1989), pp. 328-
329. Cf. de Waal, *Onze Indische financien*, 8: 62-63.

[4] Liu Huanren, *Helan Dongyindu gailan* (Singapore: n.p., 1939), p. 46.

[5] De Waal, *Onze Indische financien*, 8: 60, 63-64.

military" official, that is a military man serving in a civilian post, who retained military authority.[6] This assistant residency united all the former Chinese mine districts, including Mandor, which was removed from Pontianak. As a result, the new, enlarged district of Singkawang encompassed all those territories that had been unofficially called the Chinese Districts. The new Singkawang was divided into five subdistricts: Singkawang, Pemangkat, Bengkayang, Sambas, and Mempawah. One of these five, the *onderafdeeling* (sub-district) Pemangkat, was dissolved in 1923, at which time its territory was divided between the sub-districts of Sambas and Singkawang.[7]

As Dutch control extended to the interior in the late nineteenth century, these mostly Dayak areas came to be directly ruled by the Dutch, not subjected to Malay rulers. But the Dutch East Indies control over the interior was weak, at best. In such a vast, undeveloped territory, a handful of colonial officials could perhaps intervene, but not "rule." This situation provided resourceful and daring Chinese traders with attractive opportunities.

It was Chinese traders who promoted the considerable economic changes in the interior (as shown in chapter four). Most settlements in West Borneo that were more substantial than villages had *pasars*. *Pasars* were settlements defined by concentrations of Chinese traders living in their typical shop houses, with the business quarters situated in the front of the premises, at ground level, and family quarters located in the back of the shop or on the upper floor. *Pasars* differed from the market places for petty village traders that were prevalent in Java, in part because *"pasar"* always implied a concentration of Chinese, whether it was located in a former kongsi town, a Malay settlement, or one of the administrative centers in the interior.[8] According to the geographer Karl Helbig, who describes *pasars*, the Chinese built these compact settlements where they found concentrations of traffic (for instance, at fords in rivers, river mouths, and deltas), and these settlements "immediately acquire an urban character," even if there were as few as a dozen houses. Although the Chinese shopkeepers were thought to be relatively prosperous, the houses were weathered and neglected, devoid of comfort, according to Helbig. Along the river were the inevitable bathing places.[9] Houses were usually constructed of wood (sometimes covered with clay for fire resistance), with roofing of *alang-alang*, thatch (*atap*), or the more expensive *sirappen*, ironwood shingles.

Urban wooden construction was convenient, but risky, because it left buildings so vulnerable to fires. Although authorities attempted to convince the settlers to alter their style of building, fire remained a common and recurring threat. The extent of fire damage in certain instances shows how crowded *pasars* typically were. When Singkawang's market burned in 1927, some seventy houses, including two schools, burned.[10] Destructive fires swept through the same market in 1931 and

---

[6] Decree of Governor General, December 12, 1914, ANRI BB 461.

[7] *Encyclopaedie van Nederlandsch-Indië* (The Hague: M. Nijhoff; Leiden: Brill, 1927), p. 1114; Undated Document on Administrative Organization of Singkawang, ca. 1933, ANRI BB 1233.

[8] General Report for 1883, ANRI BW 5/14 (29).

[9] Karl Helbig, *Eine Durchquerung der Insel Borneo (Kalimantan): Nach den Tagebüchern aus dem Jahre 1937* (Berlin: Dietrich Reimer Verlag, 1982), p. 58.

[10] P. Marius van Zevenbergen, "Verwoede brand te Singkawang," *Onze Missiën in Oost- en West-Indië* 11 (1926): 156-158.

in 1937, resulting in the loss of hotels, temples, a mosque, over three hundred houses, and one hundred shops.[11] Pontianak's business district was also repeatedly prey to fires. A fire there did *f*1,000,000 damage in 1917.[12] As late as 1991, a fire in Pontianak's market—now built largely of bricks and mortar—cost lives and extensive material losses.

Plate 12. Chinese stores rebuilt after fires of 1930s in Singkawang, circa 1949.
Credit: Koninklijk Instituut voor de Tropen, Amsterdam, album 457/7, neg 475/36.
By permission.

The Chinese population was primarily concerned with commercial interests or events in China; the local administration made little impression on them. The introduction of the civil registry promised more far-reaching effects; presumably i t was a first step to making European status available to the Chinese (which never happened). Introduced earlier in Java, the official recording of births, deaths, and marriages arrived in Borneo in 1925. In fact, however, little changed as a result of the registry, and this step aroused neither compliance nor sympathy among Chinese settlers. Marrying at the civil registry took time, required papers and documents (in Dutch!), and was, in Chinese eyes, absolutely useless. Persons under thirty years of age had to show proof of parental consent, bureaucratic hours took no account of propitious days chosen by Chinese soothsayers, and the charges were the same for both Europeans and for the less wealthy Chinese. Only some

---

[11] Memorandum of transfer, Resident J. Oberman, 1938, ARA 2.10.39 MvO MMK 265, p. 20.

[12] Memorandum of transfer, Resident H. de Vogel, 1918, ARA 2.10.39, MvO MMK 261, p. 51.

prominent Pontianak Chinese expressed their appreciation for it; otherwise it was a dead letter.[13]

CHINESE OFFICERS

The number of Chinese officers and officials in West Borneo was increasing during these decades. It is not clear, however, that the quality and authority of these new officers were also on the rise:

> It may be added here that the Chinese headmen in the WAfd [Westerafdeeling, West] of Borneo, in contrast to their colleagues in Java, are almost all poor.[14]
> The capability of the Chinese headmen, with a few exceptions, is not laudable. In general, they are not attracted to taking up positions in which they can earn honor but not profit.[15]
> Authority derived only from office—without wealth—is foreign to Chinese understanding and therefore it is absurd to expect that a kapitan without any fortune could exercise personal authority over those officially placed under him.[16]

Since the early decades of the VOC, the Dutch had dealt with the Indies' Chinese residents by appointing Chinese officers as intermediaries, beginning with the first Chinese *kapitans* of Batavia. The Dutch employed this same system when they came to West Borneo. Chinese-speaking Europeans only became available to the bureaucracy in the second half of the nineteenth century,[17] so communication between the Dutch and the Chinese prior to that time was usually managed using Chinese clerks and translators or through Chinese officers who spoke Malay. One such clerk was Lim A Moy, translator for Sambas, who served the government for twenty years before being retired on a pension in 1856. He knew several Chinese dialects and wrote Malay better than some native clerks, it was said, in both Jawi and Roman letters.[18]

In nineteenth-century Pontianak, Chinese officers were appointed and served as intermediaries between the Dutch East Indies government and the Chinese minority, as was the case in Java. Little is known of officers before 1838, although it is certain they existed. In that year, three Chinese *kapitans* for Pontianak are listed in the official almanac: Hong Tjin Nie ("great *kapitan*" or *kapthai*), Lim Nie Po (*kapitan* "*tommongong*," *temenggung* being a Malay title), and Kwee Hoe

---

[13] Note about Civil Registry, Pontianak, 1948, ARA 2.21.120: 59. A colonial official summed up the experience on Java in his title, "The Fiasco of the Civil Registry for Chinese," concluding "Speak in heaven's name legal certainty, get rid of the mess at once. . . " A. J. B. Maclaine Pont, "Het Fiasco van den Burgerlichen Stand voor Chineezen," *Koloniale Studien* 8,2 (1924): 312. See chapter seven for some repercussions of the civil registry.

[14] List of persons to be rewarded for aid in suppressing Mandor revolt, in ARA 2.10.02 V. 31.5.86 (36).

[15] *Koloniaal Verslag* (1872): 13

[16] W. G. Elenbaas, "West-Borneo. Eenige mededeelingen aangaande bevolking en bestuur," *Indische Gids* 31,2 (1909): 918.

[17] See note 3 (above).

[18] Administrative Report, 1856, ANRI BW 3/12.

Toan (*kapitan "salewatan"* or *"salawatang"* [meaning unknown]). Although the titles are unexplained, we know that each individual was responsible for one of the three major speech communities: Teochiu, Hakka, and Hokkien. Hong Tjin Nie, the *kapthai,* hailed from the largest community, the Teochiu.[19]

As in Java, Chinese officers remained in office for years, far longer than most colonial officials, and were closely linked to the opium monopolies. In 1840, Song Assam became *kapitan* of Sambas. From 1844-49, he is also listed as *majoor* (major; thus Sambas had a major before Pontianak did). Song had arrived in Sambas as a poor immigrant and amassed great wealth during his twenty-one years there.[20] Also in Sambas, Liao Kang Sing was acting *kapitan* for a time before he held office as official *kapitan* from 1853-1872. He had begun his career as translator for the Dutch. His appointment, to which he brought excellent qualifications but no wealth, was a reward for his service during the negotiations with Thaikong.[21] Liao's rise from interpreter to officer was, however, an exception.

KWEE HOE TOAN AND OTHER NOTABLE OFFICERS

Perhaps more "typical" of successful officers was Kwee Hoe Toan. In 1845, this Hokkien Chinese, who was already listed as a *kapitan* in 1838, became "great *kapitan,*" and in 1859 he was promoted to *majoor.*[22] Although the Hokkiens were the smallest of the three main groups in Pontianak, Kwee was elevated over the representatives of the others; this may have happened because he was more compatible with colonial officials, who were familiar with Hokkiens from Java. Kwee advised the government during the negotiations with Thaikong. He was one of the richest Chinese in Borneo.[23] In 1856, he was guarantor of the opium farm; earlier, he had been a farmer himself. The Dutch considered him reliable and trustworthy, but "greedy." Kwee was a literate man. Although born and raised in Borneo, he was able to read and write Chinese and to speak different Chinese languages. Lt. Col. Le Bron de Vexela, head of the expedition against Monterado, arrested Kwee in 1851 and kept him in prison for two months because he had sent opium to Sungai Pinyu and Mempawah. The arrest was unjust, since Kwee, as opium farmer, was acting legally. Despite having been wronged by the authorities, and losing money in the process, Kwee continued to serve as *majoor* until 1862.

In the following year Kwee's son, Kwee Kom Beng, appears in the record as *kapitan,* and he held office until 1880, when he was discharged. The younger Kwee was repeatedly called "more Malay than Chinese," a quality that would not appear to qualify him for his job as Chinese officer, and he was known to be close to the court of Pontianak.[24]

---

[19] Political Report 1856, ANRI BW 1/7. There was no tradition of separate officers for the different speech groups in Java, where Hokkiens dominated until the twentieth century.

[20] T. A. C. van Kervel and D. W. J. C. van Lijnden, "Bijdrage tot de kennis van Borneo: De hervorming van den maatschappelijken toestand ter westkust van Borneo," *Tijdschrift voor Nederlandsch Indië* 15,1 (1853): 191, 194.

[21] Report on Chinese Society in West Borneo, 1852, ANRI BW 28/32.

[22] *Regeringsalamanak voor Nederlandsch-Indië,* various years.

[23] Chinese Conferences in Pontianak, 1852-53, ANRI BW 31/8 (87). Kwee and Kapitan Lay A Tjhok (or A Tjioh) were observers of the negotiations with kongsi representatives in December 1852 and January 1853.

[24] Political Report 1866, ANRI BW 2/4 (224).

The Kwee family later fell on hard times. Kwee Hoe Toan and the Hakka *kapitan,* Then Sioe Lin, had accumulated heavy debts to the government as a result of their involvement in the opium farms in the 1850s, a decade when the trade in opium plummeted because of smuggling and the decline of gold mining. (The fortunes of the Kwee family would decline further after 1880, when Kwee Kom Beng was discharged from office.) The finances of the *kapthai,* Lioe A Sin, of Lanfang, also suffered as a result of speculation in the farm.[25] Opportunities for Chinese who aspired to amass fortunes, and, perhaps, gain influence, by acting as revenue farmers diminished because the farm declined through the second half of the nineteenth century.

Like Kwee, Then Sioe Lin was appointed to be an officer after having proven his abilities as a trader and businessman. Then Sioe Lin acted as the Hakka *kapitan* of Pontianak from 1853–1877. A wealthy man, Then Sioe Lin was involved in trade and in revenue farming together with Kapthai Lioe A Sin of Mandor, who was also his brother-in-law. The two had common business undertakings and, although the authorities recognized Then Sioe Lin's intelligence and good service, his modernity and "cheerful nature,"[26] they knew he placed his own interests first. When Kapitan Eng Tjong Kwee of Monterado died in the late 1850s, the authorities appointed a relative of Then Sioe Lin, Lioe Tjong Sin, as Eng's successor as vice-regent or *kapitan* in the former Thaikong territory. This was an obvious attempt to increase the influence of non-kongsi Chinese there, especially since Tjang Ping remained *kapthai*-regent.

A year after Lioe Tjong Sin's appointment as *kapitan* in Monterado, Tjang Ping was suddenly removed from office, pensioned, and told to move to Pontianak, because he was suspected of involvement in an attempt on Lioe's life. Two years later, Tjang was rehabilitated, given a salary of one hundred guilders monthly, but not allowed to resume his duties—the office of *kapthai* of Monterado was abolished. The tide had turned: Lioe found himself sentenced to fifteen years' labor in chains for false charges against Tjang, although this sentence was later withdrawn. At the same time, several *laothais* were removed from office for misbehavior. Lioe, not Tjang, was the originator of the conspiracy; apparently he had hoped to take over the position of *kapthai* himself.[27] The case demonstrates how fragile Dutch intelligence was in the absence of qualified Chinese language personnel.

OPIUM FARMING

Throughout most of the Indies, the Dutch maintained "farms"—functioning commercial monopolies, administered by agents who shared in the profits—for important taxable commodities or commercial activities. By cooperating with the

---

[25] Political Report 1859, ANRI BW 1/10; General Report 1880, ANRI BW 5/11; see also chapter three, "Decline of Lanfang."

[26] Then had a happy disposition ("vrolijk van aard"), according to the Political Report for 1866, ANRI BW 2/4.

[27] Political Report 1856, ANRI BW 1/7; Political Report 1859, ANRI BW 1/10; Political Report 1862, ANRI BW 1/11 (218). ANRI BW 1/12 (219) and ANRI BW 1/13 (220) are about the Tjang/Lioe case (with Tjang's rehabilitation) and the *laothais*. Lioe, as a relative of Then, may have come from the family of Lioe A Sin of Lanfang, to which Then was linked through his sister.

"farmers" who were granted de facto monopolies over certain enterprises and who organized and directed these enterprises, the East Indies' government earned substantial sums for the colonial treasury. A number of the Chinese appointed as officers were also engaged in revenue farming and accumulated wealth and influence through this means. In the Outer Islands, the most lucrative farms were located in areas where many Chinese lived, and one of the most lucrative commodities was opium. As noted above, the influential Kwee Hoe Toan was involved with the West Borneo opium farm in different capacities for a number of years.

Throughout the first half of the nineteenth century, opium had been an important commodity in mining communities, including in the gold mines. In 1892, Buys wrote:

> Everywhere in the Indies, where I found a Chinese *kampung*, I saw a gambling house, which in many places also served as the opium den, the tavern, and the bordello.[28]

During its heyday, Monterado had had several opium dens, and most miners, many other Chinese, and some non-Chinese, were regular visitors.

The situation changed with the decline of mining. Income generated by the opium farm declined precipitously in the second half of the nineteenth century. While this regional enterprise had earned as much as ƒ400,000 before 1855, earnings dwindled to one-fifth of that amount in subsequent years.[29] The decline came unexpectedly, and it cost officers like Kwee Hoe Toan, who in 1854 won control of the farm for West Borneo, dearly. His co-farmers for the Chinese Districts were the former negotiators of Thaikong, Eng Tjong Kwee and Tjang Ping. Eng was a wealthy man, and he continued to be involved in the opium farms—a speculative activity—for some years.[30]

Soon, reduced revenues began to have an impact on the management of the farms and on the local Chinese elites who had profited from this business when it was thriving. In 1868, the right to control the West Borneo opium farm was even granted to an outsider, the lieutenant of the Chinese from the island of Belitung, Ho A Joen. Ho's lack of a firm local base resulted in a substantial financial loss, but the decline in the value of the farm would have probably taken place even if an "insider" had been granted control, since it was part of a larger trend resulting from demographic changes in the region. Between 1865 and 1874, the value of the

---

[28] Marius Buys, *Twee maanden op Borneo's Westkust: Herinneringen* (Leiden: Doesburgh, 1892), p. 192.

[29] Jacob Ozinga, *De economische ontwikkeling der Westerafdeeling van Borneo en de bevolkingsrubbercultuur* (Wageningen: N. V. gebr. Zomer en Keuning, 1940), p. 222; Political Report 1856, ANRI BW 1/7. Population decline was not the only cause for the decrease in earnings, since, as the population changed from one of miners to one of settlers, demand also dropped. In addition to fewer customers, there was also a problem of default by the opium farmers, many of whom overestimated income.

[30] Letter from Commissioner Prins to Governor General, Sambas, 1854, ARA 2.10.02 V. 1.12.54 (4). Originally, the farm was to go to Monterado directly (chapter three). Since the farms were put out at auction, and the winners had to pay the sum they offered to the colonial government, bidders had to estimate in advance what the income from the farm would be. Declining use wreaked havoc with estimates, as did smuggling.

official opium farm in West Borneo dropped from ƒ261,800 to ƒ96,900. It recovered in the 1880s and early 1890s to slightly over ƒ100,000, but then it fell again. By this time, the Pontianak opium farm was the most valuable of the farms in the region because its urban laborers were also opium users. For the residency as a whole, other revenue farms (those that managed gambling, alcohol, and the slaughter of pigs) brought in more profits than opium.[31] The fate of the opium farm reflects the changed population of the residency. With a population of settled farmers and traders, as opposed to bachelor miners, demand for the drug continued to drop.

In 1901, the West Borneo farm was rented for ƒ98,040. The much smaller territories of Bangka and Belitung islands, each of which contained about twenty thousand Chinese tin miners, sold their farms for much greater sums—ƒ279,924 and ƒ168,000 respectively—while the plantation region of East Sumatra brought the government ƒ803,600 in opium revenue.[32] In 1909, the farm "system" was finally dismantled, to be replaced by an official government monopoly that controlled the sale of opium throughout the Indies.[33]

CONDITIONS FOR THE OFFICERS

After the dissolution of Thaikong and Samtiaokioe, and with the expansion of Chinese migration to the interior, the colonial administration found it needed more officers to control the Chinese settlers residing outside major towns. The administration had, at first, chosen officers who were associated with the abolished kongsis, but thought to be pro-Dutch; later it decided, instead, to select influential Chinese townspeople who had no emotional ties or residual allegiances to the former associations. This action, however, probably left the officers with even less authority.[34]

When the substantial Lanfang Kongsi was abolished in 1884—the last of the kongsis to disappear—the Dutch found it necessary to create a new hierarchy of Chinese appointees to help govern the large area formerly administered by the kongsi. The new administration at first resembled that of the kongsi. Under the Dutch, there was a *kapitan* (but not a *kapthai*) for the whole former area of Lanfang. *Laothais* had administrative authority in smaller settlements, and villages or residential quarters were *kaptjongs* (probably *jiazhang*).

Some officers in West Borneo were paid, others were not. In the former territories of Thaikong and Samtiaokioe, *kapitans*, *laothais*, and other equivalent officers received a salary. In Pontianak, Mempawah, and Sambas, *kapitans* did not. But even in those cases where officers did receive payment, the salaries offered by the Dutch were meager and unreliable, and certainly not sufficient to insure that the officers would put colonial interests first. Salaried officers often found it necessary to hire policemen-enforcers from their modest incomes. Two

---

[31] Political Report 1867, ANRI BW 2/5; Political Report 1869, ANRI BW 2/7; Political Report 1873, ANRI BW 2/11. Ho had been the lieutenant of the Chinese in Belitung for several years. Consumption dropped, but other factors might also contribute to the decline in opium use and profit: easier smuggling and a conspiracy of the bidders to cease bidding against one another. For the farm in the 1880s, see *Koloniaal Verslag*, (1880) and ff.

[32] *Koloniaal Verslag* (1901): Appendix FF.

[33] P. M. van Meteren Brouwer, "De geschiedenis der Chineesche Districten der Wester-Afdeeling van Borneo van 1740-1926," *Indische Gids* 49,2 (1927): 1096.

[34] Political Report 1859, ANRI BW 1/10.

unsalaried *kapitans* who were too poor to meet the demands of office, the Hokkien Lay A Tjhok of Pontianak and his colleague Liao Kang Sing in Sambas, received a financial bonus in the form of free salt from the government salt monopoly. They were able to sell this commodity to raise needed funds.[35] Other officers received awards for good performance, and in time money replaced salt as a form of compensation.[36] Finally, after 1862, headmen (*kapitans*) were granted the right to exact one-third of the head tax they collected from residents in their districts and one-third of the tax levied on Chinese returning to China as reward/payment for satisfactory performance of duties.[37]

Especially in the early years of expansion, many Chinese officials chosen by the Dutch proved unfit. Finding influential Chinese men who could communicate with the Dutch and with the local Malay population was not always easy. It appears that Chinese residing in the former kongsi areas, including Singkawang, did not know Malay well, unlike their compatriots in Pontianak and Sambas, who were often fluent in Malay. Phong Seak, *kapitan* of Singkawang, asked in 1856 to be relieved of his office because he understood no Malay.[38] Some officers appointed by the Dutch were too ignorant or too greedy, others were not loyal to the colonial power, and still others feared those over whom they were expected to exercise power. Once they attained a place in the bureaucracy, Chinese officers often advanced their personal interests at the expense of either the government or the Chinese population or both.

One officer was found guilty of mistreating a number of Chinese settlers, but the colonial administration allowed him to remain in office because it could not find a replacement.[39] In 1872, the complaints about the officers, especially the lesser ones, increased. Qualified Chinese simply avoided non-paying positions.[40] In 1881, because few candidates for office could be found, the administration offered officials a salary of *f*600 to *f*1,200 yearly, but to save money, it reduced the numbers of officers.[41] This measure did not attract better quality candidates or win the appointed officers more prestige. The job could bring danger, as happened in 1912, when rebels assaulted a number of officers; a few weeks later they set fire to the house of the *kapitan* of Monterado.[42]

It becomes difficult to trace the careers of even the most prominent officers who were appointed in West Borneo after the rebellions of 1912–14. During the term of Resident H. de Vogel, the names of Chinese officers in West Borneo were not

---

[35] Political Report 1857, ANRI BW 1/8. A similar gift of 150 *piculs* of salt was made to the *kapitan* of Sambas. See Political Report of 1867, ANRI BW 2/5.

[36] Tjang Ping received the sum of one thousand guilders. Political Report 1858, ANRI BW 1/9.

[37] Political Report 1859, ANRI BW 1/10; Political Report 1861, ANRI BW 1/12; Political Report 1862, ANRI BW 1/13, citing Decree (Besluit) no. 1 of August 3, 1862.

[38] Political Report 1856, ANRI BW1/7.

[39] Political Report 1857, ANRI BW 1/8.

[40] Political Report 1872, ANRI BW 2/10.

[41] De Waal, *Onze Indische financien*, 8: 69. This refers to "troubles" with the introduction of the new tax in 1878-1879. Van Meteren Brouwer, "Geschiedenis," p. 1096, says the change occurred in 1892.

[42] Memorandum of transfer, Resident Th. H. H. van Driessche, 1912, ARA 2.10.39 MvO MMK 260, p. 56; Memorandum of transfer, Resident K. A. James, 1921, ARA 2.10.39 MvO MMK 262, p. 33.

recorded in the official almanac (*Regeringsalmanak*), although those in other residencies were listed. Some records of the officers do surface again in the mid-1920s, in the *Handboek voor de Residentie Westerafdeeling van Borneo*. The *Handboek* shows that, in 1925, there were fourteen *kapitans* with varying periods of service: two of the men had been in office since 1901, and two had been appointed in 1923. Only one *kapitan* held office in Pontianak; he was Tjia Tjeng Siang, appointed 1911[43]; in 1930, he appears in the official almanac as an honorary major. After that year, and until 1942, the main officers for West Borneo were again listed in the *Regeringsalmanak*. In the 1930s, there were only three *kapitans*—in Singkawang, Pemangkat, and Monterado—sixteen *laothais*, and twelve *kaptjongs*. In 1942, eight *kapitans* are listed in major settlements. Kwee Eng Hoe, who may have been related to the other Kwees of the capital, was *kapitan* in Pontianak from 1933 until the Japanese Occupation.[44]

After 1921, the number of Chinese officers administering West Borneo was reduced two more times. The headmen's salaries were now so low that headmen had to engage in other occupations to maintain a living, and in the 1930s, when the Depression hit, their need to earn money for themselves competed with, and often overwhelmed, their devotion to governmental duty. According to official sources, the sum of taxes collected by five Chinese headmen in 1931 was *f*24,000 lower than it should have been; the reports suggest the headmen had kept the difference. Chinese officials generally saw themselves as part of the local community rather than the administration, and many of them were probably Guomindang members. [45] Disinterested and competent leaders were rare, it appears, among the Chinese officers.

Though perhaps neither disinterested nor competent, the Chinese officers figured as a very crucial link for a colonial administration largely unable to communicate with its Chinese-speaking population. Aside from clerk-interpreters of Chinese origin, only the Chinese officers could speak both to the Chinese population and the Dutch administration (and take advantage of opportunities to manipulate information they passed on in their own favor). Only in 1860, as noted, did a European interpreter join the administration in Pontianak. These translators or "Officers for Chinese Affairs," as they were later called, were supposed to give the administration a window on Chinese society and politics untainted by local interests. Unfortunately for the administration, most of these European appointees, however competent, spent little time in the residency before moving on to other posts.[46] After 1930, two ethnic Chinese also worked as translators for the political

---

[43] G. L. Uljée, *Handboek voor de Residentie Westerafdeeling van Borneo* (Weltevreden: Visser & Co., 1925), p. 138.

[44] *Regeringsalamanak voor Nederlandsch-Indië*, various years. The reason for the hiatus is unclear. Perhaps it was de Vogel's revenge for the rebellion. In 1942, *kapitans* were in Pontianak, Singkawang, Pemangkat, Monterado, Bengkayang, Sambas, Mempawah and Sungai Pinyu, reflecting the importance of the Chinese communities in these towns. Honorary majors and other officers with honorary titles no longer existed. By the 1930s, Chinese officers had already been abolished in Java.

[45] Letter of Resident, Pontianak, March 14, 1931, ANRI BB 1233. Guomindang is the Nationalist Party of China, founded by Sun Yatsen.

[46] *Koloniaal Verslag* (1860): 51. M. von Faber became the first Chinese-language interpreter in Pontianak; see note 3. In 1862, von Faber joined Gustaaf Schlegel as interpreter at the High Court in Batavia. W. P. Groeneveldt was named to the post in August 1864; he remained until 1871, when the post appears to have fallen vacant after he moved to Padang. De Groot was

intelligence office.[47] Their work contributed to the periodic surveys of political activity in the residency.[48]

If appointees were unsuitable, the fault lay not only with the Chinese. Colonial officials feared that genuinely popular leaders might be disloyal or unreliable, and for this reason they were disinclined to appoint them or to increase the salaries or prestige of those already in office.[49] The Dutch had neither the resources nor the will to pay the officers adequately. They could assert their authority over the Chinese residents, but hardly enforce it. They collected taxes from the Chinese through the officers—in fact, Chinese were the major source of government revenue—and issued regulations, but they rarely interacted with the Chinese traders or settlers. Not surprisingly, control over the Chinese remained superficial and the influence of Dutch colonial culture on the Chinese population minor. Even in 1942, the colonial state was still in the process of establishing its authority in the province; West Borneo had no "civil society" in colonial times.

TAXES, TAXES

The nexus of Dutch-Chinese relations in West Borneo was taxes. Corvée (until the early twentieth century) and revenue farms also figured as significant sources of income for the state, but taxes predominated:

> If we examine the history of the Chinese fortresses and autonomous territories (and this history is still not completely forgotten), then we must conclude that the Government put an end to the influence of the Chinese kongsis' power with a heavy hand, but that the Government up to now has done little for the Chinese. The Chinese here knew the "Company" until recently as the institution that collected taxes and sold opium. It is really not so surprising that the Chinese has little sympathy for our Government.[50]

The colonial state's policy was to tax the Chinese as much as possible in order to meet the administrative costs of the residency, pay allowances for the native rulers, and defray the costs of improving communications and maintaining order. Normally, the Chinese officers collected and even assessed these taxes.

---

posted to the area from 1880 to March 1883. See Blussé, "Hewers of Wood," pp. 335, 344, 346; de Groot's Stamboek (personnel record) ARA 2.10.06, W113. Among others, Sinologist and writer Henri Borel also spent time in Pontianak, but none had Groeneveldt's perseverance.

[47] *Politieke Recherche*, see *Regeringsalamanak voor Nederlandsch-Indië*, 1930 and ff.

[48] The political police reports of 1927-1941 have been collated in the important *Politiek-Politioneele Overzichten van Nederlandsch-Indië*, ed. Harry Poeze, Vols. I-IV (The Hague: M. Nijhoff, 1982; Dordrecht: Foris, 1983 and 1988; Leiden: KITLV, 1994).

[49] Memorandum of transfer, Resident K. A. James, 1921, ARA 2.10.39 MvO MMK 262, p. 33; Memorandum of transfer, Resident J. H. Meijer, 1927, ARA 2.10.39 MvO MMK 263, p. 25; Memorandum of transfer, Resident J. Obeman, 1938, ARA 2.10.39, MvO MMK 265, appendix 8, p. 4a.

[50] Report on Chinese Education in West Borneo, 1916, ARA 2.10.02 V. 20.6.1917 (62). Ming Govaars-Tjia kindly made available a transcript of this report, signed by Resident de Vogel and Chinese affairs officer Snellen van Vollenhoven. "Company (*kumpeni*)" was the government, so-called in reference to the East India Company long after that was abolished.

Taxing Chinese to meet local expenses began around 1818, with the head taxes for Chinese. From 1839 to 1852, the colonial administration of Sambas had always posted losses, and Pontianak nearly always cost the Indies government more than i t earned; the Second Kongsi War left the government account with a negative balance of over *f*1.2 million, an enormous sum for the province.[51] Prins, as government commissioner after 1853, quickly established tax regulations for the newly subjected, former kongsi districts. While the Dutch imposed a general tax on imports—excepting rice—and directly administered a salt monopoly, they collected taxes on other goods and activities through farms, by granting de facto administrative and commercial monopolies to the highest bidders, who were usually Chinese. Commodity trading and commercial and recreational activities that were taxed through farms included, besides trading in opium: the brewing and sale of alcoholic beverages, the slaughter of pigs and sale of pork, gambling (the Chinese games *pho* and *topho* were run by tax farmers), running pawnshops, fishing near the shores of Singkawang, Sungai Raya, and Sungai Duri, mining gold, and collecting provincial import tariffs and exit taxes for those returning to China. Only the exit tax had not been administered by the farmers before 1855, and it was withdrawn in 1864.[52] By that time, the various revenue farms were bringing in well over *f*300,000 annually. In time, opium revenue fell, as mentioned above, but profits from other farms, except those for gold mining, increased.[53] In addition to these impositions, and apart from the government head tax, the Chinese were also expected to pay taxes of 10 percent on the collection and export of forest products, and to pay rent to native rulers for the use of the land.[54]

In 1879, the Dutch introduced a progressive replacement for the head tax; this was the *bedrijfsbelasting*, a firm or business tax, based on the amount of property one owned, including property individually held.[55] While this new system promised relief for the poorest taxpayers, in fact they continued to pay the same amount as they had when the head tax was being collected, while the wealthier Chinese paid more. The long and difficult process of assessing property in order to determine the amount of tax owed aroused strong opposition among the Chinese. Lanfang was a center of resistance, but in that area the *kapthai* and the colonial military cooperated to quash it. Throughout West Borneo, natives were exempt from the property tax, although elsewhere in the Indies some indigenous property owners were required to pay it.

This tax was assessed in 1879 at *f*39,415 for the residency, the highest in the Outer Islands, reflecting the economic importance of the Chinese community in West Borneo. Yet at the time of this assessment, the economy of West Borneo was not prospering, and population, as noted in chapter four, was declining.

In comparison, Palembang's tax was about the same (*f*38,000), but nearly two-thirds of it (*f*24,000) was paid by natives. Other areas of the Outer Islands paid

---

[51] *Koloniaal Verslag* (1854): 86.

[52] *Koloniaal Verslag* (1855): 79; *Koloniaal Verslag* (1864): 13. Apparently, the authorities thought the Chinese leaving Borneo were not so well off after all.

[53] *Koloniaal Verslag* (1869) and ff.

[54] *Koloniaal Verslag* (1865): 141. The tax on forest products also fell on natives. It was called *sepuluh-satu*, "for ten, one."

[55] *Koloniaal Verslag* (1879): 20. Beginning in 1887, Arabs were exempt from this tax, *Koloniaal Verslag* (1893): Appendix VV.

less than a third of that amount.[56] In 1887, the total assessments in West Borneo on 12,430 Chinese reached ƒ45,068, but at the end of the year over one-third of that sum remained uncollected. The opium farm, despite its falling income, brought in twice the total revenue gleaned by the property tax in that year. Most persons—in 1887, they numbered 870—were assessed at the lowest rate, two or three guilders per year (the amount of the former head tax). About one-fourth of the Chinese residents paid less than ten guilders, while only eight persons were assessed at over fifty guilders. The tax continued to climb (in 1898 it was ƒ58,333), but the average contribution per taxpayer, ƒ4.11, remained relatively low, compared to the average for Java and Madura, which was ƒ10.71, and for the Outer Islands as a whole, which was about five guilders. The numbers of Chinese in West Borneo, not their wealth, made the property tax profitable for the treasury.

The fact that Chinese officers were responsible for assessing property subject to the new tax made them, understandably, even less loved or respected. The colonial administration was collecting taxes from the Chinese with the help of badly paid Chinese officials.[57] It then left these men to their fate.

REBELLION OF 1912-1914

Beginning with an incident in 1912, the Chinese Districts, especially inland areas, suddenly posed a serious security problem for the colonial administration. The uprising was not expected by Dutch administrators:

> The attitude of the Chinese in these [rural, inland] districts is somewhat better than that at the coast. . . . It seems surprising at first glance that the rebellion began in just those districts with a more positive attitude to the government, but this is understandable if it is known that these Chinese inhabitants experienced the pressure of the corvée the most—the rich buy themselves off—and that they were stirred up by agitators from the coast, not to mention that it is rumored that rich traders from the coast provided money.[58]

The arrival in 1912 of a new, energetic resident, Henry de Vogel (in office 1912-1918;[59] see plate 13), who had plans for "developing" the largely neglected residency, certainly contributed to the unrest. At the same time, evidence suggests that trouble was brewing prior to the arrival of de Vogel. Beginning in 1906, rumors of new "secret society" activity had circulated in the residency. Administrators were also concerned that the influence of Chinese nationalism among the Chinese

---

[56] *Koloniaal Verslag* (1879): 168. ƒ12,000 was collected in West Sumatra; other areas paid less than ƒ10,000 each.

[57] A. H. Böhm, *West Borneo 1940-Kalimantan Barat 1950* (Tilburg: Gianotten, 1986), pp. 46-47.

[58] Report on Chinese Education in West Borneo, ARA 2.10.02 V. 20.6.17 (62). Ironically, Resident de Vogel is co-author of this report, although he repeatedly denied that the corvée was responsible for the rebellion (below). The report goes on to say that this "better attitude" consists not in being pro-Dutch, but in being less influenced by Chinese nationalism.

[59] Henry de Vogel M. Hzn., born in Magelang in 1862, had been in service in the Outer Islands of the Indies since 1884. He was honorably discharged from service at his own request in 1918; see his record in ARA 2.10.36.015 Stamboek B' 78.

in Southeast Asia might be spilling over into Borneo.[60] After the uprising had been quelled, the government—and above all the Resident—would blame these new political currents for the unrest, but it seems clear that official demands, not ideology, had brought some Chinese to the breaking point.[61]

Not surprisingly, given their position, Chinese officers were the first victims of the uprising. In early 1912, a Chinese officer in Buduk who had tried to arrest an agitator was forced to flee for his life. In October 1912, two lesser Chinese officers (*laothai*) in Salinse (near Bengkayang) and Benuwang (near Anjungan) were brutally murdered. Rumors of an impending, possibly widespread, uprising multiplied. Resistance involved the Chinese Districts and Tayan. In 1912, Dayaks from Landak, whose connection to the Chinese is unclear, protested violently against increased taxes, but Landak was quiet again by mid-1913.[62] Rumors circulated that China—which was proclaimed a republic on January 2, 1912—was sending warships to free the Chinese in Borneo from Dutch oppression. In some areas, posters urging Chinese not to pay their taxes appeared and resistance grew. The military had to enforce tax collection in several places.[63]

Colonial reports put the blame for these incidents partly on purported "secret society" activity and partly on Chinese nationalism.[64] Nationalist activities had introduced movements such as the Chinese chambers of commerce (M. *shanghui*) and political reading clubs (M. *shubaoshe*, literally "book and newspaper society," see below) to the area. Yet on closer examination it appears that the unrest resulted from tax increases, corvée demands, and the strict implementation of the rule that Chinese carry passes when traveling. (At one point, they were even required to carry lanterns after dark.)[65]

---

[60] Van Meteren Brouwer, "Geschiedenis," p. 1096. See also Report on Secret Society Activity among Chinese, ARA 2.10.36.03 Politieke Verslagen, Microfiche 395, V.11.5.08 (29). There was a certain overlap between the Guomindang and the "secret societies," something de Vogel's advisors emphasized.

[61] The Siauw Giap, "Rural Unrest in West Kalimantan: The Chinese Uprising in 1914," in *Leyden Studies in Sinology* (Sinica Leidensia XV), ed. W. L. Idema (Leiden: E. J. Brill, 1981), pp. 138-152, discusses the events and their causes. Colonial officials often blamed mysterious "agitators" and "ringleaders" for unrest, while economic troubles and the expansion of colonial demands were often the more obvious causes. For example, some taxes were increased under de Vogel's predecessor because appanages were being abolished and the native rulers needed income (Report on New Taxes, ARA 2.10.36.03 Politieke Verslagen, Microfiche 408, MR 1911:1737). Subsequently, de Vogel increased the financial burden through additional levies.

[62] Anonymous, "De Chineezen in West-Borneo," *Indische Gids* 35,1 (1913): 225-226. By this time, Landak was no longer a native principality. See Secret Telegram to Governor General on Murders, ARA 2.10.36.02 Politieke Verslagen, Microfiche 415, MR 1912:1941; Report on Chinese Taxes and Dayak Troubles, Microfiche 419, MR 1913:241; also Reports on End of Hostilities in Landak, Microfiche 442, MR 1913:1949; and MR 1913:2097. The Dayaks were Behe, Dait, Semarua, Seéngsatong, and Menyukei.

[63] Van Meteren Brouwer, "Geschiedenis," p. 1097; Details of Murder of Laothai, ARA 2.10.36.03 Politieke Verslagen, Microfiche 415, MR 1912:2210; Letter of Acting Assistant Resident, Pontianak, November 22, 1912 on Rebellion in Landak, Microfiche 415, MR 1912:2217; and Telegram of Resident, March 25, 1913, Microfiche 420, MR 1913:820.

[64] As does van Meteren Brouwer, "Geschiedenis," p. 1097.

[65] The, "Rural Unrest," pp. 150-151. There are no reports of corvée labor in West Borneo in the surveys of corvée published in the *Koloniaal Verslag* in the 1890s, but this must be an omission. For the lantern requirement, see Telegram of Minister of Kolonies to Governor General, ARA 2.10.36.04 V. 25.1.22 (72).

In addition, after 1900, the Chinese population experienced a strong influx of new immigrants (see graph 4.3, p. 131), and control of this growing population became a problem.[66] In the first quarter of 1913, nearly a thousand entry permits had been granted to Chinese arriving in Pontianak. De Vogel feared an "invasion" of Chinese, involving the "worst"—that is pro-republican—elements.[67] To many colonial officials—and de Vogel was one of them—the Chinese Revolution of 1911 appeared suspect and dangerous, and republican sympathizers figured as mere riffraff. Whether these immigrants were, in fact, followers of Sun Yatsen is open to question.

Plate 13. Henry de Vogel, M. Hzn., Resident of West Borneo. Credit: Collection of photographs from the career of O. Horst as Administratief Officier, Controleur, and Assistent-Resident in Riau, West Borneo, Bali and Lombok, 1912-1938.
Kroch Library Rare and Manuscript Collections, Cornell University Library.
By permission.

While the Dutch administration was eager to blame immigrants and *provocateurs* for the uprising, in fact its own actions undoubtedly contributed to Chinese resentment. Colonial demands on the Chinese had increased with de Vogel's arrival. The first burden was road-building. De Vogel was correct in his judgment that the roads of West Borneo needed repair. In 1832, according to a witness, there was "not one road worthy of the name in all of the West Coast of

---

[66] W. J. Cator, *The Economic Position of the Chinese in the Netherlands Indies* (Oxford: Blackwell, 1936), pp. 158-159.

[67] Report on Immigration to West Borneo, ARA 2.10.36.04 V. 6.1.14 (85). Arrivals increased to over six thousand in 1913, but they fell drastically during 1914-18 because the war in Europe made shipping scarcer and less reliable.

Borneo,"[68] and the situation did not change greatly in the next eighty years. For military reasons, Chinese corvée laborers had been forced to build a network of roads around Singkawang-Monterado-Bengkayang after the Kongsi War of 1850-1854. In 1885, during the war with remnants of the Lanfang Kongsi, the military had a road constructed from Pontianak in the direction of Mandor with prison labor and help from Malays and Dayaks to be used for military purposes (see chapter three). After a few decades, however, most of these roads had fallen into disrepair and been reclaimed by the jungle.[69]

Resident de Vogel had arrived in the territory with ambitious plans to promote its economic development, especially by providing better communications. Above all, he wanted a coastal road constructed linking Pontianak with Mempawah, Singkawang, and Pemangkat, a distance of over 170 kilometers. Other roads, especially in the Chinese Districts, were also to be reconstructed or improved.[70] What's more, de Vogel wanted the roads built wide enough so that two motor vehicles would be able to pass each other, although at the time West Borneo had hardly any motorized traffic. Most of these highways would be six to eight meters wide, but unsurfaced, and usable only in dry weather.

For this extraordinary task, the Chinese were called up to provide the heavy labor. Not only Chinese from the original kongsi districts (as provided by a law of 1857) were conscripted to work on the roads, but others were obliged as well. Corvée demands were extended to Dayaks and even Malays. De Vogel also demanded that the Chinese in the Chinese Districts live in prescribed quarters, not in their pepper and coconut gardens, as they were used to doing, even though this arrangement had been tolerated up to then.[71] He enforced strict regulations concerning identity cards for travelers. Every Chinese when traveling had to carry such a card, and some Chinese officials refused to issue cards to persons who were delinquent in taxes, although this action was not legal. Years later, in the Volksraad, a Chinese representative, Kapitan Tjia Tjeng Siang of Pontianak, complained that even "respectable" individuals were stopped for identity and tax checks by overzealous police.[72]

De Vogel also raised the property tax (*bedrijfsbelasting*) to 4.5 percent of annual assessed income above *f*630 and, by implementing a more careful, thorough registration of Chinese residents, he greatly increased the number of persons liable for taxation.[73] These demands on the population understandably aroused resentment. At the same time, believing that the large numbers of immigrants

---

[68] E. A. Francis, "Westkust van Borneo in 1832," *Tijdschrift voor Neêrland's Indië* 4,2 (1842): 32.

[69] Ozinga, *Economische ontwikkeling*, pp. 19-20. This was the case with the Pontianak road.

[70] According to Memorandum of transfer, Resident J. Oberman, 1938, ARA 2.10.39 MvO MMK 265, pp. 10-11, de Vogel began or completed roads totaling 1,843 kilometers or more during his term of office, an amazing record for the time.

[71] Letters on "Kampung Cards," ANRI BB 1233; Ozinga, *Economische ontwikkeling*, pp. 20-21, 91-92.

[72] Letter, Director of Civil Service to Attorney Genral, citing Minutes of Volksraad, 1933, in ANRI BB 1233. Tija was an honorary major, according to the *Regeeringsalmanak* (above).

[73] The, "Rural Unrest," p. 143.

might be a fertile base for opposition, de Vogel also tried to stem the flow of new arrivals by requiring payment of twenty-five guilders for an entry permit.[74]

Plate 14. Water containers on a street in the Chinese quarter of Pontianak, circa 1920. Credit: Koninklijk Instituut voor de Tropen, Amsterdam, Album 137/11B 001 4357 (Lonkhuyzen). By permission.

Rebellion

The unrest of 1912, which was not widespread, was followed by a more serious rebellion in 1914 in the Mempawah area that attracted support from both Chinese and Dayaks—as always, a dangerous combination.[75] In July 1914, the rebels had formed a sworn brotherhood, binding members in allegiance to each other with oath-taking and promises of secrecy. They initiated several hundred members, including Chinese, Dayaks, and Malays.[76] Anticipating unrest, many Chinese fled to Singapore, while others took to the forest. Some local rulers also abandoned their posts. A relatively small Dutch expeditionary force, however, quickly broke the back of the rebellion.[77]

---

[74] Report on Immigration to West Borneo, ARA 2.10.36.04 V. 6.1.14 (85). According to "Rural Unrest," p. 147, an additional twenty-five guilders was required as embarkation fee. Ironically, in his Memorandum of transfer in 1918, de Vogel says the twenty-five guilders admission fee for immigrants was too high, in view of the great need for laborers in West Borneo. Memorandum of transfer, Resident H. de Vogel, 1918, ARA 2.10.39 MvO MMK 261, p. 32.

[75] E. B. Kielstra, "West Borneo," in *De Indische Archipel: Geschiedkundige schetsen* (Haarlem: De Erven F. Bohn, 1917), pp. 287-288.

[76] The, "Rural Unrest," pp. 138-139.

[77] Ozinga, *Economische ontwikkeling*, pp. 90-91; van Meteren Brouwer, "Geschiedenis," p. 1097; The, "Rural Unrest," pp. 146-150.

The leader of the 1914 rebellion was Soeng Kap Sen, born in Pakbulu, Mempawah. In 1914, Soeng had just returned to Borneo after spending some years in China. After the rebellion failed, he was never captured, but escaped through Sarawak, probably to Singapore.[78] Although his history suggests that he was inspired by Chinese nationalist ideas, he and other rebels relied on secret brotherhoods to unite their membership, inviting non-Chinese as well to take the blood oath and participate in the necessary initiation rituals; these organizational techniques had been employed by Chinese in previous kongsi uprisings. The head of the political reading club (see below) in Singkawang, Lim Moi Lioek (who was discussed in chapter four in connection with the *tengkawang* trade in Landak), attracted considerable attention as a man sympathetic to the rebels, one who was inclined to use his economic power to destabilize colonial authority.

Causes

De Vogel was convinced that the reading clubs (M. *shubaoshe*, see above, "Rebellion of 1912-1914") were themselves something like "secret societies," and his Chinese affairs officer, Mouw, agreed with this assessment. They reasoned that the reading clubs were linked with the Tongmenghui, Sun Yatsen's early revolutionary organization, which itself used conspiratorial "secret society" methods. Successor nationalist organizations like the Guomindang must also be societies, something which was still strictly forbidden in the Indies. Therefore, the reading clubs and other Chinese nationalist activities, which de Vogel believed were implicated in the troubles, were to be considered illegal and must be eliminated. These reading clubs were especially popular among the Hakka residents of the Chinese Districts, a population also strongly influenced by contemporary Chinese nationalism.

An interesting sidelight on the rebellion is the role of the Sinologist Henri Borel,[79] who had been Officer for Chinese Affairs in Pontianak in 1908-1909, and who had become a strong advocate of the interests of the Chinese minority. Borel, writing in 1915 in the Netherlands, argued that Dutch bureaucrats were using the Chinese revolution as a convenient scapegoat for the troubles. The real effect of the 1911 Revolution in China was to make the Chinese in the Indies more confident of their rights and more sensitive to wrongs, he argued, but not necessarily more inclined to violence.

Nor were the "secret societies" the instigators, Borel insisted, although it was true that Chinese who felt mistreated may certainly have turned to them. Instead the corvée and the higher taxes were the chief causes of the trouble, he argued. The corvée was especially burdensome and largely unnecessary; roads that were formerly short and narrow were now being widened and straightened for no good reason. Chinese thus faced much greater corvée demands, and Dayaks, thanks to new contracts with the native rulers, were being conscripted for the corvée for the

---

[78] The, "Rural Unrest," p. 147.

[79] Borel, born in Dordrecht in 1869, served for over twenty years, with interruptions, as a Chinese language officer in the Indies, becoming Advisor for Chinese Affairs in 1911. His public speeches and writings on the Chinese question were popular with many ethnic Chinese, less so with the colonial authorities. He was honorably discharged from service in 1916 and died in 1933 in The Hague. See his personnel record in ARA 2.10.06-08 Stamboek F' 7.

first time. Given these conditions, it wasn't surprising that both Chinese and Dayaks had been moved to resist the state. Resident de Vogel had even ordered Chinese to build and maintain roads outside the Chinese Districts. Elsewhere in the Indies, corvée was being abolished just as it was being extended in West Borneo. Furthermore, Borel continued, the new officials enforced the quarter residential system among Chinese agriculturists, a legal provision that had never been enforced in the territory before. Corvée compliance became a prerequisite for gaining permission to live outside the quarters. And all these measures were imposed during a time of falling prices for major exports, including pepper and gambier, and depressed wages. The argument that the new roads would ultimately improve the economy could hardly be expected to impress the victims of these oppressive new policies.[80]

The center of this rebellion was in Mempawah, especially in the area Anjungan-Mentidung, near the old Thaikong-Lanfang Kongsi border area. Although rumors predicted that resistance would be widespread, and it was reported that people in Sambas and Pontianak were again in fear for their lives, in fact trouble never reached those places. Mandor, too, was quiet, as was Monterado. People had fled from Bengkayang's *pasar*, expecting unrest, but a contingent of troops occupied the town without incident, and then the residents began to return.

Possibly, Anjungan figured as the center of rebel activity because the rebel leader of 1912, Soeng Kap Sen, had his home in nearby Pakbulu. Furthermore, the town was the gateway to a relatively fertile area of Chinese agricultural settlement, lying at the junction of the paths connecting the former kongsi territories. This made it a strategically important area, as it had been in 1885 (see chapter three), and would be again.

Aftermath

In September 1917, the government finally withdrew the corvée requirements for Chinese. In the future, regional units[81] would pay for the construction and maintenance of all roads. Malays and Dayaks might, however, be required to perform work without pay on a daily basis.[82]

Although corvée was abolished and the quarter requirements loosened, information from the Office for Chinese Affairs shows that the pass system was still being enforced in West Borneo in 1933. Records show that a prominent Chinese man, well-known to authorities, had been arrested for traveling without his document; reverberations from the subsequent protest reached the Chinese Consul-General in Batavia. In addition, some headmen were still refusing to issue the so-

---

[80] Corvée was not only unpaid labor. Workers also had to bring their own provisions. The wealthy, however, could pay a tax instead of working. Anonymous, "De ongeregeldheden in West-Borneo," *Indische Gids* 37,1 (1915): 262-266, citing an article of Henri Borel that appeared in *De Telegraaf*. Borel had left Borneo some years earlier. The, "Rural Unrest," pp. 141-142 also draws on Borel.

[81] These were called *landschappen*, "landscapes," in practice, often the territories of the rulers. They were not necessarily co-extensive with administrative divisions, but had control of a certain budget and a few administrative responsibilities.

[82] Ozinga, *Economische ontwikkeling*, pp. 21-22, 91-92. This continued up to World War II. See General Memorandum, Bengkayang, M. Waisvisz, July 12, 1938-May 20, 1941, ANRI BB 287, pp. 16ff.

called *"kampung* card" (identity card) unless the applicant's taxes were paid up. Any policeman could demand the card, and the threat of one to three months in jail hung over a victim unable to show one. A poor laborer who went to bathe at the river found it difficult to carry identification, but he could be fined or jailed if he was caught without it. In Pontianak, one *controleur* even entered private houses looking for Chinese residents who lacked proper documentation, and when he found any individual who was not properly registered, he charged him with tax delinquency as well.[83]

G. L. Uljée, in his "handbook" for the residency, admits that the troubles with Chinese that occurred between 1906—when a "secret society" was discovered in Mempawah—and 1914 were partly a reflection of Chinese nationalism, but also partly the result of colonial interference. Most of all, Uljée blames the unruly Hakkas, who constituted a majority of the population in the "rebellious" Chinese Districts.

> The [Hakka] Chinese still try to form associations secretly, and they forge plans in conflict with our laws. They have an inexhaustible bag of tricks for this purpose and demand in every attempt and every deed on their part care and wariness.

Uljée qualifies his judgment, however, for non-Hakkas: "The Hoklos [Teochius] never fought against the Government."[84]

This bifurcation of Dutch perceptions of Chinese society in West Borneo was enshrined in colonial lore. The rebellions of 1912–14, however limited in their extent, had again convinced the authorities that the Hakka Chinese were a folk that needed to be watched. After the rebellions, the armed police—a special unit sent to regions of threatened unrest after army troops were withdrawn—were stationed in Singkawang and environs, the Hakka-dominated area, until 1926 to enforce the peace.[85]

COMMUNITY INSTITUTIONS: TEMPLES

Official Dutch reports often neglected to mention religious institutions. Before 1942, the Chinese followed the religion of their fatherland where they could. Christian missions, although they provided schools and other activities, made few converts. Large and small *toapekong* (temples) were widespread, not only in settlements, but at places notable for particular natural features. Guan Gong or Guan Di, patron of kongsis, Dabogong himself, Guan Yin, and other deities with family or homeland connections kept watch over their adherents from their shrines and addressed them through mediums.

---

[83] Letter of Procureur-General and other correspondence to and from West Borneo, December 13, 1933, ANRI BB 1233. This regulation about identity papers had been in effect on the West Coast since de Vogel's days, and applied to natives as well. It recalls the use of identity cards to control the Chinese in Malaya during the "Emergency." The affair is probably the same one referred to by Volksraad member Tjia (above).

[84] Uljée, *Handboek*, pp. 57-58.

[85] C. G. Toorop, "De krijgsverrichtingen in de Chineesche districten," *Indisch Militair Tijdschrift* 2 (1932): 881.

Annual feasts were public manifestations of Chinese beliefs and culture. The annual New Year festival (actually the festival of the fifteenth day of the New Year,[86] when a full moon appears) was the high point of the year in Singkawang. On this day, Chinese from nearby settlements poured into the town. Processions with men carrying torches and colored lanterns bore tiny temples containing figures of the gods through the town until late into the night, accompanied by deafening music. Finally, while the gods returned to their temples and shrines, the mortals spent the night in festivities. On each of the three new year's days—the European, the Chinese, and, for Muslims, on the last day of Ramadan—leaders and neighbors of the various communities visited one another to exchange good wishes.[87]

Another occasion for festivities was the arrival of a wandering theater troupe from China. These troupes usually traveled to West Borneo via Singapore. Their performances, which in the nineteenth century were generally called *wayang*, reacquainted the Chinese living abroad with the cultural traditions of their homeland.[88] Other feasts were more or less public occasions: Qing Ming, Pudu, and Chinese funerals all provided opportunities to awake the senses with gaudy colors, fragrant incense, and plenty of noise.[89]

Previous chapters have discussed, in part, the importance of the halls and temples in kongsis. In Sungai Purun, a town that formerly belonged to the Lanfang Kongsi, the present-day temple retains relics of the kongsi—these are the only known remains of Lanfang to be found in the entire province outside of Mandor itself. They include a portal inscription and a portrait of kongsi founder, Lo Fong Pak (M. Luo Fangbo).[90]

Unfortunately, the Lanfang Futhang (M. *futing*, auxiliary hall) of Pontianak (see chapter three) no longer exists. This hall initially housed an all-purpose institution that maintained worship of Lo Fong Pak, the founder of Lanfang, organized periodic festivities, housed new immigrants seeking employment in mines or in the town, and provided rooms for a school and quarters for the *kapthai* on his visits to the city. The Lanfang Futhang owned a number of houses and lent out money from a fund built up, in part, from real estate investments that increased a t an annual rate of 24 percent.[91] The hall was founded under the sponsorship of the *kapitan* of the Hakkas in Pontianak, Then Kie San, and the headman of Lanfang, Soeng A Tjap,[92] and it was completely rebuilt some forty or fifty years later, in

---

[86] Called in Java Capgomeh.

[87] P. Adriani, *Herinneringen uit en aan de Chineesche districten der Wester-Afdeeling van Borneo, 1879-1882: Schetsen en indrukken* (Amsterdam: Cambagne en Zoon, 1898), pp. 12-13.

[88] Adriani, *Herinneringen*, pp. 141-145. Compare von Faber, "Schets," p. 477 and other references to *wayang* at New Year or temple feasts.

[89] Adriani, *Herinneringen*, pp. 161ff., and von Faber, "Schets," describe Chinese funerals.

[90] Wolfgang Franke, in collaboration with Claudine Salmon and Anthony Siu, *Bali, Kalimantan, Sulawesi, Moluccas*, volume 3 of *Chinese Epigraphic Materials in Indonesia* (Singapore: South Seas Society, 1997), pp. 180-182. Franke's assertion that this is the only place outside Mandor where epigraphic evidence of a kongsi exists is certainly correct. The portrait, calling Lo "King of Pontianak," is reproduced in Liu, *Helan Dongyindu*, p. 51 and in Plate 7.

[91] Translation of statutes and description of Lanfang Futhang, ARA 2.10.10 MR 1885:293, appendix E, p. 22.

[92] According to J. J. M. de Groot, *Het kongsiwezen van Borneo: Eene verhandeling over den grondslag en den aard der chineesche politieke vereenigingen in de koloniën* (The Hague: M. Nijhoff, 1885), p. 5, Soeng was headman from 1811-1823; the Dutch first dealt with him when

1869; this time the construction project was sponsored by Kapthai Lioe A Sin of Lanfang and Then Sioe Lin, also *kapitan* of Hakkas in Pontianak.

The building was substantial and required ongoing attention and periodic renovation to meet the needs of the community. In September 1885, some members of Kapthai Lioe's family met with community leaders to discuss its reorganization, for maintenance was becoming a problem.[93] The building housed a school from its early days, but sometime after 1900, during a period when Chinese education was being modernized, a recognizably more "modern" school opened on the premises. In 1938-1939, after a fire destroyed the previous edifice, a new Lo Fong Pak building was constructed at a cost of *f*15,000 on the site in the center of Pontianak.[94] Unfortunately, this hall, an imposing and atypical two-storied edifice, fell into ruin after 1965, when most Chinese associations were closed down by the New Order government.[95]

Pontianak had at least three clan temples for the Lin, Chen, and Huang surname groups, and we know that the Huang temple was established in 1928. Dates for the other temples are unknown.[96]

Influenced by the "modernization" movement in China, the attitude to religion among Chinese in West Borneo seemed to be changing by 1930. Some temples or halls came to be used predominantly as schools rather than as places of worship. Although Chinese religion by no means disappeared, religious fervor among the Chinese in the province seemed to have weakened, especially among the educated. Other temples became headquarters for clubs of various kinds[97] or fell into disuse. In a 1939 depiction, the "Great Toapekong" (*dabogong*) temple of Pontianak appears small and shabby, compared to the appearance of the town's main temple decades later, at the end of the twentieth century.[98] The bad state of the temples

---

they returned to Pontianak. The *Regeeringsalmanak* does not list Chinese officers before 1838, so Then's term of office is unknown. He may well have been an ancestor of Then Sioe Lin.

[93] *Koloniaal Verslag* (1886): 10. Kampung Baru was the Hakka settlement on the right bank of the Landak, while Kampung Lama (as the Chinese saw it) was on the left bank of the Kapuas with the Chinese quarter and market of Pontianak. The Futhang was thus in Kampung Lama.

[94] Liu, *Helan Dongyindu*, p. 41.

[95] Translation of statutes and description of Lanfang Futhang, ARA 2.10.10 MR 1885:293, appendix E. According to Franke, the building was seized by Indonesian authorities in 1965 (*Chinese Epigraphic Materials*, p. 299). A somewhat blurry picture of the temple as it was rebuilt in 1939 is in Liu, *Helan Dongyindu*, p. 41.

[96] The Lin temple contains a sedan chair dated 1919, so this may be the oldest of the three associations, although it is possible that the object is from an earlier temple. A stone censer in the Chen temple has an ambiguous date—either 1897 or 1957. See Franke, *Chinese Epigraphic Materials*, pp. 81-84. Denys Lombard, "Guide Archipel IV: Pontianak et son arrière-pays," *Archipel* 28 (1984): 90, also mentions the Huang temple, Jiangxiatang.

[97] Kapucijn-Missionaris, "Missie onder de Chineezen," *Onze Missiën in Oost- en West-Indië* 13 (1930): 257-259. In this article, an anonymous Capuchin missionary notes that anti-Christian and anti-Western sentiments, both influences from China, affected the work of the missions, but religious skepticism applied to traditional Chinese religion as well.

[98] See Liu, *Helan Dongyindu*, p. 41. The main temple of Pontianak is here called Toapekong (*dabogong*), but as Franke reports (*Chinese Epigraphic Materials*, p. 46), it is now called Sansheng Miao for the three deities it houses, including Tianhou, Dabogong, and Guan Gong. The temple bell was cast in 1789 (not long after Pontianak's founding) in China, the earliest dated bell found so far in the Archipelago. According to Claudine Salmon, the bell was donated by the Hainanese, who are not among the larger groups in West Kalimantan, but who may have frequented the area as merchants or seamen. See Claudine Salmon, "Les Hainanais en Asie du

certainly reflected economic hard times as well, but also disinterest. Another report confirms that Landak's many small temples in its various Chinese settlements appeared neglected in 1934, although one town preserved a more elegant temple that had been built in mining times.[99]

COMMUNITY INSTITUTIONS: SCHOOLS

In 1891, according to the records, fifty-five "Chinese schoolteachers" resided in West Borneo; teaching was given as their primary occupation.[100] This was probably an underestimate of the number of teachers available to the Chinese community, as teachers might be found not only in schools, but in large families or sometimes in temples. Resident Kater emphasized the role of Chinese education in the community in 1880:

> Although the education given to Chinese children is, according to our ideas, inadequate, it stands out positively in comparison with that of the Malays. In nearly every Chinese settlement there is a school where the teachers, who are badly paid, do not as a rule come from the most cultivated part of the nation.[101]

Since early times, wealthier members of the community had supported Chinese schools or at least hired tutors for their own and certain other children. During their visit to the still isolated West Coast in 1838, the missionaries Elihu Doty and William Pohlmann found active Chinese schools even in such minor settlements as Sebawi and Sepang. Monterado had four schools and Mandor three. The missionaries reported that a number of adults in each town were literate, able and eager to read their tracts,[102] though perhaps their eagerness was due not so much to the edifying content of the materials as to the dearth of available printed matter in Chinese.

In 1899, an explorer who traversed the island found a school for a half-dozen children at the home of an extended family of planters and traders not far from Sintang. The teacher, having lost his fortune through opium use, earned his keep by giving lessons to the planter's grandchildren.[103]

Chinese hunger for education brought members of their community even into the four so-called "native" government schools. Though these schools were intended for the local elite, their pupils in the late nineteenth century were almost exclusively

---

Sud-Est: De la navigation à l'implantation (fin XVII-XIX s.)," in *Hainan: De la Chine à l'Asie du Sud-Est, Von China nach Südostasien,* ed. Claudine Salmon and Roderich Ptak (Wiesbaden: Harrassowitz Verlag, 2001), p. 211. Also in Liu (*Helan Dongyindu,* p. 41) is a photograph of Pontianak's Zhonghua Zongshanghui (Federation of Chinese Chambers of Commerce) building.

[99] Memorandum of transfer, W. J. ten Haaft, Landak, 1934, ARA 2.10.39, MvO KIT 984, p. 56.

[100] *Koloniaal Verslag* (1893): Appendix A.

[101] General Report 1880, ANRI BW 5/11 (26).

[102] E. Doty and W. J. Pohlman, "Tour in Borneo, from Sambas through Montrado to Pontianak and the Adjacent Settlements of Chinese and Dayaks, during the Autumn of 1838," *Chinese Repository* 8 (1839): 284-307.

[103] Adolphe Combanaire, *Au pays des coupeurs de têtes: À travers Bornéo* (Paris: Librairie Plon, 1910), pp. 286-287, 306.

Chinese children.[104] In 1890, the authorities knew of forty-six private Chinese schools and 263 pupils in West Borneo. In 1899, they counted fifty-four Chinese schools, which constituted more than one-third of all known Chinese schools in the colony outside Java, and that number grew to eighty in 1901, with 1,009 pupils enrolled in those institutions.[105] Even poor villagers were willing to support a "scholar" who would provide education in the mother tongue for their children, although the quality of instruction was often poor. Typically, a schoolmaster of undetermined qualifications led the pupils in reciting the primers and classics of traditional Chinese education. Members of the class called out their texts, which varied according to the pupils' different levels of skill, in unison, creating an impenetrable din.[106] After 1910, these schools continued to develop rapidly in numbers, but they adapted their curricula to accord with new ideas about education and nationalism in China. Modern schooling required that the language of instruction be Mandarin, though education in Mandarin was usually strongly influenced by Hakka or Teochiu, since teachers were often southern Chinese. Later, new teachers also arrived from China; this influx was especially notable after the Chi Nan (Ji'nan) School in Nanjing and other institutions began to offer teacher education for Chinese from abroad.[107]

Because of pressure to cut administrative costs, no Officers for Chinese Affairs were posted to the province after 1922. As a result, there were no periodic reports on Chinese education, and only occasionally did a Chinese-speaking official visit the province. In 1922, an officer did pay a visit and reported on Chinese schools. According to his observations, the content of the lessons appeared to be "steeped" in Chinese nationalism, but was not especially anti-Western. The colonial administration decided that it would be sufficient to supervise the teachers, not the schools themselves (as was the practice in the British-controlled Straits Settlements). Objectionable teachers, especially if they were suspected of Communist sympathies, could be expelled, provided they were foreigners, or otherwise forbidden to teach.[108] Repeatedly, politically objectionable teachers and others were expelled from the colony.[109]

The most important school of prewar days, the Chung Hwa (M. *Zhonghua*) School of Pontianak, was established as early as 1908 by a special school committee. In 1939, the school had about 220 pupils in five classes and was housed in the Lanfang Futhang.[110] Another school, Chen Chiang, had over two hundred pupils, while there was a special school for girls (although other modern schools practiced coeducation), the Tek Yok Girls' School (M. *Deyu Nuxiao*), with 160

---

[104] Buys, *Twee maanden*, p. 88.

[105] *Koloniaal Verslag* (1890): 106; *Koloniaal Verslag* (1900): P: IV; *Koloniaal Verslag* (1902): Appendix O.

[106] Buys, *Twee maanden*, pp. 181-184.

[107] The Ji'nan School opened to provide continuing education for Chinese children from overseas early in the twentieth century, but the institution of that name is now a university, located in Guangzhou (Canton).

[108] Report of the Service for Chinese Affairs, 1922, ARA 2.10.02 Exh. 2.1.24 (96).

[109] See references to West Borneo in *Politiek-Politioneele Overzichten*. Local-born Chinese were Netherlands subjects, and could not be expelled from the Indies. Only the foreign-born could be expelled, and they seem to have been the most politically troublesome.

[110] Liu, *Helan Dongyindu*, p. 42.

pupils in 1939. There was also at least one middle or secondary school, located in Pontianak. All the schools charged tuition, but it was adjusted according to ability to pay.[111] Continuing education was a problem, however; only a small proportion of graduates went to middle school and even fewer advanced beyond that level. Most of those traveled to China for advanced education.[112]

Although the movement for modern Chinese education in West Borneo was contemporary with that in Java, it appears that Java had little influence on the Chinese schools in West Borneo. In Java, the Tiong Hoa Hwe Koan (THHK, Chinese Association) had spearheaded the movement for modern Chinese education. The name of the Chung Hwa School ("Chung Hwa" is identical to "Tiong Hoa") of Pontianak was chosen independently of that association and independently of influences from Batavia. In fact, Nio Joe Lan's history of the THHK, written in 1940, lists no branches or other activities of the Association in West Borneo, although in the first years of the movement branches were set up in other parts of the island, and a Chung Hwa School in Banjarmasin was established by a branch of the THHK.[113] Not Java, but Singapore (or China itself) must have been the catalyst for spreading modern education in West Borneo, for many children were sent to Singapore for education or continuing education, as well as to China.[114] In fact, the main cultural and political influence in the province came, as did economic ties, from Singapore, not Batavia, and, in the twentieth century, Chinese-language newspapers from Singapore were readily available.[115]

When the Depression made it difficult to collect funds for the schools, the Chinese Chamber of Commerce in Pontianak suggested instituting a levy on all trade to support community schools and other activities. This set a precedent for other community-collected taxes in later times (see also chapter seven).[116]

WESTERN EDUCATION

In Java, at least among the *peranakans*, the opening of the Dutch-language Hollands-Chinese Scholen (HCS) in 1908 drew children from the new Chinese-language schools into Western, Dutch-language education. The HCS would itself

---

[111] Ibid., p. 43. See also Report on Modern Chinese Education in West Borneo and East Sumatra, 1923, ANRI BB 5344.

[112] Ibid. The estimate was that less than 1 percent continued their education in China, Hong Kong, Penang, or Singapore. Batavia was not a chosen destination.

[113] Nio Joe Lan, *Riwajat 40 Taoen dari Tiong Hoa Hwe Koan-Batavia (1900-1939)* (Batavia: Tiong Hoa Hwe Koan, 1940), pp. 70-77. Some authors write "Hwee Koan." See also Liu, *Helan Dongyindu*, p. 39, who, in describing the school, mentions the THHK, but not as its sponsor.

[114] *Koloniaal Verslag* (1890): 106.

[115] Liu, *Helan Dongyindu*, p. 41. Batavia's Chinese-language press did reach Pontianak, but it was deemed less interesting for the Chinese there. Compare Report on Chinese Education in West Borneo, ARA 2.10.02 V. 20.6.17 (62): "The trade of the Chinese is not directed to Java, but to Singapore. In Singapore live the traders who buy the products, from Singapore they receive their newspapers, printed in Chinese characters. . . . Nearly all wealthy Chinese have been in Singapore and have interests there; they know Batavia in name only." From 1928-29, the *Politiek-Politioneele Overzichten* refer to a Pontianak Chinese-language newspaper, *Khiaw Sang Yit Po* (Qiaosheng Ribao, Overseas Chinese Daily); its editor was deported in October 1928. (1: 454).

[116] *Politiek-Politioneele Overzichten*, 2: 328-29, from March 1930.

contribute to building *peranakan* culture and a *peranakan* elite.[117] Although the Chinese of West Borneo readily made sacrifices to give their children a Chinese education, they appear to have been immune to the lure of the HCS. When a HCS opened in Pontianak in 1912, six Chinese-language schools already existed in that city and others had opened in all the larger towns; five Chinese schools operated in the inland district of Landak alone.[118] By 1918, about one hundred Chinese schools, but only one HCS, existed in the residency.[119]

In 1921, an official Dutch report characterized the "very strange" attitude of the Chinese in the area: they preferred small schools with instruction in Chinese and sometimes English and lacked "full sympathy" for the HCS.[120] The single HCS functioning in the residency was so unsuccessful in attracting Chinese pupils to study in Dutch that the government gladly turned it over to Roman Catholic missionaries in 1924. The missionaries also took responsibility for a HCS established after 1918 in Singkawang.[121] Apparently, these schools only survived because they offered additional classes in Chinese during the afternoon, something the HCS in Java refused to do.[122]

OPTION FOR CHINESE-LANGUAGE EDUCATION

This Chinese resistance to Dutch education was related to the centrifugality of the residency's economy. Batavia was distant, and for Chinese traders in West Borneo, irrelevant. Their ties were with Singapore, where Chinese was the first language and English the second, and with China. They wanted their children to be part of New China, to have facility with the Chinese language, and, perhaps, for business or study purposes, to learn a bit of English. The colonial language did not seem important.

---

[117] See the recent study of the HCS, Ming Tien Nio Govaars-Tjia, "Hollands onderwijs in een koloniale samenleving: De Chinese ervaring in Indonesië 1900-1942" (PhD dissertation, Leiden University, 1999) and also Mary F. Somers, "Peranakan Chinese Politics in Indonesia" (PhD dissertation, Cornell University, 1965).

[118] Memorandum of transfer, Resident Th. H. H. van Driessche, 1912, ARA 2.10.39, MvO MMK 260, p. 32.

[119] Memorandum of transfer, Resident H. de Vogel, 1918, ARA 2.10.39, MvO MMK 261, p. 42.

[120] Memorandum of transfer, Resident K. A. James, 1921, ARA 2.10.39, MvO MMK 262, p. 16.

[121] Uljée, *Handboek*, p. 107. For a brief discussion of missions in West Kalimantan, see Mary Somers Heidhues, "Chinese Identity in the Diaspora: Religion and Language in West Kalimantan, Indonesia," in *Nationalism and Cultural Revival in Southeast Asia: Perspectives from the Centre and the Region*, ed. Sri Kuhnt-Saptodewo et al. (Wiesbaden: Harrassowitz, 1997), pp. 201-210.

[122] *Sejarah kebangkitan nasional daerah Kalimantan Barat* (Jakarta: Departemen Pendidikan dan Kebudayaan, Pusat Penelitian Sejarah dan Budaya, Proyek Penelitian dan Pencacatatan Kebudayaan Daerah, 1978/79), pp. 48-49. By the late 1930s, there were four HCS functioning under mission auspices. All offered several hours of voluntary instruction in Chinese; see Br. Canisius v.d. Ven, "Chinese Education at the Dutch middle school and lower school," in ARA 2.21.120 (96). Pupils learned Chinese and Chinese subjects from 2:30 to 4:00 pm, after regular instruction was completed. See B. R. Van H., "Een Chinese volksschool voor West-Borneo?," *Het Katholieke-Schoolblad van Nederlandsch-Indië* 23,19 (December 8, 1939): 223-226. This is also discussed in Heidhues, "Chinese Identity," pp. 202-206. In Java, the authorities stubbornly resisted adding Chinese instruction to the regular school curriculum.

True, the Chinese schools were, in some ways, "political," but the attitudes that shaped and influenced individual schools varied more widely than most colonial officials recognized. In Pontianak one politically more "radical" school was founded by the political reading club, another, more right-wing one, by the relatively conservative Chinese Chamber of Commerce (Siang Hwee, *shanghui*).[123]

Catholic and Protestant missionaries also established Chinese-language schools, though in general these mission schools wielded little influence compared to secular Chinese schools. A Roman Catholic mission that offered Chinese-language education had existed since the 1880s in Singkawang, and it expanded rapidly after Dutch Capuchin fathers arrived in 1906. The Catholic mission in West Borneo placed great emphasis on schools and managed not only to increase the number of its mission schools substantially during the prewar years, but also to reach and enroll a greater number of Dayak pupils, who proved extremely receptive to Western education.[124] Methodists were also at work in West Borneo. In 1907 the American Methodist Episcopal missionaries operated schools for Chinese, the so-called "Chinese-English" schools. Again, however, despite the efforts of these religious organizations, the mission schools never achieved the popularity of the local secular schools established throughout the residency by Chinese, for Chinese.

In the 1930s, Chinese-language schools in West Borneo numbered over one hundred, according to an informed estimate.[125] Even Pemangkat had four schools in 1931, two called "Chung Hua" and sponsored by the Hakkas, one from the Teochiu and one from the Fujian community.[126] (This shows again that the Chinese Districts were not entirely Hakka, only predominantly so.) Pontianak had at least eight schools, including a secondary or middle school (*zhongxue*).[127] By this time, more and more students were going to China, especially to Ji'nan School and to Xiamen University, to further their education; some also went to Singapore.[128]

Evidence shows that the Guomindang exerted strong efforts, especially after the Northern Expedition allowed it to establish a united government of China in 1927, to control the Chinese schools abroad. In November 1927, various West Bornean schools formed an association to propagate the Guomindang's ideals in education.[129] The Chung Hwa schools in Pontianak, Sintang, and Sekadau saw

---

[123] Memorandum of transfer, Resident Th. H. H. van Driessche, 1912, ARA 2.10.39 MvO MMK 260, pp. 28, 32-33, 59-60. For more on these two organizations, see below.

[124] Appendix to General Memorandum, Bangkayang, M. Waisvisz, July 12, 1938-May 20, 1941, ANRI BB 287, dated August 1941. A few dozen Catholic Chinese lived in Singkawang and elsewhere before a church was opened there in 1875; in 1882 followed the first school for Chinese children. Arn. J. H. van der Velden, *De Roomsch-Katholieke Missie in Nederlandsch Oost-Indie, 1808-1908* (Nijmegen: L. C. G. Malmberg, 1908), p. 200. For more on education, see chapter seven and epilogue.

[125] Ozinga, *Economische ontwikkeling*, p. 93.

[126] *Shenghuobao chuangkan zhounian jiniankan* (Jakarta: Sheng Huo Pao, 1955), p. 100. Individual speech groups sponsored different schools, although the language of instruction was Mandarin.

[127] Liu, *Helan Dongyindu*, pp. 42-45.

[128] The biographies in Xie Feng, *Zhanhou Nanyang Huaqiao gaikuang, Xi Poneizhou zhibu* (Singapore: n.p., 1947) show that many of the prominent but local-born Chinese spent some of their youth in China, often in elementary school years, but some attended secondary or tertiary institutions there. Those who immigrated to Borneo as young people also were China-educated.

[129] *Politiek-Politioneele Overzichten*, 1: 177.

their administrations replaced by Guomindang party members, and in the following year, boy scout organizations and obligatory gymnastics classes were introduced, following the example of Nanjing.[130]

ASSOCIATIONS

The most influential modern community association in West Borneo was the Siang Hwee, or Chamber of Commerce. It was founded in Pontianak in 1908 and later expanded to other towns. The various branches finally formed a Federation of Chinese Chambers of Commerce (Zhonghua Zongshanghui) with its headquarters in Pontianak, where the chamber represented about 40 percent of all businesses in the town.[131]

The troubles of 1914 had illuminated the activities of the politically oriented, modern, Chinese community organizations, the Chamber of Commerce (which of course was also a commercial institution), and the political reading clubs (*shubaoshe*), which now caught the attention of the colonial state. The chambers attracted business people, while the reading clubs drew those interested in politics and nationalism, including workers and small businessmen. The colonial authorities knew of reading clubs in Pontianak, Singkawang, Mempawah, Pakbulu, Mandor, Sungai Pinyu, Monterado, Bengkayang, Capkala, Pemangkat, and Sambas; all but the last three were legally incorporated under Dutch law. That of Pontianak was legally incorporated as early as 1908, the year the Chamber of Commerce was founded, and three years before the outbreak of the Chinese Revolution of 1911.[132]

Aside from its stated aim of encouraging literacy and making available Chinese-language reading matter to a wide public, the reading club in Pontianak had also helped establish modern Chinese schools. The colonial authorities, suspicious that such activities proved the reading clubs were becoming increasingly "proletarian" in character, quickly noted that reading club rules provided for the exercise of jurisdiction in criminal affairs—a sensitive matter since the abolition of the kongsis, for it might resurrect the "state within a state" they feared. Officer for Chinese Affairs Mouw, who served in Pontianak at the time of the 1914 troubles, was convinced that these clubs were in reality a branch of the Tongmenghui, which in turn, he believed, was a "secret society" and absolutely illegal.[133] After some discussion, however, the Dutch chose to leave the clubs in peace, and this proved to be a sensible policy. Over the next years, the Dutch

---

[130] *Politiek-Politioneele Overzichten*, 1: 203, 394-398. Ultimately, the model for modern Chinese schools was Japan's modern school system, with gymnastics and military exercises.

[131] Liu, *Helan Dongyindu*, p. 41; later it was simply called Zhonghua Shanghui, the Chinese Chamber of Commerce.

[132] Letter of Attorney General, December 27, 1912, ARA 2.10.02 V. 8.3.1913 (36); The, "Rural Unrest," p. 139. Legal incorporation (*rechspersonlijkheid*) was necessary for an organization to have a treasury, own property, and, for example, manage a school.

[133] The, "Rural Unrest," pp. 139-140; aside from the jurisdictional question, the Dutch understood the clubs to be foreign political organizations, and therefore "*peranakans*," in the sense of local-born Chinese, should not be members. In fact, however, many Indies-born Chinese were members and even officers. This was also true of the Chambers of Commerce, which functioned on the one hand as a representative of the Chinese abroad in the Chinese Parliament, on the other, as a representative of businessmen in the colony, both immigrant and local-born.

watched with satisfaction as the influence and importance of the Chinese reading clubs diminished, and the community lost interest in Chinese nationalist politics when economic difficulties arose in Borneo, while China itself became internally divided.

The Dutch could live more easily with the chambers of commerce, which drew their support from well-to-do businessmen of more conservative, but still China-oriented, leanings. These had the right to elect representatives to political institutions in China. Participating in foreign elections, however, was illegal for Indies-born Chinese, whom the colonial administration regarded as Dutch subjects (although China regarded them as Chinese citizens). Teochius (and some Hokkiens) made up most of the members of the chambers, which had spread to many towns. The Hakkas were considered the strongest supporters of reading clubs—another example of the greater political "radicalism" of the Hakkas.[134] No love was lost between the two types of organizations, but both were clearly oriented to China and Chinese affairs.[135]

In 1939, an observer counted some twenty to thirty community organizations (*huiguan* and kongsi) in Pontianak and Kampung Baru; these included the associations for Hainanese, Cantonese, and Hokkiens. In addition, there was a Guomindang branch in Pontianak, and other branches throughout the province.[136] Previously, some Chinese had been members of the Tongmenghui, Sun Yatsen's conspiratorial sworn brotherhood. After 1927, Guomindang activities burgeoned, but very soon the split between the party and the Communists had an impact, weakening the Guomindang branches in Borneo. Other schisms arose for various reasons, among them the Nanjing government's meddling in local affairs and its demands for financial support. With the Depression, financial worries throughout the community dampened political enthusiasm and left the Chinese of West Borneo less inclined to join politically "radical" organizations.[137]

THE "PERANAKANS"

During the colonial period, the Dutch often referred to some of the Chinese of West Borneo as *peranakans*, by which they meant "local-born." The distinction was legally significant because local-born Foreign Orientals (in this case, Chinese) were regarded as subjects of the Netherlands Indies, whatever their origin.[138]

---

[134] On this theme, see Mary S. Erbaugh, "The Secret History of the Hakkas: The Chinese Revolution as a Hakka Enterprise," *China Quarterly* 132 (1992): 937-968; and Erbaugh, "The Hakka Paradox in the People's Republic of China: Exile, Eminence, and Public Silence," in *Guest People: Hakka Identity in China and Abroad*, ed. Nicole Constable (Seattle: University of Washington Press, 1996), pp. 196-231.

[135] Van Meteren Brouwer, "Geschiedenis," p. 1097. Van Meteren Brouwer, who was head administrator of a credit bank, says the Chinese of the West Coast sent ƒ300,000 to China, even before the more substantial transfers of the 1930s (below).

[136] Liu, *Helan Dongyindu*, pp. 41-42.

[137] *Politiek-Politioneele Overzichten*, 2: 45, 146, 411, 448.

[138] Donald E. Willmott, *The National Status of the Chinese in Indonesia, 1900-1958* (Ithaca: Cornell University Modern Indonesia Project, 1961), pp. 13-15. Previously they had been defined as "citizens," then as "foreigners." A 1910 law distinguished between "citizens" and "subjects" among the inhabitants of the Indies; local-born Chinese were "subjects."

Evidence suggests that the so-called *peranakan*s of Borneo were not as ready to associate themselves with the majority culture as *peranakan*s from Java. In Java, *peranakan* Chinese had usually adopted local languages and many indigenous customs, and *peranakan* Chinese women wore a form of Malay dress, the *sarong-kebaya*, although their choice of patterns made them identifiable as Chinese. In Borneo, the Chinese were less ready to take on the dress and speech of their neighbors. Nineteenth-century reports from Borneo, at least from the kongsis, make it clear that the women wore Chinese dress—slacks—although they were not "pure" Chinese, and that the inhabitants conversed in Chinese. By the twentieth century, many Chinese women in Borneo had adopted *sarong-kebaya*, but they retained Chinese as their first language.

Malay was never the *lingua franca* of the Chinese Districts;[139] that was Hakka. Over 99 percent of Chinese in the residency, according to the census of 1920, spoke a Chinese dialect as their primary language.[140] Malay was used in coastal towns, especially in Pontianak, as evidenced by references to speakers of Malay. One such report describes the Chinese guide who accompanied van Prehn to Mandor in 1851-1852, a local man who spoke "good Malay" because he was often in Pontianak and visited other districts for trade.[141]

In their roles as traders and entrepreneurs, many Chinese found it necessary to learn a second language. In the twentieth century, in Landak, most *peranakan* Chinese were bilingual and spoke Malay, while others, active in the interior, learned Dayak languages. As mentioned earlier, many of the Chinese in the interior were themselves recent immigrants.[142] In the deepest interior, Dayaks dominated, and the Chinese were typically only occasional visitors, who came for trade.[143] As a rule, the Chinese learned the language they needed to use; they would pick up other Chinese languages or they would learn Malay or Dayak languages, depending on where they lived and did business. In turn, many Dayaks learned to speak Chinese, and of course many Dayaks spoke Malay.

In the mid-nineteenth century, according to contemporary reports, a number of prominent Chinese were fluent in Malay. Obviously, these persons were concentrated more in the Malay-influenced sultanate towns like Pontianak and Sambas. Twentieth-century reports tell us that in coastal areas, most Chinese males spoke Malay, but this does not appear to have been the case in Singkawang.[144] Malay usually took a back seat to Chinese in towns like

---

[139] Liu, *Helan Dongyindu*, p. 40, says blandly of West Borneo's Chinese, "Very few spoke Malay, but rather Chaozhou, or they spoke Hakka."

[140] Cited in Charles A. Coppel, *Indonesian Chinese in Crisis* (Kuala Lumpur: Oxford University Press, 1973), p. 158. Unfortunately, the more thorough census of 1930 did not ask about language use.

[141] R. C. van Prehn, "Aantekeningen betreffende Borneo's Westkust," *Tijdschrift voor Indische Taal-, Land-, en Volkenkunde* 7 (1858): 23. Unfortunately, the evidence does not allow a conclusion about whether Teochius were more likely than Hakkas to learn Malay, although there are a number of hints at this conclusion. For example, see the case of Phong Seak of Singkawang, above.

[142] Memorandum of transfer, anonymous description of Landak, ca. 1930, ARA 2.10.39, MvO KIT 982, pp. 29-30. The Dayak not only learned some Hakka, some of them adopted the Chinese calendar.

[143] Helbig, *Eine Durchquerung*, p. 61.

[144] Memorandum of transfer, W. Ch. Ten Cate, Mempawah, 1938, ARA 2.10.39 MvO KIT 990.

Singkawang and Pemangkat, and a report from Pemangkat in the 1950s emphasized that not only the Chinese, but many other residents, spoke Hakka.[145]

There is some evidence of tension between immigrant Chinese and local-born *peranakans*, at least from the nineteenth century. In 1873, the annual report for West Borneo noted the "continuing feud" in Pemangkat between these two groups. This tension had resulted in a number of fights and left several wounded.[146] The people Chinese once called *petompang* (M. *bantangfan*, half-Chinese barbarians, see chapter two) because of their mixed descent, and whom the Dutch called *peranakan* (because of their local birth) appear to have considered themselves to be different from the immigrant Chinese, and, even in kongsi times, they were treated with more trust and familiarity by colonial authorities and Malay elites than were most immigrant Chinese.

One outstanding *peranakan* woman was Then Sioe Kim, widow of Lioe A Sin of the former Lanfang Kongsi. In 1887, her funeral in Pontianak gave evidence of her own and the kongsi's good relations with other power centers in that area. A local-born Hakka woman who had married Kapthai Lioe in 1850 (her brother Then Sioe Lin was, as noted above, a *kapitan* in Pontianak), she was said to understand the thinking of Europeans better than most Chinese did. Then Sioe Kim had tried, after the dissolution of the kongsi in 1884, to negotiate between the Dutch and the "hotheads" of the former kongsi who had murdered the Dutch *controleur* (see chapter three). Not only did the Chinese population of Mandor attend her burial, the highest colonial civil and military authorities also appeared. The sultan himself decreed that her coffin be covered in yellow silk, a prerogative of the royal house, indicating his close relationship with her husband and her brother. Malay and Chinese musicians accompanied the procession.[147] Ethnic boundaries were still not so rigid as to prevent this kind of unified display of mourning for an individual of prominence and reputation.

THE EVE OF WAR

Administrative reform reached Borneo in 1936, when the entire island became part of a "Government of Borneo and the Great East." This region enveloped Borneo, Sulawesi, and the eastward islands, including West New Guinea. Meanwhile, the Chinese had become more politically apathetic after the Depression, when the economic difficulties forced them to concentrate on survival. One Dutch official warned his colleagues against complacency, arguing that the Chinese minority might be roused to political action again:

Although the political conditions among the Chinese population can at the moment still be termed quite good, we should not be blind to the fact that the

---

[145] *Shenghuobao*, p. 100.

[146] *Koloniaal Verslag* (1878): 23.

[147] J. W. Joung [Young], "Then Sioe Kim Njong, in de Westerafdeeling van Borneo bekend als Njonja kapthai. In memoriam," *Bijdragen tot de Taal-, Land- en Volkenkunde* 37 (1888): 149-153. Although Then Sioe Kim had relatively good relations with Dutch officials, Resident Kater (chapter three) mistrusted her, believing she was playing a double role in the tensions after the dissolution of Lanfang Kongsi. Once Kater left Pontianak, connections with the Dutch improved, and she was awarded a monthly pension of one hundred guilders, later raised to ƒ150—equal to the salary of a Chinese officer.

financial difficulties, in which by far the largest part of this group find themselves, gradually are beginning to have a deleterious influence on their mood and it may thus absolutely not be considered impossible that the old attitude of resistance be reawakened in case we should seriously offend this group of the population through one or the other [tax] measure.[148]

Plate 15. Harbor of Pontianak, circa 1935. In the foreground, oil drums are being unloaded, while in the background, the skeletons of wooden ships take shape. Credit: Koninklijk Instituut voor Taal-, Land- en Volkenkunde, Leiden, number 16.352. By permission.

Other officials confirmed that the Chinese had grown more apathetic.[149] The Guomindang's meeting places, successors to the political reading clubs, where visitors could discuss events in China and read Chinese newspapers, gradually fell into disuse. Only an engaged minority continued to follow politics in China with interest; the rest were preoccupied with making a living.

---

[148] From a letter of the director of colonial administrative service to the resident of West Borneo, 1933, ANRI BB 1233.

[149] Memorandum of transfer, Resident K. H. van Prehn, 1933, ARA 2.10.39 MvO MMK 264, p. 22, and Memorandum of transfer, Resident J. Oberman, 1938, ARA 2.10.39 MvO MMK 265, pp. 10-11.

The battle for Shanghai and the outbreak of the Sino-Japanese War reawakened political interest, especially in Pontianak, where people eagerly awaited the arrival of ships from Singapore for news of the Shanghai front.[150] Attempts to organize anti-Japanese boycotts were not very successful, but more successful was the collection of funds. Up until 1942, the Chinese in West Borneo contributed large amounts to China's war and relief funds, apart from what they otherwise remitted to home areas.

The Chinese continued to foster Chineseness in the way they lived, their language, and their religion. Their orientation to China was reflected in their political attitudes. According to a Dutch observer:

> It is still a fact that the eyes of the Chinese in this territory remain oriented to China and to the events there, and the political attitude [*richting*] among this group is a pure reflection of the attitude that is most strongly supported and propagated in the homeland.[151]

The memorandum cited here, which assesses political and economic affairs in the sub-district of Bengkayang, is the last official Dutch prewar account from West Borneo, written just months before the arrival of Japanese troops in the Indies. Chinese residents in 1941 constituted 28 percent of Bengkayang's population (7,402 persons), and all of them were considered to be Hakkas.[152] Concerning their attitude to their place of residence, the author of the report wrote:

> The Chinese is, remains, and feels himself a stranger here, although he has lived here for generations, claims rights to land, and was never in China. We could never turn him into the loyal Netherlands-Indies citizen envisioned by the ideology that gave birth to Dutch-Chinese [Hollands-Chinese] education.[153]

If the colonial power had succeeded in eliminating the kongsis as "a state within the state," it was in no position to destroy the internal independence of the Chinese community itself. Community organizations structured religious life, educated the young, tended to clan or business interests, and directed, as far as possible, political attention to China. Many Chinese had been born in West Borneo, but there was no growing sense of a West Bornean, much less a "Netherlands Indies," identity, nor did the other ethnic groups participate in such an identity.[154] If many individuals did cross ethnic boundaries, especially by learning languages or otherwise forming links with other West Bornean ethnic groups, most Chinese continued to feel they were a group apart, children of a distant homeland. The colonial administration had little reason and less ability to make them think otherwise.

---

[150] Toorop, "De krijgsverrichtingen," p. 885.

[151] General Memorandum, Bengkayang, M. Waisvisz, July 12, 1938-May 20, 1941, pp. 38-39. ANRI BB 287. The quotation is repeated from a 1933 MvO that appears to have been lost.

[152] Ibid., p. 37.

[153] Ibid., p. 39. By the time this was written, rubber prices had recovered and better incomes also led to improvement in colonial infrastructure, above all, roads.

[154] Ibid., pp. 12-18.

CHAPTER SIX

WAR AND INDONESIAN INDEPENDENCE

World War II brought devastation to West Borneo's economy and heightened interethnic tension; the immediate postwar years appear as a partial colonial restoration. The Chinese community quickly reorganized after 1945, and admiration for the New China of the Communist Party grew rapidly, but so did internal dissension.

In the 1950s, ethnic Chinese residents, farmers and craftsmen, traders and businessmen, enjoyed the fruits of an economic network built up since the nineteenth century, substantially controlling the commerce of the province. They maintained their own community organizations; above all, they looked after their schools. However, especially after 1949, political issues undermined the much sought-after unity of the minority community. A portion of the Chinese community favored the People's Republic of China, a smaller number gave their allegiance to Nationalist China, and the rest hoped for some kind of neutrality in questions of national politics. Few were consciously Indonesian citizens, although many were local-born or even third-generation residents of West Borneo. Those who held Indonesian citizenship—a group that, ironically, included some of the wealthiest businessmen—joined with the non-citizens, hoping to maintain the autonomy of their cultural, economic, and community life.

WAR AND OCCUPATION

Chinese in Borneo were well aware of the Sino-Japanese War and the tensions in East Asia, but that war became a reality a few days after the Japanese attack on Pearl Harbor. An air bombardment surprised Pontianak at midday on December 19, 1941, when nine aircraft repeatedly dropped incendiaries and fragmentation bombs and strafed the city center, killing approximately 150 civilians and injuring at least that many more. Among the victims were several Chinese children of a mission school who, not suspecting an attack, had gone out to watch the planes. The bombing of other towns—Singkawang, Mempawah, and the airfield at Sanggauledo—followed.[1]

---

[1] For a work about these years based on documents and sources in Western languages, see Remco Zeedijk, "De Chinezen in West-Borneo tijdens de Japanse bezetting en de onafhankelijkheidsstrijd 1942-1949" (Master's thesis, University of Amsterdam, 1994), p. 18. A fictional but close-to-history account is M. Yanis, *Kapal terbang sembilan: Kisah pendudukan Jepang di Kalimantan Barat* (Pontianak: Yayasan Perguruan Panca Bhakti, 1983), pp. 8-9. See also A. H. Böhm, *West Borneo 1940—Kalimantan Barat 1950* (Tilburg: H. Gianotten, 1986), pp. 12-14; *Sejarah kebangkitan nasional daerah Kalimantan Barat* (Jakarta: Departemen Pendidikan dan Kebudayaan, Pusat Penelitian Sejarah dan Budaya, Proyek Penelitian dan Pencatatan Kebudayaan Daerah, 1978), pp. 71-72.

The single battalion of KNIL (Koninklijk Nederlands Indisch Leger, Royal Netherlands Indies Army) troops and the civilian authorities had received no support from the Netherlands since its occupation by Germany in May 1940. With the exception of some Chinese and a few others, the local population was disinclined to resist Japan. Many saw the Japanese as liberators.

Deprived of the airfield, the Dutch could not even engage enemy planes. They resorted to scorched earth tactics to prevent utilization of strategically important sites and equipment—in Pontianak these included factories and smoke houses, motor vehicles, and even several markets—from falling into Japanese hands.[2] On January 28, 1942, "they just left, leaving everything in a state of ruin."[3] Japanese forces moving southwards along the coast took Pontianak on February 2, 1942. Dutch troops then retreated up the Kapuas, but surrendered with other colonial forces on March 8, 1942. Dutch nationals were quickly imprisoned, put under house arrest, or killed outright. Local people plundered the shops for rice, sugar, cigarettes, and textiles, and carried off supplies from the warehouses of import firms until the Japanese put a stop to it.[4] Some Chinese and others fled inland,[5] but it is unknown how many joined this exodus, or how long they remained in the interior. Others left the towns for their fields and rubber gardens.

Soon, a Japanese army government was in place; in August, the navy assumed responsibility for the area.[6] Before departing, the army removed Dutch military and civilian prisoners to a camp for Allied internees in Kuching, Sarawak.[7]

The navy planned to incorporate the eastern islands of the Indies, including Borneo, with their rubber and petroleum resources, as permanent Japanese possessions. There would be no talk of independence. The Occupation installed Japanese military personnel and Japanese civilians as civic officials to carry out key tasks; the new mayor of Pontianak was Japanese. Many native Indonesians were promoted to fill former Dutch posts, and the lower bureaucracy was greatly expanded.[8] The native Malay rulers, of which there were twelve in West Borneo,

[2] Letter about Policy toward Chinese, ca. 1949, ARA 2.21.120 (57). Pontianak was the first city in the Indies to be bombed.

[3] The quotation above is from Yanis, *Kapal terbang*, p. 31.

[4] Yanis says the Japanese at first urged people to loot Dutch storehouses. His account uses many autobiographical elements. On the Japanese attack, see also Böhm, *West Borneo*, pp. 12-20, 22-23; Ja' Achmad, *Kalimantan Barat dibawah pendudukan tentara Jepang* (Pontianak: Departemen Pendidikan dan Kebudayaan, Proyek Rehabilitasi dan Perluasan Museum Kalimantan Barat, 1981), pp. 5-7; *Sejarah kebangkitan*, pp. 67-72; Mawardi Rivai, *Peristiwa Mandor* (Jakarta: Pustaka Antara, 1978), pp. 26-29; Susters Penitenten Recollectinen van de Congregatie van Etten, *"En toch gaan we," na vijf en twintig jaar werken in de missie van Sambas* (Etten: privately published [1949]), pp. 73-74. A few missionaries were left to tend a leprosarium near Singkawang; one Dutch official survived, hidden by Chinese in the interior. Letter to S. Meyer from chief agricultural officer, July 30, 1947, ARA 2.21.120 (68).

[5] See, for example, Sylvia Houliston, *Borneo Breakthrough* (London: China Inland Mission, 1963), p. 86.

[6] Yanis, *Kapal terbang*, pp. 30-32; Zeedijk, "Chinezen in West-Borneo," pp. 20-21.

[7] Böhm, *West Borneo*, pp. 22-23. A discussion of the considerable literature about the camps, including that in Sarawak, is beyond the scope of this work.

[8] George Sanford Kanahele, "The Japanese Occupation of Indonesia: Prelude to Independence" (PhD dissertation, Cornell University, 1967), pp. 38-39, 43, 58-59; Zeedijk, "Chinezen in West-Borneo," p. 22, *Sejarah*, p. 59. Yanis, *Kapal terbang*, describes what must be his own experience working under a Japanese businessman he had met in prewar times. The man spoke good

were allowed to remain in office, although they were suspected of sympathy for the Dutch.[9]

Naval headquarters for Eastern Indonesia had been situated in Makassar, where its Minseifu (Civil Administration Office) was located. The headquarters for Borneo was in Banjarmasin. The system was highly decentralized, and soon Allied attacks on sea lanes had nearly isolated local authorities in Pontianak.[10]

All Dutch enterprises were seized, all Dutch schools closed, and the use of Dutch forbidden. Some schools did continue to operate, teaching lessons in Indonesian, as did some Chinese schools. Teachers and other leaders had to learn Japanese; authorities propagated Japanese songs, dances, martial gymnastics, and "voluntary" labor activities. The only newspaper, *Borneo Shimbun*, published in Malay in Banjarmasin with an edition for Pontianak, offered the public news that had been carefully screened by the occupiers. As in other countries conquered by Japan, household radios had to be exchanged for sets that could only receive official broadcasts. The Japanese were hopelessly outnumbered, but they were ready to use violence at any time to maintain their hold on the region.

WARTIME ECONOMY

During the Occupation, Japanese trading houses took control of exports and imports, eliminating many Chinese firms engaged in international trade. After 1944, monopoly organizations called *kumiai* purchased and distributed goods. These cooperatively organized traders' associations, which tried to favor native Indonesian traders over Chinese, were supposed to inhibit black marketeering in essential commodities. Because of acute shortages in imports of necessities due to Allied attacks on shipping, the system failed to meet its purpose, and the various *kumiai* were soon encouraged to engage in food production, too.[11]

In prewar times, rubber and copra exports had financed the import of food and consumer goods. Exports had been worth *f*40 million, imports *f*20 million only a few years before the invasion.[12] Rice imports for West Borneo, both from abroad and from Java, were not less than 24,000 metric tons annually, and that amount increased to over 41,000 tons in 1937, when the authorities in West Borneo began

---

Indonesian. Yanis himself was an employee of the Sumitomo lumberyards from 1943 until the war's end.

[9] Sambas and Pontianak had sultans; the others, Mempawah, Landak, Sanggau, Tayan, Sekadau, Sintang, Kubu, Simpang, Sukadana, and Matan, had *panembahans*. Achmad, *Kalimantan Barat*, p. 19. Böhm says there were thirteen native rulers (*West Borneo*, p. 10); A. Verheul, Ervaringen in oorlogstijd: Verslag van den ex-assistent-resident van Singkawang (Zeist, typescript, 1946), p. 2.

[10] Kanahele, "Japanese Occupation," pp. 62-64. Land communications between Pontianak and Banjarmasin were nonexistent.

[11] Zeedijk, "Chinezen in West-Borneo," pp. 7-8, 37; Intelligence Report on Chinese Distribution System, Nederlands Instituut voor Oorlogsdocumentatie, Indische Collectie (Netherlands Institute for War Documentation, Indies Collection, hereafter NIOD-IC) 047689-047701; A. Azahari, *De ontwikkeling van het bevolkingslandbouwbedrijf in West-Kalimantan* (Bogor: mimeo, 1950), p. 94, says these organizations had the sole function of making sure local products reached the markets at set prices, preventing illicit trade. On *kumiai* in Java and Sumatra, see Twang Peck Yang, *The Chinese Business Elite in Indonesia and the Transition to Independence 1940-1950* (Kuala Lumpur, etc.: Oxford University Press, 1998), pp. 80-85.

[12] Böhm, *West Borneo*, p. 32. For the prewar economy, see chapter four.

stockpiling rice as insurance against predicted wartime shortages. Singkawang alone imported one thousand tons a month from Java.[13] In no way could the crippled, wartime transport system meet these demands. Wartime food shortages became so severe that the Japanese encouraged people to leave the towns by offering land, money, and larger rations of sugar to those who moved to rural areas. Many complied.[14]

Clandestine inter-island shipping, often in wooden ships constructed with local timber, kept trade alive. Smuggling was now a life-saving activity, which allowed at least a few commodities to reach Borneo's shores, though the supply was insufficient to maintain basic consumption. The former captain of a Bugis sailing ship, Arena Wati, has written a lively account of plying the route from Java to Pontianak and other cities during these years, dodging mines and torpedoes, protected by a bogus letter of authorization from the Kenpeitai (the Japanese army's secret police in Java). Smuggling reflected the abnormal economy. Java wanted copra; other islands sought quinine from Java, and payments for that commodity might be made in precious stones from Borneo or Singer sewing machine needles from Singapore. In early 1945 in Pontianak, the Japanese arrested Wati, but while he was being held Allied planes bombed the city, and he managed to escape in the confusion, taking along some gold, which was exchanged for salt at the next destination.[15] Other traders, including Bugis, Chinese, and others, followed equally adventurous routes.

The Japanese employed scarcity, enforced ignorance, and terror to control the population. West Borneo's modest prosperity vanished: coconut groves and pepper gardens were choked in weeds, rubber plantations lay untended. Not a single *perahu* plied the Kapuas, and the Japanese were unable to take advantage of the strategic goods formerly produced in the province. Consumer goods disappeared. Machines were deliberately destroyed or left to rust. Education was at a near standstill, reading matter and radios tightly controlled.[16]

WARTIME ORGANIZATIONS

The Japanese Occupation of Indonesia brought a political and social de-mobilization, as previous organizations were abolished, but in some areas, particularly in Java, it gradually built up organizations to recruit and co-opt popular energies for the war effort. The occupiers' desire to utilize popular efforts resulted in an opening for nationalist leaders to propagate an anti-imperialist ideology; after 1945, they could make use of these organizations and ideas to struggle for Indonesian independence.

In eastern areas of Indonesia, the Japanese navy avoided any mobilization of this kind. Economically, of course, there were the trading monopolies, but political

---

[13] Jacob Ozinga, *De economische ontwikkeling der Westerafdeeling van Borneo en de bevolkingsrubbercultuur* (Wageningen: Zomer en Keuning, 1940), p. 351; Verheul, Ervaringen, p. 2.

[14] Intelligence Report on Chinese Distribution System, NIOD-IC 047689-047701, p. 101.

[15] Arena Wati, *Memoir Arena Wati: Enda gulingku* (Bangi: Penerbit Universiti Kebangsaan Malaysia, 1991), pp. 71-84. Arena Wati places the Allied bombing in March 1945, but other sources say it took place in April.

[16] Böhm, *West Borneo*, p. 33.

activities were strictly limited. While the army was relinquishing control of West Borneo, in July 1942, it sponsored the formation of a Partai Nisshinkai in Pontianak. Like the similar Triple-A Movement in Java,[17] Nisshinkai was open to all Asians, native Indonesians, Chinese, and Arabs; it replaced all previous political or community organizations. The party's leaders were drawn from the prewar nationalist organization Parindra (Partai Indonesia Raya), but the initiative was clearly Japanese.[18]

The navy showed little interest in continuing the activities of Nisshinkai to mobilize the population, but it did organize a youth corps, Borneo Koonan Hookudan (Borneo National Service Corps for the Southern Territory), which recruited young native men. Apparently the Hookudan was similar to Heiho, operating as an auxiliary or labor battalion, but only a few hundred youths participated. With the schools teaching a Japanese-designed curriculum, even more intensive instruction was available at *asrama*, boarding-schools for young pupils that taught West Borneo's children to be as Japanese as possible.[19]

There was no talk of independence until just before the end of the war. For the most part, people in Borneo were ignorant of the activities in Java, and especially of the building of councils to prepare for independence. In early 1945, the naval authorities did organize local councils throughout West Borneo, for they had come to acknowledge that they could not occupy the region indefinitely, as had been their plan. In August of that year, the occupiers permitted formation of a regional committee to lay the groundwork for future independence; this was just days before the Japanese surrender.[20]

On the other hand, throughout the Occupation, the military maintained a repressive local security apparatus, designed to eliminate any unauthorized political activity, which included not only various kinds of police, but also a Keibitai (surveillance corps). From the Keibitai, a Tokeitai (special police force, rather like the Kenpeitai or secret police in Java) was formed in September 1942.[21]

THE CHINESE

A fictionalized Indonesian account of the Occupation by M. Yanis recalls the pervasive sense of fear that dominated the wartime era, especially among the

---

[17] This movement, which took its name from the slogan, "Japan, the Light of Asia, Japan, the Protector of Asia, Japan, the Leader of Asia," was supposed to reflect pan-Asian solidarity in support of Japan's war efforts. Although it established regional branches and held rallies, its aims remained nebulous. In September 1945, Triple-A was quietly disbanded. See Kanahele, "Japanese Occupation," pp. 45-50.

[18] Kanahele, "Japanese Occupation," pp. 51-52, 57. Although Kanahele describes Nisshinkai as fading in October 1942, it apparently lived on. According to a later but problematic Indonesian source, some five hundred participants attended a 1943 meeting of the Nissinkai (the usual Indonesian spelling) at the Gedung Medan Sepakat in Pontianak. Because those attending were thought to be conspiring against Japan, Japanese forces surrounded the building and riddled it with machine-gun fire, taking away the survivors and imposing a curfew. See Achmad, *Kalimantan Barat*. Another source, *Sejarah*, says Nissinkai was a youth organization, with nationalist leadership.

[19] Yanis, *Kapal terbang*, pp. 71-79. Postwar accounts simply call the Hookudan Heiho.

[20] Zeedijk, "Chinezen in West-Borneo," pp. 26-27.

[21] Ibid., p. 22.

ethnic Chinese. The Japanese laid blame for wartime shortages on the Chinese shopkeepers:

> The shoppers shared the feeling of fear with the Chinese who owned the shops . . . They, who called themselves Overseas Chinese, originated from Macao or Canton (Hakkas or Khe). They came to Indonesia with a wooden pillow and a red blanket. Their clothes were only what they wore, but they were known to be hard-working and energetic. . . . It was they, or their descendants, who sat doing accounts with an abacus. . . . All the counting with the abacus and the billowing of cigarette smoke could not solve the problem of how to get new wares to replace those that had been sold, because there was no more traffic with Singapore or Jakarta and the ships that did arrive did not bring more supplies. The strategy of businessmen, who know a thousand tricks, would be either to raise prices or to hoard goods. But both could be dangerous.
>
> A few days later a trader was picked up by the [security forces] along the street and whipped. Not with a whip but with a club that could break all your bones. People said this was so people could see and hear that this person was an enemy of the people, a criminal, because he had hoarded goods or raised prices.[22]

The Chinese community had contributed generously to China since the outbreak of the Sino-Japanese War in 1937 (see chapter five), and the Japanese were aware of these activities.[23] In Singapore and Malaya, Occupation forces had many prominent Chinese promptly eliminated, but the Japanese instituted no immediate, large-scale reprisals against Chinese leaders in West Borneo.[24] In fact, they allowed them to continue doing business. Ng Ngiap Soen (M. Huang Yechun) of Pontianak, head of an export firm, became head of the Kakyo Toseikai (Overseas Chinese General Association or Huaqiao Zonghui), the single approved organization for Chinese, which was also used to distribute scarce commodities and purchase raw materials. The Japanese attempted to confiscate Chinese wealth by levying heavy taxes and demanding "voluntary" contributions. Some Chinese firms were seized, but others profited from the situation, a stroke of good fortune that alienated many Dayaks and Malays. Hostility from other quarters only made the Chinese more united.[25]

---

[22] Yanis, *Kapal terbang*, pp. 89-90.

[23] See also Verheul, Ervaringen, p. 1.

[24] According, for example, to Ian Ward, *The Killer They Called a God* (Singapore: Media Masters, 1992), p. 85, in Singapore, Japanese intelligence had "lists" of anti-Japanese Chinese to be eliminated. A Japanese text speaks of the need to "thoroughly eradicate all Overseas Chinese organizations that have been manipulated for the purposes of political movements . . . all hidden troublemakers should be eradicated," cited in *Chinese Organizations in Southeast Asia in the 1930s*, ed. George L. Hicks (Singapore: Select Books, 1996), p. 164; see also Ian Brown, "Review," *Bijdragen tot de Taal-, Land- en Volkenkunde* 153,3 (1997): 441. For West Kalimantan, compare Zeedijk, "Chinezen in West-Borneo," p. 18; Verheul, Ervaringen, p. 15 mentions that a Chinese from Mempawah who had prominently supported China's war effort was arrested and executed in the early weeks of the Occupation.

[25] Intelligence Report on Chinese Distribution System, NIOD-IC 047689-047701; Zeedijk, "Chinezen in West-Borneo," pp. 30-32.

THE PONTIANAK AFFAIR

> The reign of terror of the Japanese was probably worse in West Borneo than in any other part of the Indies.[26]

This comment in a Dutch report of 1946 sums up the experience of the people of West Borneo during the war. In early 1943, the Japanese made it known that they had discovered a rebellious "conspiracy" in Banjarmasin. The former Dutch governor of Borneo, B. J. Haga, who was interned there, was said to be the ringleader of a multi-ethnic plot against Japan. Through an Indian friend, who brought food to him in prison, the Dutch official had maintained contact with the outside world, or so it was alleged. Since the friend in turn was illegally monitoring foreign news broadcasts, according to the Japanese, Haga was in a position to organize an anti-Japanese plot. That the charges were far-fetched, even incredible, did not stop the accusers. The Japanese authorities regarded unauthorized reception of radio broadcasts as traitorous; they tortured several suspects to obtain confessions and names of others supposedly involved in the plot. Widespread arrests followed, and a few weapons came to light. Some 140 persons were executed; most of the victims were never charged with a specific crime or tried in a court.

The authorities then decided, on the basis of testimony obtained through torture, that the "Haga Conspiracy" extended to other parts of Borneo as well. The head of Japanese police in Banjarmasin visited Pontianak several times before the "Pontianak Affair" broke on October 23, 1943, with large-scale arrests of prominent persons there.[27]

It is likely that the first few persons arrested and tortured in Pontianak implicated dozens, even hundreds, of others. The matter snowballed; some two thousand persons from all communities were named as suspects, and 1,300-1,500 arrested; even several women were seized. Little attempt was made to sort out false accusations. Some victims signed blank papers or "confessions" in Japanese. The local police, mostly Malays, cooperated in arrests, interrogations, and torture.[28]

---

[26] Intelligence Report on Chinese in West Borneo, October 7, 1946, ARA 2.10.14.02 AS 3971 (32).

[27] Zeedijk, "Chinezen in West-Borneo," pp. 47-48. Zeedijk points out that the few weapons found in Banjarmasin, unsuitable for staging an uprising, had been used to prevent plundering at the beginning of the Occupation. The military leadership apparently pressured the police chief, Sasuga Iwao, to come up with information about a "plot" in Pontianak.

[28] Two thousand is the number given in the reports of the Dutch postwar administration. They investigated the killings in 1946, shortly after their return, and tried to present a full picture of what happened, in order to prosecute war criminals in the postwar tribunals in Borneo and Japan. As will be seen, the number of victims later climbed to twenty thousand, although this number seems improbably high.

Plate 16. Mandor Memorial: Japanese soldiers humiliate both native and Chinese women. Credit: the author, 1998.

Some forty-six persons (some sources say thirty-six) received a perfunctory court martial in Pontianak in June 1944. The others were "sentenced"—that is, executed—on orders of Vice Admiral Daigo Tadashigi of Balikpapan.[29] Covered trucks left by night for a secret destination near Mandor; this grim procession continued until June 29, 1944.[30] People could only speculate about what was happening. Cooperation with Japan was no protection against arrest; many of those arrested were officeholders in Japanese-sponsored organizations.

On July 2, 1944, the newspaper *Borneo Shimbun*, Pontianak edition, finally gave an explanation for the mysterious activity and the disappearances. A massive, treasonous conspiracy against the Japanese had been uncovered, it reported. The Japanese had found whole caches of weapons and other evidence. They had seized the leaders and condemned them to death.

A list of the condemned conspirators followed; they included Malays, Bugis, Javanese, Minangkabaus, Bataks, Menadonese, Chinese, Eurasians, and Dayaks. Prominent on the list were the native rulers, who were entirely wiped out in this action. Officials claimed that all of the accused were participants in a broad, multi-ethnic conspiracy of some thirteen organizations that maintained

---

[29] Zeedijk, "Chinezen in West-Borneo," p. 51. The admiral later claimed an "emergency court of war" in Balikpapan had sentenced the victims, but none of these prisoners ever even saw Balikpapan. The Pontianak court sat for one and a half hours in all; there was no defense.

[30] Documents on War Crimes, NIOD-IC 019783-84; Böhm, *West Borneo*, p. 44, citing a Chinese newspaper dated October 14, 1945.

Plate 17. Mandor Memorial: As a response to provocations, a multi-ethnic group
plans resistence to the Japanese. Credit: the author.

surreptitious ties to the imprisoned Dutch and the still-distant Allies. Some forty
thousand persons had conspired to establish a left-wing "People's Republic of West
Borneo" that would abolish government by local rulers and set itself in their place.
According to this conspiracy theory, the sultans and other local rulers were said to
be willing participants in the affair, despite the fact that the "People's Republic
of West Borneo" allegedly intended to strip them of their powers. The story
continued: after dissolution of the feeble Nisshinkai, the Islamic youth group
Pemuda Muhammadijah had provided leadership for the conspiracy, and in mid-
1943 the Chinese had joined. Even the labor battalions were implicated. The
Chinese, *Borneo Shimbun* continued, had sabotaged the economy. The newspaper
blamed the Chinese for the misery caused by Japanese policies.[31]

If the publication silenced some questions, it raised others. The fictional
account by Yanis captures a fragment of the public response:

> "Very dubious," Aspar said. "They come from all different positions in
> society. Thus they have quite different interests. There are Sultans,
> Panembahans, and in addition to them, government employees and traders."
> . . . . If indeed there had been a plan for an uprising, its background was
> very heterogeneous. If it were not true, one thing *was* clear: they were victims
> of a foreign occupation and colonization of the nation and the people. . . . [32]

---

[31] Record of Interrogation, NIOD-IC 016932-38; Zeedijk, "Chinezen in West-Borneo," pp. 42-43
and 49-50.

[32] Yanis, *Kapal terbang*, pp. 184-185.

Plate 18. The Sultan of Pontianak (seated, right) with Resident K. A. James
(presumably to his left), circa 1920. The Sultan was later killed by the Japanese.
Credit: Collection of photographs frojm the career of O. Horst as Administratief
Officier, Controleur, and Assistant-Resident in Riau, West Borneo, Bali and
Lombok, 1912-1938. Kroch Library Rare and Manuscript Collections, Cornell
University Library. By permission.

Postwar investigations of the Dutch and the Australian army confirmed "Aspar's"
suspicions. They concluded that the "plots" were either a figment of Japanese
imagination or a cynical device set in motion to eliminate local leadership. Multi-
ethnic organizations were unknown in Borneo before the war, and the Allies
themselves knew nothing of their supposed undercover contacts in West Borneo.[33] A
Japanese officer later claimed that the police had uncovered several Allied
weapons, but other military men involved admitted that the charges were trumped
up. In truth, no "deed of active resistance against the Japanese" took place.[34]

Reconstructing what happened is impossible. The only witnesses were the
perpetrators and their victims. The *Borneo Shimbun* article is the only official
explanation for the reprisals,[35] apart from the conflicting testimony of Japanese
officers at the war crimes tribunals after the war. The only physical revolt—as
opposed to imaginary ones—against Japanese rule seems to have been a Dayak
uprising around Sanggau on the Kapuas in May–June 1945. The Dayaks there killed
a number of Japanese. The violence spread, even to hunting of Malay heads. The
Upper Kapuas remained insecure for months.[36]

---

[33] Letters about War Crimes in West Borneo, undated, ARA 2.10.14.02 AS 5305 and 5306.

[34] Documents on War Crimes, NIOD-IC 019783-84.

[35] *Sejarah*, pp. 27-42.

[36] Böhm, *West Borneo*, p. 42; see also the account in L. S. E. Frans Jacobus, *Sejarah perang
majang desa melawan Jepang* (Pontianak, n.p., 1981), compiled some time later. The Dayak

The Japanese massacres devastated the local Malay elite. The elderly sultan of Pontianak died in prison; his sons Pangeran Adipati and Pangeran Agung were beheaded.[37] All the other native rulers of West Borneo were executed. Many officials and former officials, members of prewar nationalist organizations, journalists, doctors, teachers, wives of Europeans—anyone who had European legal status—were rounded up and killed. Some of these victims were wealthy Chinese businessmen who were suspected of circumventing the trade monopolies or of possessing large amounts of money. Ng Ngiap Soen of the Kakyo Toseikai died under torture.[38] Ng Ngiap Kan (Huang Yejiang), owner of an ice factory and head of the organization in Singkawang—who was probably Ng Ngiap Soen's brother or cousin—was another victim. An anonymous statement described the method of execution:

> After midnight they were taken from the prison, a sack was put over the head, they were loaded like animals onto a truck and they were taken to an unfinished airfield that lay in the neighborhood of Mandor. There they were buried alive or beheaded and thrown into pits that had been dug for this purpose.[39]

Most executions were carried out near Mandor; they took place on at least eight occasions. The executioners were drawn from the Tokeitai, the special police (Indonesian-language accounts often credit the Kenpeitai with the actual killings, but that organization was not in Borneo). Unlike the Kenpeitai, who were trained professionals, the Tokeitai members were for the most part country boys with little education or training for the job. Perhaps for this reason, they acceded willingly (it seems) to the commands to dispose of their victims, who were usually beheaded with a sword.[40]

The *Borneo Shimbun* article indicates that most arrests took place in October 1943. A second sweep on January 24, 1944, apparently set off by the arrest in Singkawang of a Chinese carrying a forbidden radio receiver, rounded up a crowd of remaining "conspirators," most of them ethnic Chinese businessmen.[41] The arrested man, tortured both by Japanese and local police, admitted participating in a conspiracy. Others were implicated in subsequent questionings or in poison pen letters. Among those arrested as a result was Tjhen Tjhong-hin (Chen Changxing), former chairman of the Chamber of Commerce, also a leader of the Kakyo Toseikai, who was accused of organizing a plot to establish an autonomous West Borneo under the authority of Chungking. Authorities claimed that the plotters in

---

uprising is mentioned in Yanis, *Kapal terbang*, p. 225. Azahari, *Ontwikkeling*, p. 94, places Dayak uprisings in Meliau, Tayan, and Sanggau.

[37] Interrogation Reports, Pontianak, February 1946, NIOD-IC 016932-38, pp. 1-2.

[38] NIOD-IC 019843, p. 6. Compare IC 016946-48.

[39] From a statement that appeared in Dutch, English, and Chinese in a Chinese newspaper in Pontianak, here translated from the Dutch in Böhm, *West Borneo*, p. 44. Yanis's version of the *Borneo Shimbun* article says the plotters had been shot, but when the corpses were disinterred in 1947, it was obvious that most had been beheaded. See Yanis, *Kapal terbang*, p. 172. The Kakyo Toseikai was the Japanese-sponsored organization of "Overseas Chinese."

[40] Zeedijk, "Chinezen in West-Borneo," p. 22.

[41] Ibid., p. 50; Achmad, *Kalimantan Barat*, pp. 22-23.

Singkawang planned to poison the Japanese. Also, it was said that these Chinese had sabotaged the economy by buying up raw materials, refusing to sell them to the Japanese. This "Chinese affair" again scapegoated the Chinese, shifting blame for wartime economic devastation onto their shoulders, when in fact it had been caused by the policies of the occupiers themselves.

Additional victims were beheaded between December 1944 and February 1945 near the airport of Pontianak, Sungai Durian, by Tokeitai and Keibitai (surveillance corps) personnel. They were buried in mass graves they had been forced to dig themselves.[42] The official search for weapons and radios had uncovered only two revolvers, but the Japanese search parties confiscated valuables, money, jewelry, and gold in the process.[43] More Chinese now left the cities for the interior, many moving to their rubber gardens, others probably becoming, as they were in parts of Malaya, "squatters."[44]

AFTERMATH

Before their removal in 1945 to Sarawak by Australian forces, the Japanese officers and men burned all documents having to do with the Pontianak massacres, and they came to agree on a consistent testimony about the "plots."[45] The Australians, acting for the Allies, had landed in West Borneo on October 17, 1945, accompanied by a few Dutch officers as the first representatives of NICA, the Netherlands Indies Civil Administration, which was to restore colonial government in the following months.

News of the massacres came to light quickly. The Chinese-language paper, *Chung Hwa Jit Pao*, in its sixth edition, dated October 16, 1945, published on its first page a letter to the Allied troops and to NICA dated October 14, copied in English, Dutch, and Chinese. The open letter explained how thousands had died as a result of Japanese mistreatment and how some prisoners, having been tortured, were taken out by trucks to be killed at the "unfinished aerodrome somewhere in the vicinity of Mandor." The paper demanded that those responsible for the killings be punished and expressed its happiness that the Allies were now arriving.[46]

In January and February 1946, some 111 lower-level Japanese military men were flown from Kuching to Pontianak to be tried at an Allied temporary war court for the killings. (Major offenders were tried in Tokyo.) It was difficult to prevent the prisoners from being lynched when they arrived in Pontianak, yet once their trials commenced, few witnesses came forward with testimony against them.

---

[42] Zeedijk, "Chinezen in West-Borneo," pp. 54-59, citing Nederlands Instituut voor Oorlogsdocumentatie, Indische Collectie documents and records of interrogations. Killings took place on at least two occasions.

[43] Interrogation Reports, NIOD-IC 016946-48.

[44] Herman Josef van Hulten, *Hidupku di antara Suku Daya: Catatan seorang misionaris* (Jakarta: Grasindo, 1992), p. 51. The Chinese farmers had leases of limited duration for their land, not ownership; the squatters had neither.

[45] Intelligence Report on Chinese Massacre, March 1, 1946, NIOD-IC 019484-019490, pp. 1-2.

[46] *Chung Hwa Jit Pao* (The Chinese Daily News), Pontianak, October 16, 1945 (in copy).

Nevertheless the press and individuals complained that the trials were moving too slowly.[47]

The prisoners finally led Dutch officials to mass graves. Some insisted that a multi-ethnic conspiracy had truly existed; others admitted they had no evidence of one. In January 1948 the court sentenced seven men to death for their involvement and another five to prison for ten to twenty years. The prosecutors themselves could not explain the extraordinary and apparently unique orgy of cruelty in West Borneo.[48]

> [The Chinese] were arrested on account of their wealth, not because they had committed any crime. . . . They were mostly wealthy and important people and therefore it was better to kill them.[49]

Only some of the dead could be identified. Early plans for a memorial were begun, and a committee formed for that purpose by Indonesians and Chinese. This Panitia Peringatan Kaum Malang (Committee for the Remembrance of the Victims), with the new sultan of Pontianak as honorary chairman, laid the cornerstone for the memorial in late 1946.[50] When in 1947 the memorial was dedicated, the numbers of victims was estimated to be about one thousand killed at Kopyang near Mandor, 270 at Sungai Durian, another 150 in Ketapang (south of Pontianak), thirteen behind the former resident's house, six at the prison, and thirteen behind one of the churches: in all about 1,500 persons. Twenty-one were identified as European, 559 as native Indonesian, eighteen as Indian, and 854 as Chinese—the largest group.[51]

Plate 19. The Mandor Memorial to victims of the Japanese massacre, built on the site after 1970. Credit: the author, 1998.

---

[47] Böhm, *West Borneo*, p. 45.

[48] Intelligence Report on Chinese Massacre, March 1, 1946, NIOD-IC 019484-019490, p. 4; Report on Reoccupying Pontianak, October 1945-March 1946, ARA 2.10.14.02 AS 3173.

[49] Zeedijk, *Chinezen in West Borneo*, p. 61, citing testimony of one Japanese involved.

[50] Böhm, *West Borneo*, pp. 57-58; Monthly Report, August 1946, ANRI AS 1313. Xie Feng, *Zhanhou Nanyang Huaqiao gaikuang: Xi Boneizhou zhibu* (Singapore: n.p., 1947), p. 34, shows a photograph of the discovery.

[51] Speech of Memorial Committee, March 15, 1947, ANRI AS 1309. The original memorial has since been replaced by a large commemorative edifice; see Plates 16, 17, and 19.

The elimination of the leadership of the entire province left a vacuum in local administration. At the beginning of 1944, the Japanese occupiers had imported some sixty Banjarese to fill the gaps in the lower levels of the Occupation administration. Pontianak had become a ghost town.[52]

COLLABORATION AND RESISTANCE

Not all Chinese were victims or opponents of the Japanese; some acted as spies or informants, some as translators, and some as speculators. Generally, however, the Chinese were perceived as less cooperative than the Malays, who were selected by the Japanese to serve as policemen and officials, as they had served in Dutch times. Japanese policy was ethnically divisive in intent and in effect. The Chinese resented Malays for collaborating with the Japanese in administrative and police tasks. Dayaks, who were the least likely to profit from interactions with the Occupation forces, sometimes saw the Malays as exploiters, and the Chinese as profiteers. Yet some Chinese found refuge with Dayaks in the interior, where Dayaks shared their meager food supplies with them.[53]

When the war turned against the Japanese, most Chinese received the news gladly. Expectations ran high, not only because it appeared that the Japanese would be forced out of West Borneo, but even more because China appeared to be one of the victors of the war. The following fictional account illustrates the Chinese reaction as perceived by their neighbors:

> Tan Si Kiang and his group often displayed their glee excessively. Admittedly, they had good reason to do so after living under oppression for so long. . . . China after all was not just a large country, but also one of those that had won the war. That country was one of the Big Three or maybe Big Four that waved the flag of victory, in the eyes of Tan Si Kiang and his group. That's what made him proud.
>
> Tan Si Kiang and his group often showed their joy openly in the form of conceit and a feeling of superiority. This attitude was not only toward Japan, . . . but toward Indonesians and even more toward the youth, who regarded this phenomenon with suppressed anger. Sometimes their attitude and their behavior surfaced in the form of negative comments. . . . In Yahya's opinion, i t would be best if Tan Si Kiang and his group would restrain their feelings.[54]

The Chinese community, divided before the war between strongly China-oriented factions and those with other concerns, was now more unified politically and more conscious of being ethnically Chinese. China became the focus of political aspirations, and Singapore soon regained its economic influence.

---

[52] Zeedijk, "Chinezen in West-Borneo," pp. 24-25, 52; Böhm, *West Borneo*, p. 33; Report on Reoccupying Pontianak, ARA 2.10.14.02 AS 3173; Yanis, *Kapal terbang*, pp. 182ff.

[53] Report on Reoccupying Pontianak, ARA 2.10.14.02 AS 3173; Secret Travel Report, West Borneo, March 15-16, 1945, ARA 2.10.29 RI 595; Attitude of Chinese to Government, Pontianak, September 15, 1946 ARA 2.10.17 PG 1194; F. H. van Naerssen, Verslag van mijn verblijf in Kalimantan Barat (Cornell University Library, typescript 1949), p. 28.

[54] Yanis, *Kapal terbang*, p. 220.

INTERIM AND DUTCH RESTORATION

When the Australian forces reached Pontianak on October 17, 1945, a full two months after the Japanese surrender, their reception reflected the new situation. In Pontianak, not a single Dutch flag welcomed the Allies. The Chinese of the town had raised Chinese flags.

When the surrender of the Japanese forces on August 15, 1945 became known in West Borneo, many Chinese confidently expected that Chinese Nationalist troops would liberate Borneo from the Japanese and integrate the Chinese Districts as an overseas province of China. In Bengkayang, Chinese secret societies had gathered some arms and used them to intimidate the Dayaks, forcing some in January 1946 to bow before the Chinese flag.[55] China was, after all, one of the Big Five and a major power.[56]

The absence of local leadership made the task of the returning Dutch—who were trying to organize a local representative council as NICA's administrative personnel began to arrive—nearly impossible. They confronted not only Chinese nationalism, but widespread Indonesian nationalism as well, for Indonesian nationalism had infected other groups of the population. When news of the Indonesian proclamation of independence (August 17, 1945) and, after that, the Indonesian revolution, reached Borneo, the reaction was relatively muted. Little open fighting took place around Pontianak or in the Chinese Districts, but Indonesian guerrillas, including about three hundred former Heiho members, were active to the south, near Ketapang,[57] and to a lesser extent in the Sambas area. In Pontianak, red-white flags appeared showing support for the Indonesian Republic. Some nationalist materials had even entered with pro-Republican Australian troops.[58]

The Japanese had passed control of local government to a certain A. Asikin, a Banjarese who had held office under the Japanese during the Occupation and who now assumed the position of resident. Since the Japanese had begun to dispose of their supplies, and the danger of banditry had increased, Asikin supported the Chinese in setting up public security forces (Penjagaan Keamanan Umum, at the time spelled "Oemum," abbreviated PKO) in most towns to guard Japanese stockpiles of commodities.[59] Most PKO supporters were Chinese; later, some people accused the Chinese businessmen of using the PKO to seize rice and sugar supplies from Japanese storehouses.[60]

---

[55] Zeedijk, "Chinezen in West-Borneo," p. 75.

[56] Report on Situation in West and South Borneo, November 1945, ARA 2.10.14.02 AS 3168, Appendices 2 and 4; Intelligence Report on the Japanese Occupation, ARA AS 3173; Report, Attitude of Chinese to Government, Pontianak, September 15, 1946 ARA 2.10.17 PG 1194.

[57] In this area, where Dutch control was almost non-existent, some Chinese were robbed, kidnapped, or raped by pro-Republican forces in the area of Air Hitam and Sukamara, Matan. ARA 2.10.14.02 AS 3651.

[58] Böhm, *West Borneo*, pp. 36-37, 41; Report on Situation, February-June 1946, ARA 2.10.14.02 AS 3651. A few Indonesian nationalists, former prisoners in Boven Digul, had spent the war years in Australia, building pro-independence sympathy there.

[59] Report of November 5, 1945, ANRI AS 1308.

[60] Yanis, *Kapal terbang*, pp. 224-227. "Among its directors sat leaders of the Siang Hwee and the Chunghua Kung Hwee," p. 225. Yanis says people resented the organization, because it was looking for goods and money to turn over to its businessmen-leaders. For a comment on

The Chinese, who had had no weapons when the Japanese searched their homes during the Pontianiak Affair, suddenly had enough to arm the PKO. This new security organization resembled the Pao An Tui (*baoandui*), the unofficial Chinese constabulary forces that grew like mushrooms in Southeast Asian cities after the war. In some parts of Java, these Chinese security forces were even partly armed by the Dutch.[61] Asikin disbanded the Chinese-dominated PKO in Pontianak on October 18, 1945, although elsewhere they continued to operate; apparently Asikin expected the Australians to maintain order. Clashes between Malays and Chinese followed. After several persons were wounded in the fighting and three died, the PKO was reinstated in Pontianak, and the arriving Dutch, needing to maintain order, supported it.[62]

Meanwhile, Dutch control expanded under NICA; prewar officials were also beginning to return from the camps in Sarawak. Asikin agreed to cooperate with NICA. Australian forces officially turned over authority to it on October 22, 1945 and departed from Borneo. NICA's authority was still tenuous. Only in January 1946 did NICA finally gain control of Singkawang. It established administrative control over Ketapang and Sintang even later, and over Bengkayang as late as October 1946.[63] This vacuum of power left Chinese communities to their own devices.

ECONOMY AND POPULATION CHANGE

In 1948, the administration estimated that Chinese in the region numbered 203,305, about 17 percent of the total population of 1,179,817. Most Chinese in West Kalimantan, as it was officially called after Indonesian independence, lived in the subdistricts of Singkawang (with a population of 73,568 Chinese residents), Pontianak (52,649 Chinese residents), and Mempawah (30,821 Chinese residents). People who had fled from the towns during the Occupation were now streaming back. Pontianak grew from a population of about 48,000 in prewar times to 85,000 in 1948; the town and territory within five kilometers of the city had a population of 110,000 people.[64] Immigration of Chinese, legal or illegal, may have added to relatively high natural growth, but identifying illegal immigrants was impossible

---

hoarding, see Report to Regional Head, S. Meyer, Pontianak, February 25, 1949, ARA 2.21.120 (83).

[61] On the Pao An Tui, see Mary F. Somers Heidhues, "Citizenship and Identity: Ethnic Chinese and the Indonesian Revolution," in *Changing Identities of the Southeast Asian Chinese since World War II*, ed. Jennifer Cushman and Wang Gungwu (Hong Kong: Hong Kong University Press, 1988), pp. 125-128. Machrus Effendy, *Penghancuran PGRS-PARAKU dan PKI di Kalimantan Barat* (Jakarta: published by author, 1995), pp. 11-13, 31, claims that the PKO acquired arms from the Japanese and used them against non-Chinese. His account is, however, not very reliable in other respects.

[62] Report of November 5, 1945, ANRI AS 1308; Report, Jakarta, December 4, and Appendix 2, ARA 2.10.14.02 AS 3168.

[63] Pontianak, Singkwang, Ketapang, and Sintang were the four district capitals in 1945. Control of the surrounding areas was probably never assured. Zeedijk, "Chinezen in West-Borneo," pp. 66-67; Saleh As'ad Djamhari et al., *Monumen Perjuangan Daerah Kalimantan Barat* ([Jakarta]: Departemen Pendidikan dan Kebudayaan, Direktorat Sejarah dan Nilai Tradisional, Projek Inventarisasi dan Dokumentasi Sejarah Nasional, 1987), p. 18.

[64] Azahari, *Ontwikkeling*, p. 95. A major reason for the shift to the towns was that scarce commodities were distributed in urban or near-urban areas only.

because so many people had destroyed their papers during the Japanese Occupation.[65] In 1953, the total population of the province was said to have reached 1,800,000, and the number of Chinese 450,000, or 25 percent of the total. This is probably a significant exaggeration, but the fact remains that the Chinese population was substantial and growing.[66]

The following report reveals the initial impression the Chinese presence made on a missionary who visited the island in 1950. It appeared to this observer that the Chinese minority had assumed such control of the economy that the rest of Kalimantan's society was of little importance:

> ... They live in the cities, the large settlements, the centers of trade, along the rivers and on the highways, everywhere where trade can be carried out, where business can be transacted. The Chinese hold the money, the capital, the goods, in their hands; they are the owners of enterprises and farms, of houses and movie theaters; of ships and buses, the gold- and silversmiths, jacks of all trades, who make money from everything and are present everywhere where money is to be made. ... They form a closed ... Chinese society in the Daerah (region) Kalimantan Barat. Their economy may have contributed a lot to the well-being of the territory, [but] that economy never had the well-being of Indonesia as its goal, nor even the well-being of Kalimantan Barat, but definitely only the well-being of the Chinese community of the region. .. [T]he Indonesians [are] only a means to their well-being ... [T]he Chinese ... in reality, have their own ministries of education and economic affairs, even if they have different titles (school *kongsis* and trade *kongsis*) ... a state within the State.[67]

Such impressions were not unusual, and they were fed by a certain inward orientation within West Kalimantan's Chinese community itself.

Disorder, devastation, and scarcities posed problems for the returned colonial administration. Since the war, some forty thousand tons of annual rice imports were now estimated to be necessary (even allowing for some substitution of cassava for rice), but imports were only 13,246 tons in 1946 and by 1948 had climbed to a still inadequate 24,821 tons.[68] Textiles, medicines, spare parts, machines, boats, motor vehicles were all rare.[69] A missionary more sympathetic to the Chinese, who had

---

[65] H. de Meel, "Het verloop van de bevolking in West-Borneo 1920-1948," *Tijdschrift van het Koninklijk Nederlandsch Aardrijkskundig Genootschap* 69 (1952): 186; Reports of September and October 1948, ARA 2.10.14.02 AS 3177. Authorities believed some of this immigration was "infiltration" from Malaya. Report, September 7-21, 1948, ARA 2.10.29 RI 588. In view of food and other rationing, perhaps some people inflated the size of their families in postwar years.

[66] K. Tobing, *Kalimantan Barat* (Bandung: Masa Baru, 1952), pp. 31-33. As will be seen, sources for West Kalimantan in the 1950s are extremely rare and, apart from Tobing's description, for the most part missionary materials. An exception is R. M. Subianto Notowardojo, *Kalimantan Barat sepintas lalu dilihat dari sudut sosial ekonomi* (Jakarta: Direktorat Perekonomian Rakjat, Kementerian Perekonomian, 1951, mimeo). (I thank Jamie Davidson for making it available.) As noted, a provincial archives was only established in the 1990s.

[67] P. Ludovicus Boddeke, *De missie in het Vicariaat van Pontianak na de Japanse capitulatie* (Bussum, mimeo, 1950), p. 20.

[68] Böhm, *West Borneo*, pp. 50, 57. Because the Japanese had confiscated firearms, hunting was difficult, and a plague of wild pigs in 1945 destroyed much of the harvest.

[69] Report, January 14, 1946, ARA 2.10.14.02 AS 3173.

lived in the province and returned to Pemangkat after the war, saw how much the devastation had affected the Chinese, too, especially the poor. He recalled that when he visited Chinese families, the children hid, for they had hardly any clothes.

The Dutch set up NIGIEO (Netherlands Indies Government Import and Export Organization), an agency intended to control the stockpiles of supplies abandoned by the Japanese, as well as all imports and exports. Rubber and copra were excepted, with control over rubber exports being assigned to NIRF (Nederlands Indisch Rubberfonds, Netherlands Indies Rubber Fund) and later to NIRUB (Nederlands Indisch Rubberuitvoerbedrijf, Netherlands Indies Rubber Export Company), and control over copra given to the Coprafonds (Copra Fund). These Dutch institutions, which were not so different from the *kumiai*, soon aroused the resentment of the Chinese traders and producers.

NIGIEO tried to monopolize all imports and exports, including those formerly in private hands. Its licences were given to Dutch firms at the expense of local businesses.[70]

> Naturally the small producer was the victim of these amazing contortions from Batavia, and trade remained quite unsettled for months, handicapping economic reconstruction.[71]

New NICA money was exchanged at a rate of Japanese 1.00 = ƒ0.03. Some Chinese and others who had hoarded the highly inflated Japanese currency now saw their "investment" evaporate. Pro-republican elements, on the other hand, encouraged people to refuse to accept NICA money and threatened those who did.[72]

NICA policy had another goal, besides restoring order and administration: they wanted control of the Outer Islands in order to earn foreign exchange for the homeland and to deny it to the Republic. Rehabilitation of rubber plantings and coconut groves was a first step; after that, producers and dealers had to be brought to collect and sell their products to official agencies at controlled prices. Not surprisingly, NICA's economic policies were distinctly unpopular; in addition, they seldom met consumer demands. In April 1946, Chinese—and later other—harbor coolies in Pontianak struck for more pay. Their dissatisfaction was understandable, given the scarcity of food and clothing and their relatively low wages.[73]

NIGIEO freed exports of non-food products, except rubber and copra, from agency control at the end of 1946. Officials wished to maintain the monopoly over rubber, but rubber exports tended to escape official control.[74] NIRF had imported needed supplies for producers (such as formic acid to treat the latex), but offered to buy rubber only at a price well below that available in Singapore. (All of West

---

[70] Netherlands, Staten-Generaal, "Borneo en de Groote Oost," part 8A of *Enquêtecommissie Regeringsbeleid, 1940-1945, Verslag* (The Hague: Staatsdrukkerij- en Uitgeverijbedrijf, 1956), pp. 582-584.

[71] Böhm, *West Borneo*, p. 56.

[72] Report, March 16-31, 1946, ARA 2.10.14.02 AS 3971.

[73] Military Report, April 1946, ARA 2.10.14.02 AS 3651.

[74] Report, October 7, 1946, ARA 2.10.14.02 AS 3971; Böhm, *West Borneo*, p. 52.

Kalimantan's rubber went to Singapore for further processing; after 1945 its quality was too poor for shipment directly to Western buyers.[75])

So long as rice prices remained high because of scarcity, NICA money and low payments were not acceptable to the people of West Kalimantan, and so they found ways to circumvent the new colonial impositions. Smuggling proliferated. The Dutch had too few boats to patrol the coast, and in 1946, for example, a trip to Singapore with a *perahu*, a small sailing boat, of fifty to sixty tons might bring a profit of *f*80,000-*f*100,000 for a smuggler. The shippers could bring in consumer goods (and sometimes weapons?) from Singapore and circumvent NIGIEO. Often these imports were shipped on to Java.

Smugglers avoided major harbors (the harbor at Singkawang had silted up by this time) and used sampans or small boats to transport their goods, departing from one of the many creeks and rivers that had served the kongsis a century earlier. They delivered the goods to larger motorized ships that waited beyond the three-mile zone, outside territorial waters, where the Dutch authorities could not intervene. Alternatively, local customs inspectors were simply bribed;[76] thus, some NIGIEO personnel were themselves implicated in illicit transactions. Each month, hundreds of tons of pigs, chickens, copra, rubber, and pepper left the province illegally. Pemangkat, where a criminal secret society was active, was an especially good base. Few legitimate goods were arriving in West Kalimantan in 1946, except for some high-priced salt.[77]

Graph 6.1:
Rubber Exports, Postwar

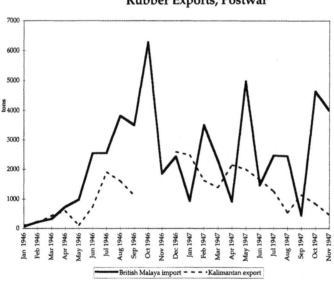

---

[75] Ng Kong Beng and Tan Kong Choon. Transcript, interviews with rubber dealers, 1980. Singapore National Archives, Oral History Department.

[76] Report, July 16-31, 1946, ARA 2.10.14.02 AS 3971; Report, March 16-31, 1948, ARA AS 3177; Excerpt from Monthly Report of Financial Authorities, April 1949, ARA 2.21.120 (113).

[77] Report on Reoccupying Pontianak, Appendix 6, ARA 2.10.14.02 AS 3173; Intelligence Report on Chinese in West Borneo, October 7, 1946, ARA AS 3971 (32); Secret Travel Report, West Borneo, March 15-16, 1945, ARA 2.10.29 RI 595; Azahari, *Ontwikkeling*, p. 97.

The preceding table for 1946-47 compares monthly NIRUB rubber purchases for export with the total imports from West Kalimantan as recorded in the official statistics for British Malaya, including Singapore. The discrepancy between the two amounts reveals the large volume of rubber that left the province "unofficially."

The colonial authorities apparently recognized that the rubber producers of West Kalimantan were reluctant to market their goods through NIRUB and that they had found other, often illegal, channels for their exports. In response, the Dutch elected to sweeten the deals offered by the agency. Toward the end of 1947, rubber sellers were given "inducements"—they were offered textiles and other goods that happened to be scarce in Singapore—in addition to the cash payment from NIRUB. Later, inducements were paid in foreign exchange. In the first six months of 1948, the official rubber exports of over three thousand tons monthly were well below the 1941 figure of 4,700 tons. The total for all of 1948, however, reached an almost "normal" 51,549 tons.[78] Smuggling was still continuing at a level of 1,000-1,200 tons monthly in August 1948-January 1949; some smuggled products were being sent overland to Sarawak. Substantial Chinese traders with close contacts among rubber "barons" in Singapore (some Pontianak firms were branches of Singapore companies) could undervalue their cargo and thus remove their profits from the grasp of tax collectors in Indonesia; they would store their illicit gain in Singapore. Smuggling and profiteering gave rise to blackmail and violence. Fearing retaliation, the victims usually would not report any crimes to the police. Only by mid-1949 had smuggling fallen significantly, but the general economic situation remained poor.[79]

Dutch export policies tended to favor producers in the Kapuas region (who were less likely to be Chinese) against those in the Singkawang area (who were predominantly Chinese). The estimated capacity of Singkawang and Sambas was nine hundred tons monthly, but in fact only about three hundred tons were officially exported from there, partly because production was lagging. The authorities tried to force all producers to export through Pontianak, despite the high costs of road transport. Consequently, the incomes of producers in the Singkawang area fell. The simplest answer to this dilemma was to smuggle, although by mid-1949 official control of shipping had improved, so that smuggling by sea had become a risky and sometimes costly alternative to legal trade.

In 1949, Officer for Chinese Affairs Steven Meyer, who had been posted to the area a few months earlier, recognized that the Singkawang-Bengkayang area was being impoverished. Meyer complained in writing that official policies were depressing the income of that area's tappers. As a result, the rubber growers and tappers of the Chinese Districts had to engage in smuggling to earn a bare living or face poverty. Official policies were so determental to this group that they were driving the people toward Communism. Since virtually "all" of Singkawang's rubber was being smuggled, tapping would completely cease if illicit trade were

---

[78] Report, June 1948, ARA 2.10.14.02 AS 3177; Böhm, *West Borneo*, p. 57.

[79] Report, June 1948, ARA 2.10.14.02 AS 3177; Report, January 1949, ARA AS 3178; Report, March, April, and June 1949, ARA 2.21.120:113; also Azahari, *Ontwikkeling*, pp. 94-96, who points out that smuggling brought a lot of cash to coastal dwellers, but at the same time, rice imports remained far below prewar levels, so some were still losing.

rigorously suppressed. Poverty in the old Chinese Districts aggravated unrest and contributed to political opposition.[80]

CHINESE COMMUNITY LIFE

In spite of the loss of its leaders as a result of the Japanese massacre, the Chinese community quickly organized in response to the restrictive measures imposed by NIGIEO, and before long a Chamber of Commerce was in operation. By 1947, Pontianak also had a Fujian Huiguan (Fujian Association) and a number of other community organizations. The restored colonial administration was unsure how to deal with this increasingly organized community. Reviving the pre-war system of government that had relied on unpopular, Dutch-appointed Chinese officers was impossible; the Chinese wanted to manage their own affairs. The Government did appoint Chinese officials to collect taxes, but press and community organizations objected strongly to the measure.[81]

Many new leaders in Pontianak were in their thirties and forties, young compared to leaders in Chinese communities in other cities, but this reflects the decimation of the older generation under the Japanese Occupation. Most business leaders were China-born, but the local-born often acted as community spokesmen. Of eighty-five prominent Chinese in Pontianak in 1947, sixty-two were China-born; at least six others had been educated in China. Only three indicated that they had a knowledge of Dutch, a situation that differed significantly from that in Java, where the Chinese leaders, at least the *peranakans*, commonly spoke Dutch.[82]

Among the newly prominent community leaders, Ng Ngiap Lian (M. Huang Yelian, thirty-eight in 1947 and Pontianak-born) was chairman of the re-instated Federation of Chinese Chambers of Commerce (Huashang Zonghui).[83] Other influential businessmen[84] included the founders of the Chinese General Association (Chung Hua Kung Hui, or Zhonghua Gonghui), which was established at the end of 1945 in Pontianak and Singkawang. The Chinese General Association was a

---

[80] Letter, July 5, 1949, ARA 2.10.14.02 AS 2780, also in ARA 2.21.120 (55); Report, June, August 1948, ARA AS 3177. A December report, also in ARA AS 3177, denied that Singkawang's rubber prices were lower than those of Pontianak. See also Situation in West Borneo, ARA AS 1313. In Sambas, one *kapitan* and his family used a private corps of enforcers to profit from smuggling and distribution of scarce goods. See Report on Visit to Sambas, ARA 2.21.120 (78).

[81] Letter of Acting Resident, January 8, 1948, ARA 2.21.120 (40). See also *Lee Ming Pao* for May 22 and 28, 1947, cited in *Chinesche Persoverzicht*, June 10, 1947.

[82] See Xie, *Zhanhou Nanyang*, pp. 12-21 for biographies of community leaders in Pontianak. Obviously the sample is not representative; nearly all are businessmen, and conceivably they earned mention in this publication by contributing to it financially.

[83] Report on Situation in West and South Borneo, November 1945, ARA 2.10.14.02 AS 3168. Ng Ngiap Lian (sometimes written Liang) is apparently a brother or cousin of the two Ngs killed by the Japanese (above); he was one of six brothers, according to Xie, *Zhanhou Nanyang*. He served as an official of the Chamber for years. Notowardojo, *Kalimantan Barat*, p. 19, lists him first among the "millionaires" of Pontianak. In January 1947, Tan Tje Oe became Chairman of the Chamber (Political and Economic Reports, West Borneo, 1947, ARA AS 3176); Ng remained a commissioner.

[84] Officials called some of them "economic collaborators" with Japan, but given Japan's economic policies, they had to collaborate to remain in business, as the discussion above shows.

community-wide umbrella organization with different internal committees involved in education, commercial activities (the local Chinese Chamber of Commerce was a member), cultural affairs, and women's affairs. Its education committee was to sponsor schools and "social institutes" for the community.[85] Other major towns in West Kalimantan had their own Chinese general associations.

The general associations claimed to represent the entire community of ethnic Chinese. Apart from the associations that joined and promoted it, every individual of Chinese descent in its territory was in theory a member of the organization. Every adult (above the Chinese age of twenty[86]) was entitled to vote in its affairs. Chinese businessmen were to provide operating funds for the association by levying an informal tax on goods sold or exported—a tax that was thus paid by all consumers in the region but which supported Chinese interests only. The general association in Pontianak at first worked closely with the Chinese consulate; both considered themselves representatives of *all* ethnic Chinese. After December 1947, leadership of the Chamber of Commerce of Pontianak, with its substantial merchants, and the leadership of the Chinese General Association were practically identical.[87]

In March 1947, Pontianak welcomed a consul of the Nationalist Republic of China, Cheng Da Hung. Local people had to pay for his house, car, office furnishings, and livelihood, since the Nanjing government was short of foreign currency. Cheng worked closely with the local Guomindang, which enjoyed considerable popularity in early postwar months. Soon, however, the civil war in China made itself felt among communities abroad, splitting the community politically.[88]

In 1947, the consul required all Chinese schools and headquarters of Chinese community organizations to display a large Chinese Nationalist flag and a portrait of Sun Yatsen. Members of the Guomindang had to swear a new oath of loyalty to the party; some complied by swearing before a *toapekong* and killing a chicken, recalling the sworn brotherhoods of the past. Organizations were offered premiums for adopting appropriate by-laws, made in China, and for contributing money to China.[89] The consul made repeated attempts to register all Chinese organizations, including data about their statutes, leaders, and finances, and even

---

[85] Statutes in Appendix 4, ARA 2.10.14.02 AS 3173; on Singkawang, see Böhm, *West Borneo*, pp. 114-115.

[86] A Chinese child is considered one year old at birth and gains another year at each Chinese New Year, so "adults" would be something over eighteen years old by Western reckoning.

[87] Report to Regional Head, S. Meyer, Pontianak, February 25, 1949, ARA 2.21.120 (83).

[88] Pamphlet, "West-Borneo/Kalimantan Barat," 12 Mei 1947, published by West Borneo Council and Information Service, Pontianak, May 12, 1947, ARA 2.21.120 (47); General Report, April 1-15, 1947, ARA 2.10.14.02 AS 3176. Cheng was probably not as effective politically as the Dutch feared. A Jiangsu man, he spoke neither Teochiu nor Hakka.

[89] Draft Note to Governor General, Pontianak, March 13, 1948, ARA 2.21.120 (69); Note, Meyer to Acting Resident, ARA 2.21.120 (70); and Notes on Role of Consulate, 1949, ARA 2.21.120 (82). The links between Guomindang and secret societies were of long standing, but this kind of oath was surely not what the consul had in mind. It was said that only a third of Guomindang members were willing to take the new oath. On killing a chicken, see chapter three and The Siauw Giap, "Rural Unrest in West Kalimantan: The Chinese Uprising in 1914," in *Leyden Studies in Sinology*, ed. W. L. Idema (Leiden: E. J. Brill, 1981), p. 150.

to register all Chinese persons in the territory.[90] As might be expected, these activities aroused great mistrust among Dutch officials.

The majority of Chinese in West Kalimantan was now local-born, which made them Dutch subjects according to colonial law (and citizens of Indonesia according to laws of the Indonesian Republic). The 1945 consular agreement between the Republic of China and the Netherlands, which controlled West Kalimantan from 1945 to early 1950, exempted these persons from the jurisdiction of the Chinese consulate, but the consul simply ignored this provision.[91]

The Chinese general associations, like the chambers of commerce, claimed to represent both local-born citizens and foreigners; membership was non-voluntary. Both the presence of Consul Cheng and the activities of these organizations thus raised the old specter of a Chinese "state within the state."[92] Consul Cheng cooperated with the Netherlands in a limited manner, not by confining his involvement to the affairs of the non-local-born (whom both sides recognized as Chinese citizens), as stipulated in the 1945 agreement, but by denouncing individuals and organizations suspected of Communist activities to the Dutch officials. The local Guomindang behaved similarly.[93]

Chinese organizations were not oblivious to the Indonesian Revolution. Small-scale fighting that often victimized Chinese took place in more isolated areas south of Pontianak.[94] The Chinese General Associations of West Kalimantan issued a common resolution asking both sides, Dutch and Indonesian, to protect the life and property of ethnic Chinese. Comments on Indonesian independence were limited to the potential effects on Chinese. The associations also appealed to the United Nations to take measures against terror. The local Chinese press reported on revolutionary affairs, but avoided taking sides. Led by the Chinese consul, many contributed funds for Chinese victims of the revolutionary violence in Java and Sumatra.[95]

COMMUNITY AFFAIRS: PONTIANAK

Although the watchword of the Chinese communities in the early postwar months had been unity, politics soon intervened. As late as May 1948, most Chinese still celebrated the election of Chiang Kai-shek as president of China; only the

---

[90] Notes on Role of Consulate, 1949, ARA 2.21.120 (82).

[91] Ibid.

[92] See also Draft Note to Governor General, Pontianak, March 13, 1948, ARA 2.21.120 (69); and Notes on Role of Consulate, 1949, ARA 2.21.120 (82). On the consul's attempts to register all CHKH, all Chinese-owned firms, property and Chinese schools, see Political and Economic Reports, West Borneo, 1948, ARA 2.10.14.02 AS 3177.

[93] On the Guomindang in 1949, see Report on Chinese Immigrants and Communism, ARA 2.10.14.02 AS 2724. Guomindang citizenship law, like that of the Qing Dynasty, regarded Chinese born abroad of Chinese fathers as Chinese citizens, which conflicted with Dutch law, making the local-born both Chinese citizens and, according to Indonesian law, Indonesian citizens.

[94] Intelligence report, February-June 1946, ARA 2.10.14.02 AS 3651.

[95] General Report, August 1947, ARA 2.10.14.02 AS 3176. There was no longer a PKO in West Kalimantan, but Chinese were setting up voluntary "fire brigades" because of their fear of arson. Compare Chinese Press Reports cited in pamphlet on Chinese education, 1949, ARA 2.21.120 (84). On this conference, see Heidhues, "Citizenship and Identity."

Chinese General Association of Singkawang took a critical stance.[96] After that time, Chiang's picture and the Nationalist flag were gradually replaced by other symbols.[97] The repercussions affected the press, organizations, and schools.

All Chinese emphasized that they desired political unity, but in fact the community was divided, not only politically but by personal rivalries, speech distinctions, family and class interests. Pontianak had three Chinese-language dailies—*Lie Ming Pao, Chen Pao*, and *Chung Hwa Jit Pao*—that reflected many of these divisions. The editorial stance of *Lie Ming Pao* tended to be anti-Guomindang and pro-Communist. In mid-1948, a new leadership took over at the daily, following an election that was probably manipulated, and as a result, the paper, which was financed by wealthy capitalists from major community organizations, became even more anti-Guomindang than it had been before. Anyone who criticized its bias was simply accused of "dividing" the community,[98] a serious charge, given the popular desire for unity. Although wealthy businessmen might be presumed to be relatively conservative, this group was closely linked to businesses in Singapore, where a pro-Communist stance among businessmen was also becoming prevalent, as will be seen below.

The newspaper *Chen* (or *Tjen*) *Pao* was originally pro-Guomindang and partially supported by a subsidy from the Nationalist government in Nanjing. With other organizations, it tried unsuccessfully to organize a boycott of LMP. Its editor was forced to resign at the end of 1948 by the paper's directors, who also came from the wealthy leadership. From that point on the daily sided with *Lie Ming Pao*. This publication seems to have disappeared sometime before 1950.[99]

This left only *Chung Hwa Jit Pao* to follow a pro-Nationalist course (though it, too, veered from this position during 1949).[100] Those who opposed the wealthy faction in the Chinese General Association retreated to the columns of *Chung Hwa Jit Pao*. The newspaper's editor, Peter Woo (probably Wu Hsiung Feng), maintained close ties to the cooperative of farmers and laborers, Long Kang Hwee (*nonggonghui*, also called "agriculture and husbandry" union), which was originally a department of the General Association and possibly Guomindang-sponsored. After 1948, Long Kang Hwee, supposedly representing workers and peasants, was increasingly at odds with the business leadership, but some of the tension was apparently personal in character.

By the end of 1948, a fight to control Pontianak's associations was underway. Two groups, superficially pro- and anti-Communist, each tried to stop the activities of the other.[101] In December, new rules for electing the governing commissioners of the General Association, adopted by a rump commission, appeared in the press. Despite the dubious origin of these new guidelines, a majority of the commission members accepted them. According to these rules, organizational

---

[96] Report, June 1948, ARA 2.10.14.02 AS 3177.

[97] Böhm, *West Borneo*, pp. 48-49; Letter of Chinese Affairs Officer Meyer, ARA 2.10.14.02 AS 2780.

[98] Report to Regional Head, S. Meyer, Pontianak, February 25, 1949, ARA 2.21.120 (83).

[99] G. William Skinner, *Report on the Chinese in Southeast Asia* (Ithaca: Cornell University Southeast Asia Program, 1950), p. 68, lists only the other two for Pontianak.

[100] Report to Regional Head, S. Meyer, Pontianak, February 25, 1949, ARA 2.21.120 (83); Chinese press reports cited in pamphlet, 1949, ARA 2.21.120 (84).

[101] This account is from Letter on Sale of Printing Press, February 15, 1949, ARA 2.21.120 (80).

members of the General Association would nominate candidates, who would then be chosen in a general vote of all members. The thirty-two incumbent commissioners were automatically candidates. Despite protests from the larger community, for many people did not approve of the new procedures, the election for commissioners took place in mid-December. It did not go smoothly. After most of the votes had been cast, unidentified individuals suddenly removed the vote boxes and took them to the consulate, where the consul sequestered them, despite protests.[102] The consul's intervention seems to have been intended to prevent an anti-Guomindang slate from gaining office. The General Association's board then expanded the number of its organizational members, including non-Pontianak organizations, creating a new, if hardly licit, majority that would support the old commissioners. On January 8, 1949, the old commission declared that it would continue in office, in contravention of the statutes. A new meeting to choose candidates was set for February 3. The elections took place from February 6-9, 1949. Only 332 of some 20,000 potential voters (out of an estimated 35,000 Chinese in Pontianak) participated; the opposition boycotted the affair. Nevertheless, the consul (apparently determined to put a good face on the situation) swore in the "successful" candidates on February 20 and promised to inform Nanjing of the new officers.

Most of the new officers were not born in West Kalimantan, so that this general association, unlike others in the province, was markedly composed of "outsiders." Those who were displeased by the results generally withdrew their support of the association. Many Chinese traders stopped delivering the informal "taxes" (as noted above) that provided the budget for the organization. At last, even the consul suggested that the association be reorganized.

Among those who opposed the consul's decision to sequester the ballot boxes were the Chinese Rubber Merchants Association, the associations of remittance shops, piece goods sellers, rice merchants, Chinese clerks (*pegawai*), tailors, teachers, the Hong Kong dealers association, the youth association, music association, boy scouts, athletes, and pupils of the Cheng Kiang school, as well as a number of other associations ("Jong Jang," "Koh-Kien," "Kau Jang"), perhaps home village or clan associations. The pro-Communist daily, *Lie Ming Pao*, led the attack on the ballot-box snatch.[103] Two groups stand out as powerful opponents of the consul in this conflict: wealthier merchants and youth groups.

Siding with the consul were the "new" rice and sugar merchants association, the fish merchants' association of Sungai Limau, the salted fish merchants, as well as the Long Kang Hwee with its branch in Siantan. Also among supporters of the consul were the board of the Fong Pak building (Lo Fong Pak Futhang; see chapter five), the association of the Lie clan (called Loeng Sie Thong), the Yung Kang association (identification uncertain), the association of graduates of the Sin Djoe school in Siantan, the Guomindang, as well as *Chen Pao*.[104] The Guomindang and the Hakkas (especially in Siantan) stood on the side of the consul and some commissioners. Soon, another "battle" broke out over control of the middle school,

---

[102] Although pro- versus anti-Communist politics were behind the maneuvers, the grounds of the dispute, and the consul's role, are not completely transparent, and personal disputes may have been involved.

[103] Report to Regional Head, S. Meyer, Pontianak, February 25, 1949, ARA 2.21.120 (83), p. 17.

[104] Ibid.

and Lie Khoi Hiun (or Lie Khai Hsiun, M. Li Kaixun), the director who had guided the school since its founding in 1938, was discharged after an acrimonious exchange of complaints.[105]

In late 1949, an observer describing the divisions among the Chinese in Southeast Asia (not just in Pontianak) expressed his opinion that they were mostly of a personal nature. It appears that personal and political factors both played a part in the unruly 1949 election, and it is clear that the squabbles diminished the prestige of the Chinese general associations and community leadership.[106] Such "battles" also occurred elsewhere, for example, in Nanga Pinoh's association in April 1948,[107] and in Singkawang. In fact, during these years pro- and anti-Guomindang forces in many towns throughout the Archipelago competed for Chinese community leadership and control over organizations. If the Chinese hoped for unity, they were frequently disappointed.

SINGKAWANG

Singkawang seems to have figured as a center of opposition to the return of the Dutch and of left-wing activity in general. The approximately 120 members of the "Anti-Nippon Society" (ANS) or "Chinese Volunteers" located in Singkawang had not been active during the war, but after the Japanese were forced out of the region, they occupied themselves with arresting so-called collaborators and retaliating against critics. Chinese radicals even set fire to a large bridge in Mempawah in September 1946, cutting communications with Pontianak.[108] An Indonesian police officer who had worked with the Japanese was murdered in Singkawang in August 1946. When the Dutch, in response, commanded citizens to fly flags at half-mast as a sign of mourning for the policeman, a group of Chinese demonstrated in protest and some soldiers fired into the crowd, wounding seven participants severely. Ultimately, few individuals who had collaborated with the Japanese were made to suffer for their actions, for although some known collaborators were arrested by the Dutch, most were freed for lack of evidence, as none would testify, either against collaborators or against the ANS itself.[109]

Rumor asserted that a Singapore organization, Bintang Tiga (Three Stars), was behind the unrest and in contact with a number of radical groups in Singkawang. One such radical group was called "Iron and Blood," a name reminiscent of a "secret society."[110] No Dutch official knew Chinese at the time, so the Dutch were unable to assess materials being distributed through the community. Nevertheless, they readily attributed Chinese anti-Dutch activity to a Communist underground and to intervention from Singapore.[111]

---

[105] On Lie Khoi Hiun, Report, ARA 2.21.120 (74); Report to Regional Head, S. Meyer, Pontianak, February 25, 1949, ARA 2.21.120 (83), p. 13.

[106] Letter about policy toward Chinese, ca. 1949, ARA 2.21.120 (57).

[107] Political and Economic Reports, West Borneo, 1948, ARA 2.10.14.02 AS 3177.

[108] Coded Telegram from Pontianak, September 8, 1946, ANRI AS 1308.

[109] Zeedijk, "Chinezen in West-Borneo," pp. 69-71; Böhm, *West Borneo*, p. 48.

[110] Zeedijk, "Chinezen in West-Borneo," p. 71.

[111] Intelligence and Other Reports, 1946, ARA 2.10.14.02 AS 3971; Report on Reoccupying Pontianak and West Borneo, October 1945-March 1946, Appendix 3, ARA AS 3173. The Anti-

In 1948, the Chinese consul was insulted by angry protesters while visiting Singkawang.[112] In April-May 1948, teachers, who were strongly leftist, went on strike because of the arrest of a colleague, Tjen Siong Tjhong (also known as Tjen Sam Sam or Tsap Tsap), who was apprehended while teaching a class. Tjen, who had entered the country illegally, was also accused of insulting Chiang Kai-shek in articles he had published in the semi-monthly publication of the Chiliu Tushuhui (or Tee See Hwee, the "Strongly Flowing Water" Library Association, a name that recalls the reading clubs of prewar days). Records show that a friend of Tjen was also expelled for distributing Communist propaganda.[113] The Chiliu Library Association offered evening classes for adults and young people. Years later, a writer would charge that Communists associated with the Chiliu Library Association had established free evening classes meeting six or seven nights a week, attracting young people for "indoctrination."[114] It is impossible to know if this assertion is accurate, but it does cast light on the library association's reputation.

While in early 1948, Pemangkat's and Singkawang's General Associations were still controlled by conservative leaders, opposition from left-wing elements was gathering below the surface. The Chambers of Commerce were reestablished at about that time, and persons with Communist sympathies, including a teacher (whose role in a chamber of commerce was not explained) were included as leaders of these organizations.[115] Schoolteachers in Singkawang and elsewhere were repeatedly accused of being pro-Communist, and apparently their politics influenced students in the Chinese schools. The Singkawang Nam Hua Middle School had expressed its support of Mao Zedong openly by September 1949, just before the establishment of the People's Republic of China.[116]

By 1951, Singkawang's Chamber of Commerce was considered to be pro-People's Republic of China, as was that of Pemangkat. In Pontianak, on the other hand, the Chamber of Commerce was still pro-Guomindang, and the much smaller chamber in Ketapang appeared to favor the Nationalists.[117]

Some of Singkawang's radical politics stemmed from its relative poverty. In 1951, the area around Sambas was profiting from the rubber trade (and probably some smuggling), but in Singkawang the economy was poor and Communist influence strong. Conceivably, the region was politically more "radical" because of the strong Hakka element, but its poverty and relative isolation seem to have been more

---

Nippon Society also "arrested" a former Chinese *kapitan* of Singkawang, holding him while the Dutch remonstrated.

[112] Report to Regional Head, S. Meyer, Pontianak, February 25, 1949, ARA 2.21.120 (83).

[113] Letter of Meyer to Resident on Guomindang, July 1948, ARA 2.21.120 (73); Letter to Acting Resident, Pontianak, May 18, 1948, ARA 2.21.120 (92); Political and Economic Reports, West Borneo, 1948, ARA 2.10.14.02 AS 3177.

[114] Houliston, *Breakthrough*, p. 18. Houliston's assessment of eight hundred participants should be taken with a grain of salt. She thought 50 percent of the Chinese in Pontianak were Communist sympathizers, and 85 percent of Chinese residents in Singkawang, while according to her, Bengkayang was a "Red stronghold" in the late 1950s. See esp. pp. 76, 85.

[115] Political and Economic Reports, West Borneo, 1948, ARA 2.10.14.02 AS 3177.

[116] Press reports, 1949, ARA 2.21.120 (84); Policy toward Chinese, 1949, ARA 2.21.120 (86).

[117] Notowardojo, *Kalimantan Barat*, p. 19. In 1951, the Chinese could still display their political favoritism openly.

significant factors.[118] In 1954, an observer asserted that 80 percent of the Chinese in the area, most of whom were not citizens of Indonesia, were pro-Communist.[119]

POLITICS AND PREFERENCES

While pro-Communist activities in Singkawang seem to have been often instigated and strongly supported by schoolteachers and youth, sympathy for the Communist cause was not restricted to these groups. As noted above, Pontianak's wealthy businessmen and rubber dealers gradually threw their support to the left-wing press and opposed the Guomindang. Singapore was the chief market for the commodities of West Kalimantan, and Pontianak's traders were closely associated with rubber "barons" there like Tan Kah Kee and Lee Kong Chian, many of whom were highly sympathetic to "New China." But while Tan and Lee also sympathized with and even aided Indonesian resistance forces during the Revolution, no evidence links Pontianak's leaders with sympathy for the Republic.[120] Chinese in West Kalimantan, up to 1949, appear to have remained non-committal in response to Indonesia's struggle for independence.

By late 1949, Chiang Kai-shek's photo and Nationalist flags disappeared from almost all Chinese shops in West Kalimantan, although Communist flags were not allowed to be raised. Not "double ten," the October 10 holiday commemorating Sun Yatsen's revolution of 1911, but October 1, the day of the founding of the People's Republic of China in 1949, became the generally celebrated holiday.[121]

CHINESE SCHOOLS

The Japanese had permitted a few Chinese schools to operate within which they integrated the Hakkas and Teochius, who had formerly maintained mostly separate schools.[122] Mission and European schools were, of course, closed. Once the war ended, Chinese schools burgeoned. According to a 1948 account, about 225,000 pupils throughout Indonesia attended these schools. This represents an estimated 80 percent of ethnic Chinese youth of school age.[123]

West Kalimantan was a center for this expansion of Chinese education, and the Chinese consul in Pontianak estimated that some 180 Chinese schools were established in the territory in the late 1940s.[124] In the capital city of Pontianak, in

[118] Interestingly, the strongly Hakka Siantan area had supported the Nationalist Chinese consul (see above), so being Hakka alone is not a sufficient explanation.

[119] Missionary report, private archive, the Netherlands. This assertion may be exaggerated. For example, many may have assented silently to the political attitudes of the more vocal, while others followed whatever they perceived as "Chinese."

[120] Compare the Report on Political Activities of Left-wing Chinese in 1949, ARA 2.10.14.02 AS 3979; this report makes no mention of West Kalimantan. See also Twang, *Business Elite*.

[121] Note on Question of Recognizing People's Republic of China, December 1949, ARA 2.10.14.02 AS 2777.

[122] Böhm, *West Borneo*, p. 47.

[123] Letter, R. Schrader, on Chinese Education, July 5, 1948, ARA 2.21.120 (93).

[124] See also Draft Note to Governor General, Pontianak, March 13, 1948, ARA 2.21.120 (69). The figure for March 1947 was 144, fifty-one of them in the Singkawang Afdeeling (district), and twenty-two in Pontianak Afdeeling. The number of pupils was well over fifteen thousand;

the first six months of 1946, 3,433 pupils were in Chinese schools (85 percent male); by the first semester of 1949, the total had climbed to 5,248 (59 percent male). To their parents, a Chinese boy, or for that matter a girl, who could not read and write "modern Mandarin" was just not really Chinese.[125] The proportion of girls climbed steadily, not only because general living conditions became more secure over time, but because parents wanted Chinese education for all children. A junior middle school opened in Pontianak in 1946, continuing the tradition of the Hua Chiao Chung Hsueh under the name Chung Hua Chung Hsueh (Zhonghua Zhongxue, Chinese middle school). Many parents sent their children to China or Singapore for continuing study in Chinese.

While most Chinese schools had been sponsored by private organizations in the prewar period, they were now usually administered by the committees for education in the General Associations.[126] Both prewar and postwar schools were clearly linked to China and to Chinese politics. The consul signed the diplomas of lower school students, and he sent the middle school diplomas to China, where they were validated by education authorities of the Nationalist Chinese government. When challenged to defend his intervention in local affairs, one which affected local-born Dutch subjects, the consul replied simply that he had his instructions. Besides, such validation gave proof of pupils' qualifications if they should choose to study in China.[127]

Instruction in these schools was conducted in Chinese, with English taught as a second language, but the Dutch authorities soon began offering subsidies to those Chinese schools that taught Indonesian four hours a week, hoping to encourage them to be more oriented to Indonesia.[128] The Dutch also directly imported Chinese-language materials and other necessities for the schools from Singapore.[129] A struggle for control over the schools came into the open in May 1948, when the daily *Lie Ming Pao* published a broadside attacking Lie Khoi Hiun, the director of the Chinese Middle School (see above). The editors were angered because Lie, in an attempt to eliminate political material from the classroom, had forbidden pupils to bring publications other than textbooks to school. The article also criticized conditions in the boarding school of the Chung Hua. If reports are representative,

---

there were over three hundred teachers (the numbers in the source, Political and Economic Reports, West Borneo, 1947, ARA 2.10.14.02 AS 3176, for pupils and teachers are incomplete).

[125] Table in an untitled publication of Wu Tung Ping, a teacher and member of the CHKH, in ARA 2.21.120 (84). The title page of this pamphlet is missing, but it is dated Pontianak, March 1949. Political and Economic Reports, West Borneo, 1947, ARA 2.10.14.02 AS 3176 gives the figure of 5,457 pupils in 1947 in twenty-five schools. Malay was not normally taught, but the Dutch authorities offered a subsidy of one guilder per pupil to those schools that taught four hours of Malay/Indonesian per week.

[126] Political and Economic Reports, West Borneo, 1947, ARA 2.10.14.02 AS 3176. The Guomindang also ran some schools. In 1958, a mission source named six thousand persons who had graduated from Catholic schools in the area, by which time the number of graduates from the various Chinese community schools must have been much higher than the 1952 estimate (below) of 45,000. See also press reports cited in Wu Tung Ping pamphlet, ARA 2.21.120 (84).

[127] Memo, February 23, 1948, ARA 2.21.120:52., and and Draft Note to Governor General, Pontianak, March 13, 1948, ARA 2.21.120 (69).

[128] Report of Abell, October 1945, ANRI AS 1308.

[129] Letter, Meyer to Regional Head, February 2, 1949, ARA 2.21.120 (98). The Dutch thus not only made available foreign exchange for these purchases, but also chose the items imported under the program.

then this criticism was justified, but it appears that the attack was prompted not so much by concerns for the students, but by political infighting: *Lie Ming Pao* did not approve of Lie's pro-Guomindang record. The school then suddenly lost its subsidy from the Chinese General Association. The conflict flared up again in September, when *Lie Ming Pao* claimed the students at the school were lazy and the teachers irresponsible. At this point the consul got involved, attacking *Lie Ming Pao* for sowing dissent in the community.[130]

In October 1948, the outgoing Association leadership—whose legitimacy remained in question—chose a new school committee and appointed Liao Eng Kheng, a prominent businessman and General Association leader, to direct it. The committee met in December 1948 and determined that it would not rehire Lie Khoi Hiun, whose contract was renewable every six months. Although some member organizations protested these methods, the wealthy leaders turned a deaf ear to complaints. A member of the old school committee, Wu Tung Ping, published a twenty-six page account, in Dutch, citing accounts in Pontianak's Chinese newspapers. Most of this document was dedicated to reiterating and expanding the attacks on Lie.[131]

Such battles for control of the Chinese schools occurred elsewhere in the Archipelago (and indeed in Southeast Asia) during postwar years. They reflected the struggle between Guomindang and Communists in the ongoing civil war in China. Outside Pontianak, West Kalimantan's Chinese teachers often proved to be even more radical. It is significant that most of these teachers (whose number climbed from 96 in 1946 to 138 in 1949, for Pontianak alone) were new arrivals who had come to West Kalimantan directly from China or from Singapore.[132]

The importance of Chinese-language schools in the province can hardly be overestimated. In 1952 it was estimated that of the total of 160,000 Chinese living in West Kalimantan, well over 45,000 (the vast majority of those who had ever attended school) had attended Chinese-language schools. This educated guess demonstrates the importance of Chinese education and language to the community.

CITIZENSHIP AND DOCUMENTS

The introduction of the civil registry (Burgerlijke Stand) of births, deaths, and marriages for Chinese in West Borneo in 1925 had been practically a dead letter.[133] Whereas in Java, prominent Chinese saw this as a step toward equality with "Europeans," in Borneo the requirements were more often ignored than welcomed. Chinese continued to contract marriage on propitious days, not when the registrar was prepared to perform a ceremony. The fact that, as late as 1948, documents were still in Dutch made things worse. Also, the fees charged by the registry for their services were a prohibitive burden for the many poor Chinese in the province. Furthermore, many documents and registers were destroyed during the Japanese

---

[130] Report to Regional Head, S. Meyer, Pontianak, February 25, 1949, ARA 2.21.120 (83).

[131] Wu Tung Ping pamphlet, 1949, ARA 2.21.120 (84); Letter, Meyer to Regional Head, February 2, 1949, ARA 2.21.120 (98).

[132] Letter about Policy toward Chinese, ca. 1949, ARA 2.21.120 (57). The statistics are from Chinese press reports cited in pamphlet, March 1949, ARA 2.21.120 (84), p. 24.

[133] See above, chapter five, "Administration after the Kongsis."

Occupation.[134] The matter was not insignificant: the lack of birth and marriage documents would plague the Chinese in later years.

Chinese diplomatic representation in the province reopened the question of Chinese nationality, only partly settled by a Dutch-Chinese consular accord of 1910 and another agreement in 1945 (see above). The government of China continued to view all ethnic Chinese, wherever they were born, as Chinese nationals. The Dutch considered all Chinese persons born in Indonesia to be Dutch subjects. Recognition of Indonesian independence on December 29, 1949 complicated the situation. Dutch subjects of Chinese origin who did not explicitly reject Indonesian citizenship within two years of that date automatically became Indonesian citizens.

As a result of their own inaction, several hundreds of thousands of ethnic Chinese now became Indonesian citizens, although they would be unable to document their citizenship. Until 1960, however, the People's Republic of China, with which Indonesia had diplomatic relations, recognized all Indonesian citizens of Chinese descent as citizens of China. In that year, the 1955 agreement on dual nationality between China and Indonesia was finally implemented, permitting Indonesian citizens of Chinese descent to choose Indonesian or Chinese citizenship.[135] Probably, about half of all ethnic Chinese in Indonesia were legally Indonesian citizens. According to the treaty, they could choose to be Chinese citizens only as this treaty was being implemented, between 1960 and 1962. In West Kalimantan, however, some observers estimated that less than 20 percent of the Chinese were Indonesian citizens, and Indonesian citizenship remained a vague concept for most. As of the mid-1950s, a mere 950 persons had applied for a document to prove their Indonesian citizenship. The rest might be suspected of being aliens, but this does not seem to have disturbed them, in spite of the many disadvantages those suspected of being aliens faced.[136]

Between 1946 and 1949, the Dutch made some efforts to get local Chinese to consider themselves part of Indonesia—for example, they encouraged instruction in Indonesian in Chinese-language schools—but these efforts met with little success. The Indonesian Republic in its first years exerted few efforts to win the allegiance of West Kalimantan's Chinese population and so failed to make its influence felt in the province.[137] Political organizations that sought to represent the Chinese

---

[134] Note about Civil Registry in Pontianak, 1948, ARA 2.21.120 (59); anonymous, "De Chinese volksplanting in Kalimantan Barat," *Schakels* 51 (December 1,1951): 22. The relevant law was Stbl. 1925 no. 92. Persons under thirty had to prove consent of their parents before marrying, something Chinese found superfluous, because marriages were usually arranged between the families involved.

[135] David Mozingo, *Chinese Policy toward Indonesia, 1949-1967* (Ithaca: Cornell University Press, 1976), pp. 88-92. On the complex issue of citizenship, which cannot be elaborated here, see Donald E. Willmott, *The National Status of the Chinese in Indonesia, 1900-1958* (Ithaca: Cornell University Modern Indonesia Project, 1961) and Mary F. Somers, *Peranakan Chinese Politics in Indonesia* (PhD dissertation, Cornell University, 1965), pp. 224-250.

[136] This estimate is from Tobing, *Kalimantan Barat*, p. 38. Chinese Affairs Officer Abell wrote in 1945 that two-thirds were local-born, ANRI AS 1308, and there is no evidence that many Chinese in West Kalimantan rejected Indonesian citizenship during the rejection period of 1949-51, so as former Dutch subjects (because local-born), they must have been Indonesian citizens. The proof of citizenship was highly unpopular. See Willmott, *National Status*, pp. 79-84.

[137] Pamphlet, "West-Borneo/Kalimantan Barat," West-Borneo Raad en R.V.D. Pontianak, West-Borneo Drukkerij, May 12, 1947, ARA 2.21.120: 47. See also, "Memo of Meeting between

minority—like the Persatuan Tionghoa (Chinese Association), formed in Jakarta in the late 1940s—also made little impression,[138] nor did their successor organizations fare significantly better.

Chinese in West Kalimantan simply felt themselves to be Chinese, a concept that combined ethnic, cultural, and national loyalties. An observer in the mid-1950s noted that, even if individual Chinese had been born in Indonesia as part of a second or third generation of settlers, China was still their country. It commanded all their allegiance; these China loyalists only encountered conflict when trying to sort out divided allegiances to the People's Republic of China and to the Nationalist Republic of China in Taiwan. With time, even this conflict subsided, as the importance of Taiwan dwindled. Although many Chinese persons had greeted the arrival of the Nationalist consul, by 1949 many were disappointed, both because of the situation in China and because he failed to bring any material advantage to West Kalimantan.[139]

Indonesia recognized the People's Republic of China in 1950; the Pontianak consulate was closed in April of that year. The new consul of the People's Republic was stationed not in Pontianak, but in Banjarmasin. To justify these actions, the Indonesian government declared that no island could have more than one consulate and that the consul ought to reside in a provincial capital (Banjarmasin was the capital of the province of Kalimantan at that time), but it was clear that they meant to limit China's influence in West Kalimantan. The new consulate opened in Banjarmasin in April 1951. Although Indonesia's official diplomatic relations with Beijing limited the Guomindang's scope, pro-Nationalist elements continued to organize openly and to maintain Chinese schools throughout Kalimantan, even as their influence waned.[140]

Only in 1958 did the Indonesian government tip the balance decisively by outlawing all Guomindang-related organizations in the country. It closed schools and organizations, seized economic assets, and made any public display of sympathies for Taiwan impossible (see chapter seven).[141]

FEDERALISM AND TRANSITION TO INDEPENDENCE

Because most Chinese of West Kalimantan considered themselves to be outsiders, the great majority of them took no part in the organization of federal states by the Dutch in 1946-49. They were "neutral," which some interpreted as a "wait and see" attitude, meaning that the Chinese would cooperate with the Dutch or the Republic when they saw which side was winning.

In the immediate postwar period, which was still influenced by a Dutch colonial legacy, Catholic Chinese and Catholic Dayaks, both graduates of mission schools, often formed the majority of the local political councils. But this influence was lost as more Malays and Javanese, some of them immigrants to the province,

---

Thio Thiam Tjong, Dr. Tan, S. Meyer, and Dr. A. H. Böhm, and other references in this file. Also see the Economic Report, October 1946, ANRI AS 1308.

[138] Letter about Policy toward Chinese, ca. 1949, ARA 2.21.120 (57).

[139] Ibid.

[140] Mozingo, *Chinese Policy*, pp. 92-97.

[141] Ibid., pp. 153-154.

took political office after independence.[142] Chinese delegates to Dutch-sponsored federal organizations like the West Borneo Council (Raad), perhaps on instructions from community organizations, cast blank votes to distance themselves from the proceedings, hoping to protect their neutrality.[143]

Most Chinese, even the local-born, viewed Indonesian politics as remote. They also regarded the divisions in community organizations with distaste, perhaps wishing that these conflicts—like the civil war in China—would just go away so that all Chinese would be able to unite under one umbrella.

CHINESE AND DAYAKS

Accounts from postwar years agree that the Chinese minority still maintained a certain influence on Dayaks with whom they had contact. Young girls in Dayak *kampungs* were wearing Chinese-style blouses and slacks for evening dress, although they wore sarongs by day. Many Dayaks, who often could not speak fluent Indonesian, as well as some Malays, spoke Chinese readily, and some could even read Chinese characters, while they were illiterate in Roman letters. Dayak families in the Chinese Districts might even have a small Chinese altar in their houses.[144]

The role of Chinese in the economy of the interior was often criticized by Dayak leaders and others, but an experiment by a Dutch agricultural expert in 1948 throws light on the trading nexus. The inhabitants of "nearly every Dayak *kampung*" he visited, most of whom lived in poverty and had expressed their conviction that the Chinese were exploiting them, had asked him to help them do business without the Chinese traders. In response, the official, J. G. de Vries, attempted to organize a purchase of one thousand kilograms of rubber himself. He paid in advance, partly in money, partly in goods, bringing rice, cloth, and formic acid to complement the payment in cash, offering what he considered to be a fair price. However, the complaints persisted, because the Dayaks who sold rubber to him, when asked what they had been paid, only named the amount of cash they received, not the goods. It appeared that the Dayaks knew they could expect to receive the full price of their rubber from the Dutchman, while the Chinese traders would withhold part of the payment to cover the sellers' ongoing debts. In fact, only four hundred kilograms of rubber were delivered to de Vries when he arrived to collect the goods, and some *kampungs* failed to show up for the transaction because of a holiday.

Furthermore, the rubber sellers were annoyed because the Dutchman had failed to bring salt, something they forgot to "order." A Chinese trader would have known about salt. Finally, the entire transaction upset the Chinese traders because they felt they had a claim to the rubber the Dayaks offered to deVries, since it was purportedly owed to them as payment for prior debts and should not have been sold elsewhere. A week later, when the official returned to buy more rubber, no one arrived at the appointed time to sell.

DeVries concluded that the Chinese-Dayak relationship was a more complex business than simply buying and selling. Much trade was in goods. The

---

[142] Boddeke, "Missie," p. 29.

[143] Political and Economic Reports, West Borneo, 1947, ARA 2.10.14.02 AS 3176.

[144] Tobing, *Kalimantan Barat*, pp. 117-118, 123; see also "Chinese volksplanting," p. 4.

comparatively low prices Chinese traders offered to the Dayak (low compared to the value of rubber in Batavia or New York) were partly justified by indebtedness, partly by poor quality and high transport costs. Furthermore, the Dayak-Chinese symbiosis was based on confidence that the Dayaks would bring in their produce and the Chinese trader, even if he was himself in debt to a larger trader, would not, in bad times, let them starve, for "When did a Chinese ever declare a Dayak bankrupt for not paying debts?" In any case, few Chinese got rich from Dayak trade.[145]

ECONOMY IN THE 1950S

Although little is known about smuggling of rubber and other goods to Singapore, this illegal traffic surely continued and probably increased when the exchange rates for the Indonesian rupiah became more and more unrealistic after the mid-1950s, making transactions in rupiah extremely unfavorable to exporters. Coastal smuggling to Sarawak from Singkawang or Pemangkat also continued, while inland regions, far from transport to Pontianak and the coast, became important centers of illicit cross-border trade with Sarawak. A border treaty with Sarawak existed from colonial times, but the exact location of this border was undetermined, and the border was unguarded on the Indonesian side. Sambas was three hours' walk along forest paths from the border.[146] Farther inland, smuggling became endemic by the late 1950s. For example, Dayak bearers carried Javanese tobacco, rubber, and pepper to the Chinese market in Mongkos in Sarawak, where trucks owned by Chinese traders waited for goods. In Sarawak, paved roads and bus connections enabled the carriers to bring their products swiftly from border crossings to buyers and exporters. A few meters from the border there would be a Chinese shop ready to do business. Some rubber crossed the border this way, but pepper was the favored commodity for smugglers, when prices were good, because it was so convenient. Luxury goods obtained in exchange for raw commodities—including radios, cigarettes, Chinese tea, and sometimes gold—could be sold for a good price in Pontianak or even Jakarta. Officials at one point estimated illicit traffic to be worth Rp. 10,000,000 annually.[147]

Pepper-growing was concentrated around Bengkayang, as chapter four has indicated, not far from Sarawak's border; most of the growers were small Chinese farmers. Planting expanded after the war, and the region produced, by 1953, an estimated five thousand tons a year. Official exports from West Kalimantan in that year were 328 tons, while Sarawak was said to export four thousand tons! Pepper prices in Sarawak were well above those in Kalimantan. The Jagoi and Lara Dayaks, who carried the pepper, earned more through this labor than by working their *ladangs* or tapping rubber. The Chinese dealers knew the bearers were dependable. Many carriers, first Chinese, then Dayaks, held Sarawak identity cards (which made it possible to purchase hunting weapons, too) or even

---

[145] Report, November 1948, ARA 2.21.120 (55). De Vries says that since the war, considerable pressure from the Dayaks to circumvent Chinese traders had built up.

[146] Houliston, *Breakthrough*, p. 37.

[147] Van Hulten, *Hidupku*, p. 153; Tobing, *Kalimantan Barat*, p. 75. The rupiah was officially worth Rp. 15 to the US dollar in the early 1950s. Pepper was an excellent smuggling commodity because of its high value per weight.

worked in Sarawak. The connections worked so well that the border area of West Kalimantan became more prosperous than areas to the east or south. It became clear that closing the border would result in economic distress and other, related problems, unless this action were followed by measures designed to offset the residents' loss of trade and income.[148]

After 1952, illegal settlers also appeared in the border area. Most of these were legal residents of Sarawak, where land was becoming scarce. They established themselves on Indonesian territory, especially in the largely unpopulated border region, Tempeduh, which, with Bau, was a favored smugglers' crossing.[149]

UNDER INDEPENDENT INDONESIA

A Chinese-language newspaper in Jakarta, *Sheng Hwo Pao*, found three groups among the Chinese population of West Kalimantan in 1957:

- first was the Chinese population of the major market towns, not very different from Chinese elsewhere in the Archipelago.
- second were the Chinese of the lowland areas near the shore. These were the coconut and sometimes rubber farmers, and other small farmers, a group practically unique in Indonesia.
- the third group were the Chinese of the "river banks" and of the interior, many of them small traders or farmers or both. Chinese rural traders were active in the collection of smallholder produce, especially in the islands outside Java, but the role of the Chinese farmers in the interior was unusual for Indonesia.

The departure of the Dutch and the arrival of Indonesian bureaucrats changed the economic base of the province very little; Chinese farmers had enlarged their holdings since the Japanese Occupation, and they maintained widespread control of productive land. K. Tobing estimated the increased influence of the Chinese in West Kalimantan's agriculture:

> ... there is an area of about 108,000 hectares ... composed of rubber gardens, and 67,000 hectares that are planted in coconuts. At least three-fourths of this area is owned by the Chinese. ... In general, *ladang* or *sawah* in [West] Kalimantan that is good and produces enough is the property of Chinese. They have been able to introduce a system of planting paddy that is very profitable, especially in the areas of Kabupaten Pontianak, Sambas and Sanggau [-Kapuas]. ... Before World War II, the Chinese inhabitants were among the farmers who were economically powerless. The Japanese period and ... the

---

[148] Tobing, *Kalimantan Barat*, pp. 75-80, 161. Just this became a problem during Konfrontasi, see chapter seven.

[149] Ibid., pp. 68, 74. Smuggling practices are also described in Soemadi, *Peranan Kalimantan Barat dalam menghadapi subversi komunis Asia Tenggara. Suatu tinjauan internasional terhadap gerakan komunis dari sudut pertahanan wilayah khususnya Kalimantan Barat*, 2nd ed. (n.p.: Yayasan Tanjungpura, 1974), pp. 99-100. Soemadi says the Malaysian dollar was the accepted currency in border areas in the 1960s.

period of Dutch occupation gave them a lot of opportunity to increase their economic power.[150]

Much of Chinese land "ownership" was in the form of long-term rental from Dutch times. With the loss of most pertinent colonial records during the Japanese Occupation, many used the opportunity to increase their claims illegitimately, or they gained control of land from natives who were indebted to them.[151] In short, Chinese were squatters on a grand scale. Attempts to measure their prosperity and determine how well off they were, however, are problematic, and some observers reported that many lived in poverty.[152]

K. Tobing, quoted above, also accused the Chinese of controlling fertile bands of land that extended up to ten kilometers on both sides of the main rivers—the best agricultural land—and of driving Malays and Dayaks into the interior. The displaced Malays and Dayaks often had to work as tappers for the Chinese. The absence of a cadastral survey, which would have taken years to complete, contributed to the problem of access to and control of land, especially since many claims to ownership or even the right to occupy the land were bogus.[153]

In addition to their control of agricultural land, the Chinese minority held the lion's share of industry during this period. They owned nineteen out of twenty rubber remilling factories, twenty-three of twenty-six rice mills, six of seven copra processing factories, and seventeen out of twenty machine-driven sawmills, as well as the great majority of consumer goods industries, and the movie houses.

The extent to which the Chinese minority dominated economic activities can by illustrated by their participation in the reconstruction of the war-damaged airfield at Sungai Durian near Pontianak. Leadership of the project was apparently assigned to a Dutch employee of a local firm, but the building contractor and supplier was a Chinese firm, Lim Yong Swa. Throughout the project, Lim Yong Swa provided financing and support when the government in Jakarta failed to meet its obligations. The site was still contaminated by unexploded bombs, and much of the work had to be done by hand for lack of machines, even though construction machinery had been promised from Jakarta. The approach of the rainy season made further postponement impossible, so the contracting firm borrowed from Lim Yong Swa some half a million rupiah, one-fourth of the final costs, which allowed work to continue. The field was opened in July 1954, although the financing promised by Jakarta did not arrive until the end of 1953. The financial problems encountered in this project were typical, it was said, of problems that bedeviled and hindered all government activities in the province.[154]

---

[150] Tobing, *Kalimantan Barat*, pp. 33, 35.

[151] Azahari, *Ontwikkeling*, p. 61, says that the Chinese are really not owners of the land, but lessees (*pachters*). These arrangements, called *hak oesaha* (*usaha*, right of use) or *huur-overeenkomst*, (hire agreement, abbreviated h.o.), although limited to twenty or fifty years, depending on the crop, were routinely extended, tending to become hereditary. They could, however, be withdrawn.

[152] Especially, of course, in the immediate postwar years, see the Report of a Visit to the Mandor Area and Ulu Sebadu, October 1948, ARA 2.21.120 (112).

[153] Tobing, *Kalimantan Barat*, pp. 64ff.

[154] Ibid., pp. 86-87. As late as 1963, when I first visited Kalimantan Barat, the runway was unpaved, covered by grass.

In the years following independence, the lack of qualified administrative personnel handicapped provincial development. Excessive centralism, competition between political parties for influence, and lack of interest from the capital added to the dilemma. Officials considered transfer to West Kalimantan a punishment, while the local population, many of them illiterate, was not qualified, or lacked connections, for official posts.[155] All of this did not bode well for the future development of West Kalimantan.

---

[155] Ibid., pp. 114, 120-125.

CHAPTER SEVEN

COMMUNITY UNDER DURESS

In spite of a history of relative ethnic harmony, mutual distrust seems to have prevailed in the postwar years among ethnic groups in West Kalimantan. This distrust seems to have been partly a result of the Japanese experience, and partly a result of rising nationalism—much of it ethnically based nationalism—in all groups. Furthermore, however proudly nationalists greeted Indonesian independence, most ethnic Chinese appear to have distrusted the new nation.

The Chinese community of West Kalimantan is very suspicious of everything that is Indonesian.[1]

The suspicion was mutual. Other ethnic groups distrusted the Chinese or resented their dominant position in the economy. An extreme example is that of an influential Dayak leader from Central Kalimantan who described the Chinese of the West Coast as greedy opium dealers and unscrupulous golddiggers.

The Chinese who came to Kalimantan Barat, in addition to trading, also brought opium from Singapore, with the intention of weakening the spirit of the Dayaks, because they really wanted to get the gold.[2]

National political pressure was building up against the Chinese minority as well.[3] Many influential leaders in Jakarta were eager to limit the economic influence of the minority; others saw the connections to China of the ethnic Chinese, their schools, and organizations as a threat to Indonesia's sovereignty. Although West Kalimantan was far from their thoughts, national politicians made policies that produced serious repercussions there.

---

[1] Comment of a Western visitor dated 1950, private archive, the Netherlands.

[2] Tjilik Riwut, *Kalimantan memanggil* (Jakarta: Endang, 1958), p. 50. Tjilik Riwut was Governor of Central Kalimantan province from 1957-67; he is considered to have helped establish the province as a kind of Dayak homeland, separate from Malay-dominated South Kalimantan. Sri Kuhnt-Saptodewo kindly provided this information. The Dayak protest against Chinese trading practices in chapter six fits with this picture of greater ethnic awareness and, sometimes, resentment.

[3] Something of this resentment can be seen in the work of a businessman of Javanese origin in Kalimantan, R. M. Subianto Notowardojo, *Kalimantan Barat sepintas lalu dilihat dari sudut sosial ekonomi* (Jakarta: Direktorat Perekonomian Rakjat, Kementerian Perekonomian, 1951), for example, pp. 11, 18-19, 31-34, and in that of a journalist of Batak origin, K. Tobing, *Kalimantan Barat* (Bandung: Masa Baru, 1952).

POLITICAL PRESSURES

Beginning in the 1950s, measures from Jakarta upset the economic life and cultural institutions of the Chinese in West Kalimantan, as the new Indonesian state extended its authority throughout the region. Apart from limitations on various economic activities by non-citizens,[4] the most far-reaching measures affected Chinese schools.

Chinese schools, whose numbers grew rapidly after 1945 (chapter six), spread to the smallest settlements of West Kalimantan, even to the Upper Kapuas. A similar expansion of Chinese education took place all over Indonesia during this time. Of course, Indonesian government schools expanded as well, but controlling or even inspecting the Chinese-language schools, above all those in remote areas, was beyond the power of an inexperienced and overtaxed bureaucracy; as a result, these schools appeared particularly disturbing. Jakarta authorities, who had attempted at least to register the schools, believed many Indonesian citizens (of Chinese origin—and sometimes even ethnic Indonesians) were receiving an education completely alien to their surroundings; perhaps they were as many as 60 percent of the pupils. This charge applied to all schools teaching in Chinese, of whatever political persuasion, pro-Communist or pro-Guomindang. In Pemangkat, for example, the middle school, with seven to eight hundred pupils, had attracted several non-Chinese children to Chinese-language education, a situation that unsettled Indonesian educational bureaucrats eager to shape a unified nation.[5]

In May 1957, the Military Governor of West Nusatenggara (Bali-Lombok), acting under special authority given him by a national state of emergency (*keadaan darurat perang*) in effect at the time,[6] decreed the closing of all Chinese-language schools in the territory. Six months later, Jakarta military headquarters eased the terms of the prohibition of Chinese schools, but extended the ban throughout Indonesia, allowing only six months for compliance. These new terms were still far-reaching, however. They required that:

1) Indonesian citizens must attend only national schools, that is, public or private schools that followed the centrally determined national curriculum. The governing boards of the national schools and all teachers must be Indonesian citizens. These schools would not offer instruction in Chinese at the elementary level, even as a second language, except during a brief transition period.

2) "Alien" schools (all those teaching in foreign languages) were limited to about 150 cities and towns in the Archipelago;[7] those in smaller towns were

---

[4] For a summary of these restrictions see Donald E. Willmott, *The National Status of the Chinese in Indonesia, 1900-1958* (Ithaca: Cornell Modern Indonesia Project, 1961), pp. 70-76. Implementation varied regionally, and there is little information about the effects of these measures in Kalimantan.

[5] Anonymous, *Shenghuobao chuangkan zhounian jinniankan* (Jakarta: Sheng Huo Pao, 1955), p. 100. An education official in Jakarta told the author in 1962 how much attendance of Indonesian children in Chinese schools was a concern.

[6] The regional rebellions against central authority had led to the proclamation of a state of emergency.

[7] That is, capitals of first- and second-level administrative areas. There were twenty-two first-level areas, the provinces and special regions like Jakarta and Yogyakarta, and about 120 second-level (*kabupaten*) areas.

closed. All teachers had to pass an examination in writing and speaking Indonesian; Indonesian language and history had to be taught. No new foreign teachers would be admitted to the country, except in those cases where there were no Indonesian citizens available to fill the positions.

All Dutch-language schools were closed by the Indonesian government in December 1957, when Dutch assets were seized during the dispute over control of West Irian. Apart from Chinese-language schools, the remaining "alien" schools were mostly for children of diplomats and of employees of foreign institutions.

In April 1958, another measure followed. Nationalist China was implicated in supporting regional rebellions against Jakarta. Schools belonging to Guomindang organizations, as well as the businesses of Taiwan citizens and all branches of the Guomindang, were closed and their property confiscated. Although the Guomindang had been steadily losing adherents, many anti-Communist or non-Communist Chinese retained sympathy for it and for Nationalist China; some continued to hold Nationalist Chinese passports. As a result of this measure, these people became "stateless."[8]

Of about 1,800 Chinese-language schools nationwide, only 510 remained in January 1959. Of an estimated 425,000 pupils who had attended Chinese- and other foreign-language schools in Indonesia, only 125,000 still attended "alien" schools by 1959, most of them Chinese schools.[9]

Although no statistics are available for West Kalimantan, these measures were certainly a blow to Chinese schools there. Wealthy Chinese with Indonesian citizenship, led by Ng Ngiap Lian of the Chamber of Commerce,[10] swiftly set up a foundation for "national" education that took over some of the private Chinese schools in Pontianak; the Catholic Church converted all its schools, including those previously teaching in Chinese, to national schools. Lack of qualified teachers and instructional materials plagued these institutions; pupils, especially advanced ones, had trouble adjusting to the new language of instruction. The ethnic Chinese were also supposed to mix with non-Chinese students in the national schools, but this rule was especially difficult to follow. Where, in the towns, could enough non-Chinese pupils be found to balance the concentrations of Chinese, or alternately, Christians, in certain neighborhoods?

Initially, afternoon classes in Chinese or instruction in Chinese (presumably Mandarin) as a *bahasa daerah* (regional language) was allowed, but in January 1959, this, too, was forbidden. The assets of schools that failed to comply with the new regulations might be seized by the authorities.

The great majority of alien children opted for the remaining Chinese schools. These schools, almost all oriented to the People's Republic of China, taught cultural and political loyalty to Beijing. Some parents deliberately rejected Indonesian citizenship so that their children could attend Chinese schools. Others—at least among the young people—left for China. During the following years, the Catholic Church, which had run Chinese-language schools, sided with those pressing for Indonesianization. These schools began to use Indonesian for

---

[8] Willmott, *National Status*, p. 43.

[9] Mary F. Somers, "Peranakan Chinese Politics in Indonesia" (PhD dissertation, Cornell University, 1965), pp. 162-166, based on official statistics.

[10] See chapter six.

instruction wherever possible, although many individual missionaries felt that retention of Chinese language and culture was necessary and justified for their flock. In time, local Indonesian officials pressed for use of Indonesian in all public worship.[11]

The Chinese, especially the alien Chinese, also bore the brunt of other nationalist measures, particularly economic ones, adopted by the Indonesian government in the 1950s. These included pressure for the Indonesianization of their enterprises (that is, the government pressed Chinese entrepreneurs to accept the participation of ethnic Indonesians in ownership and the labor force), special taxes on foreign residents, and registration and control of foreign workers.[12] The position of aliens might best be described as precarious, yet some parents were willing to tolerate it so long as their children could be raised as culturally Chinese.

ALIEN RETAIL TRADE BAN

In 1959, the Indonesian government attempted to break the Chinese hold on intermediate trade throughout the country by eliminating alien Chinese from retail trade in rural areas. A regulation of that year, PP-10 (*Peraturan Presiden*, Presidential Regulation Number Ten), forbade alien retail trade outside of second-level district capitals; as noted above, alien schools were also restricted to cities of this size.[13] In West Kalimantan, this meant that Pontianak, Singkawang (for Sambas), Sanggau and Sintang on the Kapuas, and one other inland center, were open for intermediate trade. Although in some Indonesian provinces, aliens were forced by the state to move to the larger towns, this was not the case in West Kalimantan. Some people living in the interior or along the rivers did move away, compelled to relocate by the loss of their livelihood. A few took advantage of the exceptions to the ban, which allowed activities like transport, barbering, and dentistry, to remain in the countryside. Before 1959, one missionary, describing a journey to Nanga Pinoh, three hundred miles up the Kapuas River, found "thousands" of "ubiquitous Chinese traders," "mostly aliens," in the towns and hamlets "far into the interior."[14] Attempting to make them leave would devastate the economy; closing the rural retail shops was bad enough. Visiting West Kalimantan in 1963, the author was told that PP-10/59 had been implemented in the province, but that there was no ban on alien residence outside the towns, and most aliens who could find a way to continue their activities had stayed put.[15]

---

[11] The question of "Indonesianization" of prayer and liturgy became more important to Catholics after the Second Vatican Council (1962-1965), which encouraged the replacement of Latin with vernacular languages. In West Kalimantan, with a large number of Chinese Catholics speaking Hakka, Teochiu, or Mandarin, and an even larger number of Dayak Catholics with different native languages, Indonesian was the only alternative that would reflect the unity of the Church and allow ethnically mixed congregations. Protestant denominations, often serving communities drawn from a single ethnic group, tended to use Chinese languages longer. A few Chinese- or part-Chinese-language services can still be found in the Archipelago today.

[12] Some of these measures are reported in *Warta Kalimantan Barat*, 5,8/9 (July-August 1972): 67-69. Of course, many regulations could be circumvented for a fee.

[13] Somers, "Peranakan Chinese," pp. 194-223.

[14] Sylvia Houliston, *Borneo Breakthrough* (London: China Inland Mission, 1963), pp. 113-114.

[15] Interviews, Pontianak and Singkawang, 1963.

In Indonesia as a whole, thousands of ethnic Chinese individuals, unwilling and practically unable to become Indonesian citizens, were ready to depart the nation for China. Indonesian officials were uncertain how many people would be affected by the retail trade and residence bans—they estimated there would be 25,000—but foreign news sources raised the figures to 100,000 and more. Several thousand alien rural enterprises must have existed in West Kalimantan alone, and, including family members, perhaps ten thousand or more persons were affected.[16] According to official statistics, 102,000 persons of Chinese origin left Indonesia in 1960, and, including all those who left in 1960-62, the total may well be over 120,000. The number of people who left Kalimantan is unknown, but it is known that many of those who emigrated were young people who hoped to continue their education in China, especially after the closure of so many Chinese-language schools.[17]

In February 1960, a fire destroyed the market of Pemangkat, which was, at the time, the third-largest town in the province and the "geographical centre of several predominantly Chinese villages, not to mention the great number of Chinese homes scattered throughout the extensive coconut groves and rubber plantations of that area."[18] Much of the *pasar* was reduced to ashes, rendering some six thousand people homeless, five thousand of whom soon left the country. Many expected that the town would never be rebuilt, because Chinese trade and agriculture had no future in Kalimantan, and leading pro-Beijing Chinese urged the people of Pemangkat to join the others waiting to depart for China.

The People's Republic of China sent ships to pick up the emigrants, who faced a number of restrictions (and sometimes chicanery) in their attempts to carry money and valuables with them out of the country. An undetermined number of Chinese in West Kalimantan also left for Taiwan. Finally ships from China stopped coming to pick up the emigrants, although thousands were still waiting to sail. As a result of these relocations and disruptions, the West Kalimantan economy in some places ground to a near-halt. On a visit to Michang village near Pontianak, where some five thousand Chinese had lived, a visitor observed in late 1959 only shuttered shops, and noted that many men spent the day gambling, having nothing else to do.[19]

The emigrants who fled to China faced several problems once they had arrived. China was having difficulties integrating so many new arrivals into Southeastern Chinese towns and finding study opportunities for young people. It also recognized that accepting too many Chinese refugees might encourage Indonesia to expel more of them. Lastly, there were cultural conflicts. Some "returned Overseas Chinese," as they were known in China, expected to lead privileged lives in what was still a poor homeland.[20] Not only did neighbors and

---

[16] Somers, "Peranakan Chinese," p. 208.

[17] Ibid., p. 209. Accounts in the *Beijing Review* at the time emphasized the high proportion of schoolchildren or students.

[18] Houliston, *Breakthrough*, pp. 147, 173-178; private archive. As noted above, fires were common in Kalimantan's market towns.

[19] Ibid., p. 104.

[20] Ibid., pp. 113-115. See David Mozingo, *Chinese Policy toward Indonesia, 1949-1967* (Ithaca: Cornell University Press, 1976), pp. 171-180, for China's about-face on welcoming "returning Overseas Chinese" in 1960.

party cadres resent their access to transfers of money from abroad, special housing, and other "privileges," when the Cultural Revolution broke out in 1966, many Returned Overseas Chinese bore the brunt of local violence against "bourgeois" elements. Students often had to leave schools and universities for the countryside and engage in hard physical labor instead of study.

Since Singkawang was already crowded with former rural traders and Sambas was rather small and remote, many of the stranded traders and their families finally moved to Pemangkat, a market not only for rubber and coconuts, but for rice-growers, goldsmiths, and producers of mandarin oranges (known in the Archipelago as *jeruk Pontianak*, Pontianak citrus), as well as a center of fishing and the production of fermented shrimp paste (*blacang*). Soon the town, which had been largely destroyed in the fire of 1960, was being rebuilt,[21] as it had been after the troubles of the 1850s, when people left for Sarawak and then returned. Some potential emigrants left stranded in the province even managed to get a bit of land to work there or in other locations.[22]

The effects of the economic ban fell more heavily on the poorer Chinese; wealthy members of the community had been more careful about assuring they, or someone in the family, had Indonesian citizenship. The real sufferers, however, were Dayaks and others who were dependent on Chinese retail traders, especially in the interior. Strict implementation of the ban disrupted established trading routes, and in the end the authorities were forced to relax the prohibition.

CITIZENSHIP

Enforcement of the alien retail ban overlapped with the implementation of a 1955 agreement with the People's Republic of China about the status of ethnic Chinese who were considered to be dual nationals, that is, citizens both of Indonesia and of China. The citizenship question in Indonesia is long and complicated. Both the first Indonesian citizenship law of 1946, during the Revolution, and the provisions of the Round Table Agreement of December 1949 automatically recognized all Indonesian-born Chinese (that is, former Dutch subjects of Chinese descent) as Indonesian citizens, together with indigenous Indonesians. Because the Chinese were, according to Chinese law, also citizens of China, they could reject Indonesian citizenship by an active declaration of their desire to be exclusively Chinese—and not Indonesian—citizens. Up to the end of 1951, when the opportunity for rejecting citizenship ended, some 600-700,000 of the approximately 1.5 million persons eligible had rejected Indonesian citizenship.[23] Some of those who lost their Indonesian citizenship were minors whose parents

---

[21] Houliston, *Breakthrough*, pp. 177-180. China stopped sending ships to Indonesia to pick up prospective returnees, after which the Indonesian military chartered some ships to carry the emigrants. These were insufficient to transport all who, at least initially, wanted to leave. Somers, "Peranakan Chinese," p. 211.

[22] Somers, "Peranakan Chinese," p. 212; interviews in Pontianak, 1963.

[23] Mozingo, *Chinese Policy*, p. 97, citing figures of the Indonesian ministry of justice. In an earlier paper, Mozingo gave the figure of 390,000, but the larger figure cited above may include family members. See his "The Sino-Indonesian Dual Nationality Treaty," *Asian Survey* (December 1961): 25-31. The earlier Indonesian citizenship law of 1946 and the rejection period during the Indonesian Revolution do not seem to have been implemented and would have been meaningless in West Kalimantan, which was not under Republican control.

had rejected it for them. Persons born in China were simply Chinese nationals. As a result, half or more of all the ethnic Chinese in Indonesia were designated as foreign nationals by the mid-1950s.

While all persons of Chinese descent born in the Indies or Indonesia before 1949 who had declined to reject citizenship actively were, in principle, Indonesian citizens, most had no documents to prove it. The situation in West Kalimantan was especially difficult. Civil registration of births and marriages for the Chinese in West Borneo began officially in 1925. As far as marriages were concerned, registration had been largely ignored, and the registration of births was probably also honored in the breach. The civil registry was costly and time-consuming, requiring someone who could fill out forms in Dutch. Worse yet, documents written in Dutch could be dangerously incriminating during the Japanese period, so that many persons had destroyed those they had in their possession. (The same probably applied to documents about land tenure.) In 1948, the Chinese Affairs Officer in Pontianak, aware that the civil registry was a failure, recommended simply recognizing all Chinese marriages made before that year—twenty-three years after introduction of the civil registry.[24] Yet it was not unusual for Indonesian officials to ask for an official birth certificate or even a marriage certificate of an applicant's parents to prove that the applicant had been born in Indonesia and, with that, to establish Indonesian citizenship. Bureaucrats even took offense if a name was not spelled consistently, although Chinese names were often transcribed into Latin letters in several ways. For example, in Singkawang, the court accused one man of fraud, jailed him, and deprived him of his citizenship because in his papers his mother's name was spelt Tjong instead of Tjung.[25] No wonder that in West Kalimantan less than 20 percent of the Chinese were considered citizens in the early 1950s, while a mere 950 persons had applied for an official proof of Indonesian citizenship.[26]

Naturalization was only theoretically an alternative. A law on the naturalization of aliens was introduced into parliament in 1954 and finally approved in 1958, but it required those applying for citizenship to divest themselves of their previous nationality, something impossible under Chinese law at the time. As a result, it was futile for alien Chinese to apply for naturalization

---

[24] Note about Civil Registry in Pontianak, 1948, ARA 2.21.120 (59). See also discussion in chapter six.

[25] Eddi Elison, "Kesukaran WNA Cina untuk jadi WNI di Kalbar: Ada yang jadi WNI lewat calo, tapi dihukum," *Selecta* 876 (July 3, 1978): 45. At the same time, several others "lost" their citizenship in a similar manner.

[26] This estimate is from Tobing, *Kalimantan Barat*, p. 38. Twenty percent seems far too low. The number of citizens is unknown, but Chinese Affairs Officer Abell wrote in 1945 that two-thirds of the Chinese were locally born (*peranakans*), which means at least two-thirds were eligible for Indonesian citizenship unless they rejected it officially. See "Report on the Situation of Chinese in West Borneo," Singapore, October 29, 1945, ANRI AS 1308. I know of no breakdown on rejection of citizenship in 1949-51 for West Kalimantan. The proof of citizenship certificate (SBKI, *Surat Bukti Kewarganegaraan Indonesia*) was not a required document; it was costly, of little use, and highly unpopular. People applied for it only when absolutely necessary. See Willmott, *National Status*, pp. 70ff., and Somers, "Peranakan Chinese," p. 232. When Machrus Effendy, *Penghancuran PGRS-PARAKU dan PKI di Kalimantan Barat* (Jakarta: published by author, 1995), p. 7, says that only 5 percent of the Chinese in Kalimantan Barat were Indonesian citizens, he is simply wrong.

under normal conditions.[27] Most observers assumed that in West Kalimantan, Chinese would simply not care to become Indonesian citizens. Significantly, the Consultative Body for Indonesian Citizenship, Baperki (Badan Permusyawaratan Kewarganegaraan Indonesia), a national lobby for ethnic Chinese who held Indonesian citizenship—this lobby was especially strong in Java and active throughout the Archipelago—was weakly represented in West Kalimantan, and when it campaigned for office, received no votes there in the 1955 election.[28]

Implementation of the dual nationality treaty between Indonesia and the People's Republic of China between January 1960 and January 1962 enabled those ethnic Chinese who had Indonesian citizenship either to divest themselves of Chinese nationality or to reject Indonesian citizenship. On the national level, about two-thirds of those eligible opted for Indonesian citizenship. Since the treaty did not apply to Chinese aliens, however, it was of limited applicability to the significant numbers of Chinese persons who had never been able to establish Indonesian citizenship, something felt strongly in West Kalimantan.

As late as 1978, according to official statistics, nearly 155,000 alien Chinese were registered in West Kalimantan, out of an ethnic Chinese population of about 300,000; all but 5 percent of the aliens were citizens of the People's Republic of China. The remainder were adherents of the Republic of China (Taiwan) or, according to the Indonesian government, they were "stateless." Some 50,000 aliens resided in the city of Pontianak and another 36,000 in the surrounding district (*kabupaten*) of Pontianak, with its capital at Mempawah. Another 58,000 resided in the district of Sambas, most of them around Singkawang—thus, over 90 percent were in Pontianak and the former Chinese Districts. A few thousand could be found in Ketapang (3,000) to the south and in Sanggau (6,000) and Sintang (1,600), while a mere 673 lived in the Upper Kapuas (this small population contrasts with the strong presence of ethnic Chinese around Nanga Pinoh in earlier times).[29]

---

[27] Willmott, *National Status*, pp. 40-42.

[28] Somers, "Peranakan Chinese," p. 143-173; interview with Baperki leader, Jakarta, 1963. Baperki in Java and Sumatra established national schools for children displaced from Chinese schools and propagated information on the value of citizenship. Election results from Siauw Tiong Djin, *Siauw Giok Tjhan: Perjuangan seorang patriot membangun nasion Indonesia dan masyarakat Bhineka Tunggal Ika* (Jakarta: Hasta Mitra, 1999), p. 227. Baperki always claimed it was not a political party, although it sometimes behaved like one.

[29] See Indonesia, Buro Pusat Statistik, *Penduduk Cina luar Jawa: Hasil registrasi penduduk akhir tahun 1976, 1977, 1978* (Jakarta: Buro Pusat Statistik, 1980), Tables. Soemadi, *Peranan Kalimantan Barat dalam menghadapi subversi komunis Asia Tenggara: Suatu tinjauan internasional terhadap gerakan komunis dari sudut pertahanan wilayah khususnya Kalimantan Barat* , second edition (Pontianak: Yayasan Tanjungpura, 1974), p. 39, says there were 450,000 Chinese, 350,000 of whom retained citizenship in the People's Republic of China—surely both numbers are too high. Soemadi was an officer of the Brawijaya Division of the Indonesian army who, as a lieutenant colonel, became governor of Kalimantan Barat in July 1967. He commanded operations in West Kalimantan from April 1969-March 1973. His 1974 book, a revealing account written when he was a brigadier general, may be a version of a thesis submitted in 1972 for the degree of *sarjana*, and cited by Soedarto et al., *Sejarah Daerah Kalimantan Barat* (Pontianak: Proyek Penelitian dan Pencatatan Kebudayaan Daerah, 1978), p. 229, which calls him a major general.

Table 7.1:
Alien Chinese in West Kalimantan, 1978

Location	Chinese Aliens
Pontianak City	50,000
Pontianak Kabupaten	36,000
Sambas Kabupaten	58,000
Ketapang	3000
Sanggau	6000
Sintang	1600
Upper Kapuas	693
Total	ca. 155,000
Total Ethnic Chinese	ca. 300,000

CONFRONTATION

Visiting the Monterado area in 1937, geographer Karl Helbig remarked that the Chinese were so well established and so dominant in that region that they could only be driven away by force.[30] Thirty years later, that is just what happened.

By 1962, the anti-alien measures of 1959-60 had abated somewhat. The Indonesian government was pursuing an international course that took it closer to the People's Republic of China, and it appeared to have become more favorable to the interests of the ethnic Chinese.

On September 16, 1963, Malaysia was formed by joining the independent Republic of Malaya to the former British colonies of Singapore, Sarawak, and North Borneo (Sabah). The original intent to include the Sultanate of Brunei, an oil-rich British protectorate, in the new Federation failed in December 1962 when a rebellion led by A. M. Azahari broke out in that territory, and Brunei withdrew from the project. The uprising, quickly crushed by local police and British troops, caused Indonesia to voice openly its suspicion of the new federation. After futile negotiations, President Sukarno declared Indonesia's intention to "crush (*ganyang*) Malaysia."[31]

Although Indonesia's Left—especially the Communist Party, which had already branded the creation of Malaysia as a neo-colonialist plot—rushed to support Sukarno's battle cry, large-scale fighting never emerged. For various reasons, the Indonesian Army's leadership was reluctant to provoke full-scale fighting and to withdraw troops from Java, where the political situation was becoming tense, in order to deploy them on the Kalimantan borders. However, the local military, in particular Brigadier General M. S. Supardjo, commander of the Fourth Combat Command stationed in West Kalimantan, who was more

---

[30] Karl Helbig, *Eine Durchquerung der Insel Borneo (Kalimantan): Nach den Tagebüchern aus dem Jahre 1937*, revised edition (Berlin: Dietrich Reimer Verlag, 1982), p. 80.

[31] J. A. C. Mackie, *Konfrontasi: The Indonesia-Malaysia Dispute, 1963-1966* (Kuala Lumpur: Oxford University Press, 1974); Alastair Morrison, *Fair Land Sarawak: Some Recollections of an Expatriate Official* (Ithaca: Cornell Southeast Asia Program, 1993), p. 140-141. Morrison recalls that the Brunei rebels crossed through North Borneo into Indonesia for training there; Effendy, *Penghancuran*, also mentions Azahari's use of Kalimantan Barat as a base (pp. 17, 27).

sympathetic to Sukarno's campaign, recruited Sarawak insurgents—one to two thousand of them—many of whom were from Chinese-language schools, for military and ideological training at an Indonesian military base in 1963-65. Some additional supporters came from within Kalimantan and may have included local Chinese, some of Azahari's supporters, and local sympathizers of the Indonesian Communist Party (PKI, Partai Komunis Indonesia).[32] These young people, many but not all of Chinese origin, were supposed to operate in the jungle, supporting the Indonesian military in its attacks on Sarawak territory. They linked up with armed left-wing opposition guerrillas from Sarawak, guerrillas associated with PGRS (Pasukan Gerilya Rakyat Sarawak, Sarawak Guerrilla Force) and the less important Paraku (Pasukan Gerilya Rakyat Kalimantan Utara, Guerrilla Force of North Borneo).[33]

The alteration in Indonesia's politics after October 1965, and subsequent peace with Malaysia in June 1966, left this group stranded. Brigadier General Supardjo himself participated in the attempted coup of September 30, 1965 in Jakarta, and was later imprisoned.[34] His successors were distinctly unsympathetic to the guerrillas, who were now joined by disaffected local pro-Communist elements. The number of guerrillas probably did not exceed one thousand, but they could rely on help from (or they could intimidate and compel) Chinese living in Sarawak and in Indonesian border territories.[35] In late 1966, the military did expel some Chinese

---

[32] This account follows Herbert Feith, "Dayak Legacy," *Far Eastern Economic Review* (January 25, 1968): 134-135. According to Mackie (*Konfrontasi*, p. 215), "In West Kalimantan unemployed young men from Sambas and Singkawang were said to have been rounded up *en bloc* by their village heads." Nevertheless, the numbers of rebels may be exaggerated. Soemadi (*Peranan*, p. 162) admits, "Young Chinese of Kalimantan Barat and Dayaks . . . greatly helped PGRS-PARAKU [Pasukan Gerilya Rakyat Sarawak and Pasukan Gerilya Rakyat Kalimantan Utara, the guerrilla organizations of Sarawak and North Borneo] . . . . Since the time of Konfrontasi in 1963, which 'nota bene' was pioneered (*dipelopori*) by the Old Order government, they were even trained and armed." Soemadi is otherwise at pains to deny the connection with Konfrontasi and to place PGRS-PARAKU in Sarawak—he claims it only "retreated" (*hijrah*) to Indonesian territory (p. 54). On the other hand, he relates that ten persons were given training in Bogor and another sixty in West Kalimantan (p. 56). Elison recognized the irony that, after October 1965, the military "had to take back the arms which had previously been given to [the rebels]." Not mentioning Brigadier General Supardjo, he puts the blame on an anonymous colonel in the Tanjungpura unit's staff; see Eddi Elison, "Kalbar pintu masuk komunis: Dulu gerombolan komunis menggunakan 'Amoy' sebagai pemimpin kolompok," *Selecta* 878 (July 17, 1978): 55. Effendy, *Penghancuran*, pp. 18-20, on the other hand, simply claims that Kalimantan Barat Chinese and local PKI-sympathizers supported PGRS.

[33] Feith, "Dayak Legacy"; Charles A. Coppel, *Indonesian Chinese in Crisis* (Kuala Lumpur: Oxford University Press, 1983), pp. 146-147; Wolfgang Franke, *Reisen in Ost- und Südostasien 1937-1990*, ed. Hartmut Walravens (Osnabrück: Zeller, 1998), pp. 421-422; Morrison, *Fair Land*, pp. 144-145; Morrison points out that once Malaysian and other Commonwealth forces, including Gurkhas, had permission to operate against the guerrillas in Indonesian territory, most of the fighting took place there, not in Sarawak (pp. 151-153).

[34] On Supardjo's role as a leader of the coup, see Benedict R. O'G. Anderson, Ruth T. McVey, and Frederick Bunnell, *A Preliminary Analysis of the October 1, 1965 Coup in Indonesia* (Ithaca: Cornell Modern Indonesia Project, 1971), pp. 7, 11, 33.

[35] Soemadi (*Peranan*) reports that at this time border areas (Sanggauledo, Jagoi Babang, Benua Martinus, and others, see his map, p. 171) were the center of rebel activity and, representing the official view, asserts that the guerrillas were virtually all ethnic Chinese, although he admits they had help from Dayaks. On the other hand, he names the leader of the "new PKI," Sayid Ahmad Sofyan (Soemadi, *Peranan*, p. 2). His "Chinese name" was "Tai Ko" (p. 108). (This is not a name, but a title; since kongsi days it has simply meant "boss".) Sofyan managed to organize

from rural areas, and there was talk of their repatriation to China, but no large-scale measures were implemented at this time, because the army was not up to strength in the province.

Obviously, left-wing activity was by no means limited to the Chinese community. The attempted coup of September 30, 1965—resulting in the deaths of several generals and Suharto's rise to power—had repercussions in Kalimantan as well. Many people in the province, such as lower-level Javanese clerks and some Dayaks (even army commander Supardjo himself), were sympathetic to the Communist Party. The public works service (Dinas Pekerjaan Umum) at the time employed so many Communists that its vehicles flew red flags.[36] As the military situation changed in West Kalimantan, some of these sympathizers (although not the military) may well have taken to the jungle.

When military action in late 1966 through early 1967 failed to wipe out the now stranded anti-Malaysia and pro-Communist guerrillas, the troops withdrew completely from the border area in March 1967, leaving a "vacuum of power" until new units from Military Area XII Tanjungpura consolidated their control. In July 1967, guerrillas attacked the Indonesian air force base near Sanggauledo, killing a number of officers and men, and capturing weapons and ammunition. Jakarta sent reinforcements, but not enough to crush the guerrillas. Despite the broad range of people participating in (or sympathetic to) the guerrilla movement, the new military leaders in Pontianak blamed the Chinese and were determined to drain the ethnic Chinese waters in which the guerrilla fish were presumably swimming—that is, to remove the ethnic Chinese from the interior of northwest Kalimantan. In September 1967, guerrillas had begun to prey on Dayak *kampungs*, burning, kidnapping, and killing. The Indonesian military leaders tried to drive a wedge between the guerrillas, especially between the Chinese guerrillas, and the Dayaks. A purported rebel Chinese attack on a village near Sanggauledo in September 1967, in which several Dayaks were reported killed, was one incident that rendered the Dayaks more receptive to military urgings that the Chinese ought to be driven out of West Kalimantan.[37]

---

distribution of pro-PKI pamphlets in several coastal cities in May 1972, to the consternation of the military authorities, but was killed in 1973 or 1974. Effendy (*Penghancuran*, p. 66) identifies Sofyan as a *pribumi* of part-Arab descent and an immigrant to Kalimantan; he was the military leader of the rebels. According to him, Sofyan seized control of the local PKI in 1960, putting it on a Maoist course and appealing for ethnic Chinese support. For a recent, critical analysis, see Jamie S. Davidson and Douglas Kammen, "Indonesia's Unknown War and the Lineages of Violence in West Kalimantan," *Indonesia* 73 (April 2002): 53-87. The authors emphasize that the PKI of West Kalimantan was primarily an indigenous Indonesian organization.

[36] Herman Josef van Hulten, *Hidupku di antara suku Daya: Catatan seorang misionaris* (Jakarta: Grasindo, 1992), pp. 266-267, 270, 299. Protestant missionaries Robert Peterson, *Storm over Borneo* (London: Overseas Missionary Fellowship, 1968) and *The Demon Gods of Thorny River: A True-to-Life Story of a Chinese Family in West Kalimantan, Indonesian Borneo* (London: Overseas Missionary Fellowship, 1974) as well as Houliston (*Breakthrough*) claim they and their converts were harassed by Chinese leftists. It should be emphasized that the ethnic Chinese in general were not members of the Indonesian Communist Party, but large numbers were sympathetic to the People's Republic of China at this time. Peterson was from the Overseas Missionary Fellowship, formerly the China Inland Mission.

[37] A post-Reformasi article in *Kompas* by Jannes Eudes Wawa (January 26, 2001) asserts that even the original "killing" of Dayak villagers was "engineered" by the Army, not perpetrated by PGRS/PARAKU forces. Davidson and Kammen, "Unknown War," pp. 63-64, place the

THE "DAYAK RAIDS"

Following the attacks on Dayak villagers, the blandishments of military operatives took effect, unleashing Dayak revenge:

> . . . the Dayaks were given official permission to hunt down and kill all those who had lifted their sword against them . . . the campaign soon became an "open season" against all Chinese. Even merchants and farmers who had lived side by side with the Dayaks in peace for generations were not spared.[38]

Government security forces spread the rumor that Communists were planning a "general uprising" for October 1967, accelerating tensions.[39] Contributing to the tension was the closing of the Sarawak border in 1963, which had ruined the smuggling economy from which both Chinese and Dayaks had profited. Furthermore, West Kalimantan's rubber production was in crisis since its market in Singapore had been closed off during the Confrontation between Indonesia and Malaysia, and as a result, prices were very depressed.[40] Hunger, even famine, accompanied economic troubles in the interior.

Preceding the "Dayak Raids," as Feith and Coppel call them (the Indonesian military dubbed them "demonstrations"), traditional Dayak war symbols were passed from *kampung* to *kampung*. A bowl filled with chicken blood and decorated with feathers, called *mangkok merah* (red bowl), signaled mobilization for attack. The first Dayak "retaliation" appears to have been on October 14, in Taum, south of Sanggauledo.[41]

In late October, 1967, the "demonstrations" broke out with unparalleled force, especially in the Anjungan-Mandor-Menjalin area. Dayak bands entered towns, attacking Chinese shops, piling their goods on the street, then turning to vandalize

---

attack in Taum, near Sanggauledo, in September 1967. The bodies of the victims were said to have been mutilited by "Chinese communist" attackers, but the authors suggest that the military was responsible for the mutilations. For more background, see Feith, "Dayak Legacy," p. 134; Coppel, *Indonesian Chinese*, pp. 146-148; *Kompas* (December 27, 1967); *Pembanguan* (Pontianak) (November 9, 1967); and Garth Alexander, *Silent Invasion: The Chinese in Southeast Asia* (London: Macdonald, 1973), pp. 1-5. Coppel makes a strong case for military provocation of the raids, showing how military units had made the rounds of Dayak communities in 1967, trying to incite them against the Chinese, but without results until the Dayaks themselves were attacked. Feith notes that some Dayak intellectuals felt they were being shunted aside and were eager for a return to power, perhaps by managing the violence of 1967, but it became unmanageable. Cf. van Hulten, *Hidupku*, pp. 282-283. Some people in Kalimantan today say that these Dayak leaders later felt they had been wrongly used.

[38] Peterson, *Storm*, p. 11.

[39] Coppel, *Indonesian Chinese*, p. 147; Peterson, *Demon Gods*, p. 39. Whether this rumor appeared before or after the attacks on Dayak *kampungs* is not clear.

[40] Interview, Tan Keong Choon, Singapore Archives, Oral History Project. Some rubber exports made their way through other countries (illicitly) to Singapore. On smuggling, a "traditional" occupation, see also Soedarto, *Sejarah*, p. 228, and chapter six.

[41] According to Davidson and Kammen, "Unknown War," p. 67. There is some question whether there is really a "tradition" of a *mangkok merah* or whether it dated from a time as late as the Dayak uprising in World War II.

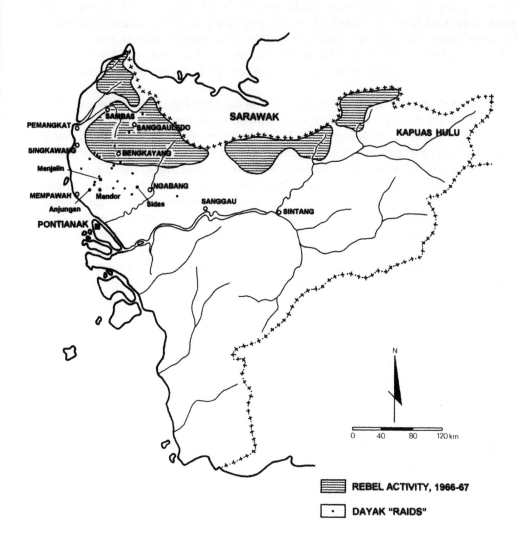

Map Eight. West Kalimantan in 1967,
showing areas of rebel activity and "Dayak Raids."

their rubber gardens and farms, and finally forcing many Chinese to flee. Yet the initial attacks on Chinese *kampungs* were not carried out by crazed hordes; witnesses recalled that the first groups were disciplined, that they gathered up the goods kept in Chinese shops and houses and destroyed them, but there was no looting. They reportedly used no firearms; their swords were convincing enough.[42] This first group of attackers was made up mostly of Sambas and Mempawah Dayaks, who had lived in usually friendly proximity to the Chinese, although there were times when the Mempawah Dayaks had fought against them.[43] The initial wave of violence continued for weeks, and tens of thousands of Chinese, who made no move to resist, fled to the coast, having lost their possessions but not their lives.

The mood changed when some young Chinese began to fight back. Some say this was the signal for the Dayaks to take up firearms, escalating the violence.

After a few weeks, on November 14, groups from the interior arrived who killed and even cannibalized their victims.[44] Under the leadership of Menyukei Dayaks, "thousands" assembled in Menjalin from all directions, moving to Toho and Anjungan and toward Sungai Pinyu. Only there did the military drive them back; Sungai Pinyu was a strategic center on the road from Pontianak to the north, and therefore the military had to prevent chaos there or see communications with the north of the province interrupted.[45] In Capkala there was also trouble, but most people fled before things got worse.[46] Although the Chinese constituted almost half of the population in some areas, where they were farmers and owners of small rubber gardens, they made no attempt to defend themselves. Initially, many menfolk remained behind, and others, who had left when the attacks broke out, tried to return to their empty houses at the end of October. In many places, women and children fled or went into hiding.[47]

When the tone of demonstrations changed in November, "demonstrators" armed with old hunting weapons began killing the Chinese and burning Chinese property. The sudden change in the level of violence is attributed in one account to the capture of a Chinese guerrilla who, as he was being taken to town, evaded his captors, killing one (a Madurese, while the other was Dayak) and stealing a gun,

---

[42] Van Hulten, *Hidupku*, pp. 280-281. The date of October 17, which is given by Hulten for the first attacks in the Menjalin area, is clearly wrong. He speaks of "Saturday, 17 October, the day before [the Feast of] Christ the King." In 1967, this would have fallen on the last Sunday in October, October 29, so the date of the attack on Menjalin must have been October 28. Military sources say October 29 (cited in Davidson and Kammen, "Unknown War," p. 67). The later date is also more likely, to allow for time after October 14 to organize the raids on a larger scale.

[43] As in the wars of the 1850s and 1880s; see chapter three.

[44] In theory the Dayaks practiced headhunting, not cannibalism. The evidence for their eating the livers of victims is, however, considerable. It appears, for example, in van Hulten, *Hidupku*, p. 165 (referring to attacks on the Japanese in 1945); interviews in Singkawang, 1996, and newspaper photographs from 1997. Van Hulten identifies the second group of attackers as predominantly Menyukei Dayak (*Hidupku*, pp. 284, 294), non-Christians, while the first, more disciplined wave, from other Dayak groups, included a number of known Christians.

[45] Van Hulten, *Hidupku*, pp. 288-289.

[46] Peterson, *Demon Gods*, p. 37.

[47] Van Hulten, *Hidupku*, pp. 290-292; private archive.

but this tale is questionable.[48] In Sebedau and Mandor, travelers reported that Chinese shops were burning and Chinese bodies lined the road.[49] In Menjalin and Anjungan, practically nothing was left of the Chinese markets. The *sawahs* Chinese had planted were harvested by Dayaks whose own harvests were still unripe.[50]

In Pemangkat, the new *pasar* had been partly burned again in 1966, and the Sambas *pasar* burned in 1967, making these towns less desirable targets for the attackers. Besides, the military protected the larger towns, as it did Mempawah and Singkawang.[51] Bengkayang was not attacked (although the environs were unsafe), and refugees fled there, too. The area of violence was "From the north via Bengkayang directly south to Anjungan and eastward to Sanggau, an area of 100-150 [square] kilometers."[52] Sanggauledo was, in some accounts, another center of violence, as was Tebas, between Sambas and Pemangkat.[53] (See map eight.)

The center of the attacks was the area inland from Mempawah and Sungai Pinyu, especially the triangle from Anjungan to Mandor and Menjalin. In 1960, Anjungan served as a central market, where people from the interior sold their fruits, especially durian, to Chinese who could not live further inland because of the ban on alien retail trade. Within seventy kilometers lived Dayaks, Javanese, Bugis, Madurese, and tens of thousands of Chinese, mostly farmers. The Javanese were official transmigrants, the Madurese mostly so-called "wild" transmigrants, who had arrived without government support. Menjalin, twenty kilometers inland from Anjungan, was the center of a Catholic parish, administered by a few Dutch

---

[48] Van Hulten, *Hidupku*, p. 292. There are many explanations, all hard to verify. Another account places the gunshots in Senakin, where Dayak revenge followed. See Davidson and Kammen, "Unknown War," p. 67.

[49] Van Hulten, *Hidupku*, pp. 292-293. Counts of immediate victims vary from several hundred to a few thousand, but van Hulten speaks of three thousand in Sebedau alone, which is probably too high.

[50] Ibid., p. 294; private archives.

[51] Private archives.

[52] Van Hulten, *Hidupku*, p. 280.

[53] Interviews, West Kalimantan, 1996; Soemadi, *Peranan*, p. 93. Soemadi lists, for the Western sector, "Seluas, Sanggauledo, Ledo, Lumar, Bengkayang (except the town itself, because there was an ABRI [Indonesian military] post there), Parigi (Perigi), Samalantan, Pekucing (Pakucing), Monterado, Capkala, Anjungan, Toho, Karangan, Darit, Mandor, Ngabang and Serimbu" as locations of Dayak "rage." Another source also mentions actions near Sosok (fifty kilometers from Sanggau), Batang Tarang, Njarumkop, and Kampung Trado, Pakumbang, Tiang, and Raba, the last four villages near Nyarumkop. *Kompas* reported that troubles began in Darit, Perigi, Samalantan, Pakucing, then Sidas, Pahauman, Mandor, Senakin (Tarap), from north to south and from the east to the coast (December 28, 1967). The market at Senakin was also destroyed and, together with that of Pahauman, it was among the worst damaged, according to *Kompas* (January 4, 1968). The reporter (J. Widodo) visited the territory from Ngabang to Pontianak, including Sidas, Pahauman, Senakin, Sebadu (Sebedau), Mandor, and the region inland from Sungai Pinyu (Anjungan, Menjalin, Tunang Darit and Perigi) and from Bengkayang to Singkawang (Serukum, Pakucing, Samalantan). All were emptied of Chinese, except for those who had fled to the forest (*Kompas*, December 6, 1967). *Pembangunan*, on November 16-18, 1967, reported incidents from Sebedau and Serukum, near Tarap/Senakin and on November 9, 1967, also in Sansalk near Bengkayang, then Serukam, Sebalai, Samalantan, Monterado, Jitrak, Aping, Pakucing, Tainam, Lohabang, Pinang Albang, Songbang, Semparit near Lohabang. *Kompas* names refugees from Bengkayang, Serukun, Pak Meong Teo, Samalantan, and Monterado in the Sambas district, and Perigi, Darit, Tunang, Karangan, Menjalin, Senakin, and Mandor in the Pontianak district. These locations are indicated by dots on map eight.

Capuchin fathers and Chinese and Dayak sisters, who maintained a small outpatient clinic.[54] Both towns were scenes of Dayak attacks against the Chinese during the fighting of 1885 and after the incidents of 1914, probably because they formed strategic links with the interior. Menjalin, administratively a *kecamatan* (sub-district, the administrative level below *kabupaten* or district), was located about one hundred kilometers from Pontianak, had a large Chinese market and a population about 45 percent Chinese in 1967. The triangle Anjungan-Menjalin-Mandor (see map three) was one of the most fertile areas in the center and a node of communications with the north, east, and south. The Chinese dominated markets and transportation in the region, but their relations with the Dayak were considered "very good." Dayak relations with the Madurese however had repeatedly led to fighting during the 1960s, fighting that recurred thereafter.[55]

The violence of 1967 was deliberately directed at all Chinese residents, on the assumption, most clearly voiced by provincial military commander Lt. Colonel Soemadi, that all Chinese, both aliens and citizens, were supporters of Communist China and the PKI.[56] While the Chinese fled, the shops, houses, schools, even a Protestant church, were all burned by the attackers.[57] Whoever was behind it, the Chinese were now being killed, not just driven away. The army openly encouraged head-taking by attackers and later rewarded with honors those who took heads.[58]

The violence did not stop at Chinese; soon it affected other ethnic groups as well. Some Madurese lived scattered in small groups through the Menjalin-Anjungan area; they were known to be fervent Muslims and good fighters. When the Dayak raids began, many Madurese fled, as did many Javanese and even Malays. In December, in Sungai Pinggam, Madurese were threatened as *"Cina hitam"* (black Chinese). Some time after the raids, a Madurese attacked the family of a local *camat* (minor official, head of a *kecamatan*), a Dayak, killing him. A group of Dayaks retaliated by killing some thirty Madurese who had not been involved in the incident, and the matter promptly escalated. Hundreds of Madurese from the neighborhood of Sungai Pinyu then approached Anjungan, armed with axes and machetes, seeking revenge, but former governor Oevang Oeray, himself implicated in the anti-Chinese violence, was able to calm the situation.[59]

The Dayak raids had emptied the inland Chinese Districts of Chinese, who had lived there since kongsi times. After about three months, things became quieter.

---

[54] Van Hulten, *Hidupku*, p. 260.

[55] Ibid., p. 265-266. Van Hulten speaks of a triangle "Anjungan-Mandor-Takong," both as the center of Chinese settlement and because of its fertility. I have been unable, even on older maps, to locate Takong, and follow here Davidson and Kammen, "Unknown War," p. 67. See epilogue for more on this region.

[56] See Soemadi, *Peranan*, and Effendy, *Penghancuran*, for repeated assertions of this.

[57] Van Hulten, *Hidupku*, p. 295. Peterson—who admits this is hearsay—blames the Dayak from the interior, Kayan and Kenyah, for the change in the level of violence (*Storm*, p. 13). Van Hulten had worked with Dayaks (Peterson worked among the Chinese) and probably knew them better. See note 44, above.

[58] In discussing events to the east, Soemadi asserts that, since head-taking is part of Dayak *adat*, it is appropriate "psychological warfare" to encourage them to decapitate their enemy. Soemadi, *Peranan*, pp. 92-96, 118, 126ff, 164.

[59] Van Hulten, *Hidupku*, p. 295; *Kompas* (December 28, 1967). On Oevang Oeray's role, see below.

Plate 20. Pasar, Anjungan, 2000. The buildings are typical of Chinese shophouses, but the Chinese themselves were driven away in 1967. Credit: the author.

As noted above, Malays, as well as Madurese, had also fled the Dayak raids; they returned to their villages only when they were sure it was safe. According to some accounts, the Dayak planned to make Anjungan a center of Dayak settlement, and they expected that their raids against the Chinese would "cleanse" the area and make it available to them, but after the Chinese were expelled, persons from many other groups—above all Madurese and some Javanese—also moved in and took over formerly Chinese rubber farms or *sawahs*. When the perpetrators saw that Anjungan had not become a purely Dayak "center," they concluded that the expulsion of the Chinese was not a success.[60] Relations between the Dayaks and the Madurese remained bad, made worse by the great increase in the numbers of "wild" transmigrants relocating from that island, a situation that the government appeared to encourage. In 1983, a missionary observed, "the Dayaks will pass around the 'red bowl' again as a sign of war."[61]

The former military commander of the territory claimed that the "western sector," where the Dayak raids had taken place, was cleared of guerrilla activity by the beginning of 1970.[62] But most of the area emptied of Chinese had nothing to do with the rebels, who were confined to border areas north of Sanggauledo or farther to the east. As map eight shows, although there may have been one or two incidents in the Sanggauledo area, the thrust of anti-Chinese violence was far south of the border areas where rebel activity was centered. This suggests that the

---

[60] Van Hulten, *Hidupku*, pp. 301-302.

[61] Ibid., pp. 296-297. Van Hulten mentions more troubles in 1974.

[62] Soemadi, *Peranan*, p. 89.

violence was not directed at the rebels at all, but simply at the Chinese farmers.[63]

The military was also convinced that the Chinese in Sanggau, Sintang, and Kapuas Hulu, the so-called "eastern sector" of the border area, were "almost all" secretly aiding the rebels. In October 1970, some seventeen thousand resident Chinese were forced to move to larger towns along the Kapuas River, at the mouths of the subsidiary rivers, where the military quartered some of them in floating houses for a time.[64] The military also took steps to reduce "Communist" influence among the Dayaks, some of whom had acted as bearers for the rebels. They were given "instruction" in the dangers of Communism.

As happened after other uprisings, new roads were built into the interior, partly for police purposes, partly in anticipation of transmigrants. In addition to allowing the introduction of thousands of transmigrants, those who now governed the province supported a project to plant oil palm (*kelapa sawit*), a large-scale, mostly plantation crop, in the Sanggau region, presumably to replace the jungle that had hidden rebels.[65] The military believed it had reason to be satisfied; any Chinese now remaining in the interior were surely Communist rebels and could be eliminated.[66] Ironically, Indonesian authorities had now implemented the old Dutch "quarter" system, making it impossible for Chinese to live in rural areas, a system never really enforced in West Kalimantan, except under the pugnacious resident de Vogel, and, in any case, abolished decades before.

REFUGEES AND ECONOMIC DISLOCATION

The Chinese refugees, some seventy thousand of them (other estimates vary from fifty thousand to eighty thousand), streamed toward the coast, coming to rest in Singkawang, Pontianak, and Sungai Pinyu. An estimated two to three thousand died in the violence, but many more—in the first weeks some four thousand—died in makeshift refugee camps, where disease and malnutrition ran rampant.[67] The lucky found refuge with family members; others were housed in churches, rubber smoke houses, warehouses, and schools. Various institutions tried to help families survive and even resettle. Help came from the International Red Cross and from UN agencies. Christian groups were able to alleviate some suffering, setting up soup kitchens with supplies donated locally or from abroad and with the backing

---

[63] Davidson and Kammen ("Unknown War," p. 68) believe that Dayaks in northern Sambas resisted violence and deliberately kept the raids from spreading to their area. Some former PKI members were active in coastal areas between Mempawah and Sungai Duri (Ibid., p. 64), but the raids did not reach the coast.

[64] Ibid., p. 91. Soemadi, in spite of everything that indicates Army provocation, still calls the Dayak "cleansing" "spontaneous."

[65] Denys Lombard, "Guide Archipel IV: Pontianak et son arrière-pays," *Archipel* 28 (1984): 84.

[66] Alexander, *Silent Invasion*, p. 3; Soemadi, *Peranan*, p. 91.

[67] Alexander, *Silent Invasion*, pp. 1-5, provides an eyewitness account of the camps, but he believes only three or four hundred persons were directly killed in the violence. Feith ("Dayak Legacy") and Coppel (*Indonesian Chinese*), whose estimates are higher, both visited the area shortly after the raids. Because the initial attacks were limited to property, and because many people fled the interior before the bloodletting began, most sources agree that the number of immediate deaths was relatively low, compared to the number of those who died in camps. Local authorities inhibited relief shipments and other aid activities from abroad, insisting that the Indonesian Red Cross (which was unprepared to handle the problem) be solely responsible. Cf. Soemadi, *Peranan*, pp. 93-94.

of some local officials' wives. An important source of aid was the Chinese surname associations (called *she,* Mandarin *shi*) in Pontianak and elsewhere, practically the only Chinese organizations still in existence.[68] They were called upon to assist refugees where they could. Local medical doctors of Chinese origin helped mobilize aid from abroad. Taiwan sent rice; the Singapore Chinese Chamber of Commerce was another benefactor. In February 1968, the government ordered refugee centers closed; by March they were empty, but the refugees' problems were hardly solved.[69] The help from abroad that arrived in the early months of the crisis soon diminished and then ended.

After the violence, no shops were open, no buses or motorboats traveled inland. The Dayaks were unable to sell their rubber, durian, and *tengkawang,* or to buy necessities. Shortages and inflation increased, and because the land abandoned by the Chinese was usually not returned (or not immediately returned) to production, famine threatened. In the former Chinese Districts, Dayaks moved into Chinese shops, homes, and fields; some began to trade on a small scale or opened coffee shops. Some people said, "In the old days, we were exploited [*dihisap,* sucked] by Chinese, but now we are exploited by our own people." And a Pontianak Chinese trader declared, " Let them say that we Chinese exploit the Dayaks. The Dayak traders not only suck their own people, they chew them up."[70] Although Dayaks and others attempted to replace the Chinese economic networks of the interior, few of the new ventures were successful.

Although Kalimantan was geographically so large, it offered no really suitable place for the refugees to go. About half of the refugees resettled in the major towns; most of the rest settled on land close to towns like Pontianak and Singkawang.[71] Some grew vegetables in a "green belt" around the capital. Others occupied simple housing on the outskirts of Singakwang and other towns. Costs were borne by Chinese businessmen and organizations—after the mayors of the these cities pressured them openly to contribute. Exploitation of forest resources soon began on a large scale, bringing new jobs; by 1970, about two-thirds of the refugee men in one settlement area were working in Kubu's lumber industry.[72]

It seems reasonable to assume that most refugees, like most Chinese in rural West Kalimantan, were Hakkas. As so often happens, those who suffer most are the weakest members. Although Hakkas were known, both in China and abroad, for respecting their women, who in turn displayed independence and initiative, the new situation victimized the women survivors especially. The Chinese in Kalimantan had, in the past, occasionally been known to "sell" their daughters (especially to Europeans or Malays), but generally observers found that the Hakka women were well-regarded by their men and honored for their capacity to do

---

[68] There were, however, about twenty funeral societies, according to Lombard, "Guide Archipel," p. 90. These provided a proper ritual burial and mourners for their subscribing members.

[69] Peterson, *Demon Gods,* pp. 33-39; interviews in Pontianak and Singkawang, 1991-96; private archives.

[70] Quotes from van Hulten, *Hidupku,* pp. 296-297.

[71] *Environment and Population,* volume 2 of *Preliminary Regional Survey for Road Network Identification in Kalimantan Barat—Indonesia* (Canberra: Government of Australia, Department of Foreign Affairs, 1973), pp. 48-50.

[72] Feith, "Dayak Legacy;" interviews; private archives.

Plate 21. Mandor, 2000. The memorial to Lo Fong Pak is almost totally overgrown.
Credit: the author.

heavy work and to engage in business, as they often managed family interests. Hakka girls were educated as well as boys, as is evident from the school statistics (see chapter six).

In this time of need, however, a different attitude toward daughters came to the fore among Hakka families. Parents sometimes abandoned their daughters when fleeing, or when departing for China, or they offered infants and young girls for "sale."[73] Older daughters were quickly married off. A visitor found many beggars and women working as prostitutes near refugee camps. Singkawang became known, and still is, for its "Amoy-Amoy" (the Hakka pronunciation of *amei*, pretty one, a common girl's name; the Indonesian plural is formed by repetition), now a synonym for a prostitute.[74]

A new wrinkle in the fate of daughters was the Taiwan bride solution. Many young women, perhaps hundreds, left for Taiwan during the 1980s and 1990s, some of them to marry retired Guomindang soldiers (who were thought to prefer simple Nanyang brides to more demanding Taiwanese girls), others perhaps to a less salutary fate as sex workers.[75]

---

[73] Van Hulten, *Hidupku*, pp. 294-295.

[74] In some contexts, "Amoy" may simply refer to a young girl, as in Zainudin Isman, "Singkawang, Kota AMOI," *Kompas* (July 5, 1987). AMOI in the title of this article is also an acronym: "*aku menjadi orang Indonesia*," "I am becoming an Indonesian." According to Indonesian and Taiwanese scholars who have done fieldwork in the Singkawang area, most of the West Kalimantan brides traveling to Taiwan are legal wives, often for men from working-class or farming areas (again, many of these in Taiwan are Hakkas). Many women transfer money from Taiwan to help their families in Kalimantan.

[75] Onghokham, "The Chinese of West Kalimantan," *Globalink* 1,3 (March-May 1996): 46.

Despite its success at destroying the network of Chinese settlements in West Kalimantan and expelling Chinese from the interior, the military seems to have been dissatisfied with its work. At the end of the 1970s, the local commander decided to disperse Chinese residents who were too "concentrated" and encourage them to contribute more to the production of food (something they were doing quite well before they were driven from their land). Some two hundred Chinese farmers were to be moved from the town of Sambas, 539 families (2,249 persons) from Mempawah, and from the larger Sambas region another 1,384 families (9,151 persons) were to be resettled, with their destination unclear.

By this time, a visiting journalist observed that virtually "98 percent" of the Chinese he met wanted to become Indonesian citizens. This included even those who did not speak Indonesian.[76]

CITIZENSHIP AND INTEGRATION

After the attacks on Chinese in rural areas, new restrictions on Chinese culture followed. New Order (as President Suharto's regime, 1965-1998, was called) policy equated Chinese culture with Communist influence and pressed the Chinese to assimilate to Indonesian culture. Assimilation or change of ethnic identity on a large scale would be difficult or impossible in a territory like West Kalimantan, where identities were multi-faceted (as discussed in chapter one), and where economic roles were so closely correlated with such identities. Nevertheless, the government propagated this policy in a number of ways after 1966, and even more strongly after 1980.

All remaining Chinese-language schools had to adopt national curricula and use Indonesian as the sole language of instruction after 1966. A few operated bilingually for a limited time, but this experiment soon ended.[77] Nearly all purely Chinese organizations were prohibited, including non-political ones. Chinese General Associations and Chambers of Commerce were special targets, while burial associations and surname organizations survived. Prohibitions extended to the open display of Chinese culture; for example, Chinese-language shop signs and advertising were forbidden, and books and newspapers could not be imported (many entered the country despite these rules).[78] Military authorities discouraged the speaking of Chinese in public, and refused to permit public displays of Chinese religious celebrations. This meant the New Order prohibited the annual Capgomeh, or Lantern Festival, that was traditionally held in Singkawang on the fifteenth day of the Lunar New Year. In the past, the festival had centered on a great procession, with festively decorated wagons and mediums in trance, which people came from miles around to see. Not until 1996 did this festival resume.[79]

---

[76] Eddi Elison, "Perlunya dididipkan penduduk Cina di Kalbar ke proyek transmigrasi," *Selecta* 877 (July 19, 1978): 58-59.

[77] According to Elison, "Kesukaran," p. 44, the use of Chinese in the schools ended in 1973.

[78] See Charles Coppel, "Contradictions of the New Order," (paper presented at workshop on "Chinese Indonesians: The Way Ahead," Canberra, February 1999), appendices, for a list of discriminatory measures. Shop signs in Chinese were probably prohibited in the early 1960s, as they were elsewhere in Indonesia.

[79] Interview, Singkawang, 1996; Onghokham, "Chinese," pp. 41-42, and illustrations there.

The 1990 census for West Kalimantan is silent about ethnicity, but it contains some data on persons above the age of five who spoke a "foreign language" as their mother tongue; almost all of these persons would have been ethnic Chinese. Of almost 600,000 urban respondents, over 167,000 (28 percent) answered that their mother tongue was a foreign language; for rural areas, the figures showed a total of 2,200,000 respondents (less than total population, because individuals younger than five years old were not included), of whom nearly 122,000 spoke a foreign language (6 percent) as their mother tongue. Normally, this "foreign tongue" would be Chinese. So almost 290,000 persons in West Kalimantan reported that they spoke a foreign language (nearly all were Chinese), and an additional number should be added for persons under five years of age. A few ethnic Chinese, but probably not many, given that the population of ethnic Chinese could be estimated at not more than 400,000, may have named Indonesian or a regional language (*bahasa daerah*) as a mother tongue. (Note that the census asked about one's "mother tongue," rather than trying to determine a person's ability to speak a foreign language, and that "foreign" languages were, by definition, non-Indonesian languages.)

As would be expected, foreign language speakers were concentrated in the city of Pontianak (96,000), in the urban areas of Sambas and Pontianak districts (40,000 and 22,000 respectively), and in the rural areas of Sambas and Pontianak. There were some 72,000 residing in the rural areas of Sambas and 31,000 in the rural areas of Pontianak district.[80] As the following table shows, the Chinese did not "return" in significant numbers to rural areas following the expulsions of the 1960s. They resided in the traditional areas of settlement and, even where "rural," stayed close to urban areas. In fact, most of the "rural" Chinese in Sambas and Pontianak lived along the coast, not in old centers like Mandor and Monterado, much less in the rural interior regions.

Table 7.2

Distribution of Chinese* in West Kalimantan, Census of 1990

Location	Urban	Rural
Pontianak Municipality	95,793	---
Pontianak District	22,131	31,107
Sambas District	39,821	72,710
Sanggau	1,667	5,705
Ketapang	104	8,527
Sintang	6,251	3,797
Kapuas Hulu	1,467	108
Total	167,234	121,954

*Chinese: persons above the age of five who gave a foreign language as their mother tongue. Included in this number could be other foreign residents, but their number would not be large, certainly less than the number of ethnic Chinese who gave an Indonesian language as their mother tongue.

Although this data might seem to suggest that an enormous number of persons spoke a foreign language in West Kalimantan in 1990, in fact, of all persons above five years old who reported that their mother tongue was a language other than Bahasa Indonesia (including those who spoke local languages or other Indonesian

---

[80] Census of 1990, Cornell University Library Fiche 887 SEI 93/50020, pp. 34-39.

languages, as well as Chinese), a mere 28,000 persons in urban areas, but 374,000 in rural areas, said they could not speak Indonesian (*tida bisa berbahasa Indonesia*). Most of these were younger than nine years old or older than fifty. Although this self-assessment says nothing about level of proficiency, it seems clear that, at least in urban areas, most of the 167,234 speakers of Chinese as a mother tongue had no problems with Indonesian. Because of aggregation of the data on Chinese with data on non-Chinese, it is less clear whether this was true in rural areas.[81]

One can conclude that, although most Chinese in West Kalimantan still retained a Chinese language as their mother tongue (including most of the 290,000 plus an indefinite number of children under five years of age), most of those who lived in urban areas—80 to 90 percent—could speak Indonesian. As far as rural areas are concerned, the amalgamation of the Chinese with Dayak respondents unable to speak Indonesian makes it difficult to reach a conclusion. Yet a trend is clear, even if we do not use the census as evidence: use of Indonesian among ethnic groups in West Kalimantan is increasing.

All the restrictions on Chinese culture did not mean that the "Chinese element" disappeared from the landscape. Shophouses, called *ruko* (short for *rumah toko*) in Indonesian, recognizably Chinese, still dominated urban commercial areas. Chinese temples were a striking feature in the towns, along the roadside, or sometimes, in the form of simple offering places with a few incense sticks, red papers, or ashes, at prominent or bizarre natural formations. Wolfgang Franke's catalog of inscriptions, made during two visits to the province in 1974 and 1980, gives evidence of several prominent temples, although it only lists those at major settlements.[82] A 1985 source claims there were 451 *vihara* (Buddhist temples, now given a Sanskrit name) and *klenteng* (the Indonesian name for Chinese temples, from Guan Yin hall or temple, *guanyinting*) in the province, most of them in the districts of Sambas and Pontianak and in the municipality of Pontianak city, the areas of greatest Chinese concentration.[83] In places cleared of Chinese, even in the traditional kongsi capitals of Monterado or Mandor, the old temples fell into ruin, but in other areas, which benefited from the prosperity of the 1980s and early 1990s, they were often freshly renovated and improved.

Most Indonesians, especially those from outside the province, still see the Chinese as an alien group, not a local *suku* (ethnic group), and the population's continuing use of the Chinese language (sometimes Mandarin, but usually Hakka or Teochiu) still arouses suspicion or resentment. Yet unquestionably, the use of Indonesian is becoming widespread. Children attend Indonesian schools; many do not have the money or energy to learn Mandarin on the side, and some of the

---

[81] Census 1990, Cornell University Library Fiche 887 SEI 93/50020, pp. 40-41. There was also a considerable number of women between twenty-five and forty-nine years old (nearly eighty thousand) who did not speak Indonesian. The strong preponderance of non-speakers of Indonesian in rural areas suggests that many of these were Dayaks. Note that this group of non-Indonesian speakers is not the same as the group in Table 7.2.

[82] Wolfgang Franke, in collaboration with Claudine Salmon and Anthony Siu, *Bali, Kalimantan, Sulawesi, Moluccas*, volume 3 of *Chinese Epigraphic Materials in Indonesia* (Singapore: South Seas Society, 1997), pp. 46-185; Franke, *Reisen*, pp. 296-302; 414-430.

[83] H. Ahmad Yunus, et al., *Upacara tradisional daerah Kalimantan Barat* (Jakarta: Departemen Pendidikan dan Kebudayaan, Proyek Inventarisasi dan Dokumentasi Kebudayaan Daerah, 1985), p. 16.

youngest may speak Indonesian more readily than a Chinese language.[84] Most older Chinese speak passable Indonesian, but still use a Chinese language to communicate among themselves, just as many Indonesians use their local language, not Indonesian, when speaking with the family or close associates.[85]

Church-run schools, common in the province, also promote integration by providing instruction in Indonesian. However, because so many of their urban adherents are Chinese, and because even non-Christian Chinese like to send their children to these schools, it remains difficult to find enough *pribumi* (as indigenous Indonesians are called) children to balance the number of Chinese pupils. Just as some residential areas are predominantly Chinese, some schools have such a high proportion of Chinese pupils that Chinese is the *lingua franca* of the playground, even if Indonesian is taught in the classroom.

Schools are not the only reason for the popularity of Christianity among Chinese. Given the widespread national perception that most Chinese were Communists in the 1960s, many Chinese decided to associate themselves with a church as a political refuge. Some Protestant missionaries reported great success in evangelizing in the first months after the Dayak terror.[86] The Catholic Church, reluctant to baptize without previous instruction, but eager to bestow political protection with some kind of church document, issued "catechumen" certificates to a number of applicants, many of whom subsequently joined the Church. The Protestant churches (3.7 percent of the population in 1971) tended to be ethnically based; Chinese Protestants may belong to denominations with all-Chinese membership. The Catholics, whose adherents in West Kalimantan were already 87 percent ethnic Indonesian in 1975 (and only 13 percent Chinese),[87] integrated Chinese, Dayaks, and other Indonesians into their ranks. This church, which represented 13.7 percent of the population, according to the 1971 census,[88] used the Indonesian language in public services after the early 1960s, and encouraged the use of Indonesian in the schools. Once predominantly an apostolate to the Chinese, the Catholic Church in West Kalimantan had long been, above all, a mission to the Dayak.

The great majority of Chinese in West Kalimantan continued to adhere to Confucianism and to Buddhism. While the New Order regime of President Suharto

---

[84] In 1996, the author observed how adults addressed a young schoolgirl in Chinese (Teochiu), while she responded consistently in Indonesian.

[85] This is a great change from the author's first visit to Pontianak and Singkawang in 1963, when Chinese shop signs had already disappeared, but when many people seemed unable or unwilling to use Indonesian in conversation.

[86] Peterson, *Storm*, p. 14, and his *Demon Gods* report that there were record conversions in 1967.

[87] According to church statistics, this trend accelerated after the war. The 11,922 Catholics in 1951 in all of West Kalimantan were already 60.5 percent ethnic Indonesian and 37.6 percent ethnic Chinese. See Huub Boelaars, OFM Cap., *Some Remarks on the Growth of the Catholic Community of West Kalimantan in the Period 1966-1985* (Jakarta: Atma Jaya Research Centre, 1976). West Kalimantan was originally a single diocese; by the 1970s, the inland territories formed three additional dioceses, another sign that the Catholic mission had become a mission to the Dayaks, not the Chinese.

[88] Cited in Boelaars, *Some Remarks*. Church statistics, based on baptisms, count less than half this number of Catholics. The census-takers extrapolated from a sample in which respondents were asked their religion. Obviously, many who were not baptized Catholics named Catholicism, whether out of sympathy or for protection.

restricted recognition of religion to Islam, Hinduism, Christianity, and Buddhism, these restrictions were rejected by his successor Abdurrahman Wahid. Both Buddhist and Confucian practices now take place openly, and there is no pressure for conversion to Christianity, at least for political reasons. As far as is known, there is no significant movement for conversion to Islam among the Chinese, although individual conversions may occur.

NOTES ON POPULATION

Extrapolating from census data on language (above) would suggest a population of Chinese descent in West Kalimantan somewhere between 350,000 and 400,000. Unfortunately, no more accurate count of ethnic groups in the province is available, although the 2000 census, when the results are tabulated, promises information on ethnicity, something not counted in official censuses since 1930. In the absence of a credible figure, sources tend to either overestimate the population of Chinese, or, in some cases, to belittle their numbers.

Although postwar estimates suggested that the Chinese in West Kalimatnan made up 20 percent or more of the region's total population, the actual proportion was probably lower and was, in any case, falling throughout the 1950s and 1960s. Between 1971 and 1980, one source put the Chinese at just under 16 percent of the population.[89] The province had a population of 2,518,705 in 1980, when Yunus estimated that 15 percent of the population were Chinese, 41 percent Dayak, and 39 percent belonged to Malay and other Indonesian ethnic groups. Nearly 87 percent of the population earned a living from farming and fishing. On the other hand, official statistics indicate a sharp decline in the proportion of aliens, especially Chinese aliens.

The number of aliens had in fact been reduced dramatically through policies that facilitated naturalization and the acquisition of citizenship documents, especially for persons born in Indonesia.[90] In 1978, the province counted, officially, 154,974 aliens. Sambas district had the largest concentration of aliens, 57,853; Pontianak city had 49,823.[91] Within two years, these numbers had dropped quickly. For example, the city of Pontianak, which in 1980 had a total population of over 300,000, had, according to Yunus, only 902 aliens.[92]

---

[89] *Hambatan*, p. 2. The Chinese represented 15.98 percent of the population, according to the estimates of those years.

[90] Indonesian citizenship is not extended automatically to persons born in Indonesia if they are not of native Indonesian (*asli* or *pribumi*) origin. See below for the discussion of citizenship measures.

[91] Indonesia, Biro Pusat Statistik, *Penduduk Cina luar Jawa: Hasil registrasi penduduk: Achir tahun 1973, 1974, 1975* (Jakarta: Biro Pusat Statistik, 1977); Indonesia, *Penduduk Cina 1976, 1977, 1978*. Kabupaten Pontianak had 36,211 alien Chinese. Other districts had altogether about sixteen thousand in 1975 and eleven thousand in 1978. Andreas Barung Tangdililing, "Perkawinan antar suku bangsa sebagai salah satu wahana pembauran bangsa: Studi kasus perkawinan antara orang Daya dengan keturunan Cina di Kecamatan Samalantan, Kabupaten Sambas, Kalimantan Barat" (PhD dissertation, Universitas Indonesia, 1993), p. 50, thinks that, after easier access to citizenship was allowed in 1980 by Presidential Decision No. 2/1980, "hundreds of thousands" of ethnic Chinese in West Kalimantan acquired Indonesian citizenship, but perhaps that number is high.

[92] Yunus, *Upacara tradisional*, pp. 9, 13, 21, 27.

Because in 1967 the Chinese were forced to move to larger cities and aliens were forbidden to engage in most retail business outside the capitals of districts, Singkawang, Pontianak, and other coastal centers experienced enormous growth. Singkawang had grown to 72,895 inhabitants in 1977. Mandor, like Monterado, declined in importance, but Pemangkat, in spite of considerable emigration (noted above), grew to 14,000 in 1977. Its coastal location, as noted, enabled it to serve the Sambas area as a commercial center.[93]

The most recent figures for provincial population, from the census of 1990, did not officially count ethnic Chinese. For 1999, the provincial government office claimed that ethnic Chinese were 17 percent of the population of 3,850,000, or over 650,000 persons. The city of Pontianak was 32 percent Chinese, Singkawang (which was to be separated from Kabupaten Sambas as an administrative city) 60 percent. Thirty percent of Kabupaten Bengkayang's population was ethnically Chinese, while Kabupaten Sambas had 22 percent, and Kabupaten Pontianak 15 percent, but in all other areas the Chinese were well under 10 percent of the population.[94] Although this seems authoritative, 17 percent appears high; other estimates are much lower.[95]

Since the Chinese are now highly urbanized, and, as a rule, urban populations increase less rapidly than rural ones, it is doubtful that they have grown faster than the other parts of the population. Chinese immigration stopped, at the latest, by 1950, and thousands of non-Chinese transmigrants have entered the province. In addition, the indigenous population has grown rapidly. Finally, the less economically prosperous years of the 1990s saw a considerable emigration of Chinese to Java, other parts of the Archipelago, or abroad. It seems appropriate, unless new census information contradicts it, to estimate that the Chinese are currently about 12 to 13 percent of the population of West Kalimantan.

ECONOMIC TRENDS

In the years after the Dayak raids and military aggressions, Chinese dealers were able to reconstruct business networks in the interior. Chinese in the larger towns recruited Dayak traders, or those of mixed descent, as their "subsidiaries." As more and more roads were built, and river traffic was better motorized, it became possible for dealers in the towns to collect and distribute supplies without living in villages or the smaller market centers, using small pickup trucks like the ubiquitous Indonesian-made Kijang.[96]

While rubber (albeit in decline), coconut, and palm oil still played an important role in the local economy, for the Chinese, mandarin oranges (*jeruk*

[93] Helbig, *Durchquerung*, pp. 41, 63.

[94] Cited in *Kompas* (January 26, 2001).

[95] Heru Cahyono ("Hubungan antaretnis dan ras: Kasus Pontianak," *Masyarakat Indonesia* 21,2 [1994]: 182) suggests a share of only 11 percent.

[96] Interviews, 1993, 1996. In 1993, the author visited Bengkayang during the rainy season, when much rubber is tapped or sold (because it is the slack season or because people need cash). While some persons carried rubber to the town themselves (for example by bicycle), selling it in one of the shops there or exchanging it for provisions, much rubber was delivered in small trucks, apparently by Chinese, to the dealers in the town. In one small town, a woman shopowner-dealer of part-Chinese descent acted as first purchaser for tappers in the neighborhood. Periodically, a larger dealer picked up the wares to take to town.

Pontianak), became a new and important cash crop. The Chinese had long planted citrus fruits for their own consumption. In the late nineteenth century, a visitor to Monterado already reported that many fruit trees lined the roads, but sale of the crops was not a significant activity.[97]

Apparently, commercial production took off in the early 1980s, and local development authorities suggested that orange groves had the potential to be developed on a large scale.[98] One center of cultivation was in Tebas, not far from Pemangkat.[99] In 1991, a traveler along the highway from Singkawang to Pontianak would, in the evening hours, pass any number of sheds where people were packing fruit, and orange groves were a common sight. Since other smallholder crops, especially coconut and rubber, were subject to strong fluctuations in world markets, while the market for oranges was not nearly as volatile, the *jeruk* provided a welcome enterprise for smallholders, especially for the Chinese, and one with a good domestic market. Local businessmen had organized the export to Java and elsewhere, some of it on refrigerated ships.

New Order development policy was extremely skewed in favor of extractive industries and exports controlled by government or joint-venture operations. An example was Kalimantan's lumber industry, with strong participation of top Jakarta businessmen who were close to President Suharto. Another economic emphasis was on Java's agriculture and anti-poverty measures there. Outer Island smallholders had no special priority; they were largely left to their own devices. This laissez-faire attitude toward the mandarin orange industry persisted until the presidential sons got wind of the profits to be made with the fruits and acquired a monopoly on their marketing. As *Tempo* reported in a review of the year 1993,

> The market for cloves and oranges just dropped (*rontoh begitu saja*), after the supporting elements, that is BPPC, led by Tommy Hutomo Mandala Putra, and PT Bima Citra Mandiri, under the command of Bambang Trihatmodjo, withdrew at the end of last September and November. These two not only made trouble for a number of bureaucrats and businessmen, but also put the farmers in a difficult situation and upset the [official government] policy of deregulation.[100]

That the Chinese farmers were the victims of this policy was apparent in 1996. Only diseased and abandoned orange trees were to be seen along the main roads

---

[97] P. Adriani, *Herinneringen uit en aan de Chineesche Districten der Wester-Afdeeling van Borneo, 1879-1882: Schetsen en indrukken* (Amsterdam: Campagne & Zoon, 1898), p. 30.

[98] *Profil Daerah Kabupaten Daerah Tingkat II Pontianak* (Pontianak: Badan Perencanaan Pembangunan Daerah, Kalimantan Barat, 1986), p. 64. Table 10 shows production and land devoted to *jeruk* increasing rapidly between 1982-1983, sometimes replacing old coconut trees. A later study, Arman, *Laporan penilitian, kondisi sosial ekonomi petani karet di desa Pasir I Kalimantan Barat: Suatu analisis komparatif* (Pontianak: Studi Pengembangan Wilayah Universitas Tanjungpura, 1991) reported that, because of high prices for oranges, farmers were felling rubber trees to plant oranges.

[99] Lombard, "Guide Archipel," p. 95.

[100] "Kilas Balik '93," photo and caption, *Tempo* (January 8, 1994). BPPC is Badan Penyangga dan Penasaran Cengkeh, Tommy Suharto's body for supporting and marketing cloves. Oranges were Bambang's monopoly.

around Singkawang. The depression in this industry coincided with problems in the lumber industry.

Economically, two other developments should be noted for the 1980s. One was the rapid growth of an extractive lumber industry, and the other immigration and settlement from elsewhere in the Archipelago, some of it under the government's policy of transmigration (on immigration, see below).

Unlike the eastern part of the island, West Kalimantan has no known petroleum reserves. In 1980, over 80 percent of the population earned a living from agriculture, and although the relative significance of agriculture had decreased during the previous decade, and would continue to fall, only about one-tenth of the population declared non-agricultural activities like trade, communications, finance, industry, or construction as their occupation.[101] Statistics show that the economy and per capita income grew rapidly in the late 1980s. Growth was over 4 percent in all but one year from 1985-1990 and reached a peak of 13.01 percent in 1988.[102]

In the mid-1990s, it was clear that the lumber industry was in crisis. Partly this was a result of over-cutting, with the supply of good trees becoming scarce. Even overaged rubber trees were felled for export. Part of the problem was in the plywood monopoly given to Bob Hasan, a Jakarta entrepreneur and confidant of President Suharto, whose levies on exports of plywood threatened to price Indonesia out of the world market.[103] By 1996, Pontianak had already lost some of the aura of prosperity it wore at the beginning of the decade.

In comparison with other provinces, West Kalimantan is now one of the poorest, deprived of the dramatic growth of the lumber and especially plywood industry. Its smallholders do not earn a good living from rubber and coconuts, which continue to be the most important crops. The "prosperity" that Dutch officials believed they observed in the 1920s evaporated in the world Depression and never really returned. True, rubber prices rose just before and after World War II, but it proved difficult to translate this into local wealth. Confrontation with Malaysia

---

[101] *Gambaran keadaan penduduk Kalimantan Barat tahun 1971 dan 1980: Hasil sensus penduduk* (Pontianak: Kantor Statistik Propinsi Kalimantan Barat, 1985), p. 26. Compare the assessment of Pulo Siahaan and Ruth Daroesman, "West Kalimantan: Uneven Development?" in *Unity and Diversity: Regional Economic Development in Indonesia since 1970*, ed. Hal Hill (Singapore: Oxford University Press, 1989), p. 538: "West Kalimantan had, in 1985, a curiously lopsided economy" that "reflects agricultural neglect."

[102] *Penduduk Indonesia selama pembangunan jangka panjang tahap I, Kalimantan Barat* (Jakarta: Kantor Menteri Negara, Kependudukan dan Lingkungan Hidup, 1992), p. 51, based on material from Kantor Statistik Kalimantan Barat.

[103] On Bob Hasan's plywood consortium, see Christopher M. Barr, "Bob Hasan, the Rise of Apkindo, and the Shifting Dynamics of Control," *Indonesia* 65 (April 1998): 1-36. Hasan's own interests were in East Kalimantan, but his organization monopolized most plywood exports. In West Kalimantan, Prayogo Pangestu (Phang Djun Phen) and his Barito Pacific exploited 5.5 million hectares of forestland throughout Indonesia, as well as other activities. Prayogo's family had to flee from their village near Bengkayang during the raids of 1967, and he attended a Chinese-language secondary school in Singkawang for a time. He began working for a logging firm belonging to a Sarawak businessman in the "*jaman smokel*" (smuggling era) of the early 1960s. See Djunaini, "Prajogo Pangestu di Kampung Halaman," *Akçaya* (Pontianak), July 21 and 22, 1993. He later purchased an East Malaysian firm himself; Doug Tsuroka, "Plywood Play," *Far Eastern Economic Review* (June 30, 1994): 53. Barito Pacific posted a member to the board of directors of Hasan's monopoly (Apkindo) in 1984. See Barr, "Bob Hasan," p. 21. Like Hasan, Prayogo was close to Suharto.

in the early 1960s cut off relations with Singapore (other than clandestine ones), and the economic development of the New Order, except for the brief flowering in the 1980s, largely passed it by. In 1996, the provincial economy showed signs of recession, well before the crisis of late 1997 shattered Indonesian dreams of prosperity.

Plate 22. Wildcat gold miners near Mandor, 2000. Credit: the author.

Perhaps no ethnic group in Indonesia is so sensitive to economic opportunity, or lack of it, as the Chinese. By the 1980s the province experienced mass emigration of the Chinese, a movement that continued into the following decade. Most of those departing, lacking skills or other assets for immigration to Western countries, headed for Jakarta.[104] Although there are no statistics on this migration, observers joked that the planes were full only when leaving Pontianak.

The movement of the Chinese from the outer provinces to Jakarta brought a less-acculturated group into the capital's crowded northern districts and led some *pribumi* Indonesians to suspect that "foreigners," perhaps even illegal immigrants, were congregating there. Ironically, these new neighborhoods failed to provide security for the immigrants. Instead, north Jakarta was the target of the anti-Chinese violence of May 1998. Some of those who had moved to Jakarta then chose to return, at least temporarily, to the apparent safety of Kalimantan.

---

[104] Citing Jakarta population data for 1986, the authors of *Hambatan dalam penbinaan persatuan dan kesatuan bangsa di Propinsi Daerah Tingkat I Kalimantan Barat* (Jakarta: Departemen Dalam Negeri, Badan Pendidikan dan Latihan, Sekolah Pimpinan Administrasi Tingkat Madya, 1986), p. 13, assert that Chinese from West Kalimantan are the fourth largest ethnic group in Jakarta. Since census-takers do not ask for information about ethnicity, this figure is questionable, but what is not questionable is that immigrants from West Kalimantan were quite numerous.

In West Kalimantan, the Chinese, on the whole, had retained their dominant role in the collection of agricultural crops and in the retail trade. Nonetheless, the economy offered few chances for prosperity for most of the inhabitants, including the Chinese. For the most part, gains from new economic activities of the 1980s and 1990s, exploitation of the forest for its lumber or expansion of oil palm and other plantation-type crops, had gone to "big players," businessmen from Jakarta with good political connections, not to local people.

The economic crisis of 1997 and the dramatic fall of the Indonesian rupiah brought producers of export crops, including smallholders, some windfall gains, at least in the short term. It is too early to know whether the devolution of more political and economic power to the regions in the reforms of the post-Suharto era might improve the economic situation of West Kalimantan, but it is difficult to imagine where new, long-term economic opportunities for the bulk of the ethnic Chinese, smallholders and small-scale traders, might lie.

CULTURAL RETENTION AND LANGUAGE

Apart from the economic situation, what cultural and political forces continue to impinge on what chapter one called the "Chinese among the Chinese"? What may be the prospects for the future?

As the preceding has repeatedly stressed, the Chinese minority in West Kalimantan have remained a distinctive group, both within Kalimantan and in comparison with other Chinese minorities in Indonesia. In spite of their relatively dispersed settlement (before 1967), their involvement in the native-dominated field of agriculture, and the frequency, in the past, of intermarriage with local women, this minority managed to remain strongly "Chinese," in their own eyes and those of others. What enabled them to be so distinctive and will they continue to be so?

An important factor in preserving Chinese culture and language was community organization. Before colonial times, the kongsis maintained Chineseness, offering a Chinese community and a state-like framework to their members. Malay rulers took no interest in the community's internal affairs. The Dutch dissolved the kongsis, but they did not eliminate the wide-ranging autonomy of the Chinese settlers.

A plethora of community organizations in social, religious, economic, and political fields gave the communities a focus. Under the Dutch, institutions that might have linked the community with the colonial power, like the wealthy and influential Chinese officers of Java, or the Dutch-language schools of the twentieth century, were unimportant in Borneo. So long as the community paid its taxes and the region remained peaceful, the Dutch left it largely to its own devices, and, indeed, the small presence of colonial officials made this the only possible policy.

Education in Chinese was also an important influence, enabling the spread of a literate, China-oriented (and sometimes Mandarin-speaking) group. Many young people chose continuing education in China, while education in Indonesia was less attractive.

Community closeness filtered local influences. In addition to formal community organizations and the educational system, Chinese religion, practiced in the home and in public on major religious festivals, helped to preserve Chinese culture.

Furthermore, in contrast to Java, where even in the twentieth century most *peranakans* did not see immigrant Chinese as cultural models, in West Kalimantan immigrants were carriers of Chinese nationalism and culture in schools, businesses, and the press, all of which in turn emphasized orientation to China.

Chinese kinship and domestic life, too, with the strong position of males, overcame influences from the surroundings, "sinifying" even children of mixed unions. Sons and daughters were integrated into the family enterprise, be it a shop, a small industry, or a farm, and expected to share in its burdens. [105]

As noted, given the strong differentiation of economic and cultural activities between ethnic groups in West Kalimantan, distinguishing Chinese, Dayaks, Malays, and others by their occupations, a basis for acculturation to local societies would have been hard to find. Particularly those Chinese who lived in rural areas, especially in predominantly Chinese settlements, where most neighbors were Chinese, would have striven to preserve their culture, tradition, and economic specializations. Their relative isolation kept them a group apart. Since 1967, Indonesian policy, by moving the Chinese to the coastal region, has removed them from rural areas, but reinforced their separation from other groups by concentrating them in urban areas near the coast. Thus, geographical isolation has continued in another form.

The question remains, insofar as rural Chinese were also Hakkas, a group with a reputation for "clannishness" and cultural persistence, were they less amenable to local influences because they were Hakkas?[106] Not necessarily. Spatial isolation and economic specialization are probably more important than "Hakka culture" itself in explaining the tendency of West Kalimantan's Chinese to retain their ancestral culture.

As far as language is concerned, the Teochiu, living more in urban communities, do seem to have learned Indonesian more quickly. Yet Hakkas who traded in the interior, in close proximity to other groups, learned local languages and adopted local ways, and the poorer Chinese especially borrowed many elements of local living styles. At the same time, their economic activities tended to keep them apart and make them more "Chinese."

Not only connections with the Chinese homeland provided a compass for the preservation of Chinese culture. Singapore, a vital economic focus for the trade of West Borneo and West Kalimantan, became not just an economic but a cultural and political center of Chineseness, mediating the influences from the homeland, and overshadowing those from Batavia or Jakarta.

Retention of Chinese language is one of the most important facets distinguishing ethnic Chinese in West Kalimantan from the *peranakans* of Java and elsewhere in the Archipelago. As noted, language is also important in

---

[105] The recent work of Bernard Formoso, *Identités en regard: Destins chinois en milieu bouddhiste thaï* (Paris: CNRS Éditions, Éditions de la Maison des Sciences de l'Homme, 2000), pp. 213-231 illustrates this mechanism very clearly for Chinese in a small town in Thailand, and it is known in other environments, too. In Java, it is often assumed that native mothers strongly formed their children into *peranakans*, but this may need closer examination.

[106] G. William Skinner, especially, has seen Hakkas as perpetuating their own culture overseas, and other authors, like Mary Erbaugh in "The Hakka Paradox in the People's Republic of China: Exile, Eminence, and Public Silence," in *Guest People: Hakka Identity in China and Abroad*, ed. Nicole Constable (Seattle: University of Washington Press, 1996), pp.196-231, stress the importance of language in preserving the distinctiveness of this group.

preserving Hakka identity. Between 1966 and 1998, and to some extent even earlier, Indonesian authorities pursued policies hostile to Chinese language, Chinese publications, and Chinese as a medium of instruction in the schools. Only after the fall of Suharto were restrictions on the import of Chinese-language materials relaxed.

Malaysia, in particular Sarawak, where ethnic Chinese residents customarily use both Mandarin and other Chinese languages (in addition to Malay and English), is an even more proximate mediator of Chinese culture than Singapore. Some parents manage to send children to school in Sarawak; others visit often. In addition, television, films, videocassettes, and other modern means of communication, originating in Singapore, Malaysia, Hong Kong, Taiwan, and China, now cross borders freely, and often did so, even during the period of restrictions on Chinese materials. These materials are mostly in Mandarin, or—in the case of Hong Kong—in Cantonese, so they would not encourage proficiency in Hakka or Teochiu.

Although many parents continue to speak Chinese, usually Hakka, Teochiu, or another southern language, in the home, over the years many also found ways of instructing their children privately in Mandarin. Only Mandarin, since the beginning of the modern school movement in the twentieth century, is considered a suitable language for education. Parents justify their efforts to have children literate in Chinese less in terms of perserving their cultural identity than because Mandarin is "important for business." The proximity of Sarawak and business ties with Singapore certainly reinforce this attitude.

One Indonesian study of Indonesian language achievement among ethnic Chinese pupils in West Kalimantan, from the 1980s, betrays a suspicion of Chinese language that is widespread among Indonesians who are not of Chinese descent. However, the study concludes that Chinese children learn Indonesian adequately, even where the language of the home and the playground is Chinese.[107]

In 1987, another study asked five hundred respondents, about half over the age of thirty, what languages they spoke. Whereas over 90 percent of the resondents could speak a Chinese language, only a small number, 35 percent, said they could read Chinese. Thirty-three percent claimed to use Indonesian in daily life, 26 percent used Chinese. Chinese language retention appears to have been greater among the Hakkas, which could be expected. Of those who spoke Chinese, the number of Hakka speakers was double that of the Teochiu, but only 1 percent said they "often" spoke Mandarin. Forty percent, however, expressed a preference for Mandarin films. More than half had a Chinese name (10 percent did not), although they used Indonesian names officially.[108]

Visiting Pontianak in early 2000, the author came across some evening classes in Mandarin, sometimes taught by former teachers from the Chinese-language

---

[107] Sutini Paimin et al., *Kemampuan berbahasa Indonesia (membaca) murid-murid sekolah dasar yang berbahasa ibu bahasa Cina di Kotamadya Pontianak* (Jakarta: Pusat Pembinaan dan Pengembangan Bahasa, Departemen Pendidikan dan Kebudayaan, 1985). The study unfortunately only compares the language achievements of Chinese-speaking school children with grade standards, not with the achievements of a control group of non-Chinese speakers. In fact, most such studies can be questioned on the grounds of their size and the representativeness of the sample, the freedom of informants to give politically nonconfirming replies, and other problems. Still, they are valuable as indications of trends and issues.

[108] Subangun, "Keturunan Cina." The author kindly gave me a printout of his results.

schools. Once the restrictions on Chinese associated with Suharto's New Order were lifted, such opportunities multiplied rapidly. Without a full-fledged Chinese-language school system, however, Mandarin is and will probably remain a foreign language. People who speak Chinese are still more likely to choose Hakka and Teochiu, which are spoken in the home, are similar to one another, and differ significantly from Mandarin.[109] It is understandable, however, that classes in Mandarin grew up so quickly. Whether for business or private use, Mandarin continues to represent the essence of Chineseness. Mandarin has a future in West Kalimantan, but a limited one, for Indonesian remains the language of schools and public life.

BEING INDONESIAN, BEING CITIZENS

The dramatic fall in the number of aliens in West Kalimantan was the result of a new policy adopted in Jakarta in 1980. Whereas in 1978 (see above), some 155,000 aliens resided in the province, these aliens virtually disappeared from the statistics in the next years. Presidental Instruction (Inpres) number 2 of 1980, propagated locally by West Kalimantan's military commander, opened an opportunity to become Indonesian citizens without red tape or cost (at least officially), and many took advantage of it. The decree was intended to apply to persons in certain areas of Indonesia with numerous ethnic Chinese, including North Sumatra, Riau, Bangka, and Belitung, parts of West Java including Jakarta, and West Kalimantan itself. If they fulfilled certain conditions, applicants could obtain proof-of-citizenship papers. These conditions included birth and current residence in Indonesia, a lifestyle similar to that of Indonesians, the ability to speak Indonesian or a regional language, and having not previously rejected Indonesian citizenship. In West Kalimantan, the language qualification was even waived in many cases. Sources report that almost the entire number of foreign Chinese acquired papers.[110] Since that number was the same as the number of aliens in the province in 1978, if this number is correct, then the number of remaining Chinese aliens must have been very small. As noted above, in Pontianak less than a thousand remained.[111]

---

[109] Hakkas often claim that their language is close to Mandarin, but linguists believe it to be more closely related to other southern Chinese languages. Some observers seem unaware of the difference. Cahyono, *Hubungan antaretnis*, criticized the Pontianak Chinese for wanting to have their language recognized as a local language and for still using Mandarin, but it is not Mandarin that they speak on a daily basis, at least not up to now.

[110] For more details, see Kelompok Kerja Pembinaan Masyarakat Cina, *Konsep pengelolaan masalah masyarakat keturunan Cina di Kalimantan Barat* (Pontianak: Badan Kerjasama Kodam XII-TPR Universitas Tanjungpura, 1982), pp. 15ff.; Tim Peneliti Fakultas Hukum Universitas Tanjungpura, *Tingkat kesadaran hukum warganegara Indonesia keturunan Cina dalam hubungannya dengan Surat Bukti Kewarganegaraan Republik Indonesia (SBKRI)* (Pontianak: Departemen Pendidikan dan Kebudayaan, Universitas Tanjungpura, 1983), pp. 3-4, and Onghokham, "Chinese," pp. 44-45. The commander mentioned was General Norman Sasono. Elison, "Kesukaran," p. 45, shows that the bureaucratic hurdles to acquiring citizenship in force before the presidential instruction came out in reality favored dubious go-betweens, who earned large sums for their services, but did not favor legitimate applicants. Nonetheless, many Chinese apparently did not know what the proof of citizenship (SBKRI) meant (Tim Peniliti, *Tingkat kesadaran*, p. 19).

[111] See Yunus, *Upacara tradisional*, pp. 9, 13, 21, 27.

Before 1980, it had been extremely difficult for any Chinese, even those born locally, to acquire Indonesian citizenship. By saddling aliens with a number of restrictive and onerous regulations, the government left them with the impression that it just wanted them to leave Indonesia, and many, especially the young, did. Although some Indonesian authors complained that the Chinese were not interested in becoming citizens, there is ample evidence that they were: some previously spent millions of rupiahs for bogus nationality papers so that they could live and do business free from bureaucratic chicanery. Similarly, a government study noted that schoolchildren whose parents were aliens were eager to become Indonesian citizens, as were the considerable number of "stateless" persons, most of them individuals with Taiwanese documents.[112]

Easier access to citizenship in the 1980s clearly brought more security to the Chinese of West Kalimantan. If not loved, or even trusted, they would at least be tolerated. An Indonesian historian who visited the area in 1996 remarked that, while in the 1980s people still seemed to feel the trauma of 1967, and were suspicious of outsiders, allowing them to obtain citizenship papers more easily had made the people seem more relaxed and open, even to outsiders, than they had been a decade earlier. It was in that year that Capgomeh was again celebrated in Singkawang.[113] Thanks to the more open policy, one could be Chinese and Indonesian, too.

BEING CHINESE INDONESIANS

New Order policies had assaulted the distinctiveness of the ethnic Chinese by restricting Chinese cultural influences and promoting what they called assimilation (*pembauran*). For some Indonesian authorities, mass adoption of citizenship was still not sufficient to prove the loyalty of the minority to Indonesia. Repeatedly, local observers asserted that the Chinese of West Kalimantan were in general unwilling or unable to adjust to local and national culture.[114] The government called into being local committees to promote assimilation and greater integration of the Chinese, inviting community leaders and others to "indoctrination" sessions on being Indonesian.

At the time of the expulsion of Chinese from rural areas in November 1967, military leaders initiated an attempt to promote assimilation of the Chinese with the founding of a Bakom (Badan Komunikasi) Urusan Cina (Communicative Body for Chinese Affairs) for West Kalimantan. Bakom undertook a number of activities to encourage Chinese to speak more Indonesian and to participate more in the larger community and public life, surviving at least into the late 1990s. Even Chinese shophouses (*ruko, rumah toko*), a distinctive feature of market towns across the Archipelago, appeared to be an obstacle to integration, and it was suggested at one point that no one should be permitted to build new ones, while the old ones would

---

[112] *Laporan singkat pelaksanaan asimilasi melalui pendidikan di Kalimantan Barat* (Pontianak: Kantor Wilayah Departemen Pendidikan dan Kebudayaan, Propinsi Kalimantan Barat, 1980), p. 7.

[113] Onghokham, "Chinese."

[114] Kelompok Kerja, *Konsep pengelolaan*, pp. 1-4.

fall into decay.[115] All of these initiatives betrayed a suspicion of Chinese culture and traditions.

Nonetheless, Kalimantan's Chinese knew well enough how to participate in local politics. When bureaucrats in Singkawang caused difficulties with citizenship papers in the 1980s, many residents, who had previously voted in national elections for Golkar, the government party, promptly gave their votes to the opposition nationalist Democratic Party (PDI, Partai Demokrasi Indonesia).[116]

The open elections of 1999 offered an opportunity for the minority to try to use their numbers to gain political influence as well. While some Chinese remained skeptical and preferred to avoid political commitment as potentially too dangerous, many seemed more than willing to express their political preferences not only in voting, but in open support for their chosen parties.

Not surprisingly perhaps, many Chinese voters favored Partai Bhinekka Tunggal Ika [sic] (Bhinneka Tunggal Ika, "out of many, one" is Indonesia's national motto), because they believed that it would represent Chinese interests, although its program spoke only of acting against discrimination. In the end, however, many voted for the PDI-P of Megawati Sukarnoputri (which won nearly half the votes in Singkawang, a town that claims to have 60 percent Chinese) or stayed with Golkar, which remained influential among the bureaucracy.[117] The fact that the "Chinese vote" was so divided suggests that the minority is not as monolithic as outsiders have often thought. If voters could disagree so readily about where "Chinese" interests lay, those interests might be quite differentiated. Perhaps more significantly, the vote shows how much "Chinese interests" lay in West Kalimantan, and with that, in Indonesia, not somewhere abroad.

CONCLUSION

The settlement of Chinese in western Borneo on a significant scale began with the gold rush days of the eighteenth century. Before then, certainly traders came from China to the West Coast, and some stayed there, but their numbers were not large, and there is little record of their coming and less of their staying. The gold miners came in tens of thousands and, although a majority died young or returned to China, they soon formed significant, settled and, under the kongsis, self-governing communities.

This study has shown how ineffectually Malay rulers tried to extend their authority over the Chinese miners. When the Dutch colonial power arrived, it needed several decades before it finally dissolved the kongsis and integrated the Chinese into its structure. However, the communities, although in theory directly ruled by the Dutch under Chinese officers, in fact remained largely autonomous, thanks to their own family and community structures. Finally, the Indonesian government, several years after independence, intervened to weaken and dissolve

---

[115] *Hambatan*, pp. 20, 28-30, 50. On these committees, see Coppel, *Indonesian Chinese*. They were directed by the Ministry of the Interior.

[116] Isman, "Singkawang."

[117] Benny Subianto, "The Politics of Chinese Indonesians after the Fall of Soeharto's New Order," unpublished paper, Jakarta, 1999, pp. 14-17. According to this author, PBI was also successful in attracting Dayak support. Voters recognized its anti-discrimination program as meaning support for Chinese interests.

most elements of community organization, including the schools, the press, the chambers of commerce, and other influential institutions. After 1967, the rural areas opened in the eighteenth century by the gold miners and still populated by Chinese farmers, the so-called Chinese Districts, were emptied of ethnic Chinese.

All three political units, whether the Malay polities, the Dutch colonial power, or independent Indonesia, tolerated for some time the independent political organization of the Chinese, more out of weakness than out of conviction, for all three lacked the men and firepower to subdue the Chinese minority. As a result, all three resorted to using Dayak violence to force the Chinese into submission, the Indonesian military's solution being the most radical, for it effectively ended Chinese settlement in the interior and closed the history of the Chinese Districts.

When the colonial power proposed an alternative education system in Dutch, the Chinese refused to submit. The Indonesian government addressed cultural hegemony in earnest after 1957, as it limited and finally prohibited Chinese schools, then went on to suppress many other expressions of Chinese culture. Yet despite measures to promote "assimilation," the Chinese of Kalimantan remained a distinct group, understandably so, given their history and the nature of local society itself.

Most autonomous community organizations were limited or eliminated during the period of military dominance during the New Order, but they had flourished previously and may be reconstituted in a more tolerant time. The national consciousness of the Chinese minority in West Kalimantan developed with reference to the Chinese homeland; only in exceptional cases did it have Indonesia as its reference point, perhaps even as late as the 1970s. This situation seems to have changed today.

Of course, many Chinese in West Kalimantan have strong local roots. Some are of part-Dayak descent, many have fathers, grandfathers, and great-grandfathers who were born on the island. By the twentieth century, many farmers had worked the land there for decades, if not for generations. Yet their Chineseness appeared to persist.

Did their Chinese descent and culture exclude them from Indonesia or was it a matter of choice? To the Malays and Dayaks, Chinese were certainly strangers. For the Dutch, they were outsiders. Indonesian politicians and administrators usually regarded them as aliens. When they accepted them as citizens after 1980, they still exerted political and cultural pressure on them to abandon Chinese cultural characteristics.

In many ways, however, these people are Indonesians and see themselves as such, although they are Chinese, too. A return to the times when West Kalimantan Chinese exerted great efforts to send their children to China or collected funds for China relief efforts seems unlikely. The still-limited opportunities Kalimantan Chinese have had to express themselves in the Indonesian political sphere, including the elections of 1999, have shown that they hope to work for their own interests within the Indonesian framework, as do other Indonesians. An elaboration of Chinese community organization would not alienate them from this framework.

While this study cannot deal with the post-Reformasi era, clearly new perspectives are opening for the ethnic Chinese of West Kalimantan. On the one hand, possibilities for preserving and displaying elements of Chinese culture have been widely restored: Chinese New Year and Capgomeh (the first full moon on the fifteenth day of the New Year) are occasions for local festivities. Capgomeh is once more a public celebration, and other religious feasts are honored openly as appropriate.

If the Chinese are rediscovering their Chineseness and savoring the opportunities to display dragon dances, celebrate Chinese festivals, or to learn Mandarin openly, they are also aware of their roots in local society. A Jakarta reporter wrote in 1987 of West Kalimantan's situation:

> If Chinese are viewed as *nonpri* [non-pribumi, non-indigenous], maybe the Javanese or Minangkabau or Madurese migrants are even more *nonpri* compared to the Chinese who have lived for four, five, and six generations at the mouth of the River Kapuas.[118]

At the same time, the field of acceptance of Chinese culture and of the ethnic Chinese themselves has widened as local people proclaim the Chinese one of the three indigenous ethnic groups (*tiga suku asli*) or three "pillars" of the province.[119] Not just the long settlement of the ethnic Chinese allows them a firm place in local communities. It is widely acknowledged that ethnic Chinese may be rich, but also poor; businessmen, but also farmers and fishermen. Their numbers may also make them a balancing force between Dayaks on the one hand, and Malays and other Islamic groups on the other. Nonetheless, the expression "three *suku*" finds adherents among all elements of Kalimantan society. In this vein, the provincial museum in Pontianak has planned an exhibit and seminar about Chinese culture in West Kalimantan. Other signs of recognition and acceptance may follow.

The history of the Chinese settlement of West Kalimantan, Indonesia, spans more than two and a half centuries. Many aspects of it remain to be told; some of those narrated here may need to be corrected. Often, violence has determined the agenda of this history, especially when the interests of the state or lesser political authorities have exacerbated interethnic tensions. In a time of reform and risk in Indonesia, it is to be hoped that the Chinese of West Kalimantan will write the next chapters of their history themselves.

---

[118] Emmanuel Subangun, "Keturunan Cina di Kalimantan Barat," *Kompas* (July 5, 1987).

[119] Interviews cited in *Kompas*, January 26 and 27, 2001; see also Edi Petebang and Eri Sutrisno, *Konflik etnik di Sambas* (Jakarta: Institut Studi Arus Informasi, 2000).

REPEATED VIOLENCE AND UNCERTAIN OUTCOME

In 1997, West Kalimantan was again rocked by large-scale terror as Dayak bands attacked Madurese and drove them from their homes, killing many. The center of the violence was not in the interior, but in the same areas from which Chinese had been expelled in 1967, and names like Sanggauledo, Anjungan, and Mandor again were key locations. Several of the same motifs that had appeared in 1967 reappeared, although in this case—unlike in 1967, when the role of the military was obvious—it is not clear who touched off the violence. Nevertheless, the two outbreaks are linked, if not by the victims, then by the perpetrators and by the location.

In early 1997, beginning in Sanggauledo in the district of Sambas, Dayaks began to attack Madurese in force, as they had once attacked Chinese.[1] The "trigger" seems to have been a fight between Dayak and Madurese youths at an event in December, probably about a perceived insult to a Dayak girl. The violence spread to other areas, to all of Sambas and Pontianak districts, finally working its way south toward the Kapuas, to Sanggau. The center of terror was in the very areas where Chinese had been expelled thirty years previously. This area is low and relatively fertile, a contrast to the hilly interior and the waterlogged coast and riverbanks, and eminently desirable for rice cultivation, a fact that suggests the violence was connected to the value of the land. If this interpretation is correct, then in 1997 the Dayaks were reasserting their claim to this strategic area.

In major towns like Sanggau-Kapuas, and in Anjungan, the military were strong enough to protect or evacuate the Madurese. In one settlement after another, truckloads of young Dayaks wearing headbands arrived. Others set up roadblocks and controlled all passing vehicles, picking out the Madurese. Helpless Madurese refugees were encouraged to leave the province or kept in camps, separating them from the Dayaks. Thousands of Madurese refugees sought help in Pontianak; some could find housing with family members, but, a few years later, thousands still

---

[1] For a collection of press reports about these events, see Institut Studi Arus Informasi and Institute Dayakology Research and Development, *Sisi gelap Kalimantan Barat: Perseteruan etnis Dayak-Madura 1997* (Jakarta: Midas Surya Grafindo, 1999). Unfortunately, officials censored press reports or held back information. Informative is Human Rights Watch, "West Kalimantan: Communal Violence in West Kalimantan," report, in http://www.hrw.org/reports/1997/wkali/Brneo97d-01.htm (September 11, 2002). See also Mary Somers Heidhues, "Kalimantan Barat 1967-1999: Violence on the Periphery," in *Violence in Indonesia*, ed. Ingrid Wessel and Georgia Wimhoefer (Hamburg: Abera, 2001), pp. 139-151, and Nancy Lee Peluso and Emily Harwell, "Territory, Custom, and the Cultural Politics of Ethnic War in West Kalimantan, Indonesia," in *Violent Environments*, ed. Nancy Lee Peluso and Michael Watts (Ithaca and London: Cornell University Press, 2001), pp. 83-116.

remained in makeshift quarters in a sport stadium and in other locations. Along the road from Anjungan to Mandor, the hulks of burned-out houses were still visible in 2000.

Following the removal of the Chinese from rural areas in the Chinese Districts in 1967, this area might have been tranformed into the "Dayak Districts" instead. Why did this not happen earlier? These fertile lowlands were not especially suited for swidden cultivation, the typical Dayak agricultural method; perhaps for this reason, Chinese-Dayak competition for territory was, historically, not great, as has been argued above. However, with more and more Dayaks practicing wet rice cultivation, both because of official policies and because of pressures on resources elsewhere, lowlands and *sawah* lands may have become more attractive to them.

If the Dayaks who participated in the 1967 Raids hoped that this territory, centering on Anjungan, would fall into their hands after the Chinese fled, they were to be disappointed. Although Dayaks moved into the area, Dayak hegemony did not last long. The New Order actively encouraged migration of settlers from crowded areas of Java, Madura, and Bali to less-populated spaces in the Outer Islands. Some of this involved large-scale, officially designed projects to open previously uninhabited (or presumably uninhabited) spaces; all government-sponsored migration was officially called "transmigration." A second kind of transmigration, called "wild" or "spontaneous," brought settlers to West Kalimantan and other areas on their own. In theory, "spontaneous migrants" would include all settlers who moved between islands over the centuries, not only those who relocated from Java-Madura and Bali, but also the Bugis, whose activities were so important along the coast of Kalimantan since the eighteenth and nineteenth century. As it turned out, of all the migrants to West Kalimantan, only the Madurese were to become a focus of resentment in 1997.

MADURESE

The Madurese have been a presence for many years in West Kalimantan, as they even participated in the colonial campaign against Monterado in the 1850s. Some migrated during the rubber boom of the 1920s as indentured laborers; some eventually managed to claim small plots of land.

They are known for living frugally and managing their money carefully. In more recent times, they have worked as boatmen, fishermen, factory workers, and petty traders, as well as farmers. Pontianak's *becaks* are driven by Madurese; they dominate the unskilled labor force in the construction industry, or did until the conflict. In 1971 and 1980, more immigrants arrived in West Kalimantan from East Java, the home province of the Madurese, than from any other Indonesian province, although in the 1990s the numbers of arrivals and departures was roughly balanced, so that transmigration apparently did not increase the numbers of Madurese living in the region during those years.[2] Of all the regions in Indonesia, West Kalimantan received, in proportion to the size of its population, comparatively large numbers of transmigrants, official and spontaneous. By the late 1990s, Madurese were estimated to constitute between 2 and 3 percent of the population.[3]

---

[2] *Hasil Sensus Penduduk 1990*, Cornell University Library, Wason Fiche 887 SEI 50359, p. 35.

[3] Human Rights Watch, "West Kalimantan," Section II.

Many Madurese moved outside the towns and settled on agricultural land, including land in the former Chinese Districts that Dayaks had first taken over. On an overland trip from Pontianak to Bengkayang following the interior route from Mandor in 1993, the author observed many Madurese agricultural settlements, sometimes juxtaposed with Dayak *kampungs*. While the Dayak *kampung* dwellers raised pigs, the Madurese Muslim settlements were easily recognized by one or more cows tethered in the yards, and by a generally neater appearance.

Given Kalimantan's limited resources and the downturn in the economy in the 1990s, not to mention the potential for conflict between the two cultures, it is perhaps not surprising that tensions led to clashes on several occasions before 1996. In that year, different informants asked about interethnic relations repeatedly ticked off on their fingers some ten incidents from the past involving outbreaks of violence between Dayaks and Madurese (not necessarily the same incidents, probably, but the number ten was important). At the same time, they insisted that Chinese-Dayak relations were good. In fact, Chinese were not harmed in the attacks of 1997, at least not intentionally.[4]

Tensions over different cultural practices, for example the presence of pigs and dogs in Dayak *kampungs*, animals which Madurese viewed as unclean, or the fact that Madurese men seemed to be quick to use a knife, were one source of trouble. In addition, Madurese competed with Dayaks for jobs in low-skilled professions, as well as in agriculture.

In 1999, Sambas Malays attacked Madurese there and above Ngabang, and, although the violence this time was primarily between Malays and Madurese, some Dayak-Madurese strife followed. Soon other local men, from other ethnic groups, joined in attacking Madurese, driving them from the interior (in those places where they had not been driven out aready, or where they had returned). The participation of Muslim Malays and others (according to some accounts, Chinese and Bugis were involved in the attacks in 1999) confirms that religious difference was not behind the incidents. Although the conflict appeared to be between an alliance of "indigenous and long-term population" against "newcomers," in fact the fury concentrated on the Madurese; other newcomers, such as the Javanese and others, were not targets. Many Madurese fled back to their home island or moved to the south, but thousands of refugee Madurese still live in Pontianak in squalid, makeshift quarters, as noted above.

POLITICIZATION OF THE DAYAKS

Missionaries had, since the early twentieth century, proselytized among the Dayak, in particular opening schools for them. In West Kalimantan, the predominant group was the Roman Catholic Capuchin fathers, but in addition, there were Catholic nuns, the Basel Protestant mission, and other Protestant groups. Especially after World War II, mission activities expanded. The efforts of the mission schools, which were welcomed by the Dayak, resulted in the creation of a group of "intellectuals" who would become leaders of and spokesmen for the community.

The Dayaks saw opportunities for bettering their situation not only in education, but also in politics. Some had participated in the local councils set up by

---

[4] Both the sources mentioned in footnote 1 and various interviewees in 2000 agreed that Chinese and their property were not deliberately harmed in the violence.

the Dutch under their "federal" policy. Under independent Indonesia, they formed an all-Dayak party, Partai Dayak, which absorbed nearly all their political energies.[5] The party was led by Oevang Oeray (a former student at the Catholic minor seminary in Nyarumkop), who in December 1959 became governor of West Kalimantan. As an ally of Sukarno, who had named him to the post, Oeray seemed to be in a good position to represent Dayak interests, although he was not quite as successful as another Dayak politician, Tjilik Riwut, of South Kalimantan, who succeeded in getting an all-Dayak province, Central Kalimantan, recognized as a political entity separate from South Kalimantan.

When in 1959 the political parties were "simplified" by Sukarno, the Dayak party was dissolved (because it was limited to one ethnic group). After an internal conflict and defections, with some former members joining the Catholic Party, Oeray and others became members of Partindo, a nationalist party that claimed to be close to Sukarno and his platform, and which was far to the left of the mainstream PNI (Partai Nasional Indonesia, Indonesian Nationalist Party). Partindo was sometimes accused of being a front for the PKI (Partai Komunis Indonesia, Indonesian Communist Party), an accusation that became dangerous after 1965, when the government initiated its deadly hunt for all Communists and Communist sympathizers. Governor Oeray and those officials who were Partindo members were replaced in 1966, and Oeray's political career appeared to be in jeopardy, a situation that threatened the interests of the Dayaks he represented. If the conflict in Partai Dayak had been traumatic, because it split Dayak unity, the abolition of Partindo and arrest of PKI sympathizers was even more so.[6] Thus perhaps it is not surprising that a number of Dayaks would be eager to demonstrate their loyalty to the nation by ridding the area of Chinese, who, the military repeatedly told them, were Communists and a threat to their security.

Both the Dayak Raids of 1967 and the Dayak uprising against the Japanese in 1945 (see chapter six) acquired a certain aura in literature written in the 1970s and 1980s. The anti-Japanese rebellion of the Dayaks is also prominently commemorated at the memorial in Mandor. Before the Dayak terror began in 1967, a Laskar Pangsuma (Fighting Force Pangsuma: Pangsuma was a leader of the action against the Japanese) appeared.[7] Military histories recall the 1967 "demonstrations," as they are euphemistically called, as a "spontaneous" response to a Communist threat of the PKI, the guerrillas, and China itself. Subsequently, Dayaks who took heads in the anti-guerrilla campaign were awarded medals; local military officials claimed head-taking was "in accordance with the [Dayak]

---

[5] *Kompas,* December 27, 1967. The party is also called Dayak Unity Party, Partai Persatuan Dayak.

[6] Feith, "Dayak Raids"; *Tempo* December 27, 1967; private archives. Some of this is confirmed by Soedarto, *Sejarah Daerah Kalimantan Barat* (Pontianak: Proyek Penelitian dan Pencatatan Kebudayaan Daerah), pp. 220-221, listing the provincial governors since Kalimantan Barat became a province in 1956.

[7] *Kompas,* December 27, 1967.

'field of experience' [sic]" and deserving of reward.[8] Violence that is rewarded and even glorified takes on a life of its own.[9]

Yet although Dayaks had participated in the anti-Communist violence of the 1960s, they received little reward for this show of loyalty; for the next thirty years their frustrations were rarely addressed by Jakarta. Rioters, apparently Dayaks, set fire to the local parliament in 1999, evidence of political frustrations accumulated under Suharto's New Order. Not only migration, but pressure on resources in general, had added to the tensions in the province. Much of West Kalimantan's forest was being exploited by firms linked to Jakarta; palm oil plantations were expanding on former forest grounds. Dayak villagers viewed much of this territory as their own reserve, but development policies rode roughshod over their interests.

The disenfranchisement of a group that sees itself as the original inhabitants of the island (a disenfranchisement they attributed to both immigrants and a distant government), the increased competition for scarce resources coupled with economic depression, and a political culture that recalls the rewards it earned for past violence against supposedly Communist Chinese in 1967—these defining elements of the Dayaks' resentments and pride proved to be an explosive mixture. In the absence of a single standard of law and ethics, tribal traditions (or what was believed to be "tradition") of violence and retribution have become the ultimate measure of right and wrong. These traditions include head-taking, the symbolism of the bloody red bowl, and the *mandau* sword.[10] All added to already volatile ingredients in West Kalimantan society.

---

[8] Soemadi, *Peranan Kalimantan Barat dalam menghadapi subversi komunis Asia Tenggara: Suatu tinjauan internasional terhadap gerakan komunis dari sudut pertahanan wilayah khususnya Kalimantan Barat*, 2nd edition (Pontianak: Yayasan Tanjungpura, 1974), p. 118.

[9] For a penetrating analysis of the events of 1997 and the role of violence and territory in building Dayak unity, see Peluso and Harwell, "Territory, Custom," pp. 100-101, and also Heidhues, "Kalimantan Barat," p. 143.

[10] The Dayak-Madurese violence of 2001 in Central Kalimantan cannot be discussed here.

GLOSSARY

Terms are identified as (I) Indonesian or Malay, (D) Dutch, (J) Japanese, (C) Chinese, and (M, Mandarin).

A
alang-alang (I), a tough tropical grass, sometimes called elephant grass.
anak bumi (I), child of the land, often Dayaks converted to Islam.
asrama (I), boarding school.
atap (I), thatched roof, usually of palm leaves.

B
bahasa daerah (I), local or regional language.
becak (I), a bicycle taxi, trishaw.
bedrijfsbelasting (D), business or property tax.
benteng (I), a fort or fortification.
bezoar (I), gallstone from a wild pig or other animal, thought to have medicinal powers.
blacang (I), a fermented shrimp paste.
bouw (D): a measure of area, especially in Java, ca. 7100 square meters.
budak (I), slave.
bungkal (I), weight of two silver dollars, used to weigh gold.

C
camat (I), a minor official, head of a *kecamatan*.
cap (C, I), seal.
controleur (D), a Dutch colonial official, below the rank of assistant resident.

D
damar (I), a tropical resin, used especially for red lacquer.
duit (I), one hundredth of a guilder, money in general.
dulang (I), a wok-shaped pan, often made of wood, used to pan gold.

H
hasil (I), result or yield, in Borneo, a tax (*hasil Dayak*) levied by Malay rulers.
hikayat (I), a Malay-language chronicle.
hui (C, M), any kind of association or grouping, often used for a "secret society."
huiguan (M), association.
hun (C, M *fen*), a share; also spelled *foen*.

I

imam (I), Islamic official, head of a mosque.

J

jeruk (I), any citrus fruit; *jeruk Pontianak* is a mandarin orange.

K

kabupaten (I), district, the administrative level below that of a province.

kain songket (I), cloth woven with gold thread, favored by Malay aristocracy.

kampung (I), settlement, village, also an urban residential quarter.

kapitan (I), captain, used for headman of a substantial Chinese settlement. The term was probably of Portuguese origin.

kapthai (C, M *jiatai*), literally great *kapitan*; also spelled *kaptai*.

kaptjong (C, M *jiazhang*?), headman of a small settlement, used in former Lanfang territory.

khie (C, M *ji*), a flag, a banner consisting of a number of troops

kiai (I), Islamic official or teacher.

klenteng (I), a Chinese temple, from M. *guanyinting*, Guan Yin temple.

koanjin (C, M *guanren*), an official or Mandarin.

kongsi (C, M *gongsi*), a cooperative endeavor, a company.

kotamadya (I), municipality, administratively below level of province.

koyan (I), a measure of weight, 27-40 *piculs*.

kumiai (J), traders'association, during Japanese Occupation.

L

ladang (I), dry field.

lansaai (C, M *lanzai*), riff-raff, good for nothing elements.

laojinshan (C, M), "old gold mountain," a name for Borneo.

laothai (C, M *laoda*), headman of a small Chinese settlement.

lila (I), a locally made portable cannon.

lin (C, M *ling*), command, commander.

M

mandau (I), a Dayak sword.

mangkok merah (I), red bowl, a bowl filled with chicken blood and decorated with feathers and other objects, passed to Dayak villages as a call to go on the war path.

mantri (I), official, minister.

masuk Melayu (I), literally "to enter Malayhood," that is, to convert to Islam.

N

nipa (I), a palm whose leaves are used for roofing.

non-pri (I), *non-pribumi*, non-indigenous, used often for ethnic Chinese.

O

orang kaya (I), nobles, literally "rich people."

orang sungai (I) people of the river, often converted Dayaks.

P

panembahan (I), title of a Malay ruler, usually a lesser ruler than a sultan.

pangeran (I), prince, son or close relative of the ruler.

panglima (I), a military leader, a general.

pansanhok (C, M, *banshanke*), literally "half-mountain-Hakka," that is, people of Hakka origin who lived in Teochiu-speaking parts of China.

pasar (I), a market area or market town

perahu (I), native sailing vessel.

peranakan (I), a person of foreign origin born in Indonesia, usually used for one speaking a local language as mother tongue

petompang (C, M *bantangfan*), literally "half-Chinese-barbarian," refers to local-born Chinese, who were usually of mixed parentage.

picul (I), about sixty-two kilograms, the load that can be carried in baskets on a shoulder pole.

pribumi (I), indigenous Indonesian, literally "child of the soil."

priyayi (I), children of the rulers, in modern Indonesia, the bureaucratic elite.

R

raadhuis (D), city hall.

raja (I), king, ruler.

rampas (I), plunder.

ruko (I), short for *rumah toko*, shophouse.

S

sarong-kebaya (I), women's dress, consisting of a long wrapped skirt (sarong) and a long blouse, worn by Indonesian and Malay women and often by Chinese *peranakan* women.

sepuluh satu (I), literally, of "ten, one," a tax of Malay rulers on natural products exported.

shubaoshe (M), reading club, literally "book-and-newspaper society," in Indonesia spellings vary, for example *soeposia*.

siang hwee (C, M *shanghui*), chamber of commerce.

silsilah (I), a Malay-language narrative emphasizing genealogy.

sirappen, from *sirap* (I), shingle, in Borneo often made of ironwood.

suku (I), an Indonesian ethnic group, as Javanese, Dayak, Minangkabau. Sometimes the Chinese are also considered to form a *suku*.

syair (I), rhymed narrative, often of a historical event.

T

tauke (C) (M *toujia*), from a Hokkien expression for businessman, boss; also spelled towkay.

tempayan (I), large earthenware jar, usually Chinese in style.

thaiko, see *tiko*.

thail (I), about 39 grams; also spelled *tahil*.

thang (C, M *ting*), a hall or temple.

tiko (C, M *dage*), literally "big brother," used for a boss of a kongsi or "secret society"; also spelled *thaiko*.

tjanto (I), a locally-made firearm.

tjoengthang (M *zongting*), a central hall, temple or meeting place.
tjong-lin (C, M *zongling*), general, commander of the troops.
tjong-saai (C, M *zongshuai*), commander of a banner of troops.
toapekong (C, M *dabogong*), title of the God of Wealth and Virtue (Fudeci), often
   used in Indonesia for an image of any Chinese deity.
towkay, see *tauke*.

V
vihara (I), a Buddhist temple.

W
wayang (I), a theatrical performance.
wijk (D), an urban residential quarter.
X
xiedou (M), feuds.

Y
yang dipertuan muda (I), a "younger ruler," second king.

Z
zhongxue (M), middle or secondary school.

BIBLIOGRAPHY

ARCHIVAL MATERIALS, MANUSCRIPT COLLECTIONS

ANRI: Arsip National Republik Indonesia (National Archives, Republic of Indonesia), Jakarta, colonial archives

AS: Archief van de Algemene Sekretarie (Archives of the Secretary-General), (1942), 1944-1950, (followed by inventory number).

BB: Binnenlands Bestuur (colonial administrative service), especially papers from the office of the Advisor for Chinese Affairs, later called Advisor, Head of the Service of Chinese Affairs and East Asian Matters. This office was responsible for CPO, Chineesche Persoversicht (Chinese Press Survey), which is found in various archives and identified by date.

BW: Borneos Westerafdeeling (district of West Borneo), with inventory number and new number.

ARA-Algemeen Rijksarchief, Eerste Afdeling (National Archives, First Section), The Hague

VOC: Vereenigte Oost-Indische Compagnie (United [Dutch] East India Company), Records.

ARA-Algemeen Rijksarchief, Tweede Afdeling (National Archives, Second Section), The Hague

2.10.01: Inventaris van het archief van het Ministerie van Koloniën (Inventory of the archives of the Ministry of Colonies), 1814-1819 (items identified by author).

2.21.120: Personal collection of S. Meyer (1912-1967), former Officer for Chinese Affairs, Pontianak, followed by document number.

AS: Inventaris van het archief van de Algemene Secretarie van de Nederlands-Indische Regering en de daarbij gedeponeerde archieven (Inventory of the archives of the General Secretary of the Netherlands Indies Government and the archives located there), (1942), 1944-1950, Inventory number 2.10.14.02, followed by file number. Part of the AS collection is in the Jakarta archive ANRI.

Collectie Schneither: Schneither collection, items from early nineteenth century. Inventory number 2.21.007.57, followed by document number.

Geh. Besluit: Secret resolution, in Resolutions of the Governors-General.

MR: Mailrapporten (mail dispatches, usually sent from the colony to the Hague every fourteen days), Index op de Mailrapporten (index of the mail dispatches), 1869-1899, 1902, Inventory number 2.10.10, followed by year and file number; Inventaris Koloniën (inventory of the colonial archives), 1900-1963, Openbare Mailrapporten (unclassified mail dispatches), 1901-1952, Inventory number 2.10.36.02, followed by year and file number. Secret Mail Reports have the inventory number 2.10.36.06.

MvO: Memorie van Overgave (memorandum of transfer by a colonial official leaving office, for his successor), Inventaris van de Memories van Overgave (inventory of the memoranda of transfer), 1849-1962, Inventory number 2.10.39, Section Westerafdeling Borneo. These are identified as MMK (Ministerie van Koloniën, Ministry of Colonies) numbers 260-265 or KIT (Collection of the Koninklijk Instituut voor de Tropen, Royal Institute for the Tropics), numbers 980-992. Items identified by author and number. This collection has been consolidated on microfiche.

PG: Inventaris van archieven van de Procureur Generaal bij het Hooggerechtshof van Indonesië (inventory of the archives of the attorney general at the high court of Indonesia) [1945-1949] Inventory number 2.10.17 followed by file number.

Politieke Verslagen: Police reports, collected from other documents such as Mailrapporten, now on microfiche. Archief Ministerie van Koloniën (Archives of the Ministry of Colonies) 1850-1900, Inventory number 2.10.36.03, identified by number of document.

RI: Rapportage Indonesië (Indonesian [intelligence] reports): Ministerie van Koloniën, Rapportage Indonesië (Ministry of the Colonies, Reports on Indonesia), 1945-1950, Inventory number 2.10.29, followed by number.

Stamboeken: Inventaris Koloniën (inventory of the colonial archives), 1900-1963, .015 burgerlijke ambtenaren (civil officials), Stamboeken Indische Ambtenaren (service records of Indies officials), 1816-1927, Inventory number 2.10.36.015, followed by number of entry. On microfiche.

Verbalen: Archief Ministerie van Koloniën (Archives, Ministry of Colonies), 1850-1900 (1932), Openbar Verbaal (V., unclassified report) or Exhibitum (Exh., displayed), Inventory number 2.10.02, identified by date and number; also Inventaris Koloniën (Inventory, Colonies), 1900-1963, Openbaar Verbaal, 1901-1952, inventory number 2.10.36.04, identified by date and number. Secret reports from the twentieth century have the investory number 2.10.26.051.

British Library, India Office Library and Records, London, European Manuscripts

Burn, J. "Manuscript on Pontianak." Papers relating to Pontianak. Mr. Burn's account of Pontianak, dated February 12, 1811 and March 12, 1811. IOLR Eur E 109.

Raffles, Thomas Stamford. "Report on the State, Revenue and Political Relations of Java..." (Report to Gov.-Gen. Minto, undated, ca. 1812). Mackensie Private Collection, IOLR. Vol. 13, item 11.

_____. Report by Raffles, ca. 1817. IOLR Raffles, Mss. Eur. D 199.

KITLV – Koninklijk Instituut voor de Taal-, Land- en Volkenkunde, Leiden, Division of Western Manuscripts

Berghuis, W. R. "Rapport aangaande de verrichtingen van Z. M. zeemagt ter Westkust van Borneo durende de krijgs-operatiën tegen Singkawang, Montrado, enz." Manuscript H254, 1854.

Berghuis, W. R. "Stukken met Betrekking tot de Expeditie ter Westkust van Borneo in 1854." Manuscript H354, 1854.

Dewall, H. van. *Opstand der Chinezen van Menteradoe, Westkust-Borneo 1853-54*. Manuscript H 83, 1854.

Leiden University Library, Western Manuscripts

Collectie Hoffman: BPL 2186 N-O; items identified below by author.

Prehn, R.C. van. "Relaas van den oorlog met de oproerige Chinezen ter West-Kust van Borneo, beginnende in 1850." BPL 2472, 1853.

NIOD, Nederlands Instituut voor Oorlogsdocumentatie (Netherlands Institute for War Documentation), Amsterdam

All items are from IC (Indische Collectie, Indies Collection) and are identified by number.

Singapore National Archives, Oral History Department

Transcripts of interviews with rubber dealers Ng Kong Beng and Tan Kong Choon (1980).

BIBLIOGRAPHIES

Avé, Jan B., Victor T. King, and Joke G. W. de Wit. *West Kalimantan: A Bibliography*. Dordrecht: Foris, 1983.

Bakker, P. A. M. de. *Klein repertorium van couranten uit voormalig Nederlands Indië*. The Hague: KITLV, 1988.

Blagden, C.O. *Catalogue of Manuscripts in European Languages Belonging to the Library of the India Office: The Mackenzie Collections*. Vol. 1(i): The 1822 Collection and the Private Collection. Oxford: University Press, 1916.

Delden, E. E. van. *Klein Repretorium: Index op tijdschriftartikelen met betrekking tot voormalig Nederlands Indië*. 7 vols. Amsterdam: Koninklijk Instituut voor de Tropen, 1986-1993.

Hooykaas, J. C., W. N. du Rieu, and Dorothee Baur, eds. *Repertorium op de koloniale literatur of systematische inhoudsopgaaf van hetgeen voorkomt over de koloniën (beoosten de Kaap) in mengelwerken en tijdschriften van 1595 tot 1865*. Continued by A. Hartman et al. 4 vols. Amsterdam: Van Kampen, 1877-81; The Hague: M. Nijhoff, 1895-1934.

Jaquet, F. G. P., ed. *Gids van in Nederland aanwezige bronnen betreffende de geschiedenis van Azië en Oceanië*. Vols. 2-8. Leiden: Koninklijk Instituut voor Taal-, Land- en Volkenkunde, 1970-77.

Müller, Werner. *Bibliographie deutschsprachiger Literatur über Indonesien*. Hamburg: Dokumentations-Leitstelle Asien, Institut für Asienkunde, 1979.

Nagelkerke, Gerard A. *Bibliografisch overzicht uit periodieken over Indonesië, 1930-1945*. Doordrecht: Foris, 1974.

Pioneers of Singapore: A Catalogue of Oral History Interviews. Singapore: Archives and Oral History Department, 1984.

Streit, Robert, and J. Dindinger, eds. *Bibliotheca Missionum*. Vol. 8: *Missionsliteratur Indiens und Indonesiens, 1800-1909*. Freiburg: Herder, 1965. Vol. 29: *Missionsliteratur Südostasiens, 1910-1970*. Freiburg: Herder, 1972.

Zeedijk, Remco. *De Chinezen in Nederlands-Indië tijdens de Japanse bezetting*. Inventory, Indonesian Section, December 1941-January 1945. Amsterdam: Rijksinstutuut voor Oorlogsdocumentatie, mimeo, 1993.

BOOKS AND ARTICLES

Achmad, Ja'. *Kalimantan Barat dibawah pendudukan tentara Jepang*. Pontianak: Proyek Rehabilitasi dan Perluasan Museum Kalimantan Barat, Depdikbud, 1981.

Adriani, P. *Herinneringen uit en aan de Chineesche districten der Wester-Afdeeling van Borneo, 1879-1882: Schetsen en indrukken*. Amsterdam: H.C.A. Campagne en Zoon, 1898.

Alexander, Garth. *Silent Invasion: The Chinese in Southeast Asia*. London: Macdonald, 1973.

Ali Haji bin Ahmad, Raja. *The Precious Gift (Tuhfat al-Nafis)*, translated by Virginia Matheson and Barbara Watson Andaya. Kuala Lumpur: Oxford University Press, 1982.

Aloysius, P., O. F. M. Cap. "De Hakka-Chineesen van Borneo." *Onze Missiën in Oost- en West-Indië* (December 1926).

Andaya, Leonard. *The World of Maluku: Eastern Indonesia in the Early Modern Period.* Honolulu: University of Hawaii Press, 1993.

Anderson, Benedict. *Imagined Communities: Reflections on the Origin and Spread of Nationalism.* London: Verso, 1983.

Anderson, Benedict R. O'G., Ruth T. McVey, and Frederick Bunnell. *A Preliminary Analysis of the October 1, 1965 Coup in Indonesia.* Ithaca: Cornell Modern Indonesia Project, 1971.

Arman. *Laporan penilitian, kondisi sosial ekonomi petani karet di desa Pasir I Kalimantan Barat: Suatu analisis komparatif.* Pontianak: Studi Pengembangan Wilayah Universitas Tanjungpura, 1951.

Avé, Jan B. and Victor T. King. *Borneo: The People of the Weeping Forest: Tradition and Change in Borneo.* Leiden: National Museum of Ethnology, 1986.

Azahari, A. *De ontwikkeling van het bevolkingslandbouwbedrijf in West-Kalimantan.* Bogor: n. p., mimeo, 1950.

Barr, Christopher M. "Bob Hasan, the Rise of Apkindo, and the Shifting Dynamics of Control." *Indonesia* 65 (April 1998).

Barth, Fredrik, "Introduction." In *Ethnic Groups and Boundaries: The Social Organization of Culture Difference,* edited by F. Barth. London: George Allen und Unwin, 1969.

"Berichten en Besluiten over staatsinstellingen der kongsi Lanfong (1857-1888)." *Adatrechtbundels* 7 (1913).

"Bijdrage tot de kennis der binnenlandsche rijken van het westelijk Borneo." *Tijdschrift voor Nederlandsch Indië* 11,1 (1849).

Blink, H. "Economische geographie van Borneo's Wester-Afdeeling." *Tijdschrift voor Economische Geographie* 12,2 (1921).

Blume, C. L. "Toelichtingen aangaande de nasporingen op *Borneo* van G. MÜLLER." *De Indische Bij* 1 (1843).

Blussé, Leonard. "Of Hewers of Wood and Drawers of Water: Leiden University's Early Sinologists (1853-1911)." In *The Leiden Oriental Connection,* edited by W. Otterspeer. Leiden: E. J. Brill, 1989.

————. *Tribuut aan China: vier eeuwen Nederlands-Chinese betrekkingen.* Amsterdam: Cramwinckel, 1989.

Blussé, Leonard, and Ank Merens. "Nuggets from the Gold Mines: Three Tales of the Ta-kang Kongsi of West Kalimantan." In *Conflict and Accomodation in Early Modern East Asia: Essays in Honour of Eric Zürcher,* edited by Leonard Blussé and Harriet Zurndorfer. Leiden: E. J. Brill, 1993.

Blythe, Wilfred. *The Impact of Chinese Secret Societies in Malaya: A Historical Study.* London: Oxford University Press for the Royal Institute of International Affairs, 1969.

Boddeke, P. Ludovicus. *De Missie in het Vicariaat van Pontianak na de Japanse capitulatie.* Bussum, mimeo, 1950.

Boelaars, Huub, O. F. M. Cap. *Perkembangan Keuskupan Agung Pontianak, 1950-1977.* Jakarta: Pusat Penelitan Atma Jaya, mimeo, 1977.

————. *Some Remarks on the Growth of the Catholic Community of West Kalimantan in the Period 1966-1985.* Jakarta: Atma Jaya Research Centre, mimeo, 1976.

Böhm, A. H. *West Borneo 1940-Kalimantan Barat 1950.* Tilburg: H. Gianotten, 1986.

Boomgard, Peter, and A. J. Goozen, comp. *Changing Economy in Indonesia. A Selection of Statistical Source Material from the Early 19th Century up to 1940.* Vol. 11. *Population Trends, 1795-1942.* Amsterdam: Royal Tropical Institute, 1991.

"Borneo en de heer Rochussen." *Tijdschrift voor Nederlandsch Indië* 16,1 (1854).

"De Borneosche expeditie en het leger in Indië." *Tijdschrift voor Nederlandsch Indië* 16,2 (1854).

Braddell, Roland. "A Note on Sambas and Borneo." *Journal of the Malayan Branch, Royal Asiatic Society* 22,4 (1949).

Brokx, Wouter. *Het recht tot wonen en tot reizen in Nederlandsch-Indië.* Bois-le-Duc, C. N. Teulings, 1925.

Bronson, Bennet. "Exchange at the Upstream and Downstream Ends: Notes toward a Functional Model of the Coastal State in Southeast Asia." In *Economic Exchange and Social Interaction in Southeast Asia*, edited by Karl L. Hutterer. Ann Arbor: Michigan Papers on Southeast Asia, 1977.

Brown, Ian. Review of George Hicks, *Chinese Organisations in Southeast Asia in the 1930s*, edited by George Hicks and *With Sweat and Abacus: Economic Roles of Southeast Asian Chinese on the Eve of World War II*, by Fukuda Shozo. *Bijdragen tot de Taal-, Land- en Volkenkunde* 153,3 (1997).

Buys, M. *Twee maanden op Borneo's Westkust: Herinneringen.* Leiden: Doesburgh, 1892.

Cahyono, Heru. "Hubungan antaretnis dan ras: Kasus Pontianak." *Masyarakat Indonesia* 21,2 (1994).

Carey, Peter. "Changing Javanese Perceptions of the Chinese Communities in Central Java, 1755-1825." *Indonesia* 37 (April 1984).

_____, ed. *The British in Java 1811-1816: A Javanese Account.* Oxford: Oxford University Press for the British Academy, 1992.

Carstens, Sharon A. "Form and Content in Hakka Malaysian Culture." In *Guest People: Hakka Identity in China and Abroad*, edited by Nicole Constable. Seattle and London: University of Washington Press, 1996.

_____. "Pulai: Memories of a Gold Mining Settlement in Ulu Kelantan." *Journal of the Malayan Branch, Royal Asiatic Society* 53,1 (1980).

Cator, W. L. *The Economic Position of the Chinese in the Netherlands Indies.* Oxford: Blackwell, 1936.

Chambert-Loir, Henri. "La demographie indonesienne." *Archipel* 51 (1996).

Chan Kwok Bun and Claire Chiang See Ngoh. *Stepping Out: The Making of Chinese Entrepreneurs.* Singapore: Prentice Hall, 1994.

Chinese Art Treasures. Geneva: Editions d'Art Albert Skira, 1961.

"The Chinese in Borneo." *The China Review* 7 (1878).

"De Chinezen op Borneo." *Tijdschrift voor Nederlandsch Indië* 15,1 (1853).

"De Chinezen op Borneo's Westkust." *Tijdschrift voor Nederlandsch Indië* 15,2 (1853). [This, like many of the other anonymous articles in TNI, must be from Baron von Hoëvell.]

"De Chinese volksplanting in Kalimantan Barat." *Schakels* 51 (December 1, 1951).

"De Chineezen in West-Borneo." *Indische Gids* 35,1 (1913).

Cohen, Myron L., "The Hakka or 'Guest People': Dialect as a Sociocultural Variable in Southeast China." In *Guest People: Hakka Identity in China and Abroad*, edited by Nicole Constable. Seattle: University of Washington Press, 1996.

Combanaire, Adolphe. *Au pays des coupeurs de têtes: À travers Bornéo.* Paris: Librairie Plon, 1910.

Comber, L. F. *Chinese Secret Societies in Malaya: A Survey of the Triad Society from 1800 to 1900.* Locust Valley, NY: J. J. Augustin for the Association for Asian Studies, 1959.

Constable, Nicole. Introduction to *Guest People: Hakka Identity in China and Abroad*, edited by Nicole Constable. Seattle: University of Washington Press, 1996.

_____, ed. *Guest People: Hakka Identity in China and Abroad.* Seattle: University of Washington Press, 1996.

Coppel, Charles A. "Contradictions of the New Order." Paper presented to the Workshop "Chinese Indonesians: The Way Ahead." Canberra, Feburary 1999.

_____. *Indonesian Chinese in Crisis.* Kuala Lumpur: Oxford University Press, 1983.

_____. "Mapping the Peranakan Chinese in Indonesia." *Papers on Far Eastern History* 8 (September 1973).

_____. *Studying Ethnic Chinese in Indonesia.* Singapore: Singapore Society of Asian Studies, 2002.

Crawfurd, John. *A Descriptive Dictionary of the Indian Islands and Adjacent Countries.* London: Bradbury and Evans, 1856.

_____. *History of the Indian Archipelago.* Edinburgh: Constable, 1820.

Crockewit, J. H. "De zoutbron aan de Spauk-rivier, landschap Sintang, residentie Westerafdeeling van Borneo," *Natuurkundig Tijdschrift voor Nederlandsch-Indië* 12,2 (1856).

"De cultuur van *hevea* in West-Borneo." *Indische Gids* 41,2 (1919).

Cushman, Jennifer W. and A. C. Milner. "Eighteenth and Nineteenth Century Chinese Accounts of the Malay Peninsula." *Journal of the Malaysian Branch, Royal Asiatic Society* 52,1 (1979).

Davidson, Jamie S., and Douglas Kammen. "Indonesia's Unknown War and the Lineages of Violence in West Kalimantan." *Indonesia* 73 (April 2002).

DeBernardi, Jean. "Epilogue: Ritual Process Reconsidered." In *"Secret Societies" Reconsidered: Perspectives on the Social History of Early Modern South China and Southeast Asia,* edited by David Ownby and Mary Somers Heidhues. Armonk NY: M. E. Sharpe, 1993.

Dijk, L. C. D. van. *Neerland's vroegste betrekkingen met Borneo, den Solo-Archipel, Cambodja, etc.* Amsterdam: J. H. Scheltema, 1862.

Dinas Pariwisata Propinso Dati I Kalimantan Barat, Indonesia: Kalimantan Barat. Pontianak, n.p., 1993.

Djamhari, Saleh As'ad et al. *Monumen Perjuangan Daerah Kalimantan Barat.* [Jakarta]: Departemen Pendidikan dan Kebudayaan, Direktorat Sejarah dan Nilai Tradisional, Projek Inventarisasi dan Dokumentasi Sejarah Nasional, 1987.

Djunaini. "Prajogo Pangesto di kampung Halaman." *Akçaya* (Pontianak) July 21 and 22, 1998.

Dong Ruizhu [pseud., Huang Dongping?]. *Chuyang qianhou* [Tale of migration]. Hong Kong: South China Press, 1979.

Doty, E., and W. J. Pohlman. "Tour in Borneo, from Sambas through Montrado to Pontianak and the Adjacent Settlements of Chinese and Dayaks, during the Autumn of 1838." *Chinese Repository* 8 (1839).

Dove, Michael R. "Living Rubber, Dead Land, and Persisting Systems in Borneo: Indigenous Representations of Sustainability." *Bijdragen tot de Taal-, Land- en Volkenkunde* 154,1 (1998).

_____. "Smallholder Rubber and Swidden Agriculture in Borneo: A Sustainable Adaptation to the Ecology and Economy of the Tropical Forest." *Economic Botany* 47,2 (1993).

Dudbridge, Glen. *China's Vernacular Cultures.* Inaugural Lecture, University of Oxford, June 1, 1995. Oxford: Clarendon Press, 1996.

Earl, George Windsor. *The Eastern Seas, or Voyages and Adventures in the Indian Archipelago.* London: W. H. Allen 1837, repr. Singapore: Oxford University Press, 1971.

Elison, Eddi. "Kalbar pintu masuk komunis: Dulu germbolan komunis menggunakan 'Amoy' sebagai pempinan kelompok." *Selecta* 878 (July 17, 1978).

_____. "Kesukaran WNA Cina untuk jadi WNI di Kalbar; ada yang jadi WNI lewat calo, tapi dihukum." *Selecta* 876 (July 3, 1978).

_____. "Perlunya dididipkan penduduk Cina di Kalbar ke proyek transmigrasi." *Selecta* 877 (July 10, 1978).

Effendy, Machrus. *Penghancuran PGRS-PARAKU dan PKI di Kalimantan Barat.* Jakarta: published by author, 1995.

Eitel, E. J. "An Outline History of the Hakkas." *The China Review* 2 (1873-74).

Elenbaas, W. G. "West-Borneo. Eenige mededeelingen aangaande bevolking en bestuur." *Indische Gids* 31,2 (1909).

Encyclopaedie van Nederlandsch-Indië. The Hague: M. Nijhoff; Leiden: Brill, 1927.

Engelhard, H. E. D. "Bijdragen tot de kennis van het grondbezit in de Chineesche Districten." *Bijdragen tot de Taal-, Land- en Volkenkunde* 51 (1900).

Enthoven, J. J. K. *Bijdragen tot de Geographie van Borneo's Wester-Afdeeling.* Supplement to *Tijdschrift Aardrijkskundig Genootschap, 1901-03.* Leiden: Brill, 1903.

Erbaugh, Mary S. "The Hakka Pardox in the People's Republic of China: Exile, Eminence, and Public Silence." In *Guest People: Hakka Identity in China and Abroad,* edited by Nicole Constable. Seattle: University of Washington Press, 1996.

_____. "The Secret History of the Hakkas: The Chinese Revolution as a Hakka Enterprise." *China Quarterly* 132 (December 1992).

Etten Zusters, Penitenten Recollectinen van de Congregatie van Etten, Noord Brabant. *"en toch gaan we,"* na vijf en twintig jaar werken in de missie van Sambas. [1949].

"De expeditie tegen de Chinezen op Borneo." *Tijdschrift voor Nederlandsch Indië* 16,1 (1854).

Faber, M. von. "Schets van Montrado in 1861." *Tijdschrift voor Indische Taal-, Land- en Volkenkunde* 13 (1864).

Feith, Herbert. "Dayak Legacy." *Far Eastern Economic Review* (January 25, 1968).

Fidler, Richard C. "Chinese-Iban Economic Symbiosis." *Southeast Asian Journal of Social Science* 6,2 (1978).

Formoso, Bernard. *Identités en regard: Destins chinois en milieu bouddhiste thaï.* Paris: CNRS Éditions, Éditions de la Maison des Sciences de l'Homme, 2000.

Francis, E. A. *Herinneringen uit den levensloop van een 'Indisch' ambtenaar van 1815 tot 1851.* Vol. 1. Batavia: Van Dorp, 1856.

_____. "Westkust van Borneo in 1832." *Tijdschrift voor Neêrlands Indië* 4,2 (1842).

Franke, Wolfgang. "Notes on Chinese Temples and Deities in Northwestern Borneo." In *Sino-Malaysiana, Selected Papers on Ming and Qing History and on the Overseas Chinese in Southeast Asia by Wolfgang Franke, 1942-1988.* Singapore: South Seas Society, 1989.

_____. *Reisen in Ost- und Südostasien, 1937-1990,* edited by Hartmut Walravens. Osnabrück: Zeller, 1998.

_____. "The Sovereigns of the Kingdoms of the Three Mountains, San Shan Guowang, at Hepo and in Southeast Asia: A Preliminary Investigation." In *Collected Papers. International Conference on Chinese Studies.* Kuala Lumpur: n. p., 1994.

Franke, Wolfgang, with Chen Tieh Fan. "A Chinese Tomb Inscription of A.D. 1264, Discovered Recently in Brunei." *Brunei Museum Journal* 3,1 (1973).

Franke, Wolfgang, in collaboration with Claudine Salmon and Anthony Siu. *Chinese Epigraphic Materials in Indonesia.* Vol. 3, *Bali, Kalimantan, Sulawesi, Moluccas.* Singapore: South Seas Society, 1997.

Freedman, Maurice, "The Handling of Money: A Note on the Background to the Economic Sophistication of Overseas Chinese." In *The Study of Chinese Society: Essays by Maurice Freedman,* edited by G. William Skinner. Stanford: Stanford University Press, 1979 (Originally published in *Man* 59 [1959]).

_____. "Immigrants and Associations: Chinese in Nineteenth-Century Singapore. " In *The Study of Chinese Society: Essays by Maurice Freedman,* edited by G. William Skinner. Stanford: Stanford University Press, 1979 (originally published in *Comparative Studies in Society and History* 3,1 [1960]).

G [name unknown]. "Bijdrage tot de kennis der Maleijers te Westkust van Borneo." *Tijdschrift voor Nederlandsch Indië* 15,2 (1853).

Gade Ismail, Mohammad, *see* Ismail.

Gambaran keadaan penduduk Kalimantan Barat tahun 1971 dan 1980: Hasil sensus penduduk. Pontianak: Kantor Statistik Propinsi Kalimantan Barat, 1985.

Gerlach, A. J. A. *Fastes militaries des Indes-Orientales néerlandaises.* Vol. 1, Zalt-Bommel: Noman, 1859. *Neerlands heldenfeiten in Oost-Indië.* Vol. 2 and 3, The Hague: Belinfante, 1876.

Golas, Peter J. *Mining.* Vol. 5, Part 13 of *Science and Civilization in China,* edited by Joseph Needham. Cambridge: Cambridge University Press, 1999.

Goor, J. van. "A Madman in the City of Ghosts: Nicolaas Kloek in Pontianak." *Itinerario* II (1985).

————. "Seapower, Trade and State Formation: Pontianak and the Dutch 1780-1840." In *Trading Companies in Asia, 1600-1830,* edited by J. van Goor. Utrecht: HES Uitgevers, 1986.

Gosling, L. A. Peter. "Contemporary Malay Traders in the Gulf of Thailand." In *Economic Exchange and Social Interaction in Southeast Asia: Perspectives from Prehistory, History, and Ethnography,* edited by Karl L. Hutterer. Ann Arbor: Michigan Papers on Southeast Asia, 1977.

Govaars-Tjia, Ming Tien Nio. "Hollands onderwijs in een koloniale samenleving: De Chinese ervaring in Indonesië 1900-1942." PhD dissertation, Leiden University, 1999.

Grijpstra, B. G. *Common Efforts in the Development of Rural Sarawak, Malaysia.* Wageningen: Centre for Publishing and Documentation, 1976.

Gronovius, D. J. van Dungen. "Verslag over de Residentie Borneo's Westkust, 1827-1829." Introduced by P. J. Veth. *Tijdschrift voor Nederlandsch Indië* 5,1 (1871).

Groot, J. J. M. de. *Het kongsiwezen van Borneo. Eene verhandeling over den grondslag en den aard der chineesche politieke vereenigingen in de koloniën.* The Hague: M. Nijhoff, 1885.

————. "Lioe A Sin van Mandohr." *Tijdschrift voor Nederlandsch Indië* 10,1 (1885).

H., B. R. van [name unknown], "Een Chinese volksschool voor West-Borneo?" *Het Katholieke-Schoolblad van Nederlandsch-Indië* 23,19 (December 8, 1939).

Haccou, J. "Fragmenten van eene reis op de Westkust van Borneo in 1830." *Tijdschrift voor Nederlandsch Indië* 1,2 (1867).

Hambatan Dalam Pembinaan Persatuan dan Kesatuan Bangsa di Propinsi Daerah Tingkat I Kalimantan Barat. Jakarta: Departemen Dalam Negeri, Badan Pendidikan dan Latihan, Sekolah Pimpinan Administrasi Tingkat Madya, 1986.

Hamilton, Alexander. *A New Account of the East Indies.* Edinburgh: John Mosman, 1727.

Harrisson, Tom. "Gold and Indian Influences in West Borneo." *Journal of the Malayan Branch, Royal Asiatic Society* 22,4 (1949).

Harrisson, Tom, ed. *The Peoples of Sarawak.* Sarawak: Sarawak Museum, 1959.

Heekeren, C. van. *Rode zon boven Borneo: West Borneo 1942.* The Hague: Bakker, etc., 1968.

Heertum, Aloysius van. "De Hakka-Chineezen van Borneo." *Onze Missiën in Oost- en West-Indië* 9 (1926).

Heidhues, Mary F. Somers. *Bangka Tin and Mentok Pepper: Chinese Settlement on an Indonesian Island.* Singapore: Institute of Southeast Asian Studies, 1992.

————. "Chinese Identity in the Diaspora: Religion and Language in West Kalimantan, Indonesia." In *Nationalism and Cultural Revival in Southeast Asia: Perspectives from the Centre and the Region,* edited by Sri Kuhnt-Saptodewo et al. Wiesbaden: Harrassowitz Verlag, 1997.

_____. "Chinese Organizations in West Borneo and Bangka: *Kongsi* and *Hui.*" In *"Secret Societies" Reconsidered: Perspectives on the Social History of Early Modern South China and Southeast Asia,* edited by David Ownby and Mary Somers Heidhues. Armonk, NY: M. E. Sharpe, 1993.

_____. "Chinese Settlements in Rural Southeast Asia: Unwritten Histories." In *Sojourners and Settlers: Histories of Southeast Asia and the Chinese in Honour of Jennifer Cushman,* edited by Anthony Reid. St. Leonards: Allen and Unwin for Asian Studies Association of Australia, 1996.

_____. "Citizenship and Identity: Ethnic Chinese and the Indonesian Revolution." In *Changing Identities of the Southeast Asian Chinese Since World War II,* edited by Jennifer Cushman and Wang Gungwu. Hong Kong: Hong Kong University Press, 1988.

_____. "The First Two Sultans of Pontianak," *Archipel* 56 (1998).

_____. "Identity and the Minority: Ethnic Chinese on the Indonesian Periphery." *Indonesia Circle* 70 (1996).

_____. "Kalimantan Barat 1967-1999; Violence on the Periphery." In *Violence in Indonesia,* edited by Ingrid Wessel and Georgia Wimhoefer. Hamburg: Abera, 2000.

_____. "Little China in the Tropics: The Chinese in West Kalimantan to 1942." In *South China: State, Culture and Social Change during the 20th Century,* edited by L. M. Douw and P. Post. Amsterdam: North-Holland for Royal Netherlands Academy of Arts and Sciences, 1996.

Helbig, Karl. *Eine Durchquerung der Insel Borneo (Kalimantan): Nach den Tagebüchern aus dem Jahre 1937.* Berlin: Dietrich Reimer Verlag, rev. ed. 1982.

"De held van Pamangkat." *Tijdschrift voor Nederlandsch Indië* 13,1 (1851).

Hicks, George L., ed. *Chinese Organisations in Southeast Asia in the 1930s.* Singapore: Select Books, 1996.

Hoëvell [W.R. Baron von Hoëvell]. "Onze roeping op Borneo." *Tijdschrift voor Nederlandsch Indië* 14,2 (1852).

Hooyer, G. B. *De krijgsgeschiedenis van Nederlandsch-Indië van 1811-1894.* 3 vols. and atlas. The Hague: van Cleef and Batavia: Kolff, 1895-1897.

Houliston, Sylvia. *Borneo Breakthrough.* London: China Inland Mission, 1963.

Hövig, P. "Overzicht van den Mijnbouw in Nederlandsch-Indië." In *Gedenkboek van de Koloniale Tentoonstelling Semarang 20 Augustus-22 November 1914,* edited by M. G. van Heel et al., vol. 2. Batavia: Mercurius, 1916.

Hsieh T'ing-yu. "Origins and Migrations of the Hakkas." *Chinese Social and Political Science Review* 13 (1929).

Huang Dongping. *Chidao xianshang.* Hong Kong: Chidao Publisher, 1979.

_____. *Qiaofeng* [Sojourning wind]. Pontianak: privately published, 1961.

Huang Kunzhang. "Taiguodi 'banshanke' [Thailand's *banshanke*]."*Huaren Life Overseas* 2 (1987).

Hullu, J. de. "De instelling van de commissie voor den handel der Oost-Indische Compagnie op China in 1756." *Bijdragen tot de Taal-, Land- en Volkenkunde* 79 (1923).

Human Rights Watch. "West Kalimantan: Communal Violence in West Kalimantan,"Report, www.hrw.org/reports/1997/wkali/Brneo97d-01.htm (accessed September 11, 2002).

Hulten, Herman Josef van. *Hidupku di antara Suku Daya: Cacatan seorang misionaris.* Jakarta: Grasindo, 1992 (Indonesian translation of *Mijn Leven met de Daya's.* Tilburg: n.p., 1983).

Hunt, J. "Sketch of Borneo or Pulo Kalamantan, Communicated by J. Hunt Esq. in 1812, to the Honorable Sir T. S. Raffles, Late Lieut. Governor of Java." Printed in *Notices of the Indian Archipelago and Adjacent Countries,* edited by J. H. Moor. Singapore: n.p., 1837, repr. London: Frank Cass, 1968.

Immerzeel, B. R., and F. van Esch, eds. *Verzet in Nederlands-Indië tegen de Japanse bezetting 1942-1945.* The Hague: B. R. Sdu Uitgeverij, 1993.

Indonesia, Biro Pusat Statistik. *Penduduk Cina luar Jawa: Hasil Registrasi Penduduk: Achir tahun 1973, 1974, 1975: Statistik penduduk dan tenaga kerja.* Jakarta: Biro Pusat Statistik, 1977.

Indonesia, Biro Pusat Statistik. *Penduduk Kalimantan Barat: Hasil Sensus Penduduk 1990* (Fiche 886 SEI 93/50020, Cornell University Library).

Indonesia, Biro Pusat Statistik. *Penduduk dan tenaga kerja, Penduduk Cina luar Jawa: Hasil Registrasi Penduduk akhir tahun 1976, 1977, 1978.* Jakarta: Biro Pusat Statistik, 1980.

Institut Studi Arus Informasi and Institute Dayakology Research and Development. *Sisi gelap Kalimantan Barat: Perseteruan etnis Dayak-Madura 1997.* Jakarta: Midas Surya Grafindo, 1999.

Irwin, Graham. *Nineteenth-Century Borneo: A Study in Diplomatic Rivalry.* The Hague: M. Nijhoff, 1955, repr. Singapore: Donald Moore Books, 1967.

Ismail, Muhammad Gade. "Trade and State Power: Sambas (West Borneo) in the Early Nineteenth Century." In *State and Trade in the Indonesian Archipelago*, edited by G. J. Schutte. Leiden: KITLV Press, 1994.

————. "Politik perdagangan Melayu di kesultanan Sambas, Kalimantan Barat: Masa akhir kesultanan 1808-1818." Jakarta: Master's thesis, Universitas Indonesia, 1985.

Isman, Zainudin. "Singkawang, Kota AMOI." *Kompas* (July 5, 1987).

Jackson, James C. *The Chinese in the West Borneo Goldfields: A Study in Cultural Geography.* Hull: University of Hull Publications, Occasional Papers in Geography, 1970.

————. "Mining in Eighteenth-Century Bangka: The Pre-European Exploitation of a 'Tin Island'." *Pacific Viewpoint* 10,2 (1969).

Jacobus, L. S. E. Frans. *Sejarah perang majang desa melawan Jepang.* Pontianak, n.p., 1981.

Jenkins, David. "The Jakarta Solution: A Million Chinese May Be Granted Indonesian Citizenship under a Bold New Plan Being Debated." *Far Eastern Economic Review* (September 21, 1979).

Jonge, J. K. J de, *De opkomst van het Nederlandsch gezag in Oost-Indië.* 13 vols. The Hague: M. Nijhoff, 1862ff.

"Kapucijn-Missionaris" (pseud.). "Missie onder de Chineezen." *Onze Missiën in Oost-en West-Indië* 13 (1930).

"Kalamantan" (pseud.). "Letters from the Interior of Borneo (West Coast)." *Journal of the Indian Archipelago* 2 (1848); 3 (1849).

Kanahele, George Sanford. "The Japanese Occupation of Indonesia: Prelude to Independence." PhD dissertation, Cornell University, 1967.

Kater, C. "Aanteekeningen op Prof. Veth's 'Westerafdeeling van Borneo,' 5de boek van het tweede deel." *Indische Gids* 5,1 (1883).

Kathirithamby-Wells, J. "*Hulu-hilir* Unity and Conflict: Malay Statecraft in East Sumatra before the Mid-Nineteenth Century." *Archipel* 45 (1993).

Kelompok Kerja Pembinaan Masyarakat Cina: *Konsep pengelolaan masalah masyarakat keturunan Cina di Kalimantan Barat.* Pontianak, Badan Kerjasama Kodam XII-TPR Universitas Tanjungpura, mimeo, 1982.

Kemp, P. H. van der. "Montrado tijdens het herstel van ons gezag in 1818." *Koloniaal Tijdschrift* 9 (1920).

————. "Palembang en Banka in 1816-1820." *Bijdragen tot de Taal-, Land- en Volkenkunde* 6, 7 (1900).

————. "De Vestiging van het Nederlandsch gezag op Borneo's Westerafdeeling in 1818-1819." *Bijdragen tot de Taal-, Land- en Volkenkunde* 76 (1920).

Keppel, Henry. *The Expedition to Borneo of H.M.S. Dido for the Suppression of Piracy: With Extracts from the Journal of James Brooke Esq. of Sarawak.* 2 vols. London: Chapman and Hall, 1846.

————. *A Visit to the Indian Archipelago in H.M. Ship Meander.* 2 vols. London: Bentley, 1853.

Kervel, T. A. C. van, and D. W. J. C. van Lijnden. "Bijdrage tot de kennis van Borneo: De hervorming van den maatschappelijken toestand ter westkust van Borneo." *Tijdschrift voor Nederlandsch Indië* 15,1 (1853).

Kessel, O. van. "Statistieke aanteekeningen omtrent het stroomgebied der rivier Kapoeas (Wester-Afdeeling van Borneo)." *Indisch Archief* 1,2 (1850).

Keyes, Charles F., ed. *Ethnic Change.* Seattle: University of Washington Press, 1982.

Kielstra, E. B. "Bijdrage tot de geschiedenis van Borneo's Westerafdeeling," Parts I-IV, *Indische Gids* 11,1 (1889); Parts V-IX, *Indische Gids* 11,2 (1889); Parts IX-XIV, *Indische Gids* 12,1 (1890); Parts XV-XVIII, *Indische Gids* 12,2 (1890); Part XIX, *Indische Gids* 14,1 (1892); Parts XX-XIII, *Indische Gids* 14,2 (1892); Parts XXIV-XXV, *Indische Gids* 15,1 (1893); Part XXVI, *Indische Gids* 15,2 (1893).

————. "West Borneo." *Onze Eeuw* 16,2 (April 1916).

————. "West Borneo." In *De Indische Archipel: Geschiedkundige schetsen,* edited by E. B. Kielstra. Haarlem: De Erven F. Bohn, 1917.

"Kilas Balik '93," *Tempo* (January 8, 1994).

King, Victor T. *Ethnic Classification and Ethnic Relations: A Borneo Case Study.* Hull: University of Hull Centre for South-East Asian Studies, 1979.

————. "Ethnicity in Borneo: An Anthropological Problem." *Southeast Asian Journal of Social Science* 10,7 (1982).

————. *The Peoples of Borneo.* Oxford: Blackwell, 1993.

Kloos, J. H. "Vorkommen und Gewinnung des Goldes auf der Insel Borneo." *Tijdschrift voor Nederlandsch Indië* 4,2 (1866).

Knaap, Gerrit and Luc Nagtegaal. "A Forgotten Trade: Salt in Southeast Asia, 1670-1813." In *Emporia, Commodities and Entrepreneurs in Asian Maritime Trade, c. 1400-1750,* edited by Roderich Ptak and Dietmar Rothermund. Stuttgart: Franz Steiner Verlag, 1991.

Kratz, Ulrich. "Silsilah Raja-raja Sambas as a Source of History." *Archipel* 20 (1980).

"Kronijk van Nederlandsch Indië, loopende van af het jaar 1816: De jaren 1824 en 1825." *Tijdschrift voor Neêrlands Indië* 7,2 (1845).

"Kultuur- en industrie-ondernemingen op Borneo." *Tijdschrift voor Nederlandsch Indië* 20,2 (1858).

Langelaan, Quirijn S. "De Chinezen van Sambas, 1850." Master's thesis, University of Amsterdam, 1984.

Laporan singkat pelaksanaan asimilasi melalui pendidikan di Kalimantan Barat. Pontianak: Kantor Wilayah Departemen P dan K, Propinsi Kalimantan Barat, 1980.

Leonard, Jane. *Wei Yuan and China's Rediscovery of the Maritime World.* Cambridge: Harvard University Press, 1984.

Leong, Sow-theng. *Migration and Ethnicity in Chinese History: Hakkas, Pengmin, and their Neighbors,* edited by Tim Wright, with an introduction by G. William Skinner. Stanford: Stanford University Press, 1997.

Lewis, Dianne. *Jan Compagnie in the Straits of Malacca, 1641-1795.* Athens: Ohio University Center for International Studies, 1995.

Leyden, Dr. [John]. "Sketch of Borneo." *Verhandelingen van het Bataviaasch Genootschap van Kunsten en Wetenschappen* 7 (1814), partly reprinted in *Notices of the Indian Archipelago and Adjacent Countries*, edited by J. H. Moor. Singapore: n.p., 1837, repr. London: Frank Cass, 1968.

Lijnden, Baron D. W. C. "Bijdragen tot de kennis van Borneo: De verhouding in welke het Gouvernement staat tot de Chinezen en Dajaks op de westkust van Borneo en voornamelijk op Sambas." *Tijdschrift voor Nederlandsch Indië* 15,1 (1853). [Text also in ANRI BW 18/2 (195), Laporan Schwaner berisi tentang perlawanan masyarakat Cina di Sambas, 1846.]

Liu Huanren, *Helan Dongyindu gailan* [Survey of the Dutch East Indies]. Singapore, n.p., 1939. Photocopy.

Lockard, Craig A. "The 1857 Chinese Rebellion in Sarawak." *Journal of Southeast Asian Studies* 9,1 (1978).

————. *From Kampung to City: A Social History of Kuching, Malaysia, 1820-1970*. Athens: Ohio University Monographs in International Studies, Southeast Asia Series, 1987.

Logan, J. R. "Notices of Chinese Intercourse with Borneo Proper prior to the Establishment of Singapore in 1819." *Journal of the Indian Archipelago* 2 (1848).

————. "Notices of European Intercourse with Borneo Proper prior to the Establishment of Singapore in 1819." *Journal of the Indian Archipelago* 2 (1848).

————. "Traces of the Origin of the Malay Kingdom of Borneo Proper." *Journal of the Indian Archipelago* 2 (1848).

Lombard, Denys. *Le carrefour javanais: Essai d'histoire globale*. Volume 2, *Les réseaux asiatiques*. Paris: Éditions de l'École des Hautes Études en Sciences Sociales, 1990.

————. "Guide Archipel IV: Pontianak et son arrière-pays." *Archipel* 28 (1984).

Lontaan, J. U. *Menjelajah Kalimantan*. Jakarta: Baru, 1985.

Lo Hsiang-lin [Luo Xianglin]. "A Chinese Presidential System in Kalimantan." *Sarawak Museum Journal*, n.s. 9,15-16 (1960), repr. of "The Establishment of the Langfang Presidential System by Lo Fang Pak in Borneo." *Kwangchow Hsueh-pao* (1937).

Ma Huan. *Ying-yai Sheng-lan: "The Overall Survey of the Ocean's Shores."* Translated and edited by J. V. G. Mills. repr. Bangkok: White Lotus Press, 1997.

Mackie, J. A. C. "Anti-Chinese Outbreaks in Indonesia, 1959-68." In *The Chinese in Indonesia: Five Essays*, edited by J. A. C. Mackie. Melbourne: Nelson for the Australian Institute of International Affairs, 1976.

————. *Konfrontasi: The Indonesia-Malaysia Dispute, 1963-1966*. Kuala Lumpur: Oxford University Press, 1974.

Maclaine Pont, A. J. B. "Het Fiasco van den Burgerlinken Stand voor Chineezen." *Koloniale Studien* 8,2 (1924).

Magnis-Suseno, Franz. "The Fear and the Fury." *Inside Indonesia* (July-September, 1997).

McBeth, John, and Margot Cohen. "Murder and Mayhem: Ethnic Aminosity Explodes in Bloodshed." *Far Eastern Economic Review* (February 20, 1997).

McKinnon, E. Edwards. "The Sambas Hoard: Bronze Drums and Gold Ornaments Found in Kalimantan in 1991." *Journal of the Malaysian Branch, Royal Asiatic Society* 67,1 (1994).

Meel, H. de. "Het verloop van de bevolking in West-Borneo 1920-1948." *Tijdschrift van het Koninklijk Nederlandsch Aardrijkskundig Genootschap* 2. ser., 69 (1952).

Meijer, P., ed. "Kronijk van Nederlandsch Indië, loopende van af het jaar 1816: De jaren 1822 en 1823: Verslagen van den Kommissaris van Borneo Mr. J. H. Tobias, anno 1822 en 1823." *Tijdschrift voor Neêrlands Indië* 4,1 (1842).

"Memoir on the Residency of the North-West Coast of Borneo." In *Notices of the Indian Archipelago and Adjacent Countries* edited by J. H. Moor. Singapore 1837, repr. London: Frank Cass, 1968. [Originally published in *Singapore Chronicle*, October-November 1827; see also "Verslag wegens de Nederlandsche bezittingen..." (below).]

Meteren Brouwer, P. M. van. "De geschiedenis der Chineesche Districten der Wester-Afdeeling van Borneo van 1740-1926." *Indische Gids* 49,2 (1927).

Meijer, J. H. "De Westerafdeeling van Borneo." Address, Indisch Genootschap, *Verslag van de Vergadering van 21 maart 1930*.

Milburn, W. *Oriental Commerce.* London: Black, Parry, and Co., 1825 [rev. ed. of 1813 volume].

Milner, A. C. *Kerajaan: Malay Political Culture on the Eve of Colonial Rule.* Tucson: The University of Arizona Press, 1982.

Mol, G. A. de. "Vier groote Landbouwwerktuigen van de Chineezen in West-Borneo." *Sin Po*, Special Issue, no. 618 (February 2, 1935).

Moor, J. H. *Notices of the Indian Archipelago and Adjacent Countries.* Singapore: n.p., 1837, repr. London: Frank Cass, 1968.

Morrison, Alastair. *Fair Land Sarawak: Some Recollections of an Expatriate Official.* Ithaca: Cornell University Southeast Asia Program, 1993.

Moser, Leo J. *The Chinese Mosaic: The Peoples and Provinces of China.* Boulder: Westview Special Studies on East Asia, 1985.

Mozingo, David. *Chinese Policy toward Indonesia, 1949-1967.* Ithaca: Cornell University Press, 1976.

_____. "The Sino-Indonesian Dual Nationality Treaty." *Asian Survey* 1 (December 1961).

Müller, G. "Proeve eener geschiedenis van een gedeelte der Westkust van Borneo," collected by E. Müller. *De Indische Bij* 1 (1843).

Muntinghe, W. H. "De bevestiging van het nederlandsch gezag op Borneo, en de vermeerdering der inkomsten van dat eiland voor de schatkist." *Tijdschrift voor Nederlandsch Indië* 12,2 (1850).

N., E. E. [Netscher, E. E.?]. "Munten der Chinezen in Sambas," *Tijdschrift voor Indische Taal-, Land- en Volkenkunde* 3 (1855).

Naerssen, F. H. van. Verslag van mijn verblijf in Kalimantan Barat (Part 2). Photocopy of typescript, 1949. Cornell University Library, Echols Collection.

Nagata, Judith. "What is a Malay? Situational Selection of Ethnic Identity in a Plural Society." *American Ethnologist* 1,2 (1974).

Nakagawa, Manabu. "Studies on the History of the Hakkas: Reconsidered." *The Developing Economies* 13,2 (1975).

Netherlands, Staten-Generaal, Enquêtecommissie Regeringsbeleid, 1940-1945. Report, Part 8A, "Borneo en de Groote Oost." The Hague, Staatsdrukkerij- en Uitgeberijbedrijf, 1956.

"Nieuwe onlusten op Borneo; door +++, dd 12 Oct 1856." *Tijdschrift voor Nederlandsch Indië* 18,2 (1856).

Nio Joe Lan, *Riwajat 40 Taoen dari Tiong Hoa Hwe Koan-Batavia* (1900-1939). Batavia: Tiong Hoa Hwe Koan, 1940.

Notowardojo, Subianto, R. M. *Kalimantan Barat sepintas lalu dilihat dari sudut sosial ekonomi.* Jakarta: Direktorat Perekonomian Rakjat, Kementerian Perekonomian (mimeo), 1951.

Nyce, Ray. *Chinese New Villages in Malaya: A Community Study*, edited by Shirle Gordon. Singapore: Malaysian Sociological Research Institute, 1973.

Ong, Aihwa, and Donald M. Nonini, eds. *Ungrounded Empires: The Cultural Politics of Modern Chinese Transnationalism.* New York and London: Routledge, 1997.

"De ongeregeldheden in West-Borneo." *Indische Gids* 37,1 (1915).

Onghokham, "The Chinese of West Kalimantan," *Globalink* 1,3 (March-May 1996).

Outer, Marilou den. "De Triade in de Indische Archipel. Een eerste verkenning van functie en beteekenis van geheimgenootschappen (ca. 1800-1940)." Master's thesis, University of Amsterdam, 1989.

Outram, R. "The Chinese." In *The Peoples of Sarawak*, edited by Tom Harrisson. Sarawak: Sarawak Museum, 1959.

Ownby, David, and Mary Somers Heidhues, eds. *"Secret Societies" Reconsidered: Perspectives on the Social History of Early Modern South China and Southeast Asia.* Armonk, NY: M. E. Sharpe, 1993.

_____. Introduction to *"Secret Societies" Reconsidered: Perspectives on the Social History of Early Modern South China and Southeast Asia,* edited by David Ownby and Mary Somers Heidhues. Armonk, NY: M. E. Sharpe, 1993.

Ozinga, Jacob. *De economische ontwikkeling der Westerafdeeling van Borneo en de bevolkingsrubbercultuur.* Wageningen: N.V. gebr. Zomer en Keuning, 1940.

Oyong, Myra. "Mencari rumah nenek moyang di RRC." *Intisari* 234 (January 1983).

Paimin, Sutini, et al. *Kemampuan berbahasa Indonesia (membaca) murid-murid sekolah dasar yang berbahasa ibu bahasa Cina di Kotamadya Pontianak.* Jakarta: Pusat Pembinaan dan Pengembangan Bahasa, Departemen Pendidikan dan Kebudayaan, 1985.

Peluso, Nancy Lee, and Emily Harwell. "Territory, Custom, and the Cultural Politics of Ethnic War in West Kalimantan, Indonesia." In *Violent Environments*, edited by Nancy Lee Peluso and Michael Watts. Ithaca and London: Cornell University Press, 2001.

Penduduk Kalimantan Barat: Hasil pencacahan lengkap sensus penduduk 1990. [Pontianak]: Kantor Statistik Propinsi Kalimantan Barat, ca. 1990.

Penduduk Indonesia selama pembangunan jangka panjang, tahap I, Kalimantan Barat. Jakarta: Kantor Menteri Negara, Kependudukan dan Lingkungan Hidup, 1992.

Peta sejarah propinsi Kalimantan Barat, edited by Drs. Soedarto, Soenarpo, et al. Jakarta: Departemen Pendidikan dan Kebudayaan, Projek Investarisasi dan Dokumentasi Sejarah Nasional, 1986.

Petebang, Edi, and Eri Sutrisno, *Konflik Etnik di Sambas.* Jakarta: Institut Studi Arus Informasi, 2000.

Peters, Charles M. "Illipe Nuts (*Shorea* spp.) in West Kalimantan: Use, Ecology, and Management Potential of an Important Forest Resource." In *Borneo in Transition: People, Forests, Conservation, and Development,* edited by Christine Padoch and Nancy Lee Peluso. Kuala Lumpur: Oxford University Press, 1996.

Peterson, Robert. *Storm over Borneo.* London: Overseas Missionary Fellowship, 1968.

_____. *The Demon Gods of Thorny River: A True-to-Life Story of a Chinese Family in West Kalimantan, Indonesian Borneo.* London: Overseas Missionary Fellowship, 1974.

Pfeiffer, Ida. *Meine zweite Weltreise.* Vol. 1. Vienna: Gerold's Sohn, 1853.

Poerwanto, Hari. "Orang Khek di Singkawang: Suatu kajian mengenai masalah asimilasi orang Cina dalam rangka integrasi nasional di Indonesia." PhD dissertation, Universitas Indonesia, 1990.

Poeze, Harry A., ed. *Politiek-Politioneele Overzichten van Nederlandsch-Indië.* Part 1, 1927-28. The Hague: Martinus Nijhoff, 1983.

_____, ed. *Politiek-Politioneele Overzichten van Nederlandsch-Indië.* Part 2, 1929-30. Dordrecht: Foris, 1983.

_____, ed. *Politiek-Politioneele Overzichten van Nederlandsch-Indië.* Part 3, 1931-34. Doordrecht: Foris, 1988.

_____, ed. *Politiek-Politioneele Overzichten van Nederlandsch-Indië.* Part 4, 1935-41. Leiden: KITLV Press, 1994.

Posewitz, Theodor, *Borneo: Entdeckungsreisen und Untersuchungen, gegenwärtiger Stand der geologischen Kenntnisse, Verbreitung der nutzbaren Mineralien.* Berlin: R. Friedländer und Sohn, 1889.

Potter, Lesley. "A Forest Product out of Control: Gutta Percha in Indonesia and the Wider Malay World, 1845-1915." In *Paper Landscapes: Explorations in the Environmental History of Indonesia*, edited by Peter Boomgaard et al. Leiden: KITLV Press, 1997.

Prehn, R. C. van. "Aantekeningen betreffende Borneo's Westkust." *Tijdschrift voor Indische Taal-, Land- en Volkenkunde* 7 (1858).

Prehn Wiese, R. C. van. "Aantekeningen omtrent de Wester-Afdeeling van Borneo." *Tijdschrift voor Indische Taal-, Land- en Volkenkunde* 4. ser, 10,1 (1861).

Preliminary Regional Survey for Road Network Identification in Kalimantan Barat–Indonesia. Vol. 2, *Environment and Population.* [Canberra]: Government of Australia, Department of Foreign Affairs, Colombo Plan, 1973.

Profil Daerah Kabupaten Daerah Tingkat II Pontianak. [Pontianak]: Badan Perencanaan Pembangunan Daerah, Kalimantan Barat, 1986.

Purcell, Victor. *The Chinese in Southeast Asia.* London: Oxford University Press, rev. ed. 1965.

Radermacher, J. C. M. "Beschrijving van het eiland Borneo, voor zoover hetzelfde tot nu toe bekend is." *Verhandelingen van het Bataviaasch Genootschap van Kunsten en Wetenschappen* 2 (1780).

Radermacher, J. C. M., and W. van Hogendorp. "Korte schets van den bezittingen der Nederlandsch Oost-Indische Maatschappij." *Verhandelingen van het Bataviaasch Genootschap van Kunsten en Wetenschappen* 1 (1779).

Raffles, Sophia. *Memoir of the Life and Public Services of Sir Thomas Stamford Raffles.* London: John Murray, 1830.

Ranken, E. A. "De niet-Europese bijdrage tot de economische ontwikkeling van West-Borneo, 1900-1940." In *Het belang van de buitengewesten: economische expansie en koloniale staatsvorming in de buitengewesten van Nederlands-Indië, 1870-1942*, edited by A. H. P. Clemens and J. Th. Lindblad. Amsterdam: NEHA, 1989.

Rees, W. A. van. *Montrado: Geschied- en krijskundige bijdrage betreffende de onderwerping der Chinezen op Borneo, naar het dagboek van een Indisch officier over 1854-1856.* Bois-le-Duc: Müller, 1858.

_____. *Wachia, Taykong en Amir.* Rotterdam: H. Nijgh, 1859.

Reid, Anthony. *Southeast Asia in the Age of Commerce 1450-1680.* Vol. 1, *The Lands below the Winds.* New Haven: Yale University Press, 1988.

Remmelink, Willem. *The Chinese War and the Collapse of the Javanese State, 1725-1743.* Leiden: KITLV Press, 1994.

Ritter, W. L., *Indische herinneringen, aantekeningen en tafereelen uit vroegeren en lateren tijd.* Amsterdam: van Kesteren, 1843.

_____. "De kanonneerboot." *De Kopiist* 1,10 (1842).

_____. *Nacht en morgen uit het indische leven.* Amsterdam: van Kesteren, 1861.

_____. "De oorsprong van Pontianak." *Tijdschrift voor Neêrlands Indië* 2,1 (1839).

Rivai, Mawardi. *Peristiwa Mandor.* Jakarta: Pustaka Antara, 1978.

Riwut, Tjilik. *Kalimantan memanggil.* Introduced by Bung Karno. Djakarta: Endang, 1958.

_____. *Kalimantan membangun.* Jakarta: Jaya Agung Offset, 1979.

Rochussen, J. J. "Redevoering, gehouden bij de overgave van het bestuur aan den heer Duymaer van Twist, in den raad van Indië, op den 12den Mei 1851." *Tijdschrift voor Nederlandsch Indië* 18,1 (1856).

_____. "Verwikkelingen met de Chinesen op de Westkust van Borneo." In *Toelichting en verdediging van eenige daden van mijn bestuur in Indië, in antwoord op sommige vragen van J.P. Cornets de Groot van Kraaijenburg.* The Hague: van Cleef, 1853.

Röttger, E. H. *Briefe über Hinter-Indien während eines zehnjährigen Aufenthalts daselbst an seine lieben Freunde in Europa.* Berlin: Enslinschen Buchhandlung, 1844.

Rush, James R. *Opium Farms in Nineteenth-Century Java: Institutional Change in a Colonial Society, 1860-1910*. Ithaca: Cornell University Press, 1990.

Rusha, Gladys. *Truth to Tell in Borneo*. London: Oliphants, 1969.

Salmon, Claudine. "Les Hainanais en Asie du Sud-Est: De la navigation à l'implantation (fin XVIIe-fin XIX^{e}s.)." In *Hainan: De la Chine à l'Asie du Sud-Est, Von China nach Südostasien*, edited by Claudine Salmon and Roderich Ptak. Wiesbaden: Harrassowitz Verlag, 2001.

————. "Taoke or Coolies? Chinese Visions of the Chinese Diaspora." *Archipel* 26 (1983).

Sandick, J. C. F. van, and V. J. van Marle. *Verslag eener spoorwegverkenning in Noordwest-Borneo*. Parts 1-3. Batavia: Albrecht, 1919.

————. "Wederwoord aan dr. E. C. J. Mohr." *Tijdschrift voor Economische Geographie* 12 (1921).

Sandick, L. H. W. van. *Chineezen buiten China: Hunne beteekenis voor de ontwikkeling van Zuid-Oost-Azië, speciaal van Nederlandsch-Indië*. The Hague: M. van der Beek's Hofboekhandel, 1909.

Schaank, S. H. "De kongsis van Montrado, Bijdrage tot de geschiedenis en de kennis van het wezen der Chineesche vereenigingen op de Westkust van Borneo." *Tijdschrift voor Indische Taal-, Land- en Volkenkunde* 35,5/6 (1893).

————. *Het Loeh-Foeng-Dialect*. Leiden: E. J. Brill, 1897.

Schipper, Kristofer. *Tao: De levende religie van China*. Amsterdam: Meulenhoff, 1998.

Schlegel, Gustaaf. *Thian Ti Hwui: The Hung-league or Heaven-Earth League: A Secret Society with the Chinese in China and India*. Batavia: Lange and Co., 1866.

————. Review of de Groot, *Het kongsiwezen van Borneo*. *Revue Coloniale Internationale* 1 (1885).

Schrieke, B. O. "De stichting van Pontianak." *Notulen van de Algemeene en Directie-vergaderingen van het Bataviaasch Genootschap van Kunsten en Wetenschappen* 59 (1921).

Schulze, Fritz. *Die Chroniken von Sambas und Mempawah: Einheimische Quellen zur Geschichte West-Kalimantans*. Heidelberg: Julius Groos, 1991.

Scott, James C. *Weapons of the Weak: Everyday Forms of Peasant Resistance*. New Haven: Yale University Press, 1985.

Sejarah kebangkitan nasional Daerah Kalimantan Barat. Jakarta: Departemen Pendidikan dan Kebudayaan, Pusat Penelitian Sejarah dan Budaya, Proyek Penelitian dan Pencatatan Kebudayaan Daerah, 1979.

Sellato, Bernard. "Myth, History and Modern Cultural Identity among Hunter-Gatherers: A Borneo Case." *Journal of Southeast Asian Studies* 24,1 (March 1993).

Senn van Basel, W. H. "Eene Chineesche nederzetting op Borneo's Westkust." *Tijdschrift voor Nederlandsch Indië* n.s., 31 (1874).

Shenghuobao chuangkan zhounian jiniankan [Sheng Huo Pao tenth anniversivary of publication, commemorative issue]. Jakarta: Sheng Huo Pao, 1955.

Siahaan, Harlem. *Golongan Tionghoa di Kalimantan Barat: Tinjauan Ekomonis Historis* Jakarta: Leknas-LIPI, mimeo, 1974.

————. "Konflik dan perlawanan kongsi Cina di Kalimantan Barat 1770-1854." PhD dissertation, Universitas Gadjah Mada, 1994.

————. "Konflik dan perlawanan kongsi Cina di Kalimantan Barat, 1770-1854." *Prisma* 23,12 (1994).

Siahaan, Pulo, and Ruth Daroesman. "West Kalimantan: Uneven Development?" In *Unity and Diversity, Regional Economic Development in Indonesia since 1970*, edited by Hal Hill. Singapore: Oxford University Press, 1989.

Siaran Perangkaan Tahunan Sarawak. [Kuching]: Jabatan Perangkaan Malaysia, Cawangan Sarawak, 1990.

Siauw Giok Tjhan. *Lima jaman perwujudan integrasi wajar.* Amsterdam: Yayasan Teratai, 1981.

Siauw Tiong Djin. *Siauw Giok Tjhan: Perjuangan seorang Patriot membangun Nasion Indonesia dan Masyarakat Bhineka Tunggal Ika.* Jakarta: Hasta Mitra, 1999.

Skinner, G. William. "The Chinese Minority." In *Indonesia,* edited by Ruth T. McVey. New Haven: Human Relations Area Files, 1963.

_____. *Report on the Chinese in Southeast Asia.* Ithaca: Cornell University Southeast Asia Program, 1950.

Smith, Anthony D. *The Ethnic Origins of Nations.* Oxford: Blackwell, 1986.

Smith, F. Andrew. "Missionaries, Mariners and Merchants: Overlooked British Travellers to West Borneo in the Early 19th Century." Paper presented to Seventh Biennial Conference, Borneo Research Council, Kota Kinabalu, July 15-18, 2002.

Soedarto. *Sejarah Daerah Kalimantan Barat.* Pontianak: Proyek Penelitian dan Pencatatan Kebudayaan Daerah, 1978.

Soemadi. *Peranan Kalimantan Barat dalam menghadapi subversi komunis Asia Tenggara. Suatu tinjauan internasional terhadap gerakan komunis dari sudut pertahanan wilayah khususnya Kalimantan Barat.* [Pontianak]: Yayasan Tanjungpura, rev. ed. 1974.

Somers, Mary F. "Peranakan Chinese Politics in Indonesia." PhD dissertation, Cornell University, 1965. *See also* Heidhues.

Spence, Jonathan D. *God's Chinese Son: The Taiping Heavenly Kingdom of Hong Xiuquan.* New York and London: W. W. Norton, 1996.

Stadt, P. A. van de. *Hakka Woordenboek.* Batavia: Landsdrukkerij, 1912.

St. John, Horace. *The Indian Archipelago: Its History and Present State.* London: Longman, Brown, Green, and Longmans, 1853.

St. John, Spenser. *Life in the Forests of the Far East.* London: Smith, Elder and Co., 1862, repr. Singapore: Oxford University Press, 1986.

Sturler, W. L. de. *Voorlezing over den innerlijken rijkdom onzer Oost-Indische bezittingen in verband met den oorsprong en den aard der zedelijke en maatschappelijke gesteldheid der bevolking van die gewesten.* Groningen: J. Oomkens, 1849.

Subangun, Emmanuel. "Keturunan Cina di Kalimantan Barat." *Kompas* (July 5, 1987)

Subianto, Benny. "The Politics of Chinese Indonesians after the Fall of Soeharto's New Order." Jakarta, unpublished paper, 1999.

Suryadinata, Leo. *Eminent Indonesian Chinese: Biographical Sketches.* Singapore: Gunung Agung, rev. ed. 1981.

Tagliacozzo, Eric. "Onto the Coasts and into the Forest: Ramifications of the China Trade on the Ecological History of Northwest Borneo, 900-1900 CE." Paper for "Environmental Change in Native and Colonial Histories of Borneo" conference, Leiden, July 2000.

Tan Yeok Seong. "Notes and Views on Sambas Treasures." In *Archeological Supplement* No. 2. Singapore: Nanyang Book Company, 1948.

Tan, Mely G., and Leo Suryadinata "The 'Special Project National Schools' in Djakarta." Paper presented to the 23rd Congress of Orientalists, Canberra, January 1971.

Tangdililing, Andreas Barung. "Partisipasi politik keturunan Cina di Kalimantan Barat: Kasus Singkawang, Kabupaten Sambas." *Jurnal Ilmu Politik* 6 (1990).

_____. "Perkawinan antar suku bangsa sebagai salah satu wahana pembauran bangsa: Studi kasus perkawinan antara orang Daya dengan keturunan Cina di Kacamatan Samalantan, Kabupaten Sambas, Kalimantan Barat." PhD dissertation, Universitas Indonesia, 1993.

Tarling, Nicholas. *Anglo-Dutch Rivalry in the Malay World, 1780-1824.* Cambridge: Cambridge University Press, 1962.

_____. *Piracy and Politics in the Malay World.* Melbourne: F. W. Cheshire, 1963.

Temminck, C. J. *Coup-d'oeil général sur les possessions néerlandaises dans l'Inde archipélagique*. Vol. 2. Leiden: Arnz, 1847.

_____. "The Geographical Group of Borneo." *Journal of the Indian Archipelago* 2 (1848).

The Siauw Giap. "Rural Unrest in West Kalimantan: The Chinese Uprising in 1914." In *Leyden Studies in Sinology* 15, edited by W. L. Idema. Leiden: E. J. Brill, 1981.

Tien Ju-k'ang. *The Chinese of Sarawak*. London: The London School of Economics, Monographs on Social Anthropology, 1953.

Tim Peneliti Fakultas Hukum Universitas Tanjungpura. *Tingkat kesadaran hukum warganegara Indonesia keturunan Cina dalam hubungannya dengan Surat Bukti Kewarganegaraan Republik Indonesia (SBKRI)*. Pontianak: Departemen Pendidikan dan Kebudayaan, Universitas Tanjungpura, 1983.

Tjen Fo-Sang. *Eenvoudig leerboekje voor het Hakka-Chineesch*. Mentok: Typ Bankatinwinning, 2nd printing, 1930.

Tobias, J. H. "Bevolkingsstaat der verschillende rijken op de Westkust van Borneo." *De Nederlands Hermes* 3,12 (1828).

Tobing, K. *Kalimantan Barat*. Bandung: Masa Baru, ca. 1952.

"De toenemende verwikkelingen op Borneo." *Tijdschrift voor Nederlandsch Indië* 15,2 (1853).

Toorop, C. G. "De krijgsverrichtingen in de Chineesche districten." *Indisch Militair Tijdschrift* 2 (1932).

Touwen, [Lourens] Jeroen. "Chinese Trade and Credit in the Outer Islands of Indonesia 1900-1940." Paper presented to Association of South-East Asian Studies in the United Kingdom Conference, London, April 25-27, 1996.

Touwen, Lourens Jeroen. "Extremes in the Archipelago: Trade and Economic Development in the Outer Islands of Indonesia, 1900-1942." PhD dissertation, Leiden University, 1997.

"Trage gang der zaken op Borneo." *Tijdschrift voor Nederlandsch Indië* 16,2 (1854).

Trocki, Carl A. *Prince of Pirates: The Temenggongs and the Development of Johor and Singapore, 1784-1885*. Singapore: Singapore University Press for the Institute of Southeast Asian Studies, 1979.

_____. *Opium and Empire: Chinese Society in Colonial Singapore, 1800-1910*. Ithaca: Cornell University Press, 1991.

Tsuroka, Doug. "Plywood Play." *Far Eastern Economic Review* (June 30,1994).

Twang Peck Yang, *The Chinese Business Élite in Indonesia and the Transition to Independence 1940-1950*. Kuala Lumpur: Oxford University Press, 1998.

Uljée, G. L. *Handboek voor de Residentie Westerafdeeling van Borneo*. Weltevreden: N. V. Boekhandel Visser & Co., 1925.

_____. "Nog eens: De economische ontwikkeling van Nederlandsch-Borneo, in 't bijzonder von West-Borneo." *Indische Gids* 51,1 (1929).

_____. "Pontianak, zijn economische beteekenis." *Tijdschrift voor Economische Geographie* 22,4 (April 15, 1931).

Velden, Arn. J. H. van der. *De Roomsch-Katholieke Missie in Nederlandsch Oost-Indië, 1808-1908*. Nijmegen: L. C. G. Malmberg, 1908.

Verheul, A. "Ervaringen in oorlogstijd: Verslag van den ex-assistent-resident von Singkawang." Zeist, typescript, 1946.

"Verslag eener reis naar Montrado, gedaan in het jaar 1844." *Tijdschrift voor Neêrlands Indië* 9,3 (1847). [The author is probably D. L. Baumgart, Assistant Resident of Sambas in 1842-44].

"Verslag wegens de Nederlandsche bezittingen op de Noord-West Kust van Borneo." *De Nederlandsche Hermes* 4,9 (1829); 4,10 (1829). [repr. in English in "Memoir on the Residency."]

"De verwikkelingen van het Nederlandsch-Indisch Gouvernement met de Chineesche bevolking op Westelijk Borneo toegelicht." *Tijdschrift voor Nederlandsch Indië* 15,2 (1853). [The author is probably Willer, Resident of West Borneo; comments are by Major General Penning Nieuwland.]

Veth, P. J. *Borneo's Wester-Afdeeling: Geographisch, statistisch, historisch, vorafgegaan door eene algemeene schets des ganschen eilands.* Vol. 1. Zaltbommel: Joh. Nomanen Zoon, 1854.

_____. *Borneo's Wester-Afdeeling: Geographisch, statistisch, historisch, vorafgegaan door eene algemeene schets des ganschen eilands.* Vol. 2. Zaltbommel: Joh. Nomanen Zoon, 1856.

_____. "Voortzetting der beraadslaging over den tegenwoordigen toestand en entwikkeling der Buitenbezittingen: Borneo; Aanteekeningen." *Tijdschrift voor Nederlandsch Indië* 4,2 (1866).

Vleming, J. L. *Het Chineesche zakenleven in Nederlandsch-Indië.* Weltevreden: Landsdrukkerij, 1926.

Nederlandsch-Indië. *Uitkomsten der in de Maand November 1920 gehouden Volkstelling.* Part 2, tables. Batavia: Ruygrok & Co., 1922.

Nederl.-Indië, Departement van Economische Zaken. *Volkstelling 1930.* Vol. 7, *Chineezen en andere vreemde oosterlingen in Nederlandsch-Indië.* Batavia: Landsdrukkerij, 1935.

Waal, E. de. *Onze Indische Financien.* Vol. 8, *West Borneo,* edited by E. A. G. J. van Delden. The Hague: M. Nijhoff, 1907.

"Waarom het advies der kommissie voor de zaken van Borneo in 1851 niet gevolgd?" *Tijdschrift voor Nederlandsch Indië* 15,2 (1853).

Wadley, Reed L. "Reconsidering an Ethnic Label in Borneo: The 'Maloh' of West Kalimantan, Indonesia." *Bijdragen tot de Taal-, Land- en Volkenkunde* 156,1 (2000).

Wang Tai Peng, *The Origins of Chinese Kongsi.* Petaling Jaya, Pelanduk Publications, 1994.

_____. "The Word Kongsi: A Note." *Journal of the Malaysian Branch, Royal Asiatic Society* 52,1 (1979).

Ward, Barbara E. "A Hakka Kongsi in Borneo." *Journal of Oriental Studies* 1,2 (1954).

Ward, Ian, *The Killer They Called a God.* Singapore: Media Masters, 1992.

Ward, M. W., and R. G. Ward. "An Economic Survey of West Kalimantan." *Bulletin of Indonesian Economic Studies* 10,3 (1974).

Warren, James F. *The Sulu Zone, 1768-1898: The Dynamics of External Trade, Slavery, and Ethnicity in the Transformation of a Southeast Asian Maritime State.* Singapore: Singapore University Press, 1981.

Warta Kalimantan Barat 5,8/9 (July-August 1972).

Wati, Arena [pseudonym of Muhammad bin Abdul Biang]. *Memoir Arena Wati: Enda Gulingku.* Bangi: Penerbit Universiti Kebangsaan Malaysia, 1991.

_____. *Syair Perang Cina di Monterado.* Bangi: Penerbit Universiti Kebangsaan Malaysia, 1989.

Werdoyo, T. S. *Tan Jin Sing, dari Kapiten Cina sampai Bupati Yogyakarta.* Jakarta: Pustaka Utama Grafiti, 1990.

West Kalimantan Regional Tourism Office, Indonesia. *West Kalimantan.* n.p., ca. 1992. [official guide to Mandor monument, in English]

Wetterberg, Anna, Sudarno Sumarto, and Lant Pritchett. "A National Snapshot of the Social Impact of Indonesia's Crisis." *Bulletin of Indonesian Economic Studies* 35,3 (December 1999).

Widodo, Johannes. "The Pattern of Chinese Settlements in Western Kalimantan." *Journal of the South Seas Society* 54 (December 1999).

Willer, J. T. [T. J.]. "Eerste Proeve eener kronijk van Mampawa en Pontianak." *Tijdschrift voor Indische Taal-, Land- en Volkenkunde* 3 (1855) and 6 (n.s. 3) (1857).

Williams, Lea E. *Overseas Chinese Nationalism: The Genesis of the Pan-Chinese Movement in Indonesia, 1900-1916*. Glencoe: The Free Press, 1960.

Willmott, Donald E. *The National Status of the Chinese in Indonesia, 1900-1958*. Ithaca: Cornell University Modern Indonesia Project, Monograph Series, 1961.

Witschi, Hermann. *Christus siegt: Geschichte der Dajak-Mission auf Borneo*. Basel: Basler Missionsbuchhandlung, 1942.

Wolters, O. W. "Southeast Asia as a Southeast Asian Field of Study." *Indonesia* 59 (October 1994).

Wurtzburg, C. E. *Raffles of the Eastern Isles*, edited by Clifford Witting. London: Hodder and Stoughton, 1954.

Xie Feng. *Zhanhou Nanyang Huaqiao gaikuang; Xi Poneizhou zhibu* [Survey of the overseas Chinese in postwar Southeast Asia; section on West Borneo]. Singapore: n.p., 1947.

Yanis, M. *Kapal Terbang Sembilan: Kisah Pendudukan Jepang di Kalimantan Barat*. Pontianak: Yayasan Perguruan Panca Bhakti, 1983.

Joung [Young], J. W. "Then Soe Kim Njong, in de Westerafdeeling van Borneo bekend als Njonja Kapthai. In memoriam." *Bijdragen tot de Taal-, Land- en Volkenkunde* 37, 5. Ser. 3,2 (1888).

Young, J. W. "Bijdrage tot de geschiedenis van Borneo's Westerafdeeling." *Tijdschrift voor Indische Taal-, Land- en Volkenkunde* 38 (1895).

Yuan Bingling. *Chinese Democracies: A Study of the Kongsis of West Borneo (1776-1884)*. Leiden: Research School of Asian, African, and Amerindian Studies, CNWS, Universiteit Leiden, 2000.

Yunus, H. Ahmad et al., eds. *Upacara tradisional Daerah Kalimantan Barat*. Jakarta: Departemen Pendidikan dan Kebudayaan, Proyek Inventarisasi dan Dokumentasi Kebudayaan Daerah, 1985.

Zeedijk, Remco. "De Chinezen in West-Borneo tijdens de Japanse bezetting en de onafhankelijkheidsstrijd 1942-1949." Master's thesis, Free University of Amsterdam, 1994.

Zevenbergen, P. Marius van. "Verwoede brand te Singkawang." *Onze Missiën in Oost- en West-Indië* 9 (1926).

Zondervan, H. "De economische ontwikkeling van Nederlandsch-Borneo." *Indische Gids* 50 (1928).

INDEX

A

Abdurachman, Sultan of Pontianak 65
aliens: Chinese 237, 238-43, 267-68; Retail Trade Ban 238-40; residence ban 238
Air Mati 108
Amoy (Xiamen) 51
Amoy (Xiamen) University 190
Amoy-Amoy 254
Andresen, Major A. J. 87, 93, 96, 99, 102, 118-20
Anjungan 108, 111, 177, 182, 273-74; Dayak center in 251
Anjungan-Mandor-Menjalin triangle 246, 249-50
Anti-Nippon Society 222
Appanage 23-25, 35, 53, 75, 83, 109, 144, 147
Arabs 28, 69, 75, 130, 135, 150, 151
Army, Indonesian 243
Asikin, A 211-212
assimilation of Chinese 40-41, 255, 268-69, 270
Australian forces 206, 211, 212

B

Badan Komunikasi Urusan Cina 268
Bangka 12, 13, 21, 37-38, 50, 61, 153, 171
Bangkok 141
Banjarmasin 19, 71, 188, 199, 228; "Haga Conspiracy" in 203
Banten, Sultanate of 19, 20, 28, 71
Baperki 242
Batavia 82, 89, 125, 142; Chinese officers in 167; Chinese schools in 188-89; kongsi negotiations with 91-98, *passim*
Bau 89, 102-03, 231
Baumgardt, Assistant Resident D. L. 83
Belitang 71, 138
Belitung 12, 21, 37-38, 153, 170, 171
Bengkayang 68, 164-65, 182, 196; Lara kongsi 63, 99; pepper growing and trade 153, 231; under Dutch control 212
Bengkulen 157
benteng 99, 118-21
bilingualism. *See* language.
blockade, naval 85, 90-91, 96-98, 118
Boeckholtz, Commissioner J. van 74
borders 18-19; with Sarawak 18, 83, 103, 230-31; Thaikong-Lanfang border area 182. *See also* boundaries.

Borel, Henri 181-82
Borneo Koonan Hookudan 201
Borsumij 160
boundaries 17-19; crossing 33; ethnic 24, 194, 196. *See also* borders, ethnicity, *masuk Melayu*.
British 51; rivalry with Dutch 69, 80; rule 17, 47-48, 73; traders 50, 67
Bron de Vexela, Lt. Col. Le 168
Brooke, James, Rajah of Sarawak 84, 89, 92, 102-03
Brunei 17, 19, 29, 33, 41, 71, 84
Buddhism 258-59
Buduk 64, 66, 81, 87, 90, 98, 177
Bugis 28, 29, 69, 71, 109, 130, 135, 160; coconut plantings 150-152; ships, 50
Bunut 136
Burn, J. 48, 50, 51, 61, 68-69, 71-73, 78

C

Capgomeh 255, 268, 270-71. *See also* New Year, religion.
Catholic Church: missions 249-50, 275-76; schools 189-190; 237-38
Canton (Guangzhou) 51
Cantonese 31, 63, 192
cash crops 33, 127-61 *passim*
Chamber of Commerce (Siang Hwee) 177, 188, 190-92, 217-18, 223, 255; leader killed 207; and schools 237
Champa 41
Cheng Da Hung, Consul 218-28 *passim*
Chiang Kai-shek 219-20, 223, 224
Chiliu Tushuhui 223
China: Hakkas in 13, 38. *See also* Nationalist China, People's Republic of China.
Chinese General Associations 217-23, 255; and schools 225
Chinese traders 97, 126-58; in interior 140-42; postwar economy 213-217
"Chinese War" 120-21
Christianity, conversions to 258
citizenship: agreement with People's Republic of China on 240-42; Indonesian policy 219, 226-28; 240-42, 255-60, 260-68
civil registry 166-67, 226-27, 241
civil society 174
coconuts 112, 134, 143, 150-53, 158, 160; Chinese farmers of 231; copra 135, 151,

153; oil 135, 146, 151; postwar exports 214, 260-63; smuggling 214
coffee 128, 138
collaboration (with Japan) 210
Combanaire, Alolphe 137-138, 186
Communist Party of Indonesia (PKI) 243, 245, 246, 250, 276-77; influence among Dayaks 252
Communists: in China 192; suspected Communists denounced 219, 220; tendencies in Singkawang 223
conflicts (of kongsis) 63, 71, 76-77, 83, 85-120. *See also* Kongsi Wars.
Confrontation 243-45, 246
Confucianism 258-59
consul (of China) 182. *See also* Cheng Da Hung.
coolies 117-18, 214
copra. *See* coconuts.
corvée 100, 118, 123, 130, 176-78, 181-82; among Dayaks 24-25, 179, 181; Malays exempt 27

D
Daeng Menambun, Upu 24, 29. *See also Hikayat Upu Daeng Menambun.*
Daeng Pamase, Upu 29
Dapu 37, 63
Dayak "Raids" 246-52; 276
Dayak trails 53
Dayaks 20-29, 36, 43, 60, 71, 98, 129, 146, 157; conflict with Chinese 25, 55, 78, 83, 114, 117; credit relations with Chinese 61, 100, 127, 132, 140-42, 158, 161, 229-30; fighters in wartime 24, 78, 87, 98-100, 102-03, 109-11, 118; head-taking 111, 118; of *hulu* 52; Malay rule over 75; miners 77; missions among 275-76; politicization of 275-77; relations with Chinese 26-27, 33, 104, 109, 121-22, 130, 137, 150, 229; uprising against Japan 206; in Western sources 44-45. *See also* appanage, intermarriage, taxes.
Depression 131-32, 141-42, 153, 155-56, 160; effect on political activity 173, 188, 192, 194
direct rule 23-24, 75, 89, 105, 124, 164; of interior 137, 165
divide and rule 31
dulang 35
Dutch East India Company (VOC) 47-48, 61, 73
Dutch subjects 192, 219
Duymaer van Twist, Governor-General A. J. 93

E
economic specialization. *See* ethnicity.
economy, crisis in 253, 264
education, Chinese 14, 32; for girls 225. *See also* schools.
elections 269
emigration (of Chinese) 158; 239-40, 260, 263
Eng Tjong Kwee 94, 97, 169-170
ethnicity: economic specialization 22, 41, 265; and identity 21-22;

Europeans 43-44, 157, 165-66; inter-preters for Chinese (Officers for Chinese Affairs) 167, 173, 181-82, 187
explorers 44-45
exports 13, 19, 67, 155; gold 48, 50, 58. *See also* rubber, pepper, coconuts.

F
federal policy (of Dutch) 211, 228-29, 276
Foreign Asiatics (Orientals) 28, 33, 150, 157, 192. *See also* Arabs, Indians.
Fujian 31, 37, 38
Fengshun 36
fires in towns, 135, 165-166, 239, 249
Fosjoen (Tjoengthang) 55, 56, 63, 65, 77-79, 81-83, 91, 102; regent of 93; as state 59-60
forest products. *See* trade, forest products.

G
gambier 149, 153, 182
gold 19, 20, 33, 128; depletion 78, 84, 102, 105, 134, 169. *See also* mining organizations, technology.
Golkar 269
government policies 41, 163-65; Indonesian 43; New Order 185. *See also* citizenship, divide and rule, Suharto.
Groot, J. J. M. de 42, 60-61, 123-24
Guan Di (Guan Gong) 107, 113-14, 116, 122
Guan Yin 122
Guangdong 31, 37, 38, 63, 64
Guangxi 37
Guomindang 173, 181, 190-92, 195, 218-28 *passim*; oath 218-19
gutta percha 138, 144-45

H
Habok 93, 122
Haga, Colonel A. 112, 115-16
Haifeng 36
Hailu: Records of Overseas 42
Hainanese 31, 37, 192
Hakka 31-32, 36-39, 104, 135, 149, 190, 194; in Bau 89, 102-103; in Bengkayang 196; cultural and language persistence 264-66; and Dayaks 14; defined by language 13, 37; gender roles, women 35, 38, 132, 194, 253-54; and minorities (She) 39; in other islands 13-14; *pansanhok* 36, 63, 72, 77; pioneers 31, 37, 125, 133, 139; radical politics and nationalism 181, 183, 192, 221, 223; refugees 253-254. *See also* China, Hakkas in; *kapitan* of Hakkas, Taiping.
Han Chinese 31
Hasan, Bob 262
Hikayat Upu Daeng Menambung 23, 29
Ho Á Joen 170-71
Hoëvell, W. R. Baron von 26
Hokkien (Fujian) 31, 37, 40, 63, 168, 190
Hoklo (Fulao). *See* Teochiu.
Hong Tjin Nie 167-68
Hoppo (Hepo) 36, 64
hui 99
Huilai 36, 63
hulu-hilir (upstream/downstream) 19-21, 24, 48, 52, 53, 74, 141

I

immigration 58, 69, 79, 80, 128, 130-33, 260; Chinese organization of 61; of Chinese prohibited 102; illegal 212, 231; immigrants, Chinese (Sinkeh) 178-80, 194, 265; and indebtedness 61-62; Malay rulers 52; of women 35, 132-33, 148. *See also* transmigration.
India: influences 21
Indians 33, 150
indirect rule 123
Indonesian Revolution 219, 224
industry: Chinese predominance in 232
initiation (in kongsis) 58, 77, 112, 123, 181
intermarriage 26, 33-36, 67, 130, 132-33; assimilation of Dayak women 38-39; Chinese-Dayak 132-33, 149
Islam 21, 29; conversion to, 33, 259; Malays as Muslims, 20, 27. *See also masuk Melayu.*

J

Jakarta, May 1998 violence in 263
Jambi 157
Japan 146
Japanese 148, 157
Japanese Occupation 43, 173, 197-208, 231-32; economy under 199-200
Java 106, 166, 176; Chinese in 40, 75, 193; influence of 19; Java Bank 142; Java War 82; trade with 50, 142, 146, 151
Jawai 152
jelutung 144-145
Ji'nan (Chi Nan) School 187, 190
Jiayingzhou. *See* Meixian.
Jieyang 36, 64
Jintang 86, 98
Johor-Riau 21, 29. *See also* Riau.

K

Kakyo Toseikai 202, 207
Kampung Baru 65, 69, 72, 104, 116, 135, 146
kapitan 94-95, 148, 164, 167-68, 171, 173; in Batavia 167; of Hakkas 94-104, 169, 184-85; in Monterado 163. *See also* officers, Chinese.
kapthai 91, 95, 97, 115, 163, 167, 169, 171; of Lanfang 94, 100, 104, 106, 123-25, 184. *See also* Lioe A Sin.
kaptjong 171, 173
Kapuas River, 20, 69, 74, 136-39, 238; kongsi ceremony on 94-95; settlements on 171; Upper Kapuas (Hulu) 155, 252
Kater, Cornelis, Resident 44, 106-12, 114-15, 130, 132, 186
Kedah 21
Keibitai 201, 208
Kenpeitai 200, 201, 207
kinship, Chinese, 265
Kioe Liong Kongsi 99
kongsi 39-40, 52, 54-68, 72; conflicts among 56; democratic 124; kongsi towns 66-68, 72, 103, 108, 110-11; leadership 54, 60-61, 92-94, 105, 124; religious functions 58-59; shareholding 54-55, 61-63, 138; states 59-60, 90, 125, 191, 196; "village republics"

60-61. *See also* Chinese sources, Kongsi Wars, mining organizations.
kongsi hall or house. *See thang.*
Kongsi Wars 78; 85-125, 160; First 80-82; Second 29, 67-68, 85-102, 128, 175, 179; Third (Lanfang) 106-17, 179
Kopian 111, 113
KPM 142, 160-61; competitors 161
Kuala Mempawah 66, 72
Kuching 102, 198, 208
Kulor 98
Kwee Eng Hoe 173
Kwee Hoe Toan 167-70
Kwee Kom Beng 168-69

L

ladang 24, 33
lake district 71, 139
Landak 18, 19, 71-72, 99-100, 189; conflict with Lanfang 71, 84; Dayaks of 109, 177; development of 134, 147-49; panembahan 71-72, 84; temples in 186
Landak River 19, 69, 71, 103, 135
landholding 134, 158-60; Arabs 28; illegal occupation and "squatting" 134, 231-32; leases 159-60
Lanfang Futhang (Lo Fong Pak Hall) 104, 106, 184-85, 187, 221
Lanfang Kongsi 55-56, 58-63, 69, 89, 101, 175, 184; conflict with Landak 71, 84, 148; decline 84, 104-06, 128, 134, 164; history of 42, 64-65; reations with Dutch 80, 82, 95, 103-17. *See also* Mandor, Kongsi Wars.
Lanfanghui 64
language: bilingualism 36-37, 149, 167, 172, 193-94, 196, 265; of Dayaks 24; Indonesian speaking ability 256-57, 266-67; Malay 21, 193-94; speech groups 31-32; use of Indonesian (in schools) 225, 227, 255, 257-58. *See also* schools, Chinese.
laothai 91, 164, 169, 171, 173, 177
Lara 63, 68, 83, 98-100, 122, 164
Lay A Tjhok 172
leadership (Chinese) 32, 210, 217-24
Lee Kong Chian 224
Liao Eng Kheng 226
Liao Kang Sing 168, 172
Liao Njie Liong 98-102, 116
Lie Khoi Hiun 222, 225-26
Lim A Moy 167
Lim Moi Lioek 148, 181
Lim Nie Po 167
Lim Yong Swa 232
Limthian Kongsi (Buduk) 64
Lioe A Sin, Kapthai of Lanfang 94, 101, 104-06, 115, 124-25, 185; widow of 106, 108, 194
Lioe En Kwon 106
Lioe Liong Kwon 105
Lioe Pang Liong 107, 109, 112, 116
Lioe Tjong Sin 169
Liong Lioe Njie. *See* Lioe Pang Liong.
Little China 12-13
Lo Fong Pak (Luo Fangbo) 64, 104, 106-07, 113-14, 116
Lo Hsiang-lin 42

Long Kang Hwee 220-21
Lufeng 36, 63
Lumar 64, 78, 81, 87, 90, 98, 101-02, 118, 164
lumber industry 127, 146, 253, 262

M
Madura 176
Madurese 28, 100, 250, 251, 273-75
Majapahit 19, 28
majoor, title of Chinese officer 168
Makassar 29
Malay courts 27-28, 43, 141
Malay Peninsula 19-21, 29, 48, 78-79
Malay principalities 55, 60, 61, 105, 125
Malay rulers 53-54, 73-76, 109, 148, 163-65, 174-75; and Chinese immigration 52; in Japanese Occupation 198-99, 205-07; land rights 158-159; in Western sources 45
Malay traders 45, 130, 140, 146
Malaya 55, 143, 187, 208
Malaysia 18, 38; East 17; Federation of 17, 243, 244. *See also* Confrontation, Malaya, Malay Peninsula, Sarawak, Sabah.
mandarin oranges 127, 240, 260-62
Mandarin, use of 257-58, 266-67
Mandor 64, 77, 114, 118, 133-34, 152, 165, 186; Hakkas in 36; massacre and memorial 204, 207, 209, 276; violence in 246, 248-50; 273-74. *See also* Lanfang Kongsi.
mangkok merah 246
Mao Zedong 223
Mas Buyang 78
masuk Melayu 22, 27
Mecca 21
Meixian 36, 37, 63-64
Melaka 19
Mempawah 20, 67-69, 80; Dayak auxiliaries from 109, 111; in Kongsi Wars 115-17; Panembahan of 23, 29, 51, 64, 74, 78-79; rebellion in 180-82; road-building 179, 181; territory of 75, 103, 105, 159, 164-65
Mempawah River 108, 111
Menado 153
Mentidung 108-09, 115, 182
Milburn, W. 67
missions and missionaries 44-45, 183, 189; to Dayaks 190; Methodist 190. *See also* Catholic Church, Christianity.
Monterado 54-56, 65-68, 130, 134, 163-64, 172-73, 182, 186; agriculture in 150-51, 153; conflict in 77-83, 85-124; history of 42-43, 62-64. *See also* Thaikong Kongsi, Fosjoen.
Mouw, Officer for Chinese Affairs 181, 191
Müller, Georg, Resident of Sambas 79-80

N
Nahuys van Burgst, Commissioner A. G. 32, 80
Nanga Badau 137, 238
Nanga Pinoh 136, 146
Napoleonic Wars. *See* British, rule.
nationalism, Chinese 176-77, 181, 183-87, 191, 211; among immigrants 178, 265; Indonesian 201, 211

Nationalist China (Republic of) 211, 218-20, 224, 228, 237
native rulers. *See* Malay rulers.
natural products, trade in. *See* trade, forest products.
naturalization 241-42, 259-60
New Year, Chinese 80, 97
Ng Ngiap Kan 207
Ng Ngiap Lian 217, 237
Ng Ngiap Soen 202, 207
Ngabang 73, 84, 109, 148-49, 152
Ngee Hin society 55, 99-100, 107
Ngee Hin-Lanfang Kongsi 100
NICA (Netherlands Indies Civil Administration) 208, 211
NIGIEO 214-216
Nisshinkai 200, 205
North Borneo 153. *See also* Sabah.

O
occupations of Chinese 66-68, 149-50
Oevang Oeray 250, 276
officers, Chinese 75, 148, 163, 167-69, 171-78, 264, 269. *See also* kapitan, kapthai, kaptjong, laothai.
oil palm 252, 260, 264, 277
opium 66-69 *passim*, 101-02, 141; Chinese dealing in 235; opium farm 75, 93-94, 97, 104-05, 124, 168-71, 174-76; smuggling 78, 85-86. *See also* revenue farms.
organizations 39-40; community, Chinese 183-92, 217-26, 264, 270; gold-mining 18, 52, 72; nationalist 201. *See also* kongsi, Chamber of Commerce, reading rooms.

P
Pa Gunang 109, 112
Pakoktin 116
Palembang 19, 33, 157, 175
Palm, W. A. 48, 61
Pangeran Anom 53-54
Pangeran Bendahara 95
Pangeran Jaya 83
Pangeran Ratu Tua Mangkunegara 85
Pangestu, Prayogo 262n
Paniraman 53
pansanhok. *See* Hakkas, *pansanhok*.
Partai Bhinekka Tunggal Ika 269
Partai Dayak 276
Partai Demokrat Indonesia (PDI) 269
Partai Nasionalis Indonesia (PNI) 276
Partindo 276
pass system 177, 182-183
Pasukan Gerilya Rakyat Sarawak 244
Pemangkat 136, 151-52, 164-65, 173, 190, 194; battle for 89-90, 240; Chinese General Association 223; economic role 68, 72, 81, 215, 260, 261; fire 239, 249; resettlement 253
Pemuda Muhammadijah 205
Penjagaan Keamanan Umum 211-212
People's Republic of China 223, 224, 228, 237, 240, 250; and Alien Retail Trade Ban 239-240; citizenship question 227; Indonesian relations with 243

pepper 33, 128, 138, 149, 182; trade and smuggling 230-31; white 153
peranakan 188-89, 192-94, 266
Perigi 84, 147
Persatuan Tionghoa 228
petompang 36, 194
Phong Seak 172
Piracy 28, 45, 47, 69, 74
Pontianak 50, 114, 116, 173, 175, 183, 185, 193; center of trade and industry 130, 134-37, 143, 149-53, 157; Chinese schools in 187-88, 190; Chinese settlers in 31-33, 36-37, 68-69; Chinese organizations 192, 217-22; during conflict with Thaikong 91-97; fires 166; founding of 65; Japanese attack 197-98; relations with Lanfang 103-07; Sultanate of 28, 73-75, 84, 95, 98, 109, 194, 207, 125
Pontianak Affair 203-10, 212
population 128-30, 212-13, 256-57, 259-60; Chinese, distribution and dispersal 18, 131, 133-39, 147-49, 171; decline 105
Prediger, C. J., Resident of Mempawah 79
Prehn, R. C. van, Assistant Resident of Sambas 85, 87, 95, 116
press, Chinese, 208, 219, 220-21, 225
pribumi 28
Prins, Commissioner A. 92, 95, 118, 175
Pulau Madjang
Putus Sibau, 136-37

Q
quarter system. *See* settlements.

R
Raffles, T. S., Lt. Governor 68
Ramadan 184
rattan 143, 145
reading clubs 177, 181, 190-92, 195
rebellions of 1912-1914 176-83
refugees 88-89, 99-100, 102-03, 252-55
religion, Chinese popular 96, 114, 264; gods 93, 122, 183; in kongsi 58-59; New Year 80, 184; Sanshan guowang 122. *See also* Confucianism, Buddhism, Taoism.
remittances to China 142, 196
revenue farms 75, 76, 85, 150, 171, 175. *See also* opium.
Riau 12, 20, 29
rice: imports 141, 156. *See also ladang, sawah.*
rivers 20; blocking of 111-12
road building 100, 111, 156, 178-79, 181-82, 252
Rochussen, J. J., Governor-General 25-26, 85
rubber 134, 145, 149, 153-58, 160; Chinese farmers 231; export tax on 155; industry 135, 260-63; in Japanese Occupation 198, 199-200; smuggling 214-16; trade and traders 224, 229-30, 260-63
ruko 257, 268-69

S
Sabah (North Borneo) 17
sago 17, 153
Saigon 141

salt 50, 52, 64, 72, 75, 78, 86, 91, 118, 137-42 *passim,* 147, 172
Sam Tiam Fui 99, 107, 115
Sambas 73-74, 79-80, 83, 157, 159, 164-65, 167-68, 193; Assistant Resident of 78, 90, 116; fire in 249; and kongsis 51, 53, 64, 72, 85, 87, 98; in Kongsi Wars 85-90, 94, 97, 103, 116;. Sultan of 51, 53, 73-74, 91-92, 98, 163; town 82. *See also* van Prehn.
Samtiaokioe Kongsi 55-57, 63, 66, 89-93, 101-03, 116; former territory 164; hostility to Thaikong 87, 96, 77-81
Sanggau 71, 136, 273
Sanggauledo 153, 245, 246, 249, 251, 273
Sarawak 68, 83-84, 96, 100-03, 113, 130, 153; cultural influences 265; insurgents (PGRS) 244; and Samtiaokioe 89, 91-92; smuggling 216, 231, 246
Sarawak Rebellion of 1857 102-03
sawah 27, 33, 68, 149, 150, 152
Schaank, S. H. 42-43, 63, 65
Schalk, van der, Resident 158
Schlegel, Gustaaf 123
schools, Chinese 66, 132, 150, 184-90, 199, 223, 255, 264; closed to Indonesian citizens 236-38; postwar expansion and control 224-26, 236, 266; teaching in Mandarin 187, 266. *See also* education, language.
schools, Western 188-89; Hollands-Chinese School 188-89, 196
schoolteachers 132, 150, 186
Sebadau 71
Sebangkau 66
Sebawi 89, 186
"secret societies" 55, 58, 62, 142, 191, 211; and kongsis 99-102, 104-05, 107, 114-15, 123; and rebellions of 1912-1914 176-78, 180-81
Sedau 53, 86, 90
Sekadau 139, 190-91
Selakau 53, 68, 72; 83, 98
Semarang, Resident of 73
Seminis 51, 64, 81, 89, 164
Sepang 64, 81-94 *passim,* 98, 100, 186
settlements: quarter system 179, 182, 252; restrictions on Chinese 26, 38-39, 100, 140, 158
shareholding. *See* kongsis, shareholding.
Siak 21
Siam 50, 69, 78, 86, 141
Siantan 69, 116
Sichuan 37
Silat 136
Silsilah Raja-Raja Sambas 29
Singapore 50, 92, 107, 123, 144, 161; focus of trade and credit 39, 78-79, 141-51 *passim,* 231, 265; political and cultural influence 184, 188, 190, 222, 225, 265; rubber trade 214-16
Singkawang 67-68, 82, 136, 153, 157, 159, 183-84, 190; administration 164-65, 172-73; Dutch reoccupation of 212; kongsi harbor 64, 66, 72, 133-34; in Kongsi Wars 98-102; language spoken 193-94; politics 181, 216-17, 222-24; refugees 240, 253; *thang* 98-99

Singkawang River 121
Sino-Japanese War 196
Sintang 71, 136, 138, 146, 163, 186, 190-91; Dayak troubles 98
Sjipngfoen Kongsi 81, 101. *See also* Lumar
Sjongbok 93, 95, 122.
Sjong-Ha-Bok Kongsoe 95
Smuggling 13, 72, 78, 83, 85-86, 93, 110, 169; in Japanese Occupation 200; postwar 215-16. *See also* rubber, opium, salt.
society, Chinese 31-37; three groups 72-73. *See also* speech groups, organizations, leadership.
Soemadi, Lt. Col. 250
Soeng A Tjap 184-85
Soeng Kap Sen 181-82
Song Assam 168
Song Dynasty 37
Sorg, Lt.Col. 89
sources: Chinese 13, 41-43, 64; Dayak 27; Western 44-45
South- and East Borneo 17-18, 157
Spice Islands 47
Srivijaya 19
Stuers, Lt.Col. H. J. J. L. de 81
Suharto 245, 255-59, 277; family 261-62
Sukadana 19, 20, 28-29, 133, 152
Sukarno 243-44, 276
Sukarnoputri, Megawati 269
suku 271
Sulawesi, 21, 28, 194
Sumatra 19-21, 29, 43-44, 48; East 12, 171; South 157
Sun Yatsen 181, 192, 218, 224
Sungai Duri 51, 78-79, 152, 175
Sungai Durian (airfield) 209, 232
Sungai Kakap 150
Sungai Peniti 65, 66, 103, 111
Sungai Pinyu 53, 72, 80, 105, 108, 111, 164, 168; in Dayak "Raids" 248
Sungai Purun 110-11, 152, 184
Sungai Raya 53, 56, 80-81, 175
Sungai Terap 103
Supardjo, Brigadier Gen. M. S. 243-45
surname associations (*she*) 253
Swatow (Shantou) 31
Syair Perang Cina di Monterado 29, 117-18, 122
Syarif Kassim, Sultan of Pontianak 74-75

T
Taiping Rebellion 32, 118, 120-21
Taiwan 228, 239, 268; brides 254. *See also* Nationalist China, Guomindang.
Tan Djin Sing 32
Tan Kah Kee 224
Tang Dynasty 41
Taoism 58
Taoism 96
taxes 78, 100, 123, 174-76, 181, 183; by Chamber of Commerce 188, 218; Chinese-Dayak 53, 60; of Chinese for Malay rulers 104; of Dayaks by Malays 24-25, 52, 74, 144; on emigration 52, 172, 175; export tax on rubber 155; head tax on Chinese 75-76, 79, 82-83, 100, 104, 130, 172, 175; on

immigration 69, 132, 180; on imports 175; in Japanese Occupation 202; property tax 175-76. *See also* appanage.
Tayan 71, 136, 179
technology, gold mining 52, 138
tempayan 41
temples, Chinese 68, 82, 93, 113-14, 183-86, 257
tengkawang 146-48
Teochiu (Chaozhou, Hoklo) 31-32, 36-37, 73, 115, 187, 192, 265; in Pontianak 14, 31-32, 72, 125, 135; officers 168
Thaikong Kongsi 42, 56, 60-83 *passim*, 120-22, 124, 170; conflict with Dutch 86-95, 98, 100-02, 130, 168; conflict with Samtiaokioe 96. *See also* Kongsi Wars, Monterado.
thang (ting) 66-67, 81, 98-99, 101-02, 106-09, 113-15; fortification of 119, 121
Then Kie San 184
Then Sioe Kim. *See* widow, Lioe A Sin.
Then Sioe Lin 104, 169, 185
Thien Thi Foei 64
Tiandihui 107
Tianhou 66, 122
Tianshi 122
Tianyu 122
tiko 65, 104; Tiko Jengut 65
Tingzhou 31
Tiong Hoa Hwe Koan 188
Tja Mien 95
Tjang Ping 91-97, 120, 169-70
Tjen Siong Tjhong 223
Tjhen Tjhong-hin 207
Tjia Tjeng Siang 173, 179
Tjilik Riwut 235n, 276
tjoengthang (zongting) 65
toapekong (Dabogong) 66, 95-96, 101,103, 113, 122, 185-86
Tobias, Commissioner J. H. 77, 81
Toho 101
Tokeitai 201, 207-08
Tongmenghui 181, 191-92
trade 20-21, 78; Chinese domination of 69, 73; Chinese networks in interior 136-139, 165; 253, 260, 264; Chinese traders 127-28, 174, 229-30; forest products 36, 41-42, 50, 125, 128, 137, 141-47, 155, 160, 175; of kongsis 64; and tribute 24, 28. *See also* smuggling, piracy.
translators, Chinese 32, 168, 173-74
transmigration 262-63, 274
Tuhfat al Nafis 29

V
Vetter, Lt. Col. J. A. 108-09, 111-12, 123
Vietnam 41, 142
VOC. *See* Dutch East India Company.
Vogel, Henry de, Resident 172-73, 176-82, 252

W
Wahid, Abdurrahman 259
warfare, 117-122
wayang (theater), 184
Wehry, Geo., 160

West Borneo Council, 229
Willer, T. J., Resident, 85-86, 89-90, 92, 94-96, 98
women, Chinese: dress, 34-35, 67-68, 193; in trade, 34-35, 67
women, Dayak. *See* Dayaks
Woo, Peter, 220
World War II, 146, 160, 197-210. *See also* Japanese Occupation
Wu Tung Ping, 226

X
Xie Qinggao, 42

SOUTHEAST ASIA PROGRAM PUBLICATIONS
Cornell University

Studies on Southeast Asia

Number 35   *Nationalism and Revolution in Indonesia*, George McTurnan Kahin, intro. Benedict R. O'G. Anderson (reprinted from 1952 edition, Cornell University Press, with permission). 2003. 530 pp. ISBN 0-87727-734-6.

Number 34   *Golddiggers, Farmers, and Traders in the "Chinese Districts" of West Kalimantan, Indonesia*, Mary Somers Heidhues. 2003. 316 pp. ISBN 0-87727-733-8

Number 33   *Opusculum de Sectis apud Sinenses et Tunkinenses (A Small Treatise on the Sects among the Chinese and Tonkinese): A Study of Religion in China and North Vietnam in the Eighteenth Century*, Father Adriano de St. Thecla, trans. Olga Dror, with Mariya Berezovska. 2002. 363 pp. ISBN 0-87727-732-X.

Number 32   *Fear and Sanctuary: Burmese Refugees in Thailand*, Hazel J. Lang. 2002. 204 pp. ISBN 0-87727-731-1.

Number 31   *Modern Dreams: An Inquiry into Power, Cultural Production, and the Cityscape in Contemporary Urban Penang, Malaysia*, Beng-Lan Goh. 2002. 225 pp. ISBN 0-87727-730-3.

Number 30   *Violence and the State in Suharto's Indonesia*, ed. Benedict R. O'G. Anderson. 2001. Second printing, 2002. 247 pp. ISBN 0-87727-729-X.

Number 29   *Studies in Southeast Asian Art: Essays in Honor of Stanley J. O'Connor*, ed. Nora A. Taylor. 2000. 243 pp. Illustrations. ISBN 0-87727-728-1.

Number 28   *The Hadrami Awakening: Community and Identity in the Netherlands East Indies, 1900-1942*, Natalie Mobini-Kesheh. 1999. 174 pp. ISBN 0-87727-727-3.

Number 27   *Tales from Djakarta: Caricatures of Circumstances and their Human Beings*, Pramoedya Ananta Toer. 1999. 145 pp. ISBN 0-87727-726-5.

Number 26   *History, Culture, and Region in Southeast Asian Perspectives*, rev. ed., O. W. Wolters. 1999. 275 pp. ISBN 0-87727-725-7.

Number 25   *Figures of Criminality in Indonesia, the Philippines, and Colonial Vietnam*, ed. Vicente L. Rafael. 1999. 259 pp. ISBN 0-87727-724-9.

Number 24   *Paths to Conflagration: Fifty Years of Diplomacy and Warfare in Laos, Thailand, and Vietnam, 1778-1828*, Mayoury Ngaosyvathn and Pheuiphanh Ngaosyvathn. 1998. 268 pp. ISBN 0-87727-723-0.

Number 23   *Nguyễn Cochinchina: Southern Vietnam in the Seventeenth and Eighteenth Centuries*, Li Tana. 1998. Second printing, 2002. 194 pp. ISBN 0-87727-722-2.

Number 22   *Young Heroes: The Indonesian Family in Politics*, Saya S. Shiraishi. 1997. 183 pp. ISBN 0-87727-721-4.

Number 21   *Interpreting Development: Capitalism, Democracy, and the Middle Class in Thailand*, John Girling. 1996. 95 pp. ISBN 0-87727-720-6.

Number 20   *Making Indonesia*, ed. Daniel S. Lev, Ruth McVey. 1996. 201 pp. ISBN 0-87727-719-2.

Number 19   *Essays into Vietnamese Pasts*, ed. K. W. Taylor, John K. Whitmore. 1995. 288 pp. ISBN 0-87727-718-4.

Number 18   *In the Land of Lady White Blood: Southern Thailand and the Meaning of History*, Lorraine M. Gesick. 1995. 106 pp. ISBN 0-87727-717-6.

Number 17   *The Vernacular Press and the Emergence of Modern Indonesian Consciousness*, Ahmat Adam. 1995. 220 pp. ISBN 0-87727-716-8.

Number 16   *The Nan Chronicle*, trans., ed. David K. Wyatt. 1994. 158 pp. ISBN 0-87727-715-X.

Number 15   *Selective Judicial Competence: The Cirebon-Priangan Legal Administration, 1680–1792*, Mason C. Hoadley. 1994. 185 pp. ISBN 0-87727-714-1.

Number 14   *Sjahrir: Politics and Exile in Indonesia*, Rudolf Mrázek. 1994. 536 pp. ISBN 0-87727-713-3.

Number 13   *Fair Land Sarawak: Some Recollections of an Expatriate Officer*, Alastair Morrison. 1993. 196 pp. ISBN 0-87727-712-5.

Number 12   *Fields from the Sea: Chinese Junk Trade with Siam during the Late Eighteenth and Early Nineteenth Centuries*, Jennifer Cushman. 1993. 206 pp. ISBN 0-87727-711-7.

Number 11   *Money, Markets, and Trade in Early Southeast Asia: The Development of Indigenous Monetary Systems to AD 1400*, Robert S. Wicks. 1992. 2nd printing 1996. 354 pp., 78 tables, illus., maps. ISBN 0-87727-710-9.

Number 10   *Tai Ahoms and the Stars: Three Ritual Texts to Ward Off Danger*, trans., ed. B. J. Terwiel, Ranoo Wichasin. 1992. 170 pp. ISBN 0-87727-709-5.

Number 9   *Southeast Asian Capitalists*, ed. Ruth McVey. 1992. 2nd printing 1993. 220 pp. ISBN 0-87727-708-7.

Number 8   *The Politics of Colonial Exploitation: Java, the Dutch, and the Cultivation System*, Cornelis Fasseur, ed. R. E. Elson, trans. R. E. Elson, Ary Kraal. 1992. 2nd printing 1994. 266 pp. ISBN 0-87727-707-9.

Number 7   *A Malay Frontier: Unity and Duality in a Sumatran Kingdom*, Jane Drakard. 1990. 215 pp. ISBN 0-87727-706-0.

Number 6   *Trends in Khmer Art*, Jean Boisselier, ed. Natasha Eilenberg, trans. Natasha Eilenberg, Melvin Elliott. 1989. 124 pp., 24 plates. ISBN 0-87727-705-2.

Number 5   *Southeast Asian Ephemeris: Solar and Planetary Positions, A.D. 638–2000*, J. C. Eade. 1989. 175 pp. ISBN 0-87727-704-4.

Number 3   *Thai Radical Discourse: The Real Face of Thai Feudalism Today*, Craig J. Reynolds. 1987. 2nd printing 1994. 186 pp. ISBN 0-87727-702-8.

Number 1   *The Symbolism of the Stupa*, Adrian Snodgrass. 1985. Revised with index, 1988. 3rd printing 1998. 469 pp. ISBN 0-87727-700-1.

SEAP Series

Number 19   *Gender, Household, State: Đổi Mới in Việt Nam*, ed. Jayne Werner and Danièle Bélanger. 2002. 151 pp. ISBN 0-87727-137-2.

Number 18   *Culture and Power in Traditional Siamese Government*, Neil A. Englehart. 2001. 130 pp. ISBN 0-87727-135-6.

Number 17   *Gangsters, Democracy, and the State*, ed. Carl A. Trocki. 1998. Second printing, 2002. 94 pp. ISBN 0-87727-134-8.

Number 16   *Cutting across the Lands: An Annotated Bibliography on Natural Resource Management and Community Development in Indonesia, the Philippines, and Malaysia*, ed. Eveline Ferretti. 1997. 329 pp. ISBN 0-87727-133-X.

Number 15   *The Revolution Falters: The Left in Philippine Politics after 1986*, ed. Patricio N. Abinales. 1996. Second printing, 2002. 182 pp. ISBN 0-87727-132-1.

Number 14   *Being Kammu: My Village, My Life*, Damrong Tayanin. 1994. 138 pp., 22 tables, illus., maps. ISBN 0-87727-130-5.

Number 13   *The American War in Vietnam*, ed. Jayne Werner, David Hunt. 1993. 132 pp. ISBN 0-87727-131-3.

Number 12   *The Political Legacy of Aung San*, ed. Josef Silverstein. Revised edition 1993. 169 pp. ISBN 0-87727-128-3.

Number 10   *Studies on Vietnamese Language and Literature: A Preliminary Bibliography*, Nguyen Dinh Tham. 1992. 227 pp. ISBN 0-87727-127-5.

Number 9   *A Secret Past*, Dokmaisot, trans. Ted Strehlow. 1992. 2nd printing 1997. 72 pp. ISBN 0-87727-126-7.

Number 8   *From PKI to the Comintern, 1924–1941: The Apprenticeship of the Malayan Communist Party*, Cheah Boon Kheng. 1992. 147 pp. ISBN 0-87727-125-9.

Number 7   *Intellectual Property and US Relations with Indonesia, Malaysia, Singapore, and Thailand*, Elisabeth Uphoff. 1991. 67 pp. ISBN 0-87727-124-0.

Number 6   *The Rise and Fall of the Communist Party of Burma (CPB)*, Bertil Lintner. 1990. 124 pp. 26 illus., 14 maps. ISBN 0-87727-123-2.

Number 5   *Japanese Relations with Vietnam: 1951–1987*, Masaya Shiraishi. 1990. 174 pp. ISBN 0-87727-122-4.

Number 3   *Postwar Vietnam: Dilemmas in Socialist Development*, ed. Christine White, David Marr. 1988. 2nd printing 1993. 260 pp. ISBN 0-87727-120-8.

Number 2   *The Dobama Movement in Burma (1930–1938)*, Khin Yi. 1988. 160 pp. ISBN 0-87727-118-6.

Translation Series

Volume 4   *Approaching Suharto's Indonesia from the Margins*, ed. Takashi Shiraishi. 1994. 153 pp. ISBN 0-87727-403-7.

Volume 3   *The Japanese in Colonial Southeast Asia*, ed. Saya Shiraishi, Takashi Shiraishi. 1993. 172 pp. ISBN 0-87727-402-9.

Volume 2   *Indochina in the 1940s and 1950s*, ed. Takashi Shiraishi, Motoo Furuta. 1992. 196 pp. ISBN 0-87727-401-0.

Volume 1   *Reading Southeast Asia*, ed. Takashi Shiraishi. 1990. 188 pp. ISBN 0-87727-400-2.

CORNELL MODERN INDONESIA PROJECT PUBLICATIONS

Cornell University

Number 75   *A Tour of Duty: Changing Patterns of Military Politics in Indonesia in the 1990s.* Douglas Kammen and Siddharth Chandra. 1999. 99 pp. ISBN 0-87763-049-6.

Number 74   *The Roots of Acehnese Rebellion 1989–1992,* Tim Kell. 1995. 103 pp. ISBN 0-87763-040-2.

Number 73   *"White Book" on the 1992 General Election in Indonesia,* trans. Dwight King. 1994. 72 pp. ISBN 0-87763-039-9.

Number 72   *Popular Indonesian Literature of the Qur'an,* Howard M. Federspiel. 1994. 170 pp. ISBN 0-87763-038-0.

Number 71   *A Javanese Memoir of Sumatra, 1945–1946: Love and Hatred in the Liberation War,* Takao Fusayama. 1993. 150 pp. ISBN 0-87763-037-2.

Number 70   *East Kalimantan: The Decline of a Commercial Aristocracy,* Burhan Magenda. 1991. 120 pp. ISBN 0-87763-036-4.

Number 69   *The Road to Madiun: The Indonesian Communist Uprising of 1948,* Elizabeth Ann Swift. 1989. 120 pp. ISBN 0-87763-035-6.

Number 68   *Intellectuals and Nationalism in Indonesia: A Study of the Following Recruited by Sutan Sjahrir in Occupation Jakarta,* J. D. Legge. 1988. 159 pp. ISBN 0-87763-034-8.

Number 67   *Indonesia Free: A Biography of Mohammad Hatta,* Mavis Rose. 1987. 252 pp. ISBN 0-87763-033-X.

Number 66   *Prisoners at Kota Cane,* Leon Salim, trans. Audrey Kahin. 1986. 112 pp. ISBN 0-87763-032-1.

Number 65   *The Kenpeitai in Java and Sumatra,* trans. Barbara G. Shimer, Guy Hobbs, intro. Theodore Friend. 1986. 80 pp. ISBN 0-87763-031-3.

Number 64   *Suharto and His Generals: Indonesia's Military Politics, 1975–1983,* David Jenkins. 1984. 4th printing 1997. 300 pp. ISBN 0-87763-030-5.

Number 62   *Interpreting Indonesian Politics: Thirteen Contributions to the Debate, 1964–1981,* ed. Benedict Anderson, Audrey Kahin, intro. Daniel S. Lev. 1982. 3rd printing 1991. 172 pp. ISBN 0-87763-028-3.

Number 60   *The Minangkabau Response to Dutch Colonial Rule in the Nineteenth Century,* Elizabeth E. Graves. 1981. 157 pp. ISBN 0-87763-000-3.

Number 59   *Breaking the Chains of Oppression of the Indonesian People: Defense Statement at His Trial on Charges of Insulting the Head of State, Bandung, June 7–10, 1979,* Heri Akhmadi. 1981. 201 pp. ISBN 0-87763-001-1.

Number 57   *Permesta: Half a Rebellion,* Barbara S. Harvey. 1977. 174 pp. ISBN 0-87763-003-8.

Number 55   *Report from Banaran: The Story of the Experiences of a Soldier during the War of Independence,* Maj. Gen. T. B. Simatupang. 1972. 186 pp. ISBN 0-87763-005-4.

Number 52   *A Preliminary Analysis of the October 1 1965, Coup in Indonesia (Prepared in January 1966),* Benedict R. Anderson, Ruth T. McVey, assist. Frederick P. Bunnell. 1971. 3rd printing 1990. 174 pp. ISBN 0-87763-008-9.

Number 51   *The Putera Reports: Problems in Indonesian-Japanese War-Time Cooperation,* Mohammad Hatta, trans., intro. William H. Frederick. 1971. 114 pp. ISBN 0-87763-009-7.

Number 50	*Schools and Politics: The Kaum Muda Movement in West Sumatra (1927–1933)*, Taufik Abdullah. 1971. 257 pp. ISBN 0-87763-010-0.
Number 49	*The Foundation of the Partai Muslimin Indonesia*, K. E. Ward. 1970. 75 pp. ISBN 0-87763-011-9.
Number 48	*Nationalism, Islam and Marxism*, Soekarno, intro. Ruth T. McVey. 1970. 2nd printing 1984. 62 pp. ISBN 0-87763-012-7.
Number 43	*State and Statecraft in Old Java: A Study of the Later Mataram Period, 16th to 19th Century*, Soemarsaid Moertono. Revised edition 1981. 180 pp. ISBN 0-87763-017-8.
Number 39	Preliminary Checklist of Indonesian Imprints (1945-1949), John M. Echols. 186 pp. ISBN 0-87763-025-9.
Number 37	*Mythology and the Tolerance of the Javanese*, Benedict R. O'G. Anderson. 2nd edition 1997. 104 pp., 65 illus. ISBN 0-87763-041-0.
Number 25	*The Communist Uprisings of 1926–1927 in Indonesia: Key Documents*, ed., intro. Harry J. Benda, Ruth T. McVey. 1960. 2nd printing 1969. 177 pp. ISBN 0-87763-024-0.
Number 7	*The Soviet View of the Indonesian Revolution*, Ruth T. McVey. 1957. 3rd printing 1969. 90 pp. ISBN 0-87763-018-6.
Number 6	*The Indonesian Elections of 1955*, Herbert Feith. 1957. 2nd printing 1971. 91 pp. ISBN 0-87763-020-8.

LANGUAGE TEXTS

INDONESIAN

Beginning Indonesian through Self-Instruction, John U. Wolff, Dédé Oetomo, Daniel Fietkiewicz. 3rd revised edition 1992. Vol. 1. 115 pp. ISBN 0-87727-529-7. Vol. 2. 434 pp. ISBN 0-87727-530-0. Vol. 3. 473 pp. ISBN 0-87727-531-9.

Indonesian Readings, John U. Wolff. 1978. 4th printing 1992. 480 pp. ISBN 0-87727-517-3

Indonesian Conversations, John U. Wolff. 1978. 3rd printing 1991. 297 pp. ISBN 0-87727-516-5

Formal Indonesian, John U. Wolff. 2nd revised edition 1986. 446 pp. ISBN 0-87727-515-7

TAGALOG

Pilipino through Self-Instruction, John U. Wolff, Maria Theresa C. Centeno, Der-Hwa V. Rau. 1991. Vol. 1. 342 pp. ISBN 0-87727—525-4. Vol. 2. 378 pp. ISBN 0-87727-526-2. Vol 3. 431 pp. ISBN 0-87727-527-0. Vol. 4. 306 pp. ISBN 0-87727-528-9.

THAI

A. U. A. Language Center Thai Course, J. Marvin Brown. Originally published by the American University Alumni Association Language Center, 1974. Reissued by Cornell Southeast Asia Program, 1991, 1992. Book 1. 267 pp. ISBN 0-87727-506-8. Book 2. 288 pp. ISBN 0-87727-507-6. Book 3. 247 pp. ISBN 0-87727-508-4.

A. U. A. Language Center Thai Course, Reading and Writing Text (mostly reading), 1979. Reissued 1997. 164 pp. ISBN 0-87727-511-4.

A. U. A. Language Center Thai Course, Reading and Writing Workbook (mostly writing), 1979. Reissued 1997. 99 pp. ISBN 0-87727-512-2.

KHMER

Cambodian System of Writing and Beginning Reader, Franklin E. Huffman. Originally published by Yale University Press, 1970. Reissued by Cornell Southeast Asia Program, 4th printing 2002. 365 pp. ISBN 0-300-01314-0.

Modern Spoken Cambodian, Franklin E. Huffman, assist. Charan Promchan, Chhom-Rak Thong Lambert. Originally published by Yale University Press, 1970. Reissued by Cornell Southeast Asia Program, 3rd printing 1991. 451 pp. ISBN 0-300-01316-7.

Intermediate Cambodian Reader, ed. Franklin E. Huffman, assist. Im Proum. Originally published by Yale University Press, 1972. Reissued by Cornell Southeast Asia Program, 1988. 499 pp. ISBN 0-300-01552-6.

Cambodian Literary Reader and Glossary, Franklin E. Huffman, Im Proum. Originally published by Yale University Press, 1977. Reissued by Cornell Southeast Asia Program, 1988. 494 pp. ISBN 0-300-02069-4.

HMONG

White Hmong-English Dictionary, Ernest E. Heimbach. 1969. 8th printing, 2002. 523 pp. ISBN 0-87727-075-9.

VIETNAMESE

Intermediate Spoken Vietnamese, Franklin E. Huffman, Tran Trong Hai. 1980. 3rd printing 1994. ISBN 0-87727-500-9.

* * *

Southeast Asian Studies: Reorientations. Craig J. Reynolds and Ruth McVey. Frank H. Golay Lectures 2 & 3. 70 pp. ISBN 0-87727-301-4.

Javanese Literature in Surakarta Manuscripts, Nancy K. Florida. Vol. 1, *Introduction and Manuscripts of the Karaton Surakarta*. 1993. 410 pp. Frontispiece, illustrations. Hard cover, ISBN 0-87727-602-1, Paperback, ISBN 0-87727-603-X. Vol. 2, *Manuscripts of the Mangkunagaran Palace*. 2000. 576 pp. Frontispiece, illustrations. Paperback, ISBN 0-87727-604-8.

Sbek Thom: Khmer Shadow Theater. Pech Tum Kravel, trans. Sos Kem, ed. Thavro Phim, Sos Kem, Martin Hatch. 1996. 363 pp., 153 photographs. ISBN 0-87727-620-X.

In the Mirror: Literature and Politics in Siam in the American Era, ed. Benedict R. O'G. Anderson, trans. Benedict R. O'G. Anderson, Ruchira Mendiones. 1985. 2nd printing 1991. 303 pp. Paperback. ISBN 974-210-380-1.

To order, please contact:

Cornell University
SEAP Distribution Center
369 Pine Tree Rd.
Ithaca, NY 14850-2819 USA

Online: http://www.einaudi.cornell.edu/bookstore/seap
Tel: 1-877-865-2432 (Toll free – U.S.)
Fax: (607) 255-7534

E-mail: SEAP-Pubs@cornell.edu
Orders must be prepaid by check or credit card (VISA, MasterCard, Discover).